Errata for Woll: *Everyday Thinking: Memory, Reasoning, and Judgment in the Real World*   ISBN 0-8058-1481-7
p. 103, paragraph 3: The reference to Fig. 3.4 should be Fig. 3.5.
p. 239, paragraph 3: The reference to Fig. 6.1 should be Fig. 6.2.
pp. 100–101, Figs. 3.1 and 3.3 should appear as follows:

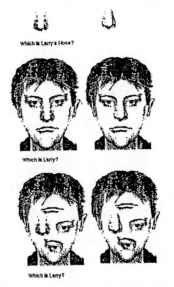

FIG. 3.1. Faces used by Tanaka and Farah in their study of configurational processes in face recognition. From "Parts and Wholes in Face Recognition" by J. W. Tanaka & M. J. Farah, 1993, *Quarterly Journal of Experimental Psychology: Human Experimental Psychology, 46A*, pp. 225–245. Copyright © 1993 by Psychology Press, LTD. Reprinted with permission of Psychology Press, LTD.

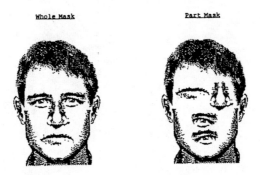

FIG. 3.3. Example of faces used in Farah et al. studies of face recognition. From "What is 'Special' About Face Perception?" by M. J. Farah, K. D. Wilson, H. M. Drain, & J. N. Tanaka, 1998, *Psychological Review, 105*, 489. Copyright © 1998 by the American Psychological Association. Reprinted with permission.

p. 462, Fig. 10.1 should appear as follows:

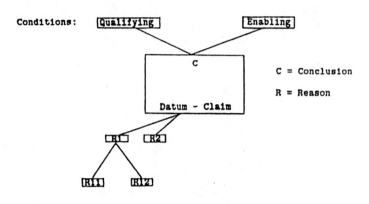

FIG. 10.1. A representation of Voss's (1985) model of informal reasoning. Adapted from "Informal Reasoning and Subject Matter Knowledge in the Solving of Problems by Naive and Novice Individuals," by J. F. Voss, J. Blais, M. L. Means, T. R. Green, & E. Ahwesh, 1986, *Cognition and Instruction, 3*, p. 273. Copyright © 1986 by Lawrence Erlbaum Associates. Reprinted with permission.

Everyday Thinking

*Memory, Reasoning, and Judgment
in the Real World*

≫ ≪

Everyday Thinking

Memory, Reasoning, and Judgment in the Real World

≫ ≪

Stanley Woll
California State University, Fullerton

LAWRENCE ERLBAUM ASSOCIATES, PUBLISHERS
2002   Mahwah, New Jersey   London

Lawrence Erlbaum Associates, Inc., Publishers
10 Industrial Avenue
Mahwah, NJ 07430

Cover design by Kathryn Houghtaling Lacey

Library of Congress Cataloging-in-Publication Data

Woll, Stanley.
    Everyday thinking: memory, reasoning, and judgment in
    the real world / Stanley Woll.
        p. cm.
    Includes bibliographical references and index.
    ISBN 0-8058-1481-7 (cloth : alk. Paper)
    1. Cognition. I. Title.
    BF311 .W63   2001
    153—dc21   00-027235
                                                     CIP

Books published by Lawrence Erlbaum Associates are printed
on acid-free paper, and their bindings are chosen for strength
and durability.

Printed in the United States of America
10 9 8 7 6 5 4 3 2 1

This book is dedicated to my parents,
Sam and Dorothy Woll,
who fostered a sense of intellectual curiosity and scholarship,
as well as a fascination with everyday cognition

Contents

Preface

As Ebbinghaus once observed about psychology in general (Boring, 1929), this book has a short history (although not nearly as short as my editor might have liked!), but a long past. I began thinking about the material discussed in this book nearly 30 years ago, back in graduate school. At that time, in studying both cognitive and social psychology, it seemed clear to me that when you introduce social or everyday content into traditional research on cognitive processes and representations, it changes things dramatically. In the process of testing out this idea, I came across examples in concept formation from Bruner, Goodnow, and Austin (1956), in conditional reasoning by Johnson-Laird, Legrenzi, and Legrenzi (1972), and in cross-cultural research by Cole, Gay, Glick, and Sharp (1971). The last two of these figure prominently in discussions in chapters 8 and 9, respectively.

My initial interest in this topic was (and still is, to some degree) the influence of *social* content and *social* context. I called this interest "social cognition" and did my dissertation on the role of social content in a propositional learning task (a combination of attribution theory with concept formation). For the following 15 years I did research on person memory, stereotypes, moral judgment, and the like. While I was doing this research, a discipline that also called itself social cognition began to develop and flourish (mostly independently of my own efforts). As I argue in chapters 1 and 2 of this book, this discipline took primarily a traditional experimental social psychology approach, which, for the most part, meant breaking cognition down into molecular units and processes, and focused on traditional experimental manipulations in rarefied laboratory situations. (There were certainly major exceptions to this, but this was the general rule.) Because my own interests lay in other ideas, I became increasingly disenchanted with "social cognition."

During this same period, I found myself drawn to studying thinking in more "real-world" situations. For example, I did several studies on impression formation in the context of a videodating service; and I also did research on political awareness and political reasoning with real political groups, and I found myself increasingly interested in topics that did not fall specifically within the social cognition area (e.g., the study of autobiographical memory and face recognition), but that seemed to me to be of great personal and social significance.

Then, around 1989, during a visit to Amsterdam, I came across an interesting book by Gillian Cohen (1989) titled *Memory in the Real World.* I began to teach seminars and undergraduate courses on everyday cognition and found that students got very excited by the content of these courses. As I began to develop these courses, I found that my knowledge in many of these areas, and for that matter the *research* in many of them, were, shall we say, skeletal at best. It was difficult to come up with books on the topic, although I was generally able to piece together combinations of books on everyday memory, practical intelligence, and autobiographical memory and the like. It struck me that a text in this area might be of some value.

It so happened that as I started writing that book, research in nearly all of the areas that I chose to include in the book started taking off. For example, the first time I taught the course, I found very little material on prospective memory. A graduate student in one of my seminars did a term paper on this topic, and she was able to find additional references; but it was still a fairly narrow area. In 1996, an entire book on this topic was published (Brandimonte, Einstein, & McDaniel, 1996), along with a number of chapters and research articles; and so when I finished writing about this topic, there was more material than I could possibly fit into the 10 or so pages allotted. Similarly, in the area of autobiographical memory the only book available when I first started teaching my Everyday Cognition class was the book by Rubin (1986). The next time I taught the course I used the book by Conway (1990a). When I started writing this book, the field mushroomed, and now it can be found everywhere (e.g., Conway, Rubin, Spinnler, & Wagenaar, 1992; Pillemer, 1998; Rubin, 1996; Thompson et al., 1998; Thompson et al., 1996). This explosion in research has made my task much more challenging than I had anticipated, but much more fascinating and rewarding as well.

In writing this book, I, like any other author, have had to make some decisions about what topics to cover, and in what depth. I have chosen some topics that are "traditional" everyday cognition ones (if that word is even appropriate in this area) such as face recognition and autobiographical memory. I have also chosen to include other topics (e.g., everyday judgment and person memory) that are not typically included under that topic, but that seem to me to be relevant to the topic of "everyday cognition." Furthermore, for the nine topics I *have* included, I chose to discuss them in some depth. As a result, I have left out some topics that may be your favorites or that you would have chosen to include. For example, I have not included research on memory for conversation or absentmindedness or the whole issue of automaticity or judgment and decision making in applied situations such as clinical, legal, or medical settings. I am prepared to be convinced that I should have covered this topic or should have left that one out. Nonetheless, my rationale, as stated in chapter 1, was to draw attention to some of the common themes and concerns that several diverse areas share; and it was that goal that shaped my selection. Comments on the book and/or suggestions for alternative topics, references, or other changes are welcomed. Feel free to email me at woll@fullerton.edu.

I believe that this book can be used in a variety of different ways. For example, it can be used as a stand-alone text for a cognitive psychology course (i.e., as a way of presenting cognitive models and concepts in a more palatable way) or it may be used as a supplement to a more traditional cognitive text. It can also be used as a text for a separate everyday cognition course or for seminars on that topic.

As far as the specific contents of the book are concerned, although I have made a concerted effort to draw connections among the different topics covered, it is clearly possible to focus on particular topics (e.g., everyday memory in chaps. 2 through 6, or everyday reasoning and judgment in chaps. 7 through 9) at the expense of others. Instructors who wish to emphasize general theories of cognition may want to expand on the brief presentations of the models of everyday cognition in chapter 1, whereas others may choose to ignore these models entirely. Similarly, those interested in showing how everyday reasoning and problem solving follow from more traditional research on those topics may want to emphasize chapter 7, or even use supplementary materials; others who are interested primarily in applied cognitive psychology may choose to ignore that chapter. Instructors who wish to teach a course that follows more common concepts of *everyday* or *applied* memory or cognition may want to leave out chapters 9 and 10; those who are interested in educational or instructional implications will obviously want to focus on chapter 10, perhaps along with chapters 7, 8, and 9.

There are a number of people who contributed to the completion of this book. First, two department chairs—Dan Kee and Dave Perkins—made life easier for me, even though I did not always seem to be making great progress on the book. A couple of the chapters were written on sabbatical at Cambridge University; and I must acknowledge Colin Fraser, Alec Broers, and Paula Halson of Churchill College for arranging for my visit there. Several people read and made comments on individual chapters or segments. These included Alan Baddeley, Michael Cole, Jennifer Devenport, Don Dulany, Baruch Fischhoff, Mike Pressley, Colleen Seifert, and John Skowronski. E-mail communications with David Berliner, Don Dulany, Deanna Kuhn, Steve Read, and Eliot

Smith helped me to clarify points, as did conversations with George Marcoulides and Bill Marelich at Fullerton. Marilynn Brewer, Martin Conway, Susan Fiske, Eliot Smith, and Michael Tarr also made preprints of chapters, talks, and difficult-to-find articles available. Finally, Chris Cozby, Dan Kee, Alison King, and Rich Mayer read and provided feedback on multiple chapters, and I am happy to acknowledge their contributions. (Chris also served, as usual, as advisor and ombudsman on many little details too numerous to mention.) Thanks also go to Shayla Markham, Hsinya Lo, Dana Carney, and Mark Montilla for working on my humongous reference list, to Paul Kieffaber and Kim Dailey for their help with the figures, and to Mark Montilla and Frances Sanchez for formatting and helping edit the final draft of the manuscript. Frances also typed 101 different tables, letters, etc. Finally, I owe a lot to Nancy Caudill and her staff in Interlibrary Loan for their efficient work and quick turnaround, and to Barbara Phillips and her staff in the CSUF Periodical Department for running interference for me too many times to mention when the system erected obstacles. Writing this book would have been much more difficult without their help.

Last, but certainly not least, I express my thanks and appreciation to Kathy Dolan and Sara Scudder and, in particular, to Judi Amsel at Lawrence Erlbaum Associates for their support in this project. Judi has been patient and encouraging when she needed to be, and appropriately insistent when she had to be. Although this book has taken much (or even much, much) longer than either of us had anticipated, Judi has always seen the value of a book in everyday thinking and has always stood behind the project.

The importance of critically examining our everyday thinking has been underlined in recent years by at least two notable political attacks on academia. The first of these was an attempt by the religious and political right, including members of Congress and well-known conservative talk-show hosts, to suppress the conclusions published in refereed journal articles because these conclusions ran counter to their own firmly entrenched, "everyday" beliefs. Unfortunately, the APA capitulated to such pressures, thus giving undue weight to religious and political beliefs to counter the results of rigorous, scientific peer review.

A second incident is the attempt by the new Chancellor of the CSU system to squelch faculty input and to replace the expertise of scholars with the everyday thinking of administrators and businessmen. Such a move would have had a significant negative impact on both faculty morale and also the quality of a college education. Fortunately, CSU faculty found their political voice and fought off such an attack, but the fight is not over by a long shot. The threats to academic scholarship come in many different forms.

Because this book is about finding common themes in diverse topics, the common theme in the foregoing two episodes is clearly threats to academics and to serious, independent scholarship and scientific research. I believe that these values are of the utmost importance and that they have served us well for the last several hundred years. I do not believe that in this new millennium we want to slip back into the Dark Ages where narrow-minded religious values govern the practice of free, open inquiry.

—Stanley Woll

Chapter 1

The Value and Appeal of Research on Everyday Thought

On July 4th of this year I woke up and found that I had no orange juice or cereal—the staples of my usual breakfast. I kicked myself because I had meant to stop off to get these groceries the day before but forgot to do so. I got dressed and got ready to run down to the store to pick up these groceries, but discovered that my car keys, as well as the key to my lab, were not in their usual place. Because all of my other keys were there, and because I usually keep the two missing keys in the same pocket, I concluded that the most likely explanation was that I'd misplaced the keys when I changed pants the evening before. Therefore, I searched in a pile of clothes in my bedroom. (I'm a notorious slob, in addition to being absentminded.) This also seemed a likely place to search because I'd lost those keys there before. I did a quick search through the pile but did not see the keys. (I did find a pair of socks that I was missing, though.)

I then started to think of all the other possible locations where I might have left the keys. It seemed unlikely that I had locked the keys in the car, because both keys were missing, but I looked through the windows of my car anyway. The keys did not seem to be there. I checked the table next to my front door, where I might have laid the keys when fumbling around trying to lock the door. The keys were not there either. I looked where I'd left the videotapes that I'd rented the night before, even though that was unlikely because I'd gotten those tapes on an earlier trip and must have had the car key after that in order to drive the car later. Then I remembered that the last trip I'd made the night before was to get some teriyaki chicken for dinner, so I looked at the spot where I'd eaten dinner. I also recalled that I'd lost my spare car key in a stack of newspapers at that spot before. (Don't ask—it's the slob thing again.) I took apart a stack of newspapers but found neither the spare key nor my recent losses. (I must go back through that stack again; I know that the spare key is there somewhere.)

Having exhausted most of my hypotheses and wanting to get some work done, I grabbed some cookies (no comment) and started grading papers from my summer school class. (I also watched a little of the Wimbledon finals—it was, after all, a holiday.) While working on those papers, I remembered that I'd picked up my mail on one of those trips last night, and had fumbled around with my keys (again) at that time, so I told myself that when I was finished with the grading, I'd check the mailbox and the surrounding area, even though I thought that was another unlikely scenario. When that possibility didn't pan out, I told myself that I really needed to find those damn keys, so I took another, closer look in the aforementioned pile of clothes. Lo and behold, my car key was hiding under another pair of socks! Strangely enough, my lab key wasn't there. (It showed up a couple of months later.) I never did go out and get the orange juice and cereal, though. (Maybe when I finish writing up this account.)

—An initial personal example of
everyday memory and problem solving

Introduction

Some Examples of Laboratory and Real-World Memory and Problem Solving

Some General Issues in Everyday Cognition

Differences Between Everyday Reasoning and Problem Solving and Their Lab Analogues

The Social and Cultural Dimensions: Some of the Differences Between the Everyday Cognition of Social and Nonsocial Objects

Some Models of Everyday Cognition

General Summary

INTRODUCTION

The subject of this book (and of the example just cited) is *everyday thought* or *cognition*. In the chapters that follow, I demonstrate that the study of everyday cognition (a) is enjoying a dramatic increase in popularity in recent years, (b) is of major significance for cognitive psychology and related disciplines, (c) merits closer examination, both conceptually and as a topic for future research, and (d) is damn interesting in its own right.

As a kind of working definition, everyday cognition refers to the ways in which we think about real-world, everyday issues in natural settings and under real-world conditions. In addition, as Banaji and Crowder (1989) and Klatzky (1991) have suggested, everyday cognition is sometimes concerned with applied problems (e.g., eyewitness testimony, how to use everyday knowledge to improve the effectiveness of instruction) and special populations (e.g., expert racetrack handicappers, blind or brain-damaged patients, decision making by firefighters or weather forecasters). As you will see, the usual contrast here—implicit or explicit—is to traditional "artificial" laboratory experiments, although much of the research that I review in this book is of the laboratory sort.

To be more specific, in this book I discuss three main topics: (a) memory for real-world experiences and objects such as people, faces, events (such as losing keys), prior intentions (such as buying orange juice or going to look in my mailbox), and one's own history; (b) informal reasoning about everyday issues such as grocery shopping, finding keys, or planning work projects or a career, and everyday, practical intelligence; and (c) everyday judgment and decision making. These topics have typically been discussed in relative isolation from each other under a variety of different labels: for example, everyday cognition (Rogoff & Lave, 1984), memory in the "real world" (G. Cohen, 1989), naturalistic decision making (e.g., G. A. Klein, Orasanu, Calderwood, & Zsambok, 1993), informal reasoning (e.g., Galotti, 1989; Voss, Perkins, & Segal, 1991), everyday reasoning (e.g., Galotti, 1989); and problem solving (Sinnott, 1989), practical intelligence (Sternberg & Wagner, 1986), and the practical aspects of memory (Gruneberg, Morris, & Sykes, 1978, 1988). In this book I point to some of the common themes and issues among these different topics and try to lay the groundwork for a more general, coherent discipline of everyday cognition.

Before I discuss some of the points at issue in the debate over the study of everyday cognition, I will give a general impression of the differences between research on this topic and traditional, laboratory research on memory and cognition. I do so by citing some examples of the sorts of tasks and topics addressed in the two areas (in addition to looking for keys).

SOME EXAMPLES OF LABORATORY AND REAL-WORLD MEMORY AND PROBLEM SOLVING

Research on Memory

As an example of a traditional laboratory study on memory, assume that you are presented with the following list of words (from Searleman & Herrmann, 1994): *dog, bus, mouse, chair, tulip, train, table, horse, rose, petunia, airplane, goat, sofa, pig, bed, boat, lilac, truck, marigold, dresser.* You are then asked to recall these words in whatever order you wish. The evidence presented by Bousfield (1953) from this sort of experiment is that participants recall words such as these in clusters corresponding to the categories built into the list, for example, animals, vehicles, furniture, flowers—hence, the term *category clustering,* or clustering in recall. Along similar lines, Tulving (1962) demonstrated that when there was no structure built into the word list, participants imposed their own structure, or what Tulving called *subjective organization,* on the list in their recall, that is, by recalling the words in a consistent order on successive trials with the same list. These two types of studies indicate that participants have, in the first case, discovered the conceptual structure built into the list or, in the second case, imposed their own structure, although we do not necessarily know what that organization is. In both cases, participants are asked to recall a word list with known, controlled properties, and the experimenter can compare their recall with this controlled list. As discussed in chapter 2, this kind of methodology has also been applied to topics in everyday cognition such as impression formation or person memory (e.g., Hamilton, Katz, & Leirer, 1980).

Contrast this type of research with the study of *autobiographical memory* (AM), which I discuss in chapters 5 and 6. In this research you may be asked to recall experiences from, say, when you were in elementary or high school, or you may receive a set of cue words, for instance, objects, activities, or emotions, and then be asked to describe a related personal memory for each word. These memories may subsequently be analyzed in terms of the relative number recalled for different time periods (e.g., adolescence vs. adulthood) or in terms of which type of cue (e.g., activities vs. emotions) elicits which kinds of and how many memories.

On the face of it, there appears to be some overlap between this type of study and laboratory studies of memory; for example, both use free or cued recall procedures (although less traditional methods such as diary keeping or think-aloud protocols have also been used in AM research). There are, however, some obvious differences between the two types of study. Specifically, traditional memory research typically involves presenting a controlled set of stimuli to participants. In the early verbal-learning tradition these stimuli consisted of nonsense syllables that explicitly controlled for meaning; in the Bousfield (1953) study, stimuli were selected to emphasize the common meaning behind the words. These stimuli are learned under controlled conditions with a relatively short interval between presentation and recall. Also, because the stimulus list is controlled, the experimenter can compare participants' recall with that original list so that recall accuracy can be calculated.

For autobiographical memory, on the other hand, there is (usually) little or no control over the remembered materials, the conditions under which they were learned or rehearsed, or over the accuracy of participants' recall—all of which are characteristics that have been considered critical by traditional memory researchers (see Pillemer, 1998). Equally important, the to-be-recalled material has personal meaning to participants; it is part of their personal life history rather than a set of relatively arbitrary syllables or general words prepared by the experimenter. Finally, AM research examines memories that participants bring into the lab, memories that may be years or decades old (see Rubin, 1996).

Mathematical Calculations

Another example of the difference between, say, standard instruction in math versus math as practiced in everyday situations, is given by Jean Lave

(1988; see also Lave, Murtaugh, & de la Rocha, 1984). First, consider the following standard arithmetic problems: $57 + 114 = ?$; $65 - 9 = ?$; $10 \times 11 = ?$; or which of these fractions is larger: $\frac{20}{35}$ or $\frac{12}{18}$? Now assume that you are shopping in a grocery store and you are trying to determine which price of each of the following pairs of products is the best buy: a 7-oz. package of canned chili for 79¢, or a 4-oz. package for 49¢; a 23-oz. jar of barbeque sauce for $1.17, or an 18-oz. jar for 89¢; a 32-oz. package of cheddar cheese for $5.29, or a 9-oz. package for $1.59?

As discussed in chapter 8, Lave (1988; Lave et al., 1984) has conducted precisely this sort of research, comparing the uses of arithmetic by American adults in standard mathematical problem-solving tasks with everyday grocery shopping. The first finding Lave reported is that performance on the comparison price problems (carried out in an actual grocery store) is unrelated to performance on the arithmetic test or to participants' years of schooling. Equally important, Lave distinguishes between mathematical calculation as a goal in and of itself and such calculations as a means toward another end—for example, finding a good buy at the grocery store. In the first case, participants try (often unsuccessfully) to use standard rules or procedures; in the latter case, people use (mostly successfully) shortcuts or heuristics and, in particular, a form of rounding and "gap-closing" approximation (see chap. 8). Once again, the emphasis is on the differences between mathematical reasoning as practiced in the classroom versus that practiced in everyday situations.

Human Judgment and Decision Making.

One final example of these differences comes from the area of human judgment and decision making. First, consider the following standard urn problem in probability theory (Bar-Hillel, 1973). You have a choice between two bets: either the chance of choosing a colored ball from an urn containing 2 colored balls along with 18 white balls, or of drawing (with replacement) four consecutive colored balls from an urn containing 10 colored and 10 white balls. In this problem, participants generally choose the latter conjunctive bet, that is, betting on the conjunction of four different events, even though the actual probability of that drawing is .06, whereas the chance for the former drawing is .10.

Or consider the following story problem example from Tversky and Kahneman (1974, p. 1125), which contains a hint of everyday content:

A certain town is served by two hospitals. In the larger hospital about 45 babies are born each day, and in the smaller hospital about 15 babies are born each day. As you know, about 50 percent of all babies are boys. However, the exact percentage varies from day to day. Sometimes it may be higher than 50 percent, sometimes lower.

For a period of one year, each hospital recorded the number of days on which more than 60 percent of the babies born were boys. Which hospital do you think recorded more such days?

The larger hospital (21)

The smaller hospital (21)

About the same (that is, within 5% of each other) (53)

(The numbers in parentheses refer to the number of participants who chose each alternative.) It is clear, then, that for this problem a majority (56%) of participants chose the third option, and an equal number (22%) chose each of the other two options, suggesting that, in general, participants ignored the sample sizes; that is, they ignored the fact that larger samples are less likely to depart from the expected value of 50% than are smaller samples.

Now consider the following account by G. A. Klein (1989, 1993) of the decision-making process of experts in a given area, for example, urban firefighters, Israeli tank commanders, and intensive care unit nurses. Klein and others (e.g., Zsambok & Klein, 1997) have described what they call *naturalistic decision making*, or decisions made on the spot in the real world by people experienced in a given area. In this view, experts do not explicitly consider and weigh all the alternatives, but rather use their background knowledge about that area to identify a particular situation as being of a certain type associated with a particular course of action. Thus, a firefighter may "know" from the pattern of the flames and from the color of the smoke that a fire is of a certain type which requires a particular sort of strategy. Or a driver may approach a curve and make an immediate judgment of this curve as of a certain sort that requires a certain reduction of speed and a particular maneuvering of the steering wheel without having to explicitly calculate the rate of acceleration or the angle of the curve or all the possible alternatives for action.

For our present purposes, the important point is that everyday judgment and decision making not only involve a richer context of environmental cues, but also draw on our everyday background knowledge of situations and are oftentimes made without great conscious deliberation. Thus, subjective utility theory, subjective value theory, or sampling theory may offer a good normative model of decision making, but they (and the numerous lab studies conducted on their behalf) do not give an adequate characterization of decision making in the real world.

SOME GENERAL ISSUES IN EVERYDAY COGNITION

Armed with a working definition of everyday cognition and a trio of examples, let me now turn to a more systematic discussion of the issues surrounding theory and research on that topic. As in the examples just presented, my emphasis is on the differences and debates between advocates of traditional lab research on memory and cognition on the one hand and those championing the study of everyday cognition on the other. For convenience, I begin with an explicit contrast drawn between these two different forms of research in the study of memory.

How Valid (and Valuable) Is Research on Everyday Memory and Problem-Solving?

A major impetus to the study of naturalistic or real-world memory, and by implication, to the current[1] study of everyday cognition in general, was a rather provocative chapter by Ulric Neisser (1978). This chapter was based on Neisser's keynote speech to the first in a series of conferences on practical aspects of memory. In an often-cited passage, and one that apparently rang true for a large number of researchers, Neisser made the following assertion: "If X is an interesting or socially significant aspect of memory, then psychologists have hardly ever studied X" (p. 4). In other words, over the last 100 years, from Ebbinghaus to the present day, traditional laboratory research on memory has seldom examined the kinds of questions that are of interest to most of us in our daily lives. In support of this position, Neisser cited such phenomena as our failure to recall the sources of quotations, our recall for lectures or speeches, students' long-term retention of what they have learned in school—all issues that we would expect to be of interest to researchers who are also educators. And yet, at least in 1976, Neisser was unable to find examples of research on these topics, or much substantial research on other topics such as memory for childhood experiences, memory (or lack thereof) for appointments, memory for names and for old, familiar places, to name just a few. In short, Neisser claimed that traditional memory research has failed to establish the *ecological validity* (cf. Brunswik, 1956), of its findings, or the applicability of these findings to the real world.

Neisser's (1978) attack on traditional memory research led to a rather heated debate over the merits and limitations of a laboratory approach versus focusing on everyday memory. The next volley in this debate came in an article by Banaji and Crowder (1989) titled "The Bankruptcy of Everyday Memory." This article in turn led to a series of articles in the *American Psychologist* (Loftus, 1991a) debating the pros and cons of the two approaches, followed by another round of debate in the book *Memory in Everyday Life* (Davies & Logie, 1993). In the sections that follow I discuss some of the central issues raised in this debate and some of the arguments on both sides of these issues.

The Issue of Generalizability. Neisser (1978) quite accurately saw that at least one major reason for the failure of memory researchers to address the question of everyday cognition is that "they [psychologists] believe they are doing something more important. They are working toward a general theory of memory, a scientific understanding of its underlying mechanisms,

---

[1]There have been a number of other schools of thought, ranging from Bartlett (1932, 1958) to Gestalt theory, to Heider's (1958) social phenomenology to Bourdieu's (1977) social practice theory, which have stressed everyday knowledge; but these approaches have not had as strong an influence on current research on everyday cognition (although Neisser, 1978, cites Bartlett as one of the few researchers who pursued the naturalistic study of memory).

more fundamental and far-reaching than any research on worldly questions could possibly be" (p. 6). In other words, most researchers in the field of memory and cognition see their task as being the search for general, universal laws of cognitive functioning. Neisser's position, however, is that there are very few meaningful principles that have held up over the many years of memory research and that laboratory research per se is incapable of establishing, or at least unlikely in principle to establish, such meaningful laws.

In response to Neisser (1978), Banaji and Crowder (1989) argued for the importance of distinguishing between two different forms of *generalizability*— namely, generalizability or ecological validity of *methods* versus the generalizability of *conclusions* arrived at by research; they argued that the two types of generalizability can, in fact, be varied independently of each other. Thus, research may be carried out in the real world, or more naturalistic methods may be used, without the results or findings of this research being more generalizable than lab results. As examples of this, Banaji and Crowder cited two naturalistic studies (i.e., Diges, 1988, on reports of traffic accidents in the real world, and Bruce & Read, 1988, on the estimated frequency of events from an actual vacation). Both of these studies showed high ecological validity, that is, in the sense that they were carried out in real-world settings; but they also were of limited generalizability because of their failure to control for a variety of other confounding factors. Conversely, there are a number of laboratory findings, a few of which I discuss in this book (e.g., research on eyewitness testimony, face recognition, transfer of training) that arguably *can* be applied to real-world settings.

Perhaps more importantly, Banaji and Crowder (1989) argued that what psychologists seek to establish is not so much *empirical* generalizability—that is, the generality of a particular set of findings—but rather *theoretical* generalizability in the form of general laws or mechanisms of memory, such as general principles of retrieval or encoding or, more generally, of reasoning, problem solving, and judgment. Of course, as I have suggested, that is what most experimental psychologists see as their ultimate purpose: namely, finding general laws of behavior or psychological functioning that apply across different contents and contexts. Shweder (1990) has put this in the following way: "General psychology presumes that there exists a general processing mechanism that can be isolated from the different particulars it might encounter, and that isolating that processing mechanism is what genuine psychological research is about" (p. 8). I argue later in this chapter, though (and Shweder has argued as well), that although such a strategy may make sense in some areas of psychology, the strategy of searching for such general, content- and context-free laws is at least open to debate in the area of higher order reasoning and problem solving (see chaps. 7 and 8; see Cole, 1996, for a discussion of the long history of proposals for a *second psychology* or *cultural psychology* for the study of higher mental processes).

I should mention in passing that a similar search for "invariants" has been pursued by Newell (1990; Newell & Simon, 1972) and Simon (1979a,

1979b, 1990) in the field of artificial intelligence in their *physical symbol systems* viewpoint. Physical symbol systems are systems that store and manipulate symbols as instantiated by a physical system such as a computer or a human brain. Such symbolic systems are assumed to be adaptive to circumstances and hence are not completely comparable with most other strict physical systems. The invariants in this view, then, consist of certain limitations on capacity and symbol manipulation, what Simon (1989) has called limited or *bounded rationality*. A result of these limitations, as will be seen in chapter 7, is that humans depend on large stores of knowledge along with mechanisms such as recognition processes and heuristic searches to reduce the processing requirements of this bounded, limited system. I return to this viewpoint later in this chapter.

Everyday memory researchers have responded to Banaji and Crowder's (1989) arguments in a variety of ways. For example, M. A. Conway (1991, 1993) and Ceci and Bronfenbrenner (1991) have argued that Banaji and Crowder and other traditional memory researchers have adopted an inappropriate model of cognitive science research—namely, a model based on the physical sciences, in which there are, in fact, "invariant mechanisms" (Banaji & Crowder, 1989, p. 1088). According to Conway (1991), this model ignores the intentional, meaning-endowing nature of human cognition. As a corollary, traditional memory research has uncritically accepted laboratory methods as *the* hallmark of the cognitive sciences. (This latter limitations does not, in general, apply to the physical systems or information processing model of Newell and Simon, 1972.)

On a different tangent, Ceci and Bronfenbrenner (1991) have argued that the aim of psychology is not necessarily to establish invariant mechanisms of memory that apply across all situations but rather to look for higher order *interactive* invariants—that is, principles that describe the way in which processes interact with situations (cf. Cole, 1996; Lave, 1988, 1991, and Resnick, 1991, for similar arguments). Thus, according to this view, the way in which we encode or retrieve information may vary depending on the situation or type of information involved; and therefore, it may not be possible to formulate principles that apply in the same way across *all* situations. At the same time, however, it *may* be possible to specify how these processes or applications vary or *interact* with the situation. For example, we may use different strategies for retrieving memories of important events in our lives from those we do for retrieving the content of lectures or the phone number of a friend; or, alternatively, experts on different topics may use different memory strategies in their areas of expertise than they do in other parts of their lives (see Chase & Ericsson, 1981, 1982). Nevertheless, it may be possible, by appealing to our knowledge of the requirements or goals that apply in any of these different contexts, to indicate how these processes will operate in that domain or situation. Ceci and Bronfenbrenner (1991) gave the example from their own research (Ceci & Bronfenbrenner, 1985) where children were allowed to play video games while waiting for cupcakes to bake or for batteries to charge in two different settings, at home or in an experimental lab. These children were found to use different strategies of "clock-checking" in the two situations; they checked the clock less frequently and used a more effective strategy in the home setting.

One implication of this point of view, of course, is that experimental situations themselves simply represent one of many different types of situation, each with its own set of rules; and, by implication, experimental situations may or may not be representative of or generalizable to other, more common situations. This same point has been made in a much stronger fashion by advocates of what has been called a *situated cognition* (e.g., Lave, 1988, 1991; Resnick, 1991) viewpoint. According to this view, cognitions vary from situation to situation or context to context, and therefore it does not make sense to talk about generalizable, "decontextualized" (Resnick, 1991) competencies, intelligences, or cognitive processes. Nor is it meaningful to look for general laws on this topic. Similarly, according to this view, the lab or classroom setting is not simply a "neutral environment ... [but rather is] a specific place ... [with] tasks and apparatuses never encountered elsewhere" (Resnick, 1991, p. 4) and with rules and expectations that may not generalize to other situations and that may even be "unavailable or unacceptable" (p. 4) to some individuals. (See Cole, 1996, and Hutchins, 1980, for similar arguments regarding the "culture" of the experiment and the degree to which such a culture or cultures do or do not generalize to other cultural contexts.) I return to this position later in this chapter.

Pillemer (1998) has pointed out another "bias" of traditional (and even some everyday) memory research: namely, the overemphasis of such research on general knowledge, as opposed to memory for specific episodes. The major reason for this preference is simple enough: It is assumed that general knowledge and general knowledge structures are of greater importance, of greater adaptive significance, and of greater educational benefit than single episodes (see the discussion of this argument in chap. 5). Nevertheless, it is clear that individuals are also influenced by single isolated events, what Pillemer refers to as "momentous events," including traumatic, inspirational, and personally significant events. In recent years there has been a decided move—particularly, but not exclusively, in the study of everyday cognition—toward the study of such single events. Pillemer traces this movement to R. Brown and Kulik's (1977) study of flashbulb memories, the increased concern with the narrative structure of memory and thought (e.g., Bruner, 1986, 1987; McAdams, 1993; Schank, 1990), and the increasing emphasis in several different areas on the effects of specific episodes on learning and memory (e.g., Nuthall & Alton-Lee, 1995; E. R. Smith, 1990; Whittlesea & Dorken, 1993). I return to this last emphasis in my discussion of the exemplar model later in this chapter.

The Importance of Experimental Control.   Another issue that is clearly related to the question of generalizability and to the laboratory versus real-world distinction is the question of *experimental control*. The viewpoint of traditional experimental psychology has been expressed by Banaji and Crowder (1989), who argued that experimental control is essential, if for no other reason than to reduce the complexity of real-world situations as well as the complexity of the causal structure in such situations. After all, one of the values of experimental studies is that they allow us to make causal statements and eliminate potentially confounding variables in a way that uncontrolled naturalistic observations cannot (though see Bahrick, Bahrick, & Wittlinger, 1975, for a good example of controls in a naturalistic study of memory for faces). Furthermore, commenting on the laboratory versus real-world debate, Roediger (1991) pointed out that many of the examples cited by advocates of everyday memory research for the value of their position (e.g., Ceci & Bronfenbrenner, 1991; M. A. Conway, 1991) entail more control than these advocates acknowledge, and in fact are sometimes actually drawn from laboratory studies—for example, research on the tip-of-the-tongue phenomenon (R. Brown & McNeill, 1966) and eyewitness testimony (e.g., Loftus & Palmer, 1974; see Poon, Welke, & Dudley, 1993, for a further discussion of the importance of lab research in everyday or applied cognition).

A rather strong opposing view has been voiced by Rubin (1988, 1996) in his chapter titled "Issues of regularity and control: Confessions of a regularity freak." According to Rubin, "it is not experimental control that is now desirable, but rather regularity of results. ... Psychology entered the laboratory too quickly. Psychology must first spend time observing and quantifying behavior in its fuller state of complexity" (1988, p. 84). In order to know what to control and what to allow to vary, you need to have collected enough data or observed enough regularity in the real world to justify such control. In the area of everyday memory, according to Rubin, we simply have not yet acquired sufficient knowledge or established the patterns of regularity to attempt such control. Along similar lines, and consistent with the arguments by Resnick (1991) reviewed earlier, Rubin argued that "less control provides more regularity" (p. 85) and "more control provides less knowledge" (p. 86). In other words, the less we try to control the information available to participants and the situation in which they are placed, the more likely we are to tap into the kinds of knowledge or processes that individuals use in their everyday life. In this sense, too strong an emphasis on experimental control can actually interfere with learning about the "normal" operation of cognitive processes by creating situations that are unrepresentative of participants' everyday worlds.

Rubin (1988) also argued that researchers should be concerned with uncovering regularity in the real world itself rather than with seeking some kind of higher order generalizations established by *theoretical* accounts. That is, researchers need to start by looking for regularity in everyday phenomena, and *then* move to the stage of theory and rigorous experimentation. It is premature to start theorizing and testing out generalizations before collecting enough data on everyday, real-world phenomena. Thus, one of the primary advantages of everyday memory research is that it may provide researchers with a compilation of real-life observations on which to base a theoretical account when they are ready to formulate one. (Of course, it may also be argued that everyone has made everyday observations too numerous to mention, so that we, as psychologists, do not need to make further ones.) Finally, in this same vein, Rubin argues that psychologists should "not be tied too strongly to any one theory or hypothesis when starting to collect data. Rather, try to think of the greatest number of theories that could be used to explain possible findings" (p. 91).

Although I disagree with Rubin's (1988) assumption that regularity is something that can be readily "discovered" or "observed" on a surface level, that is, without the aid of some kind of theoretical spectacles, his discussion of regularity does make an important point that I will return to later. Specifically, rather than designing studies to test out our prematurely formulated theories, it may be wise to spend more time being open-minded and simply collecting observations of interesting phenomena from the real world rather than strapping on our theoretical blinders too quickly and testing out our too-readily conceived hypotheses and experimental tests. In addition, as noted earlier, other psychologists have argued that creating artificial, highly controlled experimental situations or decontextualized tests or forms of instruction may not be successful in engaging the kinds of cognitive processes or knowledge that participants or students bring to bear in their everyday lives. (Instructors need only think about their experiences with students who are obviously able to think and plan in their everyday lives but who do not seem to "get with the program" when it comes to academic instruction. Here the difficulty of engaging cognitive processes and capacities is transparent; and it does not seem implausible to argue that lab experiments or standardized tests may have the same difficulty.) This is a point to which I return later in this chapter.

The Issue of Realism.   Because we are examining the topic of real-world cognition, it is not surprising that one of the points at issue is whether traditional studies of memory and cognition are sufficiently realistic to be applicable to real world settings. Can artificial laboratory studies really tell us something about real-world processing or real-world situations? As I expressed it in the last section, can experimental conditions successfully engage the cognitive processes that individuals use in everyday situations?

In response to the second of these questions, M. A. Conway (1991) argued that research on everyday memory "start[s] from the premise of prior, personally meaningful knowledge on the part of the subject and attempt[s] to understand the nature of this knowledge" (p. 20), whereas most traditional research on memory attempts to *control for* or rule out such knowledge. (This is the same point made by the autobiographical memory example given earlier.) Because higher order cognitive processes, including memory, are guided by our existing knowledge and assumptions, material that taps into that knowledge should be treated differently from material that does not. Stated differently, "the simple, or impoverished, environment of the laboratory is a stimulus that fails to exert stimulus control over behavior" (Rubin, 1988, p. 85).

On the other side of this issue, Baddeley (1993) and Crowder (1993) noted that the problem of "meaning" was one of the early and ongoing concerns of traditional verbal learning (e.g., Noble, 1952; Underwood & Schulz, 1960). In addition, Roediger (1991) suggested that Conway's argument against traditional memory research overlooks numerous laboratory studies that *have* tapped into participants' prior knowledge; and as examples of this point, he cites studies on topics such as *semantic priming*, or the facilitation of word recognition by the prior presentation of a semantically related word, category clustering, and subjective organization—topics included in our earlier examples.[2] All three of these topics entail participants' prior knowledge, of word meanings, of conceptual categories, and even of individual conceptual or semantic organization, respectively.

In the first instance, however, traditional verbal learning was primarily concerned with the associative basis of meaning as reflected in *general* norms of the frequency of such associations, rather than with individual, *personal* meanings or with the participant's *intended* meaning. In the second case, the studies mentioned by Roediger (1991) do indeed represent a significant advance over traditional research on verbal learning and memory. Nevertheless, most of the examples he cites still involve fairly basic, low-level forms of semantic or conceptual knowledge; few really get at the kind of personally meaningful, individual knowledge that is entailed, for example, in autobiographical memory or person memory or political beliefs. It is simply the case, as I illustrated in the first example, that most traditional research on memory has tried to *control* for such personal meanings and prior knowledge and has tried to focus on basic processes and basic concepts that generalize across situations and contents.

In general, the argument from realism seems compelling, and certainly it was a major point in Neisser's (1978) original call to arms. However, such an argument also runs into some inevitable problems. First, it is clearly difficult to pin down exactly what is meant by the terms *real world* and *everyday*. What is real or everyday to one person may not be for another. The everyday clearly differs from one culture to another, as I discuss in detail in chapter 8. For example, the everyday life of the rice farmers of Liberia (Cole, Gay, Glick, & Sharp, 1971) or the Puluwatan navigators of Micronesia (Gladwin, 1970; Hutchins, 1983), to be discussed in chapter 8, is clearly dif-

---

[2]Along these lines, Roediger might have cited numerous studies on discourse processing, on memory for conversation, and a whole host of research in social cognition concerned with person memory, memory for stereotypes, the impact of attitudes and political expertise on memory and information processing, to name just a few.

ferent from that of the citizens of urban America. More subtly, the real world of the ghetto black is clearly different from that of the Madison Avenue executive, which is in turn different from the real world of the midwestern farmer. The real world of the computer-literate person is certainly different from that of a remnant of the precomputer age; and the real world of university professors is often distressingly different from that of their students. Thus, any attempt to say what is and what is not realistic or everyday would seem to be doomed to failure because there exist so many different versions of the everyday.

Following Brunswik (1956), Woods (1993) suggested that instead of looking at how realistic or real-world a research situation is, psychologists should instead be examining the representativeness of that situation, that is, the degree to which the situation is related to the "class of situations that is the target of the study" (Woods, 1993, p. 231; see my later discussion of Wyer, Lambert, Budesheim, & Gruenfeld, 1992, for a somewhat similar position). This requires a careful analysis of both the task environment and the target domain or situations to determine what the effective stimuli are in the latter situation that should be duplicated in the former. Needless to say, this requires a detailed theory of what factors are and are not a consideration; and of course it also requires a clear statement of exactly what situations to generalize to. Such an examination is certainly a valuable exercise to sharpen up one's thinking about what is meant by the real world; however, it is not entirely clear to me that such a full-blown form of this is necessary for every study of everyday cognition.

Another qualification from the literature on social psychology, where realism has always been an issue, is the argument that realism for its own sake may not be of great value. Specifically, many years ago Aronson and Carlsmith (1968) distinguished between what they called *experimental* and *mundane* realism. Mundane realism refers to

> the similarity of events occurring in the laboratory to those likely to occur in the "real world." ... The very fact that an event looks like one that occurs in the "real world" does not mean that it is important to the study of human behavior. Many events that occur in the real world are boring or uninfluential. (Aronson & Carlsmith, 1968, p. 22)

Thus, for example, mindless driving on the freeway or typing at a word processor or cleaning house may all represent everyday, real-world activities for some people, as might more creative problem solving, high-level skilled performance, or exceptional feats of memory. From the point of view of Aronson and Carlsmith, the former activities would undoubtedly fit their definition of mundane realism and are probably not worthy of study. (For the record, many everyday cognitivists would *not* dismiss such activities so readily.) On the other hand, Aronson and Carlsmith also suggest that a study may have *experimental* realism "if the situation is realistic to the subjects—if they believe it, if they are forced to attend to it and take it seriously—if it has an impact on them" (p. 22). Certainly many researchers in social cognition would strive for the latter type of realism rather than or in addition to the former, whereas many everyday cognition researchers would not.

For my present purposes, the important point made by this distinction is that simply trying to recreate or capture the real world is not necessarily a worthy objective in and of itself. Some everyday situations are intrinsically interesting; others are not. Some involve intriguing or enigmatic or theoretically significant cognitive phenomena, whereas others do not. For example, it seems both intrinsically and theoretically interesting to study the thought processes of experts or people exceptional in some domain, and we will see that this has been a major topic in cognitive psychology in recent years (see Chi, Glaser, & Farr, 1988; Ericsson & Smith, 1991b). Similarly, it seems intrinsically interesting and theoretically significant to study the organization and retrieval of autobiographical memories. Thus, it may be argued that the study of everyday cognition should be restricted to phenomena that are intrinsically interesting or of some theoretical importance or that seem to shed light on cognitive processes that play a central role in our psychological functioning.

The obvious *problem* with this argument, of course, is that what is intrinsically interesting to one person may seem rather dull or irrelevant to another. For example, the study of skills in sports or chess may be of great interest to one person, whereas apprenticeships in tailoring or meat cutting (Lave & Wenger, 1989) or work in a dairy plant (Scribner, 1984a, 1986) may be fascinating to someone interested in the study of manual work. Those who are skilled in typing may find the discussion of research on that topic interesting, whereas the more academic question of the rationality or irrationality of human judgment may be more interesting to others. Clearly, it also takes a *theory*—implicit or explicit—to determine what cognitive processes or phenomena are major or central, which brings me back to the question of the role of theory and of generalizable psychological processes discussed earlier.

To summarize my discussion thus far, Table 1.1 presents the central issues that I have reviewed, along with the positions taken by both traditional memory researchers and everyday cognition researchers on each.

A Personal Viewpoint.   One of the problems with the debate over laboratory versus everyday studies of cognition is that the alternative positions have typically been stated in such extreme, even inflammatory terms—from Neisser's (1978) assertion that little if anything of practical, real-world interest has ever been studied by traditional memory researchers, to Banaji and Crowder's (1989) reference to the "bankruptcy" of everyday memory research, to Lave's view that all cognitive processes or engagements are completely situationally specific and that lab studies are practically useless—that oftentimes it seems that a lot more heat than light has been gen-

TABLE 1.1

Some of the Major Issues Regarding the Study of Everyday Cognition
and the Positions Taken by Traditional and Everyday Cognition Researchers on
These Issues

Issue	Traditional Laboratory Researchers	Everyday Cognition Researchers
1. The ability to generalize from lab research		Neisser: Such generalization is impossible, in principle (and in practice)
	Banaji & Crowder: There is a difference between ecological validity and generalizability	
	Banaji & Crowder: Researchers should be looking for theoretical rather than empirical generalizability	
		Conway, Ceci, & Bronfenbrenner: Traditional lab researchers have adopted an inappropriate model taken from the physical sciences
		Conway: Researchers should be looking at the personal meanings attached by individuals to objects and events rather than assuming that these stimuli determine thoughts
		Ceci & Bronfenbrenner: Researchers should be seeking principles describing the interactions between cognitive processes and situations rather than "invariant mechanisms"
		Situated cognitivists: Thinking and intelligence are specific to the situation, and hence cannot be generalized from lab situations
2. The importance of experimental control	Banaji & Crowder: Control is needed to reduce the complexity of a situation and its causal structure	

3. The importance of realistic content and context		
	Roediger: The evidence cited by everyday cognition researchers involves greater control that these researchers acknowledge	
		Rubin: Psychological research moved into the lab too quickly; we need to concentrate on discovering regularity rather than imposing control
		Conway, Rubin: "Realistic" or real-world materials are needed to engage the meaning and background knowledge of the participant
	Aronson & Carlsmith: There is a difference between mundane and experimental realism, and the latter is more important than the former	
		Woll: It's difficult to pin down what the "real world" is because that world differs for different people

erated by these interchanges. (There has also been a certain amount of misrepresentation of the opposing point of view.) Such extreme, controversial assertions have certainly provoked a good deal of interest in the topic; and each has apparently spoken to and, at least in the case of Neisser, galvanized a certain constituency into action (see Baddeley & Wilkins, 1984, for a description of the reaction of the Practical Aspects of Memory conference participants to Neisser's speech). At the same time, however, the strength and extremity of these assertions have also alienated others and have interfered with a rational, evenhanded consideration of the issues involved (see Klatzky, 1991, and Tulving, 1991, for similar sentiments).

As you may expect, my own viewpoint lies somewhere in between the extreme of traditional experimental psychology on the one hand, and the extreme situated-cognition and lab-research-is-useless viewpoint on the other. There is clearly merit to Neisser (1978) and Rubin's (1988) arguments that cognitive research in general, and memory research in particular, have been concerned for too long *only* with what can be experimentally controlled, operationally defined, and subsumed under higher-order theoretical principles. Experimental control is certainly desirable in order to make confident causal statements,[3] but premature control when in the process of exploring new or unclearly understood phenomena is *not* necessarily desirable. In addition, the processes that we will be examining in this book—namely, encoding, memory retrieval, reasoning, problem solving, and judgment—are generally conceived of as knowledge-based processes, that is, processes that are dependent on existing knowledge or beliefs; in addition, if overly controlled, artificial experimental situations do not engage this knowledge or belief, psychologists cannot hope to understand these processes. To be sure, controlled research has its place when researchers get to the point of trying to test out alternative causal accounts of the nature of everyday thought; in subsequent chapters I discuss a number of cases in which such competitive tests have, in fact, been helpful. Nevertheless, such controlled research clearly has its limitations.

At the same time, there seems to be little value in simply compiling catalogues of everyday examples and minutia or getting caught up in interesting everyday phenomena for their own sake, unless, of course, those phenomena have some kind of applied, practical significance in their own right. As I argued earlier, there are simply too many everyday worlds and too many different sorts of everyday knowledge to make this a fruitful exercise. In general, everyday cognition should be studied to shed light on cognitive processes or forms of knowledge representation that have some degree of generality (see Bahrick, 1991, and Banaji & Crowder, 1989, p. 1188, for similar arguments).

Exactly what these "general" processes or forms of knowledge are, and *how* general they are, remain to be seen. For example, it seems plausible that such hard-wired or semi-hard-wired processes as sensory perception, attentional and memory capacities, and the like should be general across a variety of different domains (though see Chase & Ericsson, 1981, for a theory of skilled or expanded memory capacity among experts, to be discussed in chap. 7). At the same time, it seems likely that these sorts of processes will be of less interest to researchers in everyday cognition.[4] On the other hand, there may also be flexible "control" processes (Atkinson & Shiffrin, 1968) that apply over *certain* populations, *certain* categories of situations,[5] or both—for example, the problem-solving and judgment heuristics to be discussed in chapters 7 and 9, the specific rules of pragmatic reasoning (Cheng & Holyoak, 1985) to be discussed in chapter 9, or the encoding and retrieval structures used by experts in their particular domain of expertise to be discussed in chapter 7.

---

[3]The increased use and sophistication of causal modeling now offers one major alternative to traditional experimental methods (see Bahrick & Phelps, 1988, 1996, for a discussion of the use of regression techniques in memory research).

[4]Face recognition, which will be discussed in chapter 3, is a possible exception.

[5]Even Newell and Simon (1972) argued for the importance of considering not only the invariant mechanisms of thought, but also the task requirements of the environment.

This uncertainty about the exact form that these processes and structures may take makes it all the more important to study *everyday* cognition and the knowledge that underlies it, at least in part to determine how general or context-specific such cognitive phenomena are. Given the current debate between traditional experimental psychologists such as Banaji and Crowder on the one hand, and ethnographic researchers such as Lave, or ecological psychologists such as Neisser and Ceci and Bronfenbrenner on the other, research on everyday cognition in its broadest sense—research that allows participants to bring to bear the knowledge that they use in their everyday lives—seems to me to be particularly valuable. In this sense, or measured simply in terms of its current popularity, research on everyday cognition *as a tool of contemporary cognitive science* truly appears to be, as Neisser (1982b) observed, "an idea whose time has come" (p. 4).

DIFFERENCES BETWEEN EVERYDAY REASONING AND PROBLEM SOLVING AND THEIR LAB ANALOGUES

Thus far, I have been discussing the debate between advocates of naturalistic studies of everyday memory and those who argue for traditional laboratory studies of that topic. However, there have also been numerous discussions in the area of everyday reasoning and problem solving of the related question of how everyday problems differ from more formal, academic, or laboratory materials (see Galotti, 1989; Meacham & Emont, 1989; and Wagner & Sternberg, 1986, for listings of differences). These distinctions, many of which apply to the everyday memory literature as well, include the following:

1.   Most laboratory problems (such as the urn problem described earlier, a syllogism, or a story problem) as well as most content in laboratory studies of memory are of little personal relevance (Galotti, 1989) or of little interest in and of themselves, whereas most everyday problems and topics, whether they be financial (e.g., how to stretch your weekly budget), interpersonal (e.g., how to win back a lover's affections), political (e.g., how to vote on an initiative) or whatever, *are* of either personal or general affective significance to the problem solver. Stated differently, lab problems are typically decontextualized (Resnick, 1987a, 1991) or distanced from an individual's ordinary experience (Wagner & Sternberg, 1985).

2.   Along similar lines, laboratory problems or questions on intelligence tests are solved or answered "for their own sake" (Galotti, 1989, p. 335), whereas everyday problems are solved in order to accomplish other goals—for instance, to get promoted, to keep a marriage together, to finance a vacation, or simply to avoid having to get up from your easy chair. Scribner (1986), in particular, has emphasized the fact that "practical" (i.e., everyday) thinking is "thinking that is embedded in the larger

purposive activities of daily life and that functions to achieve the goals of those activities" (p. 15). Along similar lines, as I have discussed, Lave (1988; Lave et al., 1984) has distinguished between the solving of arithmetic problems for their own sake, as in school math, and the practice of mathematics in the service of other goals, as in grocery shopping or street math. Finally, topics in everyday *memory*, such as memory for people, places, and life experiences, can also be viewed in this same context, that is, these memories serve other goals or "the larger purposive activities of daily life."

3. Laboratory problems and memory tasks are typically selected or constructed by other people (Wagner & Sternberg, 1986), such as an experimenter, a teacher, or some other authority, rather than by participants themselves or by the context (although it may be argued that many problems in everyday life are also provided by others—parents, employers, spouses—or by circumstances beyond one's control). Thus, for example, you may be given an assignment by an instructor where you have to understand a problem on her or his terms, and you may approach this problem very differently from a problem that you formulate for yourself, such as how to earn money to pay for college tuition. (It strikes me that a paradigmatic instance of Examples 2 and 3, as well as some of the other features to be listed below, is the crossword puzzle, particularly of the New York Times variety.)

4. Similarly, in everyday problem solving other people often serve as an aid in recognizing and defining the problem, searching for relevant information, and in generating solutions (see chap. 10). Meacham and Emont (1989) give the example of the Maier two-string problem (in which the task is to tie together two strings hanging from the ceiling just out of reach of each other), and they point out that the most obvious solution to this problem for most participants would be to ask the experimenter for help by holding one of the strings (rather than the prescribed solution of using a heavy object as a weight to swing one string over to where the participant is holding the other extended string). Yet help from others was not one of the solutions allowed by Maier (1930, 1931). Similarly, we frequently rely on friends, spouses, or parents to help us to "see" problems and to offer solutions or just give us information to help us solve a problem on our own.[6]

5. Along similar lines, Resnick (1987a; see also Scribner, 1986) stressed that problem solving in class (and in most lab studies) involves symbol manipulation in the head, whereas problem solving out of class typically involves the use of tools. These tools may be complex machines (e.g.,

---

[6]Ironically, one of the current movements in instruction is an emphasis on cooperative learning (e.g., Slavin, 1983).

computers, calculators) or common, everyday objects (e.g., cooking utensils, pens and pencils; see discussion in chap. 10 of the notion of intelligence being distributed over these tools and instruments).

6.   As far as the actual structure of the problem is concerned, laboratory problem-solving tasks typically provide all the necessary information and premises from the outset (Galotti, 1989), as in formal logic or mathematical problems. Everyday problems, on the other hand, often entail premises that are either implicit (as in inferring a specific political position from a candidate's position on other issues), changeable (Perkins, 1989), or are simply not provided. Therefore, everyday problem solvers must either collect or provide the necessary information for themselves (Perkins, 1989), or they may *never* have all the information (e.g., the motives and culprits in the assassination of John F. Kennedy, the source of your fears on a given topic).

7.   Lab problems and traditional memory tasks are typically well-defined (Wagner & Sternberg, 1985) and self-contained (Galotti, 1989), whereas everyday problems (and concepts in general) are typically open-ended (see Bartlett, 1958). Thus, for example, interpersonal, political, and career problems are certainly more complex and open-ended than are the kinds of well-defined, explicitly stated problems used in most lab studies of problem solving. Laboratory and formal problem solving or reasoning also involve rather clear, well-established rules or methods of inference (Galotti, 1989; Nickerson, 1991) and a single method of solution, as in math or logical reasoning, whereas everyday problems or reasoning, such as that in the interpersonal domain, does not (see Simon, 1973, for a distinction between well-structured and ill-structured problems).

8.   Laboratory and formal problems involve single correct solutions that are tested separately (Meacham & Emont, 1989), in a one-at-a-time manner. Everyday problems, on the other hand, may have a variety of solutions that "vary in quality" (Galotti, 1989, p. 335), and these problems and solutions may be interrelated. Thus, there may be many different ways in which to finance a son's or daughter's education, and these different ways may be evaluated as better or worse and may be judged in the context of other problems (e.g., the possible effect of taking on more hours at work on family relations or your own health). Along these same lines, laboratory problems are sufficiently clear-cut or well-defined so that the problem-solvers—or at least the experimenter or tester—can be certain when these problems have been correctly solved (or the material to be remembered is correctly recalled). In addition, there is often immediate feedback. In everyday problems—particularly interpersonal or social problems—it is not always clear that a problem has been solved (or that a memory has been accurately recalled—cf. the discussion in chap. 5

of autobiographical memory) or that the solution is adequate. Alternatively, feedback may be delayed for a considerable length of time (Meacham & Emont, 1989). Thus, for example, it may take weeks or even months to determine whether a surgical or exercise solution to a medical problem has been effective, and it may take years to know if a financial or child-rearing decision has had desirable results.

9. As Perkins (1985a, 1989) pointed out, in formal reasoning one must evaluate only the arguments for one side in terms of their internal consistency, whereas in informal problems there are typically arguments on both sides of an issue to be evaluated, both competitively and in terms of the consistency of each with a general position. (Kuhn, 1991, has even made the case that arguments in everyday reasoning are always, at least implicitly, two-sided.) Thus, for example, in a logical proof the problem solver need only worry about the consistency of the solution with the premises or chain of arguments, whereas reaching a conclusion on a political position (e.g., the impeachment of a President) or a personal problem (e.g., which job offer to take) requires comparing two or more positions as well as the consistency among the arguments for each position.

10. Similarly, problem-solving tasks in the lab typically allow only a limited amount of time for solution, whereas everyday problems often entail longer solution times; or as Willis and Schaie (1993) have put it, everyday problem solving is recursive and frequently requires several passes through different versions of the problem over a period of days, weeks, or even years before one arrives at a final solution (if that ever occurs). The obvious contrast here is between a participant trying to solve a laboratory problem within the allotted hour versus taking months to decide on a job change or whether to get married.

11. Finally, in keeping with our earlier observations, everyday memory and problem solving are generally much more situation- or domain-specific (Resnick, 1987a) than the general solutions involved in laboratory problem solving; and they depend more on characteristics of the environment (Scribner, 1986). Thus, the rules of math and language are assumed to apply across multiple instances and contexts (though see chap. 8), but the same is not true for, say, the rules of interpersonal problem-solving or job skills. In chapter 7, I discuss in detail the two related questions of *domain-specificity,* or the degree to which knowledge and skills are restricted to a given topic, and *transfer of training,* or the ability to apply a solution or principle learned in one context to another.

These several distinctions are summarized in Table 1.2.

TABLE 1.2

Some Differences Between Real-World and Laboratory Memory Tasks and Between Everyday and Formal Problem Solving

Difference	Example
1. Of personal interest or not	The study of your memory for your own past versus memory for an arbitrary passage or word list
2. Solved or learned for its own sake or in service of some other goal	Searching for a word to express an idea in a job application or love letter versus searching for a word in a crossword puzzle
3. Problem formulated by yourself or by some other person	Mixing ingredients on your own (e.g., brewing beer) versus conducting a chemistry experiment assigned by an instructor
4. Other people involved (or not) in recognition, definition, and solution of problem	Discussing a financial problem with family or friends versus performing alone in a lab
5. Tools or props used in problem solution or solving "in your head"	Using a calculator or unit prices (in grocery store) versus solving an arithmetic problem in your head
6. Missing information or premises versus all required information provided	An interpersonal problem in which it is not clear what all the relevant factors are versus word problems in school in which all information is provided
7. Problem involves well-defined structure and rules or not	A career or a marital decision versus a problem in formal logic
8. Problem has clear-cut solution or not, and problem solver knows when solution has been reached or not	A long-term investment decision versus an arithmetic problem to answer before next class
9. Emphasis on internal consistency of arguments on one side versus competitive test of alternative sides	Consideration of a political issue versus a problem in formal logic
10. Greater versus lesser times provided for solution	Determining the cause of an illness over a period of months or years versus a 20-minute lab problem
11. Solution is specific to situation or not	Dealing with different friends or students in different ways versus learning a general rule of logic or math

Note. Each example presents the everyday case first.

Application to Intelligence Testing and Instruction

To this point, I have discussed several differences between everyday reasoning and problem solving on the one hand, and *formal* reasoning or *laboratory* problem solving on the other. A similar case can be made for the differences between everyday reasoning and *academic intelligence* or traditional classroom instruction. For example, as I demonstrate in chapters 7 and 10, commentators in both education and mental testing have stressed the limitations of decontextualized knowledge, or cognitive processes abstracted out of their real-world settings, as occurs in most classrooms and in traditional intelligence tests. Investigators such as Brown, Collins, and Duguid (1989; see also Lave, 1988) have used the term *situated cognition* to refer to thinking and instruction that takes the situational context and individuals' everyday knowledge into account (see chap. 10). Similarly, Wagner and Sternberg have distinguished between traditional conceptions of knowledge and intelligence and what they have variously referred to as *practical intelligence* (Sternberg & Caruso, 1985; Sternberg & Wagner, 1986), *tacit knowledge* (Wagner & Sternberg, 1985), and most recently, *street smarts* (Wagner & Sternberg, 1990) or *common sense* (Sternberg, Wagner, Williams, & Horvath, 1995), all of which terms refer to a kind of real-world, informal knowledge distinct from formal school-based skills. Thus, the issue here is not only the limitations of *laboratory* research on memory and problem solving but also the limitations of traditional approaches to intelligence testing and classroom instruction.

Application to Real-World Judgment

These same distinctions have also been applied to the areas of *judgment* and *decision making*. Researchers on these topics have recently attempted to distinguish between formal decision models or tasks on the one hand and models of *everyday* decision making on the other. For example, Orasanu and Connolly (1993) identified eight features of what I earlier called naturalistic decision making, or the kinds of tasks facing firefighters, computer programmers, emergency room physicians or nurses, and others who have to make quick or difficult decisions in the real world (see Klein, 1989; Zsambok & Klein, 1997). These tasks involve *ill-structured problems* (Simon, 1973), or problems that do not have a clear solution or clear steps to such a solution. Such tasks are also characterized by "Shifting, ill-defined, or competing" goals (Orasanu & Connelly, 1993, p. 7) and by missing and uncertain information (Klein, 1989) and a changing, shifting environment. Finally, such decisions also entail "time stress," "high stakes," and "multiple players" (Orasanu & Connolly, 1993, p. 7). With the exception of the question of time pressures, which really applies primarily to the specific kinds of decision-making reviewed by Klein, all of the features outlined by Orasanu and Connelly overlap with those I discussed in connection with reasoning and problem-solving.

The Relationships Among Everyday Memory, Reasoning, and Judgment

Before moving to a discussion of some actual models of everyday cognition, it may be useful to clarify the relationship between everyday problem solving and judgment on the one hand and everyday memory on the other. First, it is clear that everyday reasoning and problem solving draw on background knowledge in long-term memory. This background knowledge may serve, for example, as a premise for problem solution (e.g., your beliefs about men or women and your knowledge about how to flirt as a basis for determining how to catch a husband or wife), as a guide for encoding or judging (or even generating) arguments and evidence (e.g., your knowledge of the nuts and bolts of politics as a basis for making sense out of a particular legislative maneuver), or as a basis for evaluating solutions or decision alternatives (e.g., which study strategy works best). Furthermore, as these examples suggest, it seems likely that this stored knowledge is typically of the informal, real-world variety. For example, a juror's interpretation and judgments of evidence and their verdicts (e.g., Pennington & Hastie, 1986) may depend on that jurist's background assumptions about, for instance, the likelihood of the police planting evidence or about the generality of domestic violence. For that matter, jurists are often instructed to use their common sense in evaluating the evidence (see Kuhn, Weinstock, & Flaton, 1994, for an alternative view of jurors' common sense).

On the other hand, as I discuss in chapters 4 and 6, a number of commentators, particularly those writing on the topic of "dynamic memory" (e.g., Kolodner, 1983a; Schank, 1982a), have argued that reasoning and problem solving are involved in the processes of understanding, building knowledge representations, and retrieval; and this would seem to be particularly true for *everyday* memory and problem-solving. Thus, for instance, recalling one's last encounter with an old high school or college friend may involve puzzling about the possible circumstances (e.g., a school reunion) under which or the location (e.g., one's old home town or that friend's home) where such an encounter might have taken place. Understanding or reconstructing the plot of a TV program or movie or even an episode from your own personal history requires problem solving and question posing; and these processes are in turn guided by additional, oftentimes common-sense background knowledge. Therefore, research on everyday memory is not only *analogous* to research on everyday reasoning; the two processes are inextricably linked. (See Fig. 1.1.)

Along similar lines, Simon (1973) and Luszcz (1989) have both discussed some of the differences between the kinds of knowledge involved in solving well-structured versus ill-structured (or informal) problems. Simon (1973), for example, pointed out that ill-structured problems require a greater amount of stored knowledge than do well-structured ones (see also Schank, 1982a); and thus a major task in solving the former problems is to sort

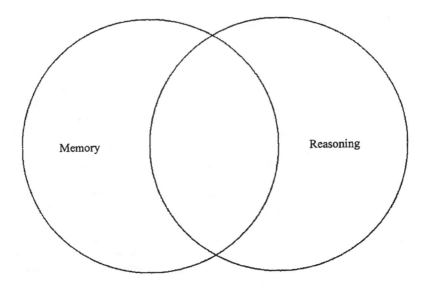

FIG. 1.1.   The overlap between everyday memory and reasoning.

through this catalog of knowledge and determine exactly what pieces of knowledge are relevant to solution. As Luszcz (1989) stated, reasoning with ill-structured or everyday problems entails a "relatively greater contribution of long-term memory in the search through the problem space" (p. 28; though see the discussions by Cole, 1996, Resnick, 1991, and Simon, 1973, of the use of external, culturally provided tools in ill-structured problems). Luszcz also noted that well-structured problems (e.g., math, logic, chess, physics) typically involve technical, and "codified" knowledge, "including a notation system that is acquired through an explicit learning experience" (pp. 25–26), whereas ill-structured or everyday problems tap into "'natural' knowledge, which lacks a notation system and usually is acquired incidentally" (p. 26). Such natural knowledge obviously corresponds, at least in part, to the kind of everyday, practical knowledge that I discussed in the first section. That is, it entails knowledge that is acquired informally and encoded imprecisely, which is difficult to articulate (see the Wagner & Sternberg, 1985, concept of tacit knowledge) and is retrieved in an unspecified way. Thus, the bottom line is that everyday problem solving typically involves the kind of memory content that I discussed earlier.

The Uses and Usefulness of Everyday Cognition Research

There are a number of ways in which research on everyday cognition can make a valuable contribution to the cognitive sciences (see Baddeley &

Wilkins, 1984; G. Cohen, 1989). First, naturalistic observations and exploratory studies of everyday cognition can serve as the basis for more controlled, parametric studies of cognitive processes and structures (see Klatzky, 1991). For example, as I discuss in chapter 8, Cole (1996; Cole et al., 1971), Scribner (1984a, 1986), and others have argued for the importance of conducting ethnographic research before designing experiments or more rigorous studies, in order to get the lay of the land, so to speak. Similarly, research on a number of topics that I will be discussing—for instance, *prospective memory* (e.g., Harris, 1984; Meacham & Leiman, 1975, 1982), or remembering to carry out intentions, *flashbulb memories* (Brown & Kulik, 1977), or individuals' recall for their personal circumstances when some significant event occurred (e.g., a presidential assassination or a major earthquake), face recognition—is partially motivated by everyday observations.

At the other end of the research process, naturalistic studies such as case histories (e.g., of patients suffering from amnesia or brain damage), diary studies (e.g., Linton, 1978, 1982; Wagenaar, 1986; Young, Hay, & Ellis, 1985a), and field studies (e.g., Baddeley & Hitch, 1977; Lave et al., 1984) can be useful as means of testing the limits or the real-world implications of established theories or laboratory-based principles of memory and cognition. As Cohen (1989) put it, "laboratory research has a tendency, left to itself, to become incestuous, endlessly exploring its own paradigms. Everyday research acts as a corrective to this tendency by opening up new lines of inquiry" (p. 14). Thus, for example, in chapter 5 I look at the implications of research on autobiographical memory for more traditional models of memory, and in chapters 8 and 9 I examine the degree to which laboratory-based models of problem solving and judgment hold up in real world, naturalistic settings. Thus, research on everyday thinking can serve a useful function at both ends of the traditional research process in cognitive psychology, or in some cases it can actually stand on its own (see chap. 8).

In addition, everyday cognition research can also help to shed light on specific, practically or socially important issues, for example, eyewitness testimony, the ways to get patients to remember to take their medicine, ways to get students to apply their everyday knowledge to academic subject matter (and vice versa). Optimally, of course, this latter function should fit into a more general theoretical context or follow from the study of more general (or more generally describable) cognitive processes, but this is not necessarily the case (e.g., Gruneberg et al., 1978, 1988). Finally, everyday cognition research provides the opportunity to study one-of-a-kind phenomena (e.g., Neisser's [1981] case study of John Dean's memories of Watergate), special populations (e.g., the study of autobiographical memory among amnesia victims), or phenomena that are difficult or unethical to reproduce in the laboratory (e.g., the recall of early childhood traumas, or the retention of material over long—i.e., years—intervals; see Bahrick & Phelps, 1988; Bahrick et al., 1975). Thus, research on everyday cognition can be useful in a number of different ways, and, as I hope you will see throughout this book, it can also be damn interesting.

THE SOCIAL AND CULTURAL DIMENSIONS: SOME OF THE DIFFERENCES BETWEEN THE EVERYDAY COGNITION OF SOCIAL AND NONSOCIAL OBJECTS

In a chapter titled "The Sovereignty of Social Cognition," Tom Ostrom (1984) has outlined a number of apparent distinctions between *social* and *nonsocial* cognition. Several of these distinctions are relevant to our present discussion, especially because it seems clear that a major defining feature of the "everyday" is its *social* content and its *social* context. For example, social objects and concepts are typically less clear-cut and generally more complex than nonsocial objects, in part because people and social institutions are more variable (see Abelson & Kanouse, 1966; Borgida & Brekke, 1981) and more individual than nonsocial objects, but also because social actors and agencies often behave in ways that belie their internal states or intentions (Ostrom, 1984). For example, it is often difficult to get a clear reading on other people's feelings and motives; and you need only sit through a political campaign (or a Presidential scandal) to realize how tricky it is to draw confident inferences about political candidates, parties, or institutions.

Second, social cognition clearly involves material that is personally relevant and, as Ostrom (1984) pointed out, *self*-relevant. As we have seen, these are qualities that apply to everyday cognition in general; but they seem less critical to our thinking about *non*social objects (if you believe that there are such things) than to our interaction with social beings. For example, relationships with other people are certainly more personal and self-relevant (for most people) than their relationship with their computer (although the internet has certainly introduced a social, and even a cultural component to computers; see my discussion in chap. 10). According to Ostrom (see also Fiske, 1992), social cognition is also concerned with action and its consequences, although to date, relatively little social cognitive research has actually focused on this topic (though see Gollwitzer & Bargh, 1996). To complicate things further, social cognition entails active participants and their *intersubjectivity*—that is, the shared, *inter*acting subjective states of the participants—a feature that is obviously unique to social cognition. However, as Ostrom pointed out, this important issue of intersubjectivity is probably the feature of social cognition on which the least amount of research has actually been done (though see the recent research on social representations theory, e.g., Breakwell & Canter, 1993; Jodelet, 1989).

This comparison of social cognition with everyday cognition points to an interesting irony in the former area. Specifically, I have suggested that social cognition is in many respects *the* most prototypical form of everyday cognition—after all, what could be more everyday or real-world than interaction with other people and social institutions? At the same time, research on social cognition has focused almost exclusively on *laboratory* research such as person memory, stereotype judgments, and causal attributions, and on verbal materials in particular (see Gilbert, 1998, for a discussion of this limitation), and has primarily been concerned with the construction of general process models (e.g., Chaiken & Trope, 1999; E. R. Smith & DeCoster, 1998a, 1998b; Wyer & Srull, 1989). In a very real sense, social cognition has seemed intent on "outsciencing" the cognitive sciences from which it has drawn its inspiration. In the process, social cognition, in general, has not only shied away from more naturalistic research outside the lab (see Skowronski, Betz, Thompson, & Shannon, 1991, and Woll & Van Der Meer, 1996, for two notable exceptions)[7] but has also paid little attention to research on everyday cognition (see the texts in social cognition by Fiske & Taylor, 1991, and by Kunda, 1999) or to the place of social cognition within this area. (In this book I chose to include two chapters—chaps. 2 and 9—that *have* been of some interest to social cognitivists, because I believe that these topics—memory for people and judgment biases—are clearly relevant to the topic of everyday cognition. However, these chapters clearly stand out from the others in terms of their style of research, and the topics will be ones that researchers in everyday cognition will least identify with.)

As one striking example of this point, consider an influential book by Wyer and Srull (1989) titled *Memory and Cognition in Its Social Context* (to be discussed in detail in chap. 3). Despite the intriguing title of this book and the authors' discussion of the differences between the concerns of cognitive psychology and those of social cognition, it is noteworthy that the book contains not one shred of nonlaboratory evidence for such a "social context." In fact, Wyer et al. (1992) have themselves acknowledged the possible limitations of the conditions under which their person memory model has been formulated and tested:

> The Person Memory model has been rigorously tested under very circumscribed instructional and information-presentation conditions. ... One can easily question the extent to which the impression formation processes that occur under these conditions resemble those that occur in other situations in which people receive information about persons. For one thing, much of the information we receive about a person is conveyed in a social context. (pp. 5–6)

At the same time, Wyer et al. (1992) also argued that "the assertion that the results obtained in one situation do not generalize to other situations is vacuous unless one can state precisely what differences exist between the situations and what specific effect these differences are likely to have" (pp. 6–7). Wyer et al. insisted that such a specification requires that a well-developed theory be available for at least one of these situations in order to iden-

---

[7]See also the *Handbook of Social Cognition* (Wyer & Srull, 1994) for examples of real-world applications of social cognitive principles and research.

tify what the critical differences should be. Such a sentiment clearly harkens back to my earlier discussion of the role of theory in establishing generalizability in cognitive processes, as well as to the Brunswikian concept of representativeness mentioned earlier. (Notice, however, that there is one subtle, but critical difference between the Brunswikian position and the argument by Wyer et al. Specifically, whereas Brunswik talked about determining representativeness in order to *do* the research, Wyer et al. asked for a justification in terms of representativeness for *critics* who would argue *against* the generalizability of experimental results.) The rather stringent requirement that an investigator be able to *specify* the critical situational conditions and their *specific* effect (i.e., rather than simply outlining the general differences listed above) also reflects the kind of premature rigor Rubin took exception to in our earlier discussion.

This exclusive focus on lab research is particularly ironic given the interest expressed by many traditional social theorists (e.g., Bartlett, 1932; Goffman, 1959; Heider, 1958) in everyday knowledge. The *restrictiveness* of social cognition is also of interest in view of the great debate in the 1970s—the so-called *crisis in social psychology* (see Gergen, 1973)—regarding the overemphasis on laboratory methods and the lack of relevance in social psychological research. As Jones (1985) described it, this crisis has proved, in retrospect, to be simply a "minor perturbation in the long history of the social sciences" (p. 100), a conclusion cited by Banaji and Crowder (1989) as a model for the current debate over the everyday relevance of cognitive psychology. Note that the arguments that I have raised are not directed simply toward the vague problem of relevance, but rather to the question of how well laboratory research can successfully engage the kinds of cognitive processes and knowledge structures that are applicable to everyday situations. Furthermore, this book is an expression of my expectation that the current everyday cognition movement will make more than a minor perturbation in social cognition as well as in cognitive psychology in general.

As a kind of footnote, I should note that a somewhat greater concern with everyday cognition has been shown by *European* social psychologists and by the recent *cultural psychology* movement (e.g., Cole, 1996; Shweder, 1990). In the former case, Potter and Wetherell (1987), among others, have proposed a *discourse psychology* that focuses on everyday speech and conversation and the function of language in helping us to find meaning in our everyday life. In addition, Moscovici (1961) has put forward an influential viewpoint referred to as *social representations* theory, which is concerned with collective, shared beliefs or knowledge within a cultural group and the effect of such beliefs on everyday topics such as the representation of gender (e.g., Duveen & Lloyd, 1993), work (e.g., Mannetti & Tanucci, 1993), and mental illness (e.g., Jodelet, 1989). In the second case, cultural psychologists have argued for the importance of considering the cultural context of cognitive phenomena, including the context of the research lab. The important point for our purposes is that these different approaches are concerned with everyday knowledge, whether it be collective or individual, and oftentimes, with research in real-world settings.

SOME MODELS OF EVERYDAY COGNITION

In this last section I will present a set of prominent models of cognition in general, and of everyday cognition in particular, which I mention repeatedly in the chapters to follow. Because each model will be applied to more than one topic (and a few will be applied to several), these models will serve as both a conceptual aid and also a means for integrating the different areas of everyday cognition that I will explore.

The Associative Network Viewpoint

One of the most traditional models of human thought, in both philosophy and psychology, is that of *associationism,* or in its most recent incarnation, the so-called *associative network* or *neo-associative model,* particularly as exemplified by J. A. Anderson and Bower's (1973) *human associative memory (HAM) model.* According to the HAM model, *declarative* or factual knowledge is represented in terms of a network of elementary units (e.g., in the HAM model, concepts or *nodes*) connected by means of associative links to form *propositions,* or sentence-like assertions. Each proposition includes (a) a fact, consisting of a subject and a predicate, plus (b) a context, consisting of time and location. The subject amounts to an agent of an action, and the predicate consists of a relation, such as a verb, comparative, or preposition, plus an object—for instance, "__loves himself," "__went to the party," "__lives in that house." Thus, a proposition that may be relevant to everyday memory is "I first met my girlfriend in my Introductory Psychology class in 1990," as an experience recalled in autobiographical memory. In this proposition, the subject is "I," the predicate is "met my girlfriend," the location is "in my Introductory Psychology class," and the time is "in 1990."

One elaboration on this model is the *spreading activation* concept of Collins and Loftus (1975), which suggests that activation of one concept or node results in the "spread" of excitation from that node to all associatively related nodes such that these related concepts also become more accessible in memory. Thus, for example, seeing a picture of your old girlfriend may activate that first meeting and make it more recallable; or simply thinking about your first year of college may also activate that same memory.

One other point to be noted is that, according to J. A. Anderson and Bower (1973), this network of propositions exists in a static, *strategy-free* component of memory, and cognitive, strategic processes operate on this knowledge. Thus, declarative knowledge is basically a passive storehouse; even spreading activation operates in an automatic, nonstrategic manner.

Although associationism has a long history in philosophy and psychology, traditional associationism and the neo-associative HAM model play a greatly reduced role in current cognitive psychology. Nevertheless, there are a number of examples of associative models and also their assumptions in the everyday memory area. For instance, I give some examples of the elementary units assumption in models of the structure of face memory in chapter 3. In addition, there are a number of applications of the associative model within *social* cognition, particularly in accounts of person memory (see Fig. 1.2 for an example), as well as some scattered examples in the areas of prospective and autobiographical memory. In addition, I look at some current versions of network models in the form of *neural* networks to be described in a later section of this chapter. Finally, the neo-associative model serves as a standard against which to compare the several other models I will examine in this book (and also serves to point out the limitations of simple passive, elemental models of memory and thought).

Procedural or Production Systems Models

One alternative to a simple associative network model and/or a simple declarative knowledge approach is what has been called a *procedural* or *production systems* model (see J. R. Anderson, 1976; 1983; Newell & Simon, 1972). As these labels indicate, this sort of model is concerned with our knowledge of procedures or how to do something, such as knowing how to operate a

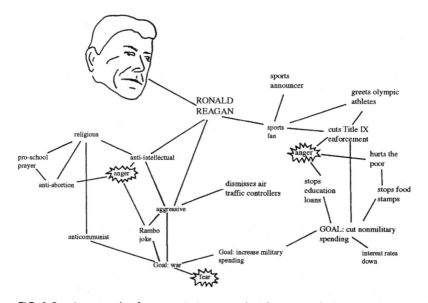

FIG. 1.2. An example of an associative network: A fragment of one person's memories for Ronald Reagan. From "A Primer of Information Processing Theory for the Political Scientist" by R. Hastie, 1986. In *Politcal Cognition: The 19th Annual Carnegie Mellon Symposium on Cognition* (pp. 11–39) edited by R. R. Lau & D. O. Sears, Mahwah, NJ: Lawrence Erlbaum Associates. Copyright © 1986 by Lawrence Erlbaum Associates. Reprinted with permission.

clutch in an automobile, how to save face in an awkward situation, or how to calculate a fraction. (A frequent way of stating this is that procedural knowledge is concerned with knowing how, whereas declarative memory is concerned with knowing that.)

The most familiar form of such a model is J. R. Anderson's (1983) revised *adaptive control of thought (ACT*)* model. According to this model, the basic unit of memory, or at least of procedural memory, is, appropriately enough, the procedure, which in this view corresponds to an "if–then" rule, where the "if" refers to a condition which must be met, and the "then" refers to an operation or action that is carried out if or when that condition is satisfied. Thus, for example, "if I shift from one gear to another, then I must depress the clutch," or "if I make a large purchase, then I use my American Express card."

J. R. Anderson (1983) makes it clear that procedural and propositional or declarative knowledge are not mutually exclusive. In fact, Neves and J. R. Anderson (1981) have argued that "all incoming knowledge is encoded declaratively; specifically the information is encoded as a set of facts in a semantic network" (p. 60), and only gradually becomes transformed into procedures by means of *proceduralization*. Proceduralization, as I develop in chapter 7, is the process by which a procedure that is simply "known" gradually or eventually becomes automatic. Again, an example here is the way in which novice drivers or novice word processors have to start off thinking carefully about what they "know" about depressing the clutch or merging documents. Over time, however, these procedures become second-nature, requiring little actual conscious thought. In fact, one of the attractions of the procedural model is that it accounts for seemingly automatic, unconscious knowledge or skills, whether they be automatic inferences about an object or behavior, about what to do in a given situation, or what mental operation to perform in thought or language.

One of the major advantages of the procedural knowledge model in the context of everyday cognition and reasoning—and again, the ACT* model is simply the best known example of that viewpoint—is that it accounts for the ease and aplomb with which individuals carry out the tasks of everyday life, and the tasks that people become expert at through daily experiences. For example, tying one's shoes, making a sandwich, driving a car, starting up a conversation with a stranger—all of these are everyday skills that were once declarative and thoughtful, but have since become second nature (for some). Similarly, each individual has also perfected his or her own particular array of proceduralized skills, whether they be typing or word processing, or physical skills such as dribbling a basketball or ice-skating, or cognitive skills such as math calculations or linguistic productions, or social skills such as being assertive or making excuses. In general, it is clear that quick, efficient, and skilled performance—both cognitive and behavioral— is both necessary to and prevalent in our daily lives, and hence the procedural viewpoint is an important one for our purposes.

I return to the topic of cognitive skills and a more detailed discussion of the process of proceduralization in chapter 7; and in chapter 8 I review some examples of research on everyday reasoning that use such proceduralized skills. Finally, in chapter 9 I discuss some of the cognitive procedures that lead to biases in judgment and reasoning.

Schema or Knowledge Structure Models

A major opposing position to the associationist viewpoint, whether it be traditional associationism or the revised neo-associative network model, is what might be called the *schema* or *knowledge structure* (Galambos, Abelson, & Black, 1986) viewpoint. The common argument of this point of view is that incoming information is encoded in terms of, and retrieval of stored information is guided by, generic, abstracted themes or structures, rather than in terms of specific items or simple inter-item links. For example, your memory for or judgment of a particular fraternity member or a female executive may be influenced by your general conception of fraternity members or appropriate roles for women or executives; and your memory for a particular experience at a party or a restaurant may be colored by your general schema for party or restaurant behavior. This point has been stated nicely by Minsky (1975) in a general observation about theories in the cognitive sciences:

> It seems to me that the ingredients of most theories in artificial intelligence and in psychology have been on the whole too minute, local, and unstructured to account—either practically or phenomenologically—for the effectiveness of *common sense thought*. The "chunks" of reasoning, language, memory, and perception ought to be larger and more structured, ... in order to explain the apparent power of mental activities. (p. 211, italics added)

Perhaps the clearest statement of this view is the *schema-copy-plus-tag* model put forward by Graesser (e.g., Graesser, 1981; Graesser & Nakamura, 1982). According to this view, incoming information that is consistent with or typical of a generic schema (e.g., a general person schema, a general event or perceptual scene) is assimilated to that generic schema, or alternatively, to a copy of that schema, whereas information that does not fit with the schema is "tagged" and stored separately. As a result, at subsequent recall or recognition, it will be difficult to discriminate between which details were actually presented and which were simply inferred or incorporated by virtue of their typicality of the generic schema. Or as schema theory has typically been presented by commentators such as Alba and Hasher (1983; see also Brewer & Nakamura, 1984, and Neisser, 1976), schemas serve a variety of functions, including selection of relevant information to attend to, abstraction of themes from the pattern of information, normalization of information (i.e., adding or deleting that information to fit the schema), integration of information into a coherent whole, and inference-based retrieval—that is, recalling information in terms of its consistency with the schema.

As an example of these notions, let's say that a voter has a political schema or stereotype about left-wing liberals or right-wing conservatives. This schema may influence what that person attends to in listening to political speeches by liberals and conservatives; it may result in adding schema-consistent information and editing out schema-inconsistent information from these speeches; it may result in selective retrieval of schema-consistent information in attempts to justify that listener's conclusions about the liberals or conservatives. (I should note that there is disagreement among schema theorists about the relative advantage of schema-consistent versus -inconsistent information—see chaps. 2 and 4.) Thus, a schema is assumed to have a major impact on information processing, as well as being an important knowledge structure in its own right.

Although schema theory has a long philosophical history, its origins in psychology are usually traced to Bartlett's (1932) classic research on the effects of prior knowledge and the "effort after meaning" (p. 20) on one's memory for stories. In current cognitive psychology and social cognition, this general viewpoint takes a number of different forms. One version is the general *constructivist* (e.g., Bransford & Franks, 1972; Bransford & Johnson, 1973), and *reconstructivist* view of memory and understanding (e.g., Kolodner, 1983a; Neisser, 1967), or the view that encoding, retrieval, or both, involve construction or reconstruction of meaning via the interaction of presented material with background knowledge. Other forms can be found in such concepts as person and role schemas (e.g., Taylor & Crocker, 1981), prototypes (e.g., Rosch, 1975), scripts or generic event schemas (e.g., Abelson, 1981; Nelson, 1986; Schank & Abelson, 1977), to the more recent knowledge structure viewpoint of Abelson, Black, and their associates (e.g., Abelson & Black, 1986; Galambos et al., 1986), with all its variations, to be discussed in chapter 4.

Schema or knowledge structure views are so common within the everyday cognition area, and within cognitive psychology in general, that I hardly need cite examples at this point. However, by way of preview I might mention that schema concepts play a prominent role in research on memory for both faces and people. Theory and research on reconstructive processes have also been popular in autobiographical memory, as have concepts of general event representations (GERs; Nelson, 1986) in the *development* of such memory. Even more clearly, script theory and the succeeding view of "dynamic memory" put forward by Schank (1982a) will play a major role in our discussion of memory for events and autobiographical memory in chapters 4, 5, and 6. Finally, I will examine the role of a particular type of schema called pragmatic reasoning schemas (Cheng & Holyoak, 1985) in my discussion of judgment and reasoning in chapter 9.

An Exemplar-Based Model

One objection to the schema viewpoint is that we remember details as well as overall themes or inferences from these details (see Alba & Hasher, 1983, for a major critique of schema theory, and Roediger, 1991, for similar reservations). E. R. Smith and Zarate (1992; see also E. R. Smith, 1998) have proposed an *exemplar-based* model of social judgment, according to which memories for specific examples of prototypes or schemas, as well as information about the prototypes themselves, may influence our social judgments. As Smith and Zarate pointed out, this model derives from various context or exemplar theories of categorization (e.g., Medin & Schaeffer, 1978; Nosofsky, 1987; see E. E. Smith & Medin, 1981, for a summary) that argue that our categorization of new stimuli is influenced by comparison with stored exemplars, amongst other things (see Barsalou, 1987). Thus, for example, our categorization and judgment of a face, person, or any new experience may be influenced by our recall of other exemplars with similar faces or personalities or experiences, as well as by the context in which that new instance is experienced. E. R. Smith and Zarate (1992) gave the example of judging Saddam Hussein by noting his similarity to Adolf Hitler, even to the point of both having a mustache. (Recently, E. R. Smith, 1988, 1991, 1998, has also related this exemplar model to the **MINERVA** model of memory put forward by Hintzman, 1986, according to which schema or prototype effects can be approximated by an accumulation of many exemplars; see also E. R. Smith's [1998] own attempt to reconcile exemplar and schema models.)

Another important kind of exemplar model is the *case-based reasoning (CBR)* viewpoint put forward by Kolodner and her associates (e.g., Hammond, 1989; Kolodner, 1993, 1994) to be examined in chapter 4. In capsule form, CBR says that an important influence on reasoning about and inferencing from events (and our resulting memory for those events) involves our store of past instances similar to the present one. Thus, for example, in trying to make sense of your current personal crisis (e.g., an accident or a loss) or a current military crisis, you may call on your memories for other similar crises or other similar events. This case-to-case matching may play as important or more important a role than general schemas of military events or of personal crises. (This accounts for what I call the *talk show effect,* that is, the fact that audience members are willing to make confident and often extreme judgments about a guest if they can relate that person's situation to one of their own in which *they* acted a certain way.)

For our purposes, the important point of this exemplar- or case-based model is that it reasserts the role of memory for *specific* instances, as well as the role of the context (including the *social* context) in our understanding of new objects or instances. The relative influence of general categories versus specific instances is clearly an issue that is of central theoretical importance for all of cognitive psychology (see E. E. Smith & Medin, 1981); but it seems of particular relevance to *everyday* cognition. Certainly much of one's everyday experience is, in fact, influenced by one's past experiences with similar objects and occurrences, whether they be of other people, faces, events, or the like. For example, a major question in the area of autobiographical memory (and its development) is whether recall starts with a generic category or time period, or whether we actually retrieve specific experiences. As we have just seen, a similar issue has been raised in the area of event memory. Similarly, face recognition research clearly raises the question of whether we remember a general facial schema or specific features or specific instances. Finally, person memory and interpersonal judgment are clearly influenced by memory for past exemplars (e.g., by comparing a new student or partner with our memory of a former one, or comparing a new acquaintance with a fictional character such as Scarlett O'Hara or Ebenezer Scrooge; see Thagard & Kunda, 1998, for a discussion of the role of analogies in parallel distributed processing models in chap. 2, as well as Andersen & Cole, 1990, for research on transference).

Information-Processing and General Computational Models

Certainly one of the most influential models in the cognitive sciences—in fact, it is the viewpoint that for a number of years *defined* the cognitive sciences—is what has been called the computer or *information-processing* viewpoint, or more generally what Pylyshyn (1979, 1984) and others (e.g., Newell, 1990; Newell & Simon, 1972) have referred to as the *computational* model. According to this viewpoint, human thinking can be viewed as analogous to the way in which a computer processes information, with certain processing and storage mechanisms operating on symbolic representations of environmental information. Whereas the associative network, procedural, and schema or knowledge structure viewpoints reviewed earlier can all be viewed as speaking to the symbolic representation level of this viewpoint, equally important is the *processing* level, and that is the point that a number of theories in cognitive psychology and everyday cognition have addressed.

The computer metaphor inherent in most computational models actually consists of at least three different assumptions that are relevant to our present discussion. The first of these is that information or symbols, in whatever form, are passed through a series of stages or information-processing systems (Newell & Simon, 1972), which analyze or transform this information in some way. As conceived of in classic information-processing models (e.g., Atkinson & Shiffrin, 1968), these stages or processes include such things as a sensory register, an attentional mechanism, short-term or working memory, long-term memory, and retrieval mechanisms (see Fig. 1.3).

The second feature of many of these computer models is that they focus on some program metaphor that represents the software that operates on the aforementioned information. The specific formulation of this program metaphor need not be discussed here (see Pylyshyn, 1984): It can be con-

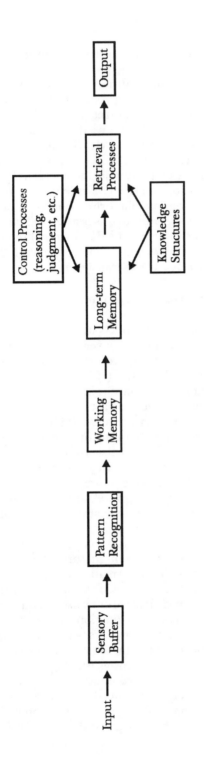

FIG. 1.3.   An example of a traditional information-processing model.

ceived of as an algorithm that can be implemented in a variety of different programming languages (Pylyshyn, 1984), a set of symbolic procedures (e.g., Graesser & Clark, 1985; Newell, 1990), problem-solving search mechanisms (Newell & Simon, 1972) or judgment heuristics (e.g., Tversky & Kahneman, 1974)—all of which operate on the symbolic representations referred to above. The critical point is simply that some sort of cognitive operation is performed on knowledge to produce some symbolic product.

Finally, the computer metaphor, at least in many versions, emphasizes the notion of capacity and capacity limitations on the information-processing system. Thus, there is the early emphasis (e.g., G. A. Miller, 1956) on the capacity limitations of short-term memory, the limits of attentional capacities, the whole discussion of judgmental heuristics, and perhaps in its most blatant form, the notion within social cognition of a *cognitive miser* (e.g., Fiske & Taylor, 1984), or the idea that we engage in various shortcuts or biased processing primarily in order to cope with our limited processing capacity. Such an assumption is clearly consistent with a model of a computer with limited RAM or processing capacity of which the human mind would seem to be a prime example.

Without trying to evaluate the plausibility of this sort of computer model (see Dreyfus, 1979, for one widely cited critique of the computer metaphor), I can identify a number of topics to which this model has been applied. For example, the information-processing model has had a major impact on research and theory on both face recognition and person memory, and a somewhat lesser impact on theories of autobiographical memory retrieval. In addition, in chapter 4 I look at a model of planning that combines procedural and computational components. Another application can be seen in the literature on judgment heuristics or shortcuts discussed in chapter 9; and in chapter 7 I look at the debate over the role of general problem-solving heuristics (vs. domain-specific knowledge) in determining "expertise."

Connectionist or Parallel Distributed Processing Models

In recent years a different kind of noncomputational viewpoint has emerged that is variously referred to as *connectionism* or *neural network* or *parallel distributed processing (PDP)* models. The major source for PDP models within cognitive science is the work of Rumelhart, McClelland, and their associates (e.g., Rumelhart et al., 1986), although the basic idea for neural networks has been around for at least 50 years (see McCollough & Pitts, 1943). Some characteristics of PDP models are as follows (Caudill & Butler, 1990; Kosslyn & Koenig, 1992; E. R. Smith, 1996, 1998):

1. These models assume that a representation is not found in any localized symbol, nor is processing centralized in a separate program or cen-

tral processor. Rather, as the label PDP suggests, both representation and processing are assumed to be distributed across a number of different, parallel units or nodes. Fiske and Taylor (1991) suggested the metaphor of a neon sign here, and Smith (1998) proposed the idea of a computer screen where each bulb (Fiske & Taylor) or pixel (Smith) can occur in a number of different patterns (although there is obviously no assumption here that the patterns of units actually form some spatial configuration).

2. As the foregoing suggests, in connectionist models the representational and processing functions are not separated from each other as they are in traditional symbolic models (and as I discuss throughout this book). The same patterns of activity account for both the representation and also the processing of the same information.

3. The units or nodes in this system are themselves interconnected via links that vary in strength or have differential weights attached to them. Kosslyn and Koenig (1992) have offered the metaphor of a set of octopi communicating by means of squeezes of their interlinked tentacles (see Fig. 1.4). Squeezes by octopi at the lowest level when their tentacles are brushed by fish are communicated to the second level, and finally result in the third level of octopi lifting their tentacles to signal to passing birds the density of fish in this area. Of course, the assumption is that these units may actually correspond to neurons —hence the term neural networks. (See Fig. 1.5 for an example of a simple network with input and output layers and an intermediate "hidden" level of units or neurons.)

4. The current representation is a joint product of the stimulus pattern and the weights on the connections. This feature is referred to as *parallel constraint satisfaction* (e.g., Barnden, 1995; Rumelhart, McClelland, et al., 1986; Thagard, 1989); that is, the representation must fit or satisfy the constraints imposed by the stimulus input on the one hand and the numerous existing weights on the other, the latter of which constitute the system's long-term memory (E. R. Smith, 1998). Furthermore, the various units and connections among these units provide parallel constraints on each other.

5. As the term neural network implies, connectionist models look, either explicitly or implicitly, for some relationship between the principles of cognitive processing and principles of neuroanatomy, neural conduction, or both—what Kosslyn and Koenig (1992) referred to as *neural plausibility*—although the most typical test of such models is in the form of computer simulations. It is certainly the case that the neurosciences are playing an increasing role in theorizing in this area (see Arbib, 1995; Gluck & Rumelhart, 1990; McClelland, McNaughton, & O'Reilly, 1995); and as we shall see in later chapters,

FIG. 1.4. Kosslyn and Koeing's (1992) metaphorical example of a neural network with nodes conceptualized as octopi. Reprinted with the permission of the Free Press, a division of Simon & Schuster, Inc., from WET MIND: The New Cognitive Neuroscience by Stephen M. Kosslyn and Oliver Koenig. Copyright © 1992 by Stephen M. Kosslyn and Oliver Koenig.

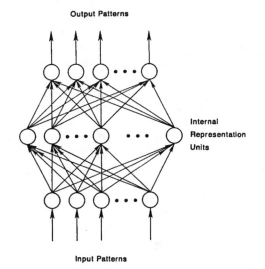

FIG. 1.5. An example of a hypothetical recurrent neural network. From "A Distributed Model of Human Learning and Memory" by J.L .McClelland, & D. E. Rumelhart, 1986. In *Parallel Distributal Processing: Explorations in the Microstructures of Cognition* (Vol. 2) edited by J. L. McClelland & D. E. Rumelhart. Cambridge, MA: MIT Press. Copyright © 1986 by MIT Press. Reprinted with permission.

appeals are often made to the cognitive effects of known neurological deficits or pathologies.

6. Although neural networks are essentially associative in nature (see Fodor & Pylyshyn) what is most important in connectionism is the overall *pattern* of activity across the many units with their various interconnections (see S. J. Read, Vanman, & Miller, 1997, for a discussion of the similarities of connectionism to Gestalt psychology on this issue) and, in some connectionist models, the pattern of feedback amongst these units. Changes in the weights attached to these different interconnections are also assumed to be a major factor in the changes in the resulting cognitive representation (Kosslyn & Koenig, 1992).

7. Changes in the network do *not* result from changes in some kind of central program or from some kind of explicit instruction, but rather from repeated, direct experiences of the system or set of elements themselves and from the resulting changes in the pattern of interconnections among these elements. As Caudill and Butler (1990) stated, some "systems [are] capable of independent or autonomous learning; some neural networks are capable of learning by trial and error" (p. 8) or by adaptation.

The *relevance* of PDP models to everyday cognition should be apparent. Although most everyday cognitivists are not particularly concerned with the neural underpinnings of everyday thought, they *are* concerned with the fact that much of our everyday knowledge and problem-solving abilities are not explicitly learned but rather are a result of our adaptation to our personal, everyday experiences. Some of this adaptation may be relatively automatic and not the result of explicit instruction (see my discussion in chaps. 8 and 9). Furthermore, the notion that such knowledge is not located in any single, higher order program, but is instead distributed across a number of different units would certainly seem to be a meaningful description of much of our everyday knowledge. For example, our knowledge of faces or persons or everyday social situations is often difficult to articulate in any explicit, symbolic manner, but it certainly may be conceived of in terms of some kind of distributed, interactive pattern (again, see Holyoak & Thagard, 1989, 1990; S. J. Read et al., 1997; E. R. Smith, 1998, for comparisons to Gestalt theory). Finally, the ability to generalize from a few instances or experiences to a category of instances, rather than learning explicit rules, is also relevant (see Bereiter, 1991; cf. also my discussion of exemplar and categorization theory).

In the chapters that follow, I show that connectionist models, although not all that prevalent in the area of everyday cognition at present, have nevertheless been applied to a few specific topics in the everyday and social cognition areas. These include, most particularly, the areas of impression formation and person memory to be discussed in chapter 2 on the one hand and of face recognition to be discussed in chapter 3 on the other. Connectionist models have also been applied to informal reasoning, as I will point out in chapter 4. I also will show that there are a variety of different types of connectionist models. It seems certain that such connectionist models will play an increasing role in everyday cognition during the next decade.

The Situated Cognition Viewpoint

A final position that has had an impact on a few areas of everyday cognition in recent years has been called the situated cognition or *situated learning* or *action* (e.g., Brown, Collins, & Duguid, 1989; Lave, 1988, 1990; Lave & Wegner, 1991) viewpoint. This perspective does not really qualify as a single coherent model but rather represents a set of both positive assertions and criticisms of other models that I have considered.

As the label suggests, and as I suggested earlier, the major assertion of situated cognition theorists is that thinking or knowing is situated; that is, it is dependent on the particular situation (physical, social, or psychological) in which one finds oneself. Thus, for example, the way in which one approaches a mathematical problem may differ depending on whether the task is balancing a checkbook or considering a sale item at a grocery store (see Lave et al., 1984). Or, to use the most frequently cited example of the situated cognitivists that we cited earlier in this chapter, people tend to view school as being a neutral, decontextualized situation in which abstract learning can occur, but in fact the classroom involves a set of social rules and assumptions that do not usually make contact with students' typical situations and everyday knowledge. Knowledge and meaning emerge out of our interaction with a particular situation. (Suchman, 1987, gives the example of a canoeist who may have a plan for a day on the river, but that plan is rapidly abandoned and improvisation takes over when the canoeist comes to the rapids on that river.)

A corollary of this argument is that knowledge does not transfer from one situation to another, for instance, from school to the real world (see chap. 7). Rather, one must negotiate understandings anew in each new situation. As a result, both traditional education, with its emphasis on general, abstract, decontextualized knowledge, and traditional experimental research on cognition, with its emphasis on general, universal principles, are doomed to failure—a sentiment that is certainly similar to some of the arguments of everyday cognition researchers, as discussed earlier in this chapter.

Perhaps the most important argument of the situated cognition position is that thinking and action need not use symbols or representations in the head. Rather, thinking involves interactions with environments, people, and objects. Knowledge or intelligence exists out there in tools and cultural artifacts or, in today's computer age, in computer software (see Salomon, 1993b), in the World Wide Web, in video technology, and the like. To focus only on symbolic processes in the head is to severely restrict the study of cognition; and for some situated cognitivists (e.g., Lave), it is a useless and completely misguided effort.

As we will see, the main influence of the situated cognition position in the study of everyday thought is in the field of education where investigators such as Resnick (1987a) have remarked on the failure of traditional education to make contact with the knowledge that students bring into the classroom and the failure of that same education to influence the way students think outside the classroom (see chap. 10). Situated cognition also has implications for the concept of everyday skills and the notion of transfer of training, as will be seen in chapter 7. In chapter 4 I examine the critique by Suchman (1987) of the cognitive sciences' conception of planning from a situated cognition point of view. Finally, in chapter 8 I review some of Lave's work on our use of arithmetic in everyday situations (e.g., grocery shopping), and the failure of that everyday math to use the mathematical skills learned in school.

It should be clear that the situated cognition viewpoint is rather different from all of the other approaches that we have examined thus far. It places the study of cognition out there in the material, cultural, and social world rather than inside the person's mind (if this kind of distinction is, in fact, a useful one). As such, it makes contact with other schools of thought, such as *ecological psychology*, which argues that important information is contained out there in the stimulus array, rather than in cognitive schemas or internal knowledge structures; see Gibson, 1966, 1979; Neisser, 1976). Both of these positions have had a major impact on the field of everyday cognition.

Summary

In this section I have reviewed seven different models of everyday cognition.[8] These different models are summarized in Table 1.3.

In the chapters that follow I look at some applications of these seven models to the different topics that I review. Then, in chapter 11, I evaluate the relative importance and effectiveness of the different models for conceptualizing everyday cognition.

GENERAL SUMMARY

In this chapter I have looked at some of the differences between everyday cognition (in its several different incarnations) and the *study* of such cognition on the one hand, versus the traditional laboratory study of memory and cognition on the other. I have examined some of the issues entailed in the debate over the relative value of the study of everyday memory, as well as

---

[8]It is interesting to note that four of these models—the associative network, schema, exemplar, and PDP models—correspond to the four models of mental representation reviewed by E. R. Smith (1998) in the most recent edition of the *Handbook of Social Psychology*.

the study of everyday, informal (vs. formal) reasoning and problem solving, of practical (vs. academic) intelligence and instruction, and of naturalistic (vs. formal) decision making. In addition, I have discussed briefly the importance of the social dimension in the study of everyday cognition. Finally, I have introduced seven models that I will be applying throughout this book. In short, I have tried to develop some tools that can be used in analyzing research and theory on particular topics in everyday cognition.

In the next chapter I begin developing one of these particular topics: namely, forming impressions of and remembering people.

TABLE 1.3

Summary of Models, Their Central Assertions, and Opposing Models

Model	Central assertion	Opposing model
1. Associative network	Knowledge begins with elementary units and is linked via simple associations to form propositional representations	Schema, constructivist
2. Procedural	Knowledge is a matter of "knowing how," and is represented in terms of a set of "if–then" procedures	The associative network model of declarative knowledge
3. Schema, constructivist	Knowledge is represented and processed in a top-down manner in terms of abstract themes or knowledge structures	Associative network
4. Exemplar, case-based	Knowledge is represented in terms of specific instances which affect our understanding, recall, and judgments of later instances (in terms of similarity)	Schema, constructivist
5. Computational, information-processing	Information or knowledge is passed through various subsystems and operated on by some kind of program	Connectionist
6. Connectionist, PDP	Both the representation and the processing of knowledge occur in parallel, distributed fashion in terms of interconnected units or neurons	Computational
7. Situated cognition	Cognition is "located" in the individual's interaction with the situation and in the use of tools and artifacts rather than in that individual's head	All of the above

Note.   PDP = parallel distribution processing.

Forming and Remembering Impressions of People

Introduction

The Units or Format for Representing Persons

The Information From Which Impressions Are Formed

The Organization of Impressions

The Processes of Impression Formation and Memory Retrieval

The Relationship Between Person Memory and Judgment

Summary

INTRODUCTION

In the next two chapters I examine research on memory and processing of faces and the people behind those faces. Clearly, faces and personalities are among the most important "objects" that people encounter in their everyday lives; and there has been considerable research and theorizing about both. Interestingly enough, although both of these topics have addressed similar topics, researchers in the two areas have seldom borrowed from each other or shared each other's literatures (see M. B. Brewer, 1988, and McArthur, 1982, for possible exceptions). Thus, one of the points of the next two chapters is to highlight some of the commonalities between these two areas.

To begin the discussion, consider the following well-known example. A name that became painfully familiar during 1998 is that of Monica Lewinsky.

Everyone repeatedly saw Ms. Lewinsky's face and figure on their television screens and heard innumerable reports about her sexual liaisons with President Clinton, her conversations with Linda Tripp, and various commentaries about her background and character. It is safe to say that most people's evaluation of Ms. Lewinsky is fairly negative. The question that arises, however, is exactly how we represent Ms. Lewinsky's personality and character to ourselves, exactly what form our impressions of her take, and how these impressions may have changed in the light of additional information about her, such as her taped deposition by the House managers, her interview by Barbara Walters, her own book, her role as spokesperson for Weight Watchers.

For example, given that TV is such a visual media, to what extent do one's impressions focus on her appearance, and to what extent does that appearance influence one's evaluations of Lewinsky? Are one's impressions primarily evaluative or are these evaluations a secondary product of more descriptive knowledge—for instance, that Lewinsky is spoiled and immature, that she learned to lie from her mother, or that she really was infatuated with Clinton? How does one's concern with determining the guilt or innocence of Clinton influence the way in which one processes information about him and Lewinsky? How do one's impressions change as a result of her grand jury testimony or with the disclosure of the taped conversations with Linda Tripp in which it became apparent how Tripp had manipulated her? To what extent are these evaluations influenced by one's view of Bill Clinton and one's political viewpoints? All of these questions relate to issues that I discuss in this chapter.

THE UNITS OR FORMAT FOR REPRESENTING PERSONS

In considering how one forms impressions and what one remembers about, say, Monica Lewinsky, or new acquaintances with whom one has direct contact, one of the most basic questions to be considered is what the basic *unit* or format of such a representation might be.

Over a half century ago, in a slightly different context, Gordon Allport (1937) proposed that *traits* offered the most meaningful, convenient "unit" for psychologists to use in describing others' personality. Although researchers in personality have raised major questions about the trait concept (e.g., Mischel, 1968) in general, researchers on person memory and impression formation have generally been in agreement with Allport's prescription. For example, in his classic research on impression formation, Solomon Asch (1946) looked at the way in which individuals form overall impressions of a person based on a list of trait descriptors (including, in particular, the role of certain *central* traits, or traits that served to organize other traits). Similarly, the influential research paradigm proposed by Norman Anderson (e.g., 1968) for studying impression formation also used traits as the primary units from which impressions are formed. Currently, the major model of impression formation and person memory—the so-called person memory model of Wyer and Srull (e.g., 1989; see also Srull & Wyer, 1989) has explicitly stressed the central role of traits in the cognitive representation of persons.

This emphasis on traits can also be found in a number of other research paradigms. For example, research on the naturalistic description of persons (e.g., Fiske & Cox, 1979; Park, 1986) has found that traits predominate in such descriptions, particularly as people become better acquainted with others. Along very different lines, Uleman (1987; Winter & Uleman, 1984) presented evidence suggesting that traits are spontaneously inferred in the encoding of social behavior; and more recently, Carlston and Skowronski (1994) reported supporting evidence for such spontaneous trait inference using an implicit memory measure.

Not everyone agrees with this viewpoint, however. For example, Andersen and Klatzky (1987) have presented evidence to suggest that *social stereotypes* or *role types* or *subtypes* (Taylor, 1981b; see also Fiske & Taylor, 1991)—for example, the egghead, yuppie, or jock—represent more reasonable units for person representations than do traits. As Fiske and Taylor (1991) put it, "there are simply too many ways to be extraverted (e.g., like a comedian, a politician, or a bully), but there apparently are fewer ways to fulfill a role schema, such as being a politician" (p. 143). (I would argue with this particular example.) Furthermore, Andersen and Klatzky (1987) have presented evidence that such social stereotypes are, in fact, closer to the kind of basic, middle-level categories described by Rosch (1978; Rosch, Mervis, Gray, Johnson, & Boyes-Braem, 1976) in her research on categorization and at least implied in Allport's account just described. For example, Andersen and Klatzky report results of a clustering analysis indicating that (a) there are numerous stereotypes associated with each trait concept; (b) participants responding to such stereotypes list a greater number of distinct attributes, including more *visual* attributes and more *tangible* qualities, than they do to trait concepts; and (c) more attributes are rated by participants as being associated with stereotypes but not with traits, than vice versa—that is, stereotypes are more distinctive. All of these are features that Rosch has proposed as characteristic of basic level concepts for describing objects. Along similar lines, M. B. Brewer and Lui (1989) have shown that participants find it easier to sort photographs of the elderly when the instructions asked them to sort them in terms of personality types than when instructed to sort in terms of traits.

Another possible alternative format is that proposed by M. B. Brewer (1988) in her *dual-process model* of impression formation. Brewer distinguished between two different forms of representation depending on whether the impression is personalized to the individual or is category-based and involves stereotyping. The former type of representation, which focuses on the individual as the basis of organization and is basically bottom-up (i.e., from the data to the impression) is assumed to involve a propositional form of representation (see chap. 1), presumably including traits, combined in network form. However, for category-based processing—that is, where the individual is treated as part of some conceptual or social group—the form of representation involved is *pictoliteral* (Klatzky, 1984) or imagery-oriented. As Brewer puts it, "images are more specific, configural, unmediated by verbal descriptions. Traits and other semantic features are assumed to be inferred from the category representation at the time judgments are made, rather than represented directly in the mental image" (p. 13). Thus, according to this view traits are a matter of output from the *real* person representation, rather than being part of that representation per se. Similarly, M. B. Brewer (1988) argued that imagery or pictoliteral representations are preferable because they "have the advantage of preserving these temporal, spatial, and configural relations among category features" (p. 13). Interestingly enough, these pictoliteral representations are assumed to refer to *categorical* representations rather than to individuals treated *as* individuals, whereas face recognition research has assumed that the imagery-oriented information is concerned with the recognition of specific persons. In fact, Brewer has presented evidence for the importance of pictorial information in the classification or stereotyping of subgroups of the elderly (Brewer, Dull, & Lui, 1981).

A related position has recently been outlined by Carlston (1992, 1994) in what he calls *associated systems theory*. In this theory Carlston proposes that person information can take a variety of different forms, ranging from memory for visual information about appearance to verbal and propositional representations primarily in the form of traits or trait labels, to affective memories, to memory for the perceiver's own behavior or actions toward the person being represented. (See Fiske & Taylor, 1991, for a similar multicode point of view.) According to Carlston, these four types of representation, which are in turn based on four different mental systems, constitute the cornerstones of a nine-element matrix (see Fig. 2.1) that also includes four *hybrid* codes: (a) categorizations, or hybrids of visual appearance or imagery and trait labels (e.g., the computer nerd); (b) evaluations, or combinations of affective and verbal labels (e.g., boring or love); (c) orientations, or a combination of affective memories and the perceiver's behavioral responses (e.g., nurture or antagonize); and (d) behavioral observations, or combinations of behavioral responses and imagery or sensory impression, such as flirting with a beautiful woman or recoiling from an intimidating glance.

Although this associated systems account does not break any major new ground, it *does* serve to systematize the various multiple-format viewpoints set forward by M. B. Brewer (1988) and Fiske (Fiske & Pavelchak (1986; Fiske & Taylor, 1991). (Fiske and Taylor have pointed out that the three major components of participants' free descriptions of other people are traits, appearance, and behavior, though this behavior refers to the behavior of the other person.) At least two of the hybrids bear on my later discussion of the representation of faces or appearance versus the representation of more substantial *person* information, as does Carlston's (1994) attempt to

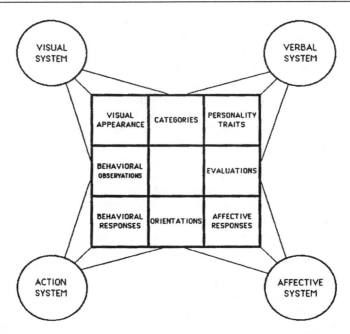

FIG. 2.1.   Carlston's Associated Systems model. From "Associated Systems Theory: A Systematic Approach to Cognitive Representations of Persons" by D. E. Carlston, 1994. In *Associated Systems Theory: A Systematic Approach to Cognitive Representations of Persons: Advances in Social Cognition* (Vol. 7, p. 7) edited by T. K. Srull & R. S. Wyer, Hillsdale, NJ: Lawrence Erlbaum Associates. Copyright © 1994 by Lawrence Erlbaum Associates.   Reprinted with permission.

link these different representations to specific types of clinical or neurological disorders. Finally, the associated systems theory also has the advantage of trying to link different representations to particular neurological systems (see Carlston, 1994, for a further discussion). Such an integrated approach does not really resolve the question of which, if any, of these codes constitutes the most dominant or most common representational format, though Carlston (1992) *does* raise the possibility of there being individual differences in the prominence of different formats (see the Monica Lewinsky example given earlier).

Given this disagreement about what constitutes the primary unit of person representations, one may ask what the exact cognitive status of traits is. It is clear, for example, that people use traits in their everyday descriptions of other people. However, that may be due to the fact that traits exist simply as summary terms used for the purpose of communication rather than as units of individual person knowledge. Certainly a number of investigators have commented on the role of semantic confoundings in the use of trait descriptors (e.g., Shweder, 1982; see also Schneider, Hastorf, & Ellsworth, 1979, for a review). Similarly, I have mentioned M. B. Brewer's

(1988) argument that, at least in the case of categorical processing, traits are not part of the actual mental representation but are simply inferred "at the time of judgment." Other investigators (e.g., Gilbert, 1998; Trope, 1986) have distinguished between traits as descriptive categories of behavior and traits as dispositions of the person; and S. J. Miller and Read (1987; Read, Jones, & L. C. Miller, 1990) argued that traits can be conceived of as "goal-based categories." Finally, Woll, Weeks, Fraps, Pendergrass, and Vanderplas (1980) suggested that traits as a form of cognitive representation have a degree of flexibility (Barclay, Bransford, Franks, McCarrell, & Nitsch, 1974) rather than a single fixed meaning, and they suggested that this meaning is constructed or reconstructed on the basis of the current context and background knowledge. Thus, *independent* may mean "without spouse or children," "able to function without other people's help," "showing a preference for being alone," "rebellious," or a variety of other things, depending on the other sorts of information that are present about a given individual.

One final point: There is clearly a difference between one's representation of a particular person and one's knowledge or beliefs about personality or person types in general (see Fiske & Taylor, 1991, for a similar distinction). I have mentioned that M. B. Brewer (1988) distinguished between the form of representation involved in individuated processing versus typing; and later I discuss how a number of other recent investigators (e.g., Fiske & Neuberg, 1990; Wyer & Carlston, 1994) have made similar distinctions. In addition, in previous research on person perception (e.g., Bruner & Taguiri, 1954; Schneider, 1973), people's general conceptions of personality have been studied under the label of *implicit personality theory*. Thus, some consideration has been given to the issue of generic versus specific person knowledge. However, the question of how these two forms of knowledge interact—for example, how generic person knowledge informs the process of forming a specific impression—remains an intriguing (and understudied) question. One notable exception to this is the work by Andersen (Andersen & Cole, 1990; Andersen & Glassman, 1996) on the "transference" of knowledge or impressions from a previous exemplar (person) to a current one.

As an example of this format or representational issue, think back to the example of Monica Lewinsky cited earlier, or think of your favorite professor or student, or a fictional character such as Sherlock Holmes. What information do you think of first? Is it the person's appearance or your affective reaction to him or her or, in the case of a person you know, your behavior toward him or her? How much of a role does that person's face play in your impression? Is your "impression" primarily affective (e.g., I like or hate him or her), or are there traits or social categories associated with that impression? Are those traits or categories accessed via exemplary behaviors or vice versa, or are these summary descriptions arrived at on their own? Finally, if you were asked to describe this person to others, what kind of information would you include and in what order?

THE INFORMATION FROM WHICH IMPRESSIONS
ARE FORMED

As I have discussed, in traditional research on impression formation (e.g., Anderson, 1968; Asch, 1946; Bruner & Tagiuri, 1954), the material presented to participants typically consisted of trait descriptors, under the implicit assumption that traits are the basic data from which impressions are formed. However, even though people certainly make *some* judgments on the basis of trait descriptions—for instance, in the form of summary descriptions from other people, or even the person's own self-description (e.g., in a job interview or on a first date)—the primary data on which person judgments are usually made is the person's actions. Most recent research on person memory and impression formation has accepted this fact, either implicitly or explicitly, in that most of the information provided to participants has been of the behavioral variety, either accompanied or unaccompanied by traits (e.g., the Hastie–Srull paradigm to be discussed later), although even here the behaviors have usually been in the form of behavioral *descriptions* (see Gilbert, 1998, for a critique of the overuse of verbal descriptions in social cognition research).

One can argue, however, that people also use many other kinds of information in forming impressions, including everything from physical appearance to clothing to nonverbal behavior to facial expression, from static cues to dynamic movements. For example, on the one extreme is Berry's (1990) evidence suggesting that individuals form fairly accurate or consensual judgments of personality on the basis of simple static photographs, whereas on the other extreme is the ecological psychology position (see McArthur & Baron, 1983) that impressions may be formed on the basis of complex dynamic cues suggesting dominance or social status or receptivity. Some early research (reviewed in Schneider et al., 1979) examined the impact of various artifacts such as glasses or makeup on impressions; and Zebrowitz (1990) reviewed more recent research on the impact of voice, gait, and stature. Finally, as we shall see in the next two sections, a number of recent formulations of impression formation (e.g., M. B. Brewer, 1988; Fiske & Neuberg, 1990) have emphasized an initial process by which we identify or categorize people automatically on the basis of salient physical cues such as race, ethnic status, gender, and age.

The bottom line is that impressions in the real world can be based on a variety of different types of information. It is probably a mistake to assume that there is one kind of stimulus material that is most "realistic," although it would be interesting to examine the differences in the process of impression formation based on verbal descriptions, still photographs, videotaped speeches, and face-to-face interactions (see Amabile & Kabat, 1982, for a comparison of verbal vs. behavioral information; see also Woll & Cozby, 1987, for a discussion of this question in the context of a study of real-world impression formation).

THE ORGANIZATION OF IMPRESSIONS

Associative Networks: The Wyer and Srull Person Memory Model

Certainly the issue that has received the most attention in the person memory literature is the organization of our person representations. Certainly the model that has received the greatest empirical support and has had the greatest impact on this area is Wyer and Srull's *Person Memory* model. According to this model (Srull & Wyer, 1989; Wyer & Srull, 1989), a target person's behaviors are encoded in terms of traits that are either provided (by an experimenter) or stored in memory. When more than one trait is applicable, behaviors are encoded in terms of the most readily accessible one. Furthermore, when an expectancy exists about which trait is applicable, only those behaviors that are relevant to that trait are encoded. At this point, associations are formed between the behaviors and the relevant trait, but no interbehavioral or intertrait associations are formed.

Next, an *evaluative person concept* or a judgment of the overall likableness (see Anderson, 1966) of the person so described is formed on the basis of the encoded behaviors. Such an evaluation is formed primarily when the observer is concerned with forming an overall impression of the target person; and this evaluation is based on only a subset of the behaviors—usually the first behaviors encountered (cf. research on the primacy effect in impression formation). Furthermore, according to Wyer (1989), even though the overall person evaluation is primarily just that (i.e., evaluative), and is itself more or less separate from the various trait concepts, this evaluation nevertheless "retains certain descriptive features of the traits on which it is based" (p. 249). Thus, there are two separate and (more or less) independent conceptions of the person. (See Fig. 2.2.)

More important for our purposes are the assumptions contained in the person memory model about how the perceiver resolves possible inconsistencies when forming impressions. First, if the perceiver cannot decide on an overall evaluation on the basis of the behavioral information provided, he or she is presumed to review the behaviors within a given trait–behavior cluster to make sure that these behaviors were interpreted correctly. This review results in an increase in the strength of the interbehavioral associations for the behaviors within that cluster. Second, when the perceiver *has* formed an overall evaluation of the person and then encounters behaviors that are *evaluatively inconsistent* with that impression (e.g., undesirable behaviors for an otherwise desirable person), then he or she gives some additional thought to those inconsistent behaviors. Such thought activity results in an increased number and strength of associations among these (inconsistent) behaviors and other behaviors and therefore an increased probability of recall for the inconsistent behaviors. Similar activity is not stimulated by the occurrence of evaluatively *consistent* or neutral behaviors. At the same

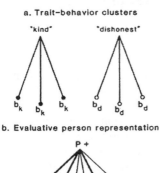

a. Trait–behavior clusters

b. Evaluative person representation

Legend
b_k = kind behavior
b_d = dishonest behavior
p + = positive evaluative person concept

FIG. 2.2.   The two different conceptions of the person in the Wyer & Srull model. From "Social Memory and Social Judgment" by R. S. Wyer, Jr., 1989. In *Memory: Interdisciplinary Approaches* edited by P. R. Solomon, G. R. Goethals, C. M. Kelley, & B. R. Stephens, New York, Springer-Verlag. Copyright © 1989 by Springer-Verlag. Reprinted with permission.

time, subsequent thought about evaluatively inconsistent behaviors also leads to a process of *bolstering,* in which further associations are formed between the consistent behaviors and the evaluative person concept in order to justify that overall evaluation.

The critical assumption in all of this is that it is primarily the person's attempts at inconsistency reduction that result in increased thought activity and deeper processing. This thought activity in turn produces an increased web of associations between inconsistent behaviors and other behaviors on the one hand and between behaviors that are evaluatively *consistent* with the overall impression of the person and the overall evaluative impression on the other hand. This processing model, combined with an associative network representational model, was initially proposed by Hastie (1980; Hastie & Kumar, 1979), and subsequently expanded upon by Srull (1981, 1983). However, as Wyer and Srull (1989) pointed out, their revised and extended person memory model differs from these earlier formulations in that the emphasis of the former is on *evaluative* inconsistencies rather than on descriptive ones stressed by Hastie and Srull.

This distinction is a critical one because it raises once again an old issue in social cognition—one that in fact dominated research on both impression formation and implicit personality theories—over the role of *descriptive* versus connotative or *evaluative* meaning (see Schneider et al., 1979, for a summary). It is also of importance because it raises a fundamental question (alluded to earlier) about one's representation of persons: Namely, are one's overall impressions based primarily on one's liking for that person, or are they based on a consideration of more semantic or descriptive meaning, with liking for that person being derived from this descriptive impression? For example, is one's impression of some political figure (choose your own) based simply on one's judgments of that figure's likableness, or is it instead a matter of assessing that figure's competence or political stance, which in turn results in a likableness judgment? (Of course, part of the answer depends on what is meant by an impression.)

Supporting Evidence.   Because one of the most impressive features of the Wyer and Srull model is the wealth of evidence that has been collected in support of its arguments, it seems appropriate to devote at least some attention to this empirical evidence. First, on the issue of trait encoding of behavioral information, some classic research by Hamilton et al. (1980) found that when participants were given instructions to form an impression of the target person on the basis of behavioral descriptions, their free recall for these descriptions clustered around a set of traits built into the stimulus list, and this clustering led to better memory than under simple memory instructions. In a similar vein, Wyer and Gordon (1982) found that when participants were asked to recall the traits provided as well as the relevant behaviors, recall of the traits led to increased recall of the related behaviors. Similarly, a good deal of research (see Stangor & McMillan, 1992; Wyer & Carlston, 1994, for reviews) has demonstrated that behavioral information inconsistent with a trait or stereotype is recalled better than consistent behaviors. Also in this connection, Srull (1981) examined the conditional recall probabilities of (descriptively) consistent and inconsistent items following other consistent and inconsistent behaviors and reported (as predicted) that consistent behaviors were more likely to be recalled following inconsistent ones, whereas inconsistent behaviors were just as likely to be recalled after *either* consistent *or* inconsistent ones (see Hamilton, Driscoll, & Worth, 1989, for contrary results; cf. also Hamilton & Sherman, 1996, for evidence of the different expectations for consistency or unity between representations for individuals and groups, the latter of which may differ in their degree of *entativity* [Campbell, 1958] or perceived unity).

On the issue of evaluative versus descriptive inconsistency, Wyer and Gordon (1982) varied these two factors independently of each other and found that the former had a greater impact on recall than did the latter. Along similar lines, Wyer, Bodenhausen, and Srull (1984) found that behaviors that were evaluatively inconsistent with either explicitly stated traits or with ones that were simply implied by the name of the target person (e.g., Einstein–intelligent, Hitler–hostile) were recalled better than evaluatively consistent behaviors and that *evaluative* inconsistency was more important than *descriptive* inconsistency. On the other hand, Hamilton et al. (1989) presented participants with multiple traits that were evaluatively consistent with each other (i.e., friendly, intelligent, and adventurous), along with behaviors that were either descriptively consistent or inconsistent with one of these traits. Participants tended to recall behaviors that were descriptively inconsistent (i.e., with the trait involved) together with the consistent behaviors *within the same trait-behavior cluster*, even though these behaviors were evaluatively *consistent* with the overall positive impression of the person. In addition, Wyer et al. (1992) recently reported that inconsistency is *not* an issue for political statements that are inconsistent with the political stance taken by the politician making the statement.

Reservations. Despite the large amount of research evidence in support of the person memory model—and I have just scratched the surface here—there are several potential problems with such an associative network model. First, as Wyer et al. (1992) have themselves pointed out, the person memory model has generally been tested under rather restricted conditions, that is, in the lab, and using rather restricted materials, such as verbal descriptions of behaviors and traits. The generalizability of these results to the real world or to other conditions is unclear. "In other words, the model ... could be a theory of the research paradigm and not of person impression formation in general" (Wyer et al., 1992, p. 6.)[1]

Second, although evaluation is certainly an important component of our person representations and also one of the primary ways in which *social* cognition differs from nonsocial cognition (see chap. 1), I must admit to having some misgivings about the resurrection of the old evaluative *versus* descriptive debate in impression formation and person representations. It seems unlikely that person representations are based primarily on *either* evaluative *or* descriptive encodings. There are some people I know, for example, about whom I have rich and detailed knowledge (and oftentimes rich and complex feelings), and then there are others about whom I know little except that I like or dislike them. (The names of some Republican congressmen come immediately to mind.) Furthermore, it seems unlikely that our representations of the numerous people whom we have formed impressions of can be reduced to a simple and crude positive–negative or likable–unlikable distinction. Are Hitler (barbaric), Mr. or Ms. Smith's last date (unattractive), an inconsiderate sales clerk, and the student who failed my last exam (unintelligent or unmotivated) all represented in the same or similar ways? (See Wyer & Srull, 1989, p. 164, for a partial acknowledgment of this point.) When we form an impression of someone in the real world, are we simply concerned with whether we "like 'em or don't like 'em"?

Such a view simply does not, in my opinion, do justice to what must be the complexity of our knowledge and our feelings about people in the real

---

[1]It should be noted that Wyer and his students have recently extended the range of application of the person memory model to the arena of political memory, memory for conversations, and impressions drawing upon real-world knowledge (see Wyer & Carlston, 1994, and Wyer et al., 1992, for reviews), however, these studies nevertheless follow the same general lines of the previous person memory research (i.e., controlled laboratory research).

world. To quote an observation made by Robert Abelson (1966)—certainly a psychologist who has demonstrated mixed feelings about the role of evaluation in social cognition—in the attitude domain, the emphasis of the person memory model on general evaluative representations of people and evaluative inconsistencies in *reasoning* about persons "gives too little scope to the possibilities of human thought, even as practiced by mediocre theorists" (p. 119). This criticism is particularly ironic in the present context because one of the themes of this book is that real-world knowledge is typically richer and practical intelligence is frequently wiser than their laboratory and academic counterparts; and yet the person memory model and other models of social cognition are typically *simpler* than the corresponding models in cognitive psychology. Stated differently, despite Wyer and Srull's attempt to formulate a general, comprehensive model of memory, as Wyer et al. (1992; see also Wyer & Carlston, 1994) themselves pointed out, it is questionable whether the person memory model actually represents a generalizable model or a generalizable paradigm for studying impression formation and person knowledge.

An Alternative Position. One final issue concerning a major assumption of the Wyer and Srull person memory model (as well as the views of a variety of other researchers—cf. Hamilton et al., 1980; Ostrom, Pryor, & Simpson, 1981) has been raised by Klein and Loftus (1990). Klein and Loftus questioned whether multiple behaviors are, in fact, encoded and clustered under a single trait node. Klein and Loftus demonstrated that, contrary to the results of Hamilton et al. (1980), when a measure of clustering is used that is unconfounded by overall recall, there is no greater clustering in terms of trait terms under impression formation instructions than under memory instructions. In addition, the degree of clustering in recall under these impression formation instructions is unrelated to amount of recall.

As an alternative to the trait-clustering account, Klein and Loftus (1990) offered what they described as a *trace elaboration model*. According to this alternative viewpoint, individual behaviors are encoded in terms of individual traits that then serve as retrieval cues for recalling these behaviors (see Fig. 2.3). In support of this view, Klein and Loftus have presented evidence that simple trait judgment instructions (i.e., instructions to use a trait of their own choosing to encode a given behavioral description) resulted in as great recall as did impression formation instructions. Further, in a second experiment Klein and Loftus showed that providing trait categories only at retrieval leads to increased clustering under impression formation but not under memorization instructions. Thus, Klein and Loftus concluded that clustering under impression formation instructions can reasonably be accounted for by retrieval processes.

The Klein and Loftus (1990) arguments are of interest for a couple of different reasons. First, their results call into question the associative, cluster-

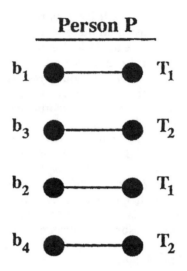

Person P

FIG. 2.3.   Trait-behavior links as conceived by S. Klein and Loftus. From "Rethinking the Role of Organization in Person Memory: An Independent Trace Storage Model" by S. B. Klein, & J. Loftus, 1990, *Journal of Personality and Social Psychology, 59*, p. 404. Copyright © 1990 by the American Psychological Association. Reprinted with permission.

ing viewpoint that has been so prominent in the person memory area. Thus, it is possible that our representations of persons do not amount to simple networks of associations between central person concepts, middle-level trait nodes, and groups of associated behaviors. In fact, these results even call into question the notion that traits are actually used as the means of encoding behaviors. Rather, traits may simply serve as retrieval cues for recalling impressions of persons. (See Wyer et al., 1992, for an acknowledgment of the need for revising some of the retrieval assumptions in the person memory model.)

The question that the Klein and Loftus results leave open, of course, is exactly how our impressions of persons are organized. Certainly these impressions are more than just a set of (redundant) traits, with, for example, the trait of extroversion being represented as many times as the number of different behaviors with which it is associated. I also find it difficult to accept that organization of person information occurs only at retrieval (though the rather artificial process of category clustering might). Furthermore, it seems certain that one comes to have an expectation about other behaviors from knowing that a person is extroverted or honest. One's intuitions also suggest, I believe, that there is a greater amount of coherence or unity to our conceptions of other persons than simply having a list of unconnected traits (though this is not really something addressed by Klein and Loftus).

Prototype and Typological Versus Exemplar Models

One major set of alternatives to associative network models are *prototype* or *typological* models such as those proposed by C. A. Anderson and Sedikides (1991) and M. B. Brewer (1988; Brewer, Dull, & Lui, 1981), both of which are ultimately based on the formulation of Rosch (e.g., 1978). In part, advocacy of a prototype model reflects the kind of preference for *categorical* over *dimensional* representations described earlier, for example, seeing someone as a member of the "man of the world" or "senior citizen" type, rather than as an individuated person with a variety of different associated attributes, or as someone located on a particular set of trait dimensions or at a particular point in multidimensional space. In this regard, recall that M. Brewer (1988) viewed the prototype as only one of two different ways of representing information about a person: namely, a categorical as opposed to an individuating approach, the latter of which is represented in much the same way as the Wyer and Srull associative network model just reviewed. Furthermore, the content or type of prototype differs from one version of this model to another, ranging from traits (Hampson, John, & Goldberg, 1986) to person types (Cantor & Mischel, 1979) to social roles or role types (Andersen & Klatzky, 1987; Fiske & Taylor, 1991).

More importantly, prototypes represent *patterns* of features arranged in some kind of *hierarchical* format, from most abstract and general to most concrete and specific, or from superordinate type to subtype. Thus, prototypes, unlike associative networks, are structured elements—for instance, the categories *feminist, redneck, jock,* and *geek* involve a constellation of different characteristics. As C. A. Anderson and Sedikides (1991) have stated, the "typological view maintains that traits composing a social category have an integrity or internal connectedness that differs from trait relations *between* categories" (p. 204, italics added). Furthermore, these configurations are typically viewed as falling in some kind of ordered sequence, with the middle-level category being conceived of as a more basic or natural one for describing or categorizing people.

Research Evidence. There has been a good deal of research on person prototypes, focusing primarily on the degree to which people's descriptions and categorizations of persons at the basic level follow the principles set down by Rosch (i.e., greater richness, distinctiveness or nonredundancy, etc.), of the sort identified earlier in this chapter (Andersen & Klatzky, 1987). As one example of a systematic research project based on these principles, consider the work of Brewer and her associates (e.g., M. B. Brewer et al., 1981; M. B. Brewer & Lui, 1989) on stereotypes of elderly people. These researchers first demonstrated that participants could, in fact, agree about how to sort preselected pictures into three subcategories (i.e., grandmotherly type, elder statesmen type, and senior citizen type) of the higher order category of elderly persons. Participants were also more likely to agree on the attributes (e.g., accepting, kindly, serene) that three pictures had in common when they came from the same subcategory (i.e., grandmotherly) than when each came from *different* subcategories. Next, these investigators showed that participants were better able to match a set of behavioral statements to one of three pairs of pictures when these pictures were judged as *good* prototypes or exemplars than when they were *poor* prototypes.

Brewer et al. (1981) also showed that the speed with which participants processed information and recalled behavioral statements associated with the pictures of the elderly depended on the degree to which those statements were consistently associated with a picture from the same *sub*category (e.g., elder statesman type) versus the appropriate higher order category (i.e., elderly persons in general). Specifically, participants in an impression formation task took a longer time to process information that combined descriptions of older and younger persons (i.e., inconsistent at the higher order category level) than they did for information from the other two conditions (i.e., information associated with pictures that were consistent at the subcategory level, or mixed information from the subcategory and the appropriate superordinate level). However, these participants later *recalled* more information from the consistent and inconsistent conditions than from the mixed condition. These latter results, along with the results for recall *intrusions* (i.e., participants misrecalling a given statement as being associated with the wrong picture) supported the notion of a type–subtype structure, that is, misrecalling information inconsistent with a given picture as having come from the alternate subcategory, and recalling information inconsistent at the higher level because more effort was put into reconciling the inconsistencies (see my discussion of the Hastie–Srull–Wyer model).

One of the advantages of the prototype viewpoint is that it is more consistent with the view for encoding faces to be described in the next chapter, although there is no reason that our representation of persons in general has to be the same as our representation for perceptual patterns such as faces. Another advantage is that the configurational emphasis of the prototype model captures, at least in part, the patterned, Gestalt-like flavor of Asch's (1946) classic formulation of the impression formation process.

As one final example, Harasty and Brewer (1995) asked participants first to generate as many names as they could in response to either a trait cue (i.e., kindness) or a category cue (i.e., woman). Not surprisingly, the latter cue generated significantly more names than did the former and also significantly shorter interitem (i.e., intername) response times for the category cue. Next, the same participants were given cards, each of which bore one of the names they had generated, and were asked to sort these cards into piles in terms of which people belonged together. Using the prior interitem response times as the dependent variable, and cue type (i.e., trait or category) and type of interitem relationship (i.e., within or between sorted categories) as independent variables, an interaction was found between these two variables. Specifically, both trait and category cues produced short and similar inter-item response times, whereas the response times for intergroup transitions were longer, and they were significantly longer for trait cues than for category cues. This latter finding is consistent with the idea that categories or subtypes have clearer connections or structure between groups than do trait categories.

Reservations.   The earlier comparison with Asch points to a potential problem with the prototype viewpoint. Specifically, prototype viewpoints tend to depict the knowledge structures involved in person memory and impression formation as being fairly static and inflexible (see Hampson, 1988, for a similar argument). This lack of flexibility applies to both the structure of individual categories themselves and the hierarchical structure *among* different *levels* of the typology. Certainly, if we are to form impressions of new people, and if we are to ever change our conceptions of existing persons or groups, then both our categories and our overall *theories* of people must be somewhat more dynamic and modifiable. Similarly, in his original discussion of the impression formation process, Asch (1946) emphasized, and later constructivists (e.g., Bransford & Johnson, 1973) have also underlined, the role of context in our memory representation (cf. Medin & Schaeffer, 1978); certainly such context effects influence our application of a prototype in any given situation. Thus, for example, one's image of a doctor as making lots of money may have to be altered when one meets a doctor who has volunteered his time to work at a family clinic in the ghetto or who works for Doctors Without Borders in Bosnia.

Still another problem with many of the categorical models is that they focus primarily, if not exclusively, on *generic* knowledge structures or on our implicit theories of people in general, rather than on our representation of concrete individuals. (The one obvious exception here is Brewer's dual process model referred to earlier.) Along somewhat similar lines, Medin (1988) suggested that despite the results of research supporting a prototypical representation, it is at least possible, particularly given some of the research methods used, that the actual encoding and initial storage of information about persons may be much more individualized, whereas the categorical viewpoint may actually apply more to retrieval or output processes.

The issue of categorical versus individualized representations brings us back to the debate raised in chapter 1 between general schema or prototype viewpoints and the exemplar position expounded by Smith and his associates (e.g., E. R. Smith & Zarate, 1992). In the present context, the exemplar position argues that our impressions of or memory for a person may be influenced by the similarity of that person to another individual whom we have known (e.g., to an ex-spouse or a previous teacher or student). Whether one is influenced primarily by categorical or individuating information will depend on how much individuating information is present (cf. Krueger & Rothbart, 1988; though see also Lockesley, Borgida, Brekke, & Hepburn, 1980) or on the degree of attention paid to these two different types of information (see Fiske & Neuberg, 1990, as well as M. B. Brewer, 1988). It is sufficient to note that individual, concrete past experiences, as well as categorical information, may have an influence on our impressions and memory.

A Schema Viewpoint

A number of different researchers (e.g., Fiske & Taylor, 1991; Taylor & Crocker, 1981) have discussed the role of *person schemas* in social cognition. Although that term has taken on a variety of different meanings, ranging from general categories or stereotypes (e.g., extraverted person, liberated woman) to specific knowledge of specific persons (e.g., Lau's [1986] example of people's impression of Ronald Reagan), a more exact definition of a person schema is that it represents a *generic* knowledge structure about a type of person (e.g., persons occupying a particular role, or having a particular temperament). A person schema differs from a prototype in that schemas summarize the typical qualities (e.g., traits, mental states), physical attributes, behaviors, and so forth, of that type of person, and, more importantly, the *relationships* or connections among these qualities (as opposed to the whole pattern). A schema is more of a conceptual summary about types of people than it is a simple pattern or configuration of attributes (though see Murphy & Medin, 1985). Furthermore, although schemas may be embedded within one another (e.g., Rumelhart & Ortony, 1977), they do not necessarily involve the assumption of a strict typological structure. As I discussed in chapter 1, schemas serve the function of guiding our encoding or interpretations of peoples' behavior and appearance, our inferences from these data, and our expectations about additional behaviors or attributes.

As an example of the difference between a prototype and a schema, consider John Wayne: For many people John Wayne represents the prototype of a the general category of western hero. In contrast, the *schema* for such a hero involves a specification of the typical features of a western hero—for example, he should be a good gun fighter, wear a 10 gallon (white) hat, and love his horse as much as the female lead. In other words, a prototype (at least on one interpretation) can be viewed as a readout or particular instantiation[2] of a general program or recipe provided by the schema. Stated differently, a prototype can be predicted from the relative *similarity* between a whole pattern (e.g., John Wayne) and other whole patterns in that particular category (Rosch, Simpson, & Miller, 1976), whereas the elements of a schema (e.g., of Western heros) can be predicted from those elements' *typicality* or representativeness of the generic schema description.

Although the term person schema has been used by a number of different writers in a variety of different ways (see Stangor & McMillan, 1992, for

---

[2]Note that there are, of course, many different conceptions of prototypes (see Smith & Medin, 1981).

a summary; see also Fiske & Linville, 1980), I shall focus on one particular explicit test of Graesser's (1981) *schema-copy-plus-tag (SC+T) model* outlined in chapter 1 as it applies to person concepts. In the first of three studies, Woll and Graesser (1982) contrasted two different conceptions of the role of person schemas. The first of these is the *filtering hypothesis* (e.g., Neisser, 1976; Taylor & Crocker, 1981), which argues that schemas filter out information that is inconsistent with expectations derived from the schema and focus attention on information that is *consistent* with those expectations. As discussed in chapter 1, the alternative SC+T model argues that information that is consistent with a schema is encoded and stored in terms of a pointer to or a copy of that generic schema (e.g., a schema of a serial killer or a social worker), whereas information that is atypical of that schema is stored separately and tagged. The result is that information that is consistent with the schema is difficult to discriminate from material inferred on the basis of this generic knowledge, whereas atypical (or inconsistent) material is distinctive and easier to discriminate on a recognition test.

Research Evidence. In a series of three studies, Woll and Graesser supported the predictions from the SC+T model. That is, participants showed better memory discrimination (i.e., the ability to discriminate between items that were or were not presented) for information that was atypical of either general person schemas (e.g., a man of the world), occupational schemas (e.g., a librarian), or general trait schemas (e.g., an introverted male). We also found a greater rate of false recognition for information that was typical of the schema. That is, participants had a harder time rejecting items that had not been presented earlier but that were typical of the schema (e.g., "enjoys reading" for an introvert). One other finding of interest is that ratings of schema typicality, or the degree to which behavioral and trait information were typical of the schema, proved to be a better predictor of false recognitions than did judgments of the similarity of the different items of information to each other (as one may expect from a prototype viewpoint—see Light, Kayra-Stuart, & Hollander, 1979; Rosch et al., 1976, in the area of face recognition).

Reservations. One question that arises regarding person schemas is if we can have a schema of a given individual, or whether schemas, as *generic* knowledge structures, are restricted to general concepts. One can certainly argue that after encountering a given person on a number of occasions, one must have constructed a generic schema of that person, whether it be Bill Clinton, Bart Simpson, a best friend, or a spouse. The questions are whether these latter knowledge structures merit the label of schema (as opposed to, say, a mere exemplar), how such schemas emerge, and how they relate to schemas of groups or categories. It is clear that such individual person schemas do not play a role in the initial formation of an impression of a person (though see Smith & Zarate, 1992), but rather individuals either apply existing generic knowledge or construct an impression on the spot from new information. The latter alternative seems implausible, that is, creating an impression in the absence of stored, generic knowledge; but it is not completely clear how our knowledge of groups and categories gets transformed into knowledge of a given individual.

One criticism raised in connection with the prototype model is also clearly relevant to the schema model: namely, the fact that people remember specific instances or features as well as generic qualities (see Alba & Hasher, 1983). Thus, one may react to a new acquaintance (or a new western hero) on the basis of some similarity in appearance, speech pattern, or life story to some other person one has known from the past (or to John Wayne). If one accepts the argument just reviewed that individuals may develop person schemas about specific individuals, then it becomes unclear exactly where exemplars leave off and schemas begin (see discussion of this topic in chap. 4).

One other problem with the application of the schema model to person concepts is that the rules of connection or the structural properties are much less clear-cut for person concepts than they are, say, for spatial schemas or event schemas. Thus, for example, in the case of event schemas, which I discuss in chapter 4, the connections between actions have a clear causal structure, temporal sequence, or both; in the case of visual schemas, there are clear spatial relationships. In the case of people, however, it is not at all clear what the relations amongst attributes are—unless, of course, you hold to some explicit theoretical model of personal functioning (e.g., psychodynamic). One attempt to specify some of these connections can be found in an article by Asch and Zukier (1984) on the resolution of inconsistencies in personal qualities, but that article covers only a few possibilities (and does not do so in a particularly rigorous way).

THE PROCESSES OF IMPRESSION FORMATION AND MEMORY RETRIEVAL

It is a virtual truism within cognitive psychology and social cognition that it is difficult, if not impossible, to evaluate structural or representational models in the absence of information about the accompanying processing assumptions. It is certainly the case that the original formulation by Asch was as concerned with the *process* of impression formation as it was with the result of that process, though this process was not clearly specified. In addition, schema theories contain explicit assumptions about the processing of information that is relevant to the schema. We now turn to a discussion of three other prominent models of the way in which we process information about persons.

The Other Half of the Wyer and Srull Person Memory Model

The representational and encoding assumptions developed earlier for Wyer and Srull's person memory model are part of a much broader processing model of social cognition. This general model is presented in Fig. 2.4.

A glance at Fig. 2.4 indicates that Wyer and Srull's model is, for the most part, a fairly standard information-processing model with a couple of distinctive features added, at least one of which is particularly relevant to social cognition and to everyday cognition in general. This feature is the *goal specification box,* which contains the kind of goals or *processing objectives* alluded to in the previous discussion of the person memory model. Specifically, these objectives refer to the goals of thinking or information processing. For example, the primary focus of research on this topic has been on the comparison of impression formation and memory goals or instructions, although a few studies have focused on the impact of anticipated interaction (e.g., Devine, Sedikides, & Fuhrman, 1989), empathy (e.g., Harvey, Yarkin, Lightner, & Town, 1980), self-reference (e.g., Rogers, Kuiper, & Kirker, 1977), and accuracy (Leyens & Fiske, 1994; Neuberg, 1989). (See C. Cohen, 1981; Hastie, Park, & Webber, 1984; and Srull & Wyer, 1986, for general reviews.)

The original motivation for this research was the argument (Hamilton et al., 1980), following Asch (1946), that impression formation involves trying to organize different pieces of information into a coherent whole; and hence it implies organization. Therefore, Hamilton et al. expected (and found) that instructions to form an impression would result in greater clustering and, by virtue of that clustering, better recall for behavioral information (though see Klein & Loftus, 1990). We have seen that laboratory research has found such impression formation instructions to have a major impact on participants' representation and recall of social information, al-

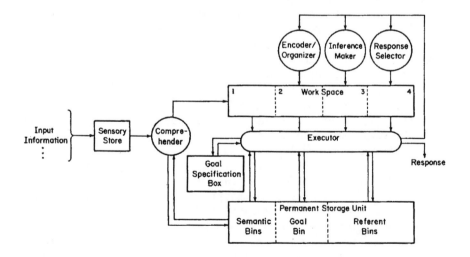

FIG. 2.4.   The original Wyer and Srull person memory model. From *Memory and Cognition in its Social Context* (p. 14), by R. S. Wyer & T. Srull, 1989, Hillsdale, NJ: Lawrence Erlbaum Associates. Copyright © 1989 by Lawrence Erlbaum Associates. Reprinted with permission.

though some contrary evidence has also been reported by Woll and Van Der Meer (1996) in a real-world videodating context. Wyer and Srull (1989) argued that knowing a person's goals is critical for understanding how that person processes social information. At the same time, however, there is evidence (e.g., Bodenhausen & Wyer, 1985; Woll & Van Der Meer, 1996; see also the ecological psychology viewpoint, e.g., McArthur & Baron, 1983) that the structure of the environment or context may have a major impact on memory and information processing as well (see Fiske, Lia, & Neubers, 1999, for a similar argument). Thus, when it comes to real-world situations, it is likely that it is the match between goals and the conditions imposed by the informational context that determines how individuals handle incoming information. (See the discussion of face processing in chap. 3 for examples of this point.)

The second feature of Wyer and Srull's model, which is an idiosyncratic feature of that model, is the specification of three *storage bins* where different sorts of information are stored. As the labels for these bins in Fig. 2.4 suggest, they are concerned with semantic information (e.g., nouns, attribute concepts), referents of this information (e.g., both specific and general persons, objects, and events), and goals. Although I will not develop this concept of storage bins in detail, the main issue addressed by the concept is that the most recently used concept or information is the one that is most likely to be recalled and used in interpreting new events. This is because information is assumed to be deposited at the top of the bin—a kind of "last in, first out" processing rule—though Wyer and Srull (1989) have also discussed the role of processing objectives in the memory search process. Although Wyer and Srull have applied this feature primarily to research—their own and others'—on *category accessibility* (Srull & Wyer, 1979, 1980), or the ease with which different concepts come to mind in interpreting new information, I also evaluate its applicability to the topic of autobiographical memory in chapter 5. As a final point, note that this bin concept does not address the question of knowledge representation, as Wyer and Carlston (1994) themselves acknowledge.

Recently, Wyer and Radvansky (1999) dropped the concept of storage bins and revised the notion of a comprehender in Fig. 2.4 to include not only semantic information but also other forms of declarative and procedural knowledge such as information about past experiences and individual persons. This past knowledge is stored in the *permanent storage unit* (see Fig. 2.5) from which it exerts its influence on the comprehension process.

In this revised model, Wyer and Radvansky addressed directly the question of knowledge representation of social information. Specifically, there are two kinds of knowledge contained in the permanent store: *situation models* of the sort described in research on text comprehension (e.g., Kintsch, 1988, 1998; Radvansky, 1999; van Dijk & Kintsch, 1983), and *generalized representations*. Situation models refer to our representation of the particular situation, including in particular the events in that situation. Generalized representa-

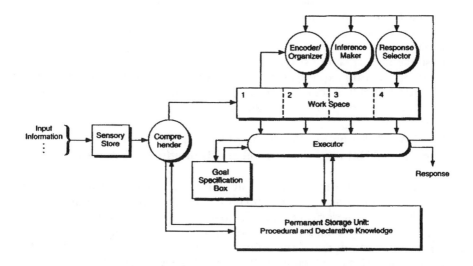

FIG. 2.5. The revised Wyer and Radvansky model. From "The Comprehension and Validation of Social Information" by R. S. Wyer, & G. A. Radvansky, 1999, *Psychological Review, 106,* p. 92. Copyright © 1999 by the American Psychological Association. Reprinted with permission.

tions, however, as the name suggests, refer to generalizations over situations and events, such as the representation of people, group stereotypes, and political institutions. It is the latter of these, of course, that Wyer and his colleagues have been concerned with in most previous formulations. In this latest version of the model, however, it is the situation models that are of primary interest.

Although the focus of this revision is on event representation, which is discussed further in chapter 4, a few features of this model are worth mentioning here. First, this formulation marks a major departure from the original associative network model discussed earlier, as Wyer and Radvansky themselves pointed out. These authors alluded to a combining of attributes to form generalized representation, and they did refer to a kind of feature comparison process (i.e., separate comparison of subject and object with components of the situation model) in both comprehension and verification of incoming social information. However, they also argued that "*relation information* provides the glue that gives structure to one's understanding of the situation" (p. 95). Second, in part because of their primary emphasis on events, Wyer and Radvansky also emphasized the role of specific examples, including specific events, over generalized categories. In fact, one of the postulates of their model is that "the referent of a situation model is more likely to be a specific exemplar of a category or concept than to the concept or category itself" (p. 98). I return to this point in chapter 4.

Finally, and most importantly for our present purposes, Wyer and Radvansky attempted to incorporate these revised conceptions of the comprehender and knowledge representation into Wyer's more general information-processing model, although in point of fact, only the comprehension and permanent storage components are really implicated. In fact, this reformulation expands the Wyer and Srull model even further into a very broad model of social information processing in general, rather than of just memory for persons and groups.

Two Other Information-Processing Models: The Distinction (Once Again) Between Categorical and Individuated Processing

Within the past 10 years, two rather similar models of impression formation have been put forward, both of which focus on the differences that we have noted between categorical and individuating processes. One of these is M. B. Brewer's (1988) dual-process model of impression formation[3] discussed earlier in this chapter, and the other is Susan Fiske's single dimension, *continuum* model (Fiske & Neuberg, 1990; Neuberg & Fiske, 1987). These two models have a great deal in common, as well as some instructive differences (see M. B. Brewer, 1988; Fiske, 1988; Fiske & Neuberg, 1990, for discussions), and so I examine them together.

The Brewer and Fiske models are presented next to each other in Figure 2.6. The first thing to note about the two models is that both are couched in information-processing terms with a sequence of processing stages and a set of decision rules associated with each, although, as M. B. Brewer (1988) has pointed out, both are clearly formulated at a lower level of generality than the expansive Wyer and Srull model. That is, both are simply concerned with impression formation and not with social cognition in general. Both models assume that the initial stage involves an automatic mode of processing in terms of salient, superficial features such as gender, race, and the like. Most importantly, both models make a basic distinction between *categorization,* or treating the individual as an example of a general category or type on the one hand, and *personalization,* or what Fiske and Neuberg (1990) referred to as *piecemeal processing,* or an attempt to understand the person as an individual consisting of a combination of attributes including category membership on the other hand. For both models, treating the person as part of a category or as an individual results in very different modes of inference or information processing, that is, top–down versus bottom–up (See Fig. 2.6a and 2.6b).

I have cited a number of examples of the categorical mode in my discussions of Andersen and Klatzky (1987) and of Brewer's (1988) research on

---

[3]There are numerous dual processing models in social psychology (see Chaiken & Trope, 1999), including Uleman's (1999) distinction between spontaneous and intentional trait inference in impression formation.

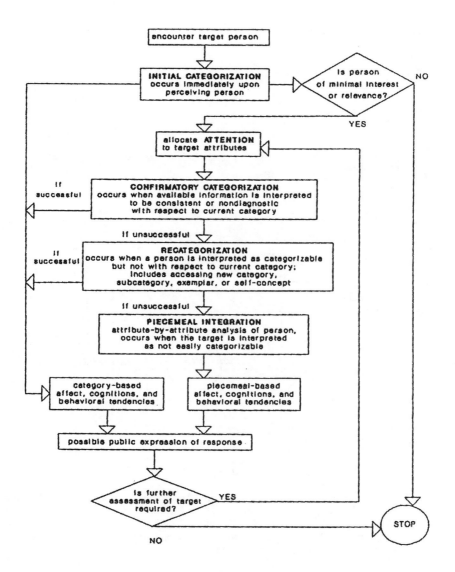

FIG. 2.6a. The Fiske and Neuberg Continuum model of impression formation. From "A Continuum of Impression Formation, From Catagory-based to Individuating Processes: Influences of Information and Attention and Interpretation" by S. T. Fiske & S. L. Neuberg in *Advances in Experimental Social Psychology, Vol 23*, edited by M. Zanna, copyright © 1990 by Academic Press, reproduced by permission of the publisher. All rights of reproduction in any form reserved.

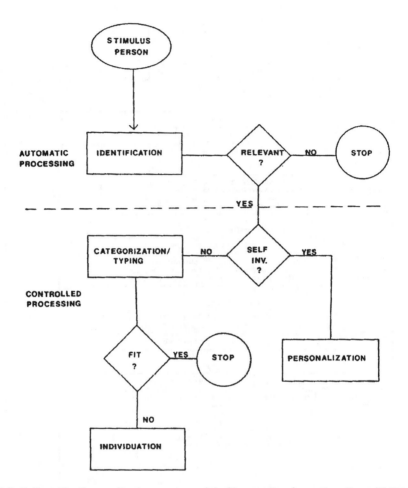

FIG. 2.6b. The Brewer Dual-process model of impression formation. From "A Dual Process Model of Impression Formation" by M. B. Brewer. In *A Dual Process Model of Impression Formation: Advances in Social Cognition* (Vol. 1, p. 5), edited by T. K. Srull & R. S. Wyer, Jr., Hillsdale, NJ: Lawrence Erlbaum Associates. Copyright © 1988 by Lawrence Erlbaum Associates. Reprinted with permission.

prototypes of the elderly; and of course, nearly all of the traditional research on impression formation (see Schneider, et al., 1979) dealt with the personalized or piecemeal mode. As one dramatic illustration of the difference between the two, Brewer and Feinstein (1999) gave the example of the Serbian and Muslim citizens of Bosnia-Herzogovina, who for 20 years had interacted with each other as individuals but then switched to a more antagonistic, categorical mode of processing and interaction.

Although these two models (contra Fiske) are very similar in many important ways, there are also a number of significant differences between them. For Brewer, the decision to approach the person in a categorical or personalized way is primarily the result of a decision about how much personal investment you have in that person, whereas for Fiske the movement from categorization to piecemeal processing depends on how successful or unsuccessful you are in confirming your categorization and recategorization of that person (e.g., as a jock or a Palestinian), that is, on how close a fit there is between your available categories and the features of the target person. Thus, as M. B. Brewer and Feinstein (1999) emphasized, the dual-process model differs from the continuum view in that the former, unlike the latter, does not assume that categorical processing necessarily takes precedence over more piecemeal processing. (At the same time, this distinction is also, in a sense, less clear-cut than it may seem because Fiske and Neuberg, 1990, also emphasized the role of motivation or *self-relevance* and, in particular, the degree of *outcome dependency* [Erber & Fiske, 1984; Neuberg & Fiske, 1987] or *interdependence* of the perceiver and the perceived, in moving the perceiver along the continuum.) As Fiske (1988) expressed it, the two models are also different in that Brewer's version assumes a branching configuration, whereas Fiske's assumes a single continuum (although as we have seen, both models assume rather different modes of processing or inference for categorization vs. personalization).

More important, for Brewer the different modes or stages of processing involve different types of representation (i.e., multidimensional space for the identification stage vs. pictoliteral prototypes for the categorization stage vs. individual schema or propositional networks for the personalization stage), whereas Fiske's model does not make such a distinction. (In fact, Fiske [1988; Fiske & Neuberg, 1990] argued that it does not make sense to suggest that images are not available for our representation of individuals or that verbal codes are not applicable to categorizations.) Finally, note that Fiske and Neuberg's model places a great deal of emphasis, both in theory and research (e.g., Fiske, Neuberg, Beattie, & Milberg, 1987), on the role of attentional processes, that is, attention to attributes, in determining which stages of the continuum are used, and in influencing affective and behavioral outcomes of the two different forms of processing.

The Brewer (1988) and Fiske and Neuberg (1990) models are of interest because, contrary to traditional viewpoints, including those of Asch and Anderson, they argue that we do not always approach the impression formation process in an individuated and personalized way but rather frequently represent the person as a member of a broad group or stereotype category. Furthermore, both models attempt to identify some of the factors, both informational and motivational, that determine the perceiver's movement through the different stages of impression formation. Finally, both models, like the Wyer and Srull (1989) model just reviewed, are backed up by extensive laboratory research.

Research Evidence. I have already reviewed studies supporting the Brewer model; and so the present discussion focuses on two representative studies illustrating the Fiske and Neuberg continuum model. In one of these studies on the effect of outcome dependency on attention and person memory (Erber & Fiske, 1984), participants were led to expect that their reward from a joint task was either dependent on their partner's performance or would be determined by their own work alone. Participants were led to believe that their partner was going to be either competent or incompetent and were later asked to recall the partner's attributes—which had been described to them prior to the task, half of which were consistent with participants' expectancy of competence or incompetence, and half of which were inconsistent. Measures were taken of the amount of time participants spent reading the consistent and inconsistent information and of their liking for the partner. The prediction was that participants who were more outcome dependent would pay closer attention to the *inconsistent* attributes because these attributes would be more informative, whereas those who were *not* outcome dependent would not focus on such inconsistent attributes. The results of the attention measure (i.e., time spent reading the different types of material) clearly supported this prediction, although no differences in recall or liking were actually found.

In a second pair of studies designed to test the degree to which attentional differences account for the relative influence of individuating information on impressions (Neuberg & Fiske, 1987), participants were led to believe that they were going to interact with a former mental patient on a joint task. These participants were then given a profile of the former patient that contained either neutral information or information inconsistent with the label provided (i.e., schizophrenia). The inconsistent information was thus individuating. In one study, participants were either dependent on this person for outcomes or were not so dependent, whereas in a second study they were either given instructions to form an accurate impression or were given no particular goal. The assumption in both experiments was that differences in attention—either measured or instructed—should mediate the effects of individuating information on memory for and impressions of the expected partner. Inconsistent information is itself individuating; and the assumption was that both outcome dependency and instructions stressing accuracy would likewise encourage participants to attend to such individuating attributes even in the absence of such inconsistencies. Such individuating information should also result in more favorable impressions (because the categorical label of schizophrenic or mentally ill was assumed to be negative).

In both experiments participants were found to show greater liking for their expected (negative) partner when they paid more attention to him, that is, in the outcome-dependent and accuracy-oriented condition given a neutral profile, as well as in the inconsistent profile condition, where the inconsistent information was, by definition, more positive. In addition, in the first study those in the inconsistent profile condition and in the neutral profile, outcome-dependent condition spent more time reading the profile (i.e., as a measure of attention) than in the neutral profile, no-outcome-dependent condition; and in this latter condition, a significant correlation was found between amount of time spent reading the profile and liking.

Reservations.   These examples suggest some of the strengths and potential problems with the Brewer and Fiske models from the standpoint of everyday cognition research. On the plus side, both research paradigms provide good examples of the strategy of experimental social psychology for studying cognitive processes—careful experimental manipulations, precise response measures, and rigorous data analyses. Both paradigms also exemplify the often complex research designs in experimental social psychology as well as the sometimes complex rationales underlying these designs.

At the same time, it is clear that the Fiske model in particular focuses primarily on information-processing mechanisms, or basic invariant *processes* (e.g., attention, categorization), to the virtual exclusion of participants' existing knowledge and representations of persons. (Brewer's model is slightly less open to criticism here in that she at least worries about the nature of and representational format for this knowledge.) To be sure, the notion of categorical processes and the attempts to tap into these processes via experimental manipulations (e.g., of the mental patient stereotype or the label of competent or incompetent) represent efforts to get at participants' knowledge of persons in an indirect way, within a rarefied, information-impoverished lab setting. However, the major emphasis here is not on the knowledge per se—no assessment of that knowledge is attempted, and even measures of recall in the Erber and Fiske (1984) experiment failed to show differences—but rather on the *process* of attention or on *general,* abstract factors in the environment (e.g., outcome dependency) that control these attentional processes.

In addition, the emphasis of both the Brewer and Fiske models is on a limited capacity system and on the influence of such limitations on our use of, for example, categorical versus individuating information. Yet in a commentary on Brewer's dual-process model, Medin (1988) made an intriguing observation about this "cognitive miser" (Fiske & Taylor, 1984) point of view:

> I confess to being very skeptical about this answer [i.e., that we categorize in order to deal with some kind of "information overload"]. To my knowledge, no one has identified a memory disorder attributable to a person's having so many items of information stored away that there is no room for any new facts. (Of course, access to this information is a different question.)
>
> I think that categorization, including social categorization, is primarily to cope with the problem of too *little* rather than too much information. We may be at a loss as to how to interact with a new person if we have no way of generating any expectation at all concerning how the person will think and act. ... If every

person were treated as absolutely unique, then there would be no basis at all for generating expectations. (pp. 121–122, italics added)

This observation has major implications for the study of everyday cognition in general and for the study of impression formation in particular. Specifically, the problem in forming an impression—and certainly this applies even more in the lab than in the real world—is *not* coping with *too much* information about that person so that we have to *simplify* the world, but rather dealing with *too little* information, so that we have to *enrich* our database (cf. Oakes & Turner, 1990, for a similar argument, and Bodenhausen, McCrae, & Sherman, 1999, for a counterargument), even if that enrichment sometimes leads to errors (see chap. 9). Thus, all impressions, whether they be category-based or individuated, involve accessing some previous knowledge structure, whether it be generic or some exemplar (which is itself probably connected with some generic knowledge). In this sense, the Fiske continuum model is probably more on target in its emphasis on more individualized, piecemeal impressions as resulting from the difficulty in correctly classifying the individual in terms of previous generalities.

Another obvious feature of Fiske's research and, to a lesser extent, Brewer's,[4] is their strong experimental flavor and their willingness to set up laboratory "microcosms," to use Fiske's terminology, to get at real-world phenomena and processes, rather than examining impression formation in real-world settings.[5] In chapter 1 I discussed some of the criticisms that have been raised against this sort of strategy. In fact, I question the degree to which principles established under impoverished lab conditions and with fairly artificial experimental manipulations really generalize to the real world. To take just one example, I wonder if the simple process of attention (or lack thereof), in the usual information-processing sense, really plays as strong a role in determining stereotyping as Fiske's (1993; Fiske & Neuberg, 1990) model suggests and whether simple measures of reading time or simple instructions to pay attention or to form accurate impressions really capture the nature and the role of attention in the real world. Without reviewing the extensive evidence on the various cognitive mechanisms involved in stereotyping (see Fiske, 1998), it seems unquestionable that stereotypes are knowledge or belief structures, that these structures guide information processing, and that such structures are not adequately captured by simple experimental manipulations or by impoverished informational environments.

As I indicated in chapter 1, there is a certain irony contained in this last criticism. Specifically, as social psychologists, both Fiske and Brewer have

---

[4]In the case of Brewer, there is clearly an attempt to use more real-world stimuli (i.e., pictures) and to use methods designed to get at the actual representation of the stimulus person, and in Fiske's case there is at least an attempt to collect think-aloud protocols.

[5]See Fiske, 1993, for an attempt to extend her research and the more naturalistic research of others (Kanter, 1977) to a real-world legal case.

explicitly attempted to place the cognitive processes of impression formation and stereotyping within a *social* context. For example, Fiske has emphasized the role of interdependence, and in recent publications (Fiske, Lin, & Neuberg, 1999; Stevens & Fiske, 1995) she has attempted to identify a variety of social motives that may influence the process of impression formation. The *irony* here, as it was for Wyer and Srull, is that although the experimental paradigms are minimally social (more so than Wyer and Srull's), these social relations are abstracted out of their real-world social context. For example, the interactions are primarily with strangers (or their facsimiles); and oftentimes these strangers are people that participants are probably not used to interacting with, such as individuals with schizophrenia. Thus, the Brewer and Fiske models appear to be more social in *theory* than they are in practice.

Another Alternative: PDP Models

In the past few years, another type of model has emerged that provides a rather different account of impression formation. This group of models can generally be called PDP or connectionist models (e.g., Kunda & Thagard, 1996; Read & Miller, 1988c; E. R. Smith & DeCoster, 1998); and as I suggested in the last chapter, these PDP models are explicitly proposed as alternatives to traditional information-processing models of the sort that I have been considering. Interestingly, as both Read et al. (1997) and E. R. Smith (1996) pointed out, these PDP models are in many ways more similar to the original Gestalt account of impression formation than the other approaches that I have discussed.

Examples of Models. The first two connectionist models (Kunda & Thagard, 1996; Read & Marcus-Newhall, 1993; Read & Miller, 1993, 1998a) focus on the concept of parallel constraint satisfaction developed in the last chapter. For example, Kunda and Thagard (1996) have taken the dual-processing models reviewed earlier and have suggested that the categorical (or what they call stereotyping) and individuating processes occur in parallel and jointly constrain each other. Stated differently, stereotypes, traits, and behavior represent nodes that are connected by excitatory and inhibitory links; and the spread of activation across this network determines the encoding of the relevant behavior or the process of impression formation. Furthermore, in keeping with the assumptions of the connectionist viewpoint in general, this model proposes that the meaning of any given construct or node in the network is not static but rather is dynamically determined by the spread of activation throughout the network (cf. Woll et al.'s [1980] emphasis on the semantic flexibility of trait meanings). As the network goes through multiple cycles of such spreading activation, weightings of the links between nodes change, and the activation levels of such nodes stabilize. Furthermore, there is no assumption that categorical or stereotyping automatically takes precedence over individuating processes, as Fiske and Neuberg (1990) assumed.

Kunda and Thagard's connectionist model of impression formation (IMP) focuses on automatic processing because, in their view, impression formation usually occurs automatically—and that is certainly one reason why PDP models are attractive in this area. The basic argument of this model is that stereotypes, traits, and behaviors are mutually constraining. That is, stereotypes influence the meaning of traits (e.g., male-assertive vs. female-assertive) and of individuating information (e.g., man hugs a friend vs. woman hugs a friend), and individuating information can influence what subtype of a stereotype is selected (e.g., "concerned with research evidence" → academic psychologist, rather than pop psychologist). In addition, though, there are interactions among these different factors in determining the value of the other. For example, Kunda and Thagard reviewed evidence that suggests that stereotypes do not have the same effect on trait interpretation when some form of individuating behavior is present; for instance, when a person is described as "abruptly" interrupting someone, it does not make much difference whether the person is female or male in interpreting that person as assertive. These authors explained this effect by the observation, backed up by a meta-analysis, that individuating information has a much stronger effect on trait interpretation than do stereotypes. At the same time, stereotypes *do* have an impact on such interpretations when the individuating information is ambiguous or irrelevant. (This latter assertion can be viewed as a modern, more precise updating of the old *change in meaning* hypothesis, Asch, 1946.) Finally, a stereotype can influence the subtype of another stereotype that is applied; for instance, a Black athlete conjures up a different subtype of Blacks than does a Black businessman (Devine & Baker, 1991).

In their most recent account, Thagard and Kunda (1998; see also Spellman & Holyoak, 1992) have incorporated another process into their account of impression formation: analogical reasoning. Specifically, Thagard and Kunda argued, correctly, that impressions often involve drawing analogies between a new person and relatives, friends, acquaintances, or even oneself. This analogy may be between the personalities or characters of two people (see the discussion of Smith & Zarate's [1992] example of Hitler and Saddam Hussein in the previous chapter) or between their circumstances (e.g., Thagard & Kunda's [1998] example of the similar circumstances of Princess Diana and Anna Karenina, in that both were in unhappy marriages where they did not love their husbands, and both loved another man; cf. the discussion of themes and case-based reasoning in chap. 4). There exists a connectionist account for such analogies (Holyoak & Thagard, 1989), though there has been relatively little research on this topic in the area of impression formation or social cognition in general (though see Read & Cesa, 1991; Read & Miller, 1993; Spellman & Holyoak, 1992).

It should be noted that the Kunda and Thagard model qualifies as a PDP model in some senses of that term, but not in others. For example, it is a PDP model in that it conceives of the processes of impression formation as operating in parallel, interacting ways rather than serially. This is the notion of parallel constraint satisfaction reviewed earlier. In addition, the postulation of inhibitory as well as excitatory links is also a feature of PDP models. Finally, Kunda and Thagard (1996) briefly described a computer simulation (i.e., IMP) in the Appendix of their article, although relatively few details are included (see Smith & DeCoster, 1998b, for a discussion and critique of this presentation).

At the same time, there is little discussion of the overall *patterns* of excitation in this model; and in fact, Kunda and Thagard (1996) themselves acknowledged that their model is a kind of localist version of connectionism in that the representations are localized in the stereotype and trait nodes rather than really being distributed,[6] even though these representations or meanings change with the context. Smith and DeCoster (1998b) argued that the Kunda and Thagard model and the Read and Miller (1993, 1998a) model (to be discussed next) have the disadvantage that they require a new structure of nodes and links for each specific task that they encounter, rather than using a general, all-purpose learning rule that applies across different tasks. In these senses, the Kunda and Thagard model is not a thoroughgoing PDP model.

Read and Miller's (1993; Read & Marcus-Newhall, 1993) *interpersonalism* model operates along lines similar to Kunda and Thagard's in that it involves networks of both excitatory and inhibitory links, successive waves or cycles of propagation throughout a network, and most importantly, parallel constraint satisfaction assumptions. The emphasis of this interpersonalism model is on the formation of a coherent model of a person and on possible explanations of that person's behavior. Like Kunda and Thagard's model, Read and Miller's concepts include traits (as well as incoming input), but also goals, plans, scripts, themes, and roles—concepts of the sort to be discussed in chapter 4. I will not develop this model in greater detail here, except to note that, like the Kunda and Thagard one, it is essentially a localist version of a connectionist model.

In a more recent version called the *social dynamics* model, Read and Miller (1998a) distinguished among four different levels of processing (roughly akin to the different levels of neurons referred to in chap. 1). The first level is the *input* or *feature* level, where, as the labels suggest, stimuli activate basic feature detectors such as orientation and movement and even such higher order features as faces (see chap. 3). The second level is the *identification* level, where the features activate nodes that identify specific or

---

[6]Kunda and Thagard (1996) argued that they did not provide a distributed representation because "no corpus of examples exists" (p. 308) that would allow them to "train" a system to provide such a representation.

general types of people and objects. These identifications in turn activate nodes at the *scenario* level (see chap. 4), which then activate nodes at the *conceptual* or *meaning* level. At this last level inferences such as the meaning of a behavior (i.e., the actor's goals, or that actor's traits) are made. Once again, this model suggests a localist representation at these different levels, although Read and Miller (1998d) indicated that this is simply a convenience for ease of presentation whereas their representation is actually assumed to be distributed. It should also be noted that activation not only flows upward but also downward from the higher levels to the lower ones.

One phenomenon (of several) that Read and Miller suggested can be accounted for by this model is the finding (reviewed earlier) that people tend to spontaneously infer traits from others' actions or from verbal descriptions of actions (e.g., Uleman, Newman, & Moskowitz, 1996; Winter & Uleman, 1984). As an example of this, in one frequently cited study Winter and Uleman (1984) presented participants with sentences such as "The secretary solves the mystery halfway through the book." After a distractor task, these participants were asked to recall the sentences when presented with one of two types of cues—namely, the implied trait (e.g., clever) or a word otherwise semantically related to the actor (e.g., typewriter, detective)—or with no cue at all. The basic finding was that the trait cues led to better recall than the semantic associates, even when participants were not explicitly asked to infer such traits or to form an impression of the actor. These results suggested to Uleman and his associates that such traits were spontaneously, automatically inferred.

According to Read and Miller's model, such spontaneous trait inference involves, first, the identification of the actor (e.g., secretary), objects (e.g., mystery, book), and actions (e.g., solves). The activation of these concepts in turn activates other features (e.g., the appearance or intelligence of secretaries) and concepts (e.g., that mysteries entail puzzles or unanswered questions). The identified concepts also activate scenarios that, in this case, amount to the setting up a frame relating the concepts to each other; for instance, the secretary does the solving involved in the sentence, and the mystery, which is a property of or is contained in the book, is the thing that is solved (see Schank's [1975] conceptual dependency analysis). On the basis of this scenario the meaning level is activated in the form of explanations for the solution, including trait concepts, intentions, and so forth. As described earlier in this chapter, Read and Miller conceive of traits as goals rather than simple dispositions, but that is really not relevant here. What *is* relevant is that traits are automatically inferred as possible explanations of the action contained in the scenario. In this sense they represent the kind of automatic inferences that are assumed by some (e.g., Graesser, Singer, & Trabasso, 1994) to be involved in text comprehension.

It should be apparent from this example that Read and Miller's model is primarily a theoretical model that represents one of many possible accounts of the spontaneous trait inference effect. To be sure, it is an account that is based on an earlier *interaction activation and competition* model of word recognition developed by McClelland and Rumelhart (1981). Nonetheless, despite their protests that the Social Dynamics model is not just "some new-fangled, gee-whiz toy" (p. 64), and that it is consistent with earlier Gestalt dynamic principles, as well as the McClelland and Rumelhart connectionist formulation, the fact remains that this model, even with its specification of learning rules and energy surfaces, is simply a speculative account that is couched in terms that could just as well be part of a traditional symbolic model as a connectionist one.[7] Its main distinctive contribution is its implication of scenario construction and event memory in the explanation of social behavior, but this is an idea that Read and Miller put forth earlier (e.g., L. C. Miller & Read, 1991; Read et al., 1990) without a thoroughgoing PDP account.

One example of a model that qualifies as a thoroughgoing PDP account is that proposed by Smith and DeCoster (1998a, 1998b). Like the Kunda and Thagard and the Read and Miller versions, the Smith and DeCoster model constitutes an autoassociative or *recurrent network* model or, in other words, a model that incorporates feedback relations. This model is intended to account for the acquisition and accessibility of social knowledge in general. It assumes a distributed representation (i.e., distributed over a number of different nodes) such that different concepts or representations may share common nodes. This commonality in turn is assumed to facilitate generalization or transfer from the one pattern to the other, thereby allowing the system to learn from experience. Such learning is represented by changes in weights for the connections between units and is a combined result of external input and past experience. In other words, each unit is affected by both external input and relationships with every other unit. In this model, then, memory can be seen as the ability of the system to reproduce previous patterns of activation and inhibition across units by means of the established connections among units in response to a given stimulus or stimulus pattern.

The two simulations by Smith and DeCoster that are of greatest relevance for this discussion of impression formation involve (a) learning to infer characteristics of one exemplar of a person from numerous encounters with (and extensive knowledge of) previous ones, and (b) learning more than one piece of knowledge at once and then combining the features of each piece to recognize a new exemplar. (As will be seen, the first of these is similar to the problem addressed by PDP models of face recognition to be discussed in the next chapter and also represents a form of an exemplar model in connectionist terms of the sort that I consider in chap. 4.) For both simulations, the criterion was the ability of that simulation to reproduce well-established findings in the person memory and stereotyping litera-

---

[7]Read (personal communication, July 21, 1999) has emphasized that the Read and Miller (1998a) model is the most detailed account in the literature on spontaneous trait inference and one that includes some novel assumptions about how trait knowledge is structured and how behavioral information activates such trait knowledge.

tures. On the first of these, Smith and DeCoster (1998a) presented a simulation demonstrating that training on a large number (1,000) of exemplars, followed by a reasonable number (200) of instances of a particular exemplar, resulted in recognition of an incomplete pattern of the latter exemplar. In the second simulation these researchers demonstrated that presenting many instances of two different overlapping patterns resulted in recognition of a new pattern that contained the two overlapping elements. Both of these simulations illustrate the *pattern completion* feature of PDP models, that is, the fact that through repeated encounters with an input pattern, the resulting pattern of activation comes to fill in missing components of that pattern.

These results are not exactly earthshaking in their own right. However, as Smith and DeCoster (1998a) pointed out, these simulations reveal some of the advantages of connectionist models over more traditional ones. For example, the traditional symbolic accounts that apply to these and other principles of social knowledge entail different models and mechanisms for the several different findings that they simulate, whereas Smith and DeCoster's connectionist model can account for all of them. Thus, the connectionist model is more parsimonious. Furthermore, according to Smith and DeCoster (1998b), the connectionist model, is, more "precise and explicit," at least on a mathematical level. Finally, the connectionist model specifically deals with the *acquisition* of social knowledge rather than just its application, as compared, for example, with schema models. In fact, this ability to *learn* is in many ways the main advantage of PDP models.

At the same time, however, a number of reservations have been raised about connectionist models in general (e.g., Fodor & Pylyshyn, 1988; Green, 1998; Massaro, 1988; McCloskey, 1991). The first of these is that connectionist accounts entail powerful and complex mathematical/computational models (see Massaro, 1988) with many free parameters, or at least parameters that are not clearly specified by a theory, as well as "constructs with no ready identification with psychological states" (Dulany, 1998, p. 2). Such models also entail random sampling of stimulus or input values (see Smith & DeCoster, 1998a).[8] These characteristics of both the models and the input raise the question of the degree to which such models are, in fact, open to falsification in any strong fashion, particularly given the criterion used by Smith and DeCoster (1998a) of a general pattern of results (as opposed to, say, recognition of a particular word or face).

Green (1998) has made a similar point in the following way:

> the apparent success of connectionism in domains where symbolic models typically fail may be due as much to the huge number of additional "degrees

---

[8]It is difficult to determine from Smith and DeCoster's (1998a) description the exact nature of the stimulus patterns they used in their study, or whether they were social or not. (They weren't.) Note that Smith and DeCoster's test of their PDP model capitalizes on chance by sampling the test pattern from the same distribution as their training stimuli.

of freedom" that connectionist networks are afforded by virtue of the blanket claim of distributed representation across large numbers of uninterpreted units, as it is to any inherent virtues that connectionism has over symbolism in explaining cognitive phenomena. (pp. 8–9)

Massaro (1988) has also commented on the power—including what he calls the *superpower*—of connectionist models:

Good models should be falsifiable. However, a single connectionist model can simulate results that imply mutually exclusive psychological processes. Thus, *results consistent with a connectionist model should not be taken as evidence for the model.* Connectionist models are too powerful. ... Some connectionist models might simulate results that have not been observed in psychological investigations and results generated by incorrect process models of performance. (pp. 219–220, italics added)

Now the major target of Massaro's criticisms of the superpower of connectionist models is those versions that include hidden units, and none of the models I have discussed in this section have that feature. (It is interesting to note, however, that Smith & DeCoster, 1998b, argued that one way of overcoming the lack of power of their limited model is to include such hidden units.) It is nevertheless the case that simply predicting a pattern of data, as Smith & DeCoster (1998a, 1998b) did, is not sufficient, particularly when the connectionist model is consistent with many different models of psychological processes (see Gregg & Simon, 1967, for a similar argument about early stochastic models of learning). In point of fact, Massaro (1988) demonstrated that the same connectionist model can simulate the different patterns of results predicted by three different process models of perception.

At the very least, some competitive test among different PDP models of, say, impression formation, is necessary in order to see which one fits the data better, although even here it may not be clear whether the superiority of one is due to differences in the mathematics or in the psychological processes involved (see Massaro, 1988, and McCloskey, 1991, for similar arguments). (Smith and DeCoster actually allude to a kind of model comparison in their claim that their model can account for several different patterns of findings whereas symbolic architectures must propose different models or different assumptions. Obviously, though, this comparison applies only to a single connectionist architecture vs. a trio of symbolic ones and is subject to the previous reservation expressed by Green.)

Massaro (1988) proposed that instead of just testing single models or even competitive testing of multiple models, investigators need to show what might be called discriminative validity, that is, showing that the model predicts the right set of findings, but not others. Thus, it is not enough to show that a model accounts for a number of different findings in a number of different areas (convergent validity); it is also important to show that the model does not also predict (or is not consistent with) findings that don't occur.

Many years ago, Gregg and Simon (1967) made a similar point with regard to mathematical models of learning:

> One point of view is that theories gain their credibility solely from the accuracy of their predictions, account being taken of their parsimony in making these predictions. ... There is another point of view on credibility, however; that the credibility of a theory depends on its plausibility as well as the accuracy of its predictions. (p. 249)

In the case of PDP models, the "plausibility" stems primarily from its rough consistency with biological, neurological observations, although the more usual test is in the form of a computer simulation. (Green, 1998, and others have noted that connectionists are typically rather vague about the degree to which their models are to be taken literally as "neural" networks.) There is certainly little *psychological* plausibility of such models, because they do not correspond to our intuitions about our mental functioning (Fodor & Pylyshyn, 1988 [see also Green, 1998], have argued that connectionism only makes sense at the neurological level). In fact, when the nodes are actually given some psychological meaning, as in the Kunda and Thagard and the Read and Miller models, they are often viewed as too localist to be true parallel *distributed* processing models. Whether that sort of neural plausibility is better or worse than psychological plausibility depends on how much of a reductionist you are. (In this connection, I recall a line from Neisser's [1967] classic book *Cognitive Psychology*, which said that "psychology is not [just] something to do until the biochemist comes" [p. 6]).

It can be argued (e.g., Read, personal communication, July 21, 1999) that some PDP models have already been falsified, rejected, or revised. On this issue, Estes (1988) has distinguished between *testability* and *sufficiency*. The former of these concepts is concerned with the degree to which the model is or can be confirmed or disconfirmed by the empirical data, whereas sufficiency refers to the ability of a given model to handle other areas or topics, that is, the generalizability of the theory or model. Estes has argued that PDP models are particularly difficult to test in view of their power, and he specifically pointed to the interactive-activation model of word recognition as a result of certain assumptions adopted for programming convenience. Sufficiency, on the other hand, which has long been a consideration in cognitive psychology (Newell & Simon, 1972), raises a different set of issues. Estes argues for a combination of the two. It is my impression that although some of PDP models have been revised in the face of falsifying data (e.g., Seidenberg), most of the revisions have been based more on sufficiency issues (i.e., the ability of a given model in one area, such as word recognition, to handle other aspects of the same topic or to generalize to other phenomena.)

McCloskey (1991) made an interesting observation about connectionist modeling in general. The thrust of McCloskey's argument is that connectionist simulations provide a *basis* for improving theorizing about the mechanisms behind, say, word recognition (e.g., by requiring the modeler to specify these mechanisms more precisely, or by spelling out the theory's predictions in greater detail); but they are not, in and of themselves, such a theory for a couple of reasons that should sound familiar. First, there are too many features of connectionist models, including many arbitrary assumptions and simplifications, for one to say which are essential to the success of the simulation and which are not. (Green, 1998, has made a similar point, arguing that it is "almost meaningless" to ask how many units are appropriate for a given phenomenon, especially "since none of the units corresponds to ANY particular aspect of performance of the network" [p. 5].) On this point, Green (1998) observed that, unlike other simulations, connectionist modeling is seldom concerned with testing specific details of the model, such as the number or nature of specific units, but rather is only testing "a network with a general sort of architecture and certain sorts of activation and learning rules" (p. 5; cf. the tests by Smith and DeCoster of their model). Green argued, however, that "this seems simply too weak a claim to be of much scientific value" (p. 5).

In addition, a simulation is incomplete as a psychological model because it fails to specify all the details of what is involved in, say, word recognition or person perception; for instance, it fails to specify exactly what knowledge is distributed across the nodes that account for such recognition (see Markman, 1999, for a similar reservation about Read & Miller's [1993] and Read & Marcus-Newhall's [1993] earlier connectionist models of dispositional inference). A successful theory must also clearly state how the simulation connects with that theory, that is, how the theory is a clear translation of the abstract theory or model. (See Seidenberg, 1993, for a response to McCloskey's criticisms.)

McCloskey (1991) put this point in the following way:

> The difficulty is not simply that Seidenberg and McClelland [1989, the successful connectionist model of word recognition] failed to describe in sufficient detail the network's encoding of knowledge and its functioning as a whole. Rather, the problem is that connectionist networks of any significant size are complex nonlinear systems, the dynamics of which are extremely difficult to analyze and apprehend. ... At present, understanding of these systems is simply inadequate to support a detailed description of the network's knowledge and functioning. (p. 390)

Some of this criticism is, of course, applicable to other simulations besides connectionist ones. However, as McCloskey (and also Green, 1998) pointed out, connectionist simulations are different in a fundamental way from most simulations of cognitive theories:

> Connectionist modeling is not simulation in the traditional sense. A modeler developing a traditional computer simulation must build in each of the crucial features of an independently specified theory. If the theory is not explicitly formulated, the simulation cannot be built. In connectionist modeling, on the

other hand, the modeler may be able to proceed on the basis of vague and fragmentary theoretical notions, because much of the work is left to the learning algorithm. ... In essence, the learning algorithms constitute procedures for creating complex systems we do not adequately understand. (p. 391)

Thus, in a fundamental irony, the learning rule, which is one of the main attractions of connectionism, is at the same time one of its major weaknesses. The bottom line, then, according to McCloskey, is that connectionist simulations should be used as a kind of model in which researchers can try out certain manipulations, in the same way that we may use, for example, animal models to test out things we cannot do with the intact human brain.

In addition to these general problems, Smith and DeCoster (1999) acknowledged that their model, along with that of Kunda and Thagard, only applies to a particular associative mode of thinking that involves fast, intuitive, automatic processing. As discussed earlier, Kunda and Thagard believe that impression formation is adequately described in terms of this sort of automatic process; and many writers in social cognition (e.g., Bargh, 1997; Bargh & Chartrand, 1999; Wegner & Bargh, 1998) believe that this process is the norm rather than the exception in everyday life.

Although it makes a certain amount of sense to suggest that impression formation, or at least *some* aspects of impression formation, involve this kind of implicit, automatic, nonrational form of processing, I think that a case can also be made that many types of impression formation, including my earlier Monica Lewinsky example or one's typical first meeting with someone or a decision of guilt or innocence, can be viewed as more thoughtful and deliberative (though see Kunda, 1999, for a contrary view). (It may also be that, as both Fiske & Neuberg, 1990, and Kunda & Thagard, 1996, have suggested, the latter form of processing occurs only when the former is somehow disrupted; but that is a separate question.) Both Smith and DeCoster (1999) and Kunda and Thagard (1996; Kunda, 1999) acknowledged that there is such a second mode of processing, a slower, symbolic, rule-based, deliberative mode for which there is, as yet, no effective connectionist account (though see McClelland et al., 1995, Seidenberg, 1997, and Smolensky, 1988, for initial attempts). Smith and DeCoster (1999) believe, and they gave a brief justification of why both of these processes can be conceived of in connectionist rather than traditional information processing terms. However, as I have indicated, there is as yet no convincing connectionist account for such higher order processes; and commentators such as Dulany (1999) have discussed some of the features of mental life (e.g., consciousness, a sense of agency, deliberative processes, metacognition) that are not easily handled by connectionist models (or may not be consistent with connectionist formulations in principle).

I shall not attempt to develop this rule-based mode in detail, except to note that the existence of such a second process makes the Kunda and Thagard and the Smith and DeCoster models another sort of dual-process model, a fact that Smith and DeCoster readily acknowledge (see Smith & DeCoster, 2000, for a review of the general psychological and neuropsychological assumptions underlying such dual processing models). Later in this chapter and in subsequent chapters, I discuss other versions of this dual-process or *separate systems assumption* (Dulany, 1997). Furthermore, it is worth noting that many of the connectionist models that I have and will examine (e.g., Burton, Bruce, & Johnston, 1990; Read & Miller, 1998a; Smith & DeCoster, 1998a, 1998b) are based on earlier models by McClelland and Rumelhart and their associates on such things as word or letter perception. Although we see in chapter 3 that such a model makes a certain amount of sense for face recognition, and it is in some sense desirable to have models that are generalizable from one phenomenon to another (Estes, 1988), I do not believe that such models are appropriate for the process of impression formation and person memory.

It is apparent from the foregoing that PDP models are starting to make inroads into the study of impression formation, and that they offer an alternative to the traditional information-processing models proposed by Brewer and by Fiske and Neuberg (which were, in turn, alternatives to the original associative and Gestalt models provided by Anderson and Asch). It should also be apparent, though, that such PDP models are at present still in a fairly primitive stage of development. It remains to be seen whether they offer, in principle as well as in fact, a viable approach to conceptualizing this area.

THE RELATIONSHIP BETWEEN PERSON MEMORY AND JUDGMENT

A final topic that has generated considerable interest and has definite significance for everyday cognition is the relationship between person memory or knowledge and judgment. One of the major motivations for research on this topic is the frequent observation that participants' judgments of a target person are unrelated to what they can remember about that person. Thus, for example, in one of the earliest studies on this topic, N. H. Anderson and Hubert (1963) found that when participants were asked to recall the descriptors that had been presented to them and on which they based their judgments, their memory for these descriptors was unrelated to the relative influence (determined empirically) of each of those descriptors on their judgments. Specifically, Anderson and Hubert found a primacy effect for the importance of the descriptor in impression formation, whereas a recency effect was found in the memory task. Similar results have also been reported by Dreben, Fiske, and Hastie (1979) and by Riskey (1979). These results suggested to Anderson and Hubert that perhaps memory and judgment are stored independently of each other such that once one has evaluated a given descriptor, one stores that evaluation separately from the piece of information itself—what Anderson and Hubert called *impression memory*.

Subsequently, one may forget the information on which that evaluation is based. Thus, for example, you may conclude that you don't trust a given individual and then forget what it was about that person that led you to feel that way.

There are a variety of studies that are consistent with some sort of separation between memory and judgment (see Hastie & Park, 1986). For example, Reyes, Thompson, and Bower (1980) examined the relation between participants' memory for the facts about a drunk driving case and their verdict in this case and found that the two were unrelated. Similarly, in a series of studies, Lingle, Ostrom, and their associates (e.g., Lingle, Geva, Ostrom, Leipper, & Baumgardner, 1979; Lingle & Ostrom, 1979; see also Carlston, 1980) demonstrated that participants often based subsequent judgments on *previous* judgments without reviewing their memory for the facts on which these judgments were based. Finally, there is the evidence reviewed earlier by Wyer, Srull, and their associates (e.g., Wyer, 1989; Wyer & Srull, 1989) that indicates that participants show better memory for behaviors that are evaluatively inconsistent with the overall person evaluation from which person judgments are made.

Note that this distinction between memory and judgment is generally consistent with the two-system model put forward by Smith and DeCoster (1999) and Kunda and Thagard (1996). Specifically, the faster associative phase is expected to be implicated in the evaluative, judgment component, whereas the slower, rule-based, symbolic phase is involved in the memory component. There is no assumption here, of course, that these two components (i.e., judgment and memory) start off as or intrinsically involve two different systems (though see Smith & DeCoster, 1999).

The On-Line Versus Memory-Based Distinction

Hastie and Park (1986) distinguished between *on-line* and *memory-based* judgments. The former of these refers to judgments made at the time of encoding (e.g., forming an impression of a person on first encountering him or her), whereas the latter refers to judgments based exclusively on *memory* for the target information. In the former case, no relationship is expected between memory and judgment, whereas in the latter a *positive* relationship is expected.

The on-line versus memory-based distinction is an important one for bringing order into the diverse literature on the memory–judgment relationship. According to this distinction, if one makes a judgment, for instance, about how much one likes a person or how guilty a suspect is, then at the time of encoding there is no reason to expect a relationship between that judgment and one's memory for the person. Because it seems likely that such judgments-at-encoding are the rule rather than the exception, one should frequently expect to observe the absence of such a relationship. On the other hand, if one acquires information about a person without the intent of judging him or her on a given dimension—for instance, without expecting to judge that person as a potential friend or without expecting to judge a colleague as a suspect in a sexual harassment case—then in this case one *would* expect to find such a relationship. Hastie and Park gave the example of returning from a convention and finding that your department has a position open and then having to review people met at the convention to see who might be a suitable candidate. Another example is a student who suddenly finds him- or herself in need of a roommate and must search his or her memory to determine which friend or acquaintance would make the best candidate.

In their seminal paper on this topic, Hastie and Park (1986) reviewed some of their own studies to illustrate this on-line versus memory-based distinction. For example, in one study participants were to make judgments, either immediate or delayed, about the suitability of a job candidate for a position as computer programmer. The investigators then looked at the correlations between these judgments and a measure of the ratio of judgment-related details recalled to total recall. In a second study they examined the relationship between memory and judgments for judgments that were either likely to be made spontaneously at encoding (i.e., sociability) or not (i.e., a judgment of the frequency with which the person engaged in cardiovascular exercise). In these and other studies Hastie and Park found evidence for the predictions made by the on-line versus memory-based distinction.

From the standpoint of ecological validity, I find it easier to think of examples of the on-line condition than of the memory-based one, just as it is easier to think of examples of the impression formation set than it is of the memory set as processing goals. This is particularly true if one accepts the notion of spontaneous trait inferences (Winter & Uleman, 1984). Thus, as in the case of the different processing objectives, I would question whether the on-line versus memory-based distinction is truly one of major real-world significance or is instead simply a description of convenient experimental manipulations. In fact, the primary everyday examples that come to mind of the memory-based case are ones in which people *change* the *type* of judgment that they originally made (e.g., in judging the honesty or reliability of someone whom one has previously judged as a friend or lover), rather than suddenly making a judgment where there was none before.

In this connection, Hastie and Pennington (1989) later added a third, intermediate condition labelled the *inference-memory-based judgment* condition, in which subsequent judgments are based on one's memory for previous inferences or judgments—for instance, basing your later judgments about whether to ask someone to be a study partner or a roommate on your earlier judgments about that person's studiousness or sociability. Another example is from N. Pennington and Hastie's own research (1986, 1993) on jury decision-making: Jurors have been found to construct a story about the case they are hearing based (loosely) on the facts they have encountered; they then judge the guilt or innocence of the suspect on the basis of which story they have constructed.

As Hastie and Pennington themselves pointed out, this third condition raises the question—one that has been raised in the text comprehension literature as well—of *when* inferences or judgments are made. In the text comprehension literature the positions range from a *minimalist* position espoused by McKoon and Ratcliff (1992), on the one hand, which says that readers make very few (automatic) inferences at encoding (i.e., just those needed to establish local textual coherence and those that are "easily available, either from explicit statements in the text or from general knowledge" [p. 440]), to a *constructionist* viewpoint (e.g., Graesser, 1981; Graesser, Robertson, & Clark, 1983) on the other, which says that individuals make a great many inferences when reading a passage and then "prune" or revise them on the basis of subsequent information. The analogous question in the area of impression formation is how many inferences or judgments are made at the outset, how or whether these inferences are revised when we encounter additional information, and, of course, how much these subsequent inferences or judgments are based on previous facts and on previous trait inferences (see Park, 1986). This question is complicated by the fact that, as noted earlier, the rules of connection or inference in the area of person memory or impression formation are more poorly-defined than in the text comprehension area, so that it is difficult to map out the process of inference in impression formation in any clear-cut way.

SUMMARY

In this chapter I have tackled the important question of how individuals form impressions of people in everyday life, how they store and represent those impressions, and how they make judgments on the basis of (or independent of) such representations. I have suggested that there are a variety of different views on the representation and organization issue, as well as some debate over the impression formation *process* and the memory–judgment relationship.

Although this review has raised many interesting substantive issues, one striking limitation of this research is that so little of it has taken place in real-world settings or used real-world materials. As I suggested in chapter 1, there is certainly nothing wrong with using experimental studies as *one* source of information on these issues, particularly when enough real-world data have been collected to warrant the formulation of rigorous models to be tested in the lab. However, it seems unlikely that the decontextualized, information-impoverished environment provided in most experiments really allows participants to use their extensive background knowledge or the strategies that they use in real life contexts.

One aspect of this—but only one—is the overuse of verbal materials. For example, Woll and van der Meer (1996) reported that when real-life[9] tapes from a videodating service were used as materials (and videodating clients served as participants), no evidence for the role of processing goals was found. It seems unlikely in the area of person memory and impression formation in particular that simple lab studies with contrived descriptions of people will be sufficient to fully engage the relevant knowledge-driven processes.

In the next chapter I discuss research and theory on the closely related topic of memory for faces. One of my aims in that chapter is to try to find some commonalities between these two areas of person knowledge and develop some of the possible implications of each for the other.

---

[9]Because these tapes can themselves be viewed as somewhat artificial (i.e., in that they involved a semistructured interview by an off-camera figure, and did not allow any form of interaction between the viewer and the target), these conditions can at best be viewed as a reasonable approximation to real-world conditions. In fact, Woll and Cozby (1987) have argued that the difference between these conditions and the conditions that videodating clients typically use in forming impressions may be one reason for the relative inaccuracy of these clients in judging target persons.

Chapter 3

Placing Faces

"I stopped a passer-by to ask directions. She looked familiar and then spoke as if she knew me. When she looked as if she knew me, I pretended to recognize her too, but didn't ask her name. After 10 minutes I stopped trying to think about who she was."

"I was in the bank, waiting to be served. I saw a person and I knew there was something familiar immediately. After a few seconds I realized she was from a shop on campus or a secretary of one of the departments. I eventually remembered by a process of elimination."

—Examples of face recognition errors
(from Young Hay, & Ellis, 1985a, p. 507)

"May I take your order, ma'am?"

—Remark occasionally made to the
(male, bearded) author at restaurants

INTRODUCTION

In chapter 2 I examined the question of how we represent and remember persons or personalities. A related and equally interesting question is how people remember and represent faces. Face recognition is of interest on both a practical, everyday level (e.g., "How is it that people remember faces from many years ago, and yet fail to recognize people whom they have just met?" or "Why do people have trouble recognizing familiar persons in unfamiliar contexts?") and a theoretical one (e.g., "How do individuals represent familiar vs. unfamiliar faces differently?"). Research on this topic also has significant implications for areas such as forensic psychology and computerized face recognition.

In this chapter I examine some of the same issues that I reviewed in chapter 2, that is, the format for representing faces, the overall structure of knowledge about faces, and the way in which individuals process facial information. I also examine some issues unique to face recognition, such as the possibility that faces have a special status among the patterns that people encounter everyday and the implications of research on face recognition for eyewitness testimony in the criminal justice system. I also try to shed some light on the kind of errors just illustrated.

THE "SPECIALNESS OF FACES" ISSUE

One question that has been hotly debated by researchers on face recognition is whether the face enjoys a special status (e.g., A. W. Ellis & Young, 1989) or constitutes a special, unique pattern for human perceivers. As several commentators (e.g., A. W. Ellis & Young, 1989; Morton & Johnson, 1989) have pointed out, the term specialness has a number of different meanings. For example, Morton and Johnson listed four different ways in which the face may be special: Namely, (a) face recognition may be found to involve an innate mechanism; (b) that mechanism or ability may be localized in a particular part of the brain; (c) that mechanism or part of the cortex is not involved in other psychological functions (the so-called modularity criterion—see Fodor, 1983); and (d) that face processing may involve some unique *form* of processing, one that distinguishes it from other forms of visual processing.

The Inversion Effect

The origin of this debate lies in a question raised by Teuber (1978) about whether face recognition is somehow uniquely dependent on the right hemisphere. Perhaps the most frequently cited (and most hotly debated) finding in support of this specialness argument comes from a study by Teuber's student Yin (1969). Yin found that even though faces are easier to recognize than most patterns (e.g., houses, airplanes) when presented right side up, such faces are *more difficult* to recognize when they are presented in inverted form. Such a finding, called the *inversion effect*, suggests that faces are processed in a unique, wholistic fashion (i.e., in a manner different from the other visual patterns) and that inversion disrupts this possibly built-in pattern. In a subsequent study, Yin (1970) found that patients with damage to the right posterior hemisphere had particular problems with face recognition, suggesting that faces are not only unique but also specifically involve the right hemisphere.

Although Yin's proposals were provocative ones and his results have been found to hold over a variety if different conditions (see Valentine, 1988), both have been subjected to a variety of different criticisms and alternative explanations (see H. D. Ellis & Young, 1989, and Valentine, 1988, for reviews). For example, Diamond and Carey (1986) found the same decrease in recognition for inversion of pictures of dogs among dog experts (but not for novices), suggesting that the inversion effect may be the result of familiarity or the development of a specialized schema and not something specific to faces. (Note that Diamond and Carey *did* argue that both face recognition and the recognition of dogs and other patterns depend on configurational properties, or what they called *second-order relational properties*,[1] as opposed to *first-order relational properties,* or the simple pairwise relations between two features.) Similarly, Shepherd (1989) reviewed evidence for practice effects in the recognition of inverted faces, and other researchers (e.g., Sergent, 1984; Toyama, 1975) have also failed to find the inversion effect when different sets of faces and houses are used as targets. Along these lines, Goldstein and Chance (1981) argued that the comparison between faces and other patterns such as houses is an unfair one because people are called on to recognize faces so much more frequently than we are for these other patterns (see Tarr, 1998, for a similar argument). Finally, Bornstein (1963; Bornstein, Sroka, & Munita, 1969) reported on patients who lost their ability to recognize faces accompanied by the concurrent loss of other acquired recognition capacities, such as the ability of an ornithologist to recognize birds, or the ability of a farmer to recognize cattle. These observations suggest that face recognition may be part of a more general pattern recognition ability[2] (though see Newcombe & de Haan, 1994).

---

[1]Rhodes, Brake, and Atkinson (1993) reported that changes in these second-order relationships produced a greater disruption in recognition of inverted faces than did changes in isolated features. Bartlett and Searcy (1993) also found, in a manner similar to Thompson (1980), that changes in relations among features that seemed grotesque in upright faces did not seem so in inverted faces, whereas changes in single, isolated features that seemed grotesque in upright faces continued to appear so in inverted faces.

[2]Gauthier and Tarr (1997) reached the same conclusion from a rather different set of findings. These investigators used a specially constructed set of rather homogeneous visual objects called *greebles,* and built expertise into naive judges by means of controlled training in visual discrimination, Gauthier and Tarr did not find an inversion effect as a function of training or expertise—an effect which they view as an artifact in previous studies resulting from using "'wrong' versions of an overlearned stimuli [sic]" (p. 1063); they did find, however, that both expert and novice judges showed better recognition accuracy for greeble parts in the context of whole figures or patterns than when these parts were viewed separately (cf. Tanaka & Farah, 1993).

Neurological Evidence

No attempt will be made to evaluate the evidence for and against Yin's case for the involvement of the right hemisphere in face recognition (see A. W. Ellis & Young, 1989, and Sergent & Bindra, 1981, for discussions). There is, however, a good deal of interesting evidence for specific neurological mechanisms involved in face processing (see Damasio, 1989, Desimone, 1991, for reviews). For example, research by Perrett (Perrett, Hietanen, Oram, & Benson, 1992; Perrett, Rolls, & Caan, 1982) found that there are specific cells in the temporal cortex—particularly in the superior temporal sulcus—of monkeys that are selectively responsive to faces and *differences* in faces (and even to different views of these faces [Harries & Perrett, 1991] though see A. W. Ellis & Young, 1989, for reservations). These cells also do not respond to a variety of other objects and features (see Desimone, 1991); in other words, these "face cells" seem to be discriminating. There is also some evidence that other cells are sensitive to different facial features (e.g., Perrett, Mistlin, & Chitty, 1987), although this evidence is less clear-cut (see Desimone, 1991) and is sensitive to such relational features as the distance between the eyes and the distance from eyes to mouth (Yamane, Kaji, & Kawano, 1988).

Rolls (1992; see also Desimone, 1991, and Gross, 1992) has emphasized the fact that responses to faces are a result of a population or group of cells, each of which has a different range of sensitivity, rather than single *grandmother* cells (Barlow, 1972), which are cells that are sensitive to specific objects or faces, such as, facetiously, your own grandmother's. (Note that the "population" view is consistent with connectionist models of face processing.) As Desimone (1991) stated, "faces may be different from other objects only in that they are so important to monkeys [i.e., for recognition of others and for recognizing facial communication], and therefore are represented by a large proportion of the cells in the temporal cortex" (p. 6). It is also apparent that such ensembles are affected by experience (Rolls, 1992) and that removal of these cells has relatively little effect on face recognition (e.g., Heywood & Cowey, 1992). Finally, Nachson (1995) has pointed out some of the difficulties in extrapolating from monkeys to humans on this topic, including the fact that the areas sensitive to faces are different in monkeys and humans. For example, recent studies (e.g., Kanwisher, McDermott, & Chun, 1997; McCarthy, Puce, Gore, & Allison, 1997) have found that cells in the fusiform gyrus are selectively responsive to face stimuli in humans.

Along these same lines, there is also interesting neuroclinical evidence from patients suffering from *prosopagnosia,* or the inability to recognize familiar faces as a result of some kind of neurological damage. Individuals suffering from such a disorder still understand faces as a generic category and recognize specific people by means of other cues, such as the example from Damasio (cited in Morton & Johnson, 1989) in which a patient learned to identify the photo of his daughter on the basis of her darkened front teeth. Recently, a number of investigators (see Bruyer, 1991, for a review) presented evidence for *covert* face recognition in prosopagnosia, as reflected in both physiological (e.g., electrodermal and evoked potential responses; Renault, Signoret, Debrville, Breton, & Bolger, 1989; Tranel & Damasio, 1985) and behavioral forms (e.g., eye movement patterns and savings scores in relearning; Rizzo, Hurtig, & Damasio, 1987; M. A. Wallace & Farah, 1992). Thus, although prosopagnosic patients cannot explicitly recognize a face and have no awareness of recognition, they *do* show covert signs of recognition in a manner similar to that found in research on implicit memory (e.g., Schacter, 1987). (See Bredart & Bruyer, 1994, for a listing of negative evidence for such covert recognition). Finally, it appears that patients can actually lose the ability to recognize familiar faces without losing the capacity for dealing with unfamiliar ones (e.g., Malone, Morris, Kay, & Levin, 1982; Warrington & James, 1967) or vice versa (e.g., Tippett, Miller, & Farah, 1997).

Recently, Farah (1996; Farah, Levinson, & Klein, 1995) reported a set of experiments performed on a patient (L. H.) who was well-educated and otherwise intelligent but who was "profoundly prosopagnosic, unable to recognize reliably his wife, children, or even himself in a group photograph" (Farah, 1996, p. 184). In a recognition memory paradigm, Farah et al. found that, unlike most participants, L. H. showed a clear *decrement* in performance for faces in comparison with other objects. Furthermore, Farah, Wilson, Drain, and Tanaka (1995) found that L. H. did not show the typical inversion effect. In fact, he actually showed an *improvement* in face recognition for inverted faces, suggesting perhaps that it was indeed an impairment of the face-specific processing that was involved in L. H.'s problem.

Essentially the same conclusion was arrived at from the opposite direction by Moscovitch, Winocur, and Behrmann (1997). These investigators recently reported a case history of a patient (CK) who suffered from extensive impairment to a variety of cognitive functions including both word and object recognition. At the same time, however, CK retained his ability to recognize faces. CK also showed a magnified inversion effect that presumably reflected his impaired ability to make the inversion.

Finally, Tarr and Behrmann (cited in Tarr, 1998) conducted research with two prosopagnosic patients that argues against the Farah et al. position. Specifically, Tarr reported that when measures other than percent correct are used (i.e., reaction times and signal detection scores), on the assumption that prosopagnosic patients may try harder to recognize objects than to recognize faces and may also be influenced by their belief that they have a deficit in face recognition, the selective impairment for face recognition is no longer found. Furthermore, on the assumption that prosopagnosic patients may have been able to discriminate between specific chairs and eyeglasses on the basis of specific features, Tarr and Behrmann found that reducing the viewing time for both such objects led to impairments in recognition similar to those found for face recognition.

Prosopagnosia is certainly a curious and interesting phenomenon. Unfortunately, such disorders are frequently not distinctive to face perception, that is, they typically involve agnosias for other objects as well. (Two exceptions here are cases reported by de Renzi, 1986, and de Renzi, Faglioni, Grossi, & Nichelli, 1991). Similarly, Sergent and Signoret (1992) noted that four different prosopagnosics whom they observed showed four different patterns of impairments on tasks involving face processing; and de Renzi et al. (1991) proposed that there are at least two different forms of prosopagnosia: namely, *apperceptive*, or perceptual (i.e., not recognizing the face), and *associative*, or semantic (i.e., not being able to connect the face with a person).

On the neurological side, prosopagnosia typically involves tumors or injuries that cover more than just a circumscribed area. In a related vein, Sergent and Signoret (1992; see also Gross & Sergent, 1992) pointed out that the location of a lesion that is responsible for prosopagnosia does not necessarily reveal which area is involved in normal face recognition, because a lesion may also have effects on other distant areas or provide input to other areas. On the latter issue, Sergent and Signoret also presented evidence that the pattern of activity found in positron-emission tomography (PET) scans of normal participants performing some of the same tasks as the four prosopagnosic patients showed the same areas of activity as those implicated in the lesions to the latter patients. Finally, as Morton and Johnson (1989) pointed out, "contemporary neuroanatomists think more in terms of circuits connecting often widely separated areas, rather than relating psychological functions to specific locales" (p. 52).

Recently, Tarr (1998) made a systematic case *against* the specialness of faces. Tarr argued that there are three major differences between face and object recognition that have not been controlled for in other studies: different levels of analysis (i.e., recognition of specific instances such as individual faces vs. general classes such as chairs), differences in experience with the object or person (where individuals have much more experience with faces than with other objects), and different degrees of similarity between or among objects or persons. Tarr's argument is that when these confounding differences are reduced, then the apparent differences between face and object recognition are reduced as well. For example, as objects become more similar (such as faces), recognition times slow down in a speed–accuracy tradeoff. In addition, the functional magnetic resonance imagery (FMRI) recordings for specific (vs. categorical) objects become more similar to the FMRI patterns for face recognition. Finally, as participants received more training on a set of patterns called "greebles" (i.e., artificial patterns partitioned in term of gender, family, and individual cases; see Gauthier & Tarr, 1997), the same inversion and transformation effects found with faces were observed (and again, the FMRI patterns supported this finding). All of this evidence suggested to Tarr that faces do not really represent a special visual pattern.

The Development of Face Recognition

Another major line of evidence focuses on the development of face recognition. There are at least two sources of developmental evidence for the specificity of such recognition, one from research on infants and one from developmental differences in face recognition. Some of the evidence from research on infants is rather dramatic, even if not universally accepted. For example, Goren, Sarty, and Wu (1975) reported that 9-minute old infants show a preference in their gaze patterns for faces versus other stimuli, such as scrambled faces and a blank face, even though there is the complication of infants' limited visual acuity at this age (A. W. Ellis & Young, 1989; M. H. Johnson & Morton, 1991; see also Carey, 1981). This result has been replicated and extended by M. H. Johnson, Dziurawiec, Ellis, and Morton (1991).

In another set of classic studies, Meltzoff and Moore (1977, 1983) reported that infants as young as a few days or even 1-hour old tend to imitate facial expressions that they see, although these results have not always been replicated, and there is also some question about the degree to which such imitation is specific to faces (see A. W. Ellis & Young, 1989, on both points). More recently, Meltzoff and his associates (e.g., Meltzoff, 1990, 1995; Meltzoff & Moore, 1994) found evidence for deferred imitation by infants as young as 6 weeks and for delay periods as long as 4 months, suggesting that infants have some kind of memory representation of faces (or even persons). All of this evidence is consistent with the notion from the attachment literature (e.g., Bowlby, 1969), as well as the ecological psychology view (e.g., McArthur & Baron, 1983) that the child should come into the world pretuned to the face and expression of the caretaker (e.g., Field, Cohen, Garcia, & Greenberg, 1984; see M. H. Johnson & Morton, 1991, for a more detailed discussion).

Unfortunately, there is a good deal of debate about the validity of these findings with infants (see Maurer, 1985, for a review), although there is also other evidence (e.g., studies of the scanning of different facial features; Carey, 1981) that *does* suggest that the face, including particularly the eyes, comes to have a special meaning to the infant around the age of 8 weeks. In this connection, M. H. Johnson and Morton (1991; see also Morton & Johnson, 1991) discussed the curious finding across a number of studies of a curvilinear trend in which sensitivity to faces occurs very early, disappears at 1 month, and returns at 2 months. This finding, along with other evidence, suggested to Johnson and Morton that infant face recognition requires both an inborn face recognition mechanism, which they have labeled CONSPEC, and also a learning mechanisms, which they have labeled CONLERN.

Still another line of evidence for specificity comes from the developmental research of Carey, Diamond, and their associates (e.g., Carey, 1981, 1992; Diamond & Carey, 1977). Specifically, Carey and colleagues suggested that although there is a clear improvement in face recognition from ages 2 to 10, there is also a slight decline at puberty, between the ages of 10 and 14, before this ability rises to its adult peak at the age of 16. Diamond and Carey's (1977) explanation for this temporary interlude at puberty is that infants and children initially depend on featural processing in face recognition, but this process proves to be relatively inefficient. During puberty, the right hemisphere, which is primarily responsible for configural processing (cf. the earlier argument by Teuber), reaches its "optimal level." Therefore, the period between 10 and 14 years is a time when perceivers are reorganizing their strategies of face processing; and this change from a featural to a configural process is at least one factor involved in the temporary decline in face recognition ability.

The important point here is that Carey and her associates argued that face processing in infancy and childhood is not configural but rather is featural in nature. One piece of evidence in favor of this position is the fact that children are not as affected by inversion of faces as adults are (though see Flin, 1985b, and Young & Bion, 1980, 1981, for contrary evidence). In any case, Carey (1981) argued that the changes in puberty are "due primarily to advances in knowledge of faces *per se,* rather then improvement in general pattern encoding" (p. 27; though see Flin, 1985, for evidence of a more general decline in pattern recognition at puberty). In fact, in her later writings, Carey (1992; Diamond & Carey, 1986) has even referred to these "advances in knowledge" as *expertise* (see discussion of this topic in chap. 7). Thus, in a sense, the Carey proposal represents an argument for the specialness of faces, in that the change is made for faces only, although this time in strictly information-processing terms.

In contrast to the Diamond and Carey position, Thomson (1986) argued that infants rely primarily on a *global, configural* process of recognition, whereas children or adolescents bring to bear more analytic, feature-testing processes—what I referred to in chapter 2 as piecemeal processing—which are involved in a more abstract, controlled process of recognition. More specifically, Thomson proposed a three-stage model of face processing consisting of an initial automatic (built-in) process that generates a feeling of familiarity, followed by a higher level problem-solving process, followed by the decision process involved in recognition memory judgments. According to this model, infants' recognition (as typically measured) is based on the more primitive familiarity process, which is itself more configural, whereas the improvement of actual face recognition throughout childhood is due to the development of the more analytic cognitive processes.

Conclusion

It is apparent from the foregoing that the evidence for specialness is complex and far from clear-cut. In their commentary on this issue, Morton and Johnson (1989) concluded that only the innateness criterion is really necessary for face processing to be considered special. As I have discussed, however, the evidence on that criterion is far from clear. More recently, Rhodes et al. (1993) proposed that even though face processing may not be special in the sense of involving a separate processing system, it also is not simply "part of a general purpose recognition system either," (p. 47) such as one involving object discrimination in general (though see Bruce & Humphreys, 1994, and Tarr, 1998, for contrary views). Similarly, Nachson (1995) concluded from his review of the literature that although face processing is not qualitatively different from other forms of object recognition, it "apparently takes place in a separate, domain-specific system; hence it is modular" (p. 267). Finally, Farah et al. (1998) recently argued that face recognition is not qualitatively different from object and word recognition, but it is quantitatively different. Once again, there does not appear to be a clear consensus on this fascinating topic.

THE FORMAT FOR REPRESENTING FACES

Probably the central issue in research on face recognition is exactly how faces are represented cognitively. The main question here is whether faces are processed and represented primarily in a feature-by-feature, piecemeal fashion, or in a more holistic, configural manner—a debate that is familiar from my discussion of the person memory or impression formation area.

Evidence for and Against the Featural Position

The *featural* position argues that faces are processed and represented in terms of specific facial features such as the eyes, mouth, hairline, and so forth, rather than as a whole. One piece of evidence for such a featural position comes from a study by Bradshaw and Wallace (1971; see also E. E. Smith & Nielson, 1970) that looked at the speed with which participants discriminated faces (using the sort of feature-by-feature, *Identikit* technique used in eyewitness identification) on the basis of 2, 4, or 7 different or distinctive features. This study found an inverse relationship between reaction time and the number of distinctive features, suggesting a kind of feature-by-feature, serial search process (though see the methodological and conceptual critiques by Sergent, 1984, and by Tanaka & Farah, 1993). Along somewhat similar lines, and using similar stimulus materials, Matthews (1978) argued that both parallel and serial processes are involved in face processing, with parallel processing involved in searching the outer parts of the face and serial processing involved in scanning the inner features (though, again, see Sergent, 1984). Finally, Tversky and Krantz (1969) presented evidence from a multidimensional scaling analysis that an overall impression of a face is a simple sum of a judge's impressions of individual impressions of particular features, with no evidence for interactions among these features.

There are a variety of arguments against the featural position. H. D. Ellis (1981; see also Bruce, 1988), for example, argued that the use of artificial faces of the sort constructed by the Identikit or other similar procedures (i.e., where schematic faces are constructed on a feature-by-feature basis) may encourage participants to use an equally artificial sort of serial processing of features that is not characteristic of their usual approach to face recognition. It is certainly true that individuals do not perform very well on artificial face recognition techniques such as the Identikit technique for witness identification. Furthermore, Woodhead, Baddeley, and Simmonds (1979) demonstrated that intensive training on facial features does not produce noticeable improvement in face recognition.

Along similar lines, G. Cohen (1989; see also Shepherd & Ellis, 1996) proposed that one reason for the substantially poorer performance on face *recall* (i.e., where participants are required to describe or reproduce faces) than on face *recognition* is that the former process is necessarily featural, that is, it involves describing the person or face involved by recounting the component features, whereas the latter is configural. In this connection, Laughery, Duval, and Wogalter (1986) looked at participants' reported strategies in face recall (using either an Identikit or sketch artist procedure) and found that a greater number of participants used a featural strategy than a holistic one, although both of these were prominent. In addition, Wells and Hryclw (1984) found that asking participants to make either trait or physical judgments about a face led to different results depending on whether recognition or recall measures were used. Specifically, trait judgments produced better recognition memory, whereas physical judgments produced superior recall, suggesting different retrieval processes (i.e., configural vs. featural processes) in the two cases. (See Davies, 1986, for an elaboration on these recognition vs. recall comparisons.)

Sergent (1984, 1989; see also Tanaka & Farah, 1993) made the important point that it is difficult to distinguish between featural and configural viewpoints, at least using reaction time data, because both positions make similar predictions, albeit for different reasons. Specifically, both featural and configural models predict that a greater number of discrepant features make it easier and faster to compare faces, the one because of a presumed serial, feature-matching search process (i.e., where the search is terminated when a discrepancy between the two faces is encountered), the other because of the greater overall dissimilarity in the facial *pattern*. In this connection, Takane and Sergent (1983) compared various multidimensional scaling models of face recognition and found support for a model that emphasizes overall configural similarity rather than an independent, feature-by-feature comparison.

In a recent set of studies, Farah, Tanaka, and their associates (Farah, Wilson, Drain, & Tanaka, 1998; Farah, Tanaka, & Drain, 1995; Tanaka & Farah, 1993) reported evidence that supports a configural interpretation of face recognition over a featural one. These investigators theorized that if faces were more likely to be encoded holistically than were other patterns, then it should be harder for participants to recognize isolated features from those faces than it is for them to recognize parts of other patterns. In these studies participants first learned pairings of a set of normal faces versus other patterns (i.e., either scrambled faces, inverted faces, or houses), with the names of the persons with those faces (or living in those houses). In the test phase participants were asked to judge which of a pair of isolated parts, whole faces (with one feature altered), or alternative patterns belonged to one of those names (e.g., "Which of these is Bill's nose?" or "... the door to Bill's house?" or "... Bill's face?"; see Fig. 3.1 for an example of these figures). In all cases participants were significantly less accurate in choosing the correct isolated feature from the normal faces than they were in selecting the whole face, whereas they were as accurate or *more* accurate in selecting these isolated features from, for example, the scrambled faces than they were in identifying the overall face. These results are consistent with the *Thatcher illusion,* in which Thompson (1980) showed that inverting the eyes and mouth of a picture of Margaret Thatcher had a major impact on participants' perception of the upright face (see Fig. 3.2), but relatively little effect on their perception of the inverted face, once again suggesting that upright face recognition involves configurational processing.

In another set of studies, Farah, Wilson, Drain, & Tanaka (1998) attempted to demonstrate that configurational processes operate in the initial encoding of faces, rather than just in memory. Farah et al. tested this by having participants compare two faces presented simultaneously in terms of one feature (e.g., the nose) while also varying another feature (e.g., the mouth; see Fig. 3.3). Once again, both normal and inverted faces were used. The rationale was that if face perception is holistic rather than piecemeal,

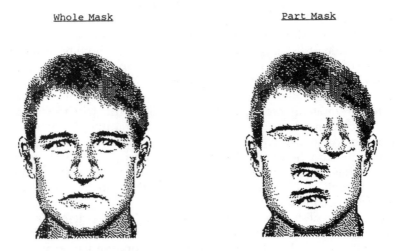

FIG. 3.1. Example of faces used in Farah et al. studies of face recognition. From "What is 'Special' About Face Perception?" by M. J. Farah, K. D. Wilson, H. M. Drain, & J. N. Tanaka, 1998, *Psychological Review, 105,* 489. Copyright © 1998 by the American Psychological Association. Reprinted with permission.

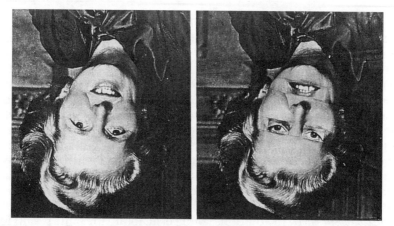

FIG. 3.2. The Thatcher illusion. From "Margaret Thatcher: A New Illusion" by P. Thompson, 1980, *Perception, 9*, p. 483. Copyright © 1980 by Pion Ltd. Reprinted with permission.

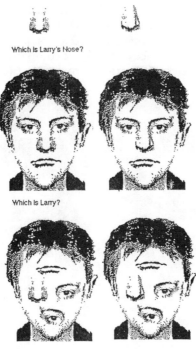

FIG. 3.3. Faces used by Tanaka and Farah in their study of configurational processes in face recognition. From "Parts and Wholes in Face Recognition" by J. W. Tanaka & M. J. Farah, 1993, *Quarterly Journal of Experimental Psychology: Human Experimental Psychology, 46A*, pp. 225–245. Copyright © 1993 by Psychology Press, LTD. Reprinted with permission of Psychology Press, LTD.

then changing a second feature should interfere with the comparison of the first one (because the features form a pattern), but this should be less true for inverted faces. That was, in fact, what Farah et al. found.

In other recent research, Young, Hellawal, and Hay (1987) reported a somewhat different sort of research evidence for configurational factors in face perception. On the basis of some of Galton's (1879) early ideas on composite faces, Young et al. developed *chimeric* or imaginary faces consisting of the top half of one celebrity face and the bottom half of another (see Fig. 3.4). Participants were then asked to make timed recognition judgments for either the top or bottom half, that is, to divide the face and indicate to whom either of the halves belongs. Participants found this to be a difficult task because they formed a new gestalt of the two halves, which essentially formed a new face. Carey and Diamond (1994) have referred to this gestalt formation as the *composite effect*. In addition, Young et al. found the same results for unfamiliar faces (in which participants were taught to attach a name to the top half). They also found that these results did not hold for inverted faces, where the same configurational processes should not hold, nor did they hold for vertically split faces. Finally, Carey and Diamond (1994) reported that the so-called composite effect held for all ages, from 6- to 10-year-olds to adults, even though the inversion effect itself *did* show an age trend.

Recently, Leder and Bruce (2000) have compared the role of simple relational versus overall configurational properties (cf. Diamond & Carey's [1986] first-order versus second-order relational properties). The results of

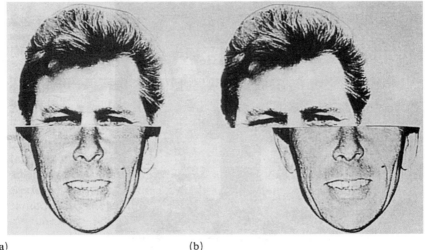

(a)   (b)

FIG. 3.4. Examples of chimeric or composite faces of Max Bygrave and Lord Snowdon. From "Configurational information in Face Perception" by A. W. Young, D. Hellawell, & D. C. Hay, 1987, *Perception, 16*, p. 749. Copyright © 1987 by Pion Ltd. Reprinted with permission.

five different experiments supported the pairwise relations over the configural interpretation.

Evidence for and Against Prototype Models

An alternative position proposed by H. D. Ellis (1981) is a *facial prototype model.* According to this viewpoint, our recognition of faces may involve "a selection of prototypical faces sampling the range of faces normally encountered. ... Incoming faces are first roughly categorized by type and then more specifically analyzed in terms of deviations from the appropriate prototypical face" (p. 180). Thus, face recognition or face processing is roughly comparable to the kind of "comparison to prototype" approach described by theorists such as Rosch (1975), Franks and Bransford (1971), and others in the areas of categorization in general, or the kind of person prototypes described by M. B. Brewer (1988), Cantor and Mischel (1979), and others in the area of person memory. The difference from these other views is that Ellis assumed *multiple* prototypes for different categories of faces.

H. D. Ellis (1981) reported a pair of studies that tested out this sort of prototype model. Both studies examined the tendency of participants to confuse specific faces with composites formed by superimposing the exemplars in a given cluster of faces. (See Fig. 3.4 for an example of a composite face.) In the first of these studies participants were shown ten exemplar faces from ten clusters of faces (established by a cluster analysis). These participants then saw groups of 50 faces made up of the ten exemplars, ten composites of these exemplars, ten unseen exemplars from the same clusters, ten distractor exemplars (from a different cluster), and ten composites of these distractor exemplars. They were then asked to pick out the faces that they had seen in the first phase. Contrary to predictions, participants did not confuse the test faces with the associated composites.

In a second study, participants learned to classify 16 faces into four clusters without learning an explicit classification rule. They then received the 16 originals, four composites, and four unpresented exemplars from the same clusters they were to classify. Classification errors and reaction times were recorded. Once again, contrary to expectations, participants were found to misclassify composite faces and to take longer to make these classifications than they did for the originals and the new exemplars.

H. D. Ellis (1981) concluded from these two studies that his results failed to support a prototype approach to face recognition. However, there are at least two ways in which the composite approach fails to capture the notion of a prototype. First, as we have seen, a prototype is a *configuration* of features rather than a simple composite (see V. Bruce, Doyle, Dench, & Burton, 1991, and Young et al., 1987, for evidence and discussions of this alternative configurational view). In other words, a prototype is, by definition, relational, and simply superimposing exemplars to form an average is unlikely to capture these relational properties (see Fig. 3.5 to verify this point). Second, a composite is a kind of artificial (though perhaps not entirely unrealistic; see the computer composite presented in Bruce & Young, 1998, Fig. 4-114) pattern that may not bear a clear similarity to any of the component exemplars. (An analogy may be drawn to the relationship of offspring to their parents. These offspring can be viewed as composites of their parents, but they certainly would not thereby be considered prototypes.)

A more recent and more appropriate test of a prototype model has been reported by V. Bruce et al. (1991; see also Malpass & Hughes, 1986). In eight different studies these investigators made subtle changes in the internal features of a set of ten prototype faces by moving individual features up or down a certain number of pixels on a computer screen to create two older and two younger versions of that prototype face. After making initial judgments about the age and masculinity–femininity of the faces, participants received a surprise recognition test in which they were to choose between one of 50 presented faces and a distractor face produced by additional manipulations of features.

In one experiment participants were found to choose the central, prototypical face over the distractor in over 90% of the cases. More important, in a second experiment participants chose that prototypical face over the distractor on 79% of the cases *even when that face had not been one of the faces presented earlier!* This tendency to choose the unseen prototype did not hold, however, when that prototype was paired with an actually seen exem-

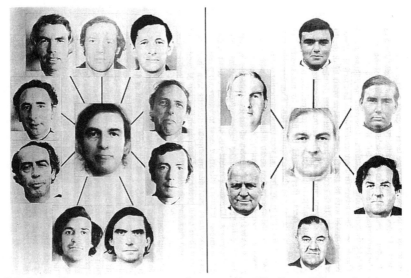

FIG. 3.5. The composite, prototype faces used by Ellis. From " Theoretical Aspects of Face Recognition" by H. D. Ellis, 1981. In *Perceiving and Remembering Faces* (p. 182), edited by G. Davies, H. Ellis, & J. Shepherd, London: Academic Press. Copyright © 1981 by Academic Press, reproduced by permission of the publisher. All rights of reproduction in any form reserved.

plar. In addition, participants showed good memory when the previously seen face came from the extremes of the set, that is, the youngest and the oldest and the distractor was the same as in the other studies. Both of these latter two findings suggest that participants remember specific exemplars as well as the (seen or unseen) prototypes.

H. D. Ellis (1981) and Goldstein and Chance (1981) reviewed other evidence consistent with a prototype position (see also Malpass & Hughes, 1986, and Valentine, 1991). For example, Goldstein and Chance pointed out that on whatever dimension of facial structure or appearance you use, faces near the end or extremes of that dimension (e.g., size of nose or pleasantness) are remembered better than faces falling in the middle (cf. Neumann, 1977), thus supporting a deviation-from-prototype position, or what Goldstein and Chance called the *singularity* or *typicality* effect (cf. earlier discussion of typicality effects in person memory). More convincingly, Light et al. (1979) showed that participants had better recognition memory for atypical than for typical faces, under a variety of different testing conditions and retention intervals. Light et al. also found significant correlations between the judged typicality of a face and the judged similarity of that face to other faces. This particular conception of prototypes obviously differs greatly from Ellis' viewpoint; also, note that Light et al.'s conception bears a greater similarity to the prototype position developed by Rosch (and by Brewer in the area of person memory) than does Ellis's. In other studies on prototypes, Malpass and Hughes (1986), Neumann (1977), and Solso and McCarthy (1981) have all found evidence for different versions of a prototype model, with Neumann's study emphasizing the role of extreme values. (See Valentine, 1991, for another version of a prototype model and for a comparison of that model with an exemplar model.)

The Notion of and Evidence for a Face Schema

Although the terms *schema* and *prototype* have often been used interchangeably in the face recognition literature (see H. D. Ellis, 1981; Goldstein & Chance, 1981), as I discussed in chapter 2, the two actually have different meanings. In the present context, a face schema may refer to one of two things: (a) the generic set of features that make up one's conception of, say, a movie villain or an intellectual or a given ethnic "type," or, in other words, a facial stereotype; or (b) if you accept the possibility of a schema for a specific individual, the commonalities among the various transformations, poses, and orientations of a given face.

The evidence for face schemas in the first sense is mostly rather indirect. For example, there is relatively good evidence (e.g., Bower & Karlin, 1974; Winograd, 1976) that when participants are asked to make abstract personality or occupational judgments about faces, they show better recall for those faces than if they are simply asked to make judgments of gender or physical appearance. Although these findings have been interpreted in terms of Craik and Lockhart's (1972) depth-of-processing model, they can also be viewed as examples of relating the given face to a person schema, as discussed in chapter 2, of which a face is one aspect (though it is perhaps more of a stretch to call this a *face* schema.)

In the second sense of the term face schema, one clearly experiences the same person or face in many different situations under different guises yet manages to form a more or less coherent impression of that person. In the same way, one views the same face in different poses and appearances and still manages to recognize that face as belonging to the same person (within limits). Davies, Ellis, and Shepherd (1978) showed that participants could readily recognize the same face when the pose was changed from full view to three-fourths view, although Ellis and Deregowski (1981) found that European participants could not do the same for African faces, nor could Africans for Caucasians. Also, Dukes and Bevan (1967) found that participants who saw multiple pictures of a target in different poses and dress were better at remembering that target than were those who saw multiple pictures of the same face in the same pose and dress, suggesting that forming a specific person schema has advantages over mere repetition of a given picture. Thus, there exists a kind of schema for a specific person, or what Bruce & Young (1986) have referred to as a face recognition unit, as well as a schema for a group of people.

A word should be said about the role of context effects in face recognition. Everyone has probably had the experience of failing to recognize a friend or teacher or student when encountered in a different setting, as in the example given at the beginning of this chapter. (Davies, 1988, cites an anecdote from his own experience where he failed to recognize a young woman whom he had just hired as a research assistant when he encountered her at a party later in the same day.) The original research by Bower and Karlin (1974) on this topic reported no effects of changes in the judgmental context (i.e., a face paired either with the same face or with a new one while making judgments of either the gender of the pair or their compatibility) on subsequent recognition, whereas additional research by Watkins, Ho, and Tulving (1976) and by E. Winograd and Rivers-Bulkeley (1977) did find context effects. Furthermore, Thomson, Robertson, and Vogt (1982) and others (see Davies, 1988, for a review) found effects of varying the background context (e.g., clothing, activities engaged in) on subsequent recognition tests (see Davies, 1988).

The Concept of a Face Recognition Unit

One explicit attempt to account for the way in which people represent information about specific individuals has been made by Bruce and Young (1986; see also Hay & Young, 1982). According to these authors, faces of known, familiar individuals are encoded in terms of distinct *face recognition units (FRUs),* each of which entails a structural representation of a specific person's face.[3] Such a face recognition unit, a concept based on Morton's (1969) concept of a *logogen* (or word recognition unit), is assumed to be set off whenever there is a match between a target face and the structural representation in that FRU. In a manner similar to Morton's logogen concept, the firing of an FRU is assumed to result in both a signal of familiarity and also the activation of a related *person identity node* (*PIN*; Hay & Young, 1982; Bruce & Young, 1986), that is, information about a specific person. *Un*like the logogen concept, an FRU is assumed to involve a judgment of relative familiarity rather than an all-or-none recognition judgment. In other words, in face recognition you can judge that a newly encountered person looks familiar or reminds you of an old friend or a movie star to a certain *degree* without being able to identify that person or concluding that that person *is* the same as that other person.

One of the sources of the face recognition unit concept was a finding by Young, McWeeny, Hay, and Ellis (1986) that reaction times (RTs) for recognizing faces as familiar were significantly faster than RTs for judging a face as, for example, that of a politician, the latter of which is assumed to involve a step beyond a simple familiarity judgment. In everyday life it is clear that individuals often judge a person as familiar without being able to "place the face" exactly. V. Bruce (1983; V. Bruce & Valentine, 1985, 1986) has also reported evidence from a priming paradigm that is consistent with the concept of a FRU. Specifically, these investigators showed that familiarity judgments were faster when the target picture was preceded by either the same or a different picture of that same target person but not when preceded by that person's name. This finding is referred by V. Bruce and Valentine (1985) as *identity* or *repetition priming.* Identity priming, which may last for minutes or even hours, can be distinguished from *associative* (V. Bruce, 1983) or *semantic priming* (V. Bruce & Valentine, 1986), in which familiarity judgments are facilitated by prior presentation of the face of a related person (e.g., a picture of Monica Lewinsky preceded by one of Bill Clinton) and from what Brennen and Bruce (1991) called *categorical* priming (e.g., Charles Bronson as a prime for Clint Eastwood). Associative priming effects are relatively short-lived and occur even at intervals between the two pictures that make it unlikely that participants are responding by name associations.

Further research on repetition priming has suggested that something other than an FRU may be required. For example, A. W. Ellis, Young, Flude, and Hay (1987) found that the amount of priming was reduced when different views of the face (ranging from completely similar to very dissimi-

---

[3]Recently, Tanaka, Giles, Kremen, and Simon (1998) have applied the concept of an *attractor field* referring in this case to the area within multidimensional space for a given face, or the area within multidimensional "face space" from which the same face can be recognized from different stimuli. Using a morphing procedure, Tanaka et al. predicted and found that atypical faces had larger attractor fields, so that when typical and atypical faces were morphed together, the resulting face was judged to be more similar to the atypical one than to the typical one.

lar) were used, though Brunas, Young, and Ellis (1990) found that priming from part of the face (e.g., internal or external features) was as effective as priming by the whole face in later whole-face recognition. More recently, Bruce et al. (1992) demonstrated that changes in the format in which the face is presented (a line drawing vs. a photograph) reduce the amount of priming as well. The conclusion reached by Bruce et al. from these results is that what are preserved in the representation of a face are "low-level properties of the image" (p. 196). What these low-level properties are is not of concern here, but these observations have convinced Bruce and her associates that some kinds of PDP model, such as those to be developed in a later section, are more appropriate in accounting for these phenomenon than the all-or-none assumption of the FRU notion (though Bruce et al., 1992, acknowledged that even their PDP model, as currently conceived, cannot account for all of their findings).

The concept of an FRU is both similar to and different from that of a face schema. It is similar in that it entails structured, generic information about a specific person's face (i.e., generic in that it involves recognition of a face that is not pose-, transformation-, or instance-specific), although the exact nature of the representation of that face is not completely clear (see the above observations by Bruce et al., 1992). However, the FRU does not refer to general categories of faces, nor does it refer to the underlying information about the person behind the face. As I discuss in the next section, V. Bruce and Young (1986) distinguished between FRUs and what they call *person identity units,* or information about the identity of the person attached to the face.

MODELS OF PROCESSING FACES AND FACIAL INFORMATION

An Information-Processing Model

Probably the most systematic and comprehensive model of face recognition is one put forward by Hay and Young (1982), and later elaborated on by V. Bruce and Young (1986; see also H. D. Ellis, 1986). The Bruce and Young version of this information-processing model is presented in Fig. 3.6. As this figure indicates, Bruce and Young distinguished among four different stages of face processing. The first is that of *structural encoding,* in which visual information is assembled to construct a facial image, a representation that remains constant across different transformations, poses, and media (e.g., pictures vs. live exposure), along with a description of the face that is independent of specific facial expressions. This structural representation is then compared with FRUs to determine whether the image is a familiar one or not. These FRUs are used to access *identity-specific semantic information* or PINs, that is, stored information about the person (what I have referred to as an individual person schema). This information in turn helps to access *name recognition,* a process that is considerably more difficult than face rec-

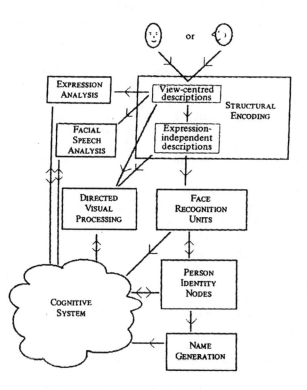

FIG. 3.6.   The Bruce and Young information processing model of face perception. From "Understanding Face Recognition" by V. Bruce, & A. W. Young, 1986, *British Journal of Psychology, 77*, p. 312. Copyright © 1986 by British Psychological Society. Reprinted with permission.

ognition, and that according to Bruce and Young, must typically be mediated by the aforementioned identity-specific nodes (see V. Bruce, 1988; V. Bruce & Young, 1986).

In addition to these four sequential stages, the Bruce and Young model also posits three subsidiary processes that enter into the process of face recognition. The first of these is an analysis of a person's facial expressions, such as happiness or surprise. The second is what Bruce and Young call *facial speech analysis or code,* which refers to the observer's representation of the person on the basis of her or his lip and tongue movements. I do not develop these two processes in greater detail.

More significantly, there is a *visually directed semantic analysis* stage. This stage involves inferences or attributions (e.g., of occupation, intelligence, honesty) from the mere appearance of the face and eye gaze direction (Campbell, Heywood, Cowey, Regard, & Landis, 1990) as well as some of the relatively "automatic" inferences of age, race, and gender mentioned in the discussion of impression formation. The important point here is that such analysis does not depend on familiarity with the person or inferences based on identity-specific information, such as knowing the identity of a friend or politician.

Finally, in addition to all of these functions and processes, Bruce and Young describe a *general cognitive system*, which includes such things as the associations among different FRUs (see later discussion), information about the person that is not directly contained in the PINs (e.g., where you met that person, what movie that particular actor was in, or even the person's address; see Bruyer & Scailquin, 1994). This system also includes control processes that receive information from and direct the functioning of visually directed processing and various decision processes, such as deciding that a person *looks* like someone familiar but is not actually that person (as opposed to the all-or-none logogen concept). (More recently, Young & de Haan, 1988, argued from evidence for semantic priming and observations on one particular prosopagnosic patient that there are probably connections between FRUs themselves.)

Given that the Bruce and Young model is primarily a model of face processing, the most important part of the model is obviously the face recognition unit. However, the component that provides the major point of contact between the *face* recognition or *face* memory component and the *person* memory systems described in chapter 2 is the PIN. The information contained in this node appears to be similar to the kind of person node referred to in some models of person memory (e.g., Hastie & Kumar, 1979; Ostrom et al., 1981), although this distinction between a central person node and the associated trait or person information is as difficult to make as is the distinction between person identity units and information contained in the cognitive system just referred to.

The arguments of the Bruce and Young (or Hay & Young) model are fairly straightforward and comprehensive (e.g., a sequential process of establishing a constant face, then establishing its familiarity, followed by attaching personal or identifying information to that face, as well as a separation between face recognition and other processes involved in mere visual search or analyses of facial expression); and, of course, these are two of the main attractions of the model. In addition, these different components also have the advantage of implying modularity as described by Fodor (1983); that is, they describe separate systems with separate functions.

Most importantly, the model provides a generally good fit to the research evidence. For example, Ley and Bryden (1979) found that participants could recognize tachistoscopically presented faces that they had just seen without being able to remember what facial expression these tachistoscopic faces had shown; and Kurucz and Feldmar (1979) reported evidence of patients who had lost the ability to recognize familiar faces yet retained the ability to analyze facial expressions and vice versa for other patients. In addition, V. Bruce (1979) showed that both semantic information (i.e., membership in the same category of politicians) and visual similarity played a role in determining reaction times in searching for target faces, but that the two factors operated in parallel. As I have discussed, judgments of whether a person is a politician or not—judgments made on the basis of identity-specific information—take longer to make than simple judgments of familiarity that presumably involve only FRUs. Along these same lines, de Haan, Young, and Newcombe (1991) presented evidence from an amnesic patient who retained the ability to recognize familiar faces but who could not access identity-specific information or names. Finally, Ellis, Flude, and Burton (1996) showed that whereas prior presentation of a face primed subsequent familiarity judgments for that same face, prior presentation of the name attached to that face did not, though the latter *did* prime face naming, suggesting again that face recognition and naming are two separable processes. (See Bredart & Bruyer, 1994, for a review of additional evidence for and against this model.)

Another source of evidence for the main sequence of stages in the Bruce and Young model is research on the kinds of everyday errors that participants report in face recognition (Young, Hay, & Ellis, 1985a, 1985b). Young et al. (1985b) had 22 participants keep diaries of the 922 errors they made over an 8-week period. These researchers divided the reported errors into seven main categories (see Table 3.1): (a) failure to recognize a familiar person; (b) misidentification of a person (including seeing an unfamiliar person as a familiar one and misidentifying a familiar person as another familiar one); (c) identifying a person as familiar without being able to identify him or her; (d) a problem in retrieving all of the details about a person (e.g., not recalling the name); (e) uncertainty whether a person is a particular person; (f) thinking that the person is not the person he or she really is; and (g) giving the wrong name to a person.

Of the 922 errors, each of the first four categories showed a substantial number (i.e., > 10%) of errors, whereas the latter three did not. More important, Young et al. showed how these incidents are consistent with the Hay and Young (1982) model (which, in fact, was partially based on these findings). For example, Category 1 errors are a function of the failure to trigger an FRU, whereas Category 3 errors can be attributed to a failure to go from an FRU to a person identity unit. Similarly, Category 7 is clearly a function of the failure to access the name generation node. Finally, some of these errors convinced Hay et al. to modify the earlier Hay and Young model. For example, Categories 1, 5, and 6 suggest that an FRU is not an all-or-none affair, but rather feeds information to the cognitive system which makes decisions about whether the face is a match or a mismatch.

Bruce, Young, and their associates also stressed the difference between the processing of familiar and unfamiliar faces (e.g., Young & Ellis, 1989), the former of which is associated with FRUs, and the latter of which involves the directed visual search process. There is clear evidence (e.g., A. W. Ellis, Shep-

TABLE 3.1

Examples of Face Recognition Errors

Category	Example
1. Failure to recognize person	I was going through the doors to B floor of the library when a friend said, "Hello." I ignored him, thinking that he must have been talking to the person behind me.
2. Misidentification of person	
Subtype A: Misidentifying unfamiliar person as familiar one	I was waiting for the phone. A lot of people were walking past. I thought one of them was my boyfriend.
Subtype B: A familiar person misidentified as another familiar one	I was outside my house, gardening and looking after the baby. I saw a person who lives near me, but I thought it was someone who used to live nearby, until I remembered he didn't live nearby any longer.
3. Person just identified as familiar	I was at the theatre when I saw someone I thought I knew. I didn't know who she was till I saw her with her sister and parents, who I knew better.
4. Problem retrieving all details	I was watching the late night film. I saw an actor who was very familiar. I know I've seen him in a television series, but I couldn't remember which one.
5. Uncertainty about whether person is right person	I was going into my house when I thought I saw Steve Duck [a British psychologist] outside. I wouldn't expect to see him there, and I decided it wasn't him, but then he spoke to me.
6. Thinking the person isn't who you thought s/he was	(See example given at beginning of this section)
7. Wrong name	I was doing a practical, and I had to get Cathy from the other side of the room. I thought her name was Jackie, but I wasn't completely sure, so I asked someone else first.

Note. From "The Faces That Launched a Thousand Slips: Everyday Difficulties and Errors in Recognizing People by A. W. Young, D. C. Hay, & A. W. Ellis, 1985, *British Journal of Psychology, 76,* pp. 495–523. Copyright © 1985 by British Psychological Society. Reprinted with permission.

herd, & Davies, 1979; Endo, Takahashi, & Maruyama, 1984) for differences in search or information-use strategies in the recognition of familiar versus unfamiliar faces—that is, participants start by searching external features for unfamiliar faces but concentrate on internal features for familiar faces. Similarly, Young et al. (1985) reported that when participants were asked to match either the internal or external features of a face with a photograph of the full face, they responded more rapidly for familiar than for unfamiliar faces when it was a matter of internal features, but showed no difference in reaction times for the external ones. These findings, however, held only when the parts of the face and the whole face were taken from different photos. Finally, in a developmental study, R. Campbell, Walker, and Baron-Cohen (1995) found that younger children (4–9 years) were more accurate in judging familiarity from *external* features, and only switched to the adult strategy of depending more on internal features after the age of 9, the period where Diamond and Carey (1977) noted a change in face-processing strategy.

There are also a number of potential difficulties with the Bruce and Young model, many of them raised by Bruce and Young themselves. For example, Bruce (1988) cited examples (such as the ones given earlier) in which recognition of familiar faces is context bound, a finding that cannot be readily accounted for by either person identity units or visually directed, semantic analysis. Bruce also pointed out that the latter process does not distinguish among the many different kinds of judgments that can be derived from a face and does not really account for how these judgments (e.g., about occupation or honesty) are made. She also observed that the Bruce and Young model is relatively silent on the critical issue of what form the representation of faces in the FRU takes, or how a face becomes familiar enough to trigger such an FRU. Finally, Ellis et al. (1987) showed that in priming experiments of the sort described earlier, the greater the degree of visual similarity between the priming and target pictures, the faster the priming effect, that is, the faster the RT to the test face. This finding is inconsistent with the original assumption, following Morton's logogen concept, of an all-or-none response of an FRU. Both Bruce and Ellis et al. have argued that these results and considerations suggest the need for an instance-based or PDP model, and it is this sort of model that I turn to next.

Rhodes and Tremewan (1993) also examined the assumption of the modularity of the different components of face recognition. I noted that the various components of the Bruce and Young model have been viewed as modular in that the different components are assumed to be *encapsulated* (Fodor, 1983) or involve separate functions. The fact that some believe that face recognition is specialized adds to this modularity view. An additional argument of the modularity position is that the perceptual systems, including, in the case of face recognition, the FRUs, occur independently of semantic or knowledge systems—that is, the latter do not influence the former. However, Rhodes and Tremewan presented evidence that semantic information (i.e., names of semantically related figures, e.g., Art Garfunkel) can indeed influence the ease of recognition of a given target face (e.g., Paul Simon); and these researchers argue that it is unlikely that processing occurring after perception mediates these effects. Thus, it appears that not only are the various components of face processing not modular, but that processing of faces is not unidirectional.

PDP or Connectionist Models of Face Recognition

The Bruce and Young model of face recognition represents what McClelland and Rumelhart (1985) have referred to as an *abstractive* model in that it assumes that the major representation of a face is in the form of an abstract unit that encompasses many different instances (e.g., different poses, encounters, appearances) of that same face. It is also an example of what I referred to in chapter 1 as a computational model in that it assumes that there are central processing mechanisms or units (e.g., FRUs, general cognitive system) that operate on information from a previous stage.

The alternative viewpoint, suggested by the Ellis et al. findings and the problems raised by Bruce, is an *instance-based* or PDP model. In this type of model, specific instances of, say, a given face, are represented in terms of different neural networks or in terms of the patterns of activity among processing units within a network. According to this view, specific facial features are stored in the individual processing units, and an instance (or possibly several instances) of the face as a whole is represented by the pattern of interconnections—more specifically, by the changing *weights* of the interconnections—among units. Thus, there is no abstract, central representation of the face—that is, no single FRU. Rather, the representation *and* processing of the face are distributed across many different units and probably different networks. Furthermore, change in these representations occur through repeated direct experiences rather than through explicit instruction (see chap. 1).

The Interactive Activation Model. One example of a PDP model that addresses the issues just raised with the Bruce and Young model is a formulation by Burton et al. (1990). Burton et al. called their position an *interactive activation model* (*IAM*) or later the *interaction activation and competition model* (*IAC*), both following from the same McClelland and Rumelhart (1981) model of letter perception that we described earlier (Read & Miller 1998a). Burton et al. acknowledged that this is not really a thoroughgoing PDP model because the representation of a face in this model is not really distributed. This model, which is illustrated in Fig. 3.7, contains three *pools* of units: one of FRUs, one of person identity units, and one of semantic information. In this model, unlike Bruce and Young's model, judgments of familiarity are assumed to be a function of the PINs rather than the FRUs, because such judgments are often based on factors other than the face, such as voice

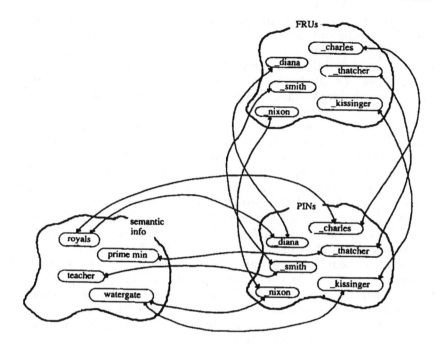

FIG. 3.7.   Burton et al.'s interaction-activation and competition model. From "I Recognize Your Face but I Can't Remember Your Name: A Simple Explanation?" by A. M. Burton and V. Bruce, 1992, *British Journal of Psychology, 83*, p. 47. Copyright © 1992 by British Psychological Society. Reprinted with permission.

or body. This model also explicitly distinguishes between the PINs and further semantic information (so that individuals may be able to recognize faces as familiar, but not recall any information about them). Within each pool, units are connected by *inhibitory* links (such that the activation of, for example, one FRU unit inhibits the activation of another), whereas connections between pools are *excitatory* (such that activation of a given FRU increases the activation of a given semantic unit).

In the IAM, activation is assumed to come through the FRUs (though these FRUs are obviously activated by perceptual inputs). Face recognition is assumed to involve the activation of a PIN that has a given threshold; and the time it takes to recognize a face is assumed to be a function of how many "processing cycles" it takes to reach that threshold level. Activation of a PIN will send excitation to a semantic unit (e.g., a picture of Bill Clinton may activate the concept of President or other concepts), which may in turn feed back into another PIN (e.g., John Kennedy). Finally, activation of a PIN by the transfer of excitation from an FRU will lead to a strengthening of the connection between these two units, in clear associative fashion.

Burton et al. (1990) used their formulation to model the nature and locus of both semantic and identity priming, as well as the nature of covert recognition in prosopagnosia (Burton et al., 1991). In the case of semantic priming, it is predicted that when one PIN activates a semantic unit, which in turn activates a related PIN (as in the Clinton–Kennedy example), the nature of the inhibitory relations between PINs (within a pool) means that the activation of the second PIN will hasten the decay of the first (while the associated PIN—such as Kennedy—continues to rise in strength). Thus, decay of the original PIN is not simply a matter of time, as other models suggest—hence, the term *interactive* activation. However, identity priming is accounted for by strengthening the links between an FRU and a PIN. As far as covert recognition in prosopagnosia is concerned, Burton, Young, Bruce, Johnston, and Ellis, (1991) proposed that such recognition can be accounted for by assuming a weakened link between FRUs and their associated PINs such that a given PIN is activated at a subthreshold level, which in this model means a lack of overt recognition. The PIN, in turn, passes some excitation to the related semantic information unit, which then passes activation to other PINs. As a result, it is possible for the participant to show signs of implicit memory—for instance, semantic priming or improved learning on subsequent trials—despite lacking awareness or a feeling of familiarity for the face. (Notice that this interpretation is inconsistent with the earlier argument that PINs have given thresholds.)

The same kind of within-pool inhibitory links that I discussed for semantic priming also account for the distinctiveness effect in face recognition. The greater the number of FRUs activated by shared features, the greater the mutual inhibition of these FRUs. Conversely, the smaller the number of shared features, and hence, the greater the distinctiveness, the better the recognition. Finally, Burton and Bruce (1992) recently extended the IAM to account for name recognition. According to this view, name recognition does not entail a separate stage, but rather names are included among the semantic information units. The reason names are often so difficult to retrieve is that (typically) a given name is relatively less common than other properties, such as occupation or nationality. As a person becomes more and more familiar with another person, other, more accessible information about that person should inhibit activation of that person's name. (See Bredart & Bruyer, 1994, for criticisms of this last argument.)

The WISARD and Kohonen Models. There are two other major connectionist models of face recognition.[4] One of these is a model called *WISARD* (for Wilkie, Stonham, and Aleksander's Recognition Device; see Stonham, 1986). WISARD, like the Burton et al. model, is not really a pure

---

[4]Tanaka et al. (1998) proposed another neural network model based directly on the software provided by McClelland and Rumelhart (1986) in connection with their own research on attractor fields.

example of a PDP model because specific faces are stored in specific locations in this model rather than being distributed throughout the system. Each face, however, is itself a combination of instances, or more precisely, a combination of responses to many different exposures or instances, so there is a kind of distribution on a smaller scale.

To be more specific, in the WISARD model, instances of faces are coded in terms of a pattern of yes–no or on–off responses. These patterns are stored in a memory bank, or *discriminator,* and this discriminator "learns," over repeated trials or exposures, to different instances, to recognize the particular patterns of responses associated with that face. Furthermore, the different discriminators for different faces can be compared in terms of how strongly they respond to any given new instance (e.g., does this face correspond to the pattern for John, Paul, George, or Ringo?). Thus, face recognition is a matter of comparing the response strengths of different discriminators.

The WISARD model has much to recommend it. It can recognize as many as 16 different faces with up to 95% accuracy without prior knowledge (Stonham, 1986) when given training on a large number of different instances (based on patterns of four features each). Furthermore, this model can be trained to discriminate particular features across many different persons as well as to recognize a particular face across many different expressions. However, the WISARD model falls short of the human capacity for face recognition in that it is restricted to 16 different faces—far less than what humans are capable of recognizing; and unlike human face recognition, WISARD is also restricted to specific lighting conditions and particular poses. Thus, the WISARD model does not really approximate our human capacity for face recognition.

The other PDP model of face recognition is one proposed by Kohonen (1977; Kohonen, Oho, & Lehtio, 1981). This model is a more standard PDP model in that a given stimulus or image of a face consists of a pattern of units interconnected by means of a set of weights (like the IAM, but unlike the WISARD models). This set of weights is established by associating the stimulus pattern with a *forcing stimulus* across the same set of units. A forcing stimulus is a pattern that produces a particular response (e.g., the name David). This association between the two stimuli causes the original set of weights to be adjusted to match that forcing stimulus. The result, then, is a kind of associative learning whereby the instance comes to elicit the same response as the forcing stimulus (i.e., recognition of a given person), and the purpose of the system is to get a number of different instances of the same face to elicit the same response as the forcing stimulus.

The Kohonen model has a number of different advantages. For one, the model can be trained to recognize novel instances of the same face (for a set of 10 different faces) presented at a number of different angles. Also, by a process of *autoassociative learning* common to PDP models (i.e., by associating a given stimulus pattern with itself), the system can learn to recognize degraded or incomplete exemplars of the same face. However, Kohonen's model works only with a restricted range of patterns (e.g., a limited number of angles) and requires a good deal of preliminary processing of the input before it is fed into the memory system per se. (This latter deficiency is a problem with all the connectionist models that we have considered, though see Burton, Bruce, & Hancock, 1999). Thus, there are a number of unspecified assumptions or procedures that are included in this processing apart from those proposed by the model itself.

The obvious advantage of PDP models of face recognition is that they are more flexible than all-or-none FRUs; also, they account for why factors such as visual similarity of various sorts influence judgments of familiarity, whereas at the same time allowing for the possibility that different poses and appearances may still be recognized as belonging to the same face (in a rather different manner from the concept of a face schema). In general, PDP models are probably more suitable than are traditional serial, symbolic architectures for pattern recognition tasks and for skills like face recognition in that such skills are either built in or are the result of mere adaptation rather than explicit instruction or programming (W. A. Phillips & Smith, 1989). Furthermore, as with most computer models, PDP models of face recognition can be evaluated in terms of how well they actually *work* in computer recognition of faces (although not all computer models of face recognition are connectionist—see R. J. Baron, 1981; V. Bruce & Burton, 1989). At the same time, as W. A. Phillips and Smith (1989) pointed out and as I noted in chapter 2, a successful computer simulation does not ensure the validity of the underlying theory. These particular PDP models or look-alikes are rather crude and simplistic versions of connectionism, and they are not specialized for face (as opposed to other pattern) recognition (with the possible exception of the Burton et al. model). Finally, as V. Bruce and Burton (1989; see also V. Bruce, 1988) have noted, neither the WISARD nor the Kohonen models (nor Burton et al.'s own model) provides a clear, detailed *front end* to show how the physical information from photographs or real faces is translated into a form that is usable by the pattern-matching system. In other words, a large part of face processing is left unspecified by these three models. (Recently, Burton, Bruce, & Hancock, 1999, added such a front end to their IAM.)

A word is also in order about how connectionist models of face recognition are similar to and different from the connectionist models of impression formation and person memory reviewed in the last chapter. The first obvious similarity is that in both cases the models are fairly primitive, with some being localist versions rather than full-scale PDP models. Second, Read and Miller's (1998a) Social Dynamics model contains basic input and identification levels that include faces as one input, although these levels are not clearly worked out in their model. Finally, with the exception of the recent updates of the Burton et al. model, the connectionist models of face recognition that I have reviewed are of decidedly earlier vintage than those reviewed in chapter 2 for impression formation.

There is a sense, however, in which such PDP models seem more appropriate for face recognition than for impression formation. In the first place, PDP models do well with pattern recognition, like word recognition; and faces are obviously more clearly patterns and simpler patterns than is personality. (It certainly is a clearer example of the automatic system than is impression formation, which is at least sometimes thoughtful and symbolic.) In fact, recall that the notion of an FRU was based on an analogy to word recognition, even if it was not a PDP model. It seems to me that face recognition is more clearly analogous to word recognition than impression formation. Second, in face recognition, like word recognition, there is a concrete test of a successful simulation (i.e., the ability of the simulation to recognize a pattern—in this case, a face) rather than simply trying to reproduce a general pattern of findings or recognition of social or nonsocial patterns.

LABORATORY VERSUS REAL-WORLD STUDIES
OF FACE RECOGNITION

Thus far I have focused primarily on laboratory research on face recognition. Although the stimuli used in most of these studies have been fairly realistic (i.e., photographs rather than line drawings or other sorts of artificial stimuli; see Shepherd, 1989), the research has nevertheless been primarily of the carefully controlled lab variety, motivated by a desire to test out basic models of memory and information processing (e.g., Bruce & Young's face-processing model). In fact, many of them (e.g.,the research by Bruce and her associates) have been explicitly modeled after laboratory research on word recognition and verbal information processing.

Face recognition has also been studied in more naturalistic settings and with nonlaboratory research designs. A particularly noteworthy example of this alternative approach is the research by Harry Bahrick (1984; Bahrick et al., 1975). In this research, Bahrick et al. examined individuals' memory, as assessed by both recall and recognition measures, for the photographs of their high school classmates at intervals ranging from 2 weeks to 57 years (see also Bruck, Cavanagh, & Ceci, 1991). This research is of interest not only because of its valuable insights into the long-term retention of real-world, personally meaningful material, but also because it exemplifies a thoroughgoing alternative to traditional experimental research on memory in which potentially confounding variables are explicitly held constant or varied systematically. Bahrick et al. referred to their alternative as a *cross-sectional design,* as opposed to the typical experimental design in which the presentation of the stimulus material is followed, after a controlled retention period, by a memory test. In this cross-sectional design, potentially confounding variables, including in particular those that cannot be adequately controlled for in the lab, are *statistically* controlled or adjusted for. Bahrick et al. (1975) described it as follows:

Examples [of variables that can't be controlled for] are a greater range of learning materials, a greater range of motivational conditions, a greater range of context effects, and most significantly, a greater range of acquisition time. If the material to be remembered must be taught in the laboratory, it usually must be taught within a few hours' time. However, much, if not most, information in the memory store essential for daily living is acquired in practice sessions which are distributed irregularly over months or years. The names and faces of friends and acquaintances, knowledge of a city in which one has lived, knowledge of a foreign language or of the rules of chess or bridge, professional skills such as those used by a surgeon or an engineer, are all examples. (p. 58)

In this study on memory for high school classmates, participants were divided into nine groups on the basis of time since graduation. A variety of uncontrolled variables were assessed, including size of graduating class, number of classes shared with given classmates, number of reunions attended, amount of time spent reviewing the yearbook, 'amount of contact with particular classmates since graduation, and the relationship with each of the figures for whom recall was assessed. In addition, participants took a number of memory tests, ranging from free recall for all names remembered within an 8-minute period, a picture recognition test (i.e., recognizing which of five pictures came from the participant's yearbook), a name recognition task (of the same format as the picture recognition task), name and picture matching tests (where names and pictures were taken from the participant's own yearbook), and a picture cuing (recall) task in which participants were to write down the name of the person whose picture they were shown.

The most significant findings of the Bahrick et al. study were that recognition performance for pictures and names, as well as name and picture matching, started at a remarkably high level of nearly 90%; and picture recognition showed almost no decline over a period of up to 35 years, whereas performance on the name recognition and the two matching tests showed a decline after some 15 years. Free and cued recall performance showed substantially lower initial levels of performance, as well as a significant, though slow decline over the 48-year period. Equally important, free recall was found to be independent of recognition performance, suggesting that the decline in the former was primarily a product of participants' inability to generate or retrieve essential information, particularly picture cues, rather than of decay or storage problems for that information. Furthermore, the independence of recall and recognition and the fairly slow decline of memory over these extended periods are inconsistent with the results of traditional lab research on memory and retention where recognition and recall are more highly correlated, and recognition shows much greater losses over considerably shorter periods of time (though cf. the results on the decline of autobiographical memory to be discussed in chap. 5). As suggested earlier, Bahrick et al. attributed the disagreement between real-world and lab results to the differences in the conditions of acquisition in the two situations.

Specifically, the slow decline is presumed to be a result of a combination of overlearning effects and distributed practice (i.e., distributed exposure to classmates), as opposed to the massed practice found in most laboratory studies. The latter difference, in particular, points to a major misconception generated by laboratory research on learning and acquisition.

Bahrick (1984a) also reported a pair of additional studies designed to test the differences between lab and real-world research on face recognition. In one of these, participants' performance on the recognition of faces encountered only in the context of the experiment were compared with these same participants' recognition of pictures of classmates repeatedly encountered in their introductory psychology classes (with other real college students from the same university as foils). The major findings of this second, shorter term study was that participants' performance on the real-world task was significantly better than in the lab study, and the two measures of recognition memory were relatively uncorrelated. Once again, both of these findings suggest that lab studies may not give a valid picture of the nature of face recognition, presumably because of differences in attentional and motivational variables in the two situations that may influence performance (though there are other differences between the two tasks as well, such as the difference between single and multiple encounters with the stimulus person).

In one final study Bahrick (1984a) examined the memory of college professors for students in their introductory classes over periods of 8, 4, or 1 years or 2 weeks. In this study some control over the age of the professor was possible, unlike the previous high school classmate study where age was necessarily confounded with time since graduation. Once again, measures of name and picture recognition, name–picture matching, and picture-cuing were included, plus a picture-cuing relearning task (for names not recalled on the other picture-cuing task).

The overall results of this study are easy to summarize. First, professors showed much poorer memory performance in general than did the students in the previous study, who had obviously encountered their classmates in different situations and on different numbers of occasions than had the professors. Second, unlike participants in the previous study, professors who had experience calling rolls in their classes actually showed *better* name recognition than they did picture recognition, whereas these professors' performance for picture recognition actually declined to near chance (20%) at the end of 8 years. Third, the relearning task revealed substantial savings even for names that professors found difficult to recall on the first occasion. Finally, the age differences in memory proved to be quite small.

Bahrick (1984a) pointed out some of the implications of naturalistic studies of memory, on the basis of his studies of both face and long-term memory for language (Bahrick, 1984b; Bahrick & Phelps, 1988; Bahrick, Bahrick, Bahrick, & Bahrick, 1993) and mathematics (Bahrick & Hall, 1991). First, as I have indicated, Bahrick's results underline the differences between laboratory and naturalistic studies, although Bahrick (1996) has recently advocated a more synergistic approach to memory research. In particular, Bahrick's findings emphasize the critical role played by attentional, motivational, and individual differences in real-world memory. At the same time, however, Bahrick (e.g., 1984a) has pointed out some of the difficulties of maintaining control (e.g., of motivational and attentional factors) in naturalistic studies, even when an assessment, multiple-regression approach is used.

APPLICATIONS OF FACE RECALL
TO EYEWITNESS IDENTIFICATION

One of the real-world settings to which research on face recognition has been usefully applied is eyewitness memory, where the witness to a crime must identify the perpetrator. For example, the findings reviewed earlier that participants are able to recognize the same face in different poses, or the finding (e.g., Malpass & Kravitz, 1969) that participants have difficulty recognizing faces of different races, or the evidence that context affects recognition—all of these seem relevant to the practical issue of how to improve (or how much confidence to place in) eyewitness recall. In addition, lab research on training in face recognition and recall, which I examine in this section, is particularly pertinent to this practical issue.

The applications of research on face recognition to eyewitness identification is also of tremendous practical significance. For instance, Devenport, Penrod, and Cutler (1997) suggested that errors in eyewitness identification "appear to be the most frequent source of erroneous convictions" (p. 1). These commentators cite research by Connors, Lundregan, Miller, and McEwen (1996) indicating that of the 28 convictions they studied that were later overturned by DNA evidence, all 28 were convicted on the basis of errors of eyewitness identification. Similarly, Huff (1987; Huff, Rattner, & Sagarin, 1996) reported that 60% of the 500 wrongful convictions he studied were due to such misidentifications.

Laboratory Simulations Versus Real-Life Lineup Studies

One question that is important to consider before reviewing evidence on eyewitness identification is the one that we have been addressing throughout this book: Are the findings obtained in the lab in fact applicable to real-life lineup or witness identification tasks? The views on this issue are mixed. For example, Deffenbacher (1988), Laughery and Wogalter (1989), and Wells (1993) have reviewed a number of findings that they feel are applicable to real-world eyewitness situations. Similarly, Kassin, Ellsworth, and Smith (1989) reported the results of a survey of experts in eyewitness testimony that suggest a variety of findings that these experts feel are well enough established to be offered as expert testimony in court cases. On the other hand, Davies (1989) has concluded that "surprisingly few of the reported effects [in a review by Laughery & Wogalter] have made this transition (to the real world) effectively" (p. 559). Certainly many judges and law enforcement officials and even some psychologists (e.g., Egeth & McCloskey, 1984; Yuille, 1993) would agree with this conclusion. Still other psychologists (e.g., Goodman & Loftus, 1989; Shapiro & Penrod, 1986) have taken a position consistent with that put forward in chapter 1: namely, that it is not so important that specific findings or phenomena generalize to the world, but rather that the underlying psychological processes do.

Along similar lines, Wells and Turtle (1986) have reviewed evidence on the differences between lab simulations and real-world studies of lineup identification. These commentators have suggested that at least one of the major differences between the two settings—namely, the finding of significantly higher false recognition of suspects as the actual culprit in the lab than in real-world situations—is due to some basic methodological differences between the two types of studies rather than to limitations or constraints on the lab simulations. (Many of these "limitations"—e.g., a shorter delay between witnessing the crime and seeing the lineup, favorable or more favorable encoding conditions in the lab, lower levels of stress—actually *favor* performance in the lab.) For example, there is the distinction between using *single-suspect* lineups in the lab versus *all-suspect* lineups in the real world. There is the need to consider the results of *target-absent* lineups (i.e., where there are no suspects present), which serve as a kind of control for guessing, as well as *target-present* ones; and there is the distinction between misidentification (i.e., mistakenly identifying a suspect as a criminal) and *false* identification (e.g., of a known *foil* as the criminal), which is not always taken into account in lab research.

With these reservations in mind, there is still much to be learned from laboratory research on face recognition and lineup identification, at least in part because such research has frequently made an effort to use more real-world materials and conditions. Some of the possible applications include the following (see Laughery & Wogalter, 1989): (a) perhaps the most obvious application is when a witness has to identify a suspect, based on that witness's own memory, from a photospread, a lineup, or simply a *showup*, where a witness has to respond "yes" or "no" to a single suspect without distractors or foils; (b) a somewhat less interesting possibility is when a police officer or law enforcement agent is asked to use a drawing, a reproduction, or even a photo or hidden camera picture of a criminal to catch him or her; (c) alternatively, the witness may be asked to *recall* the criminal by means of a verbal description, a drawing, a *Photofit*, or Identikit (i.e., kits in which faces are constructed, from a verbal description, from bits and features); (d) finally, there is research on training (e.g., of police officers or witnesses) in face identification (e.g., Baddeley & Woodhead, 1983; Malpass, 1981).

Specific Applications

Given this (far from exhaustive) list of applications, I now review some of the specific implications of laboratory research on face recognition for eye-witness recall (see Cutler & Penrod, 1995; Laughery & Wogalter, 1989; Shapiro & Penrod, 1986, for reviews). (I review additional evidence on eye-witness memory for accidents and criminal *events* in chap. 4.) As far as expo-sure and recognition conditions are concerned, the evidence (e.g., Egan, Pittner, & Goldstein, 1977; Shepherd, Ellis, & Davies, 1981) suggests that live exposure to the suspect and live lineups at recognition lead to greater recognition accuracy than do photographs or videotapes, although the sim-ilarity of exposure and recognition conditions—the well-known *encoding specificity effect* (Tulving & Thomson, 1973)—also makes a difference. Along these lines, Davies, 1989, and Schiff, Banks, and Bordas Galdi, 1986, have stressed the need for using more dynamic video materials in studies of rec-ognition, as well as using materials that focus on more than just face recog-nition because real-life eyewitness situations often involve other cues to identification[5]—(see MacLeod, Frowley, & Shepherd, 1994, and Yarmey, 1994, for discussions of the use of body and voice information, respec-tively.) I noted in my earlier discussion that context effects and context rein-statement seem to make a difference in face recognition (see Davies, 1988, Shapiro & Penrod, 1986). Although, as I discussed earlier, the evidence on this topic is not completely consistent, Shapiro and Penrod (1986) found that same versus changed context was one of the strongest influences on eyewitness identification. Along these lines, various *guided recollection in-struction* for eyewitness identification (e.g., Fisher & Geiselman, 1988; Geiselman & Fisher, 1996; Malpass, 1996) use the technique of helping wit-nesses to reconstruct the context in which they witnessed the crime, and they emphasize the role of visualization. (These recollection techniques also use another well-established memory technique, that of using as many retrieval cues as possible.)

Other features of exposure that have an impact include the fact that three-fourths poses lead to better recognition than do profiles or full-face poses (see Laughery & Wogalter, 1989). There also appears to be an effect of disguises and accessories, though the size of that effect is not clear (see Shapiro & Penrod, 1986). As I discussed earlier, more elaborative encod-ing, such as making personality judgments or forming impressions at en-coding, increases recognition performance (though see my discussion of results for recall). Another set of findings that is of great practical as well as theoretical importance is that recognition accuracy is affected by the num-

---

[5]Burton et al. (1999) recently demonstrated that people familiar with the targets shown on poor quality surveillance tapes performed very well in recognition, whereas those unfamiliar with the targets, including police officers experienced in forensic work, did very poorly. Interest-ingly, when heads, body, or gait was obscured for the familiar participants, only the obscured head (and face) led to major decrements in recognition.

ber of faces (or by the very exposure to additional faces) that the witness has seen in the interim (see Laughery & Wogalter, 1989, for a review). This means, of course, that if the witness has watched a photospread or a lineup in the period between the crime and, for example, a trial, the witness may confuse where he or she has seen the face. Deffenbacher (1988) stated this point in the following way:

> It is much easier to recognize a face as having been encountered before than it is to recall the precise circumstances of encounter. As a result, when police show a suspect's photograph to a witness in a photospread, identified or not, guilty or not, the suspect is now likely to be identified in any subsequent lineup. (p. 20)

As I discuss in chapter 4, this conclusion is consistent with the concept of *source monitoring* (e.g., M. K. Johnson, Hashtroudi, & Lindsay, 1993), according to which one may remember a piece of information but forget the *source* of that information (see Lindsay, 1994, for a specific application of this theory to eyewitness identification). Along similar lines, Davies (1989) pointed out that this problem of false identification in such situations is due, in part, to the fact that judgments are frequently made on the basis of familiarity rather then identification (cf. the distinction between FRUs and PINs), and this distinction is one of the reasons why it is difficult to apply laboratory findings, which, as we have seen, focus primarily on familiarity, to real-world eyewitness situations (though see V. Bruce's [1988] view that face *recognition* includes identification).

Other factors that play a role in face recognition and eyewitness identification (see Cutler & Penrod, 1995; Narby, Cutler, & Penrod, 1996; Shapiro & Penrod, 1986, for reviews) include the length of the delay interval, the length of exposure, the distinctiveness of the face, and the role of levels of arousal at encoding (see Christianson, 1992, for a review of the complex evidence on this topic). Recently, Shapiro and Penrod (1986; see also Chance & Goldstein, 1996) have reported strong cross- or other-race biases for both Caucasian and African American participants, and Brigham and Ready (1985) have found that these biases have an effect on lineup identifications —that is, participants selected more other-race than same-race figures to be in lineups.

One final finding that is of great practical significance for actual eyewitness identification is the relationship between the *certainty* of eyewitnesses in their judgments and the *accuracy* of these judgments. Such a finding is of importance because the evidence suggests (Wells, 1984, 1993; Wells & Lindsay, 1985) that jurors use eyewitness confidence as a major cue for judging the credibility of the eyewitness. Unfortunately, the evidence on this issue is again rather mixed (see Bothwell, Deffenbacher, & Brigham, 1987; Sporer, Penrod, Read, & Cutler, 1995; Wells, 1993). In their meta-analysis of 35 studies of the confidence–accuracy relationship, Bothwell et al. (1987) found a mean correlation of .25 but an effect size of

.52, which represents a moderate effect size (see J. Cohen, 1988). Whether "moderate" is sufficient to justify the importance attached by jurors to eyewitness confidence is not clear. (Narby et al., 1996, concluded that it is not.) In particular, Brigham (1988) pointed out that the correlations show a rather wide range and are clearly affected by a variety of other variables (see also Penrod & Cutler, 1995; Wells, 1993, on the "malleability of certainty").

In line with the research of Bahrick and his associates, it should be noted that eyewitness identification has also been examined in several naturalistic studies (or studies in naturalistic settings). For example, at least three articles (Brigham, Maass, Snyder, & Spaulding, 1982; Krafka & Penrod, 1985; Platz & Hosch, 1988) have reported studies in which clerks at convenience stores were to identify customers who had been in the store, sometimes for a substantial amount of time. These studies all showed a high rate of false identifications under a variety of different identification conditions. Pigott, Brigham, and Bothwell (1990) conducted a similar study in a bank where tellers were later asked to identify customers, and they reported similar results.

A discussion of the methods developed to improve eyewitness memory is beyond the scope of this book (see discussion in chap. 4 on eyewitness *testimony*). I should note, however, that attempts to train witnesses in recall accuracy (e.g., by hypnotic induction) have not been very effective, although the recent cognitive interview techniques developed by Malpass and Devine (1981) and expanded on by Geiselman (1988; Geiselman & Fischer, 1996), which I touched on earlier, seem to show some promise (though see Davies, 1989). In particular, Narby et al. (1996) recently concluded that training methods are particularly ineffective when they focus on "facial feature analysis. ... Generally, holistic encoding seems to be superior for later recognition ..." (p. 30).

Along these same lines, Shepherd and Ellis (1996) noted the failure of the legal system to consider the differences between face recognition and face recall in eyewitness testimony. Specifically, as I discussed earlier, facial recognition typically involves holistic processing of the entire face, whereas face recall, particularly in eyewitness testimony, is necessarily featural (at this point at least). Existing techniques such as Identikit, Photofit, various computer graphic techniques, and even artist sketches are *composite* systems, that is, composites of features (Shepherd & Ellis, 1996). These techniques, which are limited in their effectiveness for a variety of different reasons (see Shepherd & Ellis, 1996 for a review) can be contrasted with a search of mug shots, which is essentially a recognition technique, although the latter technique involves the obvious problem that looking through a number of distractor photos may obscure the witness's memory for the suspect or change the witness's criterion for resemblance (Shepherd & Ellis, 1996; see Davies, Shepherd, & Ellis, 1979, and Laughery, Alexander, & Lane, 1971, for evidence on such problems). Shepherd and his associates (e.g., Shepherd, 1986; Shepherd & Ellis,

1996) have developed a computerized system named *FACES*, which searches a large database of mugshots by comparing witnesses' verbal ratings of features with the ratings made by experts of these same features in the bank of stored photographs. This procedure, which converts a holistic recognition task into a featural recall one, has nevertheless been demonstrated to be superior to traditional mugshot review.

In a recent discussion of the role of person descriptions in eyewitness identification, Sporer (1996) suggested a link between face memory and person memory. Specifically, Sporer pointed out that verbal descriptions are typically stated in a feature-by-feature form, which must then be translated, by whatever means, into an image of the culprit. Furthermore, our language for describing faces is much less rich than that for describing the person behind the face; and in fact, Sporer's own research (e.g., 1992) found that when asked to make physical descriptions, participants typically end up describing *psychological* rather than physical characteristics. In addition, Sporer's (1996) analysis of archival records of actual witnesses' descriptions of criminals indicated that the two most frequently mentioned characteristics were hair and clothes, two features that are not very helpful because they can be changed so readily.

I began this section with the question that represents one of the central themes of this book: How valid is it to generalize from the laboratory to the real world, in this case, in the area of eyewitness identification? I have already cited Bahrick's naturalistic studies of face recognition in general. There are also a multitude of methods for studying eyewitness identification, including archival and case history methods, as well as lab and field studies. As an example of the former method, MacLeod (1985, 1987; see also Tollestrup, Turtle, & Yuille, 1994; Yuille & Kim, 1987) studied a sample of actual witness statements from police records. One finding of this research that is relevant to the application of lab research to real-world eyewitness situations is that actual victims gave more detailed information than did bystanders; yet, as Davies (1989) pointed out, participants in lab research on this topic, are, by necessity, bystanders. Similarly, Read, Tollestrup, Hammersley, McFadzen, and Christensen (1990) reported the results of five field studies of eyewitness identification which, in general, failed to find the same kind of misidentifications that have been found in lab studies. Of course, archival and field research suffer from their own problems, such as the difficulty of controlling for extraneous variables, and the difficulty in archival studies of checking on the *accuracy* of witness statements (Davies, 1989).

One of the strongest critics of the application of lab research on eyewitness testimony is John Yuille (1986, 1993). Yuille has argued that lab results do not generalize to real-world situations, and he has reported some case history studies (e.g., Cutshall & Yuille, 1989; Yuille & Cutshall, 1986) of eyewitness reports as an alternative. However, as Yuille (1993) himself acknowledges, the case history method cannot stand on its own as the only method in this area. Rather, as Davies (1989) has argued, "no one method of approaching the problem of applied facial memory enjoys a monopoly of [sic] virtue; what is required is a distillation of evidence from information acquired from all four of the differing methodologies" (p. 561).

SUMMARY AND INTEGRATION OF FACE AND PERSON MEMORIES LITERATURES

In this chapter I have reviewed some research and models of face processing and face recognition. Although the research reviewed on the specialness of faces and on eyewitness identification is unique to this topic, it should be apparent that there are also some basic connections, as well as some important differences between research and theory on face recognition in general and the research and theories reviewed in chapter 2 on impression formation and person memory. The most obvious connection is the common concern with the representation and knowledge of persons and personal identity. For example, it is clear that being able to recognize different instances as being aspects of the same face (e.g., O. J. Simpson or Johnnie Cochran with and without the cap) is critical for our understanding of persons. In addition, I have shown that the V. Bruce and Young (1986) model of face processing contains PINs, and I have suggested that these PINs are similar to the kind of person nodes contained in some models of person memory, although the latter obviously explore this node in much greater detail. It seems clear that information from the face is a major contributor to person memory and impression formation, even though current-day research on person memory has given little recognition to this fact (see M. B. Brewer, 1988, for one major exception here). At the same time, I have discussed how making attributional judgments or knowing the person behind the face facilitates face processing; and recent evidence by Rhodes and Tremewan (1993) suggests that knowledge of personal identity may even influence perceptual sensitivity to faces. On the other hand, Berry (1990) suggested that it is possible to make accurate judgments of personality on the basis of static facial expressions. Thus, it seems clear that face memory and person memory are intrinsically related and should not be pursued in relative isolation from each other.

Another obvious area of overlap is the appeal of researchers in both areas to similar models of person representation (e.g., elemental or featural vs. prototype and schema models) and processing (e.g., traditional information-processing vs. PDP models). Equally important, both areas are faced with the basic question of how readily lab research findings can be applied to everyday natural settings (and, in the case of face recognition, to applied topics as well). I have argued (and Wyer has recently acknowledged) that this question is equally relevant to both areas; and yet the response of researchers in the two areas has been quite different. Specifically, as discussed in chapter 2, researchers on person memory have generally taken the position, in a manner similar to Banaji and Crowder (1989), that controlled laboratory research can produce findings and principles that can be generalized to everyday real-world settings. This point of view is most clearly represented in the work of Wyer and his associates and by Fiske (though Fiske's "experimental microcosms" are rather different from the kinds of experimental situations defended by Banaji and Crowder). In the case of face recognition, it seems more reasonable to rely on laboratory studies because this research uses more real-world materials (though see the debate over photographs vs. videotapes or live action in the eyewitness testimony area). Nevertheless, researchers on face memory, in a manner similar to Conway and Neisser, have been quick to acknowledge the importance of real-world studies (as well as neurophysiological and neuroclinical research, computer simulations, developmental research, as well as traditional lab research.). In other words, investigators on face memory have been more open to a variety of different forms of research and a variety of different findings; and as I indicated in chapter 1, I believe that such openness is a definite plus.

It is also worth noting some of the other interesting and, I believe, instructive differences between research in the two areas. The first issue that comes to mind is that whereas research on person memory has emphasized the major role of processing goals and other conceptually-driven processes, in research on face recognition the face itself is such a natural and imposing stimulus pattern (perhaps with its own hard-wired mechanisms) that processing is more influenced by this stimulus pattern than it is by some kind of goals (although there is obviously some role of an analytic vs. global set towards encoding and retrieval). Second, there is the issue that I raised, and that was also raised by Tarr (1998), Fiske and Neuberg (1990), and M. B. Brewer (1988) in slightly different contexts, about whether people or faces are processed more at an individual, group, or category level. Whereas people may be as likely or more likely to be treated as a member of an ethnic, social, or national group than as an individual, faces are almost necessarily processed at the individual level, except perhaps in the case of the initial stage of judging race, age, gender, and the like. In fact, recall that V. Bruce (1979) found that categorical or semantic processing operated in parallel with individualized face processing. On the other hand, M. B. Brewer used photographs, interestingly, to reinforce general, categorical processing. In the next two chapters I discuss how this same issue of generality versus specificity applies to the understanding and memory for events as well.

Chapter 4

Remembering Everyday Events and Actions and Planning for Future Actions

Introduction

Event Memory and Knowledge Structures

Distortions of Event Memory

Prospective Memory and the Cognitive Representation of Planning

Conclusions

INTRODUCTION

In this chapter I look at the way in which people remember everyday events: personal or historical events, events—physical or social—people observe in their lives, or events depicted in newspapers, magazines, or novels. I begin with the work carried out over the past 25 years in psychology and artificial intelligence on the basic representation of events. In this review I focus primarily on the seminal work of Robert Abelson and Roger Schank and their students, whose conceptualizations have dominated the field. Then I move to a discussion of various distortions of event memory, focusing on the voluminous literature on one particular type of distortion—namely, eyewitness memory for crimes—and the degree to which such memory can be influenced by misleading questions or misinformation. In this area I focus on the research carried out by Elizabeth Loftus and her associates, the criticisms that have been raised against this research, and some recent evidence trying to place this research in clearer perspective. Finally, I move to a discussion of research and theorizing on the topic of *prospective memory*, or memory for carrying out plans for future action, as well as some models of the process of planning itself.

In chapter 3 I developed a personality sketch of Monica Lewinsky, one of the central figures in the Clinton White House scandal. One of the fascinating things about this news event (as is true with many political occurrences; see Abelson, 1973) is that it is open to so many interpretations. Stated differently, there are so many possible construals of Clinton and Lewinsky's actions, their respective goals, plans, and the like. As I discuss in this chapter, there are also a number of possible themes that may be used to summarize the sexual liaison—for instance, a seduction theme, a sexual harassment theme, a sexual addiction theme, a schoolgirl crush theme. Furthermore, there can be different conceptions of President Clinton's motives and the plans involved in his delays in providing information to Kenneth Starr's investigation (or of the goals of the investigation itself). Finally, it is of interest to speculate whether observers of the White House scandal are influenced more by their impressions of the participants—their person schemas—or by the particular theme or scenario that they have imposed on the events.

On a more everyday level, let's say that you just found out that you didn't get the job you interviewed for last month. You go over the details of the interview in your mind: what things you did that may have turned the interviewer off, how the interviewer responded to you, what his or her agenda may have been. In so doing, you undoubtedly try to infer the goals and plans and attributes of the interviewer, as well as trying to reproduce the actions involved in the episode. It is these kinds of events and inferences that I will focus on in the first section.

EVENT MEMORY AND KNOWLEDGE STRUCTURES

Certainly one of the critical issues in everyday cognition is what individuals remember about events and actions, and how they cognitively represent them. How does one remember historical or political events and more personal events? Do people represent them as separate, individual events or as members of a generic category, such as political revolts, economic depressions, personal accomplishments? Do individuals focus on the goals or aims of those events or the participants or the actual physical details? Are some events or types of events easier to remember than others? Do people's expectations or previous knowledge have an effect on how well they remember an event, or is it the characteristics of the event itself that determines its memorability?

Probably the most influential model of event memory, and one that addresses these sorts of questions is the script model of Schank, Abelson, and their students, and it is with this model that I begin the discussion.

The Script Model

Abelson's Initial Work on Political Scripts. Although the work of Schank and Abelson on scripts is usually traced to their seminal book *Scripts, Plans, Goals, and Understanding* (*SPGU*; 1977), one of the first discussions of these ideas can be found in Abelson's (1973, 1975) early work on belief systems. The purpose of this research was to build a computer simulation of the thinking processes (and background knowledge or beliefs) of a True Believer, such as Barry Goldwater or Ronald Reagan (or Republicans on the House Judiciary Committee), or a so-called Ideology Machine. The details of this model are not of concern to us, except to note that Abelson's fundamental argument here was that purposive action forms the basis for the cognitive representation of belief systems. Thus, the central concept of this simulation was the *molecule,* which Abelson (1973) identified as "the essential building block of all belief systems which find meaning in the purposive actions of individuals, institutions, and governments" (p. 299), for instance, studying *in order to* get good grades or fighting a war *to* secure a country's vital interests.

Of equal importance is the model's emphasis on the thematic, narrative structure of thought in general, and of political thinking in particular. For example, Abelson (1973) conceived of molecules as combining into *themes,* defined as the "interdependent molecules of two distinct actors" (p. 295), for instance, one party admiring, betraying, deceiving, or rebelling against the other. Themes were combined into *scripts,* defined as "a sequence of themes involving the same set of actors, with a change in the interdependencies from each theme to the next" (p. 295), for instance, a turncoat script or a romantic triangle or even a cold war script (or perhaps, an obstruction of justice scenario). In the next sections I discuss how this sort of conceptualization forms the basis for a general script viewpoint that is applicable to the understanding of *all* peoples' belief systems and conceptualizations of action in general.[1]

Schank and Abelson on Scripts. Of the several concepts outlined by Abelson, the one that has had the greatest impact on cognitive psychology and social cognition is that of a script. In a chapter dealing with more "mundane reality" (as opposed to political scenarios), Abelson (1975) "demoted" the script concept to the status of a "conceptual structure which explains for the believer why a specific action or sequence of actions has occurred or might occur" (p. 275). Thus, the emphasis here was on making sense of *specific,* everyday actions. In a second chapter, Abelson (1976a) argued that scripts are built from the bottom up, beginning with concrete, specific *vignettes* before abstracting out common features. Stated differently, Abelson distinguished among *epi-*

---

[1] I should also point out the interesting research by Read and his associates (e.g., Read, 1987; Read & Miller, 1993) and by Abelson and his colleagues (e.g., Abelson & Lalljee, 1988) on the role of narrative in explaining or accounting for social behavior.

sodic, categorical, and *hypothetical* scripts. Episodic scripts refer to the original, singular vignette form (e.g., one's experience or memory of a visit to a particular restaurant on a specific occasion), whereas categorical scripts refer to the generic version (e.g., restaurants in general). Finally, hypothetical scripts refer to reasoning with the generic features of scripts abstracted out of their sequence and out of any particular context. Thus, for example, deciding how much to tip a waiter who has been inept involves invoking a hypothetical script. The major point here—and one that I return to later—is that people typically use concrete, episodic scripts in making decisions[2] (e.g., previous experiences with similar situations) rather than hypothetical ones, even though they are more likely to *report* using the latter.

By far the most influential formulation of the script concept is the one presented by Schank and Abelson (1977) in their *SPGU* book. The authors' concern in this book was with natural language processing in both humans and computers. In this presentation a script was defined as a "predetermined stereotyped sequence of actions that defines a well-known situation" (p. 41). Thus, in this particular formulation the emphasis was on the *stereotyped* nature of scripts, that is, that scripts involve highly structured and predictable sequences of actions (e.g., the routinized sequence of actions— ordering, eating, and paying—at a restaurant). An emphasis was also placed on the way in which scripts are specific to, and even define a given situation (although Schank and Abelson actually distinguished *situational scripts* from other types of scripts). The importance of scripts, then, is their power in understanding and predicting actions. That is, if scripts are stereotyped and routinized and specific to situational contexts, then they should enable us to infer missing details in a description of, or in our memory for the event (e.g., that we must have paid the restaurant bill after we finished eating, or that the groom at a wedding is very likely to have given his bride a ring).

In this connection, Abelson (1981) later distinguished among three different senses of the term *script*:

> In its weak sense, it [a script] is a bundle of inferences about the potential occurrence of a set of events and may be structurally similar to other schemata that do not deal with events. In its strong sense, it involves expectations about the order as well as the occurrence of events. In the strongest sense of a totally ritualized event sequence (e.g., a Japanese tea ceremony), script predictions become infallible but this is relatively rare. (p. 717)

Thus, scripts may, but need not, entail clear ordering or sequencing of events. This is a point to which I return later.

A Brief Review of Research on Scripts.   The concept of a script, as formulated by Schank and Abelson (1977), has led to a good deal of research.

---

[2]The automaticity of scripts has led Langer (1989; see also Langer & Abelson, 1972) to suggest that many of our actions are "mindless."

One line of research alluded to in chapters 1 and 3 is the work by Graesser (e.g., 1981; Graesser & Nakamura, 1982) on the script-copy-plus-tag (SC+T) model. Graesser argued that actions that are rather typical of a given generic script are stored in terms of a copy of that script. As a result, at recall or recognition it is difficult to discriminate between these typical actions that were presented and those that were not presented but simply inferred (as default values) from the generic script. Thus, you may remember reading about a character in a narrative paying the bill at a restaurant even if that action was not mentioned because paying is part of your generic restaurant script. On the other hand, actions that are atypical or even moderately typical of that schema are assumed to be tagged and stored separately, leading to better recognition or recall of such items. Thus, for example, if you read about or observe someone taking a pill or looking for his or her glasses at a restaurant, you would be more likely to remember or discriminate that event as occurring because it is not typical (though not necessarily contradictory) of a restaurant script.

Graesser and his colleagues (see Graesser & Nakamura, 1982, for a review) have conducted a number of studies, the results of which are generally consistent with these predictions. For example, Graesser, Gordon, and Sawyer (1979) found high false alarm rates (i.e. false recognitions) and poor memory discrimination (i.e., poor ability to distinguish between items that were and were not presented in narrative passages) for items that were typical of scripts. In fact, there was virtually *no* discrimination for items that were *very* typical of the script, and there were significantly lower false alarm rates and better memory discrimination for atypical items. A similar result was reported by Graesser, Woll, Kowalski, and Smith (1980) for *recall* accuracy and recall intrusions, and these investigators also showed that the inferences made for items that *must* have been presented (because they were part of the script) occurred at encoding rather than at retrieval.

Graesser and his colleagues have also reported studies more directly relevant to everyday cognition. For example, similar results were reported (Graesser & Nakamura, 1982) when the scripted activities were presented in videotaped form. In a study that is perhaps most relevant to this discussion, Nakamura, Graesser, Zimmerman, and Riha (1985) found the same results for a behavioral enactment of a lecture script in a real-world, naturalistic setting—a classroom lecture—in which an example of a typical action was "pointing to material on the blackboard," and an example of an atypical one was "wiping one's glasses." In addition, when participants received information that was typical or atypical of either scripts or person schemas (of the sort discussed in chap. 3), script-typicality proved to be a significantly better predictor of recognition memory than did the person schema (Graesser & Nakamura, 1982; see also Woll & Clark, 1989). Finally, in one other finding that is relevant to the discussion in chapter 3, Graesser and Nakamura (1982) showed that the comprehender's processing goals do not have a significant impact on the script-typicality effect.

In one other widely cited set of studies, Bower, Black, and Turner (1979) found that participants agreed on the major components of scripts (though see Mandler & Murphy, 1983, for contrary findings), and these participants also seemed to recognize the goal–subgoal structure (e.g., ordering your food in order to eat it) of such scripts. Not surprisingly, Bower et al. also found that participants tended to recall disordered scripts back in their stereotypical order, as if scripts really do contain a clearly ordered structure that is imposed on recall. Finally, in one of their experiments, Bower et al. presented one, two, or three different versions of a given script—for instance, a doctor, dentist, and chiropractor version of a health professional script. They then asked participants to recall the actions in each of the presented passages. Bower et al. found that participants were more likely to recall having seen unstated actions from a given passage if that action was presented in another version of the same script (cf. M. B. Brewer et al., 1981, for generally similar results in the area of person memory). This finding suggested to Schank (1982a) that there may not be separate scripts for the three different types of situations. This particular finding had a major impact on later reformulations of the script concept.

Nelson's Research on the Development of Scripts and Event Memory.
One major extension of script theory is found in Katherine Nelson's (1986; Nelson & Gruendel, 1981) research on children's scripts or *general event representations* (*GERs*). Nelson's collection of protocols from young children's descriptions or recountings of common, everyday activities (e.g., lunch at the day-care center, eating at McDonalds) convinced her that children as young as 3 years of age "have well-developed event representations for familiar routine events and exhibit many of the characteristics of scripts, including generality, sequentiality, and agreement on main and central events" (Nelson & Gruendel, 1981, p. 38). That is, children showed generally good agreement about what events to include in their descriptions; they tended to leave out irrelevant details; and they agreed on what the central actions of the sequence were, as well as the order or sequence of these actions. In addition, contrary to some expectations, these children actually gave longer reports and mentioned a greater number of acts in response to questions about general than about specific events; and this was more true for children 3 years and younger than for those between 3 and 5. (See my discussion of these results and their implications for children's autobiographical memory in the next chapter.)

One of the implications of this research is that children seem to have GERs, which are assumed to have a structure, a temporal order, and a causal structure, to represent change, and to be represented hierarchically. In addition, Nelson assumed that new events or exemplars are encoded in terms of the degree to which they match these GERs, with typical events being swallowed up by or assimilated into the GER, as in my earlier discussion of the SCPT model. Nelson (1988) even suggested that specific event memory may only come *after,* and may be dependent on "the establishment of a general script for the event" (p. 248), although, she has subsequently discounted that assumption. Furthermore, specific events are assumed to be "schematized," that is, converted to generic schemas, if or when they are repeated (see further discussion of Nelson's work in chap. 5.)

The Role of Plans and Themes

Original Formulations.   Although *SPGU* is best known for its discussion of scripts, it also contained a detailed discussion of plans, goals, and themes. In this particular formulation, both plans and themes were conceptualized in terms of goals. Specifically, according to Schank and Abelson (1977), plans are conceived of as "general information about how actors achieve goals. … A plan is a series of projected actions to realize a goal" (pp. 70–71). In other words, plans involve using general knowledge of how people accomplish things to figure out the actions by which a *particular* person has or will achieve his or her goals. Plans and planning differ from scripts in that plans are more flexible, strategic structures than are the stereotyped, fairly automatic sequences involved in scripts. Scripts involve a kind of plan, but people are not aware of using the plan because it is so automatic.

As far as themes are concerned, Schank and Abelson (1977) described three different types: *role themes* (e.g., doctor, president), *interpersonal themes* (e.g., marital, parental), and *life themes,* or "the general position or aim that a person wants in life" (p. 144; e.g., personal qualities such as loyalty, or lifestyles such as jetsetter or slacker). Thus, for example, it is clear that loyalty or being a jetsetter entails a certain well-defined set of goals (though being a slacker may not!). Notice that such themes and the goals they entail represent knowledge structures that are concerned with naturalistic, real-world content, unlike the kind of concepts that most traditional memory research has been concerned with. If anything, these concepts seem almost *too* commonsensical and nonanalytic.

Reformulations of Plans, Goals, and Themes.   Although goals played a central part in the Schank and Abelson formulation—in fact, Schank (1994) suggested that goals represent the backbone of his system—the presentation of such goals in *SPGU* was fairly primitive. The authors distinguished among several different categories of goals, from satisfaction or biological goals, to enjoyment goals (i.e., those pursued for pleasure), to achievement and preservation goals (e.g., health and safety; cf. Murray, 1938, for a similar categorization). Also included were instrumental goals, that is, goals whose attainment serves as a precondition for another goal (again cf. Murray, 1938). The important point here is the interrelations among these goals, plans, and themes in the understanding of human action. (See Wilensky, 1983, for a more systematic taxonomy of goal *relationships*.)

In their later writings Schank (1982a) and Abelson (e.g., Seifert, Abelson, & McKoon, 1986) expanded on the concept of a theme. To be specific, both

Schank and Abelson introduced the concept of a *thematic organization packet* or *point* (*TOP*; see also the related concept of a *thematic abstraction unit* or *TAU*; Dyer, 1983). As in *SPGU*, thematic knowledge is presumed to be concerned with the relationships between plans and goals or among different goals (e.g., one goal subsuming another, or the competition between goals—cf. Wilensky, 1983)—rather than with mere similarities in activities. As Dyer (1983) pointed out, scripts simply involve sequences of actions with no attention paid to the goals or intentions of the actors, for instance, there is little concern in a restaurant script for *why* the person orders or pays the bill. However, TOPs or TAUs take such goals and plans[3]—the intentionality of the actors—into account. TOPs are captured by common aphorisms, such as "a stitch in time saves nine" or "better late than never," and contain "abstract, domain-independent information" (Schank, 1982a, p. 111).

TOPs serve a number of different functions. One of the most important of these is *reminding,* or the process by which a current event reminds individuals of a similar event in memory. Such remindings are of interest because they provide clues as to the form of the memory representation for that event. In the case of thematic remindings, for example, TOPs help to remind individuals of a previous story or experience with the same theme, or they help him or her to recognize an old story presented in a different form (e.g., being reminded of *Romeo and Juliet* when watching *West Side Story*; Schank & Abelson, 1995). Schank (1982a) gives the example of watching his daughter search for sand dollars in shallow water (where they would never be found) because it was "easier," and being reminded of the story of the drunk looking for his keys under a lamppost even though he lost them back in a dark alley because there's more light under the lamppost. (Everyone can probably come up with her or his own personal example of this phenomenon. In fact, one of the purposes of this book is to provide an ongoing series of remindings, though hopefully not of the "drunk looking under the lamppost" variety.) Such remindings also enable us either to predict what is going to happen in a new situation or to apply some lesson from a previous one (e.g., "Don't screw up this relationship in the same way you did the last one").

All of the examples cited thus far amount to unintentional and, one might even say, "automatic" remindings. Thematic remindings may also be intentional; that is, individuals may deliberately *try* to pose a question to themselves or establish a context in which they may find a given memory. (See the distinction in chap. 6 between intentional and unintentional probes of autobiographical memory.) Thus, one may deliberately try to remember the last time he or she dined at a particular restaurant or heard

---

[3]This distinction parallels a contrast between Abelson's early work on political scripts and an alternative approach put forward by Carbonell (1978; see also 1979) referred to as POLITICS, in which poltical beliefs were conceived of in terms of the different goals and plans of the political agents.

from a particular friend. One use of these intentional remindings (Schank, 1982a) is to take a question or comment posed in conversation (e.g., "you never bring me flowers anymore") and use it as a reminder of a similar theme in memory that may express one's own point of view (e.g., "well, you don't ever cook for me anymore").

Because TOPs are rather abstract and complex structures, it is reasonable to ask how it is that individuals detect these similarities in themes in the first place. Certainly people are not constantly on the lookout for the large variety of such themes in their everyday lives; in fact, people often fail to note these similarities (as teachers and research on analogies can certainly attest—see chap. 7). The solution offered by Schank (1982a) to this dilemma is that the remindings must be triggered by features that individuals *are* already tracking or attending to in the normal course of things. These features are ones that Schank and Abelson (1977) described in *SPGU*: namely, plans, goals, the status of goals, the conditions on goals, relationships among actors, and outcomes (see also Abelson, 1973). For example, with regard to goals, I have already discussed how there are specific goal types and goal relations. There are also the conditions for these different goals—for instance, the goal of "sexual satisfaction" usually involves the condition of "having a willing partner," whereas the goal of "getting a college degree" involves such conditions as "having tuition money" and "having needed classes available."

One thing that is apparent in the foregoing is the many changes that have occurred in the use of the concepts of script and theme (and plans) over the course of Schank and Abelson's writings on those topics. Are scripts primarily concrete, primarily abstract, or both? How stereotyped or routinized do action sequences have to be to be considered scripted? Are themes based on scripts or vice versa, and do themes (or scripts) have to do with sequences of action, sets of goals, or both? As I discuss in a subsequent section of this chapter, these and other questions have proved to be of central importance in later reformulations of the script and theme concepts as researchers in psychology and artificial intelligence have continued to grapple with these two rich and fertile concepts.

Research on Plans and Themes.   Although there has not been as much research on the understanding of plans and themes as there has been on scripts, some representative research programs on the former topics are worth noting. The first of these is research by W. F. Brewer (W. F. Brewer & Dupree, 1983; E. H. Lichtenstein & Brewer, 1980) on the cognitive representation of plans. The position taken in this research is that people's memory for purposeful actions involves *plan schemas,* which entail goal–subgoal or "in order to" relations (e.g., "he or she went to the convention to talk to a colleague to get some ideas to design a new study"). Lichtenstein and Brewer (1980) gave a simpler example, "He took his keys out of his pocket in order to open the door in order to get into his house" (cf. the similar relations in scripts).

E. H. Lichtenstein and Brewer (1980) presented action sequences in either videotaped or written form and then asked participants to recall the various actions in this sequence. The major findings of this initial study were that participants showed better recall for actions that were instrumental for accomplishing a goal than for actions that were not directly related to that goal. They also showed better recall for actions that were higher in the goal–subgoal hierarchy—that is, those that directly served a goal and that subsumed other lower goals. In addition, as in the Bower et al. (1979) study, when these actions were presented out of order, they were either not recalled or were recalled back in their stereotypical order.

In a subsequent study, W. F. Brewer and Dupree (1983) compared recognition and recall measures for plan schemas. In this study participants showed better recall for videotaped actions (e.g., *"pulled a ruler from between two books on a shelf,"* p. 120) that were part of a plan schema than they did for these same actions when they were presented outside of a schema. Such a difference was not found for a visual *recognition* measure, suggesting that plan schemas may play more of a role at retrieval than at encoding. However, when participants were tested after an extended (48-hour) delay, they *did* show better recognition memory for actions that formed part of a plan schema, suggesting that such plan schemas had an effect on more than just retrieval. Finally, in a third experiment participants were more likely to show false recognition for new *sub*ordinate instrumental actions inserted in a videotape (at recognition) to serve old superordinate actions (e.g., bending to push a trash can underneath a plant that is being watered [to catch the water] vs. kicking it under the plant with one's foot) than they did for new *super*ordinate actions inserted (at recognition) to subsume old subordinate ones (e.g., kicking the trash can underneath the plant to catch dead leaves vs. catching the runoff from watering the plant). Thus, there appears to be a clear organization to memory for planful actions, with actions lower in the hierarchy fading from memory faster than those at the top (cf. my discussion of a similar point in autobiographical memory).

Research has also been conducted on themes by Seifert and her associates (e.g., Seifert, Abelson, & McKoon, 1986; Seifert & Black, 1983; Seifert, McKoon, Abelson, & Ratcliff, 1986). Seifert and Black (1983), for example, had participants generate a new story after reading three plots exemplifying the same TAU or theme, but one with different content. Eighty-two percent of participants' stories were found to illustrate the same TAU. In a second study participants were asked to sort 36 stories written by others to illustrate six different TAUs (with six stories for each TAU). A hierarchical clustering analysis indicated that these stories fell into six different clusters corresponding to the six different TAUs. Thus, it appears that participants are able to recognize the same theme in a variety of different forms.

In another set of experiments, Seifert, McKoon, Abelson, and Ratcliff (1986) used a priming paradigm to study remindings. In the first two experiments participants were presented with a priming sentence from one story, followed by a test sentence from a second story that was either similar or different in theme. Some of these priming manipulations were accompanied by explicit discussions of themes and instructions to attend to such themes, and some were not. In these two studies, and in a second pair with a slight methodological variation, Seifert et al. found little priming except in those conditions in which explicit instructions were provided, suggesting that thematic reminding is not always automatic (see my discussion of similar results in research on transfer of training in chap. 7). Finally, in one other pair of studies, Seifert et al. presented a set of prestudy stories followed by test stories with either similar or different themes from the prestudy ones. In two different tasks participants in these two studies showed clear evidence of thematic reminding.

Some researchers (e.g., Holyoak & Koh, 1987; Medin & Ross, 1989; Reeves & Weisberg, 1994) believe that such abstract themes play much less of a role than my discussion thus far would indicate. For example, as I discuss in chapter 7, research on analogies and transfer of training has indicated that individuals do not spontaneously apply abstract rules or solutions to new problems unless their attention is explicitly called to the similarity (e.g., Gick & Holyoak, 1980, 1983). Medin and Ross (1989; Ross, 1987, 1989a, 1989b) have argued that surface features also play an important role in transfer and analogies, particularly in the *retrieval* of appropriate analogies. In general, the relative importance of surface versus structural factors in transfer—and hence, the relevance of thematic detection and reminding—is open to debate (see Reeves & Weisberg, 1994).

The Concepts of MOPs, E-MOPs, and Case-Based Reasoning: The Generality Versus Specificity of Event Knowledge

In a book titled *Dynamic Memory*, Schank (1982a) discussed some of the difficulties encountered by the original script concept. One of these was simply that the distinction between scripts and plans is not always clear. For example, going on a date can be either scripted and routinized, or it can involve a great deal of planning; it is not always clear where the line between these two possibilities is best drawn. One major difference between the two lies in the amount of background knowledge a person brings to the situation and the resulting number of inferences he or she has to make in order to make sense out of things. Scripts obviously involve very predictable sequences and hence require few inferences, whereas plan schemas are less predictable and require more inferences. At the same time, though, Schank (1982a) pointed out that attempts to program the original script-processing system required a great deal of background knowledge to account for the inferences involved in a script, whereas later attempts to get around this by creating "sketchy scripts"—shorter scripts entailing less background knowledge—led to an even greater blurring of scripts and plans. For example, are arsons, coup d'états, impeachments, and sexual encounters considered scripts, themes, plans, or what?

Another point already alluded to is that scripts were assumed to involve specific information related to particular situations. However, there is also more abstract, general knowledge that individuals bring to bear in understanding situations in general (see my discussion of the concept of plans), and much of this knowledge is based on "abstracting and generalizing from multiple experiences and from the experiences of others" (Schank, 1982a, p. 9). Of particular relevance here is the finding reviewed earlier by Bower et al. (1979) that actions from one version of a script were misremembered as being heard in another version of the same script. This finding, as well as the problem of the sheer redundancy in knowledge representations (e.g., as in three different representations for three different types of health professional visits) suggests that there must be some more general, abstract form of knowledge that ties these three scenarios together. At the same time, however, such an abstraction must take into consideration the fact that individuals are less likely to confuse a visit to a doctor's office with a visit to an accountant or a hairdresser. In other words, there must be some kind of discrimination as well as generalization.

Schank's (1982) solution to these problems was to argue that scripts do not actually exist as "one precompiled chunk," but rather are "constructed to be used as needed" (p. 16). Scripts are based on generalized structures referred to as *scenes*, such as general knowledge about waiting rooms or paying bills. According to this revised conception, scripts represent specific versions or examples of those scenes that apply in a given context (e.g., a particular type of waiting room or a particular doctor's or dentist's waiting room). Specific memories, in turn, are stored within these scripts and are "indexed with respect to how they differ from the general action in the scene" (Schank, 1982, p. 95), for instance, how one acts differently in a restaurant with a floor show or a prix fixe menu. Thus, one of the points of this reformulation is that generic knowledge is primary (even if that knowledge is initially based on individual, personal experiences), and more specific scripts and individual experiences are contained within these as deviations from the norm.

MOPs. A critical concept in this revised picture is that of a *memory organization packet* (*MOP*). MOPs are memory structures that serve to connect different scenes. Thus, to use Schank's own example, a "professional office visit" MOP connects a "waiting room" setting, a "getting service" scene, a "pay" scene, plus the action of "getting there and getting back." Defined more formally, "a MOP consists of a set of scenes directed towards the achievement of a goal" (Schank, 1982a, p. 97), where one of these scenes contains a goal that is the "essence or purpose" (p. 97) of the overall sequence of events organized by the MOP (e.g., the "getting service" scene in the previous example). Thus, MOPs include an overall goal or purpose and a set of scenes with their own goals.

One of the major features of a MOP is that the scenes it organizes must be *general* so that they can be used by other MOPs. Thus, for example, paying, ordering, and getting service are all scenes that can occur in a number of different contexts and in a number of different MOPs. This generality feature has both advantages and disadvantages for human memory. On the one hand, such multiple contexts often make it difficult to retrieve exactly where a particular scene occurred. For example, it may be difficult to remember exactly where you lost some money, because "paying" is a part of so many activities. On the other hand, sharing scenes clearly allows us to generalize from previous experiences for predicting or making sense out of new ones (see my later discussion of indexing and case-based reasoning). This is obviously an advantage that MOPs have over scripts, and it also solves the problem of redundancy alluded to earlier. Furthermore, and perhaps more important, this formulation suggests that memory is not a static repository of information, as script theory would suggest, but rather is dynamic, flexible, and reconstructive; otherwise stated, knowledge structures must be capable of change or of taking on different "colorations," as Schank (1982a) puts it, as a result of new experiences. Thus, to invoke the old Heraclitean aphorism, we never dip into or encounter exactly the same memory twice. Schank gives the example of Legal Seafoods in Boston, a restaurant where you pay *before* you receive your food; or there is the tapis or sushi bar where you do not order a main course, but rather keep ordering individual dishes.

The Concept of E-MOPs.   A further extension of Schank's theory of MOPs and dynamic memory was proposed by Kolodner (1983a, 1993; Kolodner & Simpson, 1989) and her associates (e.g., Hammond, 1989; Hammond & Seifert, 1994) in their work on event memory and case-based reasoning. Kolodner's original works (1983a, 1983b) were an attempt to produce a computer model of reconstructive memory named *CYRUS*, dealing with the diplomatic activities of the American Secretary of State, Cyrus Vance, and they were also an attempt to indicate how events from this sort of memory can be retrieved without having to search the entire store of such episodes. This model included organizational structural units called *event memory organization packets* (*E-MOPs*), which contain both general, normative information about episodes (e.g., about professional office visits or diplomatic meetings) and also more specialized episodes (e.g., visits to specific professionals). E-MOPs also contain individual events, as well as *indices* that identify "anomalous" cases or ones that deviate from the norms of that episode (e.g., the restaurant where you pay the bill before eating, the emergency room visit where you don't make an appointment in advance).

Thus, to take an example from CYRUS (see Fig. 4.1), the E-MOP "diplomatic meeting" contains normative information about the general topics and participants in such meetings, whereas the indices (represented by the triangles in Fig. 4.1) detail certain unique, discriminating information about specific versions of such meetings (e.g., the participants' nationalities, the specific topics of Vance's Middle East diplomacy) or, alternatively, about features that a given episode shares with others. For example, if one seeks to retrieve memories of the SALT agreement or an episode in which both Israelis and Arabs were involved, then the index leads him or her to follow the appropriate pathway to retrieve the desired information. Indices serve as both salient markers and also as "gates" (Kolodner, 1994) or "locks" (Kolodner, 1983a) that enable retrieval of specific information without requiring a total memory search or a consideration of the entire E-MOP with all of its generic and case-specific information. Thus, retrieval represents a kind of directed or constrained search.

A couple of features of E-MOPS should be mentioned. First, as noted in Fig. 4.1, E-MOPS have a hierarchical organization, with sub-MOPs or "spe-

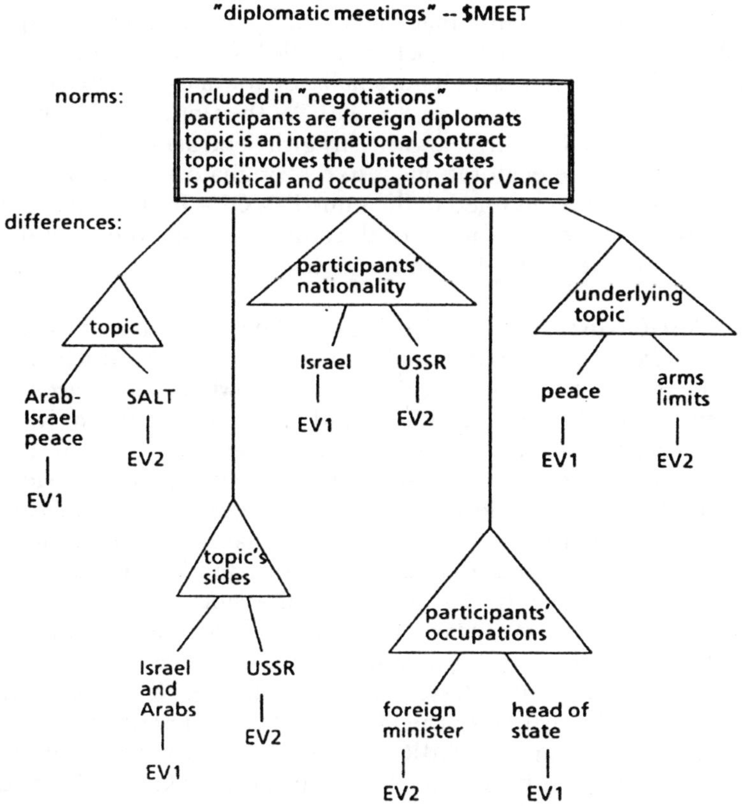

FIG. 4.1. An example of Kolodner's CYRUS model of E-MOPs. From "Maintaining Organization in a Dynamic Long Term Memory," by J. L. Kolodner, 1983a, *Cognitive Science*, 7, p. 265. Copyright © 1983 by Cognitive Science Society, Inc. Reprinted with permission.

cialized" E-MOPs and/or specific events embedded within the overall E-MOP, linked by features. Stated differently, indices divide E-MOPs into subcategories. These subcategories or specialized E-MOPs are created from single instances whenever a second instance of the same feature is encountered. At the same time, there is some redundancy in this categorization process in that the same piece of information may be stored or indexed (or "cross-indexed") in a number of different ways (e.g., in Fig. 4.1, Event 2 can be accessed through a number of different indices).

One issue addressed by the CYRUS model is that of intentional reminding. In this model it is assumed that the individual must first generate a context or elaboration from which to initiate the retrieval process. In other words, memory is reconstructive rather than simply being a matter of reviewing facts or items; and as Kolodner (1983b) put it, CYRUS views reconstruction as a process of "constructing a description of a target event, adding features to progressively differentiate it from its nearest neighbors, and finally finding its hiding place in a well-organized memory" (p. 285). For example, one might elaborate the episode "Neil Armstrong landing on the moon" with "when he said 'One small step for man …'"; or the episode "the first time I saw *Angels in America*" with "at the Cottesloe Theater at the National" and "I exchanged seats with my girlfriend at every intermission." The purpose of these elaborations is to discriminate a particular event or episode from others contained in the same E-MOP—for instance, other lunar landings or space expeditions or the other time I saw the second part of *Angels in America* or other plays in London.

Case-Based Reasoning.   This brings up the issue of *case-based reasoning* (*CBR*), or reasoning from individual instances or episodes. Much of the discussion in this first section has dealt with knowledge of *generic* events. Kolodner (1993, 1994), on the other hand, has argued that *individual* cases are "the primary generators of inferences" (Kolodner, 1994, p. 98), and that collecting such cases is "the single most useful type of knowledge acquired" (1994, p. 96), at least in the early stages of mastering an area. Kolodner (1993) defined a case as a "contextualized piece of knowledge representing an experience that teaches a lesson fundamental to achieving the goals of the listener" (p. 13). Thus, not all events qualify as "cases"; for instance, going to work everyday is not a case, but the time you ran out of gas or were bawled out for coming in late or had some other experience which taught you a "fundamental" lesson constitutes a case. Needless to say, case identification is closely tied to the idea of indexing described earlier.

As I discussed in chapter 1, CBR represents an alternative to the overemphasis on general cases by schema theory and abstract knowledge structure approaches in general (though case-based models do not rule out the use of such generic knowledge—see Kolodner, 1993, p. 74). Rather than trying to match new instances to generic scripts or scenes, individuals instead retrieve previous instances from memory on the basis of their match to a current concrete case, for example, "this is exactly like the time when ..." Such matching requires that the comprehender understand the new case in order to be able to interrogate memory, and this in turn requires an assessment or elaboration of that new case (Kolodner, 1994), that is, finding out more details about it until an appropriate memory is found. In the same way, indexing is also involved in distinguishing old cases from each other.

The important point here is that memory and retrieval are based more on individual cases—the current one and our representation of past ones—than it is on more abstract schematic representations, although the latter also play a role. There is certainly an intuitive appeal to such an account: Everyone can undoubtedly think of instances where this kind of case-to-case matching has occurred. Such a viewpoint is also consistent with some of the criticisms of schema theories (e.g., by Alba & Hasher, 1983) and with the exemplar viewpoint reviewed in chapter 1, as well as with the age-old philosophical debate over the existence of general knowledge (e.g., our knowledge of general, ideal triangles) versus knowledge of specifics (e.g., our knowledge of specific triangles). This point is also reminiscent of Abelson's (1976) distinction between episodic and categorical scripts. As I discuss in later chapters, this view is also consistent with some of ideas in the areas of human judgment and decision-making and research on transfer of training. Most importantly, this viewpoint suggests that people store individual cases without these necessarily being swallowed up by generic categories (see discussion in chap. 5) and that it is possible to retrieve these specific event memories by simply matching their features with ones in our current experience.

Some examples of everyday case-based memory are perhaps in order. Kolodner (1993, 1994) cited examples of legal arguments (i.e., referring to previous cases), medical diagnosis, and troubleshooting in automobile repair. As for more everyday examples, Abelson (1976), in his earlier discussion of episodic scripts, cited the case of graduate admissions in which applicants are often judged in terms of their resemblance to students who have been successes or failures in the past. Similarly, people undoubtedly reason about car purchases, dating selections, menu choices, and 101 other everyday decisions on the basis, at least in part, of memory for past cases.

What does all of this have to do with event memory? Well, obviously, the concept of an E-MOP and of various specialized E-MOPs is intended to describe the nature of *event* memory. In addition, the notion of individual cases as the primary unit of memory suggests that events are important at the concrete as well as the abstract level. As I discuss in chapter 6, models of event memory are particularly applicable to autobiographical memory, where, it can be argued, memory is primarily for events (although there is a good deal of debate about that claim). In fact, much of the knowledge that people deal with everyday, whether it be in the political arena, autobiographical memory, or memory for social interactions, can be viewed as event or episodic memory.

Kolodner (1993) outlined some advantages and a few disadvantages of CBR. One of the most important advantages is that CBR allows the reasoner to produce solutions quickly, by retrieving old cases rather than having to derive them on the spot. Second, CBR helps individuals understand situations or new instances that are not completely specified (e.g., medical problems, computer debugging, or personal crises) and make sense of "open-ended and ill-defined concepts" (Kolodner, 1993, p. 26). CBR also gives individuals a means for evaluating solutions in terms of their fit to previous solutions or plan failures (cf. my later discussion of this second concept). Finally, CBR allows people to focus on features of the current problem that are important (even though these cases are typically coded as a whole).

On the negative side, Kolodner (1993) suggested that individuals may often use a previous case in a rather "blind" manner, "without validating it in the new situation" (p. 26). Thus, people may give other advice based on their own experiences when that situation does not really apply, or they may see similarities between a person they just met and a former acquaintance without waiting for the evidence to come in about this new person. (See Sternberg & Frensch, 1993, for similar examples in chap. 7.) Alternatively, individuals may let previous cases bias their judgments on current ones. For example, one may let a memory of a former spouse bias his or her impressions of a new date or acquaintance. Finally, it often happens that individuals do not have an appropriate case to refer to, or they simply are unable to retrieve it. As discussed earlier, and as I discuss again in chapter 7, people do not always notice analogies between previous problems and current ones unless the similarities are explicitly pointed out to them (cf. the results of Seifert et al., 1986, reviewed earlier).

I should note that the case for CBR is not entirely speculative, as my discussion thus far may suggest. In fact, Kolodner (1993) reviewed some six different examples of computer-based, case-based reasoners, one of which I review in the next section of this chapter. In addition, in a case library presented in the index of her book, Kolodner (1993) briefly described more than 75 examples of case-based reasoners which were referred to her in a call to researchers on this topic. Thus, there are numerous computer applications of the notion of CBR. At the same time, however, there is little *psychological* evidence to date for such case-based reasoning (though see B. H. Ross, 1987, 1989a, 1989b, on the use of earlier examples rather than general principles in problem solving).

Connectionist Accounts of CBR. I should also point out that around the same time that Kolodner was formulating her model of CBR, other researchers (see Barnden & Holyoak, 1994) were attempting to show how CBR can be accounted for in terms of connectionist architectures. The basic underlying assumption of these models is that matching cases and reminding must be at least partially associative (rather than rule-based), in nature, and that connectionist models are particularly well-suited to such retrieval and matching processes, even when the cases involve the kinds of themes, plans, and goals entailed in typical event memory. Thus, for example, Domeshek (1994) designed a computer system named *Abby* that serves as an advisor to the lovelorn by matching problems to previous stories; also, Bonnisonc, Ran, and Berg (1994) developed a system named *CARS* to reason about the acquisition and mergers of corporations by matching a new case to an old one.

At the same time, however, as I discussed in the area of impression formation and face recognition; these are not *pure* PDP models. For instance, Seifert (1994) emphasized the role of processing goals (e.g., explaining vs. planning) in determining matches (cf. my discussion of processing objectives in person memory), particularly when a number of similar cases exist. Similarly, both Domeshek (1994) and Lange and Wharton (1994) have put forward models that require some sort of localist strategy or nonconnectionist mechanism in addition to the connectionist processing. In any case, it is interesting to see that such connectionist formulations developed almost simultaneously with the CBR viewpoint, even if they are not yet fully realized PDP models.

The Story Model. In their most recent statement of their viewpoint, Schank and Abelson (1995) took the extreme position that *all* knowledge and understanding involve storytelling. As in their discussions of themes, Schank and Abelson proposed that understanding a story involves relating it to the plans, goals, and themes (as well as beliefs) of some other story or stories that one holds in memory. These stories are indexed; and the more indices, the easier it is to access that story in the process of understanding. *Story-based memory*, however, is different from "generalized *event-based memory*" (Schank & Abelson, 1995, p. 35). In the first instance, one remembers the sequence and connections of different events, whereas in the second, one disconnects events from their narrative context and adds them to his or her knowledge of restaurants or doctors' offices (cf. Zukier's [1986] distinction between narrative vs. paradigmatic mode of thinking). Stories are remembered when something significant happens and individuals (consciously) want to preserve their order. "Stories are a way of preserving the connectivity of events that would otherwise be disassociated over time" (1995, p. 40; see W. F. Brewer, 1995, for a strong critique of this viewpoint).

An Evaluation of the Revisions in the Knowledge Structure Approach.
It is clear that Schank and Abelson's formulations have had a major impact on cognitive and social psychology; and in large part this is due to their willingness to put common sense back into the study of knowledge and knowledge structures. For example, their writing is always filled with interesting examples to which the reader can relate (or, in other words, they tell a good story); and of course their major interest is in studying *natural* language processing or everyday understanding. As such, their work focuses

on "unpacking" the implicit assumptions behind such understanding and remembering, and doing so in such detail that they or others can run computer simulations of their current model.

At the same time, there is still some ambiguity about the meaning of terms—for instance, what exactly is a MOP versus a scene (e.g., is a restaurant MOP a scene when it occurs as part of a dating MOP? This raises the pervasive issue of multiple levels of analysis, which I return to in the next chapter.) What sort of things are indexed and which are not (e.g., do dinners at a Mexican and a Japanese restaurant qualify as subcategories of "dinners at ethnic restaurants," and if so, what happens when you eat at a second, very different Mexican restaurant)? This question, as well as the results of the Seifert et al. (1986b) experiments, raises once again the question of exactly what is necessary for us to detect similar episodes or themes. What exactly qualifies thinking or remembering as "narrative" or storytelling? (See W. F. Brewer's [1995] and Zukier's [1986] discussions of this point.) There is once again the problem of the continual updating of concepts in Schank and Abelson's formulations—a feature that may also be seen as an asset—while at the same time feeling that readers are continually finding their way back to early conceptions. There is also, of course, the persisting question of whether it is generalities or specifics that are more important.

DISTORTIONS OF EVENT MEMORY

One implication of the knowledge structure approach to event memory is that memory is constructive or reconstructive. Individuals do not store or retrieve exact records but rather construct memories as needed. As I discussed in chapter 1, such a constructivist approach often results in apparent error or distortion (if accuracy is indeed a major consideration). In this section I focus on this issue of distortion or error in event memory (a theme I return to in chap. 9 as well). In particular, I focus on research on the distortion of eyewitness memory.

Background Research

The interest in memory distortion has a long and venerable history (see Intons-Peterson & Best, 1998a; Roediger, 1996a; Schacter, 1995; for reviews). Focusing specifically on memory for events,[4] it is clear that Freud (1924, 1953b) was one of the early proponents of a distorted memory position, particularly with reference to early childhood events (see chap. 5). However, early treatments can also be found in the classic work of Bartlett (1932) on errors in memory for the events in an unfamiliar story, which was a major influence on current-day research on memory distortion. The tra-

---

[4]There is also a substantial literature on memory distortions for objects, words, and the like (see Lynn & Payne, 1997, and Schacter, 1995, for reviews).

dition set by Bartlett was resurrected by Neisser, both in his classic reconstructivist formulation of memory and thinking (1967) and in two case studies of distorted memories: his own apparently erroneous memory of hearing about the Kennedy assassination and the errors in John Dean's recollections of his conversations with President Nixon (1982a; see chap. 5 for a discussion of both of these). This same tradition was also carried on by Bransford and Franks (e.g., 1972) in their research on constructive memory. Once again, the Schank, Abelson, and Kolodner dynamic reconstructive memory model can be seen as part of this same tradition, not to mention the whole schema model developed in chapter 1.

The memory distortion viewpoint has taken on added interest in recent years (e.g., Lynn & McConkey, 1998; Roediger, 1996; Schacter, 1995) as a result of a confluence of several different factors. Included here are developments in cognitive psychology and memory research (e.g,. M. K. Johnson, Hashtroudi, & Lindsay, 1993: Roediger, Wheeler, & Rajaram, 1993; Tulving, 1985b), social cognition (e.g., M. J. Snyder & Uranowitz, 1978), work with amnesia and brain damaged patients (e.g., Schacter, 1997; Schacter, Norman, & Koutstaal, 1998; Squire, 1997), and work on hypnosis (e.g., Lynn, Lock, Myers, & Payne, 1997; Sheehan, 1988). In fact, Roediger (1996a) recently proposed an alternative model of memory, focusing on what he calls *memory illusions,* or memories that depart from the original event (see Payne & Blackwell's [1998] description of a similar *perception–reperception* model). This model stands in contrast to the traditional *storehouse model,* which has dominated memory research historically. According to this alternative model, memory distortions, particularly those that are convincing on an experiential level, can be viewed as analogous to *perceptual* illusions and are of interest in their own right, rather than simply being viewed as "errors" (see my discussion of cognitive or judgment "illusions" in chap. 9). Similarly, Schacter (1995a) referred to the fact that "memory is simultaneously *fragile* and *powerful*; memories are often ephemeral and distorted, on the one hand, yet subjectively compelling and influential, on the other" (pp. 20–21).

Research on Eyewitness Memory

One topic in event memory (and memory distortion) that has received a great deal of attention in recent years is that of eyewitness memory. Wells and Loftus (1984) traced the resurgence of interest in this topic to the renewed emphasis on studying memory in more naturalistic contexts, an emphasis I have been documenting throughout this book. Undoubtedly, the major impetus to research in this area has been the work of Elizabeth Loftus (e.g., 1979a) on the effect of misleading questions on eyewitness memory.

Loftus' Research.   The thrust of Loftus' research paradigm has been to have participants witness an event such as an accident or a crime and then to introduce some *postevent information*—that is, some detail that did not occur in the original event. This later information usually comes in the form of a misleading question, as might be found in questioning of a witness by the police or a lawyer, or in some additional narrative. The research question is whether and how this postevent information affects participants' memory for the original event, for instance, by causing them to misrecall the postevent information or some variation on it as being part of that original event. This phenomenon is called the *misinformation* or *suggestibility effect*.

One classic example of this paradigm is an early study by Loftus (1975). In this study Loftus showed participants a film showing a car accident. This film was followed either by a question that was consistent with the events in the film ("How fast was the white sports car going while traveling along the country road?") or a misleading question ("How fast was the white sports car going when *it passed the barn* while traveling along the country road?" (Loftus, 1975, p. 566, italics added). A subsequent test question indicated that 17% of participants who received the misleading question about the barn said that they remembered seeing such a barn (which did not actually appear in the film), as compared with 3% of those receiving the control question. In a similar vein, Loftus, Miller, and Burns (1978) showed that when information was included in the misleading question that actually *contradicted* the information in the film (i.e., suggesting that the car stopped at a yield sign rather than at a stop sign, or vice versa), the accuracy of participants' recognition memory on a forced-choice question dropped from 75% to 41%. In other related studies Loftus (1977) demonstrated that it was possible to produce *compromise memories* or *blends*—that is, compromises between what actually occurred and what was suggested by a misleading question. For example, when participants were asked to recall the number of demonstrators who had disrupted a lecture, their estimates represented compromises between the actual number, 8, and the number suggested in a misleading question, 4 or 12. Specifically, participants who were asked about the 4 demonstrators later remembered seeing an average of 6.4 demonstrators versus an average of 8.9 in the 12 demonstrators condition. Similarly, when participants were asked to pick out the color from a color wheel, a green Datsun was described as blue or bluish-green when a misleading question suggested that it was blue.

A variety of other factors also have an influence on the misinformation effect. For example, Loftus et al. (1978) found that introducing the misleading information immediately prior to test produced greater problems in recognition than did presenting it immediately after the initial event, presumably because in the former case the memory traces for both pieces of information had faded, and the participant was merely guessing (though other interpretations are obviously possible). In addition, the effects of the later presentation were greater at longer delay intervals, where the memory trace for the original event had presumably weakened, whereas the effects of the earlier presentation decreased with longer delay intervals (i.e., it had its greatest impact early). Recently, Mitchell and Zaragoza (1996) demonstrated that repetition of misleading information reduces recall for the original information even further; and Roediger, Jacoby, and McDermott (1996) demonstrated that when participants are encouraged to write down the original misleading information on the first test, they tend to reproduce this material as having been in the original on a second memory test.

The explanation offered by Loftus (e.g., Loftus, 1979a; Loftus & Loftus, 1980) of this misinformation effect has been called the *overwriting, updating,* or *memory impairment position,* all of which refer to the view that the postevent information literally replaces or overwrites the original facts, which are then lost. Alternatively (as in the compromise memories studies), the two pieces of information may be melded so that, in effect, both are lost in their original form. As I have discussed, this point of view is consistent with several pieces of evidence in the memory distortion literature.

Early Critiques of Loftus' Viewpoint and Alternative Positions.   A variety of different alternative accounts have been offered for Loftus's results. For example, Bekerian and Bowers (1983) proposed an *accessibility* or *coexistence* (Loftus, 1979a) or *preclusion* (Belli & Loftus, 1996) account. This position argues that the original information is not lost, but rather coexists with the postevent information, the latter of which is more accessible because it was encountered more recently. In support of this view, Bekerian and Bowers (1983) conducted a study similar to the one by Loftus et al. (1978) reviewed earlier in which participants received postevent information that was either consistent with or contradictory to earlier information—either a stop sign or a yield sign. In this particular version participants received a recognition test in which they saw slides in either a random order, as in the original Loftus et al. study, or in the same order in which the slides had originally been presented. The rationale here was that the sequence of events in the original slide presentation contained information about the overall theme of the accident or story, information that is lost in a random presentation. Thus, participants who were asked to respond to isolated slides may have had a difficult time with retrieval because critical cues were omitted. In fact, when the items and events were presented in a nonrandom order, the percentage of correct responses was approximately equal in the misleading information condition to that in the control condition, suggesting that the original information was not actually lost when sufficient thematic context was provided. Unfortunately, McCloskey and Zaragoza (1985a) failed to replicate the Bekerian and Bowers finding.

Probably the strongest critique of the Loftus paradigm was presented by McCloskey, Zaragoza, and their associates (e.g., McCloskey & Zaragoza, 1985a; Zaragoza & Koshmider, 1989; Zaragoza, McCloskey, & Jamis, 1987), who also presented a major methodological alternative. The basic argument put forward by McCloskey and Zaragoza was that Loftus's results can be accounted for by various response biases encouraged by specific features of her paradigm. In particular, the recognition test in Loftus' studies involved a forced choice between the original event (e.g., hammer) and the postevent information or suggested event (e.g., screwdriver). One possible result of this situation is that it may have caused the misled and control groups to use different guessing strategies. That is, if the control group did not remember the original event and simply *guessed* at the right answer, they should have a 50–50 chance of correctly choosing the original event. On the other hand, if the misled group failed to remember the original event, their guessing would likely be influenced to some degree by the postevent information; and, as a result, these participants would be more likely to show errors (i.e., choosing the misleading information) than would the control group.

The solution to this problem proposed by McCloskey and Zaragoza was to use a different kind of recognition test, one that presented a forced choice between the original event or object and a new, unpresented one. Thus, for example, if the original information included a hammer, and the misleading question suggested a screwdriver, then the recognition test would involve a choice between the hammer and a wrench. The logic here is that if the original memory has, in fact, been overwritten by the postevent information, then participants in the misled condition should show lower accuracy than those in the control condition (who received no postevent information). In point of fact, the differences between the two conditions in this modified test were small and nonsignificant in six different replications, whereas the differences for the Loftus procedure remained large and significant. A similar finding was also reported by Zaragoza et al. (1987) using a recall procedure in which the postevent information was ruled out as a possible response by using postevent information that could not be plausibly confused with the original event or object, for instance, by asking participants who saw a coke bottle in the original and a 7-Up bottle in the postevent information what they remembered about a can of Planters Peanuts (which had not been presented earlier). These findings suggest that the original information was not lost; but rather the differences in the Loftus study were a product of *response biases* inherent in the procedure used, or what Belli (1989) referred to as *misinformation acceptance*.

As an aside, note that the practical implications of this criticism for eyewitness testimony are actually somewhat subtle. On the one hand, witness identifications are likely to be biased, regardless of whether this bias is due to memory impairment or response bias (see McCloskey & Zaragoza, 1985b, for an opposing argument). On the other hand, McCloskey and Zaragoza's results *do* suggest that the original memory *can* be retrieved with the proper questioning procedures. Lindsay (1994) stated the case as follows:

> The evidence suggests that the effects of misleading suggestions on ability to remember event details are likely to be small and unreliable when appropriate recognition probes are used (as in the modified test), but may be considerably larger and more robust when inappropriate recall measures are used. (p. 39)

McCloskey and Zaragoza (1985a) and Zaragoza and Koshmider (1989) also proposed two other possible explanations of Loftus's results. One of these entails the demand characteristics (although McCloskey & Zaragoza, 1985b, have voiced some objection to this term) involved in the experimenter suggesting a different version of the event or object. That is, participants in the misled condition may have thought that in introducing the misleading question the experimenter must have known more than they did, even if they (participants) correctly remembered the original event. Second, Zaragoza and Koshmider (1989) have suggested that traditional recognition memory tests do not clearly distinguish between participants believing that the misleading event is accurate (on the basis of the misleading question) and their belief that they actually saw that event (though see Tulving, 1985a, for methods for getting around this problem).

Rebuttals to the McCloskey and Zaragoza Critique and Findings. A number of rebuttals to the McCloskey and Zaragoza critique and methodological alternative have been voiced. For example, Loftus, Schooler, and Wagenaar (1985) argued that they had already presented evidence that addressed some of the issues raised by McCloskey and Zaragoza (e.g., by asking participants questions about demand characteristics during debriefing). They also argued that the modified test "is not sufficiently sensitive to detect small impairments in memory" (p. 377). For example, Lindsay (1994) suggested that misleading questions may simply reduce the strength of the original memory without eliminating it entirely (and such differences in memory strength may not be picked up on the modified test). Belli and Loftus (1996) recently referred to this as the *partial degradation* hypothesis.

Loftus et al. (1985) argued that a more sensitive test of the misinformation effect would be given by a "betting form test" (e.g., Toland, 1990), in which participants spread points out among more than two alternatives in terms of how much confidence they have in each. Such a test, according to Loftus et al. (1985), reduces the chance of being correct by sheer guessing and also "distinguishes between subjects who are confident that they are right and those who are merely guessing" (p. 377). Using such a betting procedure, Toland (1990) found that participants bet as much on the suggested items as they did on actual events, and significantly more than on novel events. Finally, Loftus et al. argued that McCloskey and Zaragoza's proposed method does not deal with the possibility of blended or compromise memories such as those described earlier. In this context, Weinberger, Wadsworth, and Baron (1983) provided a blended alternative (i.e., a red yield sign) to participants in the modified test procedure and found evidence for memory impairment.

Belli (1989) and his colleagues argued that by eliminating the postevent information as a choice in the recognition test, McCloskey and Zaragoza may have failed to uncover the effects of this information (e.g., a greater belief in the original occurrence of the misleading event). To deal with this possibility, both Belli (1989) and Tversky and Tuchin (1989) used a yes–no rating procedure (where the ratings were for both the original event and novel items). This procedure allowed them to assess both a *misinformation interference* (including both memory impairment and inaccessibility) and a misinformation acceptance (or response bias) account. Although the results of these studies are difficult to summarize, Belli obtained what were essentially mixed results; clear evidence for misinformation acceptance and also some evidence for misinformation interference in one out of his two experiments. However, Tversky and Tuchin, who also examined confidence ratings including ratings of the misleading information, found clear evidence for the memory interference or inaccessibility interpretation.

Other researchers working with McCloskey and Zaragoza's material have found results at variance with those initially reported by these researchers. For example, Loftus, Donders, Hoffman, and Schooler (1989) replicated the McCloskey and Zaragoza findings but also found that misled participants took significantly less time to respond than did controls, contrary to what may be expected if misled participants were, in fact, simply guessing. Chandler (1989, 1991) failed to replicate the McCloskey and Zaragoza results when different stimulus materials (e.g., visual postevent information) were used. Finally, Belli, Windshitl, McCarthy, and Winfrey (1992) reported evidence in support of a memory impairment position using the McCloskey and Zaragoza modified test procedure when longer retention intervals (i.e., 5–7 days) were used. In general, Belli and Loftus (1996) pointed out that those studies that have found such a result on the modified test have used longer retention intervals and most have used children as participants (though see Belli et al., 1992, and Chandler, 1989, 1991, for exceptions).

As may be expected, McCloskey and Zaragoza (1985b, 1989) disagreed with or dismissed these findings. McCloskey and Zaragoza (1985b) argued that Loftus and her associates (Loftus et al., 1985) did not really demonstrate what they claimed to demonstrate and that the emphasis on confidence in the betting form test is not acceptable as a test of memory because confidence may come from other factors or sources besides memory. In addition, McCloskey and Zaragoza (1985b) argued that the phenomenon of memory blends has not been well established.

Finally, in response to these studies, Loftus and Hoffman (1989) presented arguments against a mere guessing position, including the fact that participants are confident of their errors or suggested memories (Loftus, Korf, & Schooler, 1989; Tversky & Tuchin, 1989; see also the evidence [e.g., Lynn & Payne, 1997] of similar confidence in distorted memories in general) and the aforementioned reduction in reaction times in the misled condition. In addition, Loftus and Hoffman concluded that what Belli called the misinformation acceptance effect is of interest in and of itself (in addition to any memory impairment effects). As Loftus and Hoffman put it, "the fact that people come to accept misinformation and adopt it faithfully as their own is an important phenomenon in its own right" (p. 103). In reaching this conclusion, Loftus seems to be illustrating the "making a virtue out of necessity" effect.

Loftus and Hoffman concluded their paper with the following assertion:

> We believe that the misinformation effect is sufficiently pervasive and eventually may be so highly controllable that we are tempted to propose a Watsonian future for the misinformation effect … : Give us a dozen healthy memories, well-formed, and our own specified world to handle them in. And we'll guarantee to take any one at random and train it to become any type of memory that we might select—hammer, screwdriver, wrench, stop sign, yield sign, Indian chief—regardless of its origin or the brain that holds it. (p. 103)

In one subsequent publication Loftus (1991) expressed somewhat less bravado regarding the misinformation effect. For example, after failing to confirm predictions on an implicit memory measure and on another test, Loftus (1991b) made the following conclusion:

> Memory impairment does play some role in the misinformation effect. *It may be that the role is minor* compared to that played by the mere acceptance of misinformation by subjects who would otherwise be guessing, or compared to the role played by misremembering the source of the misleading items. (p. 211, italics added)

Nevertheless, in 1996, after reviewing some results for source misattribution effects (to be discussed next), where participants claimed *seeing* items that they actually had only *read* in a subsequent postevent narrative, Belli and Loftus (1996) referred to these errors as showing that "misinformation can alter memory by creating new visual memories for details that were presented only verbally" (p, 165). Thus, Loftus appears to have vacillated in her own confidence in the misinformation effect.

One implication of Loftus's claims, particularly this last one, is that it should be possible to *create* or *implant* false memories in individuals; in fact, Loftus (1993; Loftus & Ketcham, 1994) argued that many therapists do precisely that in "uncovering" repressed memories of childhood sexual abuse. On the first point, Loftus (1997a, 1997b; Loftus, Coan, & Pickrell, 1996) presented empirical evidence for the ability to implant a memory of being lost in a shopping mall in participants. (See also Hyman, Husband, & Billings, 1995, and Schooler, M. Bendiksen, & Ambodar, 1997, for other studies of the creation of false memories.) On the latter point, Ofshe (1992; see also Ofshe and Watters, 1994) reported on his ability to create a false memory in Paul Ingram, an alleged perpetrator of child sexual abuse, such that Ingram himself, a highly suggestible participant, actually provided elaborate detail of the suggested incident, presumably in the same way he did for the memories suggested by detectives. More generally, Loftus and Ketcham (1994) and Ofshe and Watters (1994) have reviewed numerous case histories of false memories, or at least dubious memories suggested by therapists, law enforcement officials, and others. (See Bowers & Farvolden's [1996] recent reconsideration of the issue of repressed memories; see also M. A. Conway, 1997a, Davies & Dalaleish [in press], and Pezdek & Banks, 1996, for edited books on the recovered memory debate.)

The Source Monitoring Account.   One further account of the misinformation effect is that it may result from errors or confusions in *source monitoring* (M. K. Johnson et al., 1993; Lindsay, 1990, 1993). According to this common, traditional viewpoint (Lindsay, 1994), individuals must not only remember information they have encountered, but also the *source* of that information. For example, one must try to remember whether a particular autobiographical fact was directly experienced or was told to him or her by a family member. Alternatively, one must remember whether news about a highly publicized court case or Hollywood marriage came from a respectable source or from some tabloid newspaper or TV program. Applying this notion to the research on eyewitness memory, it is possible that participants in such studies may remember both the original and the misleading postevent information (as in the coexistence hypothesis reviewed previously); but they may simply have a hard time recalling what information came from which source. In the face of such source confusions or uncertainty, participants may be persuaded to adopt a strategy in which they make judgments on the basis of the sheer familiarity of the items. Thus, when the critical test item pitting original information against the postevent information is presented, the postevent information may be chosen because it was encountered last and is therefore more familiar.

The original "source" of the source-monitoring hypothesis was Marcia Johnson's (1985; M. K. Johnson & Raye, 1981) research and theorizing on *reality monitoring,* a topic that is also relevant to the general topic of everyday memory. Reality monitoring refers to the ability to discriminate between events that actually occurred—"in reality"—and those that were self-generated, for instance, by imagination, fantasy, or by simple elaborative inference from presented material, as in the reconstructive memory tradition. Johnson's concern here was with identifying some of the ways in which individuals distinguish between these two classes of events (e.g., in autobiographical memory or in remembering a conversation with a friend or spouse). Some of these features include the number of *sensory attributes* and the amount of spatial and temporal context versus the number of *operational attributes,* or the amount of inferential or evaluative operations attached to the memory.

In the case of *source* monitoring, the question is how to distinguish among different external and internal sources of information or memory, rather than strictly with the internal–external distinction (see M. K. Johnson et al., 1993). According to M. K. Johnson et al. (1993) and Lindsay (1993), many of the same principles apply to source as to reality monitoring. For example, "the likelihood of source misattributions varies with the amount and nature of the source-specific information in the memory record, the discriminability of the potential sources, and the stringency of the decision processes and criteria used during remembering" (Lindsay, 1993, p. 87). M. K. Johnson et al. (1993) also cited some of the factors at encoding and decision making that may influence the accuracy of such source monitoring. For example, stress, incomplete attention, or the failure to adequately contextualize the event (e.g., by not seeing what led up to a fight or accident or not knowing the participants) may impair the encoding of the event and make it difficult to recall the source later.

In an initial study applying the source monitoring concept to eyewitness memory, Lindsay and Johnson (1989a) compared the results of a yes–no memory test with their own source-monitoring test. In the first of these tests, one set of participants rated items as having appeared in the original pictures or not (as in the revised version of the Loftus methodology). In the second test other participants were to indicate whether the item appeared in the pictures, the later narrative, or both. In other words, in this second test, the different sources of information were more clearly specified to participants. The main finding of this study was that participants showed the typical misinformation effect on the first test, whereas in the source-monitoring test the second set of participants correctly attributed the suggested information to the postevent narrative, presumably because these participants were given "more stringent criteria." Along these same lines, Carris, Zaragoza, and Lane (1992) found errors on a source-monitoring test when participants were asked to form an image of the postevent information (which may lead to confusions of the verbal narrative with the original [visual] slides).

In a second study, Lindsay (1990) used somewhat different methods to control for possible demand characteristics in the source-monitoring effect. Specifically, because participants may have been led to believe (e.g., by the wording of the leading questions) that the suggested information actually occurred in the original events, they may have falsely reported that they saw this information in both, even if they knew that it occurred only in the postevent information. To deal with this possibility, Lindsay used a technique taken from Jacoby (e.g., Jacoby, Woloshyn, & Kelley, 1989) called the *logic of opposition* procedure. The basic idea here was to inform participants that the postevent information did not represent a correct answer to the test questions and to instruct them at test time *not* to report this postevent information. Thus, these instructions were opposite to any possible source confusion effects, and any evidence for source confusion may therefore not be attributed to response bias or demand characteristics.

In the Lindsay study, participants were also placed in conditions in which the distinction between original and postevent information was either easy (i.e., because of a 2-day interval between the two) or difficult (i.e., because of an interval of just a few minutes and presentation under similar conditions). Using a cued recall procedure, Lindsay found that participants in the easy condition did not show source confusions (i.e., did not report postevent material in response to the test questions), whereas those in the difficult condition did. Lindsay (1994) pointed out, though, that even in the easy condition, participants were less likely to report details of the *actual* events in their recall; that is, they tended to leave the misleading questions blank or just guess. These results may suggest memory impairment (in that participants did not provide the original material either); and, in the absence of source confusions in this condition, this failure cannot be accounted for by the sort of differential guessing rates or differential response criteria proposed by McCloskey and Zaragoza. In fact, Lindsay (1994) argued that results from the opposition procedure are the only eyewitness memory results that cannot be explained in some other way. This observation also points out the degree to which traditional memory parameters play a role in everyday memory situations.

Conclusions and Evaluation.   Things have obviously become extremely complex since Loftus' original research on this topic! By now there are several separable issues involved in the debate. First, there is the question of the fate of the original memory, which is the issue that Loftus was initially concerned with and to which McCloskey and Zaragoza addressed their original critique. However, there are now several different accounts of such memory impairment. For example, Belli & Loftus (1996) have listed a blocking, preclusion, a partial degradation, and a source misattribution account—all of which specify some kind of memory impairment (although Lindsay, 1994, argued that the question of whether participants mix up the source of the suggested information is separate from the memory impairment question and probably of greater interest from a forensic point of view). Finally, all of these positions are separate from the misinformation *acceptance* factor.

All of these accounts are in turn related to the question of the correct representational format for the original event, and exactly what cognitive processes operate on that representation. Loftus et al. (1985) suggested that the representational question is potentially unanswerable, whereas McCloskey and Zaragoza (1985) argued that an examination of the underlying "cognitive mechanisms" is "required." Then there is the question of what other factors (e.g., judgmental or interpersonal) can influence a person's report, and the degree to which that report accurately reflects that participant's memory for the original event. There is also the question raised recently by Loftus as to whether individuals can actually create *new* memories that are held with some conviction (or what the meaning of such conviction is).[5]

---

[5]There is one other major issue here that I have not alluded to, and that is the question of the relative suggestibility of young children to misleading questions and, conversely, the reliability of such children in eyewitness testimony. Ceci and Bruck (1993, 1995) recently reviewed the evidence on this topic and concluded that children are more suggestible than adults but can sometimes serve as reliable witnesses. Perhaps more importantly, some of the same debate, such as over the sources (e.g., memory vs. social influences) of such increased suggestibility as I have discussed can be found in this literature as well.

Although these are all interesting questions, and ones that are of practical significance for the study of eyewitness testimony (and of memory in general), it is important to note that they are *different* questions. It is also important to note that much of the above-mentioned debate—a debate that has become increasingly adversarial in recent years—has generally focused on the first of these questions, even though the grounds of that debate have shifted in recent years. (See Ostrom, 1977, for an account of the dangers of such adversarial research in the study of impression formation.)

Recent developments in the area of eyewitness memory have also placed this phenomenon squarely back in the arena of traditional memory research and principles, for instance, of proactive and retroactive interference, of interference versus decay theory, or recall versus recognition memory. (Belli & Loftus, 1996, for example, have explicitly noted the similarity between the misinformation debate and the debate a few decades ago about retroactive interference.) One of the attractions of Loftus's research over the years has always been her ability to connect real-world phenomena to well-established laboratory findings and principles. Recently, however, attention has focused more on the latter than on the former, and on traditional principles of verbal learning at that (although Loftus, 1991a, has also tried to link her results to contemporary principles of PDP models; see also Metcalfe, 1990, for an explicit application of a PDP model to the phenomenon of blended memories in eyewitness testimony).

To those psychologists who believe in the generalizability of traditional lab research on memory (see chap. 1), this is undoubtedly a desirable turn. On the other hand, for those who are more interested in eyewitness memory as a topic in its own right, or who are concerned more with the practical implications of such research for the real-world use of eyewitness memory, these latest developments must surely seem like a retrenchment of sorts, and a sacrifice of ecological validity. For example, Chandler's (1989, 1991) studies involve nature pictures; Lindsay's (1990) studies presented misleading questions immediately after the original events. This difference in viewpoint is clearly reminiscent of the debate raised in chapter 1 between critics and advocates of research on everyday cognition in general. Although there is certainly something to be said for both points of view, the most recent attempts to sort out the exact locus of effect of misinformation seem to have made eyewitness memory research considerably less exciting than Loftus's original research.

Relating Eyewitness Memory Research to Research on Event Memory

Thus far, my discussion of research on eyewitness memory has made little contact with my earlier discussion of research on event memory; in point of fact, the two areas have had little to say to each other. One exception here is a set of studies reported by S. P. Robertson (1986; see also Lehnert, S. P.

Robertson, & Black, 1984; S. P. Robertson, Black, & Lehnert, 1985). Robertson (1986) pointed out, as I have done, that different studies on eyewitness memory have dealt with different parts of the event, such as the action or predicate (e.g., the accident itself or the act of stealing) versus an object or location involved in the action (e.g., a stop sign, a hammer). Robertson noted that different conceptual components of the event (e.g., static features such as locations or physical states vs. the predicate itself) should be differently affected by misleading questions. Specifically, the static features should be more subject to misrecall than should the actions.

In the study that is most relevant to our present concerns, Lehnert et al. (1984) varied the content of the misleading question so that it referred to either the action itself (e.g., suggesting that a character checked his hair in his rear view mirror rather than in the side window of a car) or a state (e.g., suggesting that the day was cloudy rather than sunny). Lehnert et al. also presented both direct questions and "remote" questions (i.e., questions about implied propositions) in order to examine whether the effects of the misleading question spread from suggested actions to related states or from suggested states to related actions.

The initial finding of this study was that states were, in fact, more susceptible to misleading questions than were actions, as judged by participants' answers to recall questions about actual versus implied actions or states. For instance, one pair of questions was "What did Jack do about his hair just before he sprinted across the street?" (action) and the related (state) question "Where was Jack when he checked his hair, inside or outside the car?" (Robertson, 1986, p. 159). Lehnert et al. also found that misleading questions had an effect on participants' memory for information that was related to the focus of the question (e.g., a location or physical state implied by an action), and this effect was stronger for actions implied by states than for states implied by actions. The rationale for this latter finding (Lehnert et al., 1984) is that, in Schank's (1975) early theory, memory is based on acts or predicates, and hence inferences or "internal changes to the representations are being made along conceptual links to actions and not to states" (Lehnert et al., p. 366).

Of equal importance, Robertson examined the differences among the different items in the degree to which they were subject to change and found that these differences could be interpreted in terms of Schank's (1975) conceptual rules analysis. Thus, for example, items that were peripheral to the predicate (e.g., location or a physical state such as the weather) were easier to change than were more closely related concepts (e.g., actors, objects, sources, and destinations). In part, this is because these central concepts must be "checked" in comparing the question content with one's memory representation, whereas the more peripheral ones do not need to be checked or even noticed and hence are more readily changed. Stated differently, it is easier to change modifiers of concepts (e.g., changing the green car to a blue car) than it is to change concepts or "slots" (e.g., the driver, the nature of the accident or robbery, the person hurt by the accident or victim of the robbery) in the propositional or conceptual rules structure. Research by Robertson et al. (1985) found that the exact nature of the misleading question (i.e., what parts of one's event representation it addresses) also makes a difference.

The research by Robertson and his associates adds a new wrinkle to eyewitness memory research. Although Robertson et al.'s (1985) methods differ from those of previous studies in a number of ways (e.g., different sorts of questions, different sorts of memory measures), on a conceptual level it seems reasonable to assume that different features of one's representation of an event should be more or less subject to the effects of misleading questions and that different types of questions should have different effects on memory. More important, the research that I examined earlier on event memory suggests that the nature of the memory representation *can* be addressed, contrary to what Loftus has argued, and that the nature of that representation *can* make a difference in predicting the effects of misleading questions.

PROSPECTIVE MEMORY AND THE COGNITIVE REPRESENTATION OF PLANNING

Prospective Memory

Most of what I have been concerned with in the first part of this book, and certainly what almost all traditional memory research has been concerned with, is what has been labeled *retrospective memory (RM)*, or memory for past events or previously learned material. Another type of memory that, until recently, has received relatively little attention is called *prospective memory (PM)*, or remembering to carry out future plans and actions (see Meacham & Leiman, 1982, for the introduction of this distinction and the two contrasting terms). Questions have been raised about the appropriateness of the latter term. For example, Crowder (1996) recently argued that prospective memory is a contradiction in terms (because memory, by definition, refers to past experiences),[6] and J. A. Ellis (1996) proposed *realizing delayed intentions* as an alternative term, because more is involved than just memory.

Whatever term is used, PM is obviously of great importance in everyday life; everyone has daily errands to run, dates to remember, TV programs to watch, and telephone calls to make. At least one of the reasons for the relative neglect of this topic is that, for the most part, PM does not lend itself to the same kinds of experimental controls or the same traditional experimental paradigms as RM (see E. Winograd, 1988). As Searleman and Herrmann (1994) have pointed out, the increased interest in research on PM over the past 20 years can be linked to the emergence of the area of everyday cognition and the willingness of researchers to use more naturalistic methods (e.g., diary keeping, sending in postcards, case studies), although the majority of research on PM still consists of experimental studies. In-

---

[6]This dispute over terminology is reminiscent of the old behavioristic question (e.g., Hull, 1931) about how future intentions or wishes can influence present actions.

deed, one of the motivations for research on PM has been a very practical concern with issues such as getting elderly patients to remember their medication (e.g., Levy & Loftus, 1984; Park & Kidder, 1996), or getting young children to perform tasks.

Some Examples of PM Studies. To get a flavor of PM research, consider the following two recent studies. In the first of these studies, McDaniel and Einstein (1993) had participants carry out a task (i.e., pressing a button on a keyboard) whenever they saw a particular word, which was embedded within another task involving strategies to improve short-term memory. The variables examined were the familiarity and distinctiveness of the relevant word. The major findings of this study were that both familiarity and distinctiveness played a role in participants' ability to carry out the PM task.

In the second study (Ellis & Nimmo-Smith, 1993), eight participants were asked to record the intentions they expected to satisfy on each day for 5 consecutive days. These participants were asked to indicate the time at which they expected to carry out those intentions and the personal importance of the intention. They were also asked to fill out a questionnaire in a portable booklet as soon as possible after spontaneously recalling one of those intentions. The questions on this form involved ratings of participants' physical and mental state during their spontaneous recollections and the activity they were involved in during that recollection. Participants' answers were compared with their analogous ratings during a control phase in which they were interrupted by a portable timer at random intervals in the course of their daily affairs (see the research by W. Brewer, 1988, to be discussed in chap. 6, which first used this kind of random timing device).

Simply stated, the results of this research were that participants were likely to be involved in some activity requiring less attention during the spontaneous recall periods than during their random control periods. Further, this feature was more apparent for intentions that were of greater personal importance and that could only be carried out during a limited period of time—what Ellis (1988) called *pulses*—and less so for less important intentions that could be carried out during a larger window of opportunity.

I cite these two studies as examples because they reflect some of the different types of research that fall under the label of prospective memory (and because both appeared in the same issue of the journal *Memory*). In addition, they illustrate some of the advantages and disadvantages of experimental versus more naturalistic studies, which I discuss later in this section.

Distinctions Between Retrospective and Prospective Memory. Common sense suggests that retrospective and prospective memory should be related; for instance, in order to remember to send a birthday card to a friend, one must first remember the date of that birthday, what store has a good selection of cards, and so forth. Nevertheless, a number of studies have found the two types of memory to be *un*related (e.g., Einstein & McDaniel, 1990;

Meacham & Leiman, 1982) or even *negatively* related (Wilkins & Baddeley, 1978), where RM performance typically involves some sort of free recall or recognition memory task, and the PM task requires performing some action, such as pressing a key when an agreed-upon cue is presented. At the same time, however, Bisiacchi (1996) reported that even though PM and retrospective memory loaded on separate factors for normal participants under age 70, the two loaded on the same factor for elderly participants. Similarly, Burgess and Shallice (1997) presented evidence that argues that "patients with neuropsychological deficits might reveal relationships between RM and PR [prospective memory] that do not make themselves apparent in controls" (p. 251). Consistent with this argument, these researchers reported significant correlations between the ability of 30 brain-damaged patients to remember the rules for carrying out a set of tasks and their ability to actually stick to their plans for the task, whereas the correlations for a group of control participants were not significant.

Some of the proposed differences between the two sorts of memory (e.g., Kvavilashvili, 1987; McDaniel, 1995; P. E. Morris, 1992) that might account for these findings include the intentional nature of prospective memory (i.e., the individual must intend to perform the task) and the fact that in PM individuals must remember to give *themselves* a cue to carry out the task rather than being cued by an event or an experimenter (McDaniel, 1995; E. Winograd, 1988). On the first point, Winograd (1988) has observed that "prospective memory is a goal-directed activity embedded in a hierarchy of activities" (p. 350), and this goal-directedness is certainly one reason why the failure to remember an appointment or to carry out some task is blamed on the person rather than simply being labeled as poor memory. Similarly, E. Winograd (1988) suggested that it is the "necessity to cue oneself, the self-control aspect of prospective remembering that is the distinctive feature. It is this characteristic that taxes experimental ingenuity in studying it" (p. 349). Along these lines, Shallice and Burgess (1991b) reported evidence that two out of three head injury patients showed relatively intact RM but also showed impaired performance on tests measuring their ability to schedule and carry out tasks within a restricted time period. These authors argued that one reason for the difference is that in the RM tasks the experimenter and the nature of the tasks themselves served to cue or trigger patients' memory, but in the absence of such cues in the PM tasks the patients were unable to cue themselves. However, Cockburn (1995) presented a case history of a patient who suffered a brain aneurysm but recovered PM functions while showing only very simple, primitive RM functions.

Still another proposed difference (Goschke & Kuhl, 1993) is that PM may have a higher degree of activation from the outset—that is, instructions to carry out a task may lead to greater activation than instructions to remember something. Finally, McDaniel (1995) suggested that the failure to find a correlation between the two types of memory may be due to other, simpler factors (e.g., the longer list that must be retained for retrospective tasks than for prospective ones) or the fact that the prospective task may be part of a larger task whereas the retrospective is not (see my earlier discussion of Winograd).

Research on Prospective Memory. Before I discuss research on prospective memory, it is helpful to divide the process of PM into two stages. For example, Einstein and McDaniel (1990) distinguished between a phase of remembering the action in the first place and one of remembering to *perform* that action. Both of these obviously refer to the retrieval as opposed to the initial encoding. J. A. Ellis (1996) also divided prospective memory into two (rather different and, in my opinion, more meaningful) phases. (See Fig. 4.2.) The first is a retrospective one, or perhaps more correctly, an initial phase, in which one initially encodes the action to be performed, forms an intention to carry out that action, and specifies the retrieval context (e.g., time, place) for performing that action.[7] The second phase is a prospective or follow-up one that includes recollection of the intention, the retention interval (which seems a bit out of place in either phase), the execution of the action, and an evaluation of the outcome (H. D. Ellis, 1996). Ellis proposed that the so-called retrospective phase may be represented in terms of an *action-trigger schema* (D. A. Norman, 1981; see also D. A. Norman & Shallice, 1986). According to this view, an action is represented in terms of a schema or set of schemas, which are activated by some perceptual situation. In the case of PM, the trigger is a given retrieval context or cue, which may be a time, a location, an activity, or a person. In addition, the intention itself can be viewed as influencing the degree of activation of that schema.

Along these lines, Burgess and Shallice (1997) argued that setting a retrieval context involves retrospective, or more correctly, reconstructive memory, such as remembering which post office is nearby to mail a letter or

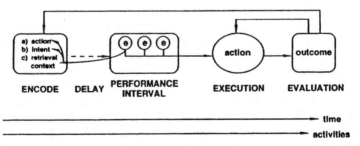

FIG. 4.2. The phases of prospective memory outlined by J. Ellis. From "Prospective Memory or the Realization of Delayed Intentions: A Conceptual Framework for Research," by J. Ellis, 1996. In *Prospective Memory: Theory and Applications* (p. 3), edited by M. A. Brandimonte, G. O. Einstein, & M. A. McDaniel, Mahwah, NJ: Lawrence Erlbaum Associates. Copyright © 1996 by Lawrence Erlbaum Associates. Reprinted with permission.

---

[7]As Burgess & Shallice (1997) have pointed out, this phase, despite Ellis's label, does not itself clearly involve recollection of earlier memories. Rather it is "retrospective" only in the sense that its components must be retrieved at the time of carrying out the intended action.

when you will go by another one. In fact, these authors (see also Koriat, Ben-Zur, & Nussbaum, 1990) present evidence on the confabulations of normal participants, which suggests that construction of retrieval contexts involves the same kind of processes that are involved in autobiographical memory (to be discussed in chap. 6). That is, thinking about a context in which you might (in the future) mail a letter is similar to the act of recalling a time in the past when you mailed a letter, which is precisely the kind of task involved in autobiographical memory. As far as context setting is concerned, the more effective context is one in which a complex set of cues or markers are set down, including both imaginal (e.g., an image of a post office or a setting in which you might interact with a friend) and sensorimotor cues (e.g., thinking of mailing the letter or making the phone call). Additionally, as I have discussed, there is also the added factor of the activated intention.

The so-called prospective phase includes a number of different components. One of these is the frequency and timing of recollections of the previous intention prior to the time that it must be enacted (J. A. Ellis, 1996; J. A. Ellis & Nimmo-Smith, 1993). The evidence from laboratory studies with short (i.e., < 15 seconds) retention intervals (e.g., Einstein & McDaniel, 1990; Harris & Wilkins, 1982) indicates that both frequency of recollection and recency are related to likelihood of carrying out a task. J. A. Ellis (1988; J. A. Ellis & Nimmo-Smith, 1993) has shown that for naturally occurring intentions and longer retention intervals (i.e., hours or days) the sheer occurrence of *any* recollection is a better predictor of the enactment of that intention than is the frequency of that recollection.

A good deal of research has also been conducted on the nature of the retention interval and the influences on retrieval during that interval. There is evidence, for instance, that the activity engaged in during the interval is a factor for both short (e.g., Brandimonte & Passolonghi, 1994; Kvavilashvili, 1987) and long intervals (e.g., J. A. Ellis & Nimmo-Smith, 1993). For example, Brandimonte and Passolonghi reported that intervening activities during a short delay led to interference, whereas Kvavilashvili found that such activities interfered only with unimportant intentions. Along these lines, J. A. Ellis (1996) observed that there are two different factors involved in retrieval of an intention: the match between the agreed-upon retrieval context and the present situation on the one hand, and the strength of the connection between that retrieval context and the intended action on the other. Thus, one must not only recognize the situation as being similar to the designated context (e.g., recognizing this store as a minimart or grocery store) but must also have established a connection between this context and an action (e.g., grocery stores as a place to purchase bottled water). In addition, one must also inhibit associations between the place and other actions (e.g., grocery stores and buying ice cream or rich pastries).

Einstein and McDaniel (1990, 1996; Einstein et al., 1996) examined differences between what they referred to as *event-based* and *time-based* tasks. As the labels suggest, time-based tasks involve remembering to execute an intention at some particular time (e.g., call back at 1:00 PM), whereas event-based tasks involve executing the intention when some event occurs (e.g., standing under a door when the next earthquake occurs). (Kvavilashvili, 1990, suggested a third type of task—namely, an *activity-based* one—or interrupting an activity in order to execute the intention, such as bringing up the issue of a raise when your boss is praising your work; and she reported evidence [Kvavilashvili & Ellis, 1996] on the ease of retrieving activity-based intentions.) One of the differences between these two, according to Einstein and McDaniel, is that event-based PM depends more on external cues than does time-based memory, which is based more on self-initiated memory processes (e.g., you have to remember to look at your watch or a clock).

One of the practical issues regarding PM is the relative value of internal versus external cues or reminders. It seems clear that many people prefer the latter to the former (see Harris, 1980; Intons-Peterson & Fournier, 1986). For example, Meacham and Leiman (1982) conducted a study in which participants were to mail back postcards on specified days (ranging up to 32 days following the experimental session), These participants were either given colored tags for their key chains or no such reminder. Although the evidence from this study was not entirely clear-cut, it did suggest that such external memory aids improved performance. In addition, a later survey of participants indicated that at least 84% of participants had used other external memory aids, such as placing the cards in a clearly visible place or keeping a calendar. Similarly, Levy and Loftus (1984; see also Morris, 1992) reviewed evidence for the role of memory aids in getting individuals to keep appointments. The evidence from this research makes it clear that reminders in the form of phone calls or postcards significantly improve appointment keeping (e.g., Gates & Colburn, 1976; Levy & Claravall, 1977)—a lesson that has clearly been learned by many physicians and dentists (though see Guynn, McDaniel, & Einstein, 1996, for a failure to find an effect of external cues per se). Finally, Meacham and Singer (1977) found that an incentive of winning $5 for sending in eight cards at given intervals increased compliance.

D. C. Park and Kidder (1996) outlined some of the implications of research on PM for increasing *medication adherence*. For example, Maylor (1990) observed that participants showed better PM when they converted a time-based task into an event-based one (e.g., taking medicine at meals rather than at specific times). Similarly, the more important the intended action or the results of not taking that action, the more likely the person is to carry out that action (Kvavilashvili, 1987). Thus, in medication adherence, individuals are more likely to adhere to a schedule of medication if the issue or illness is of particular concern to them. (This obvious finding points out once again the fact that PM is not just a memory phenomenon.) Finally, Einstein, Holland, McDaniel, and Guynn (1992) reported that PM is affected by the complexity of the task. In the case of medication adherence, where patients often are taking multiple doses of multiple medications, it is important to set up some kind of overall medication plan or schedule.

Theories and Classifications of Prospective Memory Tasks. Until recently, there has been relatively little systematic theorizing about the mechanisms of PM—a fact that clearly distinguishes this area from the other topics that I have considered in this chapter. One possible reason for this is that there are so many different types of PM tasks. In this connection, a number of different classifications have been proposed (e.g., J. A. Ellis, 1988; Kvavilashvili & Ellis, 1996; Harris, 1984). For example, Meacham and Leiman (1982; see also Harris, 1984) distinguished between *habitual* and *episodic* tasks, or tasks one performs regularly (e.g., taking vitamins in the morning or going to work out three times a week) versus those one performs only occasionally (e.g., keeping an appointment with the dentist). Presumably individuals are more likely to forget the latter than the former (although Kvavilashvili & Ellis, 1996, pointed out that it is difficult to study habitual tasks experimentally). In fact, J. A. Ellis (1988) reported that when participants were asked to keep a diary of the tasks they intended to perform, these participants typically did not mention such events as "having lunch" or "making the bed." Another distinction I have already referred to is that made by Einstein and McDaniel (1990) between event-based and time-based prospective memory tasks. Finally, Meacham and Leiman (1982; see also J. A. Ellis, 1988) distinguished between what they called *pulses* and *steps*. The former refer to actions of some personal importance that can only be carried out during a limited window of opportunity (Harris & Wilkins, 1982; e.g., keeping an appointment), whereas the latter refer to events of lesser importance that can be carried out within a longer period of time (e.g., picking up some groceries or reading a magazine article). In this connection, J. A. Ellis (1988) found in a diary study that pulses were better remembered than steps, whereas Maylor (1990) found the opposite using a field study (i.e., asking participants to phone back).

Kvavilashvili and Ellis (1996) classified studies of PM in terms of a 2 (short-term delayed vs. long-term delayed intentions) × 3 (event-, activity-, vs. time-based intentions) matrix. Not too surprisingly, all laboratory studies have been of the short-term variety, whereas research on long-term intentions has typically involved field studies. In addition, lab studies have typically involved event- or activity-based tasks, whereas research on time-based tasks has typically involved field studies (e.g. the medication compliance studies).

One theoretical account of PM that relates to the distinction between habitual and episodic tasks was proposed by Shallice and Burgess (1991a). The central concept in this account is the notion of a *supervisory system*, which serves to interrupt the routine, habitual order of activities for the enactment of a delayed intention. This interruption is accomplished by earlier formulating an alternative plan and then setting down a *marker* or *message* that a nonroutine action should be engaged in when a particular event occurs. This process involves both activation of the appropriate action schemas and the inhibition of the usual habitual ones.

On the basis of the Shallice and Burgess account, as well as research with naturally occurring intentions, J. A. Ellis and Shallice (1993) proposed two different ways in which delayed intentions may be retrieved, ways that correspond more or less to J. A. Ellis's (1988) distinction between steps and pulses. The first of these is what the authors referred to as *brute retrieval,* or retrieval involving the marker-trigger mechanisms just described. Steps are typically retrieved in this way. The second mechanism, which is more likely to be used to retrieve pulses, has been referred to as *hierarchical retrieval.* According to this view, daily activities are arranged in a hierarchy, where the superordinate nodes are referred to as *anchorpoints,* or stable, fixed activities (e.g., going to lunch or starting the day with a daily briefing) that "signal a change from one superordinate level of activity to another" (J. A. Ellis, 1996, p. 13). Thus, in this case the execution of intended activities is based on an organized hierarchy of one's daily routine.

Einstein and McDaniel (1996) described two other models of PM. The first of these, which is implied by my earlier discussion of influences on retrieval, is a *simple activation model* (see Yaniv & Meyer, 1987). According to this model, the connection between a cue and an action may be activated, but that activation dissipates over time, particularly as other activities are engaged in. Both the reactivation of the action (e.g., by rehearsal) and a reappearance of the cue or target event lead to greater activation of the action–cue pairing. (Goschke & Kuhl, 1993, proposed a similar activation model in which intentional actions are assumed to be represented with greater activation than unintentional ones.)

The alternative model, referred to as the *Noticing + Search Model* (cf., Jacoby & Kelley, 1991; Mandler, 1980), assumes that with greater experience with the target event, some feeling of familiarity is evoked or something that causes one to notice that event is evoked. This in turn leads one to engage in a directed search for the significance of that event by searching retrospective memory. Thus, for example, if you are used to getting money from the ATM on your way home from work, then when you drive home on a Friday afternoon you may "know" that you have to do something during that drive and search your memory for what needs to be done.

Burgess and Shallice (1997) "noted" the similarity of this viewpoint to various context + search models of the retrieval of autobiographical memories (to be discussed in chap. 6). Both of these are prototypical examples of "control-driven recollection" (Burgess & Shallice, 1997, p. 263), or the role of a supervisory system. Note, by the way, that such a model corresponds to a more computational viewpoint, whereas the simple activation model clearly relates to the associative network (or spreading activation) model.

There is one particularly interesting application of the simple activation model (McDaniel, 1995; McDaniel & Einstein, 1993), which has to do with the relative effectiveness of different types of cues. According to this model, some memories—in this case, connections between a cue and an action— may exist in a kind of partially activated form, such that the action is more easily elicited when the cue is presented. It follows that reminders should not have any effect on the probability of participants carrying out the planned action *except* when the reminder focuses on the link between the cue and action (e.g., "remember what you're supposed to do when the given cue is presented," rather than "remember to watch for the cue [that signals the task]"), and that is exactly what Guynn, McDaniel, and Einstein (1995) found.

McDaniel (1995) argued that the Guynn et al. (1995) results are generally consistent with the simple activation model and not with the noting + search model. However, a general problem with the models presented here (and with other conceptions of PM as well) is that, for the most part, the data collected thus far on PM do not allow for a strong, competitive test of the (underspecified) alternatives. Despite the increasing interest in and an increasing number of studies investigating prospective memory (see Brandimonte, Einstein, & McDaniel, 1996), this is still clearly an underresearched (and underconceptualized) area.

Some Criticisms of PM Research.   Recently, a number of commentators have expressed some reservations about that concept of prospective memory and the emerging area of PM. Both Crowder (1996) and Roediger (1996b) questioned whether or in what ways prospective memory differs from retrospective memory. As noted earlier, Crowder argued that memory is, by definition, retrospective; and thus, the term "prospective memory," or "memory for future actions" (Mantyla, 1996), is really an oxymoron. Both Crowder (1996) and Roediger (1996b) pointed out that no new principles have yet been demonstrated to deal with PM other than those already established from the study of retrospective memory (see the similar argument against everyday memory in general discussed in chap. 1). Roediger, for example, has suggested that PM can be seen as a subcategory of episodic memory and that PM can be viewed as memory for "lists of things to do," just as episodic memory can be viewed as memory for lists of events. (Neither of these "list" translations seems really adequate.) Roediger acknowledged, though, along with Kvavilashvili and Ellis (1996), that research on PM thus far has been rather narrow; and it is possible that different principles or phenomena may emerge when the scope of this research is expanded (e.g., to more naturalistic situations).

Another point worth noting is that, as J. A. Ellis (1996) and others have pointed out, there is more involved in PM than just cognitions and intentions.

Certainly there is some kind of motivation to recall intentions which, although not *absent* in retrospective memory, is certainly much more apparent in PM. For example, although individuals may at times be strongly motivated to recall a previous event (e.g., an early childhood experience, or a partner's birthday), there is clearly a strong motivational component in remembering to take medicine or to take a driver's license test. In this sense, the term prospective *memory* is a bit misleading. It *is* equally important to note that reducing intentions to activation does not capture all of the meaning of an intention, though there is a long history of such formulations (e.g., Lewin's [1950] classic conception of intention or will as a simple tension system).

One other criticism that can be raised against the area of prospective memory is that research on this topic has been dominated to a large degree by experimental studies. This is not just a knee-jerk reaction to the effect that everyday cognition research should be naturalistic or nonexperimental. In fact, areas such as face memory and eyewitness testimony have also been dominated by such experimental research. Rather the point is that in this particular case, experimental research may not really capture the nature of PM in the real world. For example, as I discussed earlier, Kvavilashvili and Ellis (1996) observed that experimental studies are likely to be concerned with short-term delays, whereas naturalistic studies are more likely to be concerned with long delays. These authors speculated that the processing involved in the latter may be "qualitatively different" (p. 35) from that in the former. That is, remembering to keep a doctor's appointment next month may involve very different processing demands and memory strategies than remembering to press a key after 30 seconds. Yet according to the box score of studies kept by Kvavilashvili and Ellis (1996), there have been three times as many experimental studies on PM as the number of diary, questionnaire, and case studies combined. This is clearly an area where carefully controlled experimental research needs to be supplemented (and maybe preceded) by research in real-world settings with real-world tasks.

Planning

Implicit in the study of prospective memory, and, as I have suggested, intimately related to the study of event memory is the process of planning (i.e., when or how to carry out the action). In the first section of this chapter I discussed how individuals represent other people's plans in making sense of their actions. In this section I examine how people's plans may be cognitively represented as well as the process of planning itself, and I review some recent formulations and research on this topic.

Models of the Cognitive Representation of Planning.   There are a number of different models of planning (e.g., Hammond, 1989; B. Hayes-Roth &

Hayes-Roth, 1979; Wilensky, 1983), most of which were developed in the area of artificial intelligence, although there have been a few psychological formulations as well (e.g., Barsalou, 1983; Byrne, 1977; Friedman & Scholnick, 1997). I now examine two prominent examples of these models representing two of the different approaches to everyday cognition developed in chapter 1. In addition, I look at one prominent critique (Suchman, 1987) of the concept of planning in general.

The first model is one proposed by B. Hayes-Roth and Hayes-Roth (1979). This model is an eclectic one, combining features from several of the different viewpoints. One of the central elements of the model is a set of procedures—what Hayes-Roth and Hayes-Roth referred to as "distinct cognitive *specialists* ... [that make] tentative *decisions* for incorporation into a tentative *plan*" (p. 285). These if–then procedures (e.g., "if you're near the post office, then buy some stamps") write their decisions on a central *blackboard* or limited working memory buffer, which constitutes one of the computational components of the model. Although these procedures operate in parallel (and at different levels), the blackboard also includes an executive in charge of allocating resources to the various aspects of the planning process, as well as a *meta-plan* corresponding to the planner's overall understanding of the problem, his or her general methods, and criteria for evaluating solutions (B. Hayes-Roth & Hayes-Roth, 1979). Both the executive and the meta-plan amount to traditional computational conceptions. Also included in the blackboard is a specification of the desirable features of procedures or *plan decisions,* which serve to prioritize plans. For instance, in the example of running an errand (discussed later), such features include issues of spatial proximity, efficiency, and speed of implementing that decision. Finally, the blackboard also contains a *knowledge store,* which contains information in both propositional and analogue format (e.g., knowledge of landmarks, routes, product values, in the errand-running example).

The most notable feature of the Hayes-Roth and Hayes-Roth model is its emphasis on the *opportunism* of the planning process. That is, rather than decisions being made in a top–down manner corresponding to an overall plan or goal–subgoal structure (as in earlier artificial intelligence models such as that by Sacerdoti, 1977) or proceeding in an orderly, sequential manner, the planner actually exploits various opportunities as he or she encounters them. For example, in carrying out an errand, an individual may pick up laundry if the cleaners are located near the grocery store where he or she has been shopping; or he or she may make a trip to the post office if it is near closing time. Carrying out these various subplans may lead the planner to reformulate an overall plan or at least affect later decisions in the planning sequence. A given decision may also influence decisions made at a different (i.e., higher or lower) level.

B. Hayes-Roth and Hayes-Roth (1979) give the example of a person planning an errand in which he or she is to accomplish a number of different tasks. The general problem given to participants in this task (and then simulated) is as follows:

> You have just finished working out at the health club. It is 11:00 and you can plan the rest of your day as you like. However, you must pick up your car from the Maple Street parking garage by 5:30 and then head home. You'd also like to see a movie today, if possible. Show times at both movie theaters are 1:00, 3:00, and 5:00. Both movies are on your "must see" list, but go to whichever one most conveniently fits into your plan. Your other errands are as follows:
>
> > > pick up medicine for your dog at the vet;
> > > buy a fan belt for your refrigerator at the appliance store;
> > > check out two of the three luxury apartments;
> > > meet a friend for lunch at one of the restaurants;
> > > buy a toy for your dog at the pet store;
> > > pick up your watch at the watch repair;
> > > special order a book at the bookstore;
> > > buy fresh vegetables at the grocery;
> > > buy a gardening magazine at the newsstand;
> > > go to the florist to send flowers to a friend at the hospital. (p. 277)
>
> The map of the town in which these errands must be carried out is given in Fig. 4.3.

Excerpts from one participant's think-aloud protocol for this task illustrating the role of opportunism are given in Table 4.1.

A second model of planning is based on the case-based approach to reasoning put forward by Hammond (1989; Hammond & Seifert, 1994). As Hammond (1989) put it, "Case-based planning is the idea of planning as remembering" (p. 1). In other words, planning is a matter of remembering previous plans, their successes, their failures, and their "repairs." Thus, planning is based on memory—memory for concrete instances and entire *patterns* of goals rather than for individual goals (or plans) recombined in the process of planning (though cf. the concept of a MOP developed earlier). As Hammond (1989) put it, "we want a planner that can learn and recall complex plans rather than having to repeat work it has already done" (p. 10). Thus, for example, an individual may plan a trip or, to use Hammond's (1989) example, build a car—both of these involve complex plans that are better implemented by retrieving a similar complex plan than by recalling components of that plan and reconstructing it or constructing it anew. In addition, planning involves learning from past goal failures and successes, that is, learning from experience. In fact, plans are assumed to be organized around goals and goal failures (see Schank, 1982a); and the initial formulation of a plan entails trying to anticipate

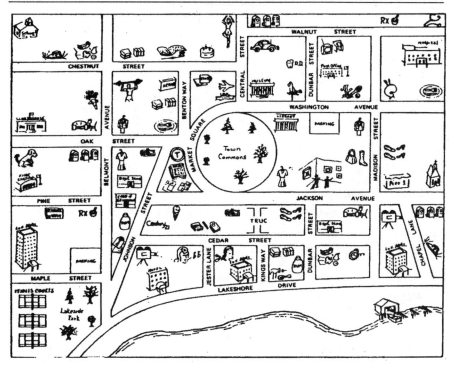

FIG. 4.3.   The map of the town given to participants by Hayes-Roth and Hayes-Roth. From "A Cognitive Model of Planning," by B. Hayes-Roth & F. Hayes-Roth, 1979, *Cognitive Science, 3,* 278–280. Copyright © 1979 by Cognitive Science Society, Inc. Reprinted with permission.

problems in order to avoid these failures. Thus, for example, you may recall that the last time you tried to get to a destination by driving on the freeway during rush hour, you arrived late. As a result, you may plan to leave earlier, or try an alternate route, or agree to meet someone halfway in between. Hammond (1989) uses the example that one may determine, on the basis of a past experience with stir-frying broccoli and beef, that trying to stir-fry chicken with snow peas will not work because the snow peas will get soggy; so you would draw on your past plan failure to determine that you must stir-fry the two ingredients separately.

The important point here is that planning is based on memory, and memory for specific cases at that. (Additionally, Hammond, 1989, also underlined the role of TOPs—in this case, general *planning* TOPs, or a description of a type of problem along with strategies for dealing with it—of which the current case is an instance.) Hammond's program is called *CHEF,* and it modifies recipes on the basis of previous plan failures. Specifically, CHEF, or case-based planners in general, have four sorts of memory: *plan*

TABLE 4.1

Excerpts from a Planning Protocol

1. Let's go back down the errand list. Pick up medicine for the dog at veterinary supplies. That's definitely a primary, anything taking care of health. Fan belt for refrigerator. Checking out two out of three luxury apartments. It's got to be a secondary, another browser. Meet the friend at one of the restaurants for lunch. All right. Now, that's going to be able to be varied I hope. That's a primary though because it is an appointment, something you have to do. Buy a toy for the dog at the pet store. If you pass it, sure. If not, the dog can play with someone else. Movie in one of the movie theaters. Better write that down, those movie times, 1, 3, or 5. Write that down on my sheet just to remember. And that's a primary because it's something I have to do. Pick up the watch at the watch repair. That's one of those borderline ones. Do you need your watch or not? Give it a primary. Special order a book at the bookstore.

2. We're having an awful lot of primaries in this one. It's going to be a busy day.

3. Fresh vegetables at the grocery. That's another primary. You need the food. Gardening magazine at the newsstand. Definitely secondary. All the many obligations of life.

4. Geez, can you believe all these primaries?

5. All right. We are now at the health club.

6. What is going to be the closest one?

7. The appliance store is a few blocks away. The medicine for the dog at the vet's office isn't too far away. Movie theaters—let's hold off on that for a little while. Pick up the watch. That's all the way across town. Special order a book at the bookstore.

8. Probably it would be best if we headed in a southeasterly direction. Start heading this way. I can see later on there are a million things I want to do in that part of town.

[The experimenter mentions that he has overlooked the nearby restaurant and flower shop]

9. Oh, how foolish of me. You're right. I can still do that and still head in the general direction.

10. But, then again, that puts a whole new light on things. We do have a bookstore. We do have ... OK. Break up town into sections. We'll call them northwest and southeast. See how many primaries are in that section. Down here in the southeast section, we have the grocery store, the watch repair and the movie theater. In the northwest section we have the grocery store, he bookstore, the flower shop, the vet's shop, and the restaurant.

11. And since we are leaving at 11:00, we might be able to get those chores done so that some time when I'm in the area, hit that restaurant. Let's try for that. Get as many of those out of the way as possible. We really could have a nice day here.

12. OK. First choose number one. At 11:00 we leave the health club. Easily, no doubt about it, we can be right across the street in 5 minutes to the flower shop. Here we go. Flower shop at 11:05. Let's give ourselves 10 minutes to

174

browse through some bouquets and different floral arrangements. You know, you want to take care in sending the right type of flowers. That's something to deal with personal relationships.

13. At 11:10 we go north on Belmont Avenue to the Chestnut Street intersection with Belmont and on the northwest corner is a grocery.

14. Oh, real bad. Don't want to buy the groceries now because groceries rot. You're going to be taking them with you all day long. Going to have to put the groceries way towards the end.

15. And that could change it again. This is not one of my days. I have those every now and again. Let's go with our original plan. Head to the southeast corner.

16. Still leaving the flower shop at 11:10. And we are going to go to the vet's shop next for medicine for the dog. We'll be there at 11:15, but out by 11:20. The vet's shop.

17. Proceeding down Oak Street. I think it would be, let's give ourselves a little short cut.

18. Maybe we'll knock off a secondary task too.

. . .

19. Third item will be the newsstand since we are heading in that direction. Often I like to do that. I know buying a gardening magazine is hardly a primary thing to do, but since I'm heading that way, it's only going to take a second. Let's do it. Get it out of the way. Sometimes you'll find that at the end of the day you've done all of the primary stuff, but you still have all of those little nuisance secondary items that you wish you would have gotten done. So, 11:20 we left the vet's office. We should arrive 11:25 at the newsstand. At 11:30 we've left the newsstand...

Note. From "A Cognitive Model of Planning," by B. Hayes-Roth & F. Hayes-Roth, 1979, *Cognitive Science, 3*, p. 278–280. Copyright © 1979 by Cognitive Science Society, Inc. Reprinted with permission.

memory, failure memory, modifier memory (or memory for means of altering plans to reach a goal), and *repair memory* (or memory for strategies for repairing plan failures). Plan memory involves assessing the similarity between past and current goals and ordering goals based on the difficulty of incorporating them into a plan, with more difficult (e.g., making the dish into a stir-fry) taking precedence over less difficult ones (e.g., making a dish taste hot).

There is another feature of Hammond's formulation that is worth noting. Specifically, not only does planning depend on memory for previous cases or plans, but *learning* also depends on planning. That is, experiences are organized and indexed in memory in a way that they can best be used in the future; and learning involves finding ways to best index experiences (plans) for future use, including plan failures (and explanations of these failures) to be avoided in the future. Such a view is consistent with the general functional emphasis of the Schank–Abelson tradition (see esp. Schank & Abelson, 1995), as well as my earlier discussion of prospective memory.

More recently, Hammond and Seifert (1994; Patalano & Seifert, 1997) proposed a model of *opportunistic planning,* derived from the notion of opportunism in the B. Hayes-Roth and Hayes-Roth (1979) model. Specifically, according to this new viewpoint, such planning involves seeing how a goal in memory is applicable to one's current circumstances. The planner draws on opportunities in the process of *executing* plans as well as in the planning itself (e.g., noticing a bookstore while driving past it and remembering that you wanted to pick up the latest John Grisham novel). In order to take advantage of these opportunities, the earlier suspended goal (e.g., reading the book) must be indexed in such a way that the suspended plans are connected to the representation of opportunities in memory. Thus, to use the bookstore example, the person who is interested in the book (but did not have it to read) must, at the time of this blockage, think about the opportunities to buy a copy of the book so that this opportunity will be noticed later. This storage of the opportunity helps to solve the problem of how to recognize opportunities as being relevant to the suspended plan when they occur. The conditions represented in memory and sought for in the new situation are familiar ones: resources, tools, locations, agents, skills, and time constraints. This monitoring of situational features bears a clear similarity to Schank's (1982a) discussion of monitoring features for noticing TOPs.

The planner–simulation that Hammond and Seifert (1994) described is a trucking system (named *TRUCKER*) that must schedule orders and assign routes to its trucks. Generally, trucks are arranged in a queue. However, opportunism is demonstrated when the central planner changes a route or constructs a new one if a previous route does not work, or sends a different truck (e.g., if that truck is closer). This simulation is of interest because of its similarity to (and differences from) that by B. Hayes-Roth and Hayes-Roth (1979).

Seifert and her students (H. M. Johnson & Seifert, 1992; Patalano & Seifert, 1997) have reported the results of several studies supporting these conceptions. For example, using a reminding paradigm (D. Gentner & Landers, 1985), Johnson and Seifert gave participants four brief stories to read (e.g., about a pregnant woman who was certain that she was going to have a boy and made preparations for that outcome, only to give birth to a girl). These stories were followed by a distractor task and then by a set of reminders that contained either the full theme (e.g., another example of "Don't count your chickens before they hatch"), a prediction of plan failure (i.e., a second story without the outcome), and one focusing on the outcome only (see Table 4.2). Participants were asked to say whether the cues reminded them of any of the earlier stories and then to recall as much of that story as they could.

TABLE 4.2

Sample Study and Test Stories from Johnson and Seifert (1992)

Study story

Judy was overjoyed about the fact that she was pregnant. She looked forward to having a baby boy, and wanted one so badly she felt absolutely certain it would be a male. As a result, she bought all kinds of toy cars, trucks, miniature army soldiers, and even arranged an extravagant "It's a boy" party. Finally, the big moment came, and she was rushed to the hospital. Everything went smoothly in the delivery room, and at last she knew. Judy's lively bouncing baby was actually a girl.

Complete-theme test story

Harrison disliked his small apartment and shabby furniture. His rich Aunt Agatha was near death, and although he hadn't seen or spoken to her in 15 years, he felt assured of inheriting a great fortune very shortly because he was her only living relative. He had already thought of plenty of ways to spend a lot of the money fixing his place up. Confident of his inheritance, Harrison began charging everything from color televisions to cars to gourmet groceries. When Aunt Agatha finally died and her will was read, she had left all her millions to the butler and now Harrison was in debt.

Predict-theme test story

Harrison disliked his small apartment and shabby furniture. His rich Aunt Agatha was near death, and although he hadn't seen or spoken to her in 15 years, he felt assured of inheriting a great fortune very shortly because he was her only living relative. He had already thought of plenty of ways to spend a lot of the money fixing his place up.

Outcome-theme test story

Confident of his inheritance, Harrison began charging everything from color televisions to cars to gourmet groceries. When Aunt Agatha finally died and her will was read, she had left all her millions to the butler and now Harrison was in debt.

Note. From "The Role of Predictive Features in Retrieving Analogical Cases," by H. M. Johnson & C. M. Seifert, 1992, *Journal of Memory and Language, 31,* 648-667. Copyright © 1992 by Academic Press, reproduced by permission of the publisher. All rights of reproduction in any form reserved.

H. M. Johnson and Seifert (1992) reported that both the prediction and the outcome reminders had an effect on memory for the stories. The outcome cue led to participants often recalling stories other than the target one (all of which had the same general theme), whereas predictive cues led to greater recall accuracy. In a second set of studies, Seifert & Patalano (1991) found that participants showed better memory for stories involving impasses or blockages of goals and that this superior memory could not be accounted for by sheer task interruption (i.e., the Zeigarnik effect). Both of these sets of findings are consistent with Hammond's emphasis on plan failures.

Recently, Patalano and Seifert (1997) presented evidence directly addressing the issue of the opportunism involved in relating a suspended intention or goal to a later circumstance. Patalano and Seifert argued in this article that the "opportunism" studied by B. Hayes-Roth and Hayes-Roth (1979) was fairly limited in that it only involved momentary diversions from a main plan, which was involved in all the different tasks, and in that participants could refer at any time to the task goals facing them (i.e., they did not have to consult their own memory). In their own studies Patalano and Seifert tested the model proposed by Hammond and Seifert, referred to as the *predictive encoding model,* in which suspended plans are represented in such a way as to make contact with the later circumstances in which the plans are to be executed.

In their research Patalano and Seifert presented participants with a set of goals[8] that they were to memorize (e.g., getting a ring off your finger), sometimes with associated plans (e.g., lubricating your finger with Vaseline), and sometimes with the requirement that these participants generate their own plans. In both cases, the plans were structured such that the objects by which the plan could be realized were provided in the plan (e.g., Vaseline). In the second phase these participants were presented with objects that were either cues that might remind them of the previous plans (e.g., Vaseline) or unrelated filler items (e.g., a bin of ice cubes). Finally, participants were asked to recall the goals they had seen during the initial phase.

The premise here was that if goals are encoded in such a way as to predict the actions that might be carried out to accomplish them, then the object reminders (i.e., objects involved in the expected action) should facilitate recall of these goals. For example, Patalano and Seifert (1997) found that participants who were given reminding objects that were relevant to the previous goals showed better recall for these goals than those who received unrelated object remindings (see the above Vaseline example). In a second experiment these researchers found the same results for relevant versus irrelevant remindings even after a 20-minute delay. Patalano and Seifert also found that participants who were asked to remember the goals without a plan and were then given reminder cues remembered fewer of the previous goals than participants who were able to see the goals throughout the study. This latter result is of interest only in that it suggests that the results by B. Hayes-Roth and Hayes-Roth (1979), where the goals were present for participants throughout the planning process, overestimated the degree of opportunism that exists in most everyday situations (where memory is typically involved).

In still another experiment Patalano and Seifert found that the success of remindings held even when new cues were used, *if* these cues were related to the same plan (e.g., consulting either medical records or a driver's license to get information about a friend's height in order to buy him or her a full-length coat), but not if the new cues applied to a different plan. The effect of the related cues, however, was not as strong as that for identical cues (i.e., identical from the plan stage to the reminding one). Finally, the different effect of relevant versus irrelevant cues and objects held even when participants were encouraged to generate abstract rather than concrete plans.

The significance of the Hammond and Seifert (1994) view is that, first, it places planning back within the knowledge structure approach reviewed ear-

---

[8]Patalano and Seifert (1997) make the interesting comment that their scenarios represent a rather sketchy information environment in comparison with the real world. Although this is obviously true, their scenarios are also much richer and more detailed than those used in most psychological research.

lier. Not only does the process of planning call on existing knowledge structures, but it also involves the monitoring of situational features similar to those encountered in the work of Schank and Abelson. The notion of reminding, of course, comes from research on TOPs, much of it carried out by Seifert herself. This research is also clearly related to the case-based-reasoning approach examined earlier. Thus, planning is not a phenomenon separate from other topics in cognition but rather is intimately related to memory for and knowledge and comprehension of events and actions in general.

A Comparison of the Two Models.   It is clear that both the Hayes-Roth and Hayes-Roth and the Hammond and Seifert models share an emphasis on the concept of opportunism, though their conception of and approach to this concept is different. Specifically, Hayes-Roth and Hayes-Roth concerned themselves primarily with spatial and temporal opportunism (e.g., being in the vicinity of a store), whereas the Hammond and Seifert model is concerned with a more general conception of opportunism as making a connection between a present circumstance and some plan in memory. In the original Hammond formulation, planning appears to be quite narrowly conceived (i.e., as simply recalling a previous prepackaged plan). In the opportunistic planning or predictive encoding model, however, planning is conceived of in the general sense of making contact with a previous plan, even if that connection involves a novel object. As I have discussed, this formulation makes clear contact with my earlier discussion of prospective memory.

One of the first things that becomes apparent in reading through these two models is that not only are they different from each other, but they both seem to encompass only a particular form of planning—undoubtedly an important form, but a restricted one nonetheless. Certainly, an individual's usual sense of planning has more to do with creative, strategic, rational "planning" (e.g., planning one's career or planning a trip or a defense strategy in a murder trial). There is undoubtedly a good deal of retrieval of previous plans and actions in these sorts of tasks, but there is a certain amount of creativity as well. Consider the following examples: On a trip to London during a recent sabbatical, I was faced with two situations that called for two very different types of planning. One involved opportunistic planning in the Hayes-Roth and Hayes-Roth sense, specifically, finding a cinema showing a movie I wanted to see that was near a theater for which I had tickets for a play, so that I would not have to travel all over London. The second task required more complex, spur-of-the-moment planning. Specifically, when my usual train line on the London underground was shut down by a bomb scare (and the train back to Cambridge was leaving in 20 minutes), I had to find an alternate route while hundreds of other commuters were trying to do the same. The latter planning undoubtedly required the retrieval of past experiences with these other lines (plus my handy underground map), but it also required putting this information together in semicreative, "planful" ways. Of course, this is precisely the type of planning that Hammond (1989) wished to downplay.

There are clearly a variety of different sorts of planning tasks (cf. G. Cohen, 1989, for a similar point); therefore, the question arises: Is there one existing model, or is there likely to be a model in the future that applies to all tasks or one that applies to the greater number of tasks? On the one hand, it would seem extremely unparsimonious to posit a large number of different models for different situations with little commonality. On the other hand, it is clear that there *is* a difference between planning a break-in at the Watergate Hotel or designing a complex experiment on the one hand, and planning a phone call or a trip to the laundromat on the other. For example, the case-based model is certainly better suited to preparing a fairly routine meal than it is to more complex, improvisational tasks such as a multifaceted errand. However, the amount of opportunism is fairly limited in preparing a simple recipe (unless you have to improvise with new ingredients) in comparison with planning or executing a complex errand.

In this connection, the best example of a task that has been approached by two different models is that of meal planning, which has been treated by both Hammond (1989) and earlier by Byrne (1977). Byrne's article is of interest because it was an explicit attempt at protocol analysis (before it was made popular by Ericsson & Simon) à la Duncker and de Groot. Also, it was an explicit attempt to come up with a study of everyday, naturalistic behavior.

A comparison of the two approaches is of interest because it involves a contrast between an abstract representation of general goals and abstract problem solving (Byrne) on the one hand, and a concrete reinstatement of a previous plan (Hammond) on the other (although Byrne's participants often reproduced meals they had made before). Even here, however, there is a difference in the meal-planning tasks studied (e.g., planning "A three course meal suitable for a dinner party" [Byrne, 1977, p. 294] vs. carrying out specific recipes). Thus, although there are certainly some features common to different planning tasks—setting goals, thinking of instrumental actions to reach these goals, and so forth—planning may also differ in significant ways from task to task (e.g., planning a military campaign vs. planning a night on the town vs. planning what to say next in a conversation).

Given this variety of plans, the question arises once again: How worthwhile is it to try to develop a single, all-purpose planning program? Might it not be of greater value to create a taxonomy of plans based not on types of goals, but on task structure (e.g., long- vs. short-term goals, multifaceted or single-minded, many obstacles vs. few, etc.). (Wilensky's [1983] account of goal interactions is one step in that direction.) At the very least, it is clear that planning is a rich, fertile area that deserves much greater conceptual and empirical attention than it has received thus far.

Suchman's Critique of the Planning Literature. Before I leave the topic of planning, let me note one major critique of the general concept of planning. Suchman (1987) argued that actions, "while systematic, are ... never planned in the strong sense that cognitive science would have it. Rather, plans are best viewed as a weak resource for what is pervasively *ad hoc* activity" (p. ix). Plans may be something that people think of *before* or *after* acting, but do not really play a causal role in the action itself (cf. Skinner, 1990). Suchman (1987) gave the example of someone rowing a canoe toward the rapids. This person may plan her or his course toward the rapids, but "When it really comes down to the details of responding to the currents and handling a canoe, you effectively abandon the plan and fall back on whatever skills are available" (p. 52). Stated somewhat differently, Suchman argued that actions always depend on situational cues and considerations—it is, in Suchman's (1987) and Lave's (1988) terms, "situated"—and cannot be planned as explicitly and systematically as many planning models suggest (though cf. my discussion of *opportunistic* planning). Furthermore, actions vary over situations; thus, general, cross- situational principles of planning are of questionable value.

I return to Suchman's general arguments in chapter 10. For now, the point of interest is that some questions have been raised about artificial intelligence models of planning, and indeed, about the concept of planning itself.

CONCLUSIONS

We have covered a number of different and important topics in this chapter, including event memory in general (which includes eyewitness memory), distortions of such memory, and memory for intentions and planning. Although there are *some* established connections between some of these different topics (e.g., Seifert's work on TOPS and her work on planning), other topics have apparently been developed in relative isolation from each other (e.g., event memory and eyewitness memory). The themes that *do* tie these various topics together are their common concern with our understanding of and memory for events, intentions, and purposive actions.

As we saw in chapter 3, it is also interesting to note the different types of research that have been used to study these different topics. For example, research on both prospective memory and eyewitness testimony has been dominated by experimental studies and traditional memory principles, supplemented in the first case by some naturalistic studies and in the second case by an explicit attempt to tie research to real-world applications. The areas of event memory and planning, however, have primarily been influenced by work in artificial intelligence, with some experimental tests of these formulations. A related difference among these different topics is that research on event memory and planning is long on theory and speculation (though these have been expressed in terms of simulations), whereas the area of prospective memory has been notably lacking in theory.

Finally, in terms of connections with other topics that I have or will discuss, I have suggested some of the similarities and differences between person schemas, as discussed in chapter 2, and generic scripts. On a more superficial level, both face recognition research and Loftus's research on misleading questions have been applied to eyewitness testimony. More important, in chapter 6 I apply some of the research on event memory, particularly Kolodner's concept of E-MOPs, to the topic of autobiographical memory. It is to this topic that I now turn.

Chapter 5

Autobiographical Memory: What, How Well, and From What Periods Do We Remember Our Own Histories?

I was in 2nd grade & my best friend was ————. I was walking over to play on the bars & she walked over to me & she had a new perm. When I was talking to her the popular kids walked by & started talking to her. She was popular and hung out with those kids after she got her perm & she never talked to me again.

I went 3 houses down to an older ladies [sic] house with my mom & my sisters. The lady had made us all dolls. I was kind of afraid of the lady. I still have the doll.

> —Childhood memories provided by participant
> in a study by Markham (1996)

I'll never forgive myself. Even if I want it, I can't. I had a brother, he was 16 or 17 years old. He was taller than I, he was bigger than I, and I said to him, "So, brother, you haven't got no working papers, and I am afraid that you will not be able to survive. Come on, take a chance with me, let's go together." Why did I take him with me? ... When I came to the gate where the selection was, the Gestapo said to me (I showed him my papers), "you go to the right." I said, "This is my brother." He whipped me over my head, he said: "He goes to the left." ... And from this time I didn't see any more my brother. ... I know it's not my fault, but my conscience is bothering me ... it's almost forty years, and it's still bothering me. I still got my brother on my conscience. God forgive me!

> —Memory of a Holocaust survivor
> (Langer, 1991, pp. 32–33)

INTRODUCTION

Certainly one of the most basic and most significant forms of real-world memory, and one that has been central to the debate over real-world versus lab studies of cognition, is what has been referred to as *autobiographical memory (AM)*. Simply stated, autobiographical memory refers to memory for some aspect of or event in one's personal history. Thus, AM includes such things as memories of childhood, college days, marriage, the birth of children, and other events, significant or trivial, in people's lives.

Interest in AM began over a century ago with the pioneering work of Galton (1883) and Ribot (1882; see Conway, 1990a, for a detailed discussion). After this initial interest, however, research and theorizing on the topic largely disappeared (with a few notable exceptions; see Conway, 1990a) for nearly a century—a period G. Cohen (1986) referred as the "hundred years of silence"—until the 1970s (e.g., Crovitz & Schiffman, 1974; Robinson, 1976). A detailed discussion of the reasons for this long "silence" is beyond the scope of this book; but one major factor, as I discussed in chapter 1, was the dominance of the Ebbinghaus tradition, with its emphasis on objectivity over phenomenology and on carefully controlled, operationally defined variables. Similarly, the resurgence of interest in this topic in the past two decades can be traced to the greater openness of the cognitive science movement to new and alternative topics and methodologies as well as the renewed emphasis (again, see chap. 1) on ecological validity and naturalistic, real-world topics and methods. As mentioned, research on AM is in many ways a barometer of the emergence of the field of everyday memory in general.

DEFINITIONS AND CONCEPTUAL DISTINCTIONS

Attempts at Definition

Despite its apparent simplicity, there has been a good deal of debate about exactly how to define the term *autobiographical* in a more formal and rigorous way. For example, what exactly is included under the term *personal*? Is my memory of the tearing down of the Berlin Wall or the assassination of President Kennedy or a friend's car accident autobiographical, even if I did not experience them directly, so long as they are *my* memories of the event (see Larsen, 1992)? If so, then *all* event or episodic memory (of the sort discussed in chap. 4) is, in a broad sense, autobiographical. Does seeing the event on television as it happened make it more autobiographical? Similarly, should only memory for past *events* be included, or should an individual's memory for his or her opinions of the Vietnam War or for his or her personality traits a decade ago? Should only events that people remember directly from their own personal experience be included, or should events in their lives related to them by others also qualify (e.g., the time as a child that you got lost and worried your parents sick)? Does the memory have to be accurate or veridical, or can it be a confabulation, so long as the individual believes that it happened?

Much of this dispute over definitions may seem nitpicky; yet the effort to stake out a separate area of autobiographical memory (vs. the traditional study of memory) and to pin down that area as clearly as possible has led to many such disputes (see Conway, Rubin, Spinnler, & Wagenaar, 1992). Each of the above questions has been raised in discussions of AM or is pertinent, explicitly or implicitly, to that concept.

Brewer's Initial Presentation. In one of the first and most instructive contemporary treatments of the concept of AM, W. F. Brewer (1986) suggested that there are two major criteria for considering a memory to be "autobiographical." The first of these is "a perceived or experienced relationship to the self" (p. 26). This is clearly Brewer's preferred criterion and one that is generally consistent with the lay definition given above. In addition, although others (e.g., Baddeley, 1992a; Conway, 1990a) have expressed reservations about this definition, such a criterion captures the experienced sense of self-involvement or self-relevance of these memories.

The second potential criterion mentioned by Brewer is to equate AM with Tulving's (1972, 1983) concept of *episodic memory*. Episodic memory, as initially conceived of by Tulving (1972), refers to "... a *personal* [italics added] experience that is remembered in its spatial–temporal relation to other such experiences" (Tulving, 1992, p. 387); and this type of memory is to be distinguished from *semantic memory,* or one's general world knowledge. Tulving (1972) also stipulated that "an integral part of the representation ... in episodic memory is its reference to the rememberer's knowledge of his *personal identity* [italics added]" (p. 389). Both of these descriptions are clearly similar to my earlier definition of AM; in fact, Tulving himself (1972, 1983) made an explicit connection between episodic memory and AM, and, as I discussed in chapter 1, many critics have equated AM with real-world memory in general. Finally, Robinson (1976) similarly defined AM as a set of "discrete experiences" involving one's own "participation in acts or situations which were to some degree localized in time and place" (p. 378).

Nevertheless, W. F. Brewer (1986) and Conway (1990a) both pointed out some difficulties raised by using these two terms interchangeably. First, the concept of episodic memory is itself too vague and controversial to serve as a basis for defining AM (which is vague enough in its own right). Second, the term episodic memory has, in actual practice, been used primarily to refer to memory for specific experiences in verbal learning studies (though see Tulving's [1983] own negative commentary on this research). Memories of this sort are hardly a representative sample of AMs in general and are, in fact, antithetical to the concept of everyday memory developed thus far in this book (see W. F. Brewer, 1996, for a similar observation). Third, as I discuss in the pages that follow, AMs do not always meet the criterion of being clearly localized in space and time (e.g., your memory of your first car or of your previous attitudes on a specific topic—see Baddeley, 1992a). Finally, memory for episodes in which individuals are themselves involved are distinguishable from those in which they are not involved but simply observe or hear about (see Larsen's [1992; see also Larsen & Plunkett, 1987] recent distinction between AMs and *narrative* memory, e.g., memory for public news events). In fact, Baddeley (1992a) cited an example (from de Renzi, Liotti, & Nichelli, 1987) of a patient who had lost her ability to remember well-known public events, but who was quite adept at remembering episodes from her own life.

Later Formulations.   In a later, more extensive treatment of the concept of AM, Conway (1990a) outlined a combination of different features that, taken together, identify the concept of AM and distinguish it from other concepts such as episodic or semantic memory. These features include self-reference, the (conscious) experience of remembering, a personal interpretation of a complex event (i.e., rather than an exact reproduction), the extended duration (of retention) of the memory (i.e., years rather than minutes or days), and context-specificity. As Conway pointed out, no one of these characteristics in and of itself distinguishes AM from the other types of memory identified by Tulving or Brewer, but the *combination* of them makes AMs distinctive. Recently, Rubin (1998) suggested another five features that represent "the minimum" requirements for a memory to be considered autobiographical: a cuing event (internal or external), a process of search or retrieval that integrates the other three components of imagery, a narrative structure, and affect. Finally, Pillemer (1998) also proposed five other defining features of AM: it involves a specific event located in space and time; "The memory contains a *detailed* account of the rememberer's *own personal circumstances* at the time of the event" (p. 50); there is the accompaniment of sensory images; these images refer to a specific "*moment* or moments of phenomenal experience" (p. 51); and "The rememberer *believes* that the memory is a truthful representation of what transpired" (p. 51).

It should be clear from these various formulations that although there is some overlap among commentators on the meaning of AM, there is also less than complete agreement on the best definition. The two most central features appear to be self-reference and location in space and time. Even on the first of these, though, Baddeley (1992a) pointed out the importance of distinguishing between the self as knower and the self as object, only the latter of which really distinguishes AM from other types of memory. On the second "criterion," I have already reviewed the reservations expressed by Brewer and Conway, and there is also the question raised at the beginning whether a memory has to be episodic to be autobiographical. For example, is my memory of my father's sunken face after he'd been suffering from Alzheimer's for 5 years autobiographical only when I retrieve it as part of a specific visit to his nursing home? Is my recollection that I hated wool pants as a kid autobiographical only when I can place that distaste within the time when I stuck toilet paper up my legs on one of my early birthdays? (See the discussion of Brewer's distinction between different types of AM in the next section.) In any case, I discuss the importance of the self-reference feature later when I discuss the development of AM as well as the emphasis on narrative structure.

Some Conceptual Distinctions

W. F. Brewer (1986) also presented a useful distinction between several different types of AMs. The first of these is a *personal memory,* or the concrete image one has of a particular episode or event in his or her life (e.g., the time you had the measles, or the ceremony in which you graduated from college, or, to use Brewer's example, the time he had a snowball fight with his sons on Mt. Palomar). G. Cohen (1989) referred to this type of memory as an *experiential memory,* a term that is perhaps somewhat more descriptive; and recently, W. F. Brewer (1992, 1996) himself, in keeping with a long tradition in philosophy (see W. F. Brewer, 1996, for a review), suggested the term *recollective memory* as another alternative. The idea behind all of these concepts is that this memory is an actual, concrete imaging or experiencing of the event—a true recollection—rather than simply a dry memory.

The second type of AM is what Brewer called an *autobiographical fact,* or what G. Cohen (1989) called a *declarative memory.* In this type of memory the individual recalls that something occurred, but without a concrete image or experience of reliving that event (cf. the Wurzburg school of imageless thought [e.g., Humphrey, 1951]). For example, one may recall that he or she saw a given movie but not have any specific image of it, or that he or she covered a topic in a class without recalling any details or images of the event. Brewer's example is that he has a memory that he drove to Mt. Palomar one time, but he cannot retrieve any images or concrete details of that experience.

Parallel to these two types of AMs are two generic forms. Specifically, Brewer talks about a *generic personal memory,* which consists of a repeated, general memory with a generic image attached. For example, I have taught the same class in the same classroom for the past several years, and I have a general image of standing in front of that class (with generic student faces) and lecturing. Similarly, W. F. Brewer (1986) gave the example of a general image of driving north on Highway 1 in the Big Sur area. This concept of a generic personal memory is an important one because (as I discuss later) the way in which similar experiences become combined is a major determinant of the accuracy or veridicality of such memories. The question also arises as to where the image attached to this generic memory comes from. Is it a mere composite of the various contributing experiences, or is it a separate concrete image generated by a generic schema formed from the repeated experience?

The second type of generic memory, paralleling the autobiographical fact described above, is what Brewer called a *self-schema*, defined as a generic, nonimaginal memory of various self-related experiences (e.g., my recollection of going through a major depression or of all the times I've helped out other people) without any kind of specific image attached. This self-schema, in other words, consists of all of the generic knowledge or stored memories that I have of my experiences that do not have any image, concrete or general, attached to them. This concept is the trickiest of the four because, as I discuss in the next chapter, the evidence reported thus far (e.g., Klein & Loftus, 1993) that simple self-judgments or generic self-knowledge is *not* related to specific memories in any direct way. In addition, the term self-schema has been used in a slightly different way in the area of social cognition (e.g., Markus, 1977). Nevertheless, the idea of generic self-related memories without associated images seems reasonable enough, even if Brewer's specific terminology is a bit problematic.

All of these types of AMs can be distinguished from semantic memory and generic perceptual memories (e.g., memory for a face or, to use Brewer's example, memory for the state of California), neither of which, presumably, involves a great deal of self-relevance.

Like Conway, Brewer also listed a number of, in this case, *phenomenological* characteristics of AM. (See W. F. Brewer's, [1992, 1996] recent arguments for studying the phenomenological aspects of memory in general.) These characteristics include the experience of reliving or replaying the experience "in one's head," the frequent accompaniment by strong visual imagery, the ability to assign a specific date and location to the event, the belief that the episode was *personally* experienced in the past, and a strong belief in the truth or veridicality of that memory. As an example of this last point, W. F. Brewer (1986) suggested that someone could convince him that his sister's wedding occurred on a date other than the one he remembers, but it would be difficult to convince him that a particular event that he remembers occurring (i.e., he and his sons soaping his sister's car) did not occur (cf. Pillemer's [1998] fifth requirement of AM, cited earlier).

On the issue of imagery (see the review by W. F. Brewer, 1996), Conway (1988; Conway & Bekerian, 1987) speculated that imagery may represent an optimal mode for searching such memories, in that images are easy to generate, and they also make possible an economical search of both their features and the relations among features. (See M. B. Brewer's [1988] similar argument in chap. 3 for the advantages of pictoliteral representations in impression formation.) Such images may also allow access to further detail—for instance, the appearance of a particular person in an image of a wedding may allow one to "probe" other facts about that person or his or her role in the wedding ceremony. Along similar lines, Rubin (1998) argued that imagery is important in "its role of increasing the specific, relived, personally experienced aspect of autobiographical memory" (p. 55; see Brewer's discussion of recollective memory and of the phenomenological characteristics of AM). As discussed in the last chapter, these kind of details, along with spatial and temporal context, are important clues to determining the external reality status of the AMs.

Now it is possible to argue that some of these characteristics are, in fact, illusory. For example, E. Loftus and G. Loftus (1980; see also Neisser, 1967, and Squire, 1987) reviewed evidence from the classic research by Penfield (e.g., Penfield & Roberts, 1959), which suggested that brain stimulation caused an exact reinstatement of permanently stored memories. However, Neisser (1967) observed that some of these memories included recent experiences, and Loftus and Loftus (1980) concluded that few of the patients' reports could be interpreted as exact reproductions. Similarly, Hyman (1999) suggested that the construction of an image is a major factor in creating false memories. Neisser (1982a) also pointed out that one of his vivid memories (that he heard about the bombing of Pearl Harbor while listening to a baseball game) subsequently turned out to be inaccurate (because there were no baseball games in December). Similarly, Conway (1990a) presented two examples of published memories that seemed vivid and accurate to those who reported them, but later proved to be largely made up or embellished. One of these is a memory reported by M. K. Johnson (1985) in a discussion of her concept of reality monitoring described in chapter 4.

> My father was driving through the San Joaquin Valley in California when we had a flat tire. We didn't have a spare, so my father took off the tire and hitch-hiked up the road to a gas station to get the tire patched. My mother, brother, sister, and I waited in the car. The temperature was over 100 degrees, extremely uncomfortable, and we got very thirsty. Finally, my sister took a couple of empty pop bottles and walked up the road to a farmhouse. The woman who lived there explained to her that the valley was suffering from a draught and she only had a little bottled-water left. She set aside a glass of water for her little boy, who would be home from school soon, and filled up my sister's pop bottles with the rest. My sister brought the water back to the car and we drank it all. I also remembered feeling guilty that we didn't save any for my father, who would probably be thirsty when he got back with the repaired tire. (p. 1)

It turns out that although the first part of this memory was accurate, the latter part (i.e., where Johnson's sister went to the farmhouse for water) was false (according to Johnson's parents). Thus, a memory that appeared to be veridical proved to be a confabulation.

It is undoubtedly true that people may be misled into thinking that false memories are true (see my discussion of Loftus's writings on false memories in chap. 4). Conversely, as I discuss later, it is also possible for people to deny autobiographical episodes that did, in fact, happen. Brewer's point, however, is not that AMs are or are not veridical, but rather that they are *experienced* as veridical, and that is an important point to note.

Still another feature of AMs noted by Nigro and Neisser (1983; see also W. F. Brewer, 1996, and Robinson & Swanson, 1993) is that some are remembered from the point of view of a third-party, outside observer. Nigro and Neisser distinguished between these *observer memories* and *field memories,* or those that are remembered from the individual's own, first-person perspective. Nigro and Neisser found that observer memories were more frequently reported for older, more distant memories, and their incidence was greatest for memories that were more emotional and in which the participant was more self-aware. Nigro and Neisser also found that some people can change perspectives in recall, and Robinson (1993) reported that this shift was accomplished more easily for more recent and more vivid AMs. Finally, Robinson and Swanson (1993) found that the changes in perspective from field to observer led to decreases in reported affect, whereas the shift from observer to field perspectives did not. These results, which actually parallel findings on perspective in dream recall (see D. B. Cohen, 1974; Weinstein, Schwartz, & Arkin, 1991), suggest that changes in perspective may serve the function of coping or coming to grips with emotion.

Inherent Difficulties in Studying Autobiographical Memory. I should also note that there are some inherent difficulties in studying AM that are not found in more controlled laboratory research on memory (or in some cases, in the study of other forms of real-world memory). I have already touched on one of these difficulties: the problem of determining the accuracy of such memories. Can the recall of an experience, such as that cited above by Johnson, even reasonably be called a memory if it is found to be made up or confabulated? (See Barclay, 1993a; Bruner, 1990; and D. Edwards & Potter, 1992, for arguments *against* the importance of establishing the empirical *truth* of AMs, and see Baddeley, 1992b; Neisser, 1992; and M. Ross, 1997, for opposing views.) Further, because the original event often occurs out of sight of a third party, how can one check on the validity of such an event? Another obvious difficulty is the lack of control over the variables that may influence such memories (e.g., the vividness of the experience, the emotion aroused by the event, its subjective or objective consequences for the individual, even the number of times the event or similar events have occurred)—all factors that have been found to influence AMs—although such factors *can* be studied as covariates (see W. F. Brewer, 1988; Thompson, Skowronski, Larsen, & Betz, 1996; Wagenaar, 1986). Another problem is the different results obtained from the various techniques used to elicit AMs (see W. F. Brewer, 1988, for a critique of some of the most frequently used methods in studying AMs). Finally, in the study of AM it is often difficult to distinguish between personal memories on the one hand, and socially or personally derived theories (e.g., of personal change and stability [see M. Ross, 1989a] or of scripts [see Ornstein, Shapiro, Clubb, Follmer, & Baker-Ward, 1997]) or information and beliefs imposed on us by other people (e.g., by our parents, a therapist, a police interrogator; see chap. 4) on the other. This final point clearly relates to my discussion in chapter 1 of the social nature of memory and cognition in general.

SOME GENERAL MODELS AND RESEARCH ON THE NATURE AND ACCURACY OF AUTOBIOGRAPHICAL MEMORY

Model 1: The Copy Model

For heuristic purposes, and for the purpose of addressing the topic of accuracy in particular, W. F. Brewer (1986) outlined three different models of AM. These three models are a simple *copy model,* a *schema* or *reconstructive memory model,* and what Brewer called a *partially reconstructive model.* The pure copy model is the sort that has dominated the memory area for most of its history. According to this viewpoint, individuals actually retrieve fairly veridical copies of the original episodes or of their experiences of them. The major attractions of this model, according to Brewer, other than its historical precedent, are the *perceived* veridicality of such memories (i.e., the experienced-reliving and perceived-accuracy features referred to above) and the fact that AMs often include seemingly irrelevant details, which would presumably be filtered out by a schema or reconstructive memory model (see Alba & Hasher, 1983; Taylor & Crocker, 1981).

One example of such a copy viewpoint is the original article by R. Brown and Kulik (1977) on *flashbulb memories,* or vivid memory for events, usually public ones (e.g., the assassination of John F. Kennedy) and individual's personal experiences of these events (see Conway, 1995, for a review of the rather extensive research literature on this topic). The term *flashbulb memory* was introduced by Brown and Kulik to describe a memory for our personal experience of an event (e.g., an assassination or an earthquake), a memory that not only includes a great deal of detail (much of it irrelevant to the event itself), but also is so clear and vivid that, as I discussed earlier, the perceiver has the impression that he or she has personally experienced the remembered event. In their original study, which was motivated in part by an *Esquire* article on peoples' clear memory for the Kennedy assassination, Brown and

Kulik presented participants with nine political events (plus one personal one) that were presumed to have differential importance or personal *consequentiality* for different participants. For example, the assassinations of Martin Luther King, Malcolm X, and Medgar Evers were assumed to be of greater consequence for Black participants than for White ones. In point of fact, Blacks *did* rate these three events as significantly more consequential than did White participants and reported significantly more flashbulb memories for these assassinations, as well as the attempted assassination of George Wallace (see Table 5.1). At the same time, both races reported the greatest number of overall flashbulb memories for the John F. Kennedy assassination, although Blacks rated the assassination of Martin Luther King as being more consequential for them. Finally, Brown and Kulik coded participants' memories in terms of six common or *canonical* categories: place, ongoing event, informant, affect in others, own affect, and aftermath. Brown and Kulik reported that participants recalled an average two to three of these categories for these public events, with an average of over four for the JFK assassination. Furthermore, the number of categories recalled was correlated with the rated consequentiality of the event.

Brown and Kulik (1977) argued that flashbulb memories are the result of a particular kind of encoding experience. Specifically, events that surprise the perceiver and are consequential lead to the formation of flashbulb memories. The degree to which such memories are elaborated is simply a function of the degree of personal consequentiality, although rehearsal also plays a role (see Woll & Breitenbach, 1998, for evidence against this account). Brown and Kulik (1977) also proposed a controversial neuroanatomical account in which the limbic system evaluates the "biological significance" of the event and then, if the event is determined to be significant, starts a sequence of events that results in a memory being formed for all "brain events" occurring at the time. Following Livingston (1967), Brown and Kulik described this discharge as a *Now Print!* mechanism developed in our evolutionary past to make sure that humans remember events that are of great personal consequence and critical for our survival. This neurobiological account is not important here, but the idea of a Now Print! mechanism is clearly consistent with the pure copy model. (See Neisser, 1982a, for an alternative, more reconstructive account of flashbulb memories, which implicates the role of the narrative format in which such memories are recounted as explaining the canonical categories described by Brown and Kulik.)

The major arguments *against* the pure copy model (and flashbulb memories), and at the same time *in favor of* the alternative schema model, include the fact already alluded to that AMs are often *not* veridical (see my discussion of the memory distortion viewpoint in the last chapter). Frequently cited examples of this observation include instances of the apparently erroneous flashbulb memory—what Neisser and Harsch (1992) labeled a *phantom flashbulb*—by Neisser (1982a) of first hearing about the bombing of

TABLE 5.1

Ratings of Consequentiality and Number of Flashbulb Memories (FMs) Reported by Blacks and Whites for Ten Different Events

Event	Black participants (N = 40)		White participants (N = 40)	
	Consequentiality	No. reporting FMs	Consequentiality	No. reporting FMs
Medgar Evans assassination	3.00	5	1.39	0
John F. Kennedy assassination	3.81	40	3.39	39
Malcolm X assassination	3.40	14	1.49	1
Martin Luther King assassination	4.34	30	2.88	14
Robert F. Kennedy assassination	3.56	20	4.08	25
Ted Kennedy (Chappaquiddick)	2.16	10	2.07	13
George Wallace shooting				
Gerald Ford shooting	1.63	16	1.88	23
Gen. Francisco Franco death	1.29	13	1.55	17
Personal, unexpected shock	4.22	32	3.68	37

Pearl Harbor (cited earlier), and a similar false flashbulb memory reported by Linton (1975) of an acquaintance of hers who implicated Linton in her memory of the JFK assassination although Linton could document that she was not in the same place as this acquaintance on that occasion. Other examples of reconstructed or inaccurate memories include Neisser's (1981) analysis of the errors in John Dean's memory for his conversations with President Nixon during the Watergate scandal, and the example given by M. K. Johnson (1985) cited earlier. Finally, there is the evidence for observer memories by Nigro and Neisser (1983) described earlier, memories that obviously cannot be completely veridical, and some more recent evidence by Neisser and Harsch (1992) suggesting numerous errors when participants tried to recall their flashbulb memories of the *Challenger* disaster 32–34 months later.

W. F. Brewer (1986) raised a number of rebuttals to these arguments. Specifically, Brewer argued that most of the evidence against the copy model is more or less anecdotal, and even some of those anecdotes are arguable. For example, in response to Neisser's Pearl Harbor story, Thompson and Cowan (1986) described an interview with the sports announcer, Red Barber, that indicated that two football teams with the same names as baseball teams (i.e., the Giants and the Dodgers) really did play a football game on December 7, 1941, a game that was interrupted by an announcement of the bombing of Pearl Harbor. Thompson and Cowan therefore argued (and Neisser, 1986, himself concurred) that Neisser's memory was actually accurate, except for the understandable mixup in the sport (see Neisser's [1986] attempt to account for this latter mixup). In addition, W. F. Brewer (1986) questioned Neisser's widely cited example of the errors in John Dean's memory for Watergate, because many of the details of Dean's account could not be validated and because other memories were the result of repeated attempts to recall events (see Hirst & Gluck's [1999] recent reconceptualization of Dean's memory in terms of conversational analysis). As I discuss later, Brewer considers such repetition to be a major source of errors in AM. Finally, it should be noted that several recent reviews of memory for personal and emotional events (e.g., Brewin, Andrews, & Gottlib, 1993; Heuer & Reisberg, 1992; Pillemer, 1998), including early childhood memories (Howes, Siegel, & Brown, 1993) have concluded that such memory is fairly accurate (as opposed to the memory distortion position reviewed in chap. 4).

Model 2: A Schema or Reconstructive Memory Model

The schema or reconstructive memory model (see chap. 1) proposes that AMs are reconstructed from memory fragments, or are generated from a general schema of, for example, baseball games or high school dances or midterm exams. The arguments for this schema alternative are essentially the same as the arguments *against* the pure copy model just reviewed; and the arguments against this schema model are the same or similar to those *for* that copy model. There is also, however, a reasonable amount of research evidence that bears directly on this reconstructive model. For instance, Barclay and his associates (e.g., C. R. Barclay, 1986, 1993a, 1996; C. R. Barclay & Wellman, 1986) conducted a series of studies examining the nature of recognition errors for AMs. Barclay and Wellman, for example, had six participants write down three memorable events in their lives, 5 days a week, for over 2½ years, with recognition tests conducted at 3-month intervals. These recognition tests consisted of 18 original memories, 9 foils with the emotion or evaluation of the original memory changed, 9 foils with some descriptive details of the original changed, and 9 taken from the experiences of other participants (see Table 5.2 for examples). The major results of this study were that the three participants who continued throughout the entire study showed high recognition accuracy for the original events over the period of 1 year, declining to a rate of .79 after 2½ years. However, these participants also showed a fairly high acceptance of the first two types (but not the third type) of foils, with no differences between those two.

C. R. Barclay (1986) concluded that these results show that "recognition of everyday events results from a tendency to identify, as one's own, memories similar to what *could* have happened in the past" (p. 92, italics added), and that "memories for most everyday events are, therefore, transformed, distorted, or forgotten" (p. 89; see chap. 4). Both of these positions are clearly consistent with the schema or reconstructive point of view developed in chapters 1 and 3, although it is not clear that they are really justified by the data. In two recent chapters, C. R. Barclay (1993a; C. R. Barclay & Smith, 1992) has taken this viewpoint a step further, arguing that "memory is ... a reconstructive process whereby what is constructed is done so as to justify feelings ... internal to the person or emergent through interaction" (1993a, p. 290). The presumed purposes of (reconstructing) AMs are to achieve a sense of personal coherence and a personal history, to establish intimate relationships, and to objectify our own history within a given cultural context. As examples of this view, C. R. Barclay (1996) used the cases of Holocaust survivors who, in his view, are unable to apply any meaningful narrative to their experience and hence experience a kind of personal fragmentation and resulting anxiety. (See C. R. Barclay, 1996, for the narratives of a Holocaust victim and of another Jew who was not placed in such a situation.)

TABLE 5.2

Examples of record types

Original	Foil evaluation	Foil description	Foil other
I went shopping downtown looking for an anniversary present for my parents but couldn't find a thing. I get so frustrated when I can't find what I want.	I went shopping downtown looking for an anniversary present for my parents but couldn't find a thing. I guess I should keep looking tomorrow.	I went shopping downtown. I must have gone to 10 stores before giving up and going home. I get so frustrated when I can't find what I want.	Spent an afternoon in the library searching material for a paper. I must have looked for a dozen journals someone else had already checked out. What a pain.

Note: An original record was used to construct only one foil in a test—either a foil evaluation or a foil description but not both. Original records were sampled without replacement and none served as both an original and a foil item. From "Schematization of Autobiographical Memory," by C. R. Barclay, 1986. In *Autobiographical Memory* edited by D. C. Rubin, p. 91. New York: Cambridge University Press. Copyright © 1986 by Cambridge University Press. Reprinted with permission.

The initial studies by Barclay and his associates had the advantage of testing out the accuracy of participants' memory for their experiences and of maintaining a certain degree of "control," or at least some degree of regularity in the eliciting and testing of these memories, unlike some of the diary and cuing studies to be discussed later. However, there are also difficulties with these studies. First, as in many studies of AM, there were relatively few participants in the C. R. Barclay and Wellman (1986) study and a rather high attrition rate—50%—as well. Further, it is not clear that the foils developed by Barclay and Wellman really constitute meaningful distractors for testing the accuracy of participants' memories (see W. F. Brewer, 1988, 1996, for similar objections). For instance, in the examples of the foils with descriptive and evaluative changes (given in Table 5.1), the alterations seem relatively subtle. Finally, the results reported can be taken as evidence for *either* the schema *or* the copy model, in that participants showed good memory for the originals but also acceptance of slightly changed foils (see Larsen, 1993, for a similar argument, and C. R. Barclay, 1993b, for a rebuttal). This finding of high rates of *both* correct and false recognition is a sure tipoff that something other than mere memory processes are involved here.

W. F. Brewer (1996) recently voiced a number of other criticisms of the reconstructive memory model. For example, in his own study of memory for randomly sampled AMs (to be reviewed in chap. 6), W. F. Brewer (1988) found very few errors that could be considered "reconstructive"; instead, most of the errors observed were due to retrieval failures (i.e., retrieving an event that actually occurred, but in response to the wrong cue). Brewer also reported evidence from the same study indicating that inferences were given moderate to low ratings on imagery. In contrast, recent research in memory for both words (e.g., Roediger & McDermott, 1995) and events (e.g., Lampinen, 1996; Loftus et al., 1996; see chap. 4) has found that participants give high confidence ratings to unpresented, inferred, or suggested material, and judge such material as "remembered" when given a choice between "remember" and "know" (see Tulving, 1985a).

Another set of studies that can be viewed as providing evidence for reconstructive memory were reported by Michael Ross and his associates (M. Ross, 1989; M. Ross & Buehler, 1994a; M. Ross & Conway, 1986) on the "construction of personal histories." As this phrase suggests, Ross's work is concerned with how individuals reconstruct their pasts. Such reconstruction is assumed to be based on two main factors: (a) one's present stance on a given dimension (e.g., of attitudes or personality traits), which serves as a standard to which past experiences can be compared; and (b) one's implicit theories of stability and change on these dimensions, including social–cultural assumptions or theories. For example, McFarland & Ross (1987) reported that participants showed biased recall for their earlier scores on a set of personality dimensions in an attempt to emphasize the consistency between their current and past personalities. This finding held particularly for those dimensions that had been pretested as being high in assumed stability. A similar result was found for recall of past behavior, which was biased to be consistent with current, recently changed attitudes (e.g., Ross, McFarland, & Fletcher, 1981).

Perhaps more interesting is the evidence reported by Ross and his associates on the exaggeration of *change* in one's life situation. In one of these studies (McFarland, Ross, & DeCourville, 1989), women who did not display the changes in mood that they expected from going through their period showed biased recall of their *previous* mood and self-evaluation in order to exaggerate the amount of (downward) change resulting from their period. In a similar manner but in the opposite direction, Conway and Ross (1984) found evidence for perceived self-improvement in participants taking a course in study skills where the expected improvement did not actually take place. As before, perceived change was accomplished by participants recalling their previous skills as being significantly worse than they had actually been.

The studies by Ross and his associates are different from other research on AM that I have been and will be reviewing, and these differences are instructive. First, the "memories" involved here are not for particular events occurring at a particular location or time, but rather for attitudes, personality traits, mood, and skills—that is, for general, abstract characteristics. These characteristics are more similar to what I later refer to as self-*judgments* than they are to episodic *memories* per se.

This distinction is of importance for a number of reasons, including its implications for how AMs are represented and organized (e.g., as specific memories or as general summary descriptions) and for the difference between AM on the one hand, and memory for or knowledge of the self on the other (see later discussion of this topic). Second, this research originates from social psychology, with its emphasis on bias and distortion (see chap. 9), rather than from the area of memory or cognitive psychology (though M. Ross, 1989, has acknowledged that much of the research in AM suggests great accuracy). This difference is reflected in the emphasis on memory for judged characteristics rather than memory for actual events, in the emphasis on construction and misrepresentation rather than on retrieval per se, and on the role of social theories or assumptions as well as social, interpersonal goals on personal conceptions of one's life history (see Ross & Buehler, 1994a). In addition, in their most recent account, Ross and Buehler (1994b) explicitly emphasized the social context and the social *goals* of recalling AM (e.g., the self-presentational goals; see Barclay, 1993a, for a similar position).

Finally, there is a recent set of diary studies by Thompson et al. (1996), to be discussed in later sections of this chapter, that also argue for a reconstructive theory of both AM itself and of estimates of the date of the original event. Thompson et al.'s view is that memory for important details of the event starts off as reproductive and later becomes more and more reconstructive, whereas memory for peripheral details is reconstructive from the outset. Along somewhat similar lines, Bahrick (1998; Bahrick, Hall, & Berger, 1996) proposed a *supplementary* view of reconstructive memory, according to which reconstructive processes are brought into play only when reproductive processes fail. Both of these viewpoints may be considered to be partially reconstructive, although it is certainly different from the model with the same label to be discussed next.

Model 3: A Partially Reconstructive Alternative

W. F. Brewer (1986, 1994) put forward a third compromise viewpoint that he labelled as a partially reconstructive model. This model essentially accepts the argument from the pure copy position that recall for AMs is fairly veridical, at least for an individual's *perception* of the experience or episode. It also argues, however, that the apparently schematizing nature of these memories can be accounted for by the distorting influence of repeated experience. Thus, for example, in her classic diary study of AM (to be reviewed later), Linton (1982) found that a major impediment to her ability to retrieve specific experiences was the *recurrence* of those or similar experiences (e.g., repeated faculty meetings). (Neisser, 1981, referred to this phenomenon as *repisodic* memory.) Conversely, the experiences that were relatively unique or distinctive were recalled more accurately and with greater facility. Further, whereas Linton made an explicit attempt to sample more memorable events, R. T. White (1982) carried out a diary study in which no attempt was made to sample in any systematic way. Not only did White find much greater forgetting than in other diary studies, but he also argued that a major source of errors was the confounding of many similar events (cf. W. F. Brewer, 1988, and M. E. Smith, 1952, for similar findings). Thus, distortion does not result from the influence of generic schemas but rather from the assimilation of similar, repeated experiences.

The upshot of Brewer's position is that memories for personal experiences are fairly accurate when they are not distorted by the effects of repetition. Brewer, who in many areas is a proponent of the schema model (see W. F. Brewer & Nakamura, 1984), was impressed in the AM area with (a) the inclusion of irrelevant details, which, as discussed, is inconsistent with a simple schema model, and (b) the perceptions of the veridicality of the memory.

THE DATING AND DISTRIBUTION
OF AUTOBIOGRAPHICAL MEMORIES

One set of issues that have preoccupied researchers in AM from the days of Galton are the questions of how these memories are distributed across a person's lifetime, the degree to which these memories can be divided into regular periods, and the extent to which these distributions and periods can be generalized across people. For example, in one of the earliest modern studies on AM, Crovitz and Schiffman (1974) used a variation on Galton's original cuing procedure by asking undergraduate students to come up with a personal memory for each of 20 cue words. These investigators found that the greatest number of memories came from recent time periods and that recall decreased for more remote time periods. This same general function was replicated by Rubin (1982) using both cued and free recall and a number of different controls, such as generalizing the findings across different cue words, different classes of cues (e.g., objects, feelings, and actions), and over participants. Furthermore, Rubin found that participants were fairly accurate at dating their memories (according to their diaries).

These results (i.e., of a recency effect) are fairly consistent, plausible, and consistent with the results of laboratory studies of list learning over much shorter periods of time. However, Conway (1990a) noted that these results not only differ from the original results of Galton (who used the cuing method on himself and found greater recall from earlier and middle periods), but they also suffer from the fact that they were obtained from a fairly restricted sample of younger college students (see also Rubin, Wetzler, & Nebes, 1986). When this research is extended to older participants (Galton himself was 57 when he conducted his self-study), rather different results are found. For example, Franklin and Holding (1977) sampled a number of different age groups (from 25 to 74). These investigators found that participants showed, with one exception, bimodal distributions in the age of their memories, with the greatest peak occurring during the most recent period, followed by a drop-off in recall until the frequency rose again during the 20–40 age range. Similarly, McCormack (1979), in a study of participants over 72 years of age, found that the greatest number of memories came from the first quarter of life and the second greatest from the latest quarter (though see Conway, 1990a, for a methodological critique of McCormack's study).

In an attempt to bring some order into these seemingly discrepant findings, Rubin et al. (1986) combined the results of three previous studies. In reviewing these combined results and plotting them in different ways, Rubin et al. noted three different trends (see Fig. 5.1). First, looking at memories for the last 20 years, regardless of current age, Rubin et al. noted that recall decreased monotonically as a function of time since the event, thus reproducing the findings reported from college participants. Second, Rubin et al. noticed a *reminiscence peak*, or a rise in memories, from ages 10 to 30, which Rubin et al. attributed to a differential sampling of memories from this period (e.g., due to more memorable events occurring during this period). Finally, the third component of the recall function was a particular lack of memories from the earliest years, a phenomenon I discuss later under the label of *infantile amnesia*.

The findings reported by Rubin et al. (1986), particularly the finding of a reminiscence peak during adolescence or young adulthood, appear to be relatively robust. In fact, Fromholt and Larsen (1992) found essentially the

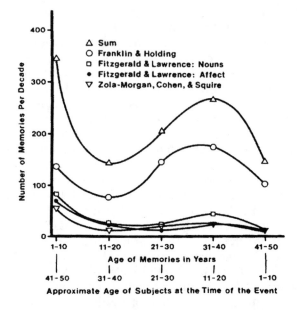

FIG. 5.1.   The distribution of autobiographical memories over the life course. From *Autobiographical Memory* (p. 221), edited by D. C. Rubin, 1986, New York: Cambridge University Press. Copyright © 1986 by Cambridge University Press. Reprinted with permission.

same function, albeit with a reduced number of overall memories, for Alzheimers' patients. There is, nevertheless, a good deal of debate over the best interpretation of these findings (see Conway & Rubin, 1993). I have already examined Rubin et al.'s (1986) *differential retrieval* account. In contrast, Fitzgerald (1988) has suggested a *differential encoding* explanation, according to which there is better memory for events during the 11–30-year-old age range because this is the period during which adolescents and young adults are forming their identities (cf. Conway's [1999; Holmes & Conway, 1999] finding of peaks at several of the different "psychosocial stages" identified by Erikson, 1950). Along the same lines, Schuman and his associates (e.g., Schuman & Rieger, 1992; Schuman & Scott, 1989) found a similar reminiscence peak during the teenage or 20s age range for important *public* events, such as the assassination of John F. Kennedy, the Vietnam War. Schuman & Rieger, 1992 and Schuman & Scott, 1989 suggested that this reflects the young adult's first major experience with a recognized political event. Finally, Benson et al. (1992) found somewhat different distributions of memories for Japanese and American participants, a finding they see as arguing for a more sociohistorical account of reminiscence phenomena, involving the different attitudes held by Japanese participants toward the elderly and the differential impact of World War II on the lives of Japanese versus American participants. At the very least, Benson et al.'s proposal (see also Neisser, 1962) underlines the importance of disentangling general developmental factors from specific social or historical events (e.g., by comparing groups of participants born in different decades). Along these same lines, Conway and Hague (1999) recently presented data from Bangladeshi participants who show a second recognition peak at the age of 40, which happened to be a time when a major political event occurred, namely, Pakistan's invasion of Bangladesh.

At the same time, it is clear that different retrieval strategies—strategies that may be greatly affected by the procedures used in any one study—can have a major impact on the observed distribution of memories. As one dramatic example of this, in the McCormack (1979) study alluded to earlier, where the results are in some way most discrepant from other studies, participants were asked to date their memories—a process that is a necessary part of all of these studies—after each of the individual memories was recalled. Most of the other studies in this area had participants date their memories only *after* they had finished recalling all the memories they could. Holding, Noonan, Pfau, and Holding (1986) argued that McCormack's approach to dating encouraged participants to search for temporal landmarks (e.g., starting or graduating from school, moving, getting married) for recovering memories. This strategy in turn encourages a search in terms of time periods, which, if the first memories are recalled from an early period (and that is a big "if"), then that in turn encourages a greater number of memories from these earlier periods, as McCormack found. Holding et al. (1986) explicitly compared the two methods of dating (i.e., simultaneous vs. afterwards) and found that the simultaneous dating procedure did, in fact, produce a greater proportion of memories for the first three quarters of participants' lives.

Recently, Rubin and Wenzel (1996) compared the temporal function that describes the distribution of AM with the functions that fit research (primarily laboratory-based) on other forms of memory or forgetting. The function for AM stands out as a clear exception to the other functions. Rubin and Wenzel cited two main reasons for the differences between AM and other memory phenomena. The first is that, as I indicated earlier, AM is more a matter of *sampling* from a very large set of memories than an attempt to *recall* a limited set of "correct" memories. The other, less obvious possibility is that AM shows a larger *range* of values for memory and forgetting than do other studies of forgetting (i.e., from 99% down to 0.1% rather than from 99% to 1%). Given the second of these explanations, Rubin and Wenzel suggested two possible conclusions: that the retention function for AM may simply be different from those for other memory data or that the functions would be identical if other memory data showed the same range as AM, both of which would be interesting findings. In either case, data on the distribution of AM clearly stand out as an exception to other data sets in the memory literature, including the results for face recognition by Bahrick et al. (1975) discussed in chapter 3.

Dating of Autobiographical Memories

One aspect of recalling AMs is being able to date such memories. How does one determine when a particular experience or event happened, and how accurate is such dating? The results of a number of different studies (e.g., Larsen & Thompson, 1995; Thompson, 1982, 1985; Thompson, Skowronski, & Betz, 1993, as well as diary studies by Linton, 1986; Wagenaar, 1986; see Thompson et al., 1996, for a summary) suggest that dating of memories is generally fairly accurate, with the *error* in such dating being a constant function of the time since the event. However, it is also clear that judging time is not simply a matter of retrieving a temporal tag or marker but rather is a matter of drawing inferences on the basis of other sorts of information (see W. J. Friedman, 1993; Larsen, Thompson, & Hansen, 1996; Thompson et al., 1996, for reviews)

One of the most important ways in which such inferences are made is by using *landmarks,* either personal or public. For example, Baddeley, Lewis, and Nimmo-Smith (1978) found that when members of the Applied Psychology Unit subject panel in Cambridge were asked when they had attended the last meeting of that panel, dating errors increased as the retention interval increased. However, fewer errors were made by those participants who related their visit to some personal experience, such as "a wedding anniversary, visits from relatives, the start of a new job, or some more unusual event" (p. 79). A similar finding was reported by Thompson (1982) in a study in which college students kept diaries of events happening to themselves and their roommates and at recall were asked to estimate the dates of these events. Those students who used a landmark strategy were more accurate in their dating. Thus, if you can relate an event to when you took an important exam or went to a notable social event, it should increase accuracy for the date of that event, at least in the short term (though see Larsen et al., 1996, for an opposing view).

An alternative dating strategy is to use *public* events as landmarks. For example, N. R. Brown, Rips, and Shevell (1985) found that well-known public events were judged to be more recent, whereas less well-known events were judged to be *less* recent, presumably because recency is judged on the basis of how easily we can recall the event—what N. R. Brown et al. (1985) labelled the *accessibility principle* (cf. my discussion in chap. 9 of the "availability heuristic"). Perhaps more important, N. R. Brown, Shevell, and Rips (1986) examined the way in which memory for public events is related to personal AMs. Using think-aloud protocols to study dating of political (e.g., "Ayatollah Khomeini takes over Iran") and nonpolitical events (e.g., "John Paul II becomes pope") from the period 1978 to 1982, Brown et al. found that participants included a good deal (40%) of personal, autobiographical information in their protocols (i.e., as landmarks; see Thompson, Skowronski, & Lee, 1988a, for similar results). In addition, participants tended to include significantly more thematically related events in their thinking about political events, presumably because, as discussed in chapter 4, a person's conception of political events has a thematic structure to it. Deciding on a date, then, is a matter of problem solving and reasonable inference. Dating of events is based on inferences in which both personal information and thematically related events play a role (see discussion of the retrieval of AMs in chap. 6).

The phenomenon of locating an event in a more recent time period is known as *forward telescoping* (Loftus & Marburger, 1983; Neter & Waksberg, 1964; Thompson et al., 1988b). As an example of this, Robinson (1986) reported a study in which participants first dated their adolescent memories (in response to cue words) without any reference to temporal landmarks. Then, when they came back 2 weeks later, they were asked to redate these memories in relation to one of two different reference points: their birthday or the school term. The idea here was that the school term would offer a structured reference system for memory dating that could both facilitate and distort recall.

In examining discrepancies in dating between the two sessions, Robinson found that participants were less consistent in the school term condition than in the birthday one. More important, participants in the school term condition were more likely to move the date forward (i.e., to date it in a later term, such as in the fall term rather than the winter or spring one of the same year or from the fall term to the winter or spring term in the next year) than were participants in the birthday condition, In addition, in the school term condition, participants' changes in dating were likely to occur in either the same or later term but not in summer, even though the summer was sometimes closer in time than to the original date than was the other term. In the birthday condition, however, the greatest number of changes occurred in the same term; but after that the changes occurred equally often in summer and in the other term. This difference in dating is presumably due to participants' use of the school term to help structure their memory in the school term condition. Larsen et al. (1996) argued that these and other results for telescoping indicate that memory for time or dates per se is fairly accurate, but that it is the knowledge of these boundaries that leads to the telescoping errors.

To clarify this point, consider the following exercise: Try to recall two different romantic, nonmarital relationships that you had (or wish you had) in high school or college. Write down the names of the people with whom you were (or wished to be) romantically involved. For the first person, try to recall whether your interest in this person began before or after your birthday for that year, and then give the actual date. For the second person, try to recall whether the event occurred during the school term or during vacation; and if during school, which term? Then try to remember the actual date for this second relationship. Although this is certainly not a well-controlled study, the argument of the Robinson study is that when you think about the dates more carefully (or check with a parent or the other person in the relationship), your dating of the second relationship should be less accurate and pushed to a more recent date than your memory for the first.

Thompson, Skowronski, and their associates (e.g., Larsen et al., 1996; Skowronski, Betz, Thompson, Walker, & Shannon, 1994; Thompson et al., 1996) also examined the issue of dating in a set of diary studies with college students (to be discussed later). One of the factors that they found to be related to dating accuracy is the ability to recall details of the event. Skowronski, Betz, Thompson, and Shannon (1991; see also Thompson et al., 1996) found a significant relation between participants' ratings of how well they recalled events and the accuracy with which they dated these events. These researchers also found that other participant ratings of their memories (e.g., emotionality, pleasantness, frequency of rehearsal, and the degree to which the event was atypical of the person) predicted dating accuracy, but that the influence of most of these variables on dating accuracy was mediated by the degree to which participants remembered the event itself. Finally, Thompson et al. (1996; see also Skowronski & Thompson, 1990) found that women were better at dating memories than were men, a finding that Skowronski and Thompson attribute to gender role differences in our society (i.e., the woman as date-keeper).

Another observation made by Skowronski et al. (1991; see also Larsen & Thompson, 1995; Thompson et al., 1996) is that participants find it easier to report the day of the week on which an event occurred than the week in which it occurred (see Huttenlocher, Hedges, & Prohaska, 1992, for a similar observation). Thompson et al. (1996) referred to this finding as the *day-of-week* (*DOW*) *effect* (see Fig. 5.2 for an illustration of this effect). This effect appears to be more applicable to personal events than to events such as earthquakes (Friedman, 1987) or news events (Friedman & Wilkins, 1985). Furthermore, Huttenlocher et al. (1992) argued that the weekday versus the weekend dis-

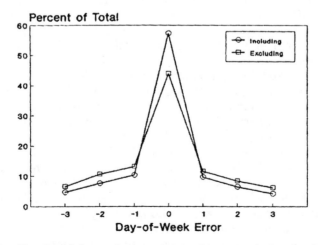

FIG. 5.2. The day-of-the-week phenomenon. From *Autobiographical Memory: Remembering What and Remembering When* (p. 15), by C. P. Thompson, J. J. Skowronski, S. F. Larsen, & A. Betz, 1996, Mahwah, NJ: Lawrence Erlbaum Associates. Copyright © 1996 by Lawrence Erlbaum Associates. Reprinted with permission.

tinction is part of a more general hierarchical structure of time (e.g., academic terms, seasons, eras in our lives; see my discussion later in this section of the more general Huttenlocher model of memory for time and space).

These findings also point to the importance of cultural conventions in estimating time; that is, individuals have a schema for a period of a week and for segments within a week (e.g., the work week vs. the weekend—see Huttenlocher et al., 1993; Thompson et al., 1996), as well as for other culturally defined units (e.g., the academic semester or term or the finding by Koriat, Fischhoff, & Razel, 1976, that Israeli participants responded more rapidly for events occurring near the Sabbath) but not for weeks within months. (There may obviously be cases where the week becomes significant, e.g., this is the week when my pension check comes.) Because the DOW effect holds up over longer periods (up to a 7-month retention interval [Larsen & Thompson, 1995] and, to a lesser extent, even through a 2.5 year period [Thompson et al., 1996]) and for memories entailing either participants themselves or other people, it appears to be based on general schematic knowledge about the structure of activities over the days. In fact, in later publications Thompson and his associates (Larsen et al., 1996; Thompson et al., 1996) focused even more on the general concept of a *temporal schema,* referring to our "general knowledge about time patterns" (Larsen et al., p. 136). The main point made by Skowronski et al. (1991; see also Thompson et al., 1996) is that people use multiple sources of information (e.g., number of details recalled, relation of event to other dated events, temporal schemas) in making their dating decisions.

The issue of forward telescoping has a number of practical implications. For example, Bradburn, Huttenlocher, and Hedges (1994; see also Loftus & Marburger, 1983) noted that on surveys, respondents are often asked to judge the frequency of an event during a period beginning with a specified date, and ending with the present (e.g., How many times have you been on a diet during the last five years?). In this context, Huttenlocher, Hedges, and Prohaska (1988) reported forward telescoping for respondents' reports of the frequency of seeing movies during either a 2-month or an 8-month period—that is, they estimated as many movies in the preceding 2 months as in the 8-month period. Similarly, Huttenlocher, Hedges, and Bradburn (1990) found forward telescoping for peoples' estimates of the time of their last doctor's visit.

A review by Friedman (1993) on memory for dates, including both lab research on memory for short-term temporal events and also research on AM and long-term memory for real-world events, has evaluated several different accounts of forward telescoping. These accounts include the theory by Bradburn, Rips, and Shevell (1987) that argues that memory dating is based on the strength or salience of the memory and that by Thompson et al. (1988b) that proposes that such judgments are based on the number of intervening events. Both of these theories hold that people assume that with the passage of time, memory for events will fade, resulting in estimates that target events that are particularly salient, or events for which the memory for intervening events has been lost, occurred later. Friedman presented evidence against both of these interpretations (e.g., the fact that not all salient memories are displaced, and the occurrence of backward as well as forward telescoping). He concluded that forward telescoping is the result of the "general imprecision of memory for time" (Friedman, 1993, p. 51), the fact that earlier events are often displaced forward but future events cannot be displaced backward—resulting in forward telescoping—as well as the tendency for people to guess that events occurred in the middle of a given period when they do not have other information.

In general, Friedman (1993) concluded that people do not really have a simple, linear, chronological sense of time, and that memory for the time or date of events is based instead on location information, that is, locating the memory by some contextual clue or some information available at encoding, rather than on the strength or vividness of the memory. In addition, rather than direct time tagging or assignment of dates at the time of the event, temporal information comes from a combination of two factors: (a) making connections between the event, other events, and context, and (b) the fact that people have a great deal of information about "the temporal structure of our lives (e.g., our years in college or the birth of our children, or the time of the day or year when we typically engage in a particular activity) and can rapidly extract the general temporal properties of some new experience" (Friedman, 1993, p. 58; see Larsen et al., 1996, for a similar viewpoint).[1]

Huttenlocher et al. (1988; see also Bradburn et al., 1994, and Huttenlocher & Hedges, 1992) proposed a model of temporal memory (as well as a similar model of spatial judgment; see Huttenlocher, Hedges, & Duncan, 1991). This model suggests that the dimension of time, like space, is represented hierarchically (e.g., years, then months, then weeks, then days). The boundaries of the higher level units (e.g., weeks or semesters) place constraints on memory for events at the lower level (e.g., 7 days, 52 weeks). The lower, more fine-grained metric is more likely to be lost with greater elapsed time between exposure and recall.[2] Under these conditions, participants' estimates will be displaced to and constrained by these coarser units, resulting in both forward and backward telescoping. Forward telescoping will occur more frequently than backward telescoping for a number of reasons: (a) Earlier events are harder to remember in general and hence are more likely to be recalled in the wrong time period; (b) events that occurred during the specified interval (e.g., a semester) that are displaced backwards will not be reported at all, whereas

---

[1]One interesting example of such a temporal schema operating at the seasonal level is the observation by W. J. Friedman and Wilkins (1985) that some of their (British) pilot participants misrecalled the Kennedy assassination as occurring during the summer because they recalled that the President was in a convertible and dressed in short sleeves.

[2]Huttenlocher and Prohaska (1997) described this hierarchical model as involving both categorical and particular or individuating information. This description points to the similarity of this model to the dual-processing model of impression formation and person memory discussed in chapter 3.

those occurring prior to the interval may be displaced forward into the interval; (c) earlier events may be displaced forward to the present, but events obviously cannot be displaced back from times beyond the present.

This emphasis on telescoping as a function of poorer memory for extended periods is consistent with the arguments presented by Skowronski, Thompson, and their associates and with a similar model proposed by Rubin and Baddeley (1989). These latter researchers presented results from a set of studies dealing with memory for colloquia to back up these arguments. In the first of these studies, Rubin and Baddeley looked at faculty's (from the Applied Psychology Unit at Cambridge) dating of colloquia over a 2-year period and found a movement of old, temporally distant events toward the middle of that period. In a second study, Rubin and Baddeley found a similar but weaker pattern for colloquia given by the faculty themselves.

To illustrate the principles proposed by Huttenlocher and her associates, consider the following example (adapted from Huttenlocher and Prohaska, 1997). Suppose that a given event occurred on October 1. This date means (according to the Huttenlocher et al. model) that there will be a distribution of scores ranging from August 1 to December 1, with October 1 as the central value. At a "higher" level you may also know that the event occurred during the Fall semester, which ranges from September 1 to December 15. As a result, the values from before September 1 will be eliminated, and hence the range of lower level values will be *truncated*. This truncation means that the central value of that new distribution will be displaced forward. If estimation of the exact date is assumed to involve sampling from this new distribution, then this estimation will also be biased in the form of forward telescoping (see Fig. 5.3). For reasons listed above, such forward telescoping will be more frequent.

In one attempt to reduce forward telescoping, Loftus and Marburger (1983) looked at the use of different types of landmarks for estimating whether a specific event (e.g., a case of criminal victimization), had occurred during a particular period. The landmarks included the eruption of Mt. St. Helens (because the studies took place at the University of Washington), New Years Day, and December 5. The participants in three different studies were passengers on airlines, shoppers at a shopping center, and respondents to a telephone survey. The results of these studies were that dating was more accurate (and there was thus less telescoping) when landmarks were used than when the question was phrased as "Did this [event] occur within the last 6 [or 8] months"? Furthermore, more salient landmarks (such as the eruption of Mt. St. Helens) were more effective than less salient ones (such as December 5).

Because forward telescoping can have such a biasing effect on survey results, other techniques have also been proposed to reduce this tendency. For example, in their early research on the topic, Neter and Waksberg (1964) tried a technique called *bounded recall*, in which individuals were first asked to report on an event in one particular time period. Although these individuals showed forward telescoping for that period, if they were then reminded of their answers for that period in reporting on a preceding period, forward

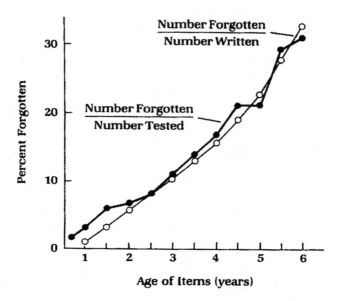

FIG. 5.3.   The forgetting curve reported by Linton. From "Transformations of Memory in Everyday Life" by M. Linton, 1982. In *Memory Observed: Remembering in Natural Contexts* (p. 84), edited by U. Neisser, San Francisco: Freeman. Copyright © 1982 by W. H. Freeman. Reprinted with permission.

telescoping was reduced. More recently, Loftus, Smith, Johnson, and Fiedler (1988) proposed a strategy of sequencing recall from broader to narrower periods in order to reduce the problem of forward telescoping.

Diary Studies of Autobiographical Memory.   One alternative to asking groups of participants to recall memories from different periods of their lives is for *individual* researchers to keep records of their *own* experiences over a more limited period of time and then testing their memory for at least a sample of these recorded experiences. Such single-participant diary studies are clearly not a method that has been encouraged by the narrow strictures of traditional lab research on memory (although Neisser, 1982b, pointed out that this sort of study is not unlike the initial research conducted by Ebbinghaus on himself). However, this sort of study has been more readily embraced by the liberal policies and eclectic interests of everyday cognition. Such a strategy has the obvious advantage of allowing the researcher to verify the accuracy of recall or recognition, as well as sampling from a large collection of memories for the memory test. The equally obvious disadvantage is that the study is (usually) based on a single nonnaive participant.

There are two classic examples of this sort of diary study (see also R. T. White, 1982, 1989). The first is a study conducted by Marigold Linton (1975, 1978, 1982) over a 6-year period. During this time Linton wrote down on cards two to three relatively unique or distinctive memories per day. These memories consisted of brief descriptions that were dated and rated on dimensions such as salience and emotionality. Every month Linton (1982) tested herself on two "semirandomly" chosen events by trying to remember the events and their order and then dating them and judging their salience again.

There are a number of significant findings from Linton's memory tests (some of which will be reviewed in chap. 6). First, Linton looked at sheer forgetting, because in the process of testing herself, she deleted cards from her file that she could not remember. On the basis of this kind of measure (see Fig. 5.3), Linton (1982) found relatively little forgetting for the first 18 months of the study and then found a steady 5–6% decrease in recall over the next 4½ years, for a total of 32% by the end of 6 years. As Linton (1982) noted, this curve is very different from the classic forgetting curve reported by Ebbinghaus (1902) using nonsense syllables; and Conway (1990a) pointed out that the finding of a fairly constant forgetting rate is also rather inconsistent with the forgetting curve established by Rubin (1982). It should be noted, however, that the events sampled by Linton were deliberately chosen to be distinctive. (Linton, 1982, in fact, observed that if you were to read her list of events, you might have no idea that she taught daily, frequently played racquet sports, frequently visited and ate with friends, etc.) In fact, in another study by White (1982), in which the selection of events over a 1-year period was less systematic (or, in White's own terms, was "haphazard," p. 175), recall was considerably reduced over that reported by Linton, ranging from 23% to 41% accuracy depending on how much of his original description of the event White read to himself. In addition, White also found that his ability to date these events was poor, as indicated by a correlation of .64 between actual and recalled sequence of events, where the chance level was .50.

A second significant finding of both the Linton and White studies was that a major factor in recall *failures* was the existence of recurrent events. That is, when the same event or a similar version of that event reoccurred, it became increasingly difficult to recall each specific event. Rather, both became assimilated into what W. F. Brewer (1986) would call a "generic personal memory" or what Nelson (1986; see later discussion) would call a "general event representation." Because Linton deliberately recorded fewer of these recurrent events, it is not surprising that her recall performance was much higher than White's. Linton (1982) also observed that there was little relationship between her initial ratings of the emotionality of an experience and her subsequent recall of it; she suggests several different explanations for this meager relationship, including changes in emotionality over time and the problem of later repetition of that event. White (1982; see also Wagenaar, 1986), on the other hand, found that "the more frequent, more vivid, and emotionally intense events are more recallable, but perceived importance and association with knowledge are not related to recall" (p. 176)

The other classic diary study of AM is that reported by Wagenaar (1986) in an article with the intriguing title of "My memory." (Imagine a traditional learning experiment with that title!) Like Linton, Wagenaar recorded events over a 6-year period, although in this case the first and sixth years served as mere pre- and posttest controls. What is perhaps most distinctive about Wagenaar's study is the fact that he systematically recorded the who, what, when, and where details of the event as well as a critical detail of the event, and he focused his recall on all of these different features rather than simply the "when," as Linton had done. (See Fig. 5.4 for an example of Wagenaar's coding of one particular event.)

Because Wagenaar had recorded the four informational details for each event, he was able to use each of these plus combinations of the four as retrieval cues in determining overall accuracy of recall. In fact, Wagenaar's procedure in recall (which occurred over the final year of the 6-year period) was to randomly choose one of the four cues for a given event and then try to retrieve the other three cues. If this procedure did not work, then Wagenaar uncovered a second cue and tried to recall the other two, and so on until the

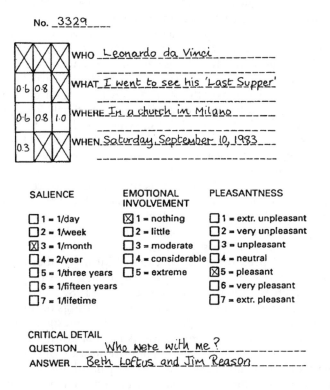

FIG. 5.4. An example of an entry from Wagenaar's diary. From "My Memory: A Study of Autobiographical Memory Over Six Years," by W. A. Wagenaar, 1986, *Cognitive Psychology, 18,* p. 230. Copyright © 1986 by Academic Press. Reprinted with permission.

event was or was not successfully recalled. (Refer to the original Wagenaar, [1986] article to see what painstaking effort he went to in order to set up this recall procedure in a systematic, unbiased way.)

The major findings of the Wagenaar study for my present purposes were as follows: (a) recall clearly increased with an increasing number of cues; also (b) overall, recall with all four cues was extremely high. In fact, Wagenaar (1986) suggested that for those few cases in which the combination of all four cues did not lead to recall, getting other people who were involved in the event to provide other cues always produced recall (by Wagenaar), suggesting that relatively few events were completely forgotten (cf. Loftus & Loftus, 1980). Furthermore: (c) the cue "when" in isolation was very ineffective for recall (see W. F. Brewer, 1988, for somewhat similar results) but was relatively effective when presented together with the "what" cue. And finally (d) Wagenaar also found little evidence for forward telescoping, except in the case of more salient events.

These results suggested to Wagenaar that AM, including memory for older events,[3] was much greater than studies using a simple, unsystematic cue-word approach would suggest. In fact, Wagenaar (1986) argued that one result of the latter procedure is that it may encourage participants to use a backward retrieval strategy, which, as I discussed, encourages recall of more recent memories over more distant ones. Thus, the traditional cue-word procedure used in many studies on AM may give a misleading picture of the distribution as well as of the overall level of recall of such AMs.

There are clearly some difficulties with the Linton and Wagenaar studies and with diary studies in general. The first of these is that the researchers themselves both selected and recorded the events, sometimes (as in Wagenaar's case) in a rather systematic manner. Such recording may have influenced researchers' memory for the events, because it provided an opportunity to rehearse the event and made it different from ordinary AMs (except perhaps for diary keepers). To his credit, Wagenaar (1986) discussed this problem. In defense of Wagenaar, Thompson et al. (1996) noted the similarity between the results of these single-person diary studies and their results for naive diary keepers.

There is also the related problem that in recording these events, the researchers–participants *knew* that they were going to be tested on this information, thus making their encoding and recall intentional rather than incidental and hence facilitating recall (Thompson et al., 1996). In defense of this procedure, there is also the finding by Thompson (1982, 1985) in the study referred to earlier on college students who recorded their own and their roommates' experiences. In this study, the sheer act of recording did

---

[3]It should be noted that the oldest memories in this study were only 6 years old.

not make a difference—the roommates recalled as much of their experiences as did those who recorded their own memories. In addition, Skowronski et al. (1991) reported a complementary finding, that these recorders remember more about their own recorded memories than they do about the memories they have recorded for a close friend.

Still another obvious problem, cited by Wagenaar (1986) himself, is that of generalizing from a single participant (or from the small samples included in many studies of AM). (This is the problem that my students typically view as a fatal flaw.) Wagenaar handles this problem by not making any claims to generalizability. One example of the difficulties involved, though, can be found in Wagenaar's note that he delayed recall for 5 months at one point during the posttest because of the emotional upheaval of a job change decision. Finally, there is the problem of inconsistent findings from different studies—most apparent in the Linton versus White results—using different procedures as well as different participants (all psychologists) sampling different sorts of memories. (See Conway, Collins, Gathercole, & Anderson, 1996, for a defense of diary studies in both the early stages of generating ideas and also for the extension or application of laboratory-produced findings to the real world.)

There is another diary study that I should mention here. Thompson et al. (1996) recently reported the results from six voluntary diary keepers, three of whom participated for 30 months or more and the others of whom participated for 25, 19, and 18 months. Thompson et al. devoted a few pages (pp. 7–18) to a separate discussion of these long-term participants. However, because here and elsewhere they treated this study as either a part of or as a boundary condition for their other 14 data sets, I defer a discussion of these results to chapter 6 in the context of Thompson et al.'s general findings.

THE CHILDHOOD OR INFANTILE AMNESIA ISSUE

One of the oldest, most interesting, and most controversial questions in the area of AM is why people have so few recollections of early childhood experiences, a phenomenon referred to as the problem of *childhood* or *infantile amnesia*. The best known approach to such memory deficits comes from Freud's (1899, 1905a, 1916–1917) theory of *repression* and *screen memories* and its modern-day equivalent of repressed traumatic childhood experiences (e.g., Bass & Davis, 1988; Bruhn, 1990). Without going into the details of either theory (see Pillemer & White, 1989; B. M. Ross, 1991; and White & Pillemer, 1979, for reviews), it is sufficient to note that Freud believed that experiences that are threatening to the young child's ego—in particular, events tied to the child's emerging sexual and aggressive feelings—are blocked or repressed. Like other threatening wishes and cognitions, these thoughts and urges are deflected from consciousness by other less threatening associated thoughts, in this case via so-called screen memories. Thus, it is the combination of amnesia for what transpired during early childhood years and the distorted recollection found in screen memories that were important to Freud. (See Crawford, Kippax, Onyx, Gault, & Benton, 1992, for a translation of the concept of repression into terms that are more consistent with current-day accounts of childhood amnesia.)

On a more mundane level, however, childhood amnesia need not deal with traumatic, painful, sexual material; it may simply refer to the well-documented finding (e.g., Crovitz, Harvey, & McKee, 1980; Wetzler & Sweeney, 1986a, 1986b; see Conway, 1990a; Pillemer & White, 1989, for reviews) that there is a clear dropoff in memory for experiences before the age of 5— a dropoff over and above the memory function observed by Rubin (1982; see Fig. 5.5). Similarly, several sources of evidence—for example, requests for recall from college students for early experiences (e.g., Crovitz & Quina-Holland, 1976; Waldfogel, 1948), requests for students to recall experiences surrounding the birth of a sibling (Sheingold & Tenney, 1982), and asking students to recall early flashbulb memories (Winograd & Killinger, 1983)—suggest that participants are seldom able to retrieve memories from before the age of 3. Thus, there seems to be a deficit in individuals' earliest childhood memories that cannot be accounted for by the memory function established in research on college students. In fact, Pillemer and White (1989) argued that there are two different periods of "accelerated forgetting" in childhood, one before the age of 3, and the other between the ages of 3 and 5 (see my later discussion of work by Nelson and her colleagues).

I should note that Usher and Neisser (1993) provided evidence for a rather different view of childhood amnesia. Specifically, these investigators

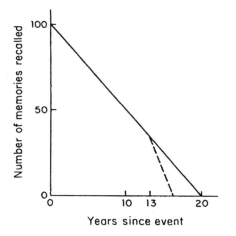

FIG. 5.5.   The dropoff in autobiographical memories for age < 5. From "Childhood Amnesia: An Empirical Demonstration" by S. E. Wetzler, & J. A. Sweeney, 1986b. In *Autobiographical Memory* (p. 193), edited by D. C. Rubin, New York: Cambridge University Press. Copyright © 1986 by Cambridge University Press. Reprinted with permission.

used a *targeted recall* procedure in which participants were deliberately chosen on the basis of their memory for one of four childhood events (i.e., the birth of a sibling, a hospitalization, the death of a family member, or moving from one home to another) at one of four or five different ages (i.e., 2, 3, 4, and 5, in one study, or 1, 2, 3, 4, and 5 in another). (This procedure is very different from the unsystematic cued recall procedure used in most studies of childhood amnesia.) Usher and Neisser found that participants showed clear memories about the birth of a sibling and their own early hospitalization from as early as 2, and they could recall experiencing the death of a family member and a family move from as early as 3 years of age. (See Loftus, 1993, for a critique of the questioning techniques used by Usher & Neisser; see also the further evidence by Eacott & Crawley, 1998, for memories of the birth of a sibling from the age of 2½ where controls were provided to eliminate these and other problems.) The accuracy of participants' memories was confirmed in at least one group by checking details of these memories with participants' mothers. Finally, the authors were able to assess the influence of the stories told by family members or of photographs about the event, which, as it turned out, had a *negative* impact (i.e., resulted in decreased memory for events occurring at ages 1 and 2). Eacott and Crawley (1998) also reported that "family knowledge" cannot account for participants' AM from this early period. These results suggest that the period of childhood amnesia may be shorter than previously thought (see the next section for similar evidence from research with young children), that this period differs for different events, and that there are a number of different influences on such amnesia.

The Cognitive Explanation of Childhood Amnesia: Theory and Research.

An alternative account of memory deficits for early childhood experiences is the possibility of some kind of cognitive deficit or difference (i.e., difference from later adult cognition) in these earlier years that makes such early experiences relatively inaccessible. For example, Wetzler and Sweeney (1986b) argued for the role of the child's encoding deficits in the inaccessibility of early childhood experiences, whereas Piaget (Piaget & Inhelder, 1973) suggested that young children lack a schema or a form of cognitive organization which might allow them to remember coherent sequences of events in the same way that adults do (see Neisser, 1962; Schachtel, 1947, for similar viewpoints).

Perhaps the most systematic version of this cognitive deficit viewpoint has been put forward by Pillemer and White (1989; see also White & Pillemer, 1989), who argued for a *dual memory system* account of childhood amnesia. According to this view, young children have a primitive private memory system that is accessed primarily through situational and emotional cues, and is "expressed through images, behaviors, or emotions" (Pillemer & White, 1989, p. 356), such as a smile of recognition. These memories are of faces, objects, and the like—more like "snapshots" (Eacott, 1999)—rather than of events or personal experiences, and these memories are situationally specific and difficult to share with others. Pillemer and White proposed that eliciting these memories requires the use of behavioral reenactment techniques (see Fivush, 1994), rather than verbal probes, as well as the "Reinstatement of situations and affective cues" (Pillemer & White, 1989, p. 327) such as returning to the original environment or using some kind of fantasy technique.

The second public memory system is one that is socially constructed and socially accessed. This system organizes memories in a narrative format, and these memories are experienced or recalled as part of one's own life history. Such memories can be retrieved intentionally and can be shared with others. At the same time, children also develop a metamemory skill for how to retrieve these memories and an awareness of the importance of sharing. Also involved here is the critical role of language and the ability of the child and adult to follow social conventions. In other words, this second memory system differs in terms of both its representational and its organizational format on the one hand and its responsiveness to social rules and social demands on the other. AM is assumed to be dependent on both of these features.

In his most recent presentation, Pillemer (1998) expressed this dualistic view in terms of both "multiple levels of representation" (p. 23) and multiple memory *systems* of the sort proposed by other memory researchers (e.g., Johnson, 1983; Schacter, 1993; Sherry & Schacter, 1987), particularly to account for dissociations between implicit and explicit memory. The particular emphasis by Pillemer is on separate imagistic and narrative memory systems. This latter proposal, as well as the original Pillemer and White formulation, bears a general similarity to the separate memory formats assumed by M. B. Brewer (1988), as well as the distinction made by both Kunda and Thagard (1996) and Smith and DeCoster (1998b) between two different learning processes based on two different neurological systems (see McClelland, McNaughton, & O'Reilly, 1995).

Nelson's Discussion of the Development of AM and the Implications for Childhood Amnesia.

The theory of the development of scripts or GERs put forward by Nelson (reviewed in chap. 4) suggests an alternative account of AM and childhood amnesia, an account that has both interesting similarities to and differences from the viewpoints discussed thus far. First, Nelson (1993a) distinguished between generic event memory and episodic memory, the latter of which, as I have discussed, refers to specific events occurring at a specific time and place. Given this distinction, Nelson viewed *autobiographical* memory as simply one subtype of episodic memory. Specifically, Nelson (1993a) defined an AM as "specific, personal, long-lasting, and (usually) of significance to the self-system" (p. 8).

The position originally taken by Nelson and her associates, as discussed in chapter 4, was that event memories in younger children are more likely to be generic and schematic than specific, and younger children are "less able to attend to and accommodate deviations [from these schemas]" (Hudson, 1986, p. 103). For example, Hudson and Nelson (1986) found that young children had an easier time responding to general questions (e.g., "What happens when you have snack at camp?") than to specific ones (e.g., "What happened when you had snack at camp yesterday?"), and the content of children's responses to these different questions did not differ significantly. Similarly, Nelson (1988, 1989) and Fivush and Hamond (1990) commented on young children's tendency to focus more on general, routine activities in their recall than on novel, atypical ones. Nelson (1988) argued that "ontogenetically, general script formation precedes episodic memory" (p. 248); also, in a recent discussion, Nelson (1993a) suggested that "The basic episodic memory system is part of a general mammalian learning-memory adaptive function for guiding present action and predicting future outcomes. The most useful memory for this function is generic memory for routines that fit recurrent situations, that is, a general event schema (or script) memory system" (p. 11).

At the same time, however, Nelson (1993a, 1994) argued that the evidence does *not* support the idea that specific episodic memories get swallowed up by GERs. Rather, the evidence suggests the existence of specific episodic memories at a very young age. Specifically, children studied *as children*, rather than as adults, report AMs as early as 2 years of age; in addition, young preschool children "are able to produce organized narratives about past episodes, either spontaneously ... or in response to experimenters' queries" (Hudson, 1986, p. 103). For example, in one widely cited study, Fivush, Hudson, and Nelson (1984) found that 3- and 5-year old children who had been on an unusual trip to a Jewish museum in New York City, in which they had engaged in such atypical activities as digging for artifacts in a sandbox and making clay models of these artifacts, showed accurate recall for these events as long as 6 weeks or even a year later. In a slightly different vein, Nelson (1989) reported observations of the pre-nap monologues of a 2½-year-old girl named Emily, which contained organized descriptions of specific events (though usually not *novel* events) as well as a temporal and causal structure previously expected only of older children. Finally, Fivush and Hamond (1990) reported that 4-year-old children can recall distinctive events or information from more than 18 months earlier that they had not reported in an interview at 2½ years old.

Hudson (1986, 1990) and Nelson (1988, 1993a) reached slightly different conclusions from these results as they apply to adults' difficulty in recalling early childhood experiences. Hudson (1986) suggested that there are two different sources of infantile amnesia, both of which I have touched on. Specifically, Hudson cited problems in cuing these early experiences and assimilating them to generic event representations. The first of these arguments, then, is that simply asking participants to recall their "earliest experience" may be insufficient to elicit childhood memories (just as Hudson herself found that cues such as "yesterday" were not sufficient to elicit specific memories in young children). In fact, the whole adult context may be inappropriate for recalling such events.[4] Some other cuing technique may be necessary, such as returning to the old situation or presenting some picture (cf. Pillemer and White's [1989] similar proposal). I have also examined the assimilation or confounding-of-multiple-experiences explanation, both in the earlier presentation of Nelson's conception of GERs and in Brewer and Linton's account of failures in the recall of adult experiences. However, Hudson (1990) also emphasized that "both novel events and distinctive episodes of familiar events ... may be retained as specific event memories ..." (p. 168).

Hudson (1986) suggested that although there are certain similarities between her account and the *cognitive reconstruction* theories of Piaget and White and Pillemer, and others,

> the important difference is that this [Hudson's] interpretation does not attribute loss in cue effectiveness or changes in organization of autobiographic memory to more general cognitive developments during childhood. Rather, changes in autobiographic memory organization are viewed as a natural result of increased real world experience that leads to richer and more elaborated representation of personal and historical events. These changes are not specific to childhood but are also characteristic of knowledge development in adults. ... (p. 118)

In other words, the shift is due to the accumulation of (everyday) experience and knowledge rather than to general maturational, cognitive changes in childhood (see Neisser, 1962, and Schachtel, 1947, for similar arguments). In fact, more recently, Hudson (1990) actually proposed a social interaction or *interactive learning* conception of the development of AM, according to which children learn two skills from their interaction or "verbal exchange" with their caretakers: (a) the skill of "independently recounting personal memories" (p. 194), rather than simply discussing them with or answering the questions posed by others; and (b) the ability to verbally "reactivate" or retrieve previous events as a result of practice at narrating those events or answering questions about them. As Hudson (1990) put it, children "are learning *how* to remember rather than *what* to remember" (p. 11).

Nelson's (1988, 1993a) account of AM shows some similarities to as well as some differences from Hudson's proposal. First, Nelson (1988) argued that children and adults have essentially the same memory systems with the exception of the child's "inability to reconstruct specific episodes and its dependence on specific cues" (p. 254). Other than that, none of the previous general differences proposed between childhood and adulthood memory or cognitive abilities really accounts for childhood amnesia. According to Nelson (1988), there *is* a basic difference between the development of general

---

[4]Conway (1999) suggested that one possible reason for childhood amnesia is that AMs are based on currently operative self-goals (see chap. 6), and the goals of early childhood are very different from those of the adult.

event memory and the development of the AM system, the latter of which is "a product of social and cultural construction" (p. 266; cf. Hirst & Manier, 1996) and is clearly facilitated by the acquisition of language, particularly *narrative* forms of language. In other words, AM develops as the child learns to share memories or experiences with others; in fact, Tessler and Nelson (1994) presented results indicating that shared talking between a mother and child during an event (i.e., either a visit to a museum or a picturebook reading) is a strong predictor of the child's memory for the event (although see Fivush, 1994b, and Goodman, Quas, Batterman-Faunce, Riddle, Berger, & Kuhn, 1994, for negative evidence). In addition, Mullen and Yi (1995) recently showed that Caucasian mothers and children engage in significantly more conversation about past events than do Korean mother–child dyads, and these differences are accompanied by Caucasian children showing earlier childhood memories than do Korean children. As Nelson (1993a) recently put it, "the initial functional significance of autobiographical memory is that of sharing memory with other people, a function that language makes possible. Memories become valued in their own right ... because they are shareable with others and thus serve a social solidarity function" (p. 12; see Barclay, 1993a, for a similar viewpoint).[5]

On the face of it, there is something ironic about conceiving of AM, which would appear to be a distinctively personal, individual form of memory, as serving primarily *social* and *cultural* functions[6] (although see Hyman & Faries, 1992; Pillemer, 1992; and Robinson & Swanson, 1990, for commentaries and research on these social functions, and Hyman, 1999, for a discussion of the possible social-evolutionary value of errors in AM). Nelson's (1993a) argument is that once AMs have been shared with others, these AMs are stored in a separate memory system. Once this happens, AMs are retained in this system throughout life without it being necessary for them to be shared again. In other words, AM is based on taking a certain perspective toward one's own memory and experience—namely, a social, shared one. In the same way that other social theorists (e.g., Vygotsky, Mead, and even Piaget himself—see Nelson, 1994) have argued for children coming to take a social, cultural, shared perspective on themselves, so did Nelson (1990, 1993a) assume that the function of "reinstating" experiences—which Nelson (1993a, 1993b) saw as one function of AM—or remembering in terms of one's own life history or autobiography is dependent on a social, intersubjective mode of thinking.

There is one other view deriving from Nelson's research that bears consideration, and that is the view of Nelson's colleague, Robyn Fivush (e.g.,

---

[5]Edwards & Middleton (1988) and Middleton and Edwards (1990) presented research and a discussion of social psychological studies of collective remembering, with a particular emphasis on parent–child reconstructions.

[6]This idea is by no means new, however (see Janet, 1928).

1988). Fivush concluded from Nelson's observations of Emily's monologues that these increasingly organized memories, and memories that cover increasingly longer time spans, reflected Emily's growing sense of self as something that is stable and extended in time (cf. Neisser's [1988] concept of the "extended self," to be discussed in the next chapter). Fivush (1988) made the following observation:

> It is the sense of self that is crucial for *autobiographical memory*. Autobiographical memory is not simply memories of previously experienced events; it is a memory of the self engaging in these activities. It is the sense of self that makes the memories cohere as a life history that expresses the essence of who we are ... autobiographical memory serves the function of organizing our knowledge about ourselves, a self-defining function. (p. 277)

Evidence from Fivush's own research discussed earlier (e.g., Fivush, Gray, & Fromhoff, 1987; Fivush et al., 1984) suggests that children as young as 2½ can recall, in a conversation with an adult, even "special one-time events" (Fivush, 1988, p. 281) from longer than 6 months before. This is obviously earlier than Nelson's research would suggest (though see Nelson, 1988), and, contrary to Nelson, such memories require a minimum of adult cuing. More recently, Fivush and Schwartzmueller (1998) have reported on the ability of 8-year-olds to recall events from age 2. In general, Fivush takes a slightly different view from Nelson's, although she *does* agree with Nelson's emphasis on the social–cultural basis of AM.

In a more recent article, Fivush and Reese (1992; see also Fivush, Haden, & Reese, 1996; and Reese & Fivush, 1993) emphasized the critical roles played both by the development of narrative forms of thought and language and by parental narrative style in particular (see Fivush & Fromhoff, 1988) in shaping AM. (Bruner, 1987, even suggested that the self is itself a product of such narrative construction.) According to this view, parents first produce the narrative, with the child simply repeating or agreeing. Then the child begins to participate more actively in the recall of AMs and in organizing and helping to create narratives. Finally, by the age of 3 or 4, the child is able to create a narrative account of past experience without parental guidance. Thus, narrative, as the culturally accepted form of communication, is internalized by the child. Furthermore, parents who provide an *elaborative* style (i.e., elaborate in their narrative to the children) have children who use "more complex and intricately detailed narrative forms for recounting their past experiences" (Fivush & Reese, 1992, p. 123) and ultimately "more complex and elaborated autobiographical memories" (p. 123) than do parents who use a more *pragmatic* or *repetitive* style (i.e., use language to serve utilitarian goals, and who simply repeat questions without elaboration; cf. Bernstein, 1958, for a somewhat similar idea). Finally, there is evidence that parents are more likely to engage in elaborative conversation with young girls, resulting in women having "richer, more embellished memories of past events and a life story that dates back further" (Fivush & Reese, 1997, p. 127).

A Related View: Howe and Courage

Howe and Courage (1993, 1997; see also M. L. Howe, 2000) recently presented a review of the literature on infantile amnesia, along with an alternative account of its origins. These writers rejected, on both neurological and perceptual grounds, Pillemer and White's (1989) conception of two different memory systems, as well as those authors' claim that preschool children can seldom remember, "on demand," memories for earlier experiences. Perhaps more important, Howe and Courage (1993) argued for a different criterion of the onset of AM (though one that is similar to Fivush's [1988]): namely, the acquisition of a stable sense of self, or "a personal frame of reference that makes memory uniquely autobiographical" (p. 329). More specifically, these authors argued that the combination of self-recognition (as exemplified by children's ability to respond to their own image in various visual forms, e.g., Brooks-Gunn & Lewis, 1984),[7] the development of language (including the ability to symbolize the self in terms of such pronouns as "I" or "me"), and the ability to speak about past events in narrative form forms the basis of AM. Thus, Howe and Courage (1993) argued that "the cognitive sense of self most likely emerges logically prior to important language developments, and that it is this sense of self that serves as the catalyst for the onset of autobiographical memory" (p. 320). Stated differently, Howe and Courage (1997) argued that "language plays an ancillary, not deterministic, role in the expression of those memories" (p. 500). Howe and Courage also argued that early childhood memory is amodal (i.e., not strictly verbal) and that language simply serves as a vehicle for *expressing* that memory in an organized (i.e., narrative) way. Notice that this emphasis on the self and a "personal frame of reference" brings our discussion back to the definition of AM discussed at the outset of this chapter. (See also Neisser, 1994a, for a further discussion of the role of the "remembered self" in AM.)

It follows from the Howe and Courage position that it should be possible to have AMs *before* being able to verbalize them. (Mandler & McDonough, 1997, have discussed this same idea in terms of a distinction between procedural, implicit memory and declarative, explicit memory.) In fact, Howe and Courage (1997; see also Howe, 2000) emphasized the continuity of memory development from birth on and argued that many of the features of AM (e.g., temporal order, spatial location, use of contextual cues) are

---

[7]Meltzoff (1990a) argued that measures of mirror recognition do not exhaust the nonverbal measures of the development of the self and that other measures (e.g., social modeling and self-practice) indicate that aspects of the self actually develop even before the 18–24 months suggested by the mirror image measure would suggest.

present much earlier than 3 or even 2 years of age (see Hartshorn et al., 1998). For example, Bauer and her associates (e.g., Bauer, 1996; Bauer & Hartegaard, 1993; Bauer & Mandler, 1989), using an elicited imitation procedure, showed that infants display event memory as early as 11 months (or even as early as 9 months—see Mandler & McDonough, 1997). Bauer (1993) also offered an anecdotal example of a vivid memory she had from before the age of 4 that she remembered without ever having shared that memory with others. However, in a recent study Howe, Courage, and Peterson (1994) concluded that although children below the age of 2 years show some limited memory for prior events (usually communicated behaviorally, such as through a fear of objects associated with a traumatic experience), more "coherent" AMs are not constructed until the age of 2.[8]

Thus, Howe and Courage (1997) argued that most of the components of the self, or the self-as-object, are present before the age of 2 (again see Neisser, 1988a). Although AM is present in some form before the age of 2½ (i.e., in the sense that children remember events from up to 23 months before; see Perris, Myers, & Clifton, 1990), later AMs are distinctive in being better structured and more "cohesive" as a result of the narrative format.

Tessler and Nelson (1994) and Fivush (1994b) outlined a number of disagreements with Howe and Courage's formulation (and with other theorizing on the development of AM in general). First, Tessler and Nelson argued that all the research evidence points to the emergence of AM at around 3½ years rather than 2. Even though children seem to be capable of remembering events from earlier than that, "these early memories are not retained in the autobiographical system of later childhood and adulthood, and it is this discrepancy that poses the paradox of infantile amnesia" (Tessler & Nelson, 1994, p. 320; though see Usher & Neisser, 1993). Along these lines, Tessler and Nelson distinguished between early event memory, which has been clearly established (e.g., Bauer, 1996; Mandler & McDonough, 1995; McDonough & Mandler, 1994) and *autobiographical* memory (see Bauer, 1993, for arguments against this distinction), where the latter refers to memories that persist beyond childhood (Nelson, 1993b). Second, Tessler and Nelson suggested that Howe and Courage failed to distinguish between the different levels of language development found at the age of 18 months to 2 years (the time implicated by Howe and Courage), in which agency and temporal location are acquired, and at 4–5, when children are capable of "connected discourse." Finally, both Tessler and Nelson (1994) and Fivush (1994b) argued that the "self" involved in children's ability to recognize themselves in a mirror is quite different from the kind of self-understanding involved in constructing "personal narratives." Similarly, Fivush has as-

---

[8]In a related study, Pillemer, Picariello, and Pruett (1994) reported that even though both 3½- and 4½-year-old children showed some memory for an emergency fire evacuation of a nursery school that had happened 2 weeks earlier, when these same children were asked to recall the same event 7 years later, only those who were 4½ years old at the time of the incident were able to recall it.

serted that it is not the self in Howe and Courage's use of that term, but rather the *narrative* self that is important for AM. (See chap. 6 for a discussion of Neisser's [1988a] distinction among five different types of selves.)

Another argument against the earlier emergence of AM was raised by Perner and Ruffman (1995). These authors argued, following Tulving's (1985a) distinction between "knowing" and "remembering," that episodic memory in general, and AM in particular, require *autonoetic consciousness,* or a self-reflective awareness of having *experienced* the event that is recalled. In particular, Perner and Ruffman emphasized the importance of remembering that one "perceived" or "saw" the event. Because this autonoetic consciousness is not available to the child before the age of 3–5, children younger than 3 cannot be said to have autobiographical memories.

Howe and Courage (1997) responded to the criticisms raised by both Tessler and Nelson and by Perner and Ruffman. Their basic argument was that even though narrative and self-reflective consciousness or the experience of remembering may be important to later forms of AM, there is no reason to believe that they are *necessary* features of AM (see Bauer, 1993, and Mandler & McDonough, 1997, for similar arguments). Furthermore, the distinctions made by Tessler and Nelson between event memory and AM and by Perner and Ruffman between autonoetic consciousness (or self-knowing) and the lack thereof do not really speak to the early development of "personalized memory," which Howe and Courage see as being at the heart of AM (see Howe, 2000, for an extended discussion of the latter point). Howe and Courage argued that although toddlers' AMs are more fragmentary and need to be cued by others, this difference from older children may reflect differences in their skills at verbal expression, particularly narrative skills, rather than differences in underlying memory. Finally, Howe and Courage (1997) argued that although language does in fact play a major role in the development of AM, language *comprehension,* or what Howe and Courage referred to as *receptive language,* and the beginnings of *gestural* forms of communication (including self-pointing) develop before (i.e., around 18 months) language *production* or *expressive language.* All of this raises once again the question of exactly how to define both AM and the self—an issue that I return to in the next section—as well as the role of language in constructing both.

Howe and Courage (1997; see also Howe, 2000) rejected, in particular, the notion (Nelson, 1993a) that AM requires the development of a separate memory system. Similarly, Bauer (1993) questioned both of Nelson's criteria for distinguishing between an episodic and an autobiographical memory system (i.e., the lack of evidence for the persistence of early memories and the necessity of outside cuing for memories at early ages). On the first of these, Bauer argued that there simply is not clear enough evidence to evaluate whether early memories persist or for how long and in what form they persist. As far as the second criterion, Bauer pointed out that older children also have to be probed sometimes. In general, Bauer questions Nelson's

(1994) notion that there are three distinct memory systems (i.e., episodic, autobiographical, and narrative).

In the preceding discussion I have focused on the differences in the views of AM taken by Howe and Courage, Nelson, Pillemer and White, and others. At the same time it is worthwhile noting some of the similarities as well. (See Table 5.3 for a summary.) For example, most of these positions share an emphasis, albeit to different degrees and in different forms, on the role of language and narrative (cf. Rubin, 1998), the self, and social, interpersonal influences on the development of AM. Similarly, despite her criticisms of the White and Pillemer two-system position, Nelson (e.g., 1993a) also came up with a two-system viewpoint, albeit of a rather different sort from Pillemer and White's. Thus, even though there are honest and meaningful differences among these different theorists, there is also a reasonable degree of commonality.

One question that arises from this review of the rapidly growing developmental literature on infantile amnesia is how much overlap there is between the results of this research and the results of retrospective studies with adults. For example, Howe and Courage (1993) criticized some of the methods for studying childhood amnesia in adults, including those that stress simple free recall (e.g., Kihlstrom & Harackiewicz, 1982; Waldfogel, 1948) or cued recall (e.g., the traditional Galtonian method; see W. F. Brewer, 1988, for additional criticisms of the cue word technique)—measures that lead to rather different age estimates from those arrived at from measures of targeted recall (Usher & Neisser, 1993). Howe and Courage (1993; see also Howe, 2000) also found fault with probed recall studies that may search for memories that the individual has never really encoded in the first place or that seem important to the adult (e.g., the birth of a sibling; see also Nelson, 1993b) but are not to the child. Similarly, Howe and Courage argued, as do so many others, that adult recall often asks for verbal memories of experiences that were never encoded in a verbal fashion. In this same vein, Howe and Courage (1997) reviewed a number of different nonverbal procedures that have been used to study infant memory. These methods include familiarization (e.g., Rovee-Collier & Bhatt, 1993), operant conditioning (e.g., Rovee-Collier & Shyi, 1992), and, in particular, deferred imitation (e.g., Mandler & McDonough, 1997; Meltzoff, 1995). Still another issue raised by Bruner (1994; see also Barclay, 1994, and Conway, Playdell-Pearce, 2000) is that adults may reconstruct childhood memories in such a way as to be consistent with a self-image or at least one's current stance. This last argument, of course, brings us back to the reconstructive memory positions of Ross and Neisser reviewed at the beginning of this chapter.

There is also the question of what exactly constitutes infantile amnesia. It has now been amply demonstrated through a variety of nonverbal measures that infants retain information for intervals ranging from minutes to 1 or 2 years, although the length of the retention interval obviously increases with

Table 5.3

Current Cognitive/Social Accounts of the Origins of Autobiographical Memory

Theorist	Distinctive Features or Criteria of Autobiographical Memory
Pillemer & White	General development of new cognitive abilities
	Socially constructed and shared*
	Narrative format*
	Metamemory and intentional recall
	Language, particularly sociolinguistic conventions*
	Experienced and remembered as part of own life*
Hudson	Ability to respond to cues and to reactivate memories
	Ability to relate specific events to general event schemas
	Accumulation of real world experiences
Nelson	Ability to retrieve or reconstruct specific events
	Narrative format and resulting ability to share with others*
	Social and cultural construction*
	Social, reflective perspective on own memory
Fivush	Narrative format*
	Extended sense of self*
Howe & Courage	Stable sense of self*
	Language as source of symbols*
	Narrative format*
Perner & Ruffman	Autonoetic consciousness, or self-reflective awareness of having experienced an event*

Note. *Characteristic shared by at least two investigators.

age (see Howe & Courage, 1997). However, if the memory does not last into later childhood or adulthood, does it constitute an AM? Nelson (1994; Tessler & Nelson, 1994) clearly believed that it does not. The complication here, of course, as suggested earlier by both Pillemer and White (1989) and by Howe and Courage (1993, 1997), is that most tests of adult AM are verbal, whereas the young infant is not capable of language. As I have discussed, however, Howe and Courage (1993, 1997) argued that verbal methods may simply reflect a superior means of expressing AM rather than a hallmark of it, and that overdependence on verbal measures may obscure memories for early childhood experiences (see my earlier discussion of Pillemer & White, 1989).

There are, to be sure, methodological limitations of the retrospective method. However, the same can certainly be said for research on young children (see Howe, 2000, for a general methodological critique). These limitations include difficulties of communicating and eliciting memories (see Mandler, 1990), the different results obtained from verbal and nonverbal methods, and the difficulty of representing the exact content of the memory through nonverbal measures. Probably the most encouraging finding is the recent convergence of evidence from the two methods on a common date for childhood amnesia—between 2 and 3 years (see Usher & Neisser, 1993).

A Reconsideration of the Definition of Autobiographical Memory

This review of the various definitions of childhood amnesia brings me back to my earlier discussion of the criteria of AM. The emphasis on the sense of self is certainly reminiscent of both Brewer's and Conway's accounts of AM, as is the emphasis on narrative and the awareness of having experienced the event in the past. On the first of these, the debate between Howe and Courage and Tessler and Nelson on the one hand, and Perner and Ruffman on the other, is a reminder of how difficult it is to pin down the "self" and the sense of self-reference, as well as the sense of the experience happening to oneself implicated in Brewer's and Conway's definitions of AM. Do AMs require an ongoing sense of self (as in the example of the amnesic patient who retained some memories of the past but did not retain a sense of self)? Do individuals have to be able to verbalize these memories or place them in narrative form in order for them to be "autobiographical" (cf. the popular distinction between explicit and implicit memory—Schacter, 1987)? For example, is the memory cited earlier of my father's sunken face autobiographical only because I can couch it in a narrative of my visit back to the Midwest over Christmas during the years that my father was in an Alzheimer's unit?

Another point of connection is the distinction made by several authors between mere episodic and autobiographical memory. Finally, there is the debate in the childhood amnesia literature regarding exactly how "extended" a period of time (e.g., a week, a month, a year, or an entire lifetime) must intervene between the experience and recall for the memory of that experience to be considered "autobiographical." For example, Mandler and McDonough (e.g., 1995; McDonough & Mandler, 1994) have shown that infants can recall an event sequence for up to a year. Is this sufficient to label these memories as "autobiographical" or at least as long-term event memory? All of these are questions that remain unresolved in the study of autobiographical memory.

SUMMARY

In this chapter I have reviewed some of the proposed definitions and criteria of autobiographical memory, along with the models put forward by Brewer (1986) to describe the relative accuracy or inaccuracy of such memory. I have also discussed research on the distribution and dating of

AMs over a lifetime, including the intriguing phenomenon labeled as childhood amnesia.

For the most part this discussion has focused on the quantitative aspects of Ams (i.e., numbers of memories from different time periods, dating, relative accuracy), rather than on the processes of encoding, representation, and retrieval. (My discussion of childhood amnesia is a partial exception here.) In the next chapter I examine these process and representation issues, as well as the relationship between AM and the self.

Chapter 6

How We Represent, Organize, and Retrieve Autobiographical Memories

E: Think of a time when you went shopping and couldn't pay for the item you wanted.

S: Um, it happens when I go shopping in Connecticut because I don't have any check-cashing privilege cards. Like, for example, Pathmark will have a special card that they issue. And so I have to pay with cash and I don't always calculate exactly what's in the carriage. So I'll have to put back, like, yogurt … yogurt's what goes. But otherwise I usually pay by check, when I'm in Massachusetts, so I don't have to, you know, worry about putting anything back.

E: Can you think of one particular experience?

S: Uh, yes, Pathmark in East Haven, I often do that.

E: Can you recall one time?

S: Yes, when I was in East Haven, I was … didn't have enough so I had to put back, I think, three yogurts. And the girl was very nice and I thought to myself, "Oh, I should ask for a subtotal next time."

—A participant's protocol from Reiser, Black, and Kalamarides, 1986, pp. 109–110

R.J.:   I sent a letter to my great aunt in South Wales when my younger brother was killed, saying just that: …

R.J.:   Dear Aunt Bertha, I am sorry to tell you that Martin has been killed in a car accident; it's all very sad and we're all terribly sorry, what can I say sort of thing, really.

B.W: It must have been very painful.

R.J.:   It was, yes.

B.W.:   Have you just got one brother?

R.J.:   I've got three now; I've got two now actually, one older and one younger.

B.W.:   What are they called?

R.J.:   Martin and James.

B.W.:   Which one was killed, then?

R.J.:   Martin.

B.W.:   So did you have two Martins?

R.J: We had actually in those days one Martin, then mother had another one and we called it Martin as well. I think she felt a bit sort of morbid about it so she called it Martin so we had two, I suppose, yes, or what would have been two.

B.W.:   So how old was your younger brother, then when he was killed.

R.J.:   He's only five now so he wasn't born then.

B.W.:   The one that was killed in the car accident that you've been telling me about, how old was he when the accident happened?

R.J.:   He would have been about 12 or 13 I suppose.

> —The confabulations of a patient (R.J.) with severe brain injury,
> reported by Baddeley & Wilson, 1986, pp. 239–240

I have a memory of being bitten by a dog when I was three. I have always remembered this: I am standing outside the closed front door when I suddenly see a big dog bounding towards me, his broken rope trailing on his left; a clear and precise picture. I see where the sun is, on my left; there is no snow or mud, the season is late spring. ... But the memory that came back after 50 years was this: the dog has knocked me over, and I am actually turning my head away and burying my face into the earth while the dog is searching between my petticoats and the long black stockings on my left leg for bare flesh to dig its teeth into ... at the time it [the second memory] came back I was actually that child of three, the 'then' was 'now,' and time stood still.

> —A personal "involuntary" memory from Salaman, 1970, p. 24

INTRODUCTION

In this chapter I take a more detailed look at AMs, including in particular their representation and organization as well as their retrieval. What format do AMs take (e.g., images, propositions, schemas), and how are different AMs interconnected (e.g., by means of a narrative or some kind of hierarchy or associative network)? How do individuals access AMs, and how is this access similar or different for memories that people actively search for versus those that come to them involuntarily? Finally, I examine the relationships alluded to in chapter 5 between AM and the self. Is self-concept or self-schema shaped by autobiographical memories or vice versa?

THE ORGANIZATION OF AUTOBIOGRAPHICAL MEMORY

In view of the importance attached by many everyday memory researchers to autobiographical memory (see chap. 1) and its differences from the memory studied in the laboratory, it is of interest to inquire how the representation of AM is similar to or different from that for other forms of memory. (See S. J. Anderson & Conway, 1997, for a discussion of three general memory models as they apply to AM.) The term *autobiographical* implies a particular type of organization: namely, a kind of historical narrative of one's life. However, it seems unlikely that memories are actually organized in terms of a full-scale narrative (or at least that this is true for *most* people; though see Conway's [1992, 1996] emphasis on themes in life history, and Bruner's [1987] and Gergen's [1994] view of "life as narrative"). Even if these memories *were* organized along such lines, a number of questions would remain unanswered; for example, how are different parts of that autobiography collated to form generalizations about oneself, exactly what parts of that autobiography take precedence over others, and who or what agency is responsible for writing that narrative? Is AM organized around chronological periods, around notable events in people's lives, or in terms of major emotional experiences? In this section I consider a number of different proposals for how AM is organized, and I review some of the arguments and evidence for each.

The Event Memory or E-Mop Viewpoint

In chapter 4 I examined Schank's conception of memory for narrative in terms of scripts or MOPs, and I also looked at Kolodner's (1983a) concepts of an E-MOP and of the indices that describe the differences among the various exemplars in a given E-MOP. Reiser, Black, and Kalamarides (1986; see also Reiser, Black, & Abelson, 1985) proposed a similar *context plus index model* to describe the organization and representation of AMs. The first argument in the Reiser et al. model is that AMs are represented in the form of generic knowledge structures or contexts used for encoding such memories in the first place (e.g., going to birthday parties or, to use Reiser et al.'s [1986] example, going to rock concerts). As Reiser et al. (1986) pointed out, the knowledge structures used for this purpose of encoding are essentially the same generic structures used in "planning and performing actions, comprehension of texts and real world events, and memory retrieval of general and specific information learned from texts and from real world experiences" (p. 102). Searching for this context entails an active problem-solving process, which I examine in greater detail in the next section.

Once this context has been located, a further search must be made *within* the context to determine the feature or index that discriminates the particular event being searched for from all other events within that context—for instance, the time I attended the birthday party for my best friend or the time I attended the Simon and Garfunkel concert in Central Park (Reiser et al., 1986). Thus, for example, I might search the birthday party context for distinguishing features of birthday parties (e.g., ages at which such parties might be given or the kinds of friends for whom or by whom such parties might be given); or I might search the rock concert context for where such concerts might take place or with which friends or in which eras of my life I might have attended such concerts). Once again, this search within context involves a directed problem-solving process in which pertinent information such as location, time, possible motivating or instigating conditions, or potential participants in the activity is probed. Thus, the indices used for searching within a context and for connecting the target event to that general context typically consist of the general forms of social and nonsocial knowledge that are used for other purposes (e.g., prediction and planning) as well.

In their initial research on this model, Reiser et al. (1985) set out to validate the premise that activities constitute the most appropriate encoding context for AMs. Reiser et al. first reviewed several other candidates for representational format. For example, one such candidate is that AMs are encoded in terms of the emotion connected to the particular experience. However, Reiser et al. (1985) pointed out that "emotions are experienced in such a wide diversity of situations that information from other sources is likely to be necessary to discriminate experiences with a given emotion" (p. 96). Thus, it is undoubtedly difficult to pin down with any degree of precision a single experience in which you felt angry or even panicky unless these feelings occurred at only one time or on one occasion. In other words, emotions are simply not distinctive enough to serve as a useful encoding contexts for AMs. The same holds for person schemas: a given person is typically associated with too many different experiences to serve as a discriminating context for representing specific AMs. Reiser et al. (1985) concluded that events are most likely to be the knowledge structures for encoding AMs, if for no other reason than the fact that an AM refers to "a set of experiences, and experiences are certainly events rather than static facts or propositions" (p. 95). I should also note that events or activities also correspond to the kind of knowledge structures proposed by Schank, Abelson, and their associates.

In two different studies Reiser et al. (1985) contrasted two different forms of event knowledge: namely, activities and general actions. Activities are defined as "a stereotyped sequence of deliberate actions undertaken to achieve one or more goals" (p. 97). Such a definition clearly bears a close similarity to the previously discussed concepts of scripts and MOPs. General actions, on the other hand, refer to the component actions within a given activity, such as paying the bill or ordering in a restaurant activity or opening presents and playing games in a birthday party activity. Like emotions and person schemas, such actions are generalized across a variety of different activities and correspond to Schank's (1982a) concept of a generalized scene. As such, actions are not necessarily associated with a particular location, are not enacted in isolation, and involve goals that are so abstract that they do not provide a sufficient basis for indexing a specific experience (e.g., the goal of paying a bill is too general to be informative in discriminating a particular personal experience). As summarized by Reiser et al. (1985), "an activity is a self-contained sequence of situation-specific actions performed in service of a goal, while a general action is a single situation-free action that occurs in various situations as part of an activity" (p. 98).

In order to determine which of these types of knowledge structures provides the more fundamental context for representing AMs, Reiser et al. (1985) borrowed a design from Freedman and Loftus (1971) for studying the organization of *semantic* memory. Specifically, Freedman and Loftus looked at the difference in reaction times for a participant to come up with a matching instance when presented with either a noun (e.g., "vegetable") followed by an attribute (e.g., "green things") or vice versa. The reasoning here was that the difference in these RTs would reflect the relative centrality of the two concepts in the organization of semantic memory (i.e., the attribute "green" is an elaboration of the category of "vegetable" rather than vice versa). In an analogous fashion, Reiser et al. presented activities (e.g., "having your hair cut") and actions (e.g., "paying at the cash register") in different orders for retrieving AMs that matched the combination of cues. As in the Freedman and Loftus study, Reiser et al. assumed that if presenting one of these cues first produces faster retrieval than presenting the other first, then it can be assumed that the former is a more fundamental form of organization than the latter, that is, that it provides a context on which the second elaborates. (As Reiser et al., 1985, expressed this, the presentation of the more fundamental cue first should give participants a "head start" in accessing a relevant memory.)[1] Other characteristics of the design were that each activity was paired with two actions and vice versa, and the resulting quartet (i.e., two activities and two actions) was presented in both orders. One final feature that is significant is that a 5-second in-

---

[1] Obviously this priority of activities over actions does not apply when the the action is itself specific to the activity, for instance, working out versus using Nautilus equipment.

terval was provided between the two cues (i.e., activity and action) to allow participants to start retrieving an AM.

The central finding of this study was that, as predicted, presenting the activity cue first produced faster RTs for retrieving AMs than did presenting the action cue first, thus confirming the proposal that activities are more fundamental organizing structures. (You need only try this out for a couple of trials of this study—e.g., going to a movie vs. paying for your ticket, or going on vacation vs. putting on your sunglasses—to confirm the finding for yourself.) Finally, in a second study, Reiser et al. found that presenting an activity cue along with an action cue led to faster RTs (again, for retrieving an appropriate AM) than did presentation of the action cue alone, but adding an action cue to an activity cue had no effect on RT. This finding again suggests that activities represent the more fundamental representational context for accessing AMs.

It is worth noting that if AMs *are,* in fact, represented in terms of activities, this is a rather different form of representation from the alternative formats I considered for person memory in chapter 2. In particular, the findings of Woll and Clark (1989) suggest that, all things being equal, individuals should have an easier time retrieving scripted actions than retrieving conceptions of persons. Thus, for example, it should be easier to retrieve the occasion of going to a dance with a given date than it is to recall the personality of that person, at least so long as that person is not well-known to you. In a later section of this chapter I explore whether the same comparison holds for AMs versus the self.

Another similar finding has been reported by Conway (1990b). Conway examined the effectiveness of taxonomic or categorical cues (e.g., animals, schoolmates) versus goal-based cues (e.g., things to take on a picnic, foods to eat on a diet; cf. the research by Hoffman, Mischel, & Mazze, 1981, on the organization of person memory in terms of the person's goals). The central finding of this study was that participants showed faster RTs in coming up with AMs for a given word when primed with the latter cues than with the former. Thus, for example, participants were quicker to respond with a memory to the word *carrot* when primed with the words *foods you eat on a diet* than when primed with the word *vegetables.* The conclusion reached by Conway was that these results support the representation of AMs in terms of goal-directed events rather than in terms of simple conceptual categories (although the division between these two sorts of categories is not completely clear—e.g., the category "sports" or, to use Conway's example, "birthday presents"). Conway and Bekerian (1987) also reported that previous semantic primes (e.g., flowers, relatives) did not affect the reaction times for retrieving related AMs. (See S. J. Anderson & Conway, 1997, for a general critique of associative network models of AM.)

In a recent article, Anderson and Conway (1997) argued that the Schank–Kolodner–Reiser et al. point of view deals with at least three out of four issues that must be considered in conceptualizing AM. Specifically, the MOP or E-MOP view addresses the observation that AM involves general as well as specific knowledge; it argues for the active effort involved in the retrieval of AMs; and it accounts for the vividness of memories in terms of the differences of those memories from the normative version. One feature that this viewpoint does not account for is the distribution of AMs over one's lifetime, discussed in chapter 5, and it is to that issue that I now turn.

Other Research and Formulations on the Organization of Autobiographical Memory

A number of objections have been raised and alternative formulations proposed to the Reiser et al. position, or what Barsalou (1988) has labeled the *activity dominance* viewpoint. For example, Robinson (1976) conducted an early study in which he gave participants three different sorts of cue words—namely, activity (e.g., throw, run, visit), object (e.g., letter, book, car), and affect or emotion words (e.g., happy, surprised, lonely)—and examined, among other things, the time taken for participants to retrieve a memory to fit that word. The finding that is of greatest interest here is that although both object and activity cues produced shorter RTs than emotion cues, the former two did not differ reliably from each other in such RTs.

On the face of it, this finding seems to argue against the activity dominance position in that it suggests that other kinds of contents can also give rapid access to AMs. The *problem* with this conclusion, however, is that the so-called activity cues used in the Robinson study were actually more like the general, decontextualized *action* cues in the Reiser et al. (1985) study than they were like Reiser et al.'s concept of activities. (I should note that Robinson's study was conducted a decade before the Reiser et al. studies so that the term *activity* was not deliberately used in the same sense that I have been applying it.)

The Concept of A-MOPs. An alternative point of view on the organization of AM was put forward in studies by Conway and Bekerian (1987) and by Barsalou (1988). In their first study Conway and Bekerian used a priming paradigm where the primes for AM consisted of either semantic category names (e.g., sports, emotions, or relatives) or lifetime periods (e.g., "in sixth form [late high school]," "lived in Italy"), and the cues consisted of general activities (e.g., "first team football," "holiday with Jenny"). The lifetime periods and events were derived from a personal memory questionnaire completed some months prior to the experiment. In the experiment itself, the same participants listed ten different periods in their lives (defined as periods with a "distinct beginning and end" [p. 123]) and then were asked to generate five general events (occurring over a period from a day to a week) for each time period. The findings of this initial study were that the time period primes produced significantly faster RTs for retrieving AMs for the general event cues than did the semantic primes. This comparison is probably not tremendously notable in and of itself, although it does raise the intuitively appealing possibility that time periods may represent a significant means for organizing one's AMs and that, as both Schank (1982a) and Reiser et al. (1985) proposed, AMs may be hierarchically organized.

In a second study along these same lines, Conway and Bekerian included sets of the activity primes and action cues used in the Reiser et al. (1985) experiment but presented the primes for only 1.5 rather than 5 seconds. Interestingly, under these conditions the activity cues no longer showed a priming effect. Conway and Bekerian's account for this difference from Reiser et al. is that a 5-second exposure in the Reiser et al. study may have allowed participants to come up with a lifetime period that cued the AM (via a general event or activity), whereas a 1.5-second exposure did not. Unfortunately, no independent evidence for this explanation is provided; and other interpretations are certainly possible—for example, it is possible that the short exposure did not allow participants to get the kind of head start for searching that they were able to get with a 5-second interval.

In another set of studies designed to test the Reiser et al. assumptions, S. J. Anderson and Conway (1994) presented pairs of actions and activities in different temporal orders. In some cases the action *naturally* preceded the activity, for example, "*going to the cinema + finding a seat*" (p. 237). In others, the activity naturally preceded the action, for example, "*parked the car + went to the cinema*" (p. 237). In this case, temporal order had a significant impact on RTs, suggesting to Anderson and Conway a possible confound in the original Reiser et al. findings and, once again, the role of temporal order in AM.

In light of their two sets of findings, Conway and Bekerian proposed the concept of an *autobiographical memory organization package (A-MOP)*. Rather than consisting of simple events or activities or even an E-MOP, A-MOPs refer to the "thematic aspects of a person's life" (Conway, 1990a, p. 116), including such things as location, activities, and particularly time period. Although this multifaceted character of A-MOPs bears some similarity to the kinds of generic knowledge structures discussed by Reiser et al., Schank, and Kolodner, it is apparent that A-MOPs represent a more general and abstract organizational unit than do activities. Thus, as I discuss later, Conway (e.g., 1990a, 1996; Conway & Bekerian, 1987; Conway & Rubin, 1993) has often argued that A-MOPs or themes index *general* events, which in turn index more specific events. Furthermore, Conway and Bekerian (1987; see also Conway & Rubin, 1993) explicitly argued that to the extent that E-MOPs or activities play a role in retrieval of AMs, they do so by participants *first accessing a time period,* which in turn provides access to the general event or activity, which then provides access to the specific memory (e.g., a time in your teens when you dated a lot, or a time when your children were growing up during which you did a lot of housework). Although the kind of memory search proposed by Conway and Bekerian bears some similarities to the kind of searches proposed by Reiser et al. (1986), there is the difference that accessing time periods in one's life has more of a personal flavor to it than some of the kinds of generic social knowledge emphasized by Reiser et al. (1986). Even here, however, Conway and Bekerian (1987) pointed out that life period themes are fairly common across people, and therefore individuals may represent these periods in terms of "culturally specified norms" (p. 130).

Despite this emphasis on organization by means of A-MOPs, Conway and Bekerian (1987) acknowledged from the outset that AMs may also be accessed through "contextual clues" such as odors, sounds, and the like (cf. my later discussion of "involuntary memories" as well as my discussion of early AMs in chap. 5). In his more recent writings, Conway (1992, 1996; Conway & Rubin, 1993) suggested the possible role of distinctive details as a major form of access to AMs, though the implication here is that these details are linked to and are indices of more general themes.

Themes.   A word is in order about Conway's (1990a, 1996, 1997a; Conway & Rubin, 1993) emphasis on thematic organization. On the one hand, Conway identifies themes with extended time periods; in fact, themes form the *basis* for such periods (e.g., the time I was without a car, the time I worked at X job). In fact, Conway (1992; Conway & Rubin, 1993; see also Barsalou, 1988) argued that a person may recall two different themes during the same chronological period (e.g., the time I went to X college, and the time I dated Y); and these different themes define two different "periods." On the other hand, themes are also involved in general events (e.g., preparing that term paper or going to a movie), but here themes refer to "events with short time spans ... time periods measured in days, weeks, and months" (Conway & Rubin, 1993, p. 108).

In a number of recent papers, Conway (e.g., 1992, 1996) argued that themes are central to AM (see the similar views by Robinson, 1992). "In general, autobiographical memories are always accompanied by ... *thematic knowledge* which provides the context for a memory" (Conway, 1992, p. 169). Without themes, an AM amounts to little more than fragments of experience, without any clear-cut, coherent meaning (see my earlier example of the memory for my father's face). Conway distinguished between thematic knowledge and what he refers to as the *phenomenological* (or experiential) *record.* These two components are assumed to be stored in separate memory systems. AMs are constructed, then, in dynamic fashion, by a central retrieval mechanism (Conway, 1997) from a combination of these two components, rather than being stored as memories in their own right. As Conway (1997) put it, "memories are not then like books in a library that we can pull down, open up, and read. Instead, they are complex transitory patterns of activation across a layered and structured knowledge base" (p. 24). In addition, themes provide *access* to event-specific knowledge, including phenomeno- logical experiences, and they also *index* that phenomenological record. This thematic indexing is critical in order to keep such experiences from being "overwritten" by other experiences. Finally, it is worth noting that such themes bear a clear resemblance to a number of other concepts in psychology, for example, Csikszentmihalkyi and Beattie's (1979) concept of *life themes,* Cantor and Kihlstrom's (1987) concept of *life tasks,* Tomkins's (1979) concept of a *script,* Schank & Abelson (1977) concept of a *life theme,* to name just a few. (See Conway, 1990a, 1996, 1997, for more detailed discussions of these concepts, including one on shared AMs within a given generation or cohort.)

An interesting contrast to these organizational concepts is provided by a *trace integrity* model outlined by Howe and Courage (1997; see also M. L. Howe, 2000, M. L. Howe & O'Sullivan, 1997), based on Brainerd and Rayna's (1993) *fuzzy trace* theory. According to this essentially associative model, memories become, in effect, unglued with the passage of time, that is, the elements of the memory become disconnected from each other. On some occasions these elements can become *reintegrated* or reorganized at recall; on other occasions elements from other memories may make contact with those from the to-be-retrieved memory and, in the process, distort that memory. Thus, there are interactions among different traces, including the elements of an AM and those of the self, but not some separate or overriding theme. Furthermore, M. L. Howe and Courage (1997) accounted for the phenomenon of childhood amnesia discussed in chapter 5 by assuming that (a) childhood memories are more likely to have lost their strength and that (b) because sampling self-elements along with memory elements is one criterion of AM, memories from before the self has really developed are less likely to be recalled.

Extended Event Time Lines. Another major alternative to the activity dominance viewpoint has been set forth by Barsalou (1988). Barsalou's critique of this activity position is based on the results of two more variations on the Reiser et al. study. In the first of these, different combinations of four types of cues were presented in counterbalanced order. These four cues were activity, person, location, and time. Although this study differed from the Reiser et al. experiment in that general actions were not used and only a 2-second exposure for the initial priming cue was provided, the important finding is that no facilitation was found for activity cues.

In a second test of this activity dominance position, Barsalou used a cued recall procedure in which participants were first asked, under the guise of a categorization task, to take 60 seconds to generate cues for each of the four categories (i.e., participants, locations, activities, and time), all in the context of their summer experiences. Participants were then asked to come back 1–2 weeks later to generate as many memories as they could for the cues they had produced. Barsalou examined the number of cues participants generated, the number of events generated per category, the number of events per cue, and the number of events remembered in the first 5 seconds. In addition, Barsalou asked participants to categorize their own memories in terms of a classification scheme developed on the basis of a previous informal free recall study of AM. These categories included summarized events, comments on the events, specific events, and extended events.

There were two major results of this second experiment. First, Barsalou found that in the final classification system 40% of participants' memories were judged to be specific events (e.g., "I went to the beach the day after graduation"), whereas 60% were classified as summarized events (e.g., "went to the beach a lot"). Such a result can be viewed as consistent with the various models of general events (e.g., Conway, 1992, 1996; Conway & Rubin, 1993; Kolodner, 1983a) and of generalized event representations (e.g., Nelson, 1986; Schank, 1982a), as well as the general activity dominance viewpoint of Reiser et al. It is worth noting, however, that these events were generated as frequently in response to location as they were to activity cues, both of which were more effective than were time and participant cues. Of equal importance, individuals were fastest in coming up with memories in response to participant cues (which were also the most frequently produced cues in general), followed by locations, and then by time and activity. Both of these results suggested to Barsalou (1988) that activities may not represent the only or most "dominant" context from which to generate AMs.

Barsalou (1988) also conducted an exercise in which participants were to simply recall all of the events that they engaged in during their summer vacation. (This and the other studies were conducted at the beginning of the fall term.) When these protocols were analyzed for content according to the classification system mentioned earlier, the most frequent type of statements (32% of participants' recall) turned out to be in the form of "summarized events" (e.g., "we went swimming a lot"), whereas statements involving instances of a *particular* kind of event (e.g., different occasions of swimming) made up only 21% of that recall. Once again, these results according to Barsalou (1988) argue against the idea that AM involves primarily memories for specific activities, although these results are certainly consistent with Kolodner's (1983a) notion of E-MOPs as summaries of events. In a further analysis of these same data in terms of organizing principles, Barsalou found that extended events, or sequences of events (e.g., "we first went to London, and from there traveled to Paris and Brussels") represented the most frequently (29%) used form of organization, with specific activities accounting for only 17% of the clusters.

Barsalou concluded from these results and from a general consideration of participants' protocols that the hierarchical organization of AM is dominated by chronological order, or what Barsalou refers to as *extended event time lines.* That is, participants' free recall of their summer vacations tended to follow the chronology of that summer rather than a classification of categorically (or thematically) related events. Furthermore, these time lines for different events may exist in parallel (cf. my discussion of themes; see the upper part of Fig. 6.1). Rather than such chronologies being subordinate to activities, as Reiser et al. proposed, Barsalou saw summarized events as being embedded within time lines. In addition, Barsalou (1988) suggested that possibly "a summarized event becomes related to an extended event only if the two are related by the logic of goal attainment," (p. 225), for in-

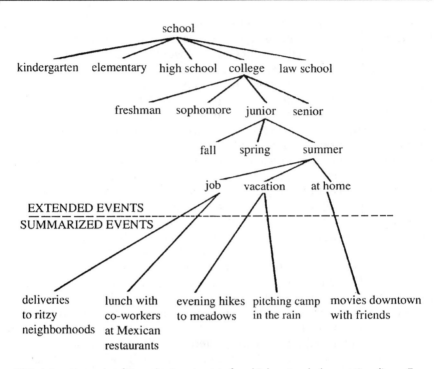

FIG. 6.1. Example of Barsalou's concept of multiple extended event time lines. From "The Content and Organization of Autobiographical Memories" by L. W. Barsalou, 1988. In *Remembering Reconsidered: Ecological and Traditional Approaches to the Study of Memory* (p. 225), edited by U. Neisser & E. Winograd, New York: Cambridge University Press. Copyright © 1988 by Cambridge University Press. Reprinted with permission.

stance, taking field trips may be related to school because the goals of the former are related to those of the latter, rather than to the goals of "playing after school with friends." (See Barsalou, 1991, for a discussion of memory for goal-directed categories.)

Barsalou (1988) acknowledged that this account of the organization of AM is "highly tentative" (p. 237). In the first place, it is primarily based on (a) the discrediting of activities or events as the primary organizing unit, and (b) the results of a rather informal exercise of participants recalling their summer vacations (a rather brief period at that). Barsalou (1988) also acknowledged that such chronological order may simply be a matter of retrieval or narrative style, rather than a true reflection of an individual's representation of AM (cf. Howe and Courage's view of the role of narrative in early AM). Obviously such time lines are not present as such at the time of encoding. Rather, Barsalou suggested that they may be "constructed in the process of reviewing, assessing, and organizing the events in one's life" (p. 219). Finally, in what is perhaps the most telling observation, Barsalou

(1987, 1988) suggested that "there are no invariant knowledge structures. Instead, people continually construct unique representations from loosely organized generic and episodic knowledge to meet the constraints of particular contexts" (Barsalou, 1988, p. 236). Along these same lines, B. H. Ross and Murphy (1999) recently demonstrated the existence of cross-classifications for an everyday domain, that is, food, where taxonomic structures were more influential than scripts, but the latter also played a role (and a greater role than ad hoc categories; see also Lancaster & Barsalou, 1997). In any case, this dynamic view of memory seems particularly relevant to the area of AM (as opposed to, say, face recognition).

At the same time, however, Barsalou's proposals are of interest for at least a couple of reasons. First, despite their tentativeness, his findings, along with Conway and Bekerian's results, *do* raise some doubts about an exclusive activity dominance viewpoint. Furthermore, there is an obvious similarity between the concept of an extended event time line and Conway and Bekerian's (1987) concept of an A-MOP (as well as Linton's [1986] concept of extendures—to be discussed later). At the very least, these different formulations suggest that there may be alternative forms of AM organization, and that, as Barsalou suggested, these may vary with context or personal requirements.

A Hierarchical Model.   One variation on this theme of multiple forms of representation is the suggestion by Conway (1990a; 1996; Conway & Rubin, 1993) that there are actually three forms of representation for AM that may form a kind of hierarchy (see the lefthand side of Fig. 6.1). At the top of this hierarchy are life periods, à la Barsalou and others, where, as I have discussed, several different themes may coexist. These units subsume another level of general events, which include periods of time ranging from hours to months. These general events include such things as playing basketball or taking psychology exams. Finally, at the lowest level is the *event specific knowledge (ESK)*, which includes phenomenological data. As I have discussed, Conway proposed that this latter knowledge may not actually be stored in AM but rather may be part of a "separate memory system," although such ESKs may be indexed and accessed by general events.

Evidence for this hierarchical view (see Neisser, 1986, to be discussed next) comes in three different forms. First, in one study S. J. Anderson and Conway (1993) asked participants to report AMs in response to cue words, then to list details of these memories in a variety of different ways, such as forward or backward listing and free recall. It was expected that the listing strategy that led to the fastest production of memory details (which turned out to be the forward, chronological strategy) would also be the one that was used to generate details in the free recall condition. As it turned out, participants in the free recall condition used the forward strategy in only 60% of the cases. In the other cases, participants' memories clustered around details that were the most salient or distinctive, e.g., "the time I nearly missed the train back to Cambridge because of a bomb scare" as a cue to "my trips to London on my last sabbatical" theme. These results suggested to S. J. Anderson and Conway (1993) that even though AMs may be *organized* in terms of their forward, chronological order, "personally important distinctive details lead to fastest access to memories" (p. 1195). Thus, access to AMs may be through the lowest level of the hierarchy as well as the top. Of course, another plausible explanation is that autobiographical knowledge is actually represented in a variety of different ways.

Another sort of evidence that is consistent with this distinction among different levels of knowledge is the everyday observation that individuals often forget specific details about their AMs, but they rarely forget the general event knowledge that lies behind these AMs. For example, one may forget the names of specific friends in college but still remember the good times he or she had with them. Conway (1996) observed that a person who demonstrated a lack of recall for one of these general events would be viewed as someone with a functional memory disorder. In fact, Conway (1996) cited evidence of participants who fail to remember general events because these events or periods are associated with traumatic affect.

Another clinical example of this hierarchical model cited by Hodges and McCarthy (1993; McCarthy & Hodges, 1995) is of a patient named PS who, as a result of a stroke, suffered from retrograde amnesia except for one period of his life in which he was on leave from the navy; he believed that he was still living in that period some 45 years later. Hodges and McCarthy interpreted this observation as an example of a disconnection between the higher (i.e., thematic and time line) and lower levels (i.e., experiential) of the AM hierarchy. Schacter (1996) took this a step further. He argued that PS's fervent belief that he is still living in this earlier period illustrates the fact that the lifetime period, which ordinarily is only activated for a short period of time (e.g., when you deliberately want to retrieve a memory from that era) may be chronically activated when there is brain damage and when this period is cut off from other information.

An additional assertion made by Conway (e.g., 1996) is that there is a basic difference between AM and *autobiographical knowledge*. Such knowledge, which up until this point I have been calling AM, is stored in long-term memory, whereas actual AMs are "temporary or transitory mental representations that only exist in the context of some specific processing episode" (Conway, 1996, p. 76; cf. Conway's [1992] earlier discussion of this point). According to this view, individuals sample autobiographical knowledge in the course of constructing AMs. For example, it may be part of (some of) one's autobiographical knowledge that he or she went to high school at a particular school during the years of the Kennedy presidency. These two facts may enable the person to reconstruct the memory of watching TV while Jacqueline Kennedy took Edward R. Murrow on a tour of the White House on the program *Person to Person*.

Such a view is strongly reconstructive, bearing a clear resemblance to both the original Bartlett (1932) and Neisser (1967) positions on the one hand, and to Schank's (1982a) dynamic memory formulation on the other. The distinction between autobiographical knowledge and AM also shows some similarity to another distinction by E. E. Smith & Medin (1981) between stored and computed knowledge. That is, autobiographical knowledge can be viewed as the "stored knowledge," whereas AMs and other inferences from this knowledge can be viewed as "computed" information. This view suggests that the AM system is economical in that it does not require storage of *too* much information. At the same time, there is the danger of being too confident of the veridicality of the products of such computations (i.e., the AMs themselves). Conway (1996) also speculated that this dynamic model implies that AMs are short-lived and unstable, both because they require a good deal of cognitive effort and resources to maintain and because repeated attempts to retrieve the same memory will be operated on by different factors on different occasions (e.g., different goals, different cues, etc.).

One problem with all of these alternative formulations of the organization and representation of AMs[2] is that each suffers from a certain amount of ambiguity in its own right. For example, in Conway's hierarchical model, it is hard to be certain exactly where general events leave off and event-specific knowledge begins. For instance, to adapt an example from W. F. Brewer (1988), if someone has gone to a Moroccan restaurant only once but has eaten out at other restaurants many times, is this event an example of event-specific knowledge on the one hand, or of *general* event knowledge on the other (see my discussion of schema- vs. case-based reasoning in chap. 4)? To muddy the waters further, Conway himself included a specific bicycle accident (1992) and an initial meeting with a future girlfriend Angela (Conway, 1996) as examples of general events (presumably because they encompass more specific events within them). In fact, Conway (1996) even described his research with Anderson (i.e., S. J. Anderson & Conway, 1993) as a study of "general events for specific, rather than extended, episodes" (p. 69); and S. J. Anderson and Conway (1993) discussed *microevents* or "extended action sequences but ones that probably took place over comparatively short time periods of minutes or possibly hours" (p. 1195), where "dancing with Angela" is one example.

In the case of Barsalou's formulation, it is not completely clear whether extended event time lines refer to a sequence of events of the form "I did X, then I did Y" or rather to a defined, constrained period such as "the time when I was vacationing at the Grand Canyon." In addition, as I have discussed, it is very difficult in free recall protocols to distinguish between organizational principles and styles of reporting on or narrating AMs. Finally, in the case of Reiser et al.'s (1985) discussion of activities, as discussed in

---

[2]S. J. Anderson and Conway (1997) recently sketched a possible connectionist approach to AM.

chapter 4, it is not clear whether such activities *have* to be "stereotyped" (e.g., going to a free clinic for the first time after many years of going to a family doctor—cf. my discussion of MOPs vs. scripts in chap. 4). Simply stated, then, before we start competitively testing different viewpoints, we need to be certain that we know exactly what each position is asserting.

The Nested Structure of AMs

An earlier version of a hierarchical model of AM was proposed by Neisser (1986). According to Neisser, both the events encoded in AM and an individual's experience of them have a hierarchical structure, with one level nested within the one above. Thus, to expand on an example given by Conway (1990a), one may remember the act of pinning a flower in a person's buttonhole on one's wedding day, which in turn may be part of the act of greeting guests, which is itself part of the overall wedding ceremony, which in turn is part of the entire celebration that took place on the day that he or she were married, and so forth.

Now the idea of a *nested structure* is not particularly radical nor innovative in and of itself (although Neisser was one of the first to state this position explicitly). The way in which Neisser's proposal *differs* from others that I have considered is that he linked this conception to the idea of nesting of objects in the real world within ecological psychology (e.g., Gibson, 1979). In fact, Neisser (1986) argued that the structure of memory *reflects* the nested structure of the environment, rather than being imposed by some kind of *cognitive* structuring. (Ncisscr, 1988b, further proposed that this nested structure is located in the hippocampus, the area where nested spatial information is encoded.) Neisser also argued that the different levels of this nested structure are represented somewhat independently in memory, although there *are* connections among them. It is possible to move up and down among these levels (e.g., it is possible to recall the greeting of guests or the exchanging of vows while recalling the wedding ceremony or vice versa). In fact, Neisser argued that "recalling an experienced event is a matter not of reviving a single record but of moving appropriately among nested levels of structure" (1986, p. 71). Neisser suggested that recall may involve either moving up from particulars or down from context, but that the particulars are more likely to be retained than the higher levels. In either case, some degree of construction or reconstruction is involved in going in either direction.

On this issue of superior memory for lower level details, Neisser's conclusion certainly does not square with my own introspections or with the position taken by other AM theorists, especially Conway and his associates (e.g., S. J. Anderson & Conway, 1993; Conway, 1992, 1996; Conway & Bekerian, 1987) or by theorists on other topics that I have considered (e.g, W. F. Brewer & Dupree, 1983; Huttenlocher et al., 1988; Lichtenstein & Brewer, 1980). Recall, though, that one of the curious features of AMs, as described by Brewer (1986, 1996) is that these memories frequently retain "irrelevant" details. In the case of Neisser's observations on *nested* structures, however, I would expect these "irrelevant" details to have a closer conceptual connection to the higher order memory than they often do. Furthermore, Conway has argued for a thematic organization of AM, a position that underlines the role of higher order sorts of organizing principles. Finally, if one accepts Conway's conception of a more dynamic memory organization, then *strict* hierarchical or nested organization seems less convincing.

RETRIEVAL

In my discussion of organizational factors in AM, I have often referred to the way in which such memories are retrieved—for instance, does retrieval involve a strategic, directed search, or is it cued by contextual factors? Does it entail a search for specific memories or a more indirect reconstruction using generic knowledge structures? Clearly, the study of retrieval and organization go hand in hand: Retrieval depends on the organization of memory (and to some extent, organization is for the purpose of later retrieval).

The Context-Plus-Index Model Again

Reiser et al. (1986) presented another set of studies in support of their *context-plus-index model* of AM as it applies to retrieval. Recall that the retrieval assumptions of this viewpoint are that individuals first search for a context and then search within that context for an index or feature that distinguishes one event from another. The first study (Reiser et al., 1986) on retrieval, then, involved collecting think-aloud protocols from a small number of college students in order to monitor the search process involved in retrieving AMs. In this study, six Yale students were presented with five major cue types: an activity, mental state, an activity that represented a subclass of a larger class (e.g., "went to a *frightening* movie"), activity plus mental state, and activity plus goal failure (i.e., where the event did not accomplish the intended goal; see chap. 4). Thus, an example of activity plus mental state might be "feeling angry when talking to a salesperson," whereas an example of an activity plus goal failure was "couldn't pay for an item while shopping" (Reiser et al., 1986, p. 105).

Reiser et al. (1986) examined and analyzed students' strategies when these students successfully retrieved a memory that matched the cues, or more importantly, when they exhibited one of a number of different types of failure to retrieve an appropriate memory. These failures included *false starts*, which were when participants began to identify a category for searching, but found that it did not contain a memory (e.g., where they thought of situations where they might have "felt cold during an exam," but couldn't locate an experience that matched that category). They also included *near misses*, which were when participants retrieved a memory that didn't quite match the requirement, (e.g., where they were searching for an example of "felt cold during an exam," but only came up with feeling cold in a classroom) or where participants actually retrieved several similar experiences.

Reiser et al. (1986) classified students' strategies for retrieving memories into several different categories. First, in accordance with their general theoretical framework, these researchers classified strategies into an initial *search-for-a-context* versus a *searching within that context.* In the former category, strategies were classified as either a *direct search* for the given activity or *finding a related activity to search.* The former was obviously used primarily when the cue was itself an activity or some variant thereof, whereas the latter was used primarily when the cue was a state, such as finding an activity related to "feeling angry." The latter strategy involved either some form of causal reasoning to link an activity to a state (e.g., thinking of some kind of activity that might generate anger) or thinking of a situation that might be the *result* of the state (e.g., getting into a fight as a result of being angry). In all cases, Reiser et al. noted that the focus of this "searching for context" was some activity.

The second and more interesting class has to do with searching *within* a context. Here Reiser et al. (1986) identified three different classes of search strategies. The first of these was either to focus initially on a *subclass* of the activity (e.g., a particular sort of restaurant or store where the activity could have occurred) or to *enumerate* the several subclasses (by accessing general information about the type of activity, e.g., the different kinds of foods that restaurants can specialize in) in order to settle on one particular class to search. The second class of strategies was to access some kind of external knowledge to guide the search. For example, students may try to think of possible participants in the activity (e.g., a friend who might have thrown or attended a birthday party), or they may try to identify a time period during which the activity might have occurred (cf. my earlier discussion of extended event time lines). Finally, participants may engage in *causal reasoning* to determine what might have motivated the activity (e.g., why they might have gone to the library in the first place) or an event or situation that might have initiated the event (e.g., what might have caused them to be cold) or the result of the activity (e.g., what might have happened if or when they went to a bank and did not have personal identification). Some examples of these different types of strategies are given in Table 6.1.

One thing to note in this reconstruction of students' retrieval strategies is the degree of problem solving and sheer causal reasoning, as well as the use of general knowledge structures involved in such retrieval. Reiser et al. (1986) argued that an active, directed search process is necessary, simply because there are "too many paths in memory associated with the cued concept for an undirected or automatic search to be successful" (p. 101). Second, in much the same way as the dynamic memory processes described by Schank and Kolodner in general, this search makes use of existing generic knowledge about causes or explanations (e.g., potential goals, initiating events, en-

TABLE 6.1

Examples of Participants' Strategies in Searching Within a Context

1. Selecting a subclass or variant of the activity or enumeration of instances

   a. Subclass: See first excerpt given at the beginning of this chapter

   b. Enumeration

   > E: Think of a time when you went to a public library.

   > P: Um ... let's see. The first thing that comes to mind is when I go to the New Haven Public Library. And I actually like that library a lot. And I also remember, I go to school in Oberlin, and I like the public library at Oberlin much better than the college library, because it has sort of a friendlier atmosphere, and there's kids, not all these studious students around. So I remember that public library very well, it was one of my favorite hangouts.

   > E: Can you think of a particular time?

   > P: Um ... one particular time I remember is when I had to pay the overdue fine in pennies because it was the only money I had. It was twenty-eight pennies. I think it was actually thirty pennies but the person let me pay with twenty-eight pennies.

   (pp. 111–112)

2. Accessing external knowledge

   a. Thinking of possible participants

   > E: Think of a time when you went to a birthday party.

   > P: Birthday surprises. [Pause] When was the last birthday? I'm trying to think through who had a birthday party last. Um, we all have summer birthdays now and everybody is away, so it's kind of hard to celebrate. Um, Amy's was in November ... that was nice, it was a real surprise. My roommate gave her a surprise party and she kept expecting it to be ... she knew she was having a party because all her really close friends ... they gave each person a surprise party. So everyone always knew that they were having a surprise party, they were just never sure when it was.

   (p. 114)

   b. Map search, for example, searching cities you've visited to find museums, or searching classes to retrieve a time when you felt "cold at an exam."

   c. Searching for time era

   > E: Think of a time when you went to a birthday party.

   > P: First of all, I thought of, like, a big birthday party and I couldn't think of any right off so I thought about, oh well, use your birthday party, then I go, wait a minute, I never have birthday parties. I don't remember them that well. So I went back to high school, we always had surprise parties, and one in particular was a surprise party for Michele, this friend of ours. Donna threw it. It was actually a surprise which was amazing because usually you can't keep them a surprise. I think I remember because party is like ... I always get really drunk at them sometimes, so this one I did get a little wasted at and everyone, it was so great, because everyone sang happy birthday and it was so out of tune that no one cared. It was wonderful.

   (p. 113)

continued on next page   **245**

3. Causal chain reasoning strategies

   a. Infer goals (of activity)

> E: Think of a time when you went to a public library. [Pause] What's going through your mind?

> P: That I always go to the library like a mile away from my home in Colorado, and it's hard to think of one particular time so I'm trying to figure out if I can think of like going for one book. And if I can remember doing like one research project, then I could put it together. Well, okay, I remember going to get a book on running, but I didn't have my card so I was talking to a man about running because I had ran [sic] up there and it's two miles back. And he was saying, "Oh, well, if you can do it, man." That's as close as I can get to my public library."

> (p. 114)

   b. Infer cause

> E: Think of a time when you felt cold at an exam.

> P: I was thinking winter first of all. I mean when or what class did I take an exam for in the winter, because I took a semester off and I took the semester off during, like, in December and so I'm trying to think, well, I couldn't have taken any finals in really cold weather so ...

> (p. 115)

   c. Infer results

> E: Think of a time when you went to a bank and didn't have proper identification.

> P: Identification ... they always ask me for identification but I usually have something. Uh, thinking ... when you said bank ... I was sort of thinking, well, last time I went to the bank and it was closed and not being ... and being annoyed that it had closed rather than not having enough money but still not being ... able to get money out.

> (p. 116)

Note. From "Strategic Memory Search Processes," by B. J. Reiser, J. B. Black, & P. Kalamarides, 1986. In *Autobiographical Memory* (pp. 111–116), edited by D. C. Rubin, New York: Cambridge University Press. Copyright ©1986 by Cambridge University Press. Adapted with permission.

abling conditions, consequences, etc), as well as temporal context, setting, possible participants, and the like. (The similarity to the earlier formulations by Schank, Abelson, and Kolodner should be apparent.) Thus, the search of AM involves asking oneself questions about general social activity and social reality. The question, of course, is to what extent this search or reconstructive process also involves more personal, individual knowledge about one's own life history and patterns (e.g., about one's own emotional reactions or motive patterns or personality characteristics) and the degree to which this use of self-knowledge varies from individual to individual.

The Cyclic Retrieval Model

The Williams and Hollan Version.   Another model of retrieval that bears a close resemblance to the Reiser et al. viewpoint is one proposed by Williams and Hollan (1981; see also Williams & Santos-Williams, 1980). This model is referred to as the *find-a-context, search, verify model* (Williams & Hollan, 1981), or the *cyclic retrieval model,* because the individual trying to retrieve a memory must first establish a context in which to locate a piece of information (e.g., a name) then search that context, evaluate or verify that search to see if the piece of information (e.g., the correct name) has in fact been retrieved, and, if not, recycle the retrieval process.

This viewpoint assumes, first, that the individual has encoded only fragmentary, partial information; and therefore it is necessary to construct a description of the target item. This involves retrieving another fact to form a new description, which is in turn used to retrieve still another fact, and so on until the target memory is found. Thus, in a manner similar to Reiser et al. (1986), Williams and Hollan assumed that retrieval is a problem-solving process in which individuals have to call on their knowledge of relevant situations and the like to locate and expand on the original fragment.

Williams and Hollan's specific retrieval task was to have four participants recall as many names from their high school graduating class as possible while the investigators collected think-aloud protocols over a period of four to nine 1-hour sessions. Thus, as an example of the retrieval process, one participant first started to think of the context of a general science class to search for classmates and their names, followed by the context of the lunch line in which classmates may be encountered, followed by people he (the participant) still runs into when he comes back to his hometown, followed by other prototypical situations. Thus, in this task the contexts that the participant searched, at least in this part of the protocol, were simply classrooms and other situations in which classmates might be encountered.

Williams and Hollan (1981) suggested that there are three sorts of problems faced by the retrieval process in general: namely, too little information in the cue or retrieval context to reconstruct a name (or other memory), too *much* information or too broad a cue to be able to pin down the memory, and false recoveries of the wrong information. In the first case, the retrieval cue provided (in this case by participants themselves) was insufficient, and thus they had to engage in some kind of elaboration to fill in the appropriate context. These elaborations included such things as *extended retrievals,* which means trying to fill in any kind of related information about a particular person (e.g., a rock band or art class that classmate was in) in order to fill in the rest of that person's name. Alternatively, participants also engaged in *systematic hypothesizing,* for example, generating all names beginning with a given letter known to be the first letter in that person's name, or *inferential recall,* where the participant remembered the person, but could not retrieve any details of the person's name, and thus had to resort to such clues as whether she was wearing the kind of dress in her graduation picture that indicated she was in the same graduating class.

A second problem in retrieval of names is when there is too much information in the cue for the participant to search, and he or she must therefore narrow the focus and select the relevant information within that context—what Williams and Santos-Williams (1980) referred to as *contextual retrievals*. Thus, for example, in response to the cue "8th grade," a participant may try to narrow the context down to a particular class or activity engaged in during that period. Once a context has been created, the participant then searches that context—for example, searching all the participants in an activity, all the people living at a given location, or all the people in a relevant picture.

Finally, *false recoveries* refer to situations in which participants continued to recall information about a person even after they had retrieved that person's name, as well as to fabrications in which the participant simply retrieved a name of someone who was not actually in the graduating class. (One of the nice features of the Williams and Hollan study was that recall could be verified by checking the high school yearbooks.)

It is apparent that the Williams and Hollan model is quite similar to the Reiser et al. one. Both models view retrieval as an effortful exercise in search, reconstruction, and problem solving. Both assume that individuals have too much memory to simply engage in an undirected search. The major difference in the two models, which results in part from the difference in the tasks that they studied, is that Reiser et al. placed a greater emphasis on the role of generic knowledge structures in retrieving AMs, whereas Williams and Hollan placed a greater emphasis on the strategies of such retrieval and on the recursive nature of retrieval (Williams & Santos-Williams, 1980). (It should be noted that Williams and Santos-Williams have made an attempt to analyze their participants' recall protocols in terms of a detailed propositional format.) Both approaches are clearly distinguishable from the models of organization and retrieval reviewed, for example, the area of person memory.

The Conway Version.   Another approach to retrieval explicitly based on the Williams and Hollan model was recently outlined by Conway (1992, 1996; see also Conway & Rubin, 1993). According to this view, a cue is first elaborated into a context by means of a *supervisory attentional system* (Shallice, 1988) or a *central executive component* of working memory (Conway & Rubin, 1993). This executive contains metamemory and other higher order knowledge as well as a "current model of the *self*" (Conway & Rubin, 1993, p. 110) or *working self* (Conway & Pleydell-Pearce, 2000; cf. Markus & Ruvolo, 1989). The resulting context, which is shaped by the themes and goal structure (Conway & Pleydell-Pearce, 2000) that are currently prominent in the self, provides entree into long-term memory as mediated by this same executive. Once this point of entry is established, a process of spreading activation leads to the retrieval of other memory or knowledge structures that are related to the point of entry. The resulting knowledge or memory is evaluated in terms of its adequacy for meeting the task requirements. If that memory is inadequate, then the process is recycled. If that memory satisfies the task requirements, then the search is terminated.

Thus, to use Conway's (1992) example, if the cue is "bicycle," the first question might be whether the respondent can cycle, and from there, the question might be when, in fact, he or she would have used a bicycle. The answer for Conway was that he used a bicycle before he got his driver's license, and the most frequent route that he took was between home and work. This in turn led (presumably by spreading activation) to the time period and the home and work theme, that is, when he worked at the Applied Psychology Unit in Cambridge, and the house he lived in on Griton at that time, which in turn accessed the fact that he used to take Huntingdon Road in going back and forth to work, which in turn accessed (again, presumably via spreading activation) the memory of the accident he had on his bicycle when he was run over by a car on one of his rides home down Huntingdon Road. (See the left side of Fig. 6.2 for a graphical description of this chain of inferences, and see Fig. 6.3 for additional details of this particular AM.)[3]

Although this retrieval process appears to be rather cumbersome, S. J. Anderson and Conway (1997) suggested that once the search process is started, the central executive need not monitor it every step of the way, but rather may switch attention back and forth between this task and others. The retrieval process also need not be fully conscious. "Rather, memories may be constructed ... in the background, and only emerge into conscious awareness at some appropriate moment or when other tasks have been completed" (p. 243). Examples of this latter point include the "remindings" discussed in chapter 4 and the "involuntary memories" to be discussed later in this chapter.

Diary Studies of Retrieval

Linton.   Another approach to studying retrieval is by means of diary keeping. In her study described in the last chapter, Linton (1986) tried at the end of each month (for a total of 69 attempts) to retrieve as many memories as possible; and she also kept track of the strategies she used during this "warm-up" exercise (i.e., a warm up for the subsequent recognition and cued recall tasks). In her review, Linton (1986) described four major strategies she used in this recall exercise. By far the most frequent one was to simply use chronological order, that is, returning to the period a year earlier and working forward to the present. Over 62% of the memories recalled were retrieved in this manner. The second strategy was to focus on some theme in her life (e.g., her love life) using what Linton calls *extendures,* or temporally bound units within a given theme (e.g., "when I was doing graduate work"; cf. Conway), and to search these extendures chronologically.

---

[3]My students' response to this exercise is that an accident such as the one reported by Conway should be so salient as to "jump out" at the retriever rather than requiring this sort of effortful, problem-solving search.

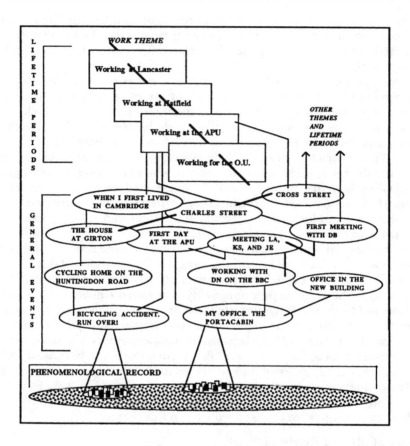

FIG. 6.2. An example of Conway's (1992) hierarchical model of autobigraphical memory. From "A Structural Model of Autobiographical Memory" by M. A. Conway, 1992. In *Theoretical Perspectives on Autobiographical Memory* (p. 179) edited by M. A. Conway, D. C. Rubin, A. Spinnler, & W. A. Wagenaar, Dordrecht, the Netherlands: Kluwer Academic Publishing. Copyright © 1992 by Kluwer Academic Publishing. Reprinted with kind permission of Kluwer Academic Publishing.

This approach accounted for another 23% of the retrievals. Finally, Linton reported using reverse chronological order on 5.8% of the retrievals, and another cryptically described graphical strategy accounted for another 5.8% of her retrievals.

A couple of other features of Linton's (1986) retrieval strategies are worth noting. First, as seen in Fig. 6.4, the frequency of chronological recall, unlike that for the other types of retrieval, increased over the 6 years, until it became the sole method used during the final year. However, when Linton went back 6 years after the end of her study and tried to recall the years in random order (unlike the previous systematic recall for the preceding year), categorical recall was preferred, and chronological strategies "are avoided. Indeed, they are difficult, if not impossible to perform for these older memories" (Linton, 1986, p. 64), although the chronology within categories remained intact. This observation has interesting implications for Conway's argument that autobiographical knowledge is ordered chronologically. Over this 12-year period, salience or relevance of memories to her current life (cf. Conway & Pleydell-Pearce, 2000; Conway & Rubin, 1993) became an increasingly important factor, as the details of memories were lost. Linton gave the example of her memory of meeting a nice, quiet man, a memory that "takes on new importance when I begin to date and decide to marry him" (Linton, 1986, p. 64). Finally, Linton also reported a general difficulty in recovering negative memories, and this difficulty increased over time.

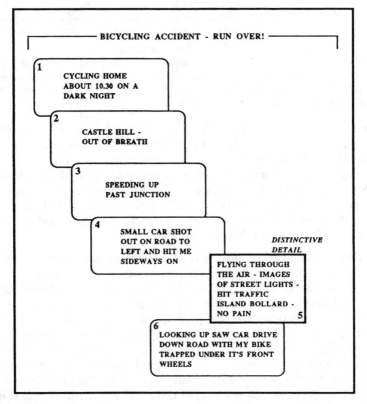

FIG. 6.3.   Temporal details for Conway's autobiographical memory. From "A Structural Model of Autobiographical Memory" by M. A. Conway, 1992. In *Theoretical Perspectives on Autobiographical Memory* (p. 181) edited by M. A. Conway, D. C. Rubin, A. Spinnler, & W. A. Wagenaar, Dordrecht, the Netherlands: Kluwer Academic Publishing. Copyright © by Kluwer Academic Publishing. Reprinted with kind permission of Kluwer Academic Publishing.

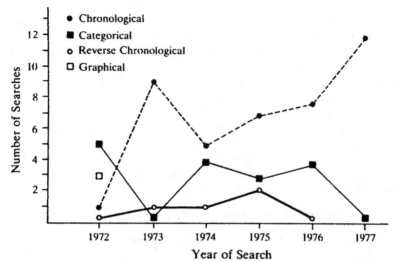

FIG. 6.4.   The time course of Linton's retrieval strategies. From "Ways of Searching and the Contents of Memory," by M. Linton, 1986. In *Autobiographical Memory* (pp. 50–67), edited by C. Rubin, New York: Cambridge University Press. Copyright © 1986 by Cambridge University Press. Reprinted with permission.

One final point should be made: Throughout her chapter on retrieval strategies, Linton (1986) distinguished between memories that are explicitly and effortfully retrieved versus "thoughts that come unbidden" (p. 53) or are triggered automatically, such as the ones studied anecdotally by Salaman (1970) in older people (to be discussed later in this chapter). As Linton pointed out, these two modes of recall in some sense represent the two ends of a memory continuum, both of which need to be studied. I return to this distinction later in this chapter.

The Diary Studies of Thompson et al.   Another ambitious set of diary studies I touched on in the previous chapter is that conducted by Thompson et al. (1996). In their book Thompson et al. reported on 15 different data sets from three different universities for retention intervals ranging from 10 weeks to 2.5 years. These studies involved participants keeping diaries in which they were encouraged to write down a variety of different events rather than just exciting or unusual ones. Participants were told to date the memory and then rate it on the following dimensions: predictions of how well they thought they would remember the event at some point in the future, the pleasantness of the event, its frequency and importance, its centrality to their lives, and their degree of emotional involvement in the event. In a few of the studies participants also made the same ratings for events in their roommates' lives.[4]

---

[4]Because the exact measure used varied from study to study (e.g., exactly what scales were and were not included, whether 5-, 6-, or 7-point scales were used), it is sometimes difficult to keep track of what data goes with what data set and what data sets or studies a given finding is based on.

Participants' diaries were collected, at least in most cases, every week at a predetermined time. At the end of the memory interval, participants were asked to respond to and rate the events, which were presented to them in random order. Their ratings (which varied somewhat from study to study) included their overall rating of how well they recalled the event (and in some cases, their roommates' event), the amount of time spent rehearsing the event, whom they were with during the event, the location of the event, the date of the event (using a blank calendar), their estimated degree of error in dating, their confidence in their dating, their strategy in making a dating estimate (sometimes), and the time of the week in which the event occurred.

I have already cited some of Thompson et al.'s (1996) findings for event dating in the previous chapter. As far as memory for the events themselves is concerned, such memory decreased gradually over the retention interval, although the slope of this curve depends on the length of the interval and the particular type of detail involved. Thompson et al. interpreted this finding, along with the finding that a more rapid decline was found for the memories rated as well-remembered (i.e., those given ratings of 6 or 7 on a 7-point scale), as indicating that participants continued to retain the gist of the events, but recall for the exact details is lost quickly over time (cf. Brainerd & Reyna's [1995] discussion of the different time course of gist vs. verbatim memory in their fuzzy trace theory). As a result, memory, in Thompson et al.'s terms, becomes less reproductive and more reconstructive.

Some of the characteristics of events that influenced participants' recall were amount of rehearsal, physical involvement in the event, strong initial *mental* involvement, event- and person-atypicality (see discussion in chap. 3 of the latter), affective intensity, and overall strength of emotion (e.g., very emotional to nonemotional). Probably none of these results is terribly surprising, although Thompson et al. (1996) also reported the interesting finding that pleasant events were better remembered than unpleasant ones for self-related events, but there was no clear relationship between this dimension and memory for other events. Participants' prediction of the accuracy of their own recall proved to be a strong predictor of actual recall. Finally, Thompson et al. found that events related to the self were better recalled than events in the news, even though the latter were often more exciting or interesting (to the general population) than the former. Along these same lines, participants who recorded their roommates' events as well as their own recalled their own better, even when their roommates' events were clearly observable. Both of these latter findings are viewed by Thompson et al. as supporting the major role played by the self-schema in recall of AMs (see my later discussion).

Although Thompson et al. (1996) are to be commended for their comprehensive data collection and for the rigor of their analyses, one difficulty in their research is their failure to focus individual attention on the six participants who kept diaries for at least 18 months (see Walter, Vogt, & Thompson, 1997, for one exception). Thompson et al. seemed to be more intent on showing how consistent the results from these participants are with the results for their various shorter term studies. Although this observation is worthy of note in and of itself, it would have been interesting to take a close-up look at these six participants in their own right.

The Retrieval of Randomly Sampled Events: The Research of William Brewer. One of the problems with diary studies of AM, apart from the small, unrepresentative samples of participants used, is their unrepresentative sampling of memories. I discussed, for example, how Linton recorded primarily unique or salient events; and certainly Wagenaar's memories were not completely random. (Although Thompson et al., 1996, instructed their participants to "give ... a variety of events from their lives" [p. 24], no evidence is presented, other than the authors' general impressions, that participants actually did engage in representative sampling.)

One attempt to get around this sort of problem was made by W. F. Brewer (1988), who asked a small groups of college students to record a random sample of their thoughts and actions. This random sampling was accomplished by having students carry around beepers with them that were activated on a random basis, but at an average rate of once every 2 hours. The exception here was that students could deactivate the beeper whenever they wanted to; they also turned the beeper off when they were asleep; and they could respond to the beeper with "private" if they were engaged in some activity that they did not want to record (e.g., exams, parties, dates). Brewer acknowledged that, as a result of this procedure, certain events were undersampled. For example, students indicated that they often did not report when they were driving or were at work. (See Thompson et al., 1996, for a critique of this feature of Brewer's study and a proposed alternative strategy.)

As described by W. F. Brewer (1988), participants were recruited for this experiment based on their ability to learn the procedures quickly, as well as on their "high motivation and legible handwriting" (p. 28). Participants were instructed to respond to the beeper by filling out a response card in which they were to give the following information: time, location, a summary statement of the thought and/or action that they were engaged in, a rating of the coordination of action and thought (i.e., to what extent were the two focused on the same or different things), and ratings of both thought and action on six scales each. The six scales were action (or thought) frequency (e.g., frequency of eating at a French restaurant), action (or thought) category frequency (e.g., frequency of eating at a restaurant), pleasantness, trivial/significant, dull/exciting, and non-goal-directedness. In addition, participants were instructed to record, at the end of the day, the most memorable event of that day in terms of the same information and scales as for the randomly sampled events.

In the first study, eight college freshmen carried the beeper for an average of 17 days. In this study a recognition memory paradigm was used in which participants were asked to indicate the degree to which they recognized either the thought or action component of one of their cards. This recognition test was administered either immediately after (the 17 days of) acquisition, or at an average interval of either 69 or 140 days later. (All eight participants took the recognition test for different cards at all three intervals, i.e., there were no repetitions.) More specifically, participants were shown either the thought or action description (in counterbalanced order) of their responses at a given time and were then asked to indicate how well they remembered the episode. No foils were included here because of questions raised by Brewer and others (e.g., W. P. Wallace, 1980) about the usefulness of such foils, as well as the inherent difficulty of coming up with such distractors in the context of AM (see my discussion in chap. 5 of the Barclay et al. studies).

As a preliminary set of findings, Brewer reported that events in general showed more rapid forgetting than was found in the diary studies of Linton and Wagenaar (see Fig. 6.5), though the forgetting curve was still shallower than forgetting curves from typical lab studies of memory. Note in Fig. 6.5 that the forgetting rate for memorable thoughts is also somewhat less shal-

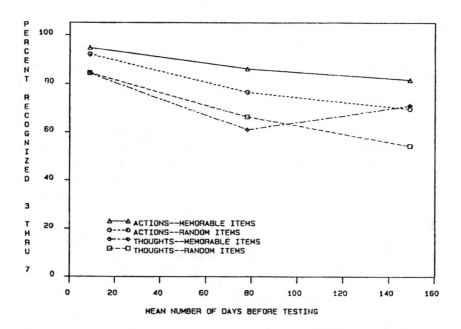

FIG. 6.5. Forgetting curves for randomly sampled autobiographical memories. From "Memory for Randomly Sampled Autobiographical Events" by W. F. Brewer (1988). In *Remembering Reconsidered: Ecological and Traditional Approaches to the Study of Memory* (pp. 21–90) edited by U. Neisser & E. Winograd, New York: Cambridge University Press. Copyright © 1988 by Cambridge University Press. Reprinted with permission.

TABLE 6.2

Memory for Memorable Versus Randomly Sampled Autobiographical Memories

Event Characteristics	Actions		Thoughts	
	Random	Memorable	Random	Memorable
Category Frequency	4.48	3.50*	3.89	3.51
Instance Frequency	2.38	1.74*	2.14	1.92
Pleasantness	3.98	4.53*	3.82	4.47*
Extreme Affect	0.82	1.60*	0.92	1.78*
Significance	2.30	2.58	2.43	2.89*
Goal-Directedness	3.53	3.31	3.32	3.24
Excitement	3.54	4.64*	3.61	4.72*
Memory	4.80	5.83*	4.24	4.70

Note. Means are based on the subject means. *Memorable versus random, $p < .05$. From "Memory for Randomly Sampled Autobiographical Events" by W. F. Brewer (1988). In *Remembering Reconsidered: Ecological and Traditional Approaches to the Study of Memory* (pp. 21–90) edited by U. Neisser & E. Winograd, New York: Cambridge University Press. Copyright © 1988 by Cambridge University Press. Reprinted with permission.

low than the curves for the other three types of items. As far as memorable versus randomly sampled actions are concerned (see Table 6.2), not only were the former recognized better than the latter (87% vs. 79%), but the memorable actions were also rated as less frequent, as coming from less frequent action categories, and as more pleasant, more exciting, and more extreme in affect than randomly sampled ones—all findings that would be expected from everyday experience and from prior research findings. In the case of thoughts, which were generally less memorable than actions (79% to 68% for randomly sampled examples), memorable thoughts were recognized slightly more readily than randomly sampled ones and were also rated as more exciting, more extreme in affect, more significant and pleasant than their random counterparts.

Amongst the randomly selected events themselves, the actions that were most clearly remembered were those that were rated lower in action category frequency and as more exciting and significant, whereas the thoughts that were most clearly remembered were those that were rated as more exciting, pleasant, and significant. Finally, when all variables were entered into a general regression equation, the only variables that predicted recognition memory, other than participant differences and retention interval, were action instance frequency for actions and excitement for thoughts.

In a second experiment using a cued recall methodology, W. F. Brewer (1988) tested 10 participants at briefer intervals (i.e., immediately, 23 days, and 46 days after acquisition). In this study, participants were shown one of five different cues at recall (i.e., time, location, time plus location, thought, and action description) and were asked to fill out the remaining information on their response cards, including the 7-point memory ratings included in Experiment 1. (This procedure is clearly similar to that used by Wagenaar, 1986.) In addition, Brewer included a questionnaire in which he assessed such qualities of the memory experience as visual, auditory, tactile, smell, and taste sensations, emotionality, and thought. (This questionnaire, in effect, completes the transition from traditional, objective laboratory research of the Ebbinghaus variety to the more phenomenological, self-rating variety of AM research.) Finally, after all the other data had been collected, participants rated their overall recognition of the event described on a given card.

An initial examination of both recognition and recall data showed rather shallow forgetting curves for both, although such curves were obviously lower for recall than for recognition. Recall for location showed very little forgetting at all, although Brewer himself pointed out that location information is probably easier to infer than the other types of information, so this result is perhaps a bit misleading.

Given the manner of data collection, Brewer was able to provide several alternative estimates of the effectiveness of different types of retrieval cues. First, there were clear differences in the effects of cue type on recognition ratings, starting with action cues (4.31), followed by thought cues (3.85), time plus location (2.92), location (2.51), and time (2.38). These results generally support the findings by Wagenaar (1986) for the ineffectiveness of "when" cues for recall and for the incremental effects of adding time to other cues. They also give some support to Reiser et al.'s (1985) findings on the effectiveness of activity cues. On the other hand, when Brewer divided up the 1–7 scale (where 7 = *certain of remembering the event*), counting any rating of 3 or above as correct, the mean percentage of correct recall, in descending order, proved to be location (92%), followed by actions (89%), thoughts (84%), emotions (78%), and time (75%). However, this latter cutoff point seems a bit arbitrary, that is, why not use a median split or the more conservative cutoff used by Thompson et al.? (See Thompson et al., 1996, for a discussion of the effects of different uses of memory scales on the observed relation between accuracy or errors and retention interval.) Once again, the results for location may be primarily a result of ease of inference.

When it comes to *recalling* information about events on the basis of different cues (where recall was scored in terms of complete vs. partial vs. no recall), it turns out that location was again recalled best overall (though the same reservation raised earlier applies here), followed by action and thought. Recall accuracy for different types of information was also a function of recall *cue*. Specifically, recall accuracy for actions was highest with thought cues (58%) and lowest with location (33%) and time cues (25%), whereas recall accuracy for thoughts was highest with action cues (42%) and again lowest with location (9%) and time (7%). These findings suggest that thought and action may be related; however, in general (in terms of characteristics of each that make them memorable), Brewer concluded that his data speak against an overall correlation. Finally, recall for location is fairly high for all cues (from 51% for time to 91% for action cues), again presumably because of the easy inference of location.

An analysis was also carried out for the different kinds of recall *errors* made for different types of information and different cues. For example, Brewer distinguished between four different types of errors: *overt errors* (i.e., remembering something that clearly contradicted a detail on the response card), remembering the *wrong event* (i.e., recalling a thought or action that was different from the original response, but that did not contradict that response), remembering the *wrong time slice* (i.e., remembering an event that is slightly off in time or sequence from the one actually recorded), and *correct with detail* (i.e., including more detail in recall than was included in the original response). (Recall could also be classified as correct, omission, or inference.) In general, recall errors for actions tended to involve remembering the wrong event, omissions, or inferring the wrong event, whereas for thoughts, the errors consisted primarily of omitting that thought. In neither case did participants show many overt errors ($N = 4$).

As indicated earlier, this second experiment also included an analysis of the phenomenological dimensions of participants' memories, based on Brewer's belief that memory researchers in general, and researchers on AM in particular, need to take a closer look at this kind of information. In general, Brewer found that participants' confidence in their memories was associated with a report of strong phenomenological qualities, that is, high ratings on visual imagery, thought, auditory, and motor "reexperiencing." (The experiential scales were all couched in terms of the degree to which a participant was "reexperiencing" the sensation in question.) This finding is obviously consistent with Brewer's earlier discussion of AM as having the flavor of reliving or reexperiencing the event.

The results for visual imagery are rather informative. Specifically, participants reported high visual imagery for experiences they recalled correctly and especially for experiences they recalled correctly with detail. They also reported high visual imagery for experiences that were classified as "wrong time slice"—that is, recalling an actual event, but in a different sequence or context. On the other hand, participants reported very low imagery when they wrote nothing down on the response card or when they recalled the wrong event. Thus, it appears that, in general, the level of imagery was a good predictor of the accuracy of participants' recall.

Brewer also argued that his results do not support a strong reconstructive memory model of AM (see my discussion in chap. 5; see also W. F. Brewer, 1993, for a similar conclusion from a review of work on flashbulb memories, as well as the diary study and opposing commentary by Thompson et al., 1996). For example, although 50% of all responses were classified as errors, in the broad sense of that term, only four responses, or 1.5% of the total, actually represented overt errors. Rather, 90% of the errors were what Brewer classified as wrong time slices or wrong events, both of which, Brewer argued, are more a matter of retrieval errors than of reconstructions, although I would question this argument in the case of wrong events (see Hyman, 1999, for a discussion of other findings of wrong time slice errors). Finally, another 8.5% of the errors were classified as "correct plus detail," which are errors only in the sense that they contained details not included on the response cards.

Now the question arises as to whether the methods used by Brewer are likely to have detected reconstructions if and when they did occur. Brewer himself acknowledged that the lives of his participants were sufficiently routinized that reconstructions may actually be so similar to the events on the response cards as to be scored as correct. In addition, he speculated that the details of participants' personal or recollective memories, such as visual details, may be remembered better and longer than their linguistic counterparts that are typically tested for in traditional laboratory research on memory.

At the same time it should be noted that when omissions are added to the other types of errors, at least 50% of participants' recall is incorrect, and the forgetting rates in both experiments, although low in comparison with findings from lab research, were much higher than those reported by Linton and Wagenaar and higher even than the figures reported by White in his study of more mundane experiences. Another consideration is that Brewer's study only covered 2–3 weeks, in contrast to the very long-term studies by the other diary researchers I have reviewed. Nevertheless, it is clear that memory for these randomly sampled events is considerably below that for events rated as most memorable, suggesting again that the results from the Linton and Wagenaar studies may overestimate individuals' memory for everyday experiences.

Another issue addressed by Brewer's study is the role of distinctiveness versus duplication in AM. In chapter 5, I noted that Brewer's partially reconstructive model argues that the main source of inaccuracy in recalling AMs is the distorting effect of duplicated experiences. Conversely, I have pointed out that distinctive or infrequent locations and actions play a strong role in the recall of both thoughts and actions, and such infrequency also accounts for why actions such as talking to a faculty member or TA, a card game, and taking drugs received the highest memory scores. In fact, an overall correlation of –.45 was found between frequency and overall memory. These results are collectively referred to by W. F. Brewer (1988) as the *distinctive-representation hypothesis*.[5] Brewer also labels his theoretical account

---

[5]See however, my discussion in chapter 9 of some of the problems with the concept of distinctiveness.

of how events become distinctive as the *dual-process theory of repetition,* which says that repetition leads to an increase in the strength of semantic memory, but a *decrease* in episodic memory. W. F. Brewer (1988) acknowledged, however, that his results "provide little insight into the mechanism that underlies the repetition effect" (p. 76). These results and Brewer's account are consistent with his earlier discussion (W. F. Brewer, 1986) of his partially reconstructive viewpoint and are also clearly related to my discussion in chapter 5 of memory for specific versus general or repeated events in children.

Finally, following Neisser (1986), Brewer argued that many of his results can be accounted for by the ecology of the students' environments. For example. since these students spent a lot of time in one particular location (i.e., their room), this location was not a good predictor of the variety of different actions that took place there, but the actions were good predictors of that location. On the other hand, infrequent locations (e.g., a particular restaurant) were good predictors of the actions that occurred there. The same holds for frequently versus infrequently encountered people. In addition, because recurrent times (e.g., Monday and Wednesday at 9:00 a.m.) tend to be related to certain activities (e.g., taking a psychology class), these times will be good predictors of such events. In this way, knowing the regularities and the unusual aspects of our environment can help to understand our memories with respect to that environment.

Brewer's study offers an important, albeit somewhat unwieldy antidote to the studies of self-selected memories that I have considered. In effect, Brewer's study places a kind of boundary condition on these previous studies by examining what individuals remember about the more mundane, everyday events and thoughts in their lives. Ironically, the study is also a commentary on both the complexity and the repetitive, routine nature of everyday cognition. (I assume that college students are not the only ones whose lives are mundane and routine.) Brewer's results are sometimes hard to get a firm grasp on, just as the fabric of our everyday lives is often hard to capsulize or bring into clear relief. Stated differently, the study offers some important theoretical and empirical insights, but does not a coherent story make.

"INVOLUNTARY" MEMORIES
OR "THOUGHTS THAT COME UNBIDDEN"

Thus far in my discussion of both organization and retrieval, I have focused on the deliberate, strategic recall of AMs; in fact, Bekerian and Dritschel (1992), in a critique of AM research, argued that every reported controlled study of AM has used the same pattern of conditions, namely, intentional retrieval plus direct tests of memory, and usually awareness of the source of that memory. (See Jacoby, 1988, for a similar criticism.) There is obviously another type of AM that is more difficult to study and on which there has been little research: namely, memories that are elicited passively and apparently involuntarily by some cue. Everyone has probably had the experience of hearing a song or seeing a sight that brings to mind some long-forgotten event in our lives. The classic literary example of this sort of phenomena is found in Proust's *Remembrance of Things Past*, in which the character Marcel dips his madeleine pastry into a cup of tea and suddenly is overwhelmed by a sense of "well-being," and eventually recalls that when he was young, he took delight in visiting his aunt, who used to give him crumbs of madeleine dipped in tea. A similar (though less eloquent) real-life example has been presented by Lucchelli, Muggia, and Spinnler (1995), in which a patient suffering from both retrograde and anterograde amnesia suddenly recalled a hernia operation from 25 years ago while undergoing an operation to install a pacemaker. This memory led to a flood of memories from that patient's past as well as a renewed sense of self.

The main source of information about such *passive* (Spence, 1988) or *involuntary memories* is a book by Ester Salaman (1970) entitled *A Collection of Moments*. As the title suggests, this book is a collection of various authors' and artists' memories that had an impact on their own artistic productions. For example, speaking of her own experiences, Salaman observes:

> For many years my experience of involuntary memories was unpredictable, sporadic, and elusive. Only in maturity, when a large number came back within a comparatively short period of time, did a pattern of their general nature begin to appear. But I was too preoccupied by the submerged ship of childhood, adolescence, and early youth, which was rising to the surface, to concentrate on the nature of memories as an end in itself. It was not until some years later that I began to decipher my own observations about memories, and to understand other writers' passing remarks. It was then that I became certain that one can gather much knowledge about the nature of memories from writers. (p. 2)

Salaman's (1970) book consists of many examples, several from her own experience (see the example given at the beginning of this chapter), and many others from writers such as Proust, De Quincey, and Chateaubriand, as well as anecdotes from Tolstoy, Stendahl, Darwin, and others. Some of the examples she gives are like dreams or trances, and she argues that these memories always involve some strong feeling, and "give a sensation of living in the past" (Salaman, 1970, p. 45). They may be either whole memories or fragments. For Salaman, these memories are to be distinguished from the "innumerable other floating fragment memories—of faces, names, numbers—which are easily distinguishable from the [other] kind of precious fragments ... by the fact that they carry no strong emotions, do not give the feeling of living in the past, and never come back involuntarily" (Salaman, 1970, p. 45). Salaman was particularly interested in how these "precious fragments" inform the writing of authors. She argued that "the involuntary memory has this in common with a moment of inspiration: it is unexpected, surprising, and yet we claim it as our own at once, sure of its validity" (p. 135). A number of these features should sound familiar from our discussion of Brewer's view in chapter 5, and there is also an apparent similarity between Salaman's descriptions and the accounts given earlier by Pillemer and White and others of early childhood memories.

Pillemer (1998), in fact, discussed the phenomenon of "intrusive memory images" (p. 162), including in particular examples of memories of patients suffering from posttraumatic stress disorder (PTSD). For example, Pillemer cited the case of tennis star Monica Seles who was stabbed in the back by a crazed spectator during a match in Hamburg. Seles continued to be haunted by sensory images of the attack, of her own voice screaming out during the attack, and of the episodes in the hospital when she was shown the knife and her bloody shirt. Other anecdotal examples cited by Pillemer are cases of the memories of World War II veterans for their experiences 50 years after the war, the intrusive memories of Holocaust victims, and the memories of survivors of earthquakes. Finally, in keeping with his own model of AM, Pillemer makes the case that one of the functions of (some forms of) psychotherapy is to provide a narrative format for recovering these unintegrated images (cf. Barclay, 1996).

Although Salaman's and Pillemer's books are filled with very interesting and compelling examples, both of their approaches are nevertheless unabashedly anecdotal. The memories Salaman recounted come from a very select sample of writers and an even more select sample of their own memories, neither of which are at all representative of the population as a whole (which, in Salaman's view, is probably just as well). Pillemer's examples come from a wider variety of sources, but once again they are simply anecdotal, coming from a variety of newspaper stories and biographies.

In contrast, Roberts and McGinnis (1998; Roberts, McGinnis, Clark, & Reyes, 1996) reported results of two diary studies in which college students and community volunteers kept diaries for a week of their "passive memories." The findings of these two studies were that some 54% of the passive memories reported were more everyday and "inconsequential." These memories were also less intense than Salaman (1982) proposed (more like what Spence, 1988, described as a "whisper"), and over 47% of these memories were of relationships.

In related research, Berntsen (1996, 1998) compared the nature and the sources of voluntary and involuntary memories. The latter memories were collected from a diary study (Berntsen, 1996), whereas the former were gathered in a cued recall task (Berntsen, 1998), where the cues were taken from those listed by respondents in the earlier diary study. The first relevant finding, which harkens back to my discussion in the last chapter, was that both voluntary and involuntary memories were more likely to be specific than they were to be general; and the specificity was more apparent for the involuntary than for the voluntary memories (though see the somewhat different results reported by Roberts and her associates). Similarly, both groups were more likely to report distinctive or unusual events than common ones, though there was not a difference between the groups on this dimension. Memories from the involuntary group were more recent than those from the voluntary one, although memories in both groups were skewed toward recency.

Other characteristics of involuntary memories were that such memories proved to be significantly more positive than did voluntary ones, although both types showed more positive and neutral memories than negative ones. Participants were more likely to rehearse voluntary memories than involuntary ones, and rehearsal in both groups was related to emotional intensity regardless of whether that emotion was positive or negative. Finally, in reanalyzing the results of her earlier diary study, Berntsen (1998) pointed out that fully two thirds of the involuntary memories were reported under conditions of "diffuse [i.e., unfocused] attention" and were elicited in response to external rather than internal cues (unlike the voluntary retrieval of memories). This last finding contrasts with the assumption of some researchers on the stream of consciousness (e.g., Singer, 1993), who argue that it is primarily internal cues that elicit involuntary memories.

Berntsen (1998) concluded from these results that voluntary and involuntary memories "may access different samples of autobiographical memories" (p. 113). More specifically, she argued that at least one possible interpretation is that involuntary memories are drawn directly from sensory, phenomenological experience, or what Conway (1996; Conway & Rubin, 1993) called event-specific knowledge (see also W. F. Brewer's [1996] emphasis on phenomenological details). Although Conway championed a hierarchical view of AM, which is the other possible viewpoint reviewed by Berntsen, it will be recalled that Conway also suggested that ESK may exist in a different knowledge store and that Anderson and Conway (1993) argued that "personally important distinctive details" may be the easiest way of accessing AMs. Such a view also follows from the point raised earlier that people obviously do not encode experiences in terms of lifetime periods at the time that they are experiencing them (see Berntsen, 1998, for a similar point). Berntsen also suggested a connection to arguments by G. Mandler (1994) that successful retrieval of some memories may depend on a relaxed state of awareness and the lack of a deliberate retrieval strategy, the latter of which may even block access to some memories. (Note the similarity here to arguments from psychoanalytic theory, as well as to research on dreaming and daydreaming.) Finally, Berntsen noted the similarity to Schank's (1982a) view of "remindings" and to his suggestion that some remindings are unintentional.

It is certainly of interest to note that involuntary memories have different phenomenological properties from voluntary ones. It is not clear, however, that it is necessary to posit two different systems or sources of memories, although I have certainly pointed out many suggestions of a two-system model in previous chapters. It is also the case, as Berntsen herself acknowledged, that this is not an entirely fair comparison because the cues for the voluntary memories were mere verbal descriptions, and fairly general descriptions at that, of the original cues in the involuntary condition. Furthermore, the cues in the voluntary memory study were clearly generated by the experimenter (albeit from cues reported by the participants themselves), whereas the cues for the involuntary memories were more ecologically valid. (Notice that this distinction takes us back to the fundamental distinction between experimental and everyday memory studies discussed in chap. 1.) Finally, given our discussion of the relative reconstructive versus reproductive nature of AM, and Hyman's (1999) account of why people believe false memories, it is not completely clear whether these involuntary memories are indeed exact copies of the original experience.

It would certainly be interesting to study both the mundane and also more exotic forms of "involuntary memories" in a more systematic, scientific way—to examine the conditions that evoke them, individual differences in their frequency and style, their organization, their accuracy or embellishment, and their phenomenology. Diary studies are certainly a good start, or at the opposite end of the spectrum, researchers may use priming or individualized cued recall tests to get at them (though see Berntsen's [1998] results on this), although even here it would be difficult to clearly distinguish between automatic and voluntary, calculated memories. One thing is certain: The phenomenon of passive or involuntary memories will be much more difficult to study than those memories that are voluntary or "bidden." As Bekerian and Dritschel (1992) argued, however, our account of AM retrieval will be severely restricted if we do not also pay attention to these other forms of AM.

AUTOBIOGRAPHICAL MEMORY AND THE SELF

One final question that arises from this discussion of both the theoretical and empirical literatures on AM is how such memories relate to individuals' conception of or knowledge about themselves. For example, in the last chapter I discussed how W. F. Brewer (1986) referred to generic knowledge about one's past unaccompanied by imagery as the "self-schema"; in the previous and current chapters I discussed the increased emphasis on the self placed by Barclay (1994, 1996) and Conway (e.g., 1992, 1995; Conway & Playdell-Pearce, 2000; Conway & Rubin, 1993). In addition, during the past two decades there has been considerable research within social psychology on the *self-schema* (e.g., Markus, 1977), the *self-reference effect* (e.g., Rogers et al., 1977), *possible selves* (Markus & Nurius, 1986), to name just a few. Also, as I discuss in this section, Neisser (1994b, Neisser & Fivush, 1994; Neisser & Jopling, 1997) recently edited three volumes on the different aspects of the self.

Neisser's Conception of the Self.   In his initial article on the self, Neisser (1988b) distinguished among five different forms of self-knowledge, "aspects which are so distinct that they are essentially different *selves*:

they differ in their origins and developmental histories, in what we know about them, ... and in the manner in which they contribute to human social experience" (p. 35). These five forms of self-knowledge are (a) the *ecological self,* or the self perceived in terms of time, place, and activity; (b) the *interpersonal self,* or the self involved in a particular form of interaction; (c) the *extended self,* or the self "based primarily on our personal memories and anticipations" (p. 36); (d) the *private self,* or the part of the self that is not presented to or shared with others; and (e) the *conceptual self,* or the self which "draws its meaning from the network of assumptions and theories in which it is embedded" (p. 36). (See Neisser, 1994b, for a symposium on the first of these two types of self-knowledge, Neisser & Fivush, 1994, for a discussion of the extended or remembered self, and Neisser & Jopling, 1997, on the conceptual self.)

The major point of this distinction for my purposes is that the extended self is the one that is related to AM. It is obvious that for most people the extended self is also connected to the ecological or physically present self, although in the extreme case of amnesia, that link may be broken (see Hirst, 1994, and Tulving, Schacter, McLachlan. & Moscovitch, 1980, for examples of this discontinuity). In addition, and more important for my purposes, the extended self, or the set of AMs, is influenced by and often distorted by an individual's self-concept or self-schema (Markus, 1977), or, in Neisser's terminology, the conceptual self. Examples that I examined in chapter 5 are the work of Barclay (e.g., 1994; Barclay & Subrumanian, 1987) and Ross (1989), as well as the work by Fivush (1988) and M. L. Howe and Courage (1993) on the development of AMs. In addition, I discussed the increasing emphasis by Conway (1992, 1996; Conway & Playdell-Pearce, 2000; Conway & Rubin, 1993) on the influence of the self on the themes that shape AMs. For example, Conway (1992) has stated this point as follows:

> It is assumed that the self is the main source of themes and that as the self changes over time themes are discarded and replaced by other themes. In this way, a theme which was previously used to structure knowledge but was subsequently discarded and of which no explicit representation remains, may nonetheless be implicitly retained in preserved thematic knowledge structures. (p. 175)

As noted earlier, Conway and others (e.g., Singer & Salovey, 1997) have also implicated the goals or "goal structure" of the working self and the plans for reaching those goals in the encoding and retrieval of autobiographical memories. These concepts of themes, goals, and plans clearly relate back to the discussion of event memory in chapter 4. However, here these concepts appear to refer to the self-as-knower rather to the knowledge or memories as such (though see Conway's [1992; Conway & Pleydell-Pearce, 2000] reluctance to make such a distinction).

Given this newfound emphasis on the self in both social and cognitive psychology, it is somewhat surprising that relatively little research has been carried out on this fundamental question of the relationship between self-knowledge and AM. One recent research program that has, in fact, addressed this topic is the work of S. B. Klein and Loftus (1993; S. B. Klein, Loftus, & Burton, 1989; S. B. Klein, Loftus, Trafton, & Fuhrman, 1992).

The main question addressed in this research is whether retrieval of AMs is necessary for making self-judgments or, stated differently (S. B. Klein & Loftus, 1993), whether remembering specific behavioral or event exemplars is necessary for making abstract trait judgments about oneself. Thus, for example, is it necessary or helpful to recall examples of your extroverted behaviors to judge whether or not you are an extrovert? The central paradigm used in this research is the task facilitation design adapted earlier by Reiser et al. (1985) from Freedman and Loftus (1971). Specifically, participants were asked to make either trait descriptive judgments (i.e., how well a given trait described them) followed by a behavioral event recall task (i.e., recalling a behavior relevant to that trait) or to perform these tasks in the reverse order. As a control condition, Klein and Loftus used a task in which participants were asked to define the trait adjective under consideration, and this task was paired, in both orders, with either the trait-description or the AM task. The idea here was to see whether making an abstract trait judgment required first coming up with a specific behavioral exemplar, in which case a preceding trait judgment should lead to faster RTs for the succeeding AM task, and whether retrieving an AM first facilitates subsequent trait judgments.

The results of this basic paradigm are straightforward. Making an abstract trait judgment did *not* facilitate retrieval of AMs, presumably because trait judgments are represented at an abstract level rather than as groups or clusters of exemplars. Furthermore, making an AM judgment did *not* facilitate subsequent trait judgments. These results are similar to the results discussed in chapter 2 on the relationship between trait judgments and memory for behavioral exemplars. Nelson (1993c) also drew a rough analogy between Klein & Loftus's distinction and her own distinction between generic event memory and episodic memory for specific events in childhood, as discussed in chapter 5. These results held even when degree of self-descriptiveness (of the trait descriptors) was controlled for.

S. B. Klein and Loftus (1993) couched these results in terms of a contrast between a *pure abstraction model,* in which traits are represented by a summary or abstraction from a set of exemplars (in this case, AMs) that define that category, versus a *dual exemplar/summary model,* in which traits are represented in terms of *both* exemplars and abstract traits. Both of these models can be contrasted with a *pure exemplar model* in which traits are represented primarily in terms of their exemplars. The results of the facilitation task, as well as a subsequent encoding specificity task (S. B. Klein, Loftus, & Plog, 1992) and a comparison of the effects of AM and trait description task performed separately or together on free recall (Klein et al., 1989) are all inconsistent with a pure exemplar model (though see Keenan, 1993, for a variation on an exemplar model that can account for the Klein & Loftus findings). S. B. Klein and Loftus (1993) also pointed out that their results are inconsistent with an associative network model, according to which traits are simply one node linked to behavioral exemplars (see S. B. Klein & Loftus, 1990).

S. B. Klein et al. (1992; S. B. Klein & Loftus, 1993) also proposed a compromise account to both the pure abstraction and pure exemplar models. This compromise argues that whether individuals use exemplar information in making self-referent judgments depends on how much information they have available about themselves on that particular quality. Specifically, the less information one has about a given topic, the more likely he or she is to depend on a review of relevant exemplars. S. B. Klein et al. (1992) tested out this mixed exemplar–abstraction model by varying the time period for which participants could make their judgments. Specifically, these investigators asked their first-year college students to make their self-judgments on the basis of either the limited time that they had spent in college (low experience condition) or on the basis of their lives prior to coming to college (high experience condition). Using the same task facilitation paradigm, S. B. Klein et al. (1992) found support for their mixed model in that the trait judgment task facilitated RTs for retrieval of AMs under the low experience condition, where students presumably had a small enough amount of information to be able to search exemplars, whereas no facilitation was found in the high experience condition. These results suggest that individuals may, in fact, rely more on AM exemplars when they have little experience from which to form abstract trait judgments. As an example, consider how you might go about making a judgment of how "charismatic" you are versus a judgment of how "outgoing" you are.

One of the questions that arises from this discussion of autobiographical versus self-knowledge is how (or if) these two sorts of knowledge are represented differently from each other or from knowledge about, say, other people. On the first of these questions, I have suggested that researchers in AM (e.g., Conway, 1990a, 1996, 1997a) have tended to emphasize thematic representations in a manner similar to researchers in event memory. Researchers on the self-schema, on the other hand, have emphasized more static traits or abstracted qualities (see Bruner, 1987; and Gergen, 1994, for notable exceptions) in a manner similar to researchers on person memory. (See Woll, 2000, for a more detailed discussion of this distinction.)

S. B. Klein and Loftus (1993) raised a similar issue in the more limited context of why exemplar and associative network models work in other areas but not for the self. Their response is an interesting one, and one that is relevant to the study of everyday cognition in general. (Also note the similarity to the rationale provided by Bahrick et al., 1975, in chap. 3):

> Most of the research supporting these [i.e., exemplar and associative network] models examines memory for information that is small in amount, recently learned, and devoid of context: Typically a list of statements composed by the experimenters about a supposed person. Subjects are presented with

this information and then tested shortly thereafter (often within minutes) to determine how the information is represented in memory. Knowledge of self, by contrast, includes a vast amount of information that has been acquired across a variety of meaningful contexts over the course of a lifetime. (p. 32)

In other words, traditional laboratory studies of memory, whether it be on person memory or other more "basic" memory topics, fail to capture the fact that much everyday memory is based on multiple episodes over extended periods of time and over a variety of different contexts. Clearly, this point holds for all areas of everyday memory, including memory for other people, faces, and events, although no person, face, or event is encountered as frequently or in more different situations nor do we have more knowledge about than ourselves. In any case, it is interesting to note that models that have been successfully applied to laboratory research on memory do not necessarily capture the real-world phenomena of AM or the self (see S. J. Anderson & Conway, 1997, for a similar observation).

SUMMARY

In this chapter I have reviewed some of the research conducted during the last decade and a half on the organization and retrieval of AM. In so doing, I have highlighted the debate between Reiser et al. and both Barsalou and Conway on the basic organizational format for AM. I have also reviewed some models and research on the active versus passive retrieval of such memories, including the extensive diary studies by Thompson et al. and by Brewer. Finally, I have examined the small amount of literature on the relationship between the self and autobiographical memory.

It is interesting to see how much (and what varied) research and theory have been published on this topic within a very short period of time, particularly since, for the most part, such research was not even accepted into traditional journals of memory until around 1986, which saw the publication or Rubin's book *Autobiographical Memory* (see also Schooler & Herrmann, 1992, for a discussion of their experiences in this area). It is also apparent that there is still a good deal of disagreement on matters of theory and that there is a good deal of research that needs to be done on some topics (e.g., involuntary memories, the role of themes, the relationship between the self and AM). Nevertheless, this is one area of everyday cognition in which some systematic research has been done, and a core group of theorists and researchers exists (see Conway et al.'s [1992] report of a NATO conference on this topic) who believe in the importance of this topic. In that sense, AM represents something of a model for other areas of everyday memory.

Chapter 7

Skills, Expertise, and Their Generality: The Backgrounds of Practical Intelligence and Everyday Reasoning

INTRODUCTION

In the previous five chapters I have examined some of the similarities and differences between research on everyday memory on the one hand, and laboratory studies on that topic on the other. In the next three chapters I consider some of the reasoning and judgment processes that operate on this knowledge and on information from the environment. Are the processes or skills involved in practical, everyday reasoning different from those involved in *formal* and/or academic reasoning, or are the processes the same but simply operating on different representations or databases (see Abelson, 1976b, for a similar distinction)? Can the results of lab research on reasoning and problem solving and from the psychometric study of intelligence be meaningfully applied to everyday reasoning? Are there differences in reasoning processes and in knowledge representations between people who are more or less expert at a given task? Are these skills general across tasks (i.e., across formal and informal reasoning tasks, or across different types of practical problems), or are they task- or domain-specific? It is these sorts of questions that I consider in this chapter.

Before I begin discussing these issues, recall that many researchers, especially those conducting research on so-called "dynamic memory" (e.g., Kolodner, 1983a; Schank, 1982a, 1982b), argued that it is impossible to disentangle knowledge representations and the process of remembering on the one hand, from reasoning and problem-solving on the other. Such a distinction is difficult to make because problem solving is influenced by one's background knowledge and one's representation of the problem (see my later discussion of the study of expert knowledge and reasoning) and because reasoning is intimately involved in the process of understanding and retrieval. As I discuss in the next section, this distinction is even more difficult to make in the case of informal, everyday cognition. Furthermore, as I have suggested, theorists such as the connectionists also argue that a clear separation between processing and representation cannot really be made. Thus, although it is useful to distinguish between memory and reasoning for expository purposes, such a distinction is by no means a hard and fast one.

SOME DIFFERENCES BETWEEN FORMAL
AND INFORMAL REASONING

In chapter 1 I reviewed a number of differences between everyday cognition and more traditional laboratory approaches to memory and cognition, including some specific differences between formal and informal *reasoning* and *problem solving*. At this point it may be useful to review some of the latter distinctions, which have been raised by a variety of commentators (e.g., Galotti, 1989; Meacham & Emont, 1989; Wagner & Sternberg, 1990), including some whose work will be reviewed in the subsequent two chapters.

To begin with, Galotti (1989) observed that formal reasoning involves explicitly stated premises (as in syllogistic reasoning) or components (in, for example, traditional problem solving), whereas informal reasoning incorporates the individual's ability to generate or retrieve the relevant premises (e.g., what are the relevant considerations in resolving a marital conflict or in planning a third-down play in football?). This suggests that informal reasoning skills, for better or worse, depend more on the individual's background knowledge and experience than does formal reasoning; certainly this is true in many familiar, everyday situations. Thus, parents of a young baby must be able to distinguish among which factors and behaviors or symptoms are noteworthy and which ones are not; similarly, racetrack handicappers must be able to separate between track conditions that make a difference in race results and those that do not. In fact, Galotti (1989) argued that valid everyday reasoning involves greater breadth and depth of knowledge, as well as "a more thorough and less biased search for arguments and evidence" (p. 389), although it may be argued that *typical* everyday reasoning just as often involves a more *biased,* motivated search. (You need only recall the differences between the arguments of the Republican House Managers and those of the White House defense team in the recent trial of Bill Clinton to validate such a biased search; cf. Perkins, Farady, & Bushey's [1991] distinction between pursuing "my-side" versus "other-side" arguments).

Along similar lines, Galotti (1989) argued that emotional issues may come into play in evaluating the premises, conclusions, or both, in informal reasoning (see also Nickerson, 1991; Ostrom, 1984), although this obviously holds true for some topics (e.g., political reasoning, marital problem solving) more so than for others (e.g., the routinized or well-practiced decision making of experts in a given area—see Ceci & Liker, 1986a, 1986b; Scribner, 1984a, 1986—or the practice of everyday mathematics). In addition, the problem solver's personal goals may affect the problem-solving or reasoning process over and above the goal of problem solution itself (cf. Nickerson's [1991] discussion of the impact of goals in informal reasoning). Such goals may include anything from wanting to maintain a relationship or support a legal position to simply trying to save physical or mental effort (see discussion of Scribner's [1984a, 1986] research on dairy workers).

Other differences mentioned by Galotti (1989) include the fact that formal reasoning typically involves a single correct answer or conclusion and a standard, agreed-upon method of reasoning (e.g., a syllogism or Bayes's theorem), whereas informal reasoning allows for more than one conclusion. Furthermore, almost by definition, informal reasoning does not involve a single, consensual "form" or method (though see Voss, Blais, Means, Greene, & Awesh, 1989, for a model of the format for informal reasoning), although many of the examples of everyday reasoning that I discuss later involve a fairly regular, predictable procedure or format. The conclusions of formal reasoning are clear and unambiguous, whereas those of informal reasoning typically (but not always) are not. Problems requiring informal reasoning typically have personal relevance, whereas those involving formal reasoning typically do not (and when personally relevant material is added, changes in the reasoning process or conclusions may result—see Evans, 1989). Finally, informal reasoning typically occurs as part of a larger context (see Saxe, 1991; Scribner, 1986), whether it be deciding on one of several advertised products in a grocery store (see Lave et al., 1984) or solving a political problem within a broader national or international context (see Voss, Greene, Post, & Penner, 1983), whereas formal reasoning is usually self-contained and engaged in for its own sake. A prominent part of this "context" is the role of social influences and concerns (see Meacham & Emont, 1989), as I discuss in chapter 8. In the same vein, it seems reasonable to assume that informal reasoning is more context-specific than formal reasoning (though see my later discussion of the domain-specificity of problem-solving or cognitive skills in general). Thus, the way in which you reason about your career may be very different from the way you reason about your relationships, which in turn may differ from the way you reason about other peoples' relationships. Similarly, as I discuss in chapter 8, people may use math differently in their everyday grocery shopping or in their sales transactions than they do, for example, in balancing their checkbook or in a school context.

As I noted in chapter 1, Neisser (1976) and Wagner and Sternberg (1985, 1990) raised similar points in distinguishing between the tasks used for assessing *academic intelligence* or IQ and those involved in practical intelligence. For example, Neisser (1976) observed that tasks on IQ tests are typically removed from their real-world context and from the test-taker's short- and long-term goals (though see the recent movement toward "authentic tests" to be discussed in chap. 10). In addition, these problems are formulated by other people, have little intrinsic, personal interest for the test-taker, and are self-contained. Similarly, Wagner and Sternberg (1985, 1990) pointed out that the tasks presented in academic settings, unlike those encountered in real-world settings, are well-defined and, as described above, have one right answer and method of solution. In addition, as I discuss in chapter 8, Wagner and Sternberg (1985, 1986) argued that much of the knowledge involved in practical intelligence is "tacit," that is, not explicitly articulated or directly taught (see Evans & Over, 1996, for a further discussion of the tacit knowledge involved in "practical reasoning").

Galotti (1989) and Wagner and Sternberg (1986) also reviewed some of the empirical evidence on the relationship between formal and informal reasoning and between academic and practical intelligence. First, Wagner and Sternberg argued that IQ tests are limited in their ability to predict real-world occupational performance, whereas Ericsson and Smith (1991a) noted a similar lack of success in predicting accomplishments in the arts and sciences and "advanced professions" (p. 5), and Sternberg and Williams (1997) demonstrated the failure of the Graduate Records Exam to predict any measure of performance in graduate school other than grades. Along similar lines, Ericsson, Krampe, and Tesch-Roemer (1993; see also Ericsson & Charness, 1994; Ericsson & Smith, 1991a) reviewed evidence that fails to find a relationship between skilled performance in areas such as music or chess on the one hand, and performance on standard tests or laboratory measures of cognitive ability on the other. Galotti (1989) also reviewed the evidence for a lack of relationship between standard tests of intelligence and tests of informal or everyday reasoning. However, Galotti (1989) herself pointed out that IQ tests obviously involve other types of skill and knowledge besides formal reasoning. In addition, despite possible reservations about their predictive validity, IQ tests have psychometric properties that are known and have been extensively researched, whereas most tests of everyday reasoning and practical intelligence, including those to be reviewed in the next chapter, do not. (See Ceci & Liker, 1988, and Wagner, 1987, for defenses of the reliability and validity of their particular measures of practical intelligence.)

THE STUDY OF EXPERTISE

One of the most active areas of research in current-day cognitive psychology, and one that is clearly relevant to my present concern with cognitive skills, is the study of *expert–novice differences* in knowledge and skill, or "what distinguishes outstanding individuals in a domain from less outstanding individuals in that domain, as well as from people in general" (Ericsson & Smith, 1991a, p. 2). The origins of this research can be found in the work of such researchers as de Groot (1965) and Chase and Simon (1973a, 1973b) on chess masters and in subsequent research by Chi, Larkin, and their associates (e.g., Chi, Feltovich, & Glaser, 1981; Larkin, McDermott, Simon, & Simon, 1980) on expertise in physics and on other well-structured (Reitman, 1965; Simon, 1973) problems (e.g., computer programming, medical diagnosis, electronics). For the most part, this research has not dealt with "everyday knowledge," nor with the kinds of ill-defined or ill-structured problems that are characteristic of such everyday situations. (Exceptions to this rule are the research by Voss on social studies and international relations [e.g., Voss, Greene, Post, & Penner, 1983; Voss, Tyler, & Yengo, 1983] and other examples such as sports, dance, and music discussed in Ericsson, 1996b, and Ericsson & Smith, 1991b). In chapter 8, I talk about how researchers on practical intelligence have often framed their research in terms of this expert–novice distinction; however, with a few exceptions, actual comparisons of experts and novices even in this area have used more well-structured problems such as mathematics or filling of well-defined orders in a milk-processing plant (Scribner, 1984a, 1986).

Before I describe some of the traditional research on expert–novice differences in detail, it is worthwhile to review some of the general conclusions from this research as outlined by Glaser and Chi (1988; see also Bedard & Chi, 1992; Berliner, 1994; Ericsson & Smith, 1991b). First, experts obviously have more knowledge in their area of expertise than do novices; but this knowledge or expertise is *domain-specific*, that is, it is restricted to one specific topic (e.g., chess, physics, Soviet agriculture, etc.) rather than being an ability that is generalizable across diverse topics. (This is an issue I return to later in this chapter.) In fact, the evidence (e.g., Ericsson & Smith, 1991a) suggests that expertise, say, in chess, is *not* related to general intelligence or to specific components of intelligence.

Second, experts are better able to see meaningful patterns in the data, as evidenced by the ability of chess masters to encode meaningful (but not random) chess configurations (see Chase & Simon, 1973a), by the ability of experts in radiological diagnosis to see patterns in X-rays (e.g., Lesgold et al., 1988) and to detect inconsistencies (e.g., Feltovich, Johnson, Moller, & Swanson, 1984; P. E. Johnson et al., 1981), or the ability of experts in baseball or international relations to see meaningful patterns in what they observe. This ability is attributable to the more clearly organized knowledge base of the experts, although G. A. Klein and Hoffman (1993) emphasized that changes in this knowledge base also lead to actual perceptual-cognitive differences (see the discussion of Scribner's [1986] research on the visual strategies of expert inventory takers in a dairy).

Third, along these same lines, experts show better memory, both short- and long-term, for content in their domain of expertise than do novices. As I discuss later, this was one of the first, classic findings in the study of chess masters (e.g., Chase & Simon, 1973a, 1973b; de Groot, 1965, 1966) and has been developed in greater detail by Chase and Ericsson (1981, 1982; see also Ericsson & Kintsch, 1995; Ericsson & Staszewski, 1989). For example, chess masters are not only able to reproduce configurations they have just seen (e.g., Chase & Simon, 1973a), but they are also able to reconstruct games they have played months or years earlier (see Charness, 1991). This knowledge is also easier for the expert to access (see Feltovich et al., 1984; P. E. Johnson et al., 1981; Voss, Greene, et al., 1983a). Fourth, experts are faster at solving problems and performing their skills than are novices, in part because experts have their skills more automatized (see J. R. Anderson, 1982), and in part because the organization of their knowledge frees up processing capacity for taking in new information or for performing other parts of the task (see D. R. Gentner, 1988). They also perform these skills with fewer errors. In fact, Salthouse (1991) conceptualized expertise as the "process or processes of circumventing normal limitations on human information processing" (p. 290).

Fifth, even though they are faster overall, experts spend more time during the initial stages of problem solution in analyzing that problem on a qualitative level. This feature is perhaps clearest in the solution of physics problems (e.g., Larkin et al., 1980) and in chess masters (de Groot, 1965); however, in many different areas novices tend to "jump in," applying rules or equations without much thought, whereas experts spend some time trying to understand the structure and deeper meaning of the problem. Sixth, along similar lines, experts represent a problem at a deeper level, whereas novices represent the same problem more superficially. This is found in the way in which experts classify problems or objects (e.g., Chi et al., 1981) according to principles and conceptual rules rather than according to superficial appearances or similarities (though see my earlier discussion of the role of surface similarities in case-based reasoning). Finally, experts are better at monitoring their progress in problem solution. They ask more questions, at least on more difficult problems (e.g., Miyake & Norman, 1979), are less likely to start down blind alleys (Larkin, 1983), and are better at predicting their own performance and the difficulty of the problem (e.g., Chi, 1978).

Some Examples of Expert Performance

To illustrate some of these characteristics as well as some of the research methods used to study expertise, let me describe three different areas of expertise research: namely, the classic, seminal research on chess, research on baseball and other sports, and research on the skill of typing.

Chess. The modern study of expertise can be traced to the classic research by de Groot (1965) and the equally classic follow-up research by Chase and Simon (1973a). In his initial research de Groot, a chess master himself, collected think-aloud protocols from chess players at various levels of expertise (ranging from experienced amateurs to grandmaster and even two world champions[1]) as they planned their best next move for varying chess positions. Not surprisingly, the more skilled chess players invariably chose better moves than those lacking in expertise. Both masters and grandmasters spent considerable time planning their moves, including evaluating the strengths and weaknesses of their current position, plus a review of possible moves and an in-depth analysis of a few of these moves. Interestingly, and to de Groot's surprise, higher ranking players did *not* seem to plan farther ahead (i.e., a longer sequence of planned moves) than did players of lesser rank, nor did they consider a greater number of moves or go into a more in-depth analysis. On the other hand, experts *did* seem to recognize the best move in the very process of acquainting themselves with the position.

de Groot's conclusion from these observations was that grandmasters operated not by reasoning and higher level planning, but rather by comparing positions with their extensive store of knowledge of previous moves and games.[2] (In this regard, de Groot wrote about the role of "intuition" in chess, referring to knowledge of moves for which the player cannot give a thorough, conscious justification, but is nevertheless completely "reproductive" and based on past experience; cf. my later discussion of Dreyfus and Dreyfus's [1986] model of the development of expertise.) To support this argument, de Groot showed participants chess configurations for a brief time (i.e., 2–10 seconds) and then asked them to reconstruct their thought processes while evaluating their position and to recall that position. Grandmasters and masters were found to take in the position in larger chunks or integrated wholes than were less experienced players; these experts noticed unusual features of the position more readily, and they showed near perfect memory for the chess configuration (see Fig. 7.1 for examples of the relative memory of a grandmaster, master, expert, and amateur chess player for a given configuration).

de Groot attributed this superiority to the chess masters' extensive (but "dynamic")[3] memory for previous positions, along with their greater ability

---

[1]de Groot (1965) also included two "lady players" (p. 87).

[2]At one point, de Groot's (1965) description of the thought processes of chess masters sounds a lot like our discussion of directed thought in chapter 4: the process of "position management ... can itself be split up into (a) recognizing the position as one of a certain general type and (b) noting certain individual, characteristic features of the position" (p. 156).

[3]It should be noted that de Groot's (1965) book starts off with a discussion of the limitations of associationism in accounting for thought in general, and for directed thought in particular.

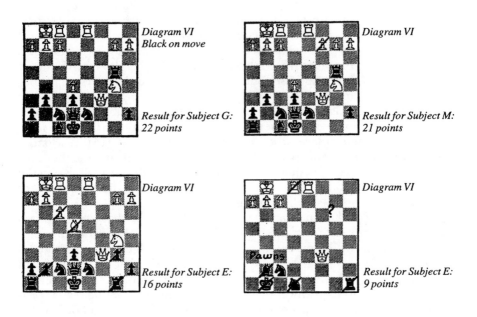

FIG. 7.1. Relative memory for chess configurations by grandmaster, master, expert, and amateur chess players. From *Thought and Choice in Text* (pp. 326–327), by A. D. de Groot, 1965, New York: Basic Books. Reprinted with the permission.

to access these experiences from their perception of the current chess position. Hence, chess expertise is more a matter of perception and memory than of reasoning. In this connection, Chase and Simon (1973a, 1973b) estimated that chess masters know some 50,000 chunks, whereas more recent estimates by Gobet and Simon (1995) are in the range of 50,000 to 100,000 or even higher. de Groot (1966) and Tikhomirov and Poznyanskaya (1966) both reported data on the eye movements of chess masters thinking about what moves to make when faced with a particular chess configuration; these data support the idea that chess masters perceive or scan the chessboard in terms of meaningful patterns. Specifically, chess masters do not scan all

squares equally, but rather fixate on pieces and squares that play a significant role in planning the next move.

In support of this position, Chase and Simon (1973a; see also, Jongman,
1968), using a more standardized memory task, found that players with
greater expertise showed better memory for brief (5-second) presentations of
chess positions, so long as these positions were meaningful ones. Stated differently, chess masters did *not* show greater memory than did novices for chess
positions that were arranged in a random manner. This finding reinforced the
idea that experts rely on past knowledge of chess positions. Of equal importance, Chase and Simon showed that masters recalled positions in larger
"bursts" or chunks (i.e., groupings of positions) followed by brief pauses before recalling another chunk. Stated differently, these investigators found
that experts and novices did *not* differ in the *number* of chunks they recalled,
but did differ in terms of the *size* of these chunks. Chase and Simon also argued that these chunks are stored in long-term memory and are transferred
to short-term memory to match the current chess configuration, which in
turn is encoded in terms of a label referring to that chunk (e.g., a castled
king–pawn formation). This procedure enables chess masters to exceed the
assumed limits on short-term memory (i.e., G. A. Miller's [1956] "7 plus or
minus 2 items" measure).

As a result of this and subsequent research on chess, a variety of different
explanations of the superior talents of chess experts have been proposed,
accounts that are assumed to be generalizable to a variety of different tasks.
The first and most prominent of these is that put forward by Chase and Simon (1973a) themselves. As I have indicated, these investigators suggested
that masters and grandmasters have a larger store of knowledge or of previously encountered chess positions and the moves that follow from them. In
addition, this knowledge is organized in terms of larger chunks. Finally, experts are able to access this knowledge more readily and more quickly.
(Ericsson & Staszewski, 1989—see also Barsalou & Bower, 1984; E. E.
Smith, Adams, & Schorr, 1978—have described this as the *paradox of expertise,* that is, the fact that experts have more knowledge to search but nevertheless make that search and retrieval more rapidly than novices.) Thus,
this viewpoint focuses on the role of sheer memory as the basis for skill and
expertise and emphasizes the role of working memory.

One problem with this memory → skill position is the finding by Ericsson
and Harris (1989) that it is possible to train superior memory for chess positions and to do so within 50–100 hours (as compared with the 10,000–
50,000 hours or 10 years of practice estimated by Simon & Chase, 1973, to
be required to reach master status) without the need for actual expertise in
playing chess. (See Chase & Ericsson, 1982, for similar results for digit
memory vs. actual expertise in mental calculation.) Along similar lines,
Holding and Reynolds (1982) reported that recall for chess positions was
unrelated to quality of move selection. In addition, Charness (1976) found
that participants' memory for chess configurations was disrupted to only a

minor degree by interfering chess or nonchess tasks, such as repeating random digits. (Holding, 1985, gave an example of Sir George Mitchell, "who played Bach fugues at the organ while winning a blindfold [chess] game behind his back" [p. 48]). Thus, it appears that skill or expertise in a given domain cannot be based on short-term memory alone.

A related viewpoint that places less emphasis on short-term memory is the *skilled memory* position put forward by Chase and Ericsson (1981, 1982), which is examined in greater detail later in this chapter. According to this view, the superior memory of experts, including those who are expert in chess, is due to the construction at encoding of retrieval structures and associated retrieval cues by which these structures are accessed. That is, experts use their long-term memory advantages to facilitate encoding and subsequent retrieval of incoming information. Thus, this position focuses more on long-term memory (or what Ericsson & Kintsch, 1995, recently labeled *long-term working memory,* or LT-WM) and on retrieval from such long-term memory than on perception and short-term or working memory. Thus, for example, Ericsson and Staszewski (1989) reported results from a chess player rated just below the level of master who was asked to read a verbal description of a sequence of chess moves and then specify the chess positions that came in between given pairs of moves. This near-master was able to produce these positions as fast mentally as if he were actually playing a game, and when quizzed about what piece fell on which square during this mental chess game, he could identify this position quickly and accurately as well. Further, when this near-master received a brief presentation of a middle-game position, he was able to quickly name the piece on a given square, and he also showed a clear, knowledge-based estimation of all pieces that were threatening that position. All of these results implicate the role of long-term, easily accessed memory structures.

One final position on this topic is that chess skill involves an ability to plan moves farther ahead. Recall that in his initial research de Groot failed to find a superior ability of grandmasters to plan future moves as compared with other chess experts. On the other hand, Charness (1981; see also Gruber, 1991) later demonstrated that such differences in planning do exist at levels below that of expert (see Charness, 1989, for similar observations on expertise in bridge). Similarly, Holding (1985; cf. Binet, 1894) showed that chess masters can play chess blindfolded with little decrement in their performance. On the other hand, it has also been demonstrated (Holding & Reynolds, 1982) that move selection is impaired when chess players are faced with a "demanding secondary task" while considering a move. Needless to say, such planning requires superior memory skills as well. On the other hand, Gobet and Simon (1996) reported evidence from world champion Gary Kasparov playing several games (4–8) simultaneously with little time (3 minutes on average for making 4–8 moves) for reflection or planning. In these games Kasparov performed nearly as well as he did under single-game conditions, a finding Gobet and Simon interpreted as supporting the recognition-memory interpretation over the "planning ahead" one.

Baseball.   A second, more common form of expertise is knowledge of and skill in baseball. Baseball expertise has been studied as both a body of declarative knowledge possessed by spectators and as an athletic skill or form of procedural knowledge acted on by participants (see K. T. Thomas, 1994). In fact, during the past decade the study of athletic skill in general has become a popular topic within the field of expertise (e.g., Shea & Paull, 1996; Starkes & Allard, 1993; Starkes, Deakin, Allard, Hodges, & Hayes, 1996).

On the spectator side, Spilich, Vesonder, Chiesi, and Voss (1979; see also Chiesi, Spilich, & Voss, 1979; Voss, Vesonder, & Spilich, 1980) looked at memory differences between participants who are knowledgeable and those who lack knowledge of baseball after a 5-minute description of a baseball game. Not surprisingly, knowledgeable participants recalled more and made fewer errors or confusions than did less knowledgeable ones. Voss et al. found this difference held even when the text had been generated by the low-knowledge participants themselves. In addition, knowledgeable participants recalled different types of information. For example, they recalled more actions that were instrumental in affecting the outcome of the game. Further, they were more likely to recall these significant actions and changes of state in the correct sequence. Thus, knowledgeable participants showed a better grasp of the goal structure of the described baseball game.

Similar findings have been reported by P. E. Morris (P. E. Morris, Gruneberg, Sykes, & Merrick, 1981; P. E. Morris, Tweedy, & Gruneberg, 1985) regarding memory for soccer scores. Specifically, participants knowledgeable about soccer showed better memory for sets of real scores than did less knowledgeable ones, and this superiority was clearer for real than for simulated ones (where participants were informed beforehand of this difference).

On the participation side, researchers have examined both differences in procedural knowledge and differences in response selection and execution. For example, on the knowledge issue Hanson (1992) reported the results of an interview with Hank Aaron, the Major League Baseball world record holder in home runs and total bases. This interview underlined the explicit mental preparation Aaron put in for each new pitcher, because each pitcher is somewhat different. This preparation, which began the day before the game and continued through the game (e.g., on the bench and when on deck), involved not only calling on existing knowledge, but also visualizing himself batting against that pitcher, focusing on the angle at which the pitch was likely to come in (p. 58), as well as the various situations (e.g., number of players on base) in which he might find himself. Thus, such preparation involved both knowledge and response selection, and it results in greater concentration and focus.

With regard to response selection, J. R. Thomas, French, and Humphries (1986) proposed that the mechanisms for response selection may be structured in the same way as individuals' recall of text for a baseball game; and Abernethy, Thomas, and Thomas (1993) suggested that think-aloud protocols may be useful in studying the former. Building on these ideas, McPherson (1993a, 1993b) asked expert (collegiate) baseball players and novices (volunteers from physical education classes) to watch an edited tape (without sound) of part of a collegiate baseball game and to think aloud while a pitcher threw to three batters in preparation for participants taking the role of a fourth batter in that half inning. Participants' protocols were coded in terms of different categories of conditions (e.g., batter and/or pitcher characteristics, defense and/or offense), actions, and goals. This sort of protocol analysis was explicitly motivated by work on expertise by Chi and Bassok (1989).

McPherson (1993a, 1993b) reported that experts included significantly more conditions and actions but not more goals than did novices. In their condition concepts, experts specifically focused more on pitcher and batter characteristics. More important, among their action concepts experts showed a significantly greater consideration of tactics, such as focusing on gathering information from earlier batters, statements about the probability of certain pitcher behaviors and their own (participants') probable responses. The actions generated by experts were more likely to focus on visual and motor components (McPherson, 1993a), for example, "[you've got to keep] picking up arm angle [of the pitcher], where everybody's hitting the ball, checking velocity" (p. 316) versus "You got to watch it, gotta keep your eye on the ball" (p. 316). Experts included significantly more connections among concepts (e.g., between conditions and actions or between different actions), and they also showed greater monitoring of their predictions (i.e., noting whether these predictions came true). As far as final solutions (or batting in the fourth position) are concerned, experts were more likely to mention previous pitches and more "sophisticated analysis of the current situation" (p. 318). In general, experts showed a "more advanced knowledge structure" and greater attention to a variety of internal and external cues. They were better at accessing relevant information and knowing which factors were relevant. Experts, in effect, used more domain-specific strategies for bat preparation, whereas novices used more general baseball issues (e.g., looking for stolen bases).

On the response selection side, Paull and Glenncross (1997) reported that expert batters reacted faster than novices to an interactive simulation of pitching, and these experts showed further decreases in decision times without a reduction in accuracy when they knew the game situation. Similarly, Shank and Haywood (1987) found that whereas novice baseball players focused on both the pitcher's eyes and his arm in preparing to bat, expert players fixated only on the point of release of the pitch. Similarly, Hyllegard (1991) found that expert batters predicted the type of pitch better and that accuracy in predictions was improved when batters could see the seams of the pitched ball better, although the interaction here was not significant. These, along with observations from a variety of other sports (see Starkes & Allard, 1993), speak to some of the cognitive differences between experts and novices in the actual practice of sports.

Given the variety of different forms of sports knowledge and the variety of possible representations of this knowledge (e.g., by spectators vs. participants, declarative vs. procedural), the question arises how interchangeable these different forms of knowledge are (see the observation by J. R. Thomas et al., 1986, cited previously). For example, would an expert player in baseball, basketball, golf, or the like also show superior ability at computer game versions of these sports? Or a familiar question in sports is whether a top player necessarily would be able to become a similarly talented coach? Do coaches at a given sport show greater knowledge than their players (as McPherson, 1993a, 1993b, found for a single coach), and might this difference reflect differences in representations or simply in the ability to articulate that knowledge?

Typing. One final everyday skill that entails both a perceptual-cognitive and a motor skills component is transcription typing. Such a skill obviously requires manual dexterity, but it also involves the ability to take in information in chunks that must then be broken down into specific keystrokes. Furthermore, typing is clearly a skill that can reasonably be studied in its "natural" form in the laboratory.

The skill of typing has been studied extensively by Salthouse (1984, 1986) and by D. R. Gentner (1987, 1988). For example, Salthouse (1984) and others (see Salthouse, 1986) have shown that the speed of expert typists is greater when they are typing words versus random letters, but typing speed does not increase further when the words appear in meaningful text. Along these lines, Salthouse (1984) has also found that there is little relationship between comprehension of the text and typing speed, and no relation between memory span and typing speed (Salthouse, 1984). Typists obviously *do* hold the text in working memory, as evidenced by the fact that typing speed is reduced when typists are limited in the amount of text they are allowed to preview (Salthouse, 1991; see also Shaffer, 1973). Another set of studies described by Gentner (1988) involved making the perception of the text more difficult for typists to determine whether they do indeed have unused cognitive resources while typing. Gentner found that although obscuring the printed word by dot patterns of varying densities made the text harder to read (as shown by a clear decrease in the typists' reading speed), such difficulty did not have an effect on typing speed. Essentially the same result has been reported by Shaffer (1975) who found that reciting nursery rhymes or shadowing an auditory message had relatively little effect on typing patterns. Both of these results are presumably due to the fact the expert typists had sufficient resources left over to devote to this perceptual processing problem.

In addition to these clear perceptual-cognitive changes, expert typists also show equally clear improvements in cognitive-motor skills. For example, expert typists not only show greater overall speed, but they also show less variability in the intervals between different keystrokes. In addition, skilled typists show less variability in the speed of both the same and different keystrokes (Salthouse, 1986), and they show increases in the speed of sequential keystrokes by two fingers on the same hand and on different hands. In fact, whereas such repetitive strokes are the fastest for novice typist, they are the slowest for experts (Gentner, 1988). Finally, experts show particular improvement in the typing of digraphs involving overlapping movements, that is, where the typist can start on the second or third letter while completing the first (Gentner, 1988).

Given these different components of typing skills, Gentner (1988) has drawn a number of conclusions about expert-novice differences in these skills. First, Gentner argues that "The performance of student typists is limited primarily by cognitive constraints, whereas the performance of expert typists is limited primarily by motoric constraints" (p. 18). In other words, the acquisition of typing skills is more a matter of refining the cognitive components than it is of improving motoric ones. In addition, instead of expert typists becoming more rigid or routinized, they actually show greater adaptability to different types of text, again suggesting greater cognitive sophistication rather than simply improved motoric skills.

Thus, although typing seems to be a fairly simple skill, it clearly involves a complex combination of perceptual, cognitive, and response selection and execution mechanisms (which, of course, is one reason for including a discussion of it here). In this connection, Salthouse (1984) put forward a four-component information-processing model of transcription typing (see Fig. 7.2). These four components are a perceptual or encoding mechanism that translates the transcribed input into meaningful words, a parser that divides the word into individual ordered characters, keypress schemas that specify the corresponding movements for typing, and a response selection mechanism that translates these keystrokes into action, informed by knowledge about the location of one's fingers on the keyboard.

According to this view, keypress schemas are activated by the parsing schema and by the other keypress schemas—that is, a given keypress schema is actually inhibited for a time by those that immediately precede it, in the same way that PDP models in general stress the role of inhibitory processes. In fact, Rumelhart (cited in D. R. Gentner, 1988) reported a simulation in which increases in inhibitory strength parallel the findings for the movement from novice to expert typing status. A given keystroke is performed when its activation is the highest of all keystrokes and when the relevant finger is located within a given distance of the relevant key. Such a model accounts for the various interstroke intervals described earlier. As D. R. Gentner, Grudin, and Conway (1988) pointed out, however, Rumelhart's model does not take into account observed differences in the latencies of different pairs of letters.

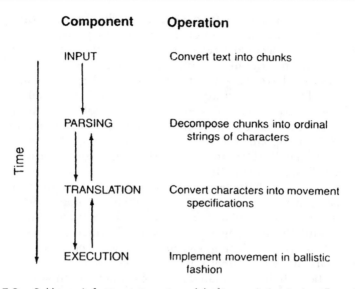

FIG. 7.2.   Salthouse's four component model of transcription typing. From "Percep-tual, Cognitive, and Motoric Aspects of Transcription typing" by T. A. Salthouse, 1984, *Psy-chological Bulletin, 99*, p. 304. Copyright © 1986 by the American Psychological Association. Reprinted with permission.

For example, Grudin and Larochelle (1982) found that skilled typists showed better coordination for high-frequency letter pairs. In general, Gentner et al. found different speeds for letter pairs in Dutch versus English, depending on their frequency in that language.

Summary.   I have reviewed three different areas of expertise that in-volve rather different skills. Chess expertise is almost entirely perceptual-cognitive; baseball is entirely cognitive for the spectator, but cognitive-mo-tor for the participant; and typing includes perceptual, cognitive, and mo-tor or response selection and activation. There are undoubtedly certain commonalities in the skills, particularly in their development, as I discuss in a later section, but there are certainly differences as well. In fact, Ericsson and Smith (1991a) proposed that researchers establish a taxonomy of dif-ferent forms or areas of expertise in order to explore some of the different factors involved in these different skills.

Application to Everyday Expertise

In light of my discussion of research on expertise, the question arises as to whether some of the general characteristics of expertise that I have de-scribed also apply to expertise in more everyday or informal tasks. Does it make sense to talk about everyday expertise or skills? I address this question in greater detail in the next chapter after I review some direct evidence on this topic. However, a cursory review of the seven characteristics of expertise suggests that they do, in fact, apply to some degree to everyday skills.

To begin with, I have argued that baseball (in both spectator and participant form) and typing constitute skills possessed by large numbers of people and hence in some sense represent everyday skills. Research has also been conducted on such fundamental, everyday skills as reading (e.g., Stanovich & Cunningham, 1991; Wagner & Stanovich, 1996; see also West, Stanovich, & Mitchell, 1993) and writing (Bryson, Bereiter, Scardamalia, & Joram, 1991; Scardamalia & Bereiter, 1991).

As far as the seven characteristics are concerned, it seems clear that experts in, say, music (e.g., Ericsson et al., 1993; Krampe, 1994; Sloboda, 1985, 1991), sports (e.g., Allard & Starkes, 1991; Starkes & Allard, 1993; Starkes, Deakin, Allard, Hodges, & Hayes, 1996), video games (e.g., Allard & Starkes, 1991), racetrack handicapping (Ceci & Liker, 1986a), or politics (e.g., Voss, Greene, et al., 1983; Voss et al., 1983; Woll & Loukides, 2000), know more about their areas than do novices, that their knowledge is more organized or systematic, and most importantly, that such knowledge is, for the most part, likely to be domain-specific, that is, there is no reason to expect expertise in baseball or racetrack handicapping to generalize to other areas (though such generalizability certainly applies to reading and writing skills; see my later discussion of transfer of training).

It also seems reasonable to assume that experts in these areas see patterns that novices do not notice, whether they be configurations of factors in horse racing, or "high-strategy" sports (K. T. Thomas, 1994; e.g., baseball, basketball), or international politics. For example, G. A. Klein (e.g., 1993) described some of the differences between novice and expert urban firefighters, including the ability of the latter to see patterns of features (e.g., color of the smoke, heat or intensity of the fire) to pinpoint a fire in making rapid decisions about how to combat it. In a rather different domain, Dawsen, Zeitz, and Wright (1989) have reported similar results for experts' (i.e., members of the supervisory staff of a residential home for emotionally disturbed boys) predictions of patterns of aggressive behaviors. It is also likely that, with their greater store of knowledge and its greater organization, experts in these areas should show better memory, greater and quicker access to that memory, and faster information processing and problem solving in their particular domains (e.g., memory for details of sporting events, speed and efficiency of analyzing political events).

It seems somewhat less likely that there is, in all areas of practical intelligence, a greater preanalysis of the problem prior to embarking on problem solution. For example, much of the practical intelligence that I examine in the next chapter (e.g., street math, product assembly, navigation) seems rather rote and automatized. Other areas such as political reasoning would seem to invite automatic, party-line (knee jerk liberal or conservative) responses (see the House and Senate hearings on impeachment; though see Voss, Greene, et al.'s [1983] evidence in the area of international relations). Similarly, G. A. Klein (e.g., 1989) has studied a number of real-life situations (e.g., firefighting) in which experts must make rapid decisions without extensive analysis (see chap. 10). It is also not clear that practical, everyday problems are always represented at deeper, more principled levels (see my later discussion or research on street math and expert navigation), though there is certainly evidence (e.g., Tetlock, 1985; Woll & Loukides, 2000) of deeper representation in the area of political expertise. Finally, although some degree of self-monitoring and self-regulation may be involved in everyday expertise (see Glaser, 1996), it remains to be seen how highly developed or successful these skills are in different areas of practical reasoning. (It certainly seems reasonable to assume that individuals with an everyday expertise in social skills might, at least, in some cases, be adept at self-monitoring; cf. Riggio, 1986; M. J. Snyder, 1974.)

A word is also in order about the methodology of expertise research and how such methods apply to research on everyday expertise. Ericsson and Smith (1991a; see also Ericsson & Lehmann, 1996) suggested that the first step in studies of expert–novice differences is to find tasks on which experts show outstanding performance *under fairly standard conditions* (e.g., reconstruction of chess positions). For some forms of expertise (e.g., typing) it is possible to reproduce the real-life context in the lab, whereas for others (e.g., medical decision making or racetrack handicapping) some kind of standardized task simulating real conditions must be used. In this regard, Shiffrin (1996) took the strong position that the antecedents of expertise can only be examined by means of lab research, often involving breaking complex skills down into simpler components; and Ericsson and Lehmann (1996) argued that "investigators strive for the minimum of complexity necessary to successfully reproduce the relevant expert performance" (pp. 281–282).

Ericsson and Smith (1991a) pointed out that "there are few instances of real-life experience on which superior performance can be demonstrated under standardized conditions" (p. 14). This is due, in part, to the fact that for many real-life experiences (e.g., talking, walking, eating) there are no clear expert–novice differences (as opposed to a mere range of abilities), and certainly there is nothing like the kind of 10 years of *deliberate* practice (Ericsson et al., 1993) implicated in expertise (Simon & Chase, 1973). It is also true, however, as I have discussed, that research on everyday reasoning and problem solving quite often does not rely on standardized laboratory conditions. Indeed, studies of everyday cognition typically eschew such laboratory studies, although an attempt *is* frequently made to maintain *some* control over the conditions in the real world under which "expert" performance is elicited. It may even be (and, in fact, *has* been) argued that attempting to take some of these everyday skills, such as sports (see McPherson, 1993a) or firefighting (G. A. Klein, 1993) or social skills out of their everyday contexts or to study isolated components or simulations of them is to alter the skill entirely (see my discussion in chap. 1). In any case, as a result of these and other considerations, Ericsson and Smith (1991a) concluded that to study real-life expertise "we need to broaden our approach. Indeed, in many cases we may well be forced to rely on correlational methods" (p. 33; see Bahrick et al., 1975, as well as the recent research by Ericsson et al., 1993, on the correlation between musical expertise and years of practice).

Some Alternative Views of Expertise

In my discussion of chess expertise, I discussed three different accounts of chess expertise. Ericsson and Pennington (1993) discussed three broader views of expertise in general, including the *innate talent*, the *knowledge*, and the *acquired mechanism* viewpoints. Ericsson and his associates (e.g., Ericsson & Charness, 1994; Ericsson & Lehmann, 1996; Ericsson & Pennington, 1993) gave rather short shrift to the first of these, primarily based on the observation that "deliberate practice" (Ericsson et al., 1993) has such a strong impact on expertise as well as the physiological systems (e.g., heart size, muscle movements) that underlie these skills. In addition, as discussed earlier in this chapter, tests of general abilities typically do not strongly predict performance in particular skill areas. (See Howe, Davidson, & Sloboda, 1998, for a more recent argument against the innate talent point of view.)

The second knowledge model is the one that has dominated research in memory since Ebbinghaus. This position argues that expert performance is simply the result of adding existing knowledge to a set of invariant mechanisms and general laws of memory (see chap. 1). However, Ericsson and Pennington suggested that experts actually have acquired domain-specific *mechanisms* for encoding and retrieval for overcoming ordinary capacity limitations. Thus, "in addition to having vastly larger and more organized amounts of knowledge than novices: [sic] experts have reliable and rapid access to their knowledge, while novices retrieve individual facts in a piecemeal fashion and generate results sequentially" (Ericsson & Pennington, 1993, p. 248). This retrieval includes the recovery of strategies and solutions as well as knowledge per se.

The acquired mechanisms view is based in large part on Chase and Ericsson's (1981, 1982) *skilled memory* theory of expert performance referred to earlier. One of the original findings that motivated the formulation of skilled memory theory was a study by Chase and Ericsson (1981) in which participants were able, with extensive practice, to increase their memory span for digits from 7 to 80, suggesting that expert memory is not limited to the brief memory span associated with short-term or working memory. This and other results concerning memory for chess positions (e.g., Charness, 1976) and mental multiplication (Chase & Ericsson, 1982; Staszewski, 1988) led Chase and Ericsson to propose that for experts in a given area, both encoding and retrieval involve making contact with prior knowledge contained in long-term memory (or LT-WM). These ideas were summarized by Chase and Ericsson (1982) in terms of a set of three principles described as the *meaningful encoding*, the *retrieval structure*, and the *speed up* principles, the latter of which refers to the fact that for experts both encoding and retrieval increase in speed such that "their speed and accuracy approach the speed and accuracy of STM [short-term memory] storage" (Ericsson & Staszewski, 1989, p. 240).

To illustrate, there were participants in Chase and Ericsson's (1981) memory span study who were collegiate runners; and these runners tended to treat the sequences of numbers as running times (e.g., 4 minutes 10.5 seconds for a mile run). Furthermore, these mnemonic encodings can be related to each other in the form of a higher order structure (e.g., a story or an organized picture of spatial locations), which increases memory still further. In this and other cases, participants used some existing knowledge to encode (and retrieve) incoming information (see the similar evidence for mnemonists). Specifically, links are made between encoding and retrieval by "associating the encoded information with special retrieval cues belonging to a *retrieval structure* at the time of the original presentation" (Ericsson & Pennington, 1993, p. 252, italics added). (See Fig. 7.3 for an illustration of such a retrieval structure.)

Thus, in the example of the runners cited earlier, the knowledge or retrieval structures consisted of the runners' knowledge of meaningful running times. Similarly, in a study by Ericsson and Polson (1988a, 1988b) verbal protocols provided by a waiter with exceptional memory for food orders indicated that he used a variety of mnemonic structures for encoding and retrieving such orders—for instance, by remembering a sequence of letters for the salad dressings (e.g., TOB for thousand island, oil and vinegar, and bleu cheese) and points on a visual thermometer for the temperatures (e.g., rare vs. well done) of steaks. Still another example cited by Ericsson (1996a) is research by Saariluoma (1989, 1991) on chess masters' memory for nonvisually presented chess positions. For example, Saariluoma (1989) showed that chess masters can play six games in their heads simultaneously when the moves of the opponent are presented on a computer screen. Similarly, masters can recall a chess configuration when the individual chess positions are presented to them verbally in terms of the exact board location of each piece, and can do so even in the face of interference by simultaneously presented visually or verbally presented secondary tasks (Saariluoma, 1991).

Knowledge plays a variety of different roles in expert memory. For example, it seems clear that experts remember more relevant but not more irrelevant information. This selective advantage at encoding can be accounted for by greater chunking of information and the greater ability to produce new memory traces (e.g., by making meaningful connections between numbers encoded as soccer scores). At retrieval, the trick is to access retrieval cues stored at encoding by means of links to existing knowledge structures—for example, the mnemonic cues established by the expert

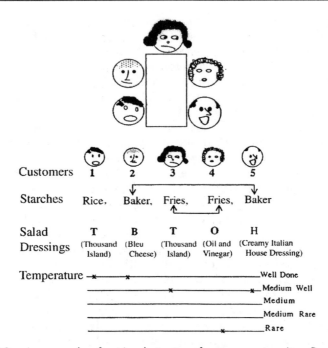

FIG. 7.3. An example of retrieval structure for an expert waiter. Reprinted from Ericsson and Pennington (1993), The Structure of Memory Performance in Experts: Implications for Memory in Everyday Life. In *Memory in Everyday Life* edited by G. M. Davies & R. H. Logie. Copyright © 1993, p. 253, with permission of Elsevier Science.

waiter or chess masters' ability to recall multiple chunks based on their encoding of such chunks in terms of their higher order relations (cf. the discussion in chapter 4 of setting down a "marker" for a later action in prospective memory). In addition, expert knowledge allows for greater and more extensive planning, for example, in bridge (Charness, 1989) or chess (e.g., Charness, 1981; Ericsson & Polson, 1988b). In general, skilled memory or LT-WM theory disputes the idea that memory capacity, or at least working memory capacity, is limited by universal, fixed memory mechanisms and suggests instead that there may be domain-specific differences in memory and cognitive skills (see Ericsson & Kintsch, 1995, for a discussion of this point.)

Ericsson and Pennington (1993) suggested some implications of research on expert memory for everyday cognition or performance. According to the acquired mechanism point of view, the same mechanisms should apply to both expert and everyday performance, but not to traditional lab research (i.e., because such research does not engage existing knowledge structures). At the same time, Ericsson and Pennington (1993) argued that expert–novice differences are typically found in areas where one group has a minimum of knowledge; this kind of separation between novices and experts is unlikely to be found in most everyday performance (see my earlier discussion of this point). Further, these authors argued that the kind of lengthy, intensive training found in most areas of expertise is not seen in everyday life.

I would argue with both of these last two positions. For example, I can think of people who are exceptionally skilled at everyday social interaction and small talk versus those who are relatively unskilled, or people (e.g., con men) who are exceptionally good at manipulating others versus those who are poor at it. Similarly, it is possible to identify expert drivers or expert cooks versus those who are totally unskilled in these areas. Although such skills may not involve the kind of extensive "deliberate practice" emphasized by Ericsson et al. (1993; Ericsson, 1996b), they *do* involve lots of practice and probably are only accomplished after years of such practice.

Some Criticisms of Research on Expertise

A variety of different criticisms have recently been raised concerning research on expert–novice differences. I have already cited the position taken by Shiffrin (1996) that simple correlations (e.g., between length of practice and expertise) do not provide conclusive evidence and that it is obviously not feasible to try to build 10 years of practice into an experimental design (although longitudinal studies of expertise have been initiated). One solution offered by Shiffrin is to break complex skills down into smaller subskills that can then be studied experimentally. It should be clear from my previous discussions that I believe that carefully controlled laboratory studies are not a sine qua non of research on everyday cognition, particularly in view of the sophisticated multivariate techniques currently available (see my discussion of the research by Bahrick and his associates in chaps. 1 and 3). In this connection, Ericsson and Charness (1994) cited evidence that failed to find a relationship between these sorts of laboratory tasks (e.g., simple RT tasks) and actual expert performance (e.g., typing, music). Furthermore, breaking complex skills down into their subcomponents may alter the skills themselves, particularly if one believes that these skills are based on complex, integrated knowledge representations (e.g., a pitching motion in baseball or piano playing; see Ericsson & Charness, 1994, for a similar point, and also see chap. 10 for a debate over whether it is best to learn skills component by component or all at once).

Sternberg (1996) raised a different set of criticisms of research on expertise. Specifically, Sternberg argued that research on expert–novice differences and, in particular, the role of deliberate practice has ignored the overwhelming evidence on the importance of genetic differences in intelligence or skills (see Plomin, 1998, and Rowe, 1998, for similar arguments). In addition, in the case of studies of deliberate practice, by using only groups of experts without control groups or taking into account dropouts (i.e., those who do not persist for the necessary 10 years) there remain alternative accounts of the correlation between deliberate practice and skill, including the fact that individuals who are better at a given task are more motivated to continue practicing that skill. In fact, Sternberg, like Shiffrin, argued that correlations are not sufficient to show causation. (I should note that in most studies of expert–novice differences, a kind of control group—the novices—is built in. Also note that Sternberg's criticisms are primarily concerned with the issue of deliberate practice, which I examine in the next section; and even on this topic Ericsson et al.'s [1993] research has included control groups of less proficient musicians).

THEORIES OF SKILL ACQUISITION

Now that I have examined the research evidence on expertise and skills—a topic that I pursue in greater detail in chapter 8—it is important to also take a look at research and theory on the acquisition of such skills.

It should be noted at the outset that most of the evidence on the development of expert performance suggests that acquisition takes place over an extended period of time and through a process of what I have referred to as *deliberate practice* (Ericsson et al., 1993) or "individualized training on tasks selected by a qualified teacher" (Ericsson & Charness, 1994, p. 738). For example, Chase and Simon (1973a) estimated that the acquisition of master level chess skills required some 10 years of intense practice—the so-called *rule of 10*; more recently, Ericsson et al. (1993) confirmed this 10-year estimate in the field of chess, as well as in other areas such as sports, the arts, and science. Such extended training is obviously rather difficult to duplicate in the lab (though see Chase & Ericsson's [1982; see also Staszewski, 1987] findings on the training of digit recall, and Staszewski's [1988] research on training expert calculators). Perhaps of greater interest for our purposes, Ericsson and Charness (1994) also argued that there is no reason to expect that the process and changes that occur in the acquisition of expert performance should be any less applicable to the acquisition of everyday skills, although the latter process is obviously less structured and more difficult to evaluate in terms of ultimate standards of excellence.

Stage Theories

There have been a number of different descriptive accounts that have attempted to identify stages in the development of expertise (e.g., Dreyfus & Dreyfus, 1986; Ericsson et al., 1993; Taylor & Winkler, 1980). For example, Ericsson et al. (1993; following Bloom, 1985) identified three "phases" in the development of expertise, phases distinguished by the type of practice and the speed of learning (see Fig. 7.4). The first phase involves casual learning with relatively nonintensive practice before the individual initiates *deliberate* practice. According to Ericsson et al., deliberate practice, which begins during the second phase, involves "a well-defined task with an appropriate difficulty level for the particular individual, informative feed-

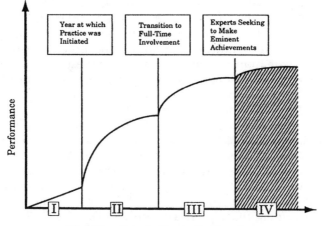

FIG. 7.4. Three stages in the development of expertise. From "The Acquisition of Expert Performance: An Introduction to Some of the Issues," by K. A. Ericsson, 1996a. In *The Road to Excellence: The Acquisition of Expert Performance in the Arts and Sciences, Sports, and Games* (p. 19) edited by K. A. Ericsson, Mahwah, NJ: Lawrence Erlbaum Associates. Copyright © 1996 by Lawrence Erlbaum Associates. Reprinted with permission.

back, and opportunities for corrections of errors" (Ericsson, 1996a, pp. 20–21). During this second phase, performance improves dramatically. Finally, during the third phase the individual undertakes a full-time commitment to the skill, and performance improves even more dramatically. One finding observed in a variety of different skill areas is that experts are people who begin deliberate practice at an earlier age and show more intensive practice (Ericsson et al., 1993).

A somewhat different stage theory has been proposed by Dreyfus and Dreyfus (1986; Dreyfus, 1997) who have outlined five stages of skill acquisition, ranging from novice to expert. In the *novice* stage the individual has little experience in the situation or with the task and therefore depends on objective, context-free features and rules (i.e., rules that are independent of the particular context) in making decisions. For instance, Dreyfus and Dreyfus (1986) cited the example of the beginning driver being told the exact speed at which to shift gears, without regard for other features of traffic or the environment, or the beginning nurse being taught a formula for what to do when certain measures of, for example, blood pressure or respiration rates are read. In the second, *advanced beginner* stage, the individual has had enough experience in situations or tasks to have abstracted out, on his or her own, situational rules or "aspects," such as engine sounds or traffic patterns for gear-shifting or breathing patterns to distinguish between different medical problems. The emphasis here is on *global* features (e.g., general patterns of characteristics indicating anger or distress in a friend or spouse) rather than on precisely defined or specifiable features. In the third, *compe-tent* stage, the individual chooses a perspective or "plan" and as a result is sensitive to the overall configuration of features in a given situation, can distinguish between the significant and nonsignificant features in that situation, can anticipate future situations in terms of these significant features. Dreyfus (1997) gave the example of a competent driver getting off the freeway on a curved off-ramp who must take into account speed, road conditions, and so forth in deciding whether to slow down, brake, or the like.

In the fourth, *proficient* stage, the basis for responding to the situation changes fundamentally. As Dreyfus (1997) summarized this difference, "intuitive behavior gradually replaces reasoned responses" (p. 21). Here the individual responds, in an intuitive, nondeliberative way to a typical situation as a whole, based on its similarity to past situations, rather than analyzing the situation into components or features (cf. my discussion of case-based reasoning in chap. 4). Dreyfus and Dreyfus (1986) referred to this type of pattern recognition as *holistic similarity recognition* (cf. G. A. Klein's [1989] "recognition primed decision" model to be discussed in chap. 9). On the basis of this recognition, the decision maker is assumed to formulate plans (or "maxims," i.e., instructions based on "nuances" of the situation; Benner, 1984, p. 29) that are appropriate for that situation; alternatively, he or she alters plans in terms of changes in that situation. Thus, for example, a driver "knows" when she or he is rounding a curve too fast, or a basketball player "knows" when she or he must switch hands to avoid a defender blocking her or his shot. To cite an example given by Berliner (1994), the great hockey player, Wayne Gretzky, when asked the secret of his success, replied, "I simply go to where the puck is going to be" (see Ericsson & Charness, 1994, for a review of the evidence for experts' ability to anticipate events).

Finally, at the *expert* level, the individual again responds intuitively to the situation without having to analyze it into parts and focuses immediately on the important parts of the problem. At the same time, the expert's *performance* follows fairly immediately or automatically from his or her perception of the situation, and that performance is "fluid and flexible and highly proficient" (Klein & Hoffman, 1993, p. 206). Dreyfus and Dreyfus (1986) stated it thus:

> With enough experience in a variety of situations, all seen from the same perspective or with the same goal in mind but requiring different tactical decisions, the proficient [expert] performer seems to group together situations sharing not only the same goal or perspective, but also the same decision, action, or tactic. (p. 32)

Thus, in the expert stage the decision or action follows immediately from the perception, rather than involving the formulation of some rule or principle. (See Benner, Tanner, & Chesla, 1996, for the results of a study using narrative interviews with nurses that support the Dreyfus and Dreyfus model.)

The final two (and to some extent, the third) stages of the Dreyfus and Dreyfus model of expertise are assumed to be more intuitive and to represent a level of thinking over and beyond that accounted for by traditional theories of problem solving, including those (e.g., Newell & Simon, 1972) that were largely responsible for the interest in the topic of expert–novice differences in the first place. Dreyfus and Dreyfus (1986) explicitly took issue with the view that all intelligence involves explicit problem solving and rule following. In fact, one of Dreyfus and Dreyfus's (1986) arguments on this issue is particularly relevant to our present discussion of everyday reasoning and practical intelligence:

> Clearly we are not *conscious* of solving problems, that is, of selecting goals and combining elements by rule to reach them, during much of our life's activity. When we ride a bicycle, recognize a face in a crowd, exhibit common sense, use natural language, or cope skillfully with the great bulk of everyday situations, are we acting on the basis of rules? If not, are those activities therefore somehow not intelligent? (p. 27, italics added)

Rumelhart and Norman's Schema Approach

Rumelhart and Norman (1978) presented an extension of schema theory in which they proposed three different mechanisms of schema change believed to be involved in learning or knowledge acquisition. The first of these is the mechanism or principle of *accretion,* or simply adding new information to the schema without changing the basic principles (e.g., adding the results of a new study to your schema concerning violence and crime, or adding a new piece of knowledge about a President being tried for impeachment to your person schema for that individual). The second mechanism is that of *tuning,* or *fine tuning,* a process that maintains the essential structure of the schema while changing some of its components in order to fit some new situation or feature of the data (e.g., inserting a new wrinkle into an old football or basketball play, or generalizing your schema of "ballet" to include some of the more gymnastic movements of modern dance). Finally, there is the mechanism of *restructuring,* or the formation of new schemas on the basis of some contradiction, inconsistency, or "troublesome information" (Rumelhart & Norman, 1978, p. 45) encountered by the old one (e.g., modifying your schema of abortion on the basis of some personally experienced or indirectly communicated information, or formation of a new schema for "art" as a result of your exposure to abstract expressionist or minimalist paintings). Thus, knowledge acquisition occurs in a number of different ways, rather than exclusively through accretion. In fact, the process of restructuring is probably a more significant mechanism in the development of expertise than either simple accretion or tuning.

Anderson's Proceduralization Model

Certainly the most popular and most influential model of skill acquisition is J. R. Anderson's (1983; Neves & Anderson, 1981) ACT* model. As developed in chapter 1, Anderson's model argues that in the initial stage of skill acquisition, knowledge is encoded in the form of declarative knowledge. However, if such knowledge is to be applied skillfully and quickly, as it is by experts or proficient users, it must be turned into "if–then" procedures. The process by which a declarative fact or proposition is transformed into an easily implemented procedure is called *proceduralization*.[4] Thus, a typing stroke, shifting gears, a mathematical operation, a chess move, or social or everyday inferences may all start off as pieces of knowledge that one needs to think about or explicitly represent to oneself, but eventually such knowledge must become automatic. In addition, one needs to combine procedures into sequences that can be run off smoothly and efficiently, as in typing or shifting and depressing the clutch or combining various mathematical operations. This second process is labeled *composition,* and the two processes of proceduralization and composition together make up a second stage of *knowledge compilation.*

The final stage of skill acquisition, according to J. R. Anderson (1983), is that of *tuning* (not to be confused with the tuning mechanism proposed by schema theory), whereby procedures or productions are refined. The three mechanisms involved in this stage are familiar: *strengthening,* or making procedures (e.g., gear shifting or a particular chess move) more easily activated as a result of success; *generalization,* or making the same procedure applicable to more than one content (e.g., applying the same mathematical operation to more than one quantity); and *discrimination,* or the process of placing restrictions on or limiting the range of application of a procedure as a result of failure (e.g., learning where a rule for forming the past tense or an otherwise winning chess strategy or rule of etiquette does not apply).

You may note that these mechanisms sound similar to some of the processes identified earlier by behaviorists and conditioning theorists. Although skills do bear some similarity to habits, in that they are often "doings" that are strengthened by practice and refined by their consequences, there are also important differences. Specifically, procedures, unlike habits, are *cognitive* operations with a *cognitive* representation, and they typically apply to fairly general, abstract conditions rather than to specific stimuli or objective conditions. In addition, procedures are initially governed by declarative knowledge rather than being acquired directly, as is assumed in most traditional

---

[4]It should be noted that not all researchers agree with Anderson's proposal that knowledge must first be represented declaratively (e.g., Broadbent, 1989; Wellington, Nissen, & Bullemer, 1989) and that the learner loses contact with that declarative representation after the knowledge has been proceduralized (see Gordon, 1993; Sanderson, 1989). Anderson (1993) has subsequently restated his belief in the declarative-procedural distinction and the role of declarative knowledge in "supporting" that procedural learning.

theories of conditioning. At the same time, procedures are like habits in that they do not require full attention or retrieval of all necessary information from long-term memory (C. A. Anderson, 1983).

In recent years J. R. Anderson (1986; D. Lewis & Anderson, 1985; Singley & Anderson, 1989) has added another mechanism to his theory of skill acquisition: namely, *analogy*. Analogizing is a major process of learning or skill acquisition, one that takes the place of the generalization and discrimination processes proposed in earlier versions of the ACT* model. Although participants generally have a difficult time with analogical reasoning and analogical transfer, Anderson's position is that research on this issue has generally used declarative-to-declarative transfer (e.g., one problem description presented as an analogy to a second one), whereas Anderson's approach is procedure-to-procedure transfer (e.g., from one mathematical operation or one programming function to another). This is a topic I return to in the next section.

Relation to Research on Expertise

It is important to note some of the ways in which these theories of skill acquisition relate to the phenomenon of expertise. First, it is obvious that the acquisition of expertise involves changes in the sheer amount of knowledge or information available. However, this is certainly not the most important change that occurs. Rather, there are changes in the degree and the form of *organization* of this knowledge, whether it be in the form of composition, restructuring, becoming more intuitive and less rule-bound, or some other alternative. As pointed out by Ericsson and Smith (1991a; see also Ericsson et al., 1993), practice by itself is not sufficient to become an expert (though see J. R. Anderson, 1983); oftentimes some correction or restructuring or change in strategy, not to mention feedback, is required. Furthermore, this knowledge becomes more accessible or more automatized, and in accessing this knowledge, experts are better able to distinguish between what is relevant and what is not (see Ericcson & Smith, 1991a, and also Dreyfus & Dreyfus, 1986). Frequently, this greater accessibility and organization result in a facilitation of information processing, as reflected in the fact that the performance of chess masters is less disrupted by the time constraints of "speed" chess than is that of less skilled players (Calderwood, Klein, & Crandall, 1988) and by the ability of expert typists and chess masters to carry on concurrent activities while engaged in skilled performance (e.g., Charness, 1976; Gentner, 1987).

Finally, Ericsson and Smith (1991a) pointed out that there is a good deal of evidence that experts from several areas engage in higher order reasoning based on their knowledge representations. For example, I mentioned earlier that Charness (1981) found that chess masters and experts plan their moves at a greater depth than do chess players with a rating below that of expert; it also seems likely that experts in, for example, the areas of law, medicine, and the sciences, engage in such planning and informed reasoning as well. Thus, it appears that more is involved in expertise than simply an extensive and easily accessed knowledge base.

TRANSFER OF TRAINING AND THE DOMAIN-SPECIFICITY ISSUE

In my discussion of research on expertise I raised the question of whether such expertise is specific to a particular domain or topic or is generalizable across different content areas. This question has been referred to as the *domain-specificity* issue. Such an issue is clearly relevant to my discussion of the relation between formal and informal reasoning and between academic and practical intelligence, as well to the generality of so-called common sense or practical intelligence to be discussed in the next chapter.

A related issue that is equally relevant to the study of practical, everyday reasoning is that of *transfer of training*, or the transfer of knowledge in general. Transfer can be defined more formally as "the use of knowledge or skill acquired in one situation to the performance of a new novel task, a task sufficiently novel that it involves additional learning as well as the use of old knowledge" (N. Pennington & Rehder, 1995, p. 223). For example, in chapter 10 I examine the degree to which cognitive skills learned in the classroom transfer to individuals' everyday lives, and vice versa. Alternatively, how well does the knowledge gained from one experience, for instance, one relationship (Sternberg & Frensch, 1993) or one sport, transfer to another experience of the same or different sort?

Although the transfer and domain-specificity issues are clearly related, the two have somewhat different histories. The transfer-of-training issue can be traced within psychology back to the classic research by Thorndike and Woodworth (1901; Thorndike, 1913) debunking the *exercise of faculties* view of education (i.e., the view that formal training in Latin or Greek served to "exercise" general faculties of the mind). Interestingly, the transfer issue has made something of a comeback in the past two decades as a result, in part, of the increasing interest of cognitive scientists in the acquisition of cognitive skills (e.g., J. R. Anderson, 1981, 1982), including, in particular, the idea (e.g., Papert, 1980) that the skill of computer programming may transfer to other domains (see Pea & Kurland, 1984, and Perkins, Schwartz, & Simmons, 1988, for negative evidence on this issue) and in part as a result of the debate over the concept of situated cognition (e.g., Lave, 1988; see chap. 10).

As described by Perkins and Salomon (1989), on the other hand, the history of the domain-specificity debate can be traced to problems encountered by the original attempts by theorists in problem solving and artificial intelligence (e.g., Ernst & Newell, 1969; Newell & Simon, 1972; Polya, 1957)—the so-called first wave of research on expertise (Holyoak, 1991)—to establish general principles of problem solving that apply across diverse types of problems. One major difficulty with this first wave was that it proved to be impossible to account for or simulate skill in a given area such as chess by using only these general, *weak methods* (Newell, 1973), that is, general methods that do not entail knowledge of specific domains. Rather, as I discussed in the last section, accounts of chess expertise require that the master have an extensive store of knowledge of past games and of chess strategies. For example, a computer using general methods without an extensive knowledge base could not beat chess masters (whereas the computer *Deep Blue*, which uses chess-specific knowledge, recently defeated the world chess champion, Gary Kasparov).

I begin with a discussion of the transfer literature, followed by a discussion of the domain-specificity issue.

Transfer of Training

Before addressing research on transfer of training, I must make some distinctions among different types of transfer. The most important distinction is between *near* and *far* transfer. As its name suggests, near transfer refers to transfer of knowledge to similar tasks or situations (e.g., from one algebra problem to another similar one), whereas far transfer refers to the applicability of existing knowledge or skills to dissimilar tasks or situations (e.g., from a statistics course to everyday problems that illustrate such principles—see chaps. 9 and 10). In most everyday situations, as well as in most educational settings, the concern is primarily with far transfer, although as the earlier examples suggest, such situations actually range on a continuum from nearer to farther. Another distinction that is relevant to the discussion that follows is that between *surface-oriented* and *deep* transfer, that is, transfer based on surface features versus deeper, underlying principles (see my discussion of themes in chap. 4). Once again, most of the concern with transfer of training has to do with the latter sort, though much of the research on this topic has dealt with superficial similarities. (This distinction also captures the original debate between Thorndike and the Gestalt psychologists on the nature of transfer, as well as more recent research emphasizing the role of inferential or causal reasoning in transfer, e.g., A. L. Brown, 1990; Chi, Bassock, Lewis, Reimann, & Glaser, 1989; Gentner, 1983.)

Another similar distinction proposed by Perkins & Salomon (1988, Salomon & Perkins, 1989) is that between *low road* and *high road* transfer. The former of these refers to "the automatic triggering of well-practiced routines in circumstances where there is considerable perceptual similarity to the original learning context" (Perkins & Salomon, 1988, p. 25), for instance, from typing to word processing or from one car to another. High road transfer, on the other hand, refers to a more "deliberate, mindful abstraction" (p. 25) of ideas, concepts, or skills from one context to the other (e.g., seeing the connections between some historical or fictional event and some current situation in the political world or in your personal life). (I return to this distinction later in this section.) One can also distinguish between *specific* transfer, or the transfer of some specific element or point, and *general* or nonspecific transfer, or the transfer of general principles or skills. Although the major concern in both educational and everyday settings here is with general transfer, much of the research, going back to Thorndike and Woodworth's (1901) identical elements theory, has focused on more specific transfer. Finally, one can distinguish, at least conceptually, between transfer of knowledge on the one hand, and transfer of cognitive or motor skills or general abilities on the other.

As examples of this debate, consider the following: You have learned to drive a high-powered car with lots of bells and whistles. To what extent will that knowledge or skill transfer to learning, for example, to fly a plane or even to learning to operate another similar car (see Perkins & Salomon, 1988)? To what extent will experience, interpersonal or sexual, in one relationship help you out in a new relationship (Sternberg & Frensch, 1993)? How about the transfer of skill from a typewriter to a word processor, or from one computer language or one word processor to another? How about the transfer from one sport, such as American football, to another, such as soccer, or from one language to another? All of these are examples where the transfer of skills or knowledge becomes an issue. In addition, there is the equally important question of how skills learned in school (e.g., mathematics, physics, problem solving) will transfer to people's everyday lives. I examine a number of examples of this last sort of transfer (or lack thereof) in chapter 8.

One example of an extreme position on this issue is found in a chapter by Detterman (1993). Detterman, like many other writers on this topic, was impressed by how little transfer has been found and to what lengths researchers have had to go to find transfer (e.g., prompts, reminders, and explicit instructions that transfer is to be sought for). Detterman (1993) indicated that the overwhelming nature of this negative evidence, from Thorndike and Woodworth to the present, compelled him to change his philosophy of teaching from "teaching for transfer" to teaching exactly what students need to know:

> [Before] I thought the discovery of principles was a fundamental skill that students needed to learn and transfer to new situations. Now I view education, even graduate education, as the learning of new information. ... In general, I subscribe to the principle that you should teach people exactly what you want them to learn in a situation as close as possible to the one in which the learning will be applied. I don't count on transfer and I don't try to promote it except by explicitly pointing out where taught skills may apply. (p. 17)

It is certainly true that the optimistic view of many educators that transfer occurs readily and without effort—what Perkins and Salomon (1988) referred to as the Bo Peep theory (i.e., "Let them alone and the cows will come home")—is rather naive. It is certainly true that numerous studies on a variety of different topics, ranging from crossing out zeros (Thorndike & Woodworth, 1901) to analogical reasoning (e.g., Gick & Holyoak, 1980, 1983; Reed, Ernst, & Banerji, 1974), have reported failures to find transfer. Thus, for example, Perkins and Salomon (1989) concluded that "to the extent that transfer does take place, it is highly specific and must be cued, primed, and guided; it seldom occurs spontaneously" (p. 19).

The Identical Elements Viewpoint. The original position put forward by Thorndike and Woodworth (1901) was the *identical elements* theory, which argued that transfer will occur to the extent that the training and transfer tasks or situations share common features. As I discuss later, one of the major theories of transfer today (Singley & Anderson, 1989) represents a variation on this identical elements theme.

The notion of identical elements certainly makes a good deal of sense. Clearly one would expect to find greater transfer between two problems or situations that share a greater number of features, common perceptual features or common mathematical operations. However, as several commentators (e.g., Gage & Berliner, 1988; Larkin, 1989; Singley & Anderson, 1989) have pointed out, there are a number of ways of conceptualizing the "elements" in this position. For example, Gage & Berliner (1988) distinguished between *identity of substance,* or similarity in the specific materials in the training and transfer tasks, and *identity of procedures* which operate on knowledge (e.g., grammatical rules or operations in computer programming). Thus, to take the relationship example cited above, similarity in the characteristics of your two partners would represent identity of substance, whereas similarities in the "principles" or "strategies" you use in approaching the two partners (e.g., trying to dominate or "please" your partner) would represent the identity of procedures. Similarly, Larkin (1989) outlined several possible sorts of common elements in problem-solving tasks. These possibilities include commonalities in problem-solving strategies having to do with either general or domain-specific knowledge, commonalities in subgoals (i.e., involved in solving a problem), in problem representations, in metacognitive skills, and in "skills for learning" (Larkin, 1989, p. 296; e.g., for acquiring knowledge relevant to the problem).

Singley and Anderson (1989) recently proposed a new identical elements approach to transfer that is clearly modeled after the original Thorndikean viewpoint. This new approach represents an application of Anderson's ACT* model of procedural knowledge and skill acquisition developed earlier. According to this account, transfer is a matter of the number of common *procedures* or productions shared by the two tasks, rather than of specific, shared, concrete features of the stimulus material or specific habits or responses. That is, as I pointed out earlier, procedures are abstract and context-independent. At the same time, however, procedures have the important property of being *use-specific*—that is, knowledge shows transfer only to the extent that it serves the same use in different tasks. Thus, for example, Singley and

Anderson (1989) cited the expected (and observed) lack of transfer between language comprehension and language generation, both of which involve the same syntactic rules, but also involve different *uses* of these rules. A more obvious, everyday example is the failure of children and adults to use school math in their everyday activities (e.g., Lave et al., 1984; Nunes et al., 1994) because of differences in use (e.g., between applying rules in a rote manner in school vs. finding the easiest, most convenient rules in calculating buys in the grocery store). Alternatively, such use-specificity can be seen in the failure of the skills involved in answering multiple choice questions to transfer to active problem-solving situations.

To illustrate this idea of use-specificity, Singley and Anderson (1989) cited a study involving the learning of calculus. Calculus is of interest for the study of transfer because the two major skills of integration and differentiation involve some, but not all of the same operations and because the stages of translating word problems and their solutions do not share operations. Singley and Anderson provided high school students with a basic computer tutor for a particular kind of calculus problem (i.e., related rates problems) where the tutor provided information about the basic operators involved. These practice problems were presented in three different forms: as geometry problems, as problems in economics, or neither. In addition, students were tutored in either integration, differentiation, or neither; and the practice problems involved either the translation (i.e., interpretation) or solution (i.e., integration or differentiation) of the problem. As a transfer problem, students received either the same or different cover story, the same or different set of operations (i.e., integration or differentiation), and the same or different phase of the problem (i.e., translation or solution). In all cases, the transfer task was a geometry-differentiation problem; only the practice problems differed.

Singley and Anderson (1989) found that although there was complete transfer across different cover stories (i.e., problems originally presented as exercises in economics vs. geometry) there was no transfer between practice on different stages of problem solution (i.e., practice on translating verbal problems into equations did not influence these students' performance on solution strategies, such as differentiating or integrating these equations). The latter finding can be attributed to the fact that translation and solution do not share common operations. Finally, and perhaps most important, integration and differentiation showed a high degree of transfer (64% for integration to differentiation and 58% for differentiation to integration), and this transfer can be accounted for entirely by the common operators used in the two skills.

Following J. R. Anderson (1983), Singley and Anderson distinguished between two types of knowledge—namely, procedural and declarative—which in turn result in four different types of transfer: procedural-to-procedural, declarative-to-procedural, procedural-to-declarative, and declarative-to-declarative. Singley and Anderson's main interest was in the transfer of cognitive skills, and hence their research focused on procedural-to-procedural transfer, although they acknowledged that most previous research on transfer, particularly in the verbal learning tradition, has been concerned with declarative-to-declarative transfer, which, from their point of view, is more problematic. It should be noted that Singley and Anderson *do* acknowledge the role of declarative-to-procedural transfer in the form of *structured analogy*. Such analogies are assumed to operate during the initial stage of skill acquisition. In keeping with the research evidence discussed in chapter 4 though, Singley and Anderson (1989) argued that such analogical transfer occurs only when an explicit example is provided or the source of the analogy is pointed out.

As an example of procedural-to-procedural transfer in everyday problem solving, consider the following: You are trying to learn a new version of your word processor. You know the earlier version pretty well, so an obvious strategy for you to use is to look to this earlier version for examples of the procedures for, say, cutting and pasting or creating margins. In most cases, such an approach will lead to positive transfer—that is, make it easier for you to learn the new system—whereas in others, such a strategy will produce negative transfer (i.e., interfere with such learning). To be more specific, Singley and Anderson argued that so-called negative transfer is really just a matter of the transfer of "nonoptimal methods" (p. 114).

You may note that Singley and Anderson's examples all involve well-structured problems, that is, problems with clearly defined rules or procedures, such as text editing, calculus, computer programming. As I discussed earlier, however, most everyday problems are likely to be *ill*-structured—the rules or "methods" are not clear or well-defined. Thus, it is more difficult to know exactly which elements can be appropriately transferred from one relationship to another, from one business venture to another, or from one political situation to another. Clearly, there *are* procedures involved in everyday thinking and activity; for instance, there are procedures for conducting yourself and treating your partner in a relationship, for business investments, and for political decisions. However, humans and social institutions are certainly more variable than calculus problems or text editors; therefore, the degree to which specific procedures in these three areas successfully transfer is an open question. (You need only think about the different interpretations of the [relatively] clear constitutional rules for impeachment displayed in the trial of Bill Clinton to see how this is so.)

An Alternative Position: The Greater Role of Declarative Knowledge. In a recent chapter, Pennington and Rehder (1995) proposed a *componential view of transfer* similar to that of Singley and Anderson (1989). According to this alternative view, a transfer task can be broken down into component processes to determine which component accounts for the degree or lack of transfer for that particular task. Pennington and Rehder (1995) argued that it is important to identify and control these different components in any given situation lest individuals be misled into thinking that overall transfer did or did not occur.

More importantly, Pennington and Rehder (1995) argued that Singley and Anderson (1989) underestimated the role of declarative knowledge in producing transfer. Pennington and Rehder reported the results of a study comparing two groups of participants, both of whom were given some instruction in LISP programming: One of them practiced generating LISP expressions, and the other practiced *evaluating* such expressions. The transfer task in this study was the alternative one—that is, evaluation for the generation task and generation for the evaluation one. According to the use specificity principle propounded by Singley and Anderson, there should be no transfer between these two tasks because procedural transfer is much more important than declarative transfer, and the two tasks do not share common procedures (cf. the earlier calculus example). In point of fact, however, Pennington and Rehder found considerable transfer between the two tasks (in both directions). They argued that this transfer was due to the common declarative knowledge involved in the initial instruction in LISP programming, and they backed up this argument with the results of a second experiment in which they collected think-aloud protocols from a small subset of participants and examined the degree of declarative knowledge elaboration shown in these protocols. In general, Pennington and Rehder reported that these protocols and the resulting knowledge maps support the elaboration of declarative knowledge and the function of this declarative knowledge in producing transfer in this area of limited background knowledge. It certainly seems likely that in areas involving a richer store of such background knowledge, declarative transfer may play a greater role (so long as that knowledge has not thoroughly practiced and hence proceduralized).

As Pennington and Rehder (1995) pointed out, their evidence, although inconsistent with the results of Singley and Anderson (1989), is consistent with a number of other findings in the problem-solving literature. For example, Chi and her associates (e.g., Chi et al., 1989; Chi & Van Lehn, 1991; see also King, 1994) have demonstrated that participants who engage in "self-explanations" while learning physics or computer programming problems also show better learning and transfer on these sorts of problems. Similarly, numerous studies of learning science concepts from a conceptual model (see Mayer, 1989, for a review) have shown that using such a model facilitates transfer while at the same time reducing dependence on sheer verbatim recall.

The debate over procedural versus declarative knowledge bases of transfer (particularly when the latter involves some elaboration) bears a resemblance to another distinction that I have already mentioned, namely, Perkins and Salomon's (1989) distinction between low road and high road transfer. In this particular case, the sharing of specific, overlearned procedures, amounts to the low road. The elaboration of declarative knowledge, particularly when that elaboration involves higher order conceptual models or "deeper" understanding or involves metacognitive skills or general problem-solving heuristics (see Perkins & Salomon, 1989), resembles the high road. In addition to these two forms of transfer, Pennington and Rehder (1995) argued for a more "middle-of-the road" form of transfer resulting from "strategies of intermediate level of abstraction that apply to a limited set of tasks, but tasks that nonetheless appear in different content domains ... [or] tasks of the same abstract *type*" (p. 269). Such strategies include the "pragmatic reasoning schemas" alluded to in chapter 1, the general social science reasoning schemas identified by Voss, Greene, et al. (1983), and other skills at argumentation, statistical reasoning (see chap. 10), and the like. The common feature of all these different schemas and skills is that they all show transfer over a limited range of problems or situations.

On the basis of evidence from research in artificial intelligence on expert systems, especially research by Hayes-Roth, Waterman, and Lenat (1983) on different types of tasks, Pennington and Rehder (1995) proposed that the skills of diagnosis, prediction, and design in computer programming represented reasonable candidates for the kind of intermediate or middle-of-the-road skills that may be the source of transfer. These authors cited two particular computer simulations that embody these kind of skills. One is a model of physics problem solving called FERMI (Larkin, 1989), which includes both general problem-solving strategies (i.e., general across different physical science domains) and domain-specific knowledge (i.e., specific to "fluid statics" and particular types of circuits). The second example is an expert systems model of medical diagnosis called NEOMYCIN, put forward by Clancey (1988). In this model a separation is made between the knowledge base, and a model of reasoning involving general heuristic rules such as "gather information," "formulate hypotheses," "test hypotheses," and so forth. The idea here is that NEOMYCIN represents a general model that can be applied to other domains such as computer debugging given that the individual can acquire the requisite domain knowledge.

Pennington and Rehder (1995) classified these two examples as models of competence insofar as they assume domain-independent processes. These investigators carried out an experiment themselves on transfer from computer debugging to electronic troubleshooting, and vice versa (see earlier research by Gott, Hall, Pokorny, Dibble, & Glaser, 1993). In this study Pennington and Rehder compared the performance of a group of participants experienced in computer debugging on an electronic troubleshooting task (with which they were unfamiliar) with the performance on that task by a group of participants inexperienced in both. In all cases participants were given necessary domain knowledge and had an opportunity to ask questions and therefore receive additional information. The major result of this experiment was that the participants experienced in computer program debugging showed spontaneous transfer (i.e., without cuing) to the electronics problem in comparison with the performance of the inexperienced participants.

The general conclusion reached by Pennington and Rehder from their research is that there is evidence for transfer at both the middle-of-the road and high transfer levels. As a corollary to this conclusion, these investigators are also much more positive about the possibility of transfer than are some of the commentators I referred to earlier.

The Relevance of the Declarative-Procedural Distinction for Everyday Cognition. The question that undoubtedly has crossed your mind is how this distinction between declarative- versus procedural-based transfer is relevant to everyday knowledge or skills. To begin with, it is clear that both procedural and declarative knowledge are involved in everyday cognition (e.g., in routine, highly practiced activities and judgments versus less familiar ones). For example, fixing dinner, driving a car, shaving, applying makeup, making stereotyped judgments—all of these are examples of well-practiced procedural knowledge—whereas finding your way in an unfamiliar landscape, interacting with people you don't know, solving a relationship problem, or trying to master computer software are all examples of the use of declarative knowledge (as is writing a book). Learning to fix a *new* meal (though see my discussion of Hammond's [1989] case-based approach) or to drive a *new* car or to shave with a *new* razor—each of these is an example of procedure-to-procedure transfer—whereas learning to navigate a *new* environment or a *new* relationship or *new* software are all examples that depend on accessing declarative (as well as some procedural) representations.

Which form of knowledge and transfer is most prominent will, of course, depend on lifestyle. Those who live a humdrum, routinized existence will depend on more procedural, "mindless" (Langer, Blank, & Chanowitz, 1978) knowledge, whereas those who are more adventurous, whose lives involve new challenges, intellectual or otherwise, and whose everyday lives are more "mindful" (Langer, 1989; Salomon & Perkins, 1989) rely more on declarative knowledge and transfer. In any case, it is undoubtedly true that procedural knowledge plays a rather large role in all of our lives, and that its transfer—for example, from driving one car to driving another or from using one eyeliner to using another—also plays a major role, perhaps more than many people would like to acknowledge. (The same can be said for low road transfer.) At the same time, however, the fact that I (and, hopefully, you) am trying to draw connections among different topics in this book, as well as trying to think up everyday examples, or that individuals explicitly think about lessons from raising one child or making one investment or taking one class to another, suggests that declarative-to-declarative transfer also plays a role (as does high road and middle-of-the-road transfer).

The Role of "Noticing" Similarity. One factor involved in transfer is the degree to which individuals notice the similarity between the training and the transfer problems. For example, Singley and Anderson (1989) argued for a two-step model of transfer consisting of a noticing phase followed by a mapping phase (see Gentner & Gentner, 1983; cf. Einstein & McDaniel's [1996] Noticing + Search model discussed in chap. 4), in the latter of which the rules from the first problem are applied to the second. Similarly, Sternberg and Frensch (1993) outlined four components of transfer, the first of which is based on the concept of *encoding specificity* (Tulving & Thomson, 1973), or the argument that the likelihood of retrieving (or transferring) a piece of information depends on the match of the retrieval context to the context in which that information was encoded in the first place. Thus, one of the possible obstacles to transfer is that the knowledge may be "encapsulated" (Bransford, Nitsch, & Franks, 1977) so that it is inaccessible for transfer. Sternberg and Frensch suggested that this may be the case for much knowledge learned in school that is not tied to or encoded in terms of everyday, real-world situations.

One of the best examples of such an emphasis can be found in the writings of Bassok and Holyoak (1993). According to these authors, transfer depends at least in part on the individual's ability to see the *pragmatically relevant* aspects of the training and transfer problems, or in other words, those aspects that are relevant to the solution of both problems. On the one hand, I have pointed out that some past research (e.g., Gick & Holyoak, 1980) has suggested that individuals have a hard time *spontaneously* noting the similarities between isomorphs of a given problem unless those similarities are explicitly pointed out to them. Other research (e.g., Holyoak & Koh, 1987; B. H. Ross, 1989a) has demonstrated that it is more difficult for individuals to *access* prior knowledge than it is to *use* it. In other words, it appears that when similarities are pointed out to participants, they have little problem applying or using that knowledge. A good example of this can be found in a study by Ceci and Ruiz (1993) to be discussed later. In this study two participants who were experts at racetrack handicapping (see my discussion in chap. 8) were asked to solve an isomorphic problem in stock market prediction. These handicappers were unable to solve the latter problems even after some 600 trials spaced over 18 months. (See Fig. 7.5).

A major problem with noticing similarity, as I have discussed, is an overreliance on surface similarities. Or, as Bassok and Holyoak (1993) stated this, "the impact of similarity on transfer can be understood if people use the default option (either explicitly or implicitly) that salient similarities and differences are correlated to the important, pragmatically relevant properties" (p. 70). At the same time, Bassok and Holyoak argued that individuals, particularly experienced or expert ones, are also sensitive to deeper properties of the problem, in particular to goal-related or pragmatically relevant properties. For example, those with some expertise at physics were better able to classify physics problems according to basic principles (e.g., the law of conservation of energy) rather than superficial characteristics (e.g., pulleys; Chi et al., 1981). In the same way, Novick (1988) showed that people with greater experience in math are able to ignore superficial

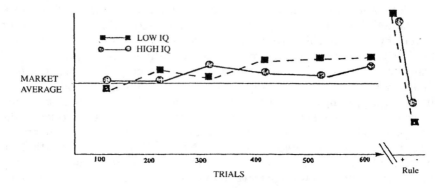

FIG. 7.5. Transfer from racetrack handicapping to stock market discussions. From "Transfer Abstractness and Intelligence" by S. J. Ceci & A. Ruiz, 1993. In *Transfer on Trial: Intelligence, Cognition, and Instruction* (p. 183), edited by D. K. Detterman & R. J. Sternberg, Westport, CT: Greenwood Publishing Group. Copyright © 1993 by Greenwood Publishing Group. Reprinted with permission of Greenwood Publishing Group, Inc. Westport, CT.

similarities in math problems and show positive and negative transfer based on the actual underlying problem structure.

Bassok and Holyoak's (1985, 1989, 1993) own research on transfer has looked at the transfer of skill at solving equations from one content area (algebra) to a different one (physics). Specifically, high school students were trained to solve either arithmetic progression problems in algebra or problems in physics regarding acceleration in a straight line. These two types of problems are structurally isomorphic, but the content and format of the two are very different. That is, algebra problems are abstract and contentless and are solved for their own sake, whereas physics problems obviously have content, have more specific terms and concepts, and use algebraic equations that are solved as a means to an end. (See Table 7.1 for examples of the two types of problems used by Bassok and Holyoak, 1989.) The prediction based on these differences is that students should show positive transfer from the algebra word problems to the physics problems but not vice versa (because the latter is more content-specific). Such an asymmetry in transfer was, in fact, found in two initial studies, one with existing groups of high school students who had training in one or the other domain (Bassok & Holyoak, 1985), and the other in the form of a more traditional laboratory study of transfer. At the same time, though, Bassok (1990) found that using domain-specific content from the area of banking or finance did not have the same effect on transfer as did the physics problems—that is, it did not inhibit transfer to algebra or geometry as much as the physics problems did.

To bring this discussion back to the original issue, it appears that the way in which the problem or content domain is represented makes a major difference in the degree to which individuals notice the relevant similarities

TABLE 7.1

Examples of the Two Types of Problems Used by Bassok and Holyoak (1989)

Algebra	Physics
1. A boy was given an allowance of 50 cents a week beginning on his sixth birthday. On each birthday following this, the weekly allowance was increased 25 cents. What is the weekly allowance for the year beginning on his 15th birthday?	1. An express train traveling at 30 meters per second (30 m/s) at the beginning of the 3rd second of its travel, uniformly accelerates increasing in speed 5 m/s each successive second. What is its final speed at the end of the 9th second?
2. During a laboratory observation period it is found that the diameter of a tree increases the same amount each month. If the diameter was 8 mm at the beginning of the first month, and 56 mm at the end of the 24th month, by how much does the diameter increase each month?	2. What is the acceleration (=increase in speed each second) of a racing car if its speed increased uniformly from 44 meters per second (44 m/s) at the beginning of the first second, to 55 m/s at the end of the 11th second?
3. A mechanic has to cut 9 different length metal rods. The shortest rod has to be 6 ft. long and the longest rod has to be 10 ft. long, and each rod has to be longer than the one before by a constant amount. What is the total length of metal required to prepare these rods?	3. A jumbo jet starts from rest and accelerates uniformly during 8 seconds for takeoff. If it travels 25 meters during the first second and 375 meters during the 8th second, what distance does it travel in all?
4. Kate O'Hara has a job that pays $7,500 for the first six months, with a raise of $250 at the end of every six months thereafter. What was her total income after 12 years?	4. An object dropped from a hovering helicopter falls 4.9 meters during the first second of its descent, and during each subsequent second it falls 9.8 meters farther than it fell during the preceding second. If it took the object 10 seconds to reach the ground, how high above the ground was the helicopter hovering?

Note. From "Interdomain Transfer Between Isomorphic Topics in Algebra and Physics" by M. Bassok & K. J. Holyoak, 1989, *Journal of Experimental Psychology: Learning, Memory, and Cognition,* 15, p. 156. Copyright © 1989 by the American Psychological Association. Reprinted with permission.

between problems. This in turn influences the success of transfer between the problems. In other words, the problem representation and the detection of similarities and differences are closely related. These representation and pattern recognition abilities are themselves influenced by the expertise of the problem solver. It is an interesting question to speculate about the degree to which everyday knowledge or skills are "encapsulated" or represented in such a way as to facilitate transfer.

In one other discussion of transfer, Sternberg and Frensch (1993) offered a number of everyday examples of that process (or lack thereof). For instance, these authors cited the example of a student who writes well in

English but cannot bring the same "talent" to bear on writing papers for her science course. Another example referred to throughout this section is the case of a woman who feels that she has "learned her lesson" from a previous relationship, but when she tries to apply this learning to a new relationship, it results in disaster. Finally, there is the example of an executive lured from one company to another to work his magic in corporate restructuring, but whose strategy does not work with the new company. The point of these and other examples that may come to mind (e.g., the student who finds that the study strategies he or she used in one course do or do not work in another, or the actor who finds that the technique he or she used for a character on a TV series does not work in live theater, or the salesman whose sales technique works for one type of product but does not work for another) is that transfer operates in a variety of different everyday situations as well as in the transfer of academic skills to these everyday situations.

One other approach to transfer that focuses on both noticing similarity and the role of domain-specific knowledge is that referred to earlier by Ceci and Ruiz (1993). The main concern of these investigators, as I discuss in the next chapter, is to call into question the assumption that transfer is the hallmark of (and the result of) intelligence, as well as the assumption that such transfer is ubiquitous. Like many of the other researchers whose work I have reviewed, Ceci and Ruiz cited several examples of research in which investigators failed to find transfer. One of these studies that is relevant to my emphasis in this book is by Leshowitz (1989). In this study students who had taken introductory social science courses as well as math and science courses failed to transfer principles from these courses (e.g., the need for a control group) to everyday situations. In general, Ceci and Ruiz, like so many other commentators I have discussed, argued that transfer requires high domain-specific knowledge in both areas.

To test out these notions, Ceci and Ruiz examined the ability of two expert racetrack handicappers (taken from a study of everyday expertise to be discussed in chap. 8) to transfer their complex handicapping strategies to an isomorphic problem dealing with predicting stock prices. Specifically, these two handicappers, one with a high IQ and one with a low one, were given 600 trials to predict which stocks would show the best earning-to-price ratio, where the rule for such prediction was the same one that they had previously used successfully to predict winners in horse races. The significant finding of this study (see Fig. 7.5) is that these participants failed to show transfer over those 600 trials (although they did show greater than chance performance) at which time the isomorphism was pointed out to them, and they were given 25 more trials. At that point both participants showed marked improvement in their performance, with each showing ceiling effects within these 25 trials. Although the major conclusion reached by Ceci and Ruiz from these results is that intelligence or cognitive complexity does not generalize across different domains (i.e., is domain-specific), it is also clear that individuals do not necessarily notice similarity or isomorphism when two different problem-solving domains are involved. (See Reed, Ernst, & Banerji, 1974, for similar results with lab problems.)

Critique. Lave (1988) criticized the recent wave of research on transfer (as well as studies of thinking and problem solving in general) on the grounds that such research abstracts these processes out of their real world context, including the context of everyday *activity* (see chaps. 8 and 10). Thus, such research (as well as that on the topic of domain-specificity) artificially equates "context" or "situations" with types of problem *content* or with the reified concept of a knowledge domain, rather than with *social* situations or with the context of activity. Lave also raised some of the points reviewed in the first section of this chapter, such as the fact that the problems involved in these experiments are designed by others without any contribution by the participants themselves, that these problems (unlike real-life problems) are formulated in such a way that there is a single, well-defined, normatively described right answer, that research on transfer ignores the role of participants' motivation for solving problems or for transferring their knowledge to new problems. Thus, Lave questioned the degree to which the results of these studies really shed much light on real-world problem solving (see Lave's own research and commentary on the latter topic in chap. 8.) This is an issue that I return to in the next chapter.

The Domain-Specificity Issue

Perkins and Salomon (1989; see also Holyoak, 1991) provided a valuable overview of the history of the domain-specificity issue. This issue originally arose (at least under that label) in the area of problem solving and artificial intelligence (e.g., Newell & Simon, 1972; Polya, 1957) and the resulting research on expertise. In particular, Newell and Simon (1972; Ernst & Newell, 1969) proposed in their *General Problem Solver (GPS)* model that certain general heuristics or general problem-solving strategies such as means–ends analysis (i.e., finding subgoals and operators that will reduce the gap between your current state and a desired goal state) or working backwards (i.e., moving from your goal to a preceding subgoal) could be used to solve problems in a variety of different areas, such as logic, algebra, chess, story problems. Thus, the ability to solve problems in one domain should be related to the ability to solve problems in other domains.

This original proposal, however, or what Holyoak (1991) referred to as the *first generation* of research on expertise, ran into a number of difficulties. First, as I noted in my review of the expertise literature, it became apparent that expertise in most areas depends on a rich and extensive database of domain-specific knowledge rather than simply on general, rational rules of calculation or strategies of problem solving. In addition, in the area of artificial intelligence it became apparent that the use of general heuristics alone could not adequately account for performance in areas such as chess, physics, or medical diagnosis. For example, I have already referred to the finding that chess programs that use only "weak" or generalized methods are incapable of beating chess masters or grandmasters. Such observations cast doubt on the notion of a *general* problem solver. Finally, as I have discussed, research on the transfer-of-training issue failed to find evidence for transfer across different content areas. All of these observations led to what Holyoak (1991) referred to as the *second generation* of research on expertise.

In the past several years the specificity–generality pendulum has swung at least partway back to the other side. Although much of this evidence is not immediately relevant to the current discussion, I should note at least a few of the developments that *are* pertinent. For example, Clement (1989) reported that when experts in physics are confronted with unfamiliar or unusual physics problems, they resort to some general heuristics of the sort discussed by Polya and Newell and Simon, such as the use of analogies from well-known areas, or the use of extreme case arguments, although these heuristics do not appear to transfer to other areas besides physics. Second, there is increasing evidence that general problem-solving methods sometimes do, in fact, work. For example, and most relevant to this discussion, Schoenfeld (1982, 1985; Schoenfeld & Herrmann, 1982) demonstrated that general heuristics aid in mathematics learning when these heuristics are contextualized—that is, when they make contact with students' existing knowledge (see chap. 10 and the discussion of street math in chap. 8), although, again, there is little evidence of transfer of these heuristics. In addition, current general models of thought such as Anderson's ACT* and Newell's (1990; Rosenbloom, Newell, & Laird, 1991) SOAR system master a given area by starting with weak, generalized methods and then, through experience, gradually build up a set of domain-specific rules or methods. (See Holyoak, 1991, for an alternative *symbolic connectionist,* or *third generation* model of expertise, which combines the kinds of production systems or computational models just described with a connectionist model).

As I have discussed, there is also evidence for the transfer of skills under certain conditions. For example, Perkins and Salomon (1989) summarized a number of studies that indicate that transfer occurs "when general principles of reasoning are taught together with self-monitoring practices and applications in varied contexts" (p. 22; cf. my discussion of the principles of expertise). Similarly, as I referred to earlier, Perkins and Salomon (1989; see also Salomon & Perkins, 1989) distinguished between two different conditions under which transfer does occur (see Hatano, 1986, for a similar distinction). The first of these is the so-called low road, where the skill is learned to the point of automaticity in a variety of different situations, resulting in the application of the skill to situations that are (perceptually) similar. There are several instances of everyday cognition that come to mind in which this low road (or what Hatano, 1988, has referred to as *routine* expertise) may be applicable, such as the motor skills involved in sports or driving, or some of the blue collar skills described by Scribner (1984a, 1986) in her research on dairy workers (see chap. 8), or Hatano's (1986) example of learning the abacus. In their discussion of this particular form of transfer, Salomon and Perkins (1989) pointed to skills or attitudes that result from cultural socialization as prime examples of such low road transfer.

At the same time, however, Perkins and Salomon (1988) also argued that the conditions for low road transfer (i.e., a good deal of practice in many different situations to a point of mastery and automaticity) do not occur very often in either natural or laboratory settings. In particular, it is probably the condition that practice occurs "in a variety of different situations" such that the "ability gradually becomes more and more detached from its original context and more and more evocable in others" (Salomon & Perkins, 1989, p. 120) that is difficult to meet in everyday cognition, as I discuss in the next chapter (and as Lave suggested in her critique outlined earlier).

The second, or so-called high road (or *adaptive* expertise—Hatano, 1988), involves the "deliberate mindful application of a principle" (Perkins & Salomon, 1989, p. 22) from one situation to another, either by keeping the principle in mind when entering into the new situation or by reviewing past experiences to induce principles that may be applied to this situation. Salomon and Perkins (1989) labelled the first type of high road transfer *forward-reaching* because the principle is formulated prior to encountering the new situation, whereas the latter is referred to as *backward-reaching* transfer. An example of the latter condition is found in the studies by Gick and Holyoak (1980) and Ceci and Ruiz (1993) cited earlier in which a reminder or instructions to go back and try to remember a relevant principle increased the likelihood of transfer. Unfortunately, it is questionable how frequently such high road transfer (whether self-initiated or instructed by others) occurs in everyday cognition (or in most educational settings for that matter—see chap. 10).

Perkins and Salomon (1989) concluded from their review of the literature on domain-specificity that cognitive skills are a combination of general cognitive abilities or operations on the one hand, and domain-specific knowledge on the other (cf. Anderson, 1987, for a similar view). They used the metaphor of general cognitive skills as "gripping devices for retrieving and wielding domain-specific knowledge" (p. 23). Thus, these cognitive skills or operations (e.g., means–ends analysis or use of counterexamples) can be applied in a variety of different content areas, but the application requires that the individual have a reasonable amount of domain-specific knowledge (e.g., knowledge of chess configurations and sequences, knowledge of math or law or the social sciences, or even different areas of sales or sports; see chap. 8) to which these operations can be applied. Cognitive operations cannot be "wielded" in the absence of such knowledge, and in that restricted (but significant) sense, skills are domain-specific. However, this does not mean that they are not usable across different topics. Whether the same skills or heuristics are readily transferred among different forms of everyday intelligence or between everyday and more formal or academic forms of reasoning is another question—the first of which I examine in chapter 8 and the second of which I address in chapter 10.

SUMMARY

In this chapter I have reviewed research and theory on a number of basic issues in cognitive psychology that are essential for understanding practical, everyday reasoning and intelligence. Specifically, I have discussed the extensive research on expertise, the competing models of skill acquisition, and the rather mixed evidence on transfer and domain-specificity. In addition, I have looked at some "everyday" examples of each of these topics. Finally, I have also reexamined some of the differences between formal and informal or everyday reasoning.

It is perhaps useful to take the "high road" and go back and try to find some of the common threads in these different areas of research. One clear thread is the importance of an extensive knowledge base, in both expertise and in successful transfer, a base that is at least equal with, if not more important than general principles. An obviously related thread is the relative domain-specificity of knowledge and skills. Finally, there is the question of the relative role of declarative versus procedural knowledge or of explicit versus implicit thought processes in both skill acquisition and transfer of learning.

In the next chapter I discuss several different research programs dealing specifically with practical intelligence and everyday reasoning. In the process, I try to apply some of the lessons learned in this chapter.

Chapter 8

From the Workplace to the Racetrack and Beyond: Representative Research on Everyday Reasoning and Practical Intelligence

INTRODUCTION

In this chapter I review some representative research projects on different forms of practical reasoning and problem solving, ranging from everyday uses of mathematics to specific job-related skills to the specialized abilities developed by particular cultures to more general forms of knowledge involved in occupational success. In this review I once again try to highlight some of the common themes and concerns of this research, as well as some of the ways in which these concerns and research results relate to the general conceptual issues developed in chapter 7. My aim in this review is to demonstrate that there is a growing and, despite the diversity of topics, an increasingly interconnected literature on the topic of practical intelligence.

PRACTICAL PROBLEM SOLVING IN THE WORKPLACE

Probably the most complete and systematic account of practical problem solving has been provided by Sylvia Scribner (1984a, 1986). Scribner's interest in this topic grew out of her lifelong concern with the importance of work in people's lives (see Kapelman, 1996), as well as her research with Michael Cole (Scribner & Cole, 1981) on the impact of literacy on cognitive skills. One of the findings of this latter research was an observed connection between certain cultural activities (such as memorizing the Koran in a particular ordered fashion among the Vai of Liberia) and particular cognitive skills (such as the ability to remember information in the correct order). This sort of observation led Scribner and Cole to formulate a *practice* account of thinking, or a view emphasizing the relation of thinking to cultural activities and goal-directed activities in general. It is this theoretical concern to which I now turn.

Scribner's Account of Practical Thinking

Scribner's (1983, 1986) account begins with the age-old distinction between *theoretical knowledge* or *intelligence* on the one hand, and *practical intelligence* on the other. Theoretical intelligence is the kind of knowledge that has been most valued in Western thought and that has been the focus of most traditional psychological research and testing (i.e., intelligence and achievement testing), whereas practical thought is the sort that is involved in everyday goal-directed action and "instrumental" activity (cf. Leont'ev, 1979). The focus of Scribner's research has been on this latter form of thought, and she distinguished this emphasis from that of traditional cognitive science, which is concerned with the former and which "portrays mind as a system of symbolic representations and operations that can be understood in and of itself, in isolation from other systems of activity ... [and] abstracted from tasks and separated from one another" (Scribner, 1986, p. 15). In addition, carrying out these tasks is viewed as an end in itself. In contrast, practical intelligence is concerned with "thinking that is embedded in the larger purposive activities of daily life and that functions to achieve the goals of these activities" (Scribner, 1986, p. 15). This distinction clearly hearkens back to some of the distinctions made in chapters 1 and 8 between formal and informal reasoning. In general, the emphasis of practical thinking is on action or activities, goals or purposes, and everyday tasks and activities. In addition, these activities are assumed (Scribner, 1983) to be constructed and organized by social–cultural forces.

Scribner's Research on Dairy Workers

The primary focus of Scribner's research (e.g., 1983, 1984a, 1986) has been on work settings, and in particular the kinds of everyday thinking and problem solving engaged in by workers at a dairy plant. The choice of a work environment in general was dictated by the aforementioned significance of work in people's lives, and by the fact that the work environment—or at least the environment of the dairy plant studied in this research—is highly structured, and hence allows for a clear definition of the tasks required and the behavioral outcomes of those tasks. In other words, it allows for a clearly defined naturalistic study. In addition, the study of such factory workers may help to shed light on some of the differences between practical, working intelligence and more traditional academic intelligence (cf. Neisser, 1976).

Scribner's research focused on three different types of dairy workers: (a) product assembly workers, who retrieve dairy products from a large ice box in order to fill orders; (b) wholesale drivers, who fill orders for and deliver products to customers; and (c) inventory takers. The general procedure for researching these different tasks or workers was to begin with a general ethnographic analysis of the dairy environment to decide on which tasks to examine, followed by observations under typical working conditions in order to arrive at accounts of the strategies used by workers and a set of hypotheses. These hypotheses were in turn investigated by simulated tasks and task modifications, as well as by more careful, more focused observations. In addition, experiments examining expert–novice differences were also run, where the experts were experienced workers at a particular task (e.g., pricing deliveries), and novices consisted of workers from other areas of the plant (e.g., product assembly workers for the pricing task), office workers, and students with no experience at the task in question. Thus, Scribner's strategy in this study and in general was to combine initial ethnographic and observational methods with later more controlled simulations and experiments (Scribner, 1983; see Laufer & Glick, 1996, for a similar strategy in a study focusing on the work of managers and telephone sales representatives of a distribution company for industrial precision parts).

Research on Product Assembly Workers.   The first group to be studied was the product assembly workers or "preloaders" whose job was to take the orders taken by drivers and fill them by pulling out the requested number of products (e.g., quarts of milk) from the refrigerated compartment with a hook. There was a clear incentive for these workers to perform their work quickly and accurately because they were to work until they finished the day's orders and because inaccurately filled orders were returned for them to fill again.

The major problem faced by such assemblers was that the orders they received had been converted into case "equivalencies" (a case consists of 16 quarts of milk) by computer, and thus they had to work with mixed orders (e.g., a case plus or minus 6 quarts). Because these mixed orders required the assemblers to engage in some kind of goal-directed problem solving, they held the greatest interest for the study of practical intelligence. Hence, the initial observations with these product assemblers involved setting up an observation post across from the products that were most likely to entail partial orders (e.g., buttermilk or chocolate milk). These observations included mini-experiments in which the researchers added or subtracted quantities to test out particular hypotheses.

As summarized by Scribner (1984a, 1986), the major finding of these observations was that the product assemblers always performed their task in the most efficient way, employing the smallest number of moves (e.g., subtracting 2 quarts from a partial case of 14 units to fill an order of 1 case minus 4, rather than moving 6 of those quarts and adding them to another partial case of 6 quarts) and without error, even though these solutions frequently deviated from the literal format of the order (e.g., simply subtracting 4 units from a full case to fill an order of 1 case minus 4). Thus, Scribner, Gauvain, and Fahrmeier (1984) calculated the number of steps that would have to be taken to fill a list of orders in the sequence given. By these calculations, the product assemblers, who typically deviated from that sequence in order to take advantage of spatial proximities, filled the orders by traveling significantly less distance (10,922 vs. 13,279 feet). In addition, these assemblers were very flexible in their solutions; for instance, they sometimes added units, sometimes subtracted them, or subtracted a smaller number from a partially filled case (as in the above example)—all depending on the quantities available as well as the requirements of the task. Scribner (1984b) viewed this flexibility as one of most significant, and in some sense the most surprising, features of the assemblers' strategies—that is, rather than carrying out routine work in a mindless, routinized way, they continued to adapt their solutions to the specific conditions with which they were faced.

In general, preloaders' actions seemed to follow a *least effort principle* (Scribner, 1984a, 1984b, 1986), as evidenced by the fact that they frequently filled more than one order at the same time. Scribner (1984a) also described preloaders' behavior in terms of a *law of mental effort*; that is, "mental effort will be expended to save physical effort" (p. 21). These results were confirmed in a simulation in which product assemblers were found to use a nonliteral strategy that was optimal on 70% of the trials.

An additional set of comparisons of product assemblers with novices (i.e., high school students, inventory takers, drivers, and office workers) indicated that the students were the least efficient, were extremely literal, sometimes making nonoptimal moves in filling the orders. For example, Scribner (1984b) cited the case of a student who, when asked to fill an order of 1 case minus 6 quarts (or 10 quarts), took 4 quarts from one partially filled case (of 7 quarts) and 6 quarts from another case (of 6 quarts) and placed them in an empty case. This strategy is clearly "nonoptimal" because it involved moving the full 10 quarts, where the simplest move would have been to move the 4 quarts from the first case and add it to the second partially filled case. The office workers, who had no specific experience with the task, were the next least efficient, followed by drivers and inventory takers, both of whom had some experience at product assembly.

Because product assembly is clearly a skill that can be learned or perfected with practice—and in fact, novices *did* become more efficient within a small number of trials—these results for accuracy and efficiency are not all that surprising. Perhaps of greater interest is the fact that there was a clear difference in the *strategies* used by, for example, office workers versus preloaders. Office workers filled orders by counting and by explicit numerical calculations, whereas preloaders tended to use visual inspection strategies—that is, they "knew" how many units there were in a partially filled case by simple inspection without having to count them. The similarity of this distinction to the observations made on chess masters (e.g., Chase & Simon, 1973a; de Groot, 1966) and by G. A. Klein (e.g., 1989) on firefighters, as well as to Dreyfus and Dreyfus's (1986) general account of expertise should be apparent. In fact, Scribner (1988) reported a test in which college students were shown a product order followed by a briefly presented picture of an array and were asked to indicate whether the picture met the order. Students who participated in this task were significantly more likely to *start off* using nonliteral strategies from the beginning when they were placed in the assembly task.

The Study of Drivers.   Whereas the main concern of the product assemblers was to minimize physical effort (or to maximize physical efficiency), the concern of the drivers was strictly symbolic. That is, the task of these drivers was to come up with the fastest, most efficient calculation of a price for an order. It is interesting to note that even though the drivers made numerous errors on standard multiplication tests, they made no errors in their calculations on the job. It is also noteworthy that these drivers frequently used cases as the units in their calculations, even though their price lists were expressed in units (i.e., quarts), and the amount of each product on the orders or delivery tickets was to be expressed in units as well. An illustration of this is given in a protocol cited by Scribner (1984a). Specifically, when asked to calculate the price of 120 gallons of homogenized milk, the driver explained his calculations in the following way:

> All right, so it's nine [dollars] thirty-two [cents] a case and we have four [gallons a case] into a hundred and twenty [quarts] is thirty cases. So, I'll take thirty times nine thirty-two. I'll figure that's the easiest way to do it. Two seventy-nine sixty. See, in other words, it's two thirty-three a gallon, there's four gallons to a case, that's how you get nine thirty-two. (p. 31)

Thus, these drivers operated in much the same way as product assemblers, substituting the case as their unit of analysis, although in this instance the case was being used as a strictly *symbolic* unit. As Scribner (1984a) put it, this is a case in which "an object which first possesses instrumental value in physical activity begins to serve a sign function and becomes incorporated in mental operations" (p. 29). In subsequent simulations, think-aloud protocols were collected as experts and novices went over orders within the plant offices. In these protocols all of the drivers used the case-price strategy on some occasions. The younger drivers who sometimes used calculators were more likely to use a unit-price strategy than were older drivers, although even the younger drivers used the case-price strategy when even-case orders were encountered (e.g., 32 quarts) and when drivers knew the case-equivalencies. In general, the drivers, like the product assemblers, were very flexible in their calculations, shifting their strategies on the basis of what computational aids were available; and like the product assemblers, they always made their calculations in the least (mentally) effortful way.

In a further simulation involving expert–novice comparisons, participants were presented with orders entailing new but analogous products (e.g., iced coffee) and were asked to calculate the total price. In this sort of transfer problem, drivers still showed the most flexible and efficient strategies, and students were still the most literal and inflexible. The students seldom used the case-price strategy, and when they *did* use it, they "applied it indiscriminately to all problems, regardless of their numerical properties ..." (Scribner, 1984a, p. 33), regardless of whether the problem lent itself to such a strategy. Once again, preloaders and office workers (who in this case had some knowledge of the prices) showed an intermediate level of performance, with one third of each group using more flexible strategies.

The Study of Inventory Workers.   Finally, the inventory workers, who were required to perform their work in the icebox under rather severe constraints (e.g., limited room for walking, large displays with unseen containers for which quantities had to be estimated) nevertheless had to do their job accurately. As expected, these inventory takers used various heuristics in which they used certain fixed dimensions of the storage space and arrays to estimate quantities instead of actually counting or enumerating. These workers also used various mental transformations of the arrays (e.g., filling in gaps in the array and then subtracting out equivalent quantities later) in order to make their estimation task easier. Finally, when they *did* use counting or enumeration strategies, the unit used was the stack or number of cases in a stack rather than the case itself (even though the inventory form required them to express total counts in terms of the number of cases).

Conclusions From Scribner's Research.   On the basis of her observations and simulations, Scribner (1984b, 1986) attempted to identify a number of general characteristics of practical problem solving. First, workers learn techniques for reformulating or redefining problems in such a way as to allow them to apply shortcuts or to use some "preferred mode of problem solving" (Scribner, 1986, p. 21), even when that problem has well-defined constraints. (See Laufer & Glick, 1996, for a similar observation about expert sales clerks.) This feature clearly distinguishes practical problem solving from laboratory tasks where, as emphasized in chapter 7, the format of the problem is clearly stated, and there are clear restrictions on what constitutes an acceptable method of problem solution. In fact, Scribner (1984b) stressed the amount of creativity involved in this sort of seemingly routine, environmentally constrained activity. This sort of difference between practical problem solving on the one hand, and more formal reasoning or academic intelligence on the other, is clearly illustrated in the differences between the dairy workers and their student counterparts, as well as in the discrepancy between the performance of drivers on the job versus on standard multiplication tests. This difference is also apparent in my later discussion of everyday versus school math.

A second feature of practical problem solving (referred to earlier) illustrated in Scribner's observations is its flexibility, a flexibility that is less clearly observed in lab studies (cf. Duncker's [1945] research on "functional fixedness"). In the case of the dairy workers, this flexibility or adaptiveness primarily serves the principle of least effort. The dairy workers were typically concerned with finding the simplest path to reaching a goal or to solving a problem within existing constraints (e.g., physical, social, or cognitive), although Scribner (1984a, 1984b) acknowledged that it is not clear how general this principle of least effort is, or whether it simply results from, as Scribner (1984b) put it, "a particular configuration of institutional and personal goals" (p. 39). Certainly such a principle underlies a good deal of current research on mental heuristics (to be discussed in chap. 9) and in the area of social cognition (see Taylor's [1981b, Fiske & Taylor, 1991] formulation of the *cognitive miser* model), as well as research on street math to be reviewed in the next section.

Another feature that is clearly illustrated in the research with dairy workers is the everyday problem solvers' use of the environment—including the socially constructed environment (Scribner, 1985)—in reaching a solution. The most obvious examples of this point are the product assemblers' use of the case as a unit, even though the case was not intended for that purpose, and the inventory takers' use of the dimensions of the storage area and array size. According to Scribner (1986), this emphasis on the role of the environment suggests that cognitive models that focus primarily or exclusively on internal, mental representations of the world, or on stored knowledge that is not responsive to the environment or to changes in that environment, are necessarily incomplete. (See Hutchins, 1995, for a similar emphasis on the way in which modern navigators' cognitions are partly contained in the charts that they consult, and also see my discussion of distributed cognition in chap. 10.) In addition, this reliance on the environment suggests once again that skills may be rather task- or situation-specific (see Scribner, 1984b). I return to these points in the next section (and in chap. 10) when I examine Lave's research on supermarket shopping and her "situated cognition" position in general.

Evaluation of Scribner's Research. Scribner's research is an excellent example of both the possibilities and the limitations of everyday cognition research. On the one hand, this research has the advantage of being conducted in a naturalistic, real-world setting with a modicum of control. It is on a topic that is of great relevance and is not typically touched on by traditional cognitive psychology (though see Vera, Lewis, & Lerch, 1993). At the same time, Scribner also attempted to place this research in the context of more general issues for a psychology of practical problem solving.

On the negative side, Scribner's research is not the most rigorous in the world. Like other everyday cognition research, it involves relatively small numbers of participants (e.g., five product assemblers, four inventory takers, and 10 drivers), simple descriptive statistics as the primary results, and a rather cursory, unsystematic presentation of these results (i.e., often in mere lists of general conclusions without actual data).

Scribner (1984a, 1984b) herself listed at least three different limitations of her research: namely, the nonrandom sampling of participants (i.e. only those who were willing to participate were used), the difficulty of conducting more fine-grained analyses in the absence of multiple (and more controlled) studies on dairy workers' strategies and performance, and the problem of validity and generalizability of findings. To this list one may add that Scribner does not really present a very precise or coherent theory of practical problem solving, but rather simply describes some general features that distinguish such thinking from academic or theoretical problem solving.[1] A final question that is raised by Scribner's research is the degree to which the tasks carried out by the problem solvers really provide a representative sample of the kinds of "problems" that people face in the world in general (or even of the world of work). For example, in one definition of a problem, Newell and Simon (1972) emphasized that the problem solver "doesn't know immediately what series of actions he can perform to get it" (p. 72), for example, a desired state. The solutions implemented by product assemblers and drivers, on the other hand, constitute more routinized procedures with little uncertainty involved. (Scribner, 1984b, actually argued that her research may not even be generalized to more routinized, "mindless" tasks such as work on an automobile assembly line). Clearly many of the tasks individuals engage in everyday are similar to these procedures, but whether such routines should be called "problem solving" is open to question.

---

[1]In her defense, it should be noted that, according to Tobach, Falmagne, Parlee, Martin, and Kapelman (1996), Scribner was working on a book to synthesize her work when she died in 1991.

MATHEMATICS IN THE GROCERY STORE
AND ON THE STREET

A second area of research that has a number of features in common with Scribner's is the studies and formulations by Lave (1988; Lave et al., 1984), Saxe (1988, 1991), and by Carraher, Schliemann, and their associates (e.g., Nunes, Schliemann, & Carraher, 1994; Schliemann & Acioly, 1989) concerning the use of arithmetic in everyday activities such as grocery shopping, street vending, and bookmaking. The common theme in this research, as in Scribner's work, is that practical uses of math, or math as a part of everyday practice, frequently departs in significant ways from the math taught in school.

Lave's Work on Arithmetic in the Grocery Store

Probably the most thoroughgoing treatment of the everyday use of arithmetic is found in Jean Lave's (Lave, 1988; Lave et al., 1984) writings on the dialectic of grocery shopping. Lave's work on this topic was motivated by a more general concern with the way in which situations or settings—defined as the point of contact between the physical situation (in this case, the layout of the grocery store) and the individual's own plan or agenda (in this case, the shopper's grocery list or plan)—influence thinking and problem solving. Thus, according to this point of view, the actual practice of calculation in grocery shopping should be viewed as an "activity-in-setting," rather than as "a cognitive function and its context as merely a stage on which action occurs" (p. 154; cf. Scribner, 1988).

The Research Study. Lave's primary observations (Lave et al., 1984) were made on a group of 25 shoppers in supermarkets in southern California. These observations involved tape-recording conversations between the shopper and a researcher in the actual context of the grocery store and the actual process of grocery shopping. This *in situ* approach is important to note in comparing Lave's findings with other research on the use of math in grocery shopping to be reviewed later.

One of the first conclusions that Lave et al. reached from their observations was that shoppers used arithmetic in a fairly small percentage of their purchases. When they did use arithmetic, it was primarily for the purpose of price comparisons when other factors failed to produce a singular choice. As Lave et al. (1984) put it, "This kind of calculation [i.e., price comparisons] occurs at the end of largely qualitative decision-making processes [e.g., involving brand, taste, size, etc.] which smoothly reduce numerous possibilities on the shelf to single items in the cart" (pp. 80–81). Specifically, of 803 observed purchases, only 16% involved arithmetic calculations, and 62% of these calculations involved price comparisons. In general, price comparisons are viewed as justifications or as a "rational accounting" for selections when there are otherwise no strong preferences on other bases. (It may be argued, of course, that for shoppers in less affluent areas, price may play a more central role in their decision-making process, rather than simply being an end-of-the-line justification.)

Another finding from Lave et al.'s research was that the use of math in the grocery store was unrelated to shoppers' performance on standard tests of arithmetic. Specifically, shoppers were only able to solve 59% of the problems correctly on a standard arithmetic test, whereas they accurately selected the best bargain in 98% of their grocery store purchases. There was no correlation between shoppers' performance on the math test or their years of schooling or years since school on the one hand, and their use of arithmetic in grocery shopping on the other. (It was impossible to compute a correlation with accuracy in grocery shopping because there was no variation in shoppers' accuracy.) The accuracy of shoppers' selections was the result of the use of multiple calculations and checks in the selections of a product in the process of "gap closing." Lave (1988) gave the example of a shopper trying to decide between two packages of noodles, one of which she decided to purchase at the price of 32 ounces for $1.12, versus a second at 64 ounces for $1.98. Her expectation was that the larger package should be a better buy; but in her first calculation, in which she rounded $1.98 up to $2.00, and $1.12 down to $1.00, there did not seem to be a difference. However, in part because this solution did not conform to her expectations, and in part because of probing by the observer, she recalculated by transforming 32 ounces to two pounds and 64 to four pounds, and such a simplification made division easier so that "less than 50¢ a pound" is clearly a better buy than "greater than 50¢ per pound" (or closer to 60¢). Finally, accuracy is also ensured in grocery shopping calculations by the fact that if the problem becomes too difficult, the option always remains of "abandoning" a calculation entirely.

As the foregoing example points out, one of the things that Lave et al. observed in their conversations with grocery shoppers was that these shoppers, like the drivers in Scribner's study, used various shortcuts or heuristics to avoid the mental effort of formal calculations. Lave et al. provide anecdotes of shoppers who engaged in various rounding procedures to allow simpler calculations (e.g., rounding $1.93 up to $2.00, or rounding 18 ounces up to 20 or down to a pound).

Lave (1988) also reported the results of simulations in which shoppers, among other things, were to determine the best buy among competing products (see Table 8.1 for some examples of these simulation problems.) In these studies Lave and her associates found three major strategies for calculating the best bargain. These included a *difference* strategy, in which shoppers subtracted the smaller quantity from the larger, then subtracted the lower price from the higher, and compared the latter difference with the former to see if the larger quantity product was worth it. Thus, for example, one bottle of salad dressing may contain 15 ounces and cost $2.35,

TABLE 8.1

Examples of Simulated "Best Buy" Problems

Product	Ratios (larger package vs. smaller package)			
	I		II	
refried beans	$ .57	20-1/2 oz.	$ .49	17 oz.
canned chilis	.79	7 oz.	.49	4 oz.
rice	2.16	28 oz.	1.21	14 oz.
syrup	2.26	36 oz.	1.63	24 oz.
canned fruit mix	.82	30 oz.	.69	29 oz.
tuna	1.89	12-1/2 oz.	1.39	9-1/4 oz.
BBQ sauce	1.17	23 oz.	.89	18 oz.
celery	.79	2 lbs.	.23	1 lb.
mustard	.75	24 oz.	.79	16 oz.
paper towels	.93	100 ft.	.62	85 ft.
cheddar cheese	5.29	32 oz.	1.59	9 oz.
peanut butter	2.21	40 oz.	1.05	18 oz.
honey	3.00	2 lbs.	1.64	24 oz.
frozen fish	1.72	12 oz.	3.13	8 oz.
paper towels	.93	11 × 14	.59	11 × 10

Note. Adapted from *Cognition in Practice: Mind, Mathematics and Culture in Everyday Life* (pp. 772–773), by J. Lave, 1988, New York: Cambridge University Press. Copyright © 1988 by Cambridge University Press. Adapted with permission.

while another bottle may contain 8 ounces and cost $1.80. The difference in quantities is 7 ounces, and the difference in price is only 55¢—considerably less than the $1.80 for 8 ounces (though this last step involves going beyond a simple difference strategy). A second strategy, illustrated in the packages of noodles example cited earlier, was a *ratio* strategy where the ratio of quantities was compared with the ratio of prices. Thus, to take another example from Lave, one can of peanuts may contain 10 ounces and cost 90¢, whereas a second contains 4 ounces and costs 45¢. Because the first can costs twice as much as the second and contains more than twice as many ounces, it is clearly the "best buy." Finally, a third, last resort strategy is for a shopper to calculate a unit price.

Of particular interest here is the frequency with which different strategies were observed, both in the naturalistic setting of the supermarket and in the simulations, which explicitly posed the problem in written form. In the supermarket setting, the most common strategy was the ratio strategy (35%), followed by the difference strategy (22%), with the unit price strategy coming in a distant third (5%). In the simulation study, on the other hand, the order of the second two strategies was reversed, with the ratio strategy still coming in first (47%), followed by the unit pricing strategy (39%), followed by the difference strategy (9%). This finding suggests that when arithmetic problems are presented in the form of word problems, they are more likely to elicit an algorithmic strategy. In general, it seems that shoppers in a real-life setting find different strategies and different ways to represent problems, ways that depart significantly from the algorithmic solution learned in school settings. (At least part of the difference here, as observed by Leont'ev [cited in Lave et al., 1984], is the distinction between math as an activity or goal that is focused on for its own sake vs. math as an operation in service of a more basic goal, such as finding the best buy.) This discontinuity between supermarket activity and school-based procedures points to the situational specificity or lack of transfer from one context to another on the one hand, and to the difficulty of predicting real-world performance from results of traditional academic tests on the other. This is a point I return to later in this chapter.

A Comparison With a More Traditional Study. The results presented by Lave (1988) from the best buy simulations are at variance with results of earlier "real-world" studies by Capon and Kuhn (1979, 1982). Like Lave, Capon and Kuhn interviewed people about to shop in a supermarket; and they also presented these shoppers with a set of best buy problems, although their emphasis was on the degree to which such real-world problem solving reflected different stages of Piaget's theory of cognitive development. In contrast to Lave and her associates, Capon and Kuhn found a much lower solution rate (44% vs. 93%), and they also found that shoppers used similar strategies across problems, whereas Lave found substantial differences across problems, with shoppers adjusting their solutions to the type and difficulty of the problem.

Lave (1988) pointed out a number of differences between the Capon and Kuhn study and her own, many of which are relevant to the more general comparison between lab studies and the research on everyday cognition that I have been considering throughout this book. First, Lave (1988) argued that the difference in generality or specificity between problem solution in the two studies can be traced to the fact that Capon and Kuhn used only two somewhat more difficult ratio problems, whereas Lave and her associates included a wider variety of different problems, in terms of both type and difficulty level. More important, Capon and Kuhn were concerned with a particular theoretical position (i.e., Piagetian theory) and with examining the applicability of cognitive research on that position to real-world settings. This Piagetian framework and the resulting concern with proportional reasoning and formal operational thought dictated the choice of settings and tasks—that is, the supermarket in general, and unit price problems in particular, are situations in which such proportional reasoning and formal operations should be observable. Furthermore, this concern led them to set up a kind of experiment at a card table outside a supermarket rather than making observations of actual shoppers doing their shopping within the supermarket.

Lave and her associates, on the other hand, were concerned with studying real-world problem solving, using an observational–interview study followed by a simulation to better determine some of the specific strategies used by shoppers. In addition, Capon and Kuhn were primarily concerned with certain universal cognitive processes and certain normative judgments about level of cognitive sophistication, whereas Lave and her associates were less concerned with universal methods or procedures than they were with the way in which these procedures are adapted to and structured by particular situations.

Research by Saxe on Street Math in Brazil

Another set of studies that examined real-life street math and the way in which it departs from school math were reported by Geoffrey Saxe (1988a, 1991) and by Carraher, Schliemann, and their associates (e.g., Nunes et al., 1994). Both of these teams of researchers pointed out that mathematics learning does not only occur within the classroom, but rather is more frequently acquired from "participation in cultural practices as children and adults attempt to accomplish pragmatic goals" (Saxe, 1988a, pp. 14–15). Thus, people learn math from shopping, from buying and selling, from work activities (such as those studied by Scribner), from cultural activities such as games and stories, and so forth. In these nonschool contexts, "math often has only a distant resemblance to classroom mathematics: Individuals usually do not use a written symbolic system to produce mathematical computations but rely, instead, on invented procedures that may include mentally regrouping terms to arrive at sums or manipulating objects in computations" (Saxe, 1988a, p. 14).

A major research project that illustrates these alternative forms of representation and problem solution is Saxe's (1988a, 1988b, 1991) study on the candy sellers of Recife, Brazil. The sellers in this study were young boys ranging in age from 6 to 15 with varying degrees of schooling whose motive in selling these candies (and a variety of other products) was strictly economic. Specifically, these children came from poor families, most of whom lived in the shanty towns of Recife. These children engaged in selling in order to help themselves and their families to survive in an extremely inflationary economy. Thus, their selling reflects not only cognitive processes, but also social, cultural, and economic considerations. In addition, Nunes et al. (1994) pointed out that the several deficiencies in the Brazilian school system (i.e., the number of students not in school, the slow progress of other students through the system) make street math a particularly significant phenomenon. As they put it, "street mathematics develops mostly when there is a discrepancy between people's need in problem solving and the amount of mathematics they have learned in school" (Nunes et al., 1994, p. 14).

Saxe (1988a, 1991) identified four main phases of the candy selling practice: a phase of purchasing candy from wholesalers, preparing the boxes of candy for sale, the actual sale of the candy, and a "preparation-to-purchase" phase in which a decision must be made about what kinds of candy (or other commodities) are selling well and what wholesalers to purchase the candies from. All four stages involve mathematical calculations and transactions in some form. For example, such calculations are obviously involved in the purchase and sale phases, but they are also involved in the prepare-for-sale phase, where the seller must translate prices of large quantities of candy (from the wholesaler) to the price for individual units and decide how much mark-up to make. In addition, as indicated above, there are clearly a variety of social and cultural factors that influence the sales procedure, including the high and rapidly changing inflation rate, certain social conventions (e.g., the pricing convention of selling a given number of boxes for 1000 cruzeiros, a standard unit of Brazilian currency), and the impact of social interactions (e.g., bargaining with customers, the impact of the territoriality of various street sellers on sales).

Like Scribner, Saxe (1991) reported a number of preliminary observational and interview studies focusing on, for example, the nature of the social interactions in the selling and purchasing phases. Of greater importance for the purposes of this section, however, are the more structured tests conducted by Saxe (1988a, 1991) of sellers' representation of large monetary values, their ability to calculate these values or units, and their ability to compare ratios of prices to see which offers the better profit. For the first issue, Saxe examined the ability of three groups of children—namely, urban sellers and nonsellers and rural children—to understand standard symbols of simple numbers versus their ability to recognize different units of currency. In the number identification test, none of the three groups of children performed very well. No group scored above 50% (of the 67% of the responses that were even scorable across the three groups) on the number identification task. On the currency identification tasks, on the other hand, in which children were to identify either standard bills, bills with the numerical value covered up, or photocopies of the bill currency numbers separate from the bill itself (see Fig. 8.1), children scored at nearly 100% accuracy on the first two tasks and significantly better on these two tasks than on the test of numerical values alone, suggesting that they could master the currency system (i.e., on the basis of the sheer figurative qualities of the bills) without mastering the numbers per se.

In addition, all children showed that they understood the ordinal and multiplicative relations among currency types (i.e., which values were

FIG. 8.1. The standard bills used in the currency identification problems for Brazilian street sellers. From *Culture and Cognitive Development* (p. 30), by G. Saxe, 1991, Hillsdale, NJ: Lawrence Erlbaum Associates. Copyright © 1991 by Lawrence Erlbaum Associates. Reprinted with permission.

higher or lower than others and how many of a lower value currency were required to make up a higher denomination), although nonsellers did better on the multiplicative relations tasks for higher denominations than for lower ones, whereas sellers performed equally well on both denominations. Finally, in a task in which the children were required to ask for the correct change for a given bill, both sellers and nonsellers performed well for lower denomination bills, but sellers performed better for higher denomination bills than did nonsellers. Sellers also required fewer attempts than nonsellers at determining the right change for both higher and lower denomination bills. Thus, it appeared that sellers had a greater facility with the currency system in general than did nonsellers, and both did better in the identification and representation of currency than of numerical values in their own right.

A related study on five Brazilian street vendors was reported by Carraher, Carraher, and Schliemann (1985). This study began with an informal test of math ability in which the researcher acted as a customer asking the vendor to calculate the cost of the sale of coconuts, lemons, and the like. This test was followed by a more formal test consisting of word problems and a formal test of mathematical operations, both of which were based on problems posed in the initial informal study. In general, Carraher et al. (1985) found that the vendors performed better on the informal problems than on the formal ones. More important, the procedures used for solving the informal problems differed from those for the formal ones, with the former involving informal *grouping* techniques (e.g., instead of multiplying the price of one lemon by 12 to get the price of 12 lemons, a vendor multiplied the former price by 2 and then added the product 6 times), as well as *decomposition* techniques (e.g., instead of adding 35 to 195 directly, a vendor first added 3 tens followed by 5 units), whereas the formal problems were solved by more school-based procedures. As discussed earlier, the sellers were less successful at the latter than at the former. Thus, formal mathematical procedures are not always superior to more informal procedures, although the latter are obviously more limited in their applicability (e.g., to larger numbers) than are the former.

Another more important task in Saxe's (1988a, 1991) research required vendors to perform arithmetical calculations on bills. Specifically, the same children were asked to add a fairly large set of bills, followed by instructions to purchase a box of candy from this total and then figure out the correct change. On the addition task, urban sellers performed better on two different problems, varying in complexity, than did urban nonsellers, who in turn did better than rural children. More interesting, both the urban sellers and the nonsellers tended to shift their strategy of calculation for the more complex of the two problems (i.e., by grouping similar bills, such as Cr$500 or Cr$1000), to make calculations easier. The sellers showed this shift more clearly than did the nonsellers. Furthermore, none of the children used paper-and-pencil strategies for solving the problem.

When it came to subtraction, there was again evidence of an interaction between problem difficulty and group (see Fig. 8.2). Specifically, on a less complex problem, both urban sellers and nonsellers performed significantly better than did rural children. On a second, more complex problem, on the other hand, sellers did significantly better than did urban nonsellers, again suggesting the role of selling experience on facility with numerical operations. Again, the children generally did not use paper-and-pencil strategies on these problems.

A third set of tests administered by Saxe (1988a, 1991) required children to indicate which of two ratios was more profitable. For example, which is more profitable, one Pirulito (a type of candy) for Cr$200 or three Pirulitos for Cr$500? The obvious solution for this kind of problem is to appeal to some "common term," such as the Cr$200 unit. However, many children

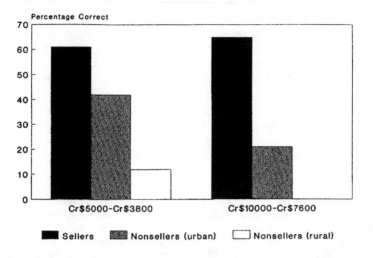

FIG. 8.2. Interaction between problem difficulty and group (sellers, urban nonsellers, and rural nonsellers). From *Culture and Cognitive Development* (p. 84), by G. Saxe, 1991, Hillsdale, NJ: Lawrence Erlbaum Associates. Copyright © 1991 by Lawrence Erlbaum Associates. Reprinted with permission.

seemed to have difficulty seeing this strategy, as illustrated in the following protocol:

> S No. 910. 10-year-old rural nonseller, first grade. ... In comparing one for Cr$200 to three for Cr$500, he states that three for Cr$500 will bring the most profit "BECAUSE YOU WILL MAKE MORE MONEY. SELLING IT FOR Cr$200 YOU WILL MAKE LITTLE AND SELLING IT FOR Cr$500 YOU WILL MAKE MORE." (Saxe, 1991, p. 85)

The major finding from these tests is that sellers were significantly more likely to use the "common terms" solution than were either the urban nonsellers or the rural children.

On the issue of the relationship between schooling and performance on practical math tests, Saxe (1991) reported a comparison of 12–15-year-old sellers with little or no schooling to another group of the same age level, but moderate (3rd–4th grade) or greater (5th–7th grade) schooling. This comparison indicated that as sellers acquired more schooling, their performance on the numerical representation problems improved significantly, but their level of problem solution did not. In addition, schooled sellers increasingly came to use mathematical algorithms (e.g., multiplication of a unit price to get at a total multi-unit price) rather than the "count by price ratio" strategy described earlier (i.e., using the price convention of, for example, X units per Cr$1000, and then dividing the total number of units up into multiples of X and counting by Cr$1000 to get to the total price).

In a further comparison of 2nd and 3rd grade sellers versus nonsellers, sellers arrived at solutions almost entirely by using regrouping strategies. That is, they changed the order of operations or of the values on which these operations were performed by regrouping them into common groups (e.g., adding 35 plus 47 by first adding 30 and 40, followed by the addition of 5 and then 7). Such regrouping simplified the task for these less schooled sellers. In addition, the improvements made by nonsellers between grades 2 and 3 came in the form of both better regrouping and better algorithmic strategies.

An example of a solution that combines both regrouping and more algorithmic strategies is given in the following protocol:

> S No. V309. Seller, third grade ... is provided with the problem 790 + 470 = ? in computation form, and solves it correctly. ... When questioned about his solution strategy, he explains, referring first to the units column, "0 PLUS 0 EQUALS 0"; then referring to the tens column and using a regrouping strategy, "NINE (of 790) MINUS THREE [the amount required to make ten out of the 7 from 470] IS SIX, AND THREE PLUS SEVEN [from 470] IS 10 AND 10 PLUS SIX IS 16." He writes down the six and carries one to the hundreds column. Again he uses a regrouping strategy to add the numbers in the hundreds column. "FOUR MINUS THREE [the number required to make a ten of the 7 from 790] IS ONE, AND THREE PLUS SEVEN [from 790] IS 10. TEN PLUS ONE PLUS ONE IS 12," and he writes down the number 12. While his final answer is correct, he reads the value as 10,260, making a place value error. (Saxe, 1991, pp. 168–169)

This observation of the interaction between street math and school math underlines the importance of understanding the former in designing instruction in the latter. Saxe (1988a) stated this point in the following way:

> Many researchers now recognize the pedagogical importance of using linkages as means of strengthening children's mathematical intuitions ... and recommend appropriate classroom techniques to facilitate and build on these linkages ... These results ... point to the need to examine how we can better make classroom mathematics more readily accessible and transparent to children as they approach and pursue problems in the course of their everyday out-of-school activities. (pp. 20–21)

This is a point that I discuss in detail in chapter 10.

In general, these results suggest that selling and schooling have different but interrelated effects on children's mathematical understanding, as well as on the *practice* of mathematics. For example, sellers are often not concerned with exact mathematical calculations, particularly when it comes to small denominations (e.g., Cr$100, which is relatively worthless in a highly inflated economy). On the other hand, "in school, mathematics is an object of study without a pragmatic end. ... The pedagogical objective in many mathematics classes is for children, when doing mathematics, to appeal to mathematical norms of correctness without worldly constraints" (p. 136; cf. my earlier discussion of Lave). In addition, there are major difference in the social structure and social interactions involved in the two settings. Many of the interactions in selling are among peers and leave the seller in control of his calculations and selling practices, whereas the rules and practices in school are set by the teacher and by the authoritative standards set by a formal discipline (see chaps. 1 and 7) with a long cultural history.[2]

Research by Carraher and Associates on "Street Math"

T. Carraher (aka Nunes), Schliemann, and their associates have reported a number of different studies contrasting *street math,* or math learned and practiced in everyday activities or work settings, with school or written math, again using a Brazilian population. A common theme in this research is that street math has the advantage of preserving the meaning of the particular situation, materials, and units being worked with, while sacrificing a degree of generality, whereas school math sacrifices exact, specific meaning (e.g., 2.15 can refer to 2.15 of anything) in the interest of greater generality. Stated differently, school math separates or distances the mathematical operations from the representation of the concrete situation to which these operations apply, whereas oral math represents these two components together.

The Research Studies. To illustrate this point, consider a study by Carraher (1986) in which she compared the responses of Brazilian construction foremen and students to a set of blueprints that depicted a scale value (e.g., 3 cm) and the actual dimensions (e.g., 3 m) of one wall. Both groups were then asked to infer the dimension of a second wall from the scale value (e.g., 2.8 cm) for that wall. This task is the inverse of what the foremen usually have to solve. That is, they typically must apply a known scale (e.g., 1:100) to a scale value (e.g., 3 cm) to infer the actual dimensions of a wall (e.g., 3 m), whereas in these problems they must actually *infer* such a scale from two values (e.g., 3 cm:3 m). The problems presented in this study involved both familiar (e.g., 1 cm:100 cm) and unfamiliar scales (e.g., 1 cm:40 cm).

The major findings of this study were that the foremen were more likely to arrive at correct solutions for the familiar scales than were the students, whereas no differences were found between groups for the unfamiliar scales. As far as problem-solving strategies were concerned, none of the foremen and only one of the 16 students used the algebraic ratio solution (i.e., $a/b = x/c$) taught in schools, presumably because the blueprint problem did not bear an obvious resemblance to the form in which ratio problems are typically presented in school. For the foremen, the most frequent strategies were

---

[2]Ironically, Lave (1988) pointed out that instruction in school math was originally motivated by the demands of commerce and the marketplace—see P. C. Cohen (1982).

(a) *finding-the-relation* strategy, in which participants looked for the relation between the first two numbers (e.g., 3 cm:3 m) and then applied that to the third value in order to come up with the fourth, and (b) *hypothesis testing* strategy, in which they generated a succession of values for the fourth term until they zerod in on the correct one. These two strategies were used equally often when the scale was a familiar one, but the finding-the-relation strategy was more common for the unfamiliar scale problems where there were no ready, familiar hypotheses available. For students, who did not have a store of hypotheses about scales available, the hypothesis-testing strategy was not used at all, whereas the finding-the-relation strategy was used by more than 80% of them in both familiar and unfamiliar scale problems.

As conceived of by Carraher (1986), a common feature of the hypothesis-testing and finding-the-relation strategies is that they both stick fairly close to the actual situation and the meaning of that situation. In this connection, Carraher (1986) interpreted her results as arguing against the traditional Piagetian (e.g., Inhelder & Piaget, 1958) conception of proportionality as an abstract, context-free mathematical schema.

One of the questions that arises from these studies, as well as from other examples to be discussed in chapter 10, is whether the foremen have simply learned a concrete, rote strategy that they can only apply to familiar problems (though the foremen's ability to perform a slightly different task from the one they are used to provides one argument against this possibility). Thus, in one additional study Schliemann and Nunes (1990) studied the ability of Brazilian fishermen to transfer their ability to perform a familiar calculation to another sort of computation that they do not typically make. Specifically, the fishermen negotiate, on a daily basis, a price for their catch. This negotiation is with a middleman, who in turn processes the fish for sale in the market. The fishermen are thus accustomed to calculating a price for their fish, taking into account inflation; but they do not typically calculate the price for which the fish processor will have to sell *his* product, even though the same kind of multiplicative pricing procedure would be used in this case. Thus, the purpose of the study by Schliemann and Nunes (1990) was to determine if fishermen had simply developed a kind of rote, procedural knowledge for calculating prices, or had instead developed a more abstract knowledge of the relationship between price and weight so that they could actually invert or reverse this calculation (as in the above example with construction foremen), or had even developed a more abstract schema of proportionality in general that could be applied to new situations or problems besides mere pricing.

A group of fishermen were given sets of problems corresponding to these three possibilities, with all three involving calculation of the prices for fish. (The interviews here were even conducted on the beach!) The first finding from these interviews was that the fishermen were significantly more accurate on the problems involving the kinds of calculations they typically made than they were on the inverse of these (i.e., calculating a unit price from the total product and total price), though there was still high accuracy (> 70%) for the latter problems. On the first type of transfer problem in which they were to make calculations on the *processed* fish, the fishermen performed as well, or even slightly better (79%) than on the initial inverse problem. However, on a more complex transfer problem involving a full set of proportions (i.e., given a particular ratio of unprocessed to processed fish, how much unprocessed fish would be necessary to get, say, 16 kilos of processed fish)—the kind of problem typically presented to schoolchildren—the fishermen showed significantly poorer performance (60%).

In a second study fishermen were found to show great accuracy for a set of problems isomorphic to the ones just reviewed, but involving farm content—that is, having to do with the processing of cassava (a starchy plant used in these peoples' diet and one that is processed in a manner analogous to the fish described above). This result suggests that the fishermen's mathematical skills are not just restricted to the products that they ordinarily deal with, but can be generalized to an analogous product that is familiar to them. This result is consistent with the finding of Scribner (1984a, 1986) on the ability of drivers to transfer their strategies to new products (though cf. Ceci & Ruiz, 1993). On the other hand, Schliemann and Nunes (1990) also found that another group of teacher trainees who had learned proportions in school performed more poorly on the unfamiliar fisherman problems than on ones with more familiar content, and they continued to use everyday strategies rather than school-based ones even when these strategies were not the easiest or most appropriate ones. Nunes et al. (1994) argued that an everyday strategy is more likely to be used:

> They [the teacher trainees] understood it [the familiar solution] better. It is a solution that preserves meaning. ... It also seems safe to conclude that when school-taught procedures come into conflict with a previously known out-of-school model for proportionality, school procedures are poorly learned and quickly forgotten. (Nunes et al., 1994, p. 126)

This conclusion is clearly consistent with that reached by Lave et al. (1984).

One final, particularly interesting research project reported by Schliemann and Acioly (1989) focused on adults' performance as bookies in a popular Brazilian lottery game called the Animals Game. In this game, animals' names are given to a group of numbers (e.g., numbers 01 to 04 correspond to ostrich, up to 97-00 for cow). Bets are made on a set of four-digit numbers, five sets of which are drawn at the end of the day. These bets can be made on the full four-digit number, or on three- or two-digit ones. Bets can also be made on a single or on all five winners, the latter of which costs five times as much as the former. Finally, bets can be made on several numbers by asking for all permutations of a given four- (or three- or two-) digit number, a bet that is called for by asking for a given number *inverted*.

As an example of a bet in this game and the required calculations by the bookie, consider the following (from Schliemann & Acioly, 1989): "I want to bet 2 *cruzeiros* ... in the thousand and hundred inverted of 582492 (i.e., in all possible three-digit and four-digit permutations of the digits in 583492), from the first to the fifth (i.e., in any of the five four-digit numbers to be drawn)" (p. 190).

In order to determine the full amount of the bet, a bookie must first consult reference tables that list the total number of permutations for any subset of digits (e.g., three or four digits) from an n-digit number. Thus, in the above example, after adding up the total number of four-digit (i.e., 360) and three-digit permutations (i.e., 120), the bookie must then multiply this sum by 5 (i.e., the number of numbers to be drawn), and multiply the resulting product by 2 (i.e., the number of cruzeiros per number), for a total of 4800 cruzeiros (or a little less than $1.00). It follows that the bookie must have some understanding of addition and multiplication, along with some knowledge of combinatorial principles (although the permutations are determined primarily by consulting the reference tables) and some understanding of probability (because the value of a bet is determined by the probabilities of a certain number occurring, and bettors must take this into account, though they are also influenced by superstitions and other less rational considerations).

The study reported by Schliemann and Acioly involved 20 adult bookies with varying degrees of schooling. As in the previous studies, Schliemann and Acioly began with an ethnographic study in which bookies were observed doing their work during the peak hour. These observations were followed by interviews with these bookies about their computation strategies. Finally, 2 months later, these same bookies were asked to solve three series of problems, one in which they were to transfer their combinatorial knowledge to other materials such as letters or colors, a second in which they were to apply their skills to bets using nonround numbers, and a third in which they had to solve betting problems that involved division rather than multiplication. Examples of these three types of problems are given in Table 8.2.

In the observational part of the study, it was found that only 24% of the bets actually required computations. (Others involved a bet on only a single number.) Of these 609 problems requiring some type of calculation, 88% yielded an immediate solution, suggesting that bookies had a memorized answer that did not require calculations. Of the remaining 57 problems that involved identifiable forms of computation, the most frequent strategy was that of decomposition (cf. Carraher et al., 1985), in which a quantity involved was broken down into subtotals that were easier to work with, and these subtotals were then recomposed. For example, a bookie who had to deal with 1 cruzeiro and 50 broke the bet down into calculations for the 1, and then divided that total in half to come up with the 50 or half cruzeiro, which was then summed with the previous total (i.e., rather than multiplying by 1.5) as he might be taught to do in school. Another strategy (which I discussed earlier) was a regrouping one in which bookies transformed multiplication into addition (e.g., 12, 12, 12, and 12, rather than 4 × 12). Still

TABLE 8.2

Examples of Three Types of Problems Used in Schliemann and Acioly
(1989) Betting Study

1. Permutation problems

   a. Let's suppose that you have cloth of three colors: red, blue, and black; and you want to make shirts for different soccer teams. Each team must have a different kind of shirt made with the three colors. You can make different shirts, arranging the colors so that for one team you might use red on the top, blue in the middle, black on the bottom. For another team you might use black on the top, red in the middle, blue on the bottom. How many different shirts can you make in that way? Show me the different ways you can find.

   b. Number of ways of rearranging letters in word casa (see text)

2. Problems with nonround numbers

   a. Thousands and hundreds from the first to the fifth

   I want to bet on 6 thousands and hundreds, from the first to the fifth. On each thousand I want to put 18 cruzeiros and on each hundred, 34. How much do I have to pay?

   b. Inverted thousands and hundreds from the first to the fifth

   I want to bet on the inverted thousands and hundreds of 2233456 and 4455678, from the first to the fifth, at 12 cruzeiros each. How much do I have to pay?

3. Problems requiring division

   a. Thousands and hundreds from the first to the fifth

   I have 1500 cruzeiros, and I want to bet on the thousands and the hundreds of 4721, 6534, and 6745, from the first to the fifth. How much does each bet cost?

   b. Inverted thousands and hundreds from the first to the fifth

   I have 2400 cruzeiros, and I want to bet on the thousands and hundreds of 2345 and 7542, from the first to the fifth. How much does each bet cost?

Note. From "Mathematical Knowledge Developed at Work: The Contribution of Practice Versus the Contribution of Schooling," by A. D. Schliemann & N. M. Acioly, 1989, *Cognition and Instruction,* 6, pp. 195–196. Copyright © 1989 by Lawrence Erlbaum Associates. Reprinted with permission.

another technique used was to make difficult problems less difficult by convincing the bettor to accept a slightly different version of the problem (cf. Lave et al.'s notion of "abandoning" a problem). Thus, for example, when a bettor wanted to bet 50 cruzeiros on a problem that came to 48 cruzeiros using round numbers (2 cruzeiros per number), a bookie convinced the bettor to place the extra 2 cruzeiro on a second bet rather than his having to calculate an uneven number. Interestingly, even though bookies all had calculators that could be used to solve such difficult problems, they never used these calculators, perhaps because fractions of a cruzeiro are so worthless as to not be worth worrying about (Schliemann & Acioly, 1989). Finally, years of schooling did not have an effect on the bookies' performance, primarily because only two errors were made in the 609 problems involving calculation, though schooling did seem to have an effect on bookies' ability to *explain* their calculations.

This observational phase, of course, did not allow a determination of what the bookies actually knew and understood versus, for example, what they had simply memorized. The investigators therefore posed a set of structured problems to bookies that were designed to address this question. For example, in one series of problems involving the number of letters or colors, schooling played a major role in the ability of bookies to see the similarities between these new problems and those involving permutations of numbers. Those without schooling either did not see all the possible permutations with these varied materials or simply refused to tackle the problem. An example of the latter response is given in the following excerpt from a bookie with no schooling:

E.: I want you to tell me how many different ways you can combine the letters in the word *casa* without leaving any letter out and without putting any other letter in.

S.: This one is even worse because I don't know how to read.

E.: But you don't have to read. I want you to find out how many different ways there are to change the places of the letters.

S.: This I can't do.

E.: What if you tried to as you do in the game.

S.: This is too complicated because to read is more difficult than to deal with numbers. I know how to do a few computations but I can't read at all. I don't even know how to write my name.

E.: What if you do it like this: The c stands for number 1, the a for number 2, the s for number 3, and the a for number 2? Couldn't you do it?

S.: No, because one thing is different from the other. (Schliemann & Acioly, 1989, p. 206)

When it came to more difficult versions of betting problems (i.e., problems with nonround numbers) bookies with more schooling were significantly more likely to solve the problems correctly, primarily because those without schooling simply refused to try to solve many of these problems. More important, with these particular problems bookies were most likely to use written, algorithmic calculations, either alone or in conjunction with mental calculations or calculators. Interestingly enough, these written calculations were also most likely to lead to errors.

As far as the problems requiring division are concerned (i.e., determining the number of cruzeiros per number given an overall total), the results were essentially the same as those just reviewed. The explanation that was typically given for solutions was in terms of multiplicative operations rather than division. The major type of alternative multiplicative solution here was the hypothesis-testing approach described earlier, in which bookies tried out successive values per bets until they zeroed in on the correct total. Thus, for example, in a protocol cited by Schliemann and Acioly (1989), a bookie tried out 5, then 10, and then 15 cruzeiros before settling on 20 per number in order to come up with a total bet of 9600 cruzeiros on inverted thousands and hundreds. Interestingly enough, even though bookies were less likely to use school-based written procedures for these division problems—in fact, most bookies said that they did not know how to do division—in this case they made *fewer* errors than in the problems with nonround numbers.

Two Types of Rules.   The effects of schooling, then, are rather mixed. Schooling does not seem to have an effect on problem solution within the constraints of the work setting, nor does it affect peoples' use of written, algorithmic procedures.

> However, school experience has an effect on how people deal with more academic problems, such as explaining their everyday procedures or making explicit the mathematical structures implicit in their everyday activities. School experience is also related to better performance on solving problems that differ from those usually encountered at work. (Schliemann & Acioly, 1989, pp. 218–219)

By way of summary, Nunes et al. (1994) distinguished between two sets of rules entailed in *street math*: namely, *mathematical rules* and *social rules* (cf. the similar distinction made by Saxe). Although the former, as generally conceived, are to be judged in terms of formal correctness, such judgments are elicited by a particular social context or social interaction (cf. my discussion of Lave). As I have discussed, the particular social context of street math encourages a stance of evaluating math problems in terms of personal experience and observations rather than in terms of formal rules. As I point out in a later section of this chapter, this observation is consistent with a good deal of cross-cultural evidence (see Cole et al., 1971; Cole & Scribner, 1974; Luria, 1976) suggesting that unschooled individuals frequently use personal experience to judge mathematical or logical conclusions—that is, if it is implausible in terms of their personal experience, then it is judged to be invalid. When the judgment refers to the same situation or pertains to those experiences, then such empirical observations may, in fact, be helpful. When it does not, such experiences are limiting at best.

As one final point, Nunes et al. (1994) drew a connection between the mathematical versus social rules distinction and the concept of pragmatic reasoning schemas (Cheng & Holyoak, 1985) touched on in chapter 1. For the present purposes, it is sufficient to note that such schemas are assumed to combine social rules (e.g., of permission or propriety "induced from everyday life experiences"; Cheng & Holyoak, 1985, p. 395) with more abstract, fairly general reasoning structures, with the former presumably eliciting the latter. I return to this concept of pragmatic reasoning schemas and its implications for instruction in chapter 10.

Evaluation of Alternative Math Studies

It is clear from this review that the study of alternative math has enjoyed a good deal of popularity in recent years. From the vantage point of the transfer of training literature reviewed in chapter 7, it is of interest to see that even individuals schooled in math frequently fail to apply that knowledge in their everyday activities; and it is fascinating to look at the numerous strategies (e.g., difference and ratio comparisons, regrouping and decomposition, hypothesis testing) that individuals, both schooled and unschooled, devise as alternatives to school math. Perhaps of greatest importance is the distinction, made particularly by Lave and by the activity theorists (e.g., Wertsch, 1981) between math as an end in itself, as in school math, and math as embedded in some larger goal-directed activity, as in grocery shopping or betting. In this connection, it is also of interest to consider some of the social, cultural, and practical concerns that affect the use of different strategies, as well as the decision to use school math or not. Finally, as I observed in the research by Scribner, the combination of real-world, informal observations followed by more precise experimental and/or simulation studies makes for an oftentimes compelling demonstration of both external and internal validity of these findings.

At the same time, a number of questions arise in interpreting the results of these studies. For example, a major theoretical issue that I discussed in the last chapter is the domain- or situational-specificity versus generality of abilities, or whether such generality is in any way expected for street math. The fact that sellers, construction foremen, and bookies perform accurately on problems from their own area of expertise when they cannot solve school math problems, and that they use different strategies for these familiar problems is of some interest. It is not clear, however, whether these skills or strategies generalize in any meaningful way to other kinds of activity or that they should even be viewed as "skills" (e.g., as opposed to rote procedures). Unlike Scribner's research, there is little evidence provided for the *flexibility* of these strategies, and the primary evidence for generality comes from the findings by Schliemann and Nunes on the ability of fishermen to solve analogous problems dealing with a different product (i.e., cassava) or requiring them to perform inverse operations on less familiar material. But how much generality or abstraction is required by the first of these, particularly given that cassava is part of the fishermen's daily meals, or on the latter, in that all fishermen are familiar with the fact that processed fish must be sold in a similar way as their own unprocessed fish (and hence could have simply reasoned by analogy here)? For that matter, it is not clear from Nunes et al.'s formulation exactly how much abstraction is expected or desirable. Certainly commentators such as Lave do not believe in such generality because a major feature of street math is that in involves a situational "model" or "scheme," as well as an abstract mathematical one. In this regard, Nunes et al. (1994) argued that their studies indicate that "there is a need to make the distinction between general and particular forms of knowledge less rigid" (p. 140).

From a methodological standpoint, questions can be raised about the rigor of much of the research described in this section. For example, although questioning participants in more natural settings, with more familiar materials, and with real-world experts is certainly an attractive feature—and in fact, is one of the *defining* features of research on everyday cognition—I can't help but have some reservations about the validity of some of these interviews. Let me take the interviews by Carraher and her associates as an example. To begin with, the very fact that the questions, as well as participants' responses, were exclusively verbal is certainly problematic. That is, it is not clear that the young participants (or the older ones) completely understood the questions posed to them by the interviewer, or could always explain their answers clearly (see my later discussion of the cross-cultural observations by Cole et al. and by Scribner, 1975, 1977). The most blatant examples of these are the refusals of young children (e.g., in the Schliemann & Acioly, 1989, study) to even tackle some problems and the difficulty encountered by some of the younger children in Saxe's research to understand the concepts of addition, subtraction, and ratio comparisons, but there may also be other cases where unschooled participants had difficulty fully explaining their strategies. Other questionable features of the studies by Carraher and her associates include (a) their sometimes ad hoc selection of derived dependent variables—for instance, the number of unreasonable solutions and the number of strategies falling in different categories such as those illustrating the finding-the-relation strategy; and (b) their sometimes arbitrary interpretation of findings—for instance, their interpretation of similar performance levels as high (e.g., 69% correct) or low (e.g., 60% correct), depending on their purpose.

I now turn to another real-world study of the reasoning involved in betting. The study by Ceci and Liker (1986a, 1986b) to be discussed next addresses once again the issue of the relationship (or lack thereof) between academic intelligence and practical intelligence in the real world.

CECI AND LIKER'S STUDY OF RACETRACK HANDICAPPING

Ceci and Liker's (1986a, 1986b) study of racetrack handicapping represents both an excellent example of a particular type of real-world research on reasoning and also an explicit challenge to traditional views of intelligence. On the second point, Ceci and Liker argued that intelligence or cognitive ability in any given domain should not be equated with IQ or the results of IQ tests, as many psychologists have done. IQ simply measures the kind of intelligence involved in and fostered by formal schooling. (Ceci, 1991, even argued that IQ is the *product* of such schooling rather than an ability that we bring to it.) According to Ceci and Liker (1986b), "there exist multiple intelligences, each an underlying capacity to acquire knowledge, detect relationships, and monitor our ongoing cognitions for a given cognitive domain" (p. 119). Thus, intelligence or cognitive ability varies with the situation or domain (see my discussion of domain-specificity in chap. 7), as well as with the "environmental challenges, opportunities, and motivation" (p. 119) that individuals face in this domain.

To demonstrate this position, Ceci and Liker (1986a, 1986b) conducted a study with racetrack handicappers, people who were clearly knowledgeable about harness racing and motivated to pick winners, but who were not necessarily well-educated and did not necessarily score high on IQ tests. Participants were chosen from a group of 110 individuals at the racetrack who were observed buying the Early Form of the racetrack program, which presented statistics on the past racing performances of the horses in the next day's races, but did not present odds or explicit evaluations of the horses. From this set of 110, a group of 14 experts and 16 nonexperts were chosen on the basis of their ability to pick the favorites, as well as the top three horses in the next day's races. Thus, those classified as experts were found to predict 93% of horses with the best post time odds and 53% of the top three rated horses in correct order, whereas the nonexperts averaged 55% and 6% for these same two measures—still well above the chance values of 12% and .00025%, respectively. Thus, expert versus nonexpert status was determined by an objective performance measure; correct predictions of post time favorites.

The Handicapping Task

In order to examine more precisely the relationship between handicapping success and IQ, as well as the strategies of expert handicappers, Ceci and Liker designed a complex simulation task in which handicappers were given 50 paired comparisons between a challenging horse and a standard one and were then asked to estimate the odds of the one over the other. The challenging horses were described in terms of 14 different characteristics (e.g., lifetime speed, purse size, position of finish); the values of which varied from comparison to comparison, whereas other factors (e.g., breeding) were held constant. The standard horse, on the other hand, was described in terms of a standard set of values of these dimensions; in all cases these values described a horse of "average caliber."

Because it was impossible to systematically sample all of the possible levels of the 14 variables (where the number of values per variable ranged from 3 to 29), an alternative factorial survey design (Rossi & Nock, 1982) was used in which values for the 14 variables were sampled in a more or less random fashion. However, in an attempt to simulate more realistic racing conditions, the values of the 14 variables were sampled from actual racing programs; as a result, the sampling was not entirely random, and some of the variables were correlated with each other. Further, in spite of their attempts to make the handicapping task as realistic as possible, Ceci and Liker (1986a) acknowledged that there were a variety of ways in which their task departed from a completely naturalistic judgment for handicappers—for instance, it involved paired comparisons rather than comparisons of eight horses at a time, and it included some comparisons of challengers and standard horses which were very unlikely in actual practice.

In addition to the 14 variables referred to above, Ceci and Liker also included a complex interactive variable intended to capture the fact that handicappers seemed to take as many as seven different factors (and their interactions) into account in making their predictions. Ceci and Liker attempted to model this presumed higher order reasoning factor by taking seven different variables from the challengers' last race (e.g., last race speed, closing speed, track conditions) based on interviews with expert handicappers, and then using their own sense of how this variable operated to rate the 50 horses on a 7-point scale of likelihood of beating or losing to the standard horse. Although this judgment variable does not correspond to an interaction effect in the statistical sense, Ceci and Liker (1986a) did attempt to confirm its validity by comparing it with the commentary of a professional handicapper with his own TV racing program, and with interviews with their own expert handicappers about the reasoning involved in their choices, and also by examining the predictive strength of this term in a regression equation (i.e., in predicting the winner and the odds).

In this regression equation the 14 different variables were entered first, followed by the interaction term, in predicting the handicappers' stated odds of the challenger beating the standard horse. The central results of this analysis were, first, that the overall regression equations produced good predictions of handicappers' odds estimation, for both experts and nonexperts ($R^2 = .79$ and $.74$, respectively). More important, the interaction term proved to be the strongest predictor for both experts and novices, although this term was more than twice as large for the former as it was for the latter. Finally, in a set of separate regressions for each participant (because the initial analyses had treated each prediction by each participant for each comparison as a separate, independent case), the size of the interaction term proved to be significantly greater for the experts than for the nonexperts.

On the critical issue of the relationship between success at handicapping and IQ, Ceci and Liker offered two major arguments. First, they presented evidence that IQ was uncorrelated with success at handicapping winners, even when years of experience at such handicapping (which is significantly negatively correlated with IQ) was controlled for. Second, as I just indicated, expert handicappers were more likely to use higher order combinations in making their judgments than were nonexperts. Most important, the use of such presumably higher order reasoning was found to be uncorrelated with IQ. Thus, even though experts were more likely to engage in higher level reasoning than were nonexperts, this reasoning was not clearly assessed by IQ tests.

CHAPTER 8

To summarize, Ceci and Liker (1986a, 1986b) argued from these results that both expert and nonexpert handicappers use higher order, complex rules in making their predictions, that experts are significantly more likely to use such higher-order reasoning, and that the use of these rules is unrelated to and does not *require* high IQ. Furthermore, Ceci and Liker (1986b) made the following arguement.

> The sheer volume of raw data processed by experts and nonexperts was quite impressive, but even more impressive is the cognitive sophistication of the algorithms experts used to weight each variable and sometimes consider them in combination with others. ... We doubt that any profession—be it scientists, lawyers, or bankers—engages in a more intellectually demanding form of decision-making than these expert handicappers (pp. 131–132)

Some Reservations About Ceci and Liker's Results

Although Ceci and Liker make an apparently compelling case for the sophistication of practical, domain-specific reasoning and for the independence of such reasoning from IQ, a closer inspection of their study raises a number of questions about their methodology and conceptual rationale. First, as I have noted, the so-called "interaction model variable" is not really an interaction term in the statistical sense of that term. (In keeping with the literature on human judgment—e.g., Camerer & Johnson, 1991; Goldberg, 1968—it is probably more appropriately called a configural rule or term.) Rather, it is simply a judgment on the part of the experimenters (rather than the handicappers themselves) intended to capture the way in which the handicappers combine several variables in making their predictions.

Ceci and Liker (1986a) presented a couple of pieces of impressionistic evidence to confirm that this form of combination really is the one used by handicappers (i.e., the consistency of this rationale with impressions of a professional handicapper and with the participants' own comments); but the only real piece of *concrete empirical* evidence for this assumption is that this configural term successfully predicts the handicappers' odds estimation. However, there are a number of other possible reasons why this term may predict the criterion (e.g., because it is the only variable for which the values were not randomly sampled, or the only predictor scaled in terms of the likelihood of winning—the same variable on which the criterion was scaled).

What makes this finding particularly problematic is that research in the area of human judgment (e.g., Camerer & Johnson, 1991; Goldberg, 1968), including research on gambling (e.g., Fryback & Edwards, 1973; Lichtenstein & Slovic, 1973) and stockbrokering (e.g., Slovic, 1969) has demonstrated fairly clearly that regression models with (statistical) interaction terns—even two-way interactions—are seldom if ever better than simple additive models in predicting either objective outcomes or the judge's own overall judgment, at least in part because of the "robust beauty" of the general linear model (see Dawes, 1979; Dawes, Faust, & Meehl, 1993; Goldberg, 1968). It is thus rather surprising that in this one study where the interaction term was calculated in such an indirect way and in which such an unusual task (i.e., a set of paired comparisons) was used, this interaction term should prove to be significant (though Slovic, 1969, reported "substantial" configural factors in the decisions made by stockbrokers, and Fryback & Edwards, 1973, found significant context effects in gambling).

Perhaps a more important consideration is that Ceci and Liker's analysis shows only *indirectly* that this interaction or configural term accounts for the higher accuracy of the expert over the nonexpert handicappers. That is, the experts were shown to make greater use of the interaction term in computing the odds in the paired comparison task, and experts are obviously better at predicting the post-time odds than are nonexperts in the preliminary task; but there is no direct evidence that the kind of thinking presumably captured by the interaction term is what *accounts* for the predictive accuracy of the experts, nor evidence of how well that accuracy translates into prediction of actual winners. (Ceci & Liker, 1986a, 1988, have given a number of explanations of why they did not use actual race results as a criterion.) Thus, for example, it is possible that the constant comparison to a standard horse in the central experimental task may have encouraged handicappers to be less analytical and more configural (i.e., because they did not have to keep in mind each of the specific dimensions on which that standard and comparison horse were contrasted). For this or other reasons it is possible that the interaction term may have played a major role in participants' odds-making in the particular experimental task used, but that some other singular variable may have accounted for their predictive superiority.

Over and above these reservations, there are a couple of more general conceptual and methodological issues raised by this study. First, there is the assumption that an ability to consider several different variables at once, or more specifically, the significance of an interaction term, is somehow equivalent to higher-order reasoning. There is a certain plausibility to this assumption, but it is equally possible that handicappers, with their superior knowledge about harness racing, simply talk a good game[3] (cf. Nisbett & Wilson's [1977] argument that self-reports of judgment policies are often just reiterations of "public theories"). Thus, there is reason to question whether these stated policies do, in fact, offer an accurate account of the way in which the handicappers estimate odds. It seems clear that more systematic studies need to be done, as Ceci and Liker (1986a) themselves argued, with verbal protocols and their relation to actual predictive performance by handicappers.

A second question that arises is just how "naturalistic" the Ceci and Liker study is. On the one hand, the use of actual racetrack handicappers and

---

[3]Ceci and Liker (1986b) argued that the handicappers were actually not very articulate in describing their judgment policies.

data from actual racing forms, the presentation of information in the form of a racing form—these represent attempts to make the study more naturalistic, in comparison with most lab studies of gambling (see Ceci & Liker, 1986a, for a similar argument). On the other hand, the paired comparison format of the handicapping task, the inclusion of certain comparisons that were unlikely in actual practice, and the fact that a standard, unchanging horse was used as the comparison horse in all judgments—all of *these* are factors that seem less than "natural." Thus, although Ceci and Liker's study involves a simulation that is roughly analogous to that reported by Scribner and the research reviewed on street math, the former study represents a greater departure from the usual task encountered by participants than do the latter.

CROSS-CULTURAL RESEARCH ON EVERYDAY REASONING AND PROBLEM SOLVING

Another area of research that is related to our earlier discussion of street math and to the topic of everyday, practical reasoning in general is the study of cross-cultural[4] differences in cognitive skills and forms of reasoning. The question here, as in the earlier discussion of street math and Scribner's research, is how specific cultural practices or the requirements of a specific ecological niche promote the development of particular cognitive skills, styles, or both. Do different cultures develop particular cognitive abilities or forms of reasoning as a practical adaptation to the needs of their economy or ecology, and how specific or general are these differences in cognition?

Rather than attempting an exhaustive review of cross-cultural differences in everyday cognition (see J. W. Berry & Irvine, 1986; Cole, 1996; Cole & Scribner, 1974, for reviews), in this section I focus on three prototypical examples of research on the particular cognitive abilities of particular cultural groups. Specifically, I examine Gladwin's classic study of the navigational skills of the Puluwatans of the Caroline Islands (and a reconceptualization of Gladwin's results by Edwin Hutchins, 1983, 1995), Hutchins's (1980) own study of land tenure decisions among the Trobriand Islanders, and the observations by Cole and his associates (e.g., Cole et al., 1971) on the abilities and apparent cognitive limitations of the Kpelle of Liberia.

Research on Puluwat Navigation

One of the most interesting and frequently cited cross-cultural studies of practical intelligence is the investigation of navigational skills among the Puluwatans of Micronesia by Gladwin (1970). These abilities are also of in-

---

[4]I have chosen to use the traditional term "cross-cultural" here despite Cole's (1996) position that the term connotes comparisons of cultures on experimental or Western materials and tasks and that "cultural psychology" has gone beyond that sort of research.

terest for our present purposes because they represent a rather different form of cognitive skill from those we have been considering.

The Puluwatans were faced with the task of traveling back and forth by canoe among a set of islands at some distance (20–150 miles) from each other (see Fig. 8.3, for a map of the Caroline islands), often without any landmarks in sight. Because of the importance of such navigation to the Puluwatans, a complex set of navigational skills developed, along with a rather complicated, detailed course of instruction in such navigation and the assignment of a special status to masters of these skills.

One interesting feature of the process of teaching navigation is that it involved a good deal of complex formal (and explicit) instruction on land before any kind of practice in actual navigation took place. This instruction began with learning star positions (i.e., the rising and setting of stars) and the course and pattern of such star positions as the canoe moves in a particular direction. This pattern of star positions or *star compass* (see Fig. 8.4 for a drawing of this compass) served as the major guide to navigation, as we see later. Other issues include knowledge of currents, wave patterns, weather forecasting, and "the system for keeping track of distance ...; navigation in storms; ... [and] techniques for locating, even in the dark, passes through the reefs of various islands" (Gladwin, 1970, pp. 131–132). This formal instruction, along with the teaching of more esoteric mythological knowledge, is followed by further instruction on both land and sea.

The actual course of navigation, according to Gladwin (1970), consists of three different phases: namely, setting down a course plan and direction, maintaining that direction while sailing, and actually locating the destination island. The first of these steps involves the selection of a destination and a process of *backsighting*, in which the navigator establishes a line from his destination back to some landmark or view of the shore from which the journey started. The second phase entails a complex system of "dead reckoning ... [where] one's position at any time is determined solely on the basis of distance and direction traveled since the last known location" (p. 144). Involved in such dead reckoning are a number of the types of knowledge acquired through formal instruction, including, in particular, monitoring the star positions, as well as a process of *etak*, whereby the navigator charts his position by keeping track of certain unseen reference islands. (According to Gladwin and others, these islands are conceived of as moving while the canoe is thought of as standing still under the equally unmoving stars.) Finally, the third phase involves repeated changes of direction (called *tacking*) to zero in on the destination, as well as taking note of the types of birds flying overhead, the wave patterns, the odors and sounds, and so forth.

Hutchins (1983) suggested that the process of etak is of particular interest for a number of different reasons. First, the process of etak is assumed to be a fairly sophisticated form of expertise, even though early anthropologists believed the Puluwatans to have a "primitive" (i.e., non-Western) mentality. Second, there are a several different theories (e.g., Gladwin, 1970;

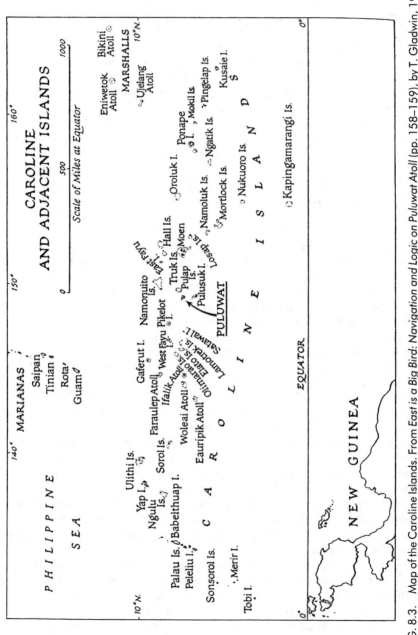

FIG. 8.3.   Map of the Caroline Islands. From *East is a Big Bird: Navigation and Logic on Puluwat Atoll* (pp. 158–159), by T. Gladwin, 1970, Cambridge, MA: Harvard University Press. Copyright © 1970 by Harvard University Press. Reprinted with permission.

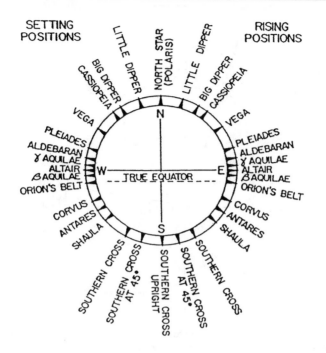

STAR COMPASS

FIG. 8.4.   Star (sidereal) compass used by Puluwatan navigators. From "Understanding Micronesian Navigation" by E. Hutchins, 1983. In *Mental Models* (p. 195) edited by D. Gentner & A. Stevens, Hillsdale, NJ: Lawrence Erlbaum Associates. Copyright © 1983 by Lawrence Erlbaum Associates. Reprinted with the permission.

Hutchins, 1983; Sarfert, 1911), but no agreement on the exact nature of this process. Finally, this is a case where it is of little use to question the expert navigators themselves. As Hutchins (1983) put it, "as is the case with any truly expert performance in any culture, the experts themselves are often unable to specify just what it is they do while they are performing" (p. 200). In fact, Puluwat navigators have a hard time understanding the questions posed by Western investigators (and of course, Western investigators have had a difficult time understanding the Puluwatans' skills).

On the first issue, Sarfert (1911) and Gladwin (1970) agreed that navigators use a combination of the presumably moving and typically unseen islands, and the bearing of the star patterns to calculate distance (see Fig. 8.5 for an example of this relationship). Gladwin saw a given island as a reference point to divide the voyage into segments and thereby to calculate distance traveled. Hutchins (1983), on the other hand, argued that this and other earlier positions assumed, erroneously, that the Puluwat navigators

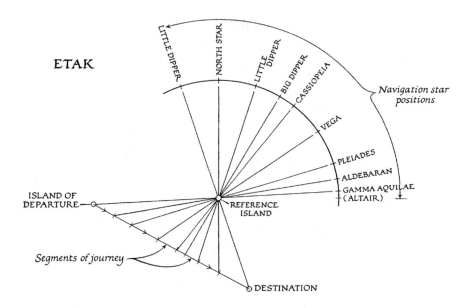

FIG. 8.5.   Gladwin's conceptioin of Etak. From *East is a Big Bird: Navigation and Logic on Puhuwat Atoll* (p. 185), by T. Gladwin, 1970, Cambridge, MA: Harvard University Press. Copyright © 1970 by Harvard University Press. Reprinted with permission.

take the same birds-eye, map-like point of view that Western navigators take. In point of fact, when Lewis (1972) questioned two expert navigators about a particular reference island and presented a diagram for locating that island based on the intersections of two etack bearings, these navigators seemed to have no conception of this kind of abstract geometric representation. Rather, one expert navigator could only partially grasp the idea when he attempted to take his *own* view of the star bearings from the island of origin and also the destination island. In other words, he understood this when he took into consideration *his own two perspectives*. Thus, according to Hutchins, Gladwin (and other commentators) were wrong in their attempts to understand Puluwatan navigation from a Western perspective. Furthermore, Hutchins argued that the Puluwatan "egocentric" perspective is not all that different from our own everyday conception of the sun as moving in the sky from dawn to noon.

Hutchins (1983; Hutchins & Hinton, 1984) proposed an alternative model in which Puluwat navigators do not deal with units of distance or engage in numerical calculations, but rather use the star bearings and the reference island to determine *temporal* duration. That is, the navigators begin with a conception of how long the voyage should take, and they then visualize the reference islands moving along the horizon from star pattern to star pattern. The navigator must then keep track, without instruments, of the rate at which the canoe is moving and use that information to modify the duration estimates.

The point of this rather abbreviated account is that the navigation process is based on a fairly sophisticated form of practical intelligence, one that involves a system of abstract knowledge—a schema or mental model— rather than simply rote memorization or mere technique or procedures. It is a system that is actually taught via formal instruction, and one that clearly stands the Puluwatans in good stead. At the same time, Gladwin (1970) argued that the type of intelligence involved in navigation is rather different from Western conceptions of intelligence (and in fact, it is not even conceived of as "intelligence" by the Puluwatans themselves) in that it is also characterized by concrete procedures or automatic inferences, and is relatively noninnovative. That is, it does not involve coming up with novel insights or conclusions; rather, the kinds of information available to the navigators (e.g., wave patterns and star positions) and the kinds of plans and decisions that these navigators must make are preestablished.

It should be apparent, however, that such closed-ended thinking is not all that different from other forms of practical reasoning that I have discussed in this chapter (e.g., Scribner's account of product assemblers, the calculations of street mathematicians). I have already alluded to the analogy drawn by Hutchins (1983) between Westerner's commonsense, egocentric view of the movement of the sun across the sky and the Puluwatans' view of the moving island; Gladwin (1970) himself drew an analogy between this (navigational) knowledge and the skill of driving in which most, if not all of the relevant information is present from the outset, in which both abstract and concrete knowledge and planning are involved, and in which few novel, innovative problems must be solved or decisions must be made. Furthermore, driving is an activity that is engaged in by both educated and uneducated people of all social classes. In this sense, driving, and by extension, Puluwat navigation, can be seen as a kind of prototype of practical intelligence in general, or at least of one major form of such intelligence.

Hutchins on Land Tenure Decisions Among the Trobriand Islanders

Another widely cited study of the specialized reasoning processes engaged in by a seemingly "primitive" culture is Edwin Hutchins's (1980) systematic cognitive analysis of the land tenure decisions made in the village courts of the Troobriand Islanders. The Trobriand land tenure system involves a rather complicated network of social, traditional, institutional, and economic considerations that make judgments a rather complex form of problem solving indeed. Yet previous accounts of Trobriand reasoning (e.g., Lee, 1940, 1949) have portrayed it as primitive and lacking in essential logical relations. In commenting on his own observations, Hutchins (1980) noted that "whereas my daily interactions with people [in New Guinea] told me that they were quite capable of elaborate reasoning strategies, the battery of intelligence tests we administered showed the unschooled village adults to be performing at the level appropriate for an elementary school child in our society" (p. vii; see Cole et al., 1971, for a similar observation).

As indicated, the Trobriand farming system is a complicated one. First, within a given village, there are numerous fields or groves, only some of which are being cultivated at any given time. Within those fields, there are different plots that are owned by a particular clan. A distinction is made between ownership and *use rights*, where use rights refer to the agreement by which a man is allowed to farm the land of a given owner. Such use rights are important because they not only enable the male gardener to provide food for his own household, but also allow him to gather food to serve as a gift for another head of a family, usually a superior. Offering a gift to another has a social significance in that the giver typically hopes for some kind of return (e.g., some magic or the rights to a garden). One frequent recipient of such gifts is a kinsman, especially one who is dying, with the giver hoping to receive some sort of bequest of gifts, including land, on that kinsman's death. The important thing to note is that such gifts or transfers are not contractual agreements, but rather are *social* transactions. As Hutchins (1980) put it, "every exchange is a communication from one person to another of both an artifact (item exchanged) and a social message" (p. 37).

In terms of the legal context of these rights and exchanges, there are two sorts of disputes that are heard in the village courts: namely, disputes between clans over the proper ownership of a piece of land and disputes over user rights. Settlement of the first type of case involves tracing the genealogy of the land (i.e., who has passed it down to whom), whereas the latter are settled in terms of a history of transactions through which the land is exchanged or transferred.

What is particularly significant about this account, apart from the intriguing nature of the whole land tenure system, is Hutchins's attempt to construct a model of reasoning to account for the arguments and decisions made in this system. This model involves combining propositions into schemas via interconnections or relations dealing with such issues as reciprocity (i.e., an expectation of reciprocation for a gift) or ownership or the transfer of land rights. It is these interconnections or the "cultural grammar" of these propositions that is critical because the purpose of the model is to account for and evaluate inferences (i.e., determining the truth value of an unstated proposition by tracing it to another proposition via these interconnections).

This kind of model addresses a fundamental criticism raised by Hutchins (1980) against other approaches to knowledge and reasoning in cognitive psychology and cognitive anthropology. Specifically, many traditional cognitive psychologists (e.g., some of the reasoning studies to be discussed in chap.

9) focus on reasoning without taking into consideration the knowledge representation on which such rules of reasoning operate, whereas others (e.g., anthropologists attempting to represent cultural knowledge in static, taxonomic form—see D'Andrade, 1995; Tyler, 1964) focus on the representations in isolation from the processes that operate on them. This dichotomy clearly relates to the distinction between knowledge representations and cognitive operations that I have been developing throughout this book.

The crux of Hutchins' presentation is his application of his cultural model to three different court cases, only one of which—a dispute over allocation of use rights—is examined here. In general, the analysis of the courtroom testimony by means of the cultural model indicates that in this case much of the testimony was "profoundly incomplete," requiring background knowledge and use of interconnections within the model to make inferences about the meaning of statements—that is, by interpreting an event as an instance of a particular concept (see chap. 4 on event representation) and by tracking the further links of that concept within the network of propositions. Thus, for example, the critical event in the history of the dispute—a gift of an arm of bananas—was interpreted in different ways by the two litigants, and as a result, different conclusions about land rights were reached.

In part, the interpretation of testimony is essentially driven by the evidence (e.g., by noting the clan membership of the participants or the direction of the exchange of land or gifts), whereas other parts are knowledge driven (e.g., application of existing knowledge of the social structure and of the "prior distribution of the titles to the land"; Hutchins, 1980, p. 113). The model also contains cultural scripts that tie together groups of propositions about events. Most important, the model enables problem solving or decision making about the outcome of a dispute by tracing the path from a past event to the present one and by interpreting these events in terms of a particular schema. For example, in the case analyzed in the Hutchins book, the case made by one litigant regarding ownership of land is demonstrated to be more compelling than that of the other because the former traces ownership to a previous court decision, whereas the latter's case is based on mere plausible inferences.

Hutchins (1980) drew a number of strong conclusions from this study on practical intelligence, and these conclusions are of relevance to this book in general. First, Hutchins argued that the critical issue in this and other studies of reasoning is the particular representation of the task or situation that the individual brings to the problem. In an experimental situation or simulation, the experimenter attempts to establish a representation by his or her experimental design or tries to probe the participant's own representation, whereas in cross-cultural research (including the studies of street math described earlier) the representation is given by the culture or group itself. When it comes to comparing cultures, the differences lie primarily in the different worldviews of these cultures rather than in the logical operations or cognitive processes that are applied to those representations or the inferences that follow from such operations (Hutchins, 1980, p. 128).

Cole et al.'s Observations on "Indigenous Activities"

One of the most interesting accounts of cross-cultural differences in practical thinking is that provided by Michael Cole and his associates in their book on the Kpelle of Liberia (Cole et al., 1971). Cole himself has long been a major advocate of a truly *cultural psychology* (Cole, 1990, 1996), or the study of mind and activity in context;[5] but his initial experience in this area came in his work with Gay, Glick, and Sharp on the Kpelle of Liberia. Like Hutchins, Cole et al. were initially struck by the differences between the Liberians' performance on traditional reasoning and concept formation (as well as memory and classification) tasks and their performance in naturally occurring situations and activities. For example, although the Kpelle appeared to have a hard time with mathematics in the classroom (Cole, 1996, in fact had originally been brought to Liberia as a consultant on a project for teaching the new math to the Kpelle), they nevertheless proved to be skillful in mathematical calculations when trading at the marketplace and in negotiating the fare for a taxi ride. Similarly, even though the Kpelle were usually considered to have a hard time with measurement, when they were asked to estimate quantities of their main subsistence crop (i.e., rice), they performed at a much higher level than their American counterparts. As another example, Cole et al. cited a divorce case in which the litigants used hypothetical arguments and the judge decided the case by noting a contradiction in the arguments of one of the litigants, despite the Kpelle's presumed deficiencies in this area. Specifically, the wife in this case complained that her husband had not provided for her in the marriage (e.g., he had not started a farm for her) but also mentioned that she had been gone for a year and a half visiting her family. The judge denied the complaint because her husband could not have provided for her during the time that she was away.

As a final example, Cole et al. cite the game of *malang*, a board game like *worri*, in which the goal is to distribute one's pieces over a set of holes so as to land in one of those holes containing one's opponent's pieces and thereby capture those pieces. As Cole et al. (1971) pointed out, this game

> depends on a set of strategies. The winning player makes sure that he has solid defenses, that he catalogues the possibilities of every move, that he reserves time to himself, that he lures the opponent into making premature captures, that he moves for decisive, rather than piecemeal victories, and that he is flexible in redistributing his forces in preparation for new assaults. (p. 184)

---

[5]It is interesting to note that Cole (1996, p. 104) stated that one of the principles of this cultural psychology is that the study of psychology should be "grounded" in everyday activities.

In other words, this game requires a good deal of cognitive sophistication, mathematical ability, planning, and strategy—and this from a people who generally perform poorly on tests of these kinds of cognitive skills.

Cole (1996; see also Cole & Bruner, 1971) also drew a connection between these findings and the results of studies with American participants. For example, Cole cited the research of Labov (1972) on language differences demonstrated by African American children in different situations. Labov demonstrated that when an 8-year-old boy was questioned by a large White male experimenter, the boy answered in monosyllables and only when prodded by the interviewer. On the other hand, when this same child was interviewed by an African American experimenter who sat down on the floor, who brought in potato chips and the boy's best friend, and who used taboo language and talked about topics such as street fighting, this child engaged in active, spontaneous conversation and demonstrated a variety of different grammatical forms in nonstandard (Black) English. (See Bennett & Woll, 1980, for evidence that African American teenagers are able to switch from nonstandard to standard English when confronted, for example, with a courtroom situation.) Cole, Dore, Hall, and Dowley (1978) replicated these results by comparing the speech of children in a preschool versus the supermarket. Looking at 3-minute excerpts from speech in these two situations, Cole et al. found that children not only spoke more and in longer sentences in the supermarket than in preschool, but they also showed differences in the *types* of speech acts they engaged in. That is, whereas children in preschool spoke primarily in response to questions, in the supermarket they were as likely to initiate conversations (with a familiar researcher) as they were to respond. (See Cole, 1996, for a discussion of additional research along these lines.)

Cole et al. (1971), following Luria (1931, 1971, 1976), also cited a number of examples of the different approaches taken by unschooled and schooled Liberians toward the same problems. For example, in trying to solve conjunctive and disjunctive (syllogistic) problems, unschooled Kpelle had no problem evaluating the conclusions reached by others, but when it came to generating their *own* conclusions on the basis of premises provided by others, these unschooled Kpelle faced quite a different situation. Specifically, in the latter case the Kpelle relied on the specific content of the problem in drawing their conclusions. Thus, for example, consider the following:

EXPERIMENTER: At one time spider went to a feast. He was told to answer this question before he could eat any of the food. The question is:
Spider and black deer always eat together. Spider is eating. Is black deer eating?

SUBJECT: Were they in the bush?

EXPERIMENTER: Yes.

SUBJECT:	They were eating together?
EXPERIMENTER:	Spider and black deer always eat together. Spider is eating. Is black deer eating?
SUBJECT:	But I was not there. How can I answer such a question?
EXPERIMENTER:	Can't you answer it? Even if you were not there you can answer it.
SUBJECT:	Ask the question again for me to hear.
EXPERIMENTER:	[repeats the question]
SUBJECT:	Oh, oh black deer was eating.
EXPERIMENTER:	Black deer was eating?
SUBJECT:	Yes.
EXPERIMENTER:	What is your reason for saying that black deer was eating?
SUBJECT:	The reason is that black deer always walks around all day eating green leaves in the bush. When it rests for a while it gets up again and goes to eat. (Cole et al., 1971, p. 187)

On the other hand, such content did not have an effect on the conclusions reached by schooled Kpelle children. In a similar study on the evaluations of riddles, one of the primary forms of sport among the Kpelle, unschooled children were again dependent on the specific content of the riddles (and the familiarity of this content), whereas schooled children simply relied on the logical structure of the riddle itself. Finally, Sharp, Cole, and Lave (1979) found similar results regarding syllogistic reasoning among Mayan and Mestizo children and adults from the Yucatan with differing amounts of education. Specifically, amount of education was a strong predictor of the tendency to rely more on problem content (what Scribner, 1975, called *theoretical reasoning*) rather than prior knowledge (or *empirical reasoning*).

These observations, along with a number of other pieces of evidence on cross-cultural differences in memory, led Cole et al. (1971) to some general conclusions about cross-cultural research on cognition and learning. The first of these was a methodological one. Specifically, consistent with observations I have made in other sections of this chapter, Cole et al. (1971) argued for the importance of beginning with an *"ethnographic analysis prior to experimentation in order to identify the kinds of activities that people often engage in and hence ought to be skilled at dealing with"* (p. 217). Different cultures have different skills or areas of expertise based on their different experiences (cf. the earlier discussion of Scribner and Cole's position on literacy), just as experts in different areas have different learning experiences; these cultural or group differences need to be taken into account before conducting a cognitive assessment. Finally, and most important, in a widely cited passage Cole et al. spoke to the nature of cultural differences in cognition: such differences "*reside more in the situations in which particular cognitive processes are applied than in the existence of a process in one cultural group and its absence in another*" (p. 233). That is, rather than looking for general, fundamental differences in underlying cognitive processes in different cultures, the more appropriate strategy is to look for the specific situations or domains in which these processes are expressed in these cultures (cf. Cole & Bruner's [1971] discussion of the *difference* versus the *deficit* hypothesis.)

General Comments on Cross-Cultural Research

I have barely scratched the surface of research on cultural differences in cognitive skills (see J. W. Berry & Irvine, 1986; Cole, 1996; Laboratory for Comparative Human Cognition, 1988, for reviews). Nevertheless, it should be clear from the three examples I have cited that such studies have a number of distinct advantages and disadvantages. On the one hand, cross-cultural studies of practical intelligence help to illustrate the wide variety of different forms (many of them unfamiliar to Westerners) that such "intelligence" can take, as well as the ways in which these skills vary with the ecological context. This emphasis on context, which is the major defining feature of the new cultural psychology, is consistent with Ceci and Liker's (1986a, 1986b) contextual account of intelligence, as well as with Scribner's (1986) emphasis on the use of the environment in problem solving. In addition, cross-cultural evidence underlines the discrepancy between traditional measures and experimental demonstrations of problem-solving abilities on the one hand, and an experimental approach based on a prior ethnographic analysis, or what Cole et al. (1971) called an *experimental anthropology*, on the other. Finally, and perhaps most important, cross-cultural research adds a critical cultural dimension to the study of activity—mental and behavioral—one that is frequently ignored by traditional cognitive psychology, as well as by many current studies of everyday cognition.

   On the downside, most cross-cultural research, like other studies of practical intelligence that I have considered, lacks the kind of rigorous experimental control that allows researchers to rule out alternative explanations—for instance, the possibility that the judge in the court case cited by Cole et al. may have simply been looking for an excuse to reach a sexist verdict (see Cole et al.'s discussion of this alternative), or the possibility that the unschooled Kpelle in the syllogistic reasoning task, like their Brazilian counterparts, simply did not understand the task or the researchers' questions. On the other hand, the observations of expert performance *do* provide a kind of "extreme case" analysis, similar to case histories of mnemonists, savant skills, or expert calculators (see Gardner, 1983, for a discussion of the use of these different kinds of evidence in pinning down intelligence). In this case, as well as in the study of Brazilian street math, there is also the danger of romanticizing or idealizing "talents" that are either very different from our own or that stand out from the seeming "primitiveness" for that group, just as early anthropologists were criticized for overemphasizing the cognitive *deficiencies* of these cultures. This concern is in turn related to the obvious problem that these researchers are generally outsiders who must rely on master navigators or expert intermediaries or special examples (e.g., court cases).

RESEARCH BY WAGNER AND STERNBERG ON TACIT KNOWLEDGE

One final, rather different approach to practical intelligence—in fact, the approach that coined the term—is that put forward by Wagner and Sternberg. The general framework for this approach is Sternberg's (1985) triarchic theory of intelligence. This theory proposes a contextual definition of intelligence with an emphasis on the role of such intelligence in adapting to the *"real world environments relevant to one's environment"* (Sternberg, 1988, p. 45). One important form of this intelligence is practical intelligence, defined as "procedural information that is useful in one's everyday life" (Sternberg & Caruso, 1985, p. 134). In other words, practical intelligence involves knowledge of how to do or accomplish things and, like other types of procedural knowledge developed in earlier chapters, is represented in terms of if–then productions, with the restriction that such productions be "useful in one's everyday life." Thus, knowing that sufficient doses of strychnine may cause death is of little practical significance (unless you are contemplating homicide or suicide); or, as I discussed earlier, many practitioners of street math also find school math to be of little personal relevance.

A key to such practical intelligence, and of particular importance for the purposes of this chapter, is what Wagner and Sternberg (1985, 1986) referred to as *tacit knowledge*. As the term suggests, tacit knowledge is information that is neither explicitly stated nor directly taught and that extends beyond mere academic intelligence. Although the concept of tacit knowledge is discussed in a general fashion by philosophers such as Polanyi (1966, 1973), Wagner and Sternberg have been particularly interested in the role of such knowledge in career success. That is, to what extent does implicit, unstated knowledge about how to get ahead enter into job success? At least part of the motivation for this interest is the observation (Wagner & Sternberg, 1985, 1986) that scores on IQ tests do not correlate very highly (0.2) with job performance, suggesting that job success involves something more than mere academic intelligence. Wagner and Sternberg have therefore attempted to construct tests of tacit knowledge that provide stronger predictions of job performance.

Wagner and Sternberg (1985, 1986) argued that there are three major types of tacit knowledge, at least in the job setting. These three types are (a) the ability to *manage yourself* (i.e., in terms of setting priorities and goals, managing your time effectively, etc.), (b) the ability to *manage others* (e.g., getting the most out of employees and colleagues, how best to reward or sanction others for their work), and (c) the ability to *manage your career* (e.g., knowing what is important in your field, knowing how to convince others of the value of your work, gaining visibility in your field, etc.). (In his later writings, Wagner, 1987, referred to the third component or an analogous skill as *managing tasks*.) As the last of these descriptions suggests, these "abilities" are assumed to be varieties of *knowledge*. In subsequent publications Wagner (1987; see also Wagner & Sternberg, 1986) also distinguished between two different contexts (i.e., local vs. global) within which such knowledge can be applied. A *local context* refers to a concern with short-term goals and accomplishments, whereas the *global context* refers to a concern with the "bigger picture" or more long-terms goals. In addition, Wagner distinguished between an *actual* or *pragmatic orientation* and an *ideal* one, the former of which refers to a practical, nuts-and-bolts concern, whereas the latter refers to a more idealistic point of view.

Research Findings

Initial Research on Tacit Knowledge. In their initial research on tacit knowledge, Wagner and Sternberg (1985) constructed a set of 12 scenarios, each with multiple response options, on the basis of interviews with five Yale psychologists, theory, and a review of the literature. A parallel set of 12 scenarios was also constructed for business managers. Examples of scenarios and items from each of these tests are given in Table 8.3. The first test, consisting of 123 items, was sent out to a nationwide sample of psychology faculty (54 individuals from 20 schools), psychology graduate students (104 individuals from 21 departments), and a group of 29 Yale psychology undergraduates. The psychology departments were divided up into those within the top 15 ranked departments in the country versus those taken from lower-ranked departments. In the case of the business managers, a 143-item test was sent to business managers taken from either the top 20 companies in the Fortune 500 or from randomly chosen companies not within the top 500. For the business graduate students, the division was again between those from top-ranked schools and those from lesser ranked ones.

There are three major sets of findings from this initial study. First, the tests for both psychologists and business managers discriminated between experts and novices in these two occupations, as defined by either group differences (i.e., the distinction among faculty or managers, graduate students, and undergraduates), or by the distinction between more successful and less successful members of the profession (i.e., as defined by the ranking of the department or the company). It should be noted, however, that not all of the items discriminated among the groups. For example, 25% of the managing career versus 51% of the managing self items discriminated among the psychology faculty, graduate students, and undergraduate students.

TABLE 8.3

Sample Items From Wagner and Sternberg's Tacit Knowledge Test

This questionnaire asks you about your views on matters pertaining to the work of an academic psychologist.

The questions ask you to rate the importance you would assign to various items in making work-related decisions and judgments. Use a 1 to 7 rating scale, with 1 signifying "not important," 4 signifying "moderately important," and 7 signifying "extremely important."

1	2	3	4	5	6	7
not important			moderately important			extremely important

Try to use the entire scale when responding, although not necessarily for each question. For example, you may decide that none of the items listed for a particular question are important, or that they all are. There are, of course, no "correct" answers. You are encouraged to scan briefly the items of a given question before responding to get some idea of the range of importance for the items. Remember, you are being asked to rate the importance you *personally* would assign each item in making the judgment or decision mentioned in the question stem.

1. It is your second year as an assistant professor in a prestigious psychology department. This past year you published two unrelated empirical articles in established journals. You don't, however, believe there is yet a research area that can be identified as your own. You believe yourself to be about as productive as others. The feedback about your first year of teaching has been generally good. You have as yet to serve on a university committee. There is one graduate student who has chosen to work with you. You have no external source of funding, nor have you applied for funding.

   Your goals are to become one of the top people in your field and to get tenure in your department. The following is a list of things you are considering doing in the next two months. You obviously cannot do them all. Rate the importance of each as a means of reaching your goals.

   _____ a.   Improve the quality of your teaching.

   _____ b.   Write a grant proposal.

   _____ c.   Begin long-term research that may lead to a major theoretical article.

   _____ d.   Serve on a committee studying university–community relations.

   _____ e.   Participate in a series of panel discussions to be shown on the local public television station.

   _____ f.   Write a paper for presentation to an upcoming American Psychological Association convention.

   _____ g.   Adjust your work habits to increase your productivity.

   _____ h.   Write an integrative literature review chapter for a soon to be published book (due in six weeks).

2. A number of factors enter into the establishment of a good reputation among scholars in one's field. Consider the following factors and rate their importance:

_____ a.   teaching ability

_____ b.   judged quality of research

_____ c.   quantity of research published

_____ d.   involvement in public service and charitable organizations

_____ e.   a tendency usually to be the initiator of research projects

_____ f.   having written popular books on psychology for the general public

_____ g.   visibility (being well known to the scientific community)

3. An undergraduate student has asked for your advice in deciding to which graduate programs in psychology to apply. Consider the following dimensions for rating the overall quality of a graduate program in psychology and rate their importance:

_____ a.   teaching ability of the faculty

_____ b.   job placement of recent graduates of the program

_____ c.   number of required courses

_____ d.   number of graduate students in the program

_____ e.   percentage of faculty time spent on formal teaching

_____ f.   extracurricular and athletic facilities

_____ g.   flexibility of program

_____ h.   equipment and facilities (computers, labs, and so on)

_____ i.   amount of research currently being conducted by faculty

Note. From *Intelligence Applied: Understanding and Increasing Your Intellectual Skills* by R. J. Sternberg, 1986. New York: Harcourt Brace. Reprinted with permission of the author.

Second, both the psychology and the business manager tests (and their respective subscales) were correlated with a variety of outside criteria of success in the two fields. For example, the tacit knowledge test for psychologists was positively correlated with research-related criteria (e.g., number of publications, amount of time spent in research) and negatively correlated with non-research-related criteria (e.g., amount of time spent in teaching and/or in administrative duties). In the case of psychology graduate students, the tacit knowledge test was correlated with number of publications and number of research projects involved in. Similarly, scores on the business management test were significantly correlated with such criteria as salary and level in the company. At the same time, the tests were *un*correlated with other interesting criteria. For example, the tacit knowledge test for psychology was not correlated with rank or years since obtaining one's PhD, suggesting to Wagner and Sternberg (1985, 1986) that tacit knowledge is not something that is automatically obtained simply by years of experience. Similarly, tacit knowledge for business managers was not related to years of management experience or number of employees supervised. Furthermore, none of the criteria for the business graduate students were related to outside criteria.

Finally, perhaps most important, the scores on both tacit knowledge tests proved to be uncorrelated with measures of verbal IQ, although this result is only applicable to undergraduate students, who were the only ones to whom the IQ test was administered. Related to this finding is the observation that the correlations of tacit knowledge with the various criterion measures were 1½ to 2½ times the size of those typically found between IQ and measures of job performance. These two findings, plus the fact that tacit knowledge scores discriminate among a group of participants (e.g., the faculty in psychology) assumed to be relatively homogeneous in intelligence suggested to Wagner and Sternberg that their tacit knowledge test really does tap knowledge or skills that are unrelated to IQ.

Additional Research. In a subsequent study, Wagner (1987; Wagner & Sternberg, 1986) tested an expanded model of tacit knowledge using a slightly different assessment tool. Specifically, as I indicated earlier, this revised model includes a distinction between the local and global contexts of such knowledge and also a pragmatic versus ideal orientation. In addition, in this study the scoring of tacit knowledge was based on a *deviation-from-prototype* criterion where the answers of a set of recognized "experts" in psychology or business management were used as the prototypes, and the greater deviations of participants' responses (to the scenarios) from these experts' responses were assumed to indicate less tacit knowledge. A major advantage of this approach is that it enables the researcher to use all of the items in the assessment of tacit knowledge rather than determining after the fact which items distinguish between experts and novices and which do not.

The areas of expertise studied in this second set of studies were once again those of psychology and business management. The experts in the first case consisted of 11 faculty members from top-ranked psychology departments, whereas the prototype sample in the second case consisted of "13 executives who (a) were employed by companies on the Fortune 500 list, (b) had titles higher in status and responsibility than vice-president (e.g., executive vice-president, chairman, president), and (c) reported annual salaries of $100,000 or more" (Wagner, 1987, p. 1244). The responses of these experts to the previous 12 scenarios constituted the "prototypes" for the two studies.

The results of this second set of studies essentially confirm those from the first. Specifically, there was a decreasing deviation from prototype (indicating a greater agreement with the experts) from the undergraduate to the graduate student to the faculty samples. Second, a similar pattern of correlations with outside criteria was found, as in the first set of studies. Third, unlike the previous studies, a significant correlation was found between verbal IQ and tacit knowledge for the psychology undergraduates, but not for the business undergraduates. Finally, a group of undergraduates who took both the psychology and the business knowledge forms showed significant correlations between scores on the two scales, suggesting at least some degree of generality of tacit knowledge across domains.

Along these lines, Wagner (1987) also reported a number of pieces of evidence for the generality and internal consistency of tacit knowledge. For example, there were clear intercorrelations among the three different types of tacit knowledge, between the actual and ideal scales, and between the local and global orientations. In addition, a similar pattern of findings was observed for the different subscales and orientations in terms of between-group differences and correlations with outside criteria. Perhaps most important, Wagner found from factor analyses and structural equations modeling that a two-factor model, with a single general factor for tacit knowledge, seemed to account for the commonalities in participants' responses.

In recent years, Sternberg, Wagner, and their associates (e.g., Sternberg & Wagner, 1993; Sternberg et al., 1995) expanded their research on tacit knowledge to the study of sales (Sternberg, Wagner, & Okagaki, 1993; Wagner, Sujan, Sujan, Rashotte, & Sternberg, 1999), management (e.g., Wagner & Sternberg, 1990), the military (Horvath et al., 1999), and success in school and teaching (Sternberg & Horvath, 1995; Sternberg, Wagner, & Okagaki, 1993; Torff, 1999). For example, Wagner and Sternberg (1990) carried out a study of business managers in a leadership development program and found that tacit knowledge was the best single predictor of performance on a managerial simulation and that such knowledge produced significant changes in R^2 values when entered last in a series of regressions including variables such as IQ, scores on two personality scales, and measures of job satisfaction. In addition, research on the Practical Intelligence for Schools (PIFS) curriculum (Okagaki & Sternberg, 1993; Sternberg et al., 1993) for teaching tacit knowledge in schools has proved to be quite effective, resulting in improvement in reading, writing, test taking, and the like.

One of the attractions of these more recent studies is that they help to clarify the relationship between tacit knowledge and IQ. For example, Eddy (1998) found a correlation of –.07 between the tacit knowledge test and a measure of cognitive ability from the Armed Services Vocational Aptitude Test. Similarly, Wagner and Sternberg (1990) found a correlation of –.14 between IQ and tacit knowledge for managers. Thus, even in a more diverse sample, tacit knowledge seems to be a different factor from IQ.

Evaluation of Research on Tacit Knowledge

The General Concept. There is certainly some appeal to the concept of tacit knowledge. It makes sense that people acquire a lot of knowledge by doing or by emulating role models (see Sternberg, 1994) rather than by direct, explicit instruction. Likewise, it seems clear that much of an individual's everyday knowledge for getting along in the world is implicit, unarticulated, and not declarative.

At the same time, however, it is also clear that Wagner and Sternberg use the term *tacit knowledge* in a rather restricted way. That is, the tacit knowledge assessed by their scales clearly refers solely to knowledge of how to manage one's own career (professional or academic) and to manage oneself and others in pursuit of success in that career. Although this is certainly an important type of tacit knowledge, it does not even begin to cover the various areas of tacit knowledge in people's lives. For example, people have tacit knowledge of how to raise children, of how to be popular in their social life, how to deal with relationships, and how to manage their physical appearance in order to make a good impression, to name just a few. Furthermore, tacit knowledge need not refer to the self: It may be tacit knowledge of politics or of "what men or women really want," or the like. The point is that the term *tacit knowledge* is slightly misleading (as is the more recent term *street smarts* [Wagner & Sternberg, 1990] or *common sense* [Sternberg et al., 1995]) when it is equated with the restricted domains studied by Wagner and Sternberg.

Another question that arises is whether Wagner and Sternberg's tacit knowledge tests actually measure knowledge or values. That is, it is one thing not to *know* what behavior or strategies are required for success, and it is quite another thing to know but not *endorse* those behaviors. For example, one response option on the business management test that is endorsed by successful business managers is "the need to win at everything no matter what the cost." Now it is certainly possible to *know* that such a quality is related to success without necessarily *endorsing* such a quality. Because the instructions to the tacit knowledge test specify that "you are being asked to rate the importance *you personally* would assign in making the judgment or decision ..." (Sternberg, 1986, italics added), it could very well be that a person's personal values conflict with his or her knowledge of what succeeds.

This distinction between knowledge and values does *not* mean that the tacit knowledge test is an invalid way of predicting success in a given field. It *does* mean, however, that the test may not be measuring primarily *knowledge*—and Wagner and Sternberg (1985, 1986) emphasized that their's is a "knowledge-based" approach—but rather some combination of knowledge and values. (It should actually be simple enough to test out this distinction by varying the instructions that accompany the test.)

Another point of concern in Wagner and Sternberg's formulation is that they provide little theoretical justification for the basic concept of tacit knowledge and relatively little systematic rationale for the construction of their test. For example, why did they choose to concentrate on Managing Self, Managing Others, and Managing Career? These components certainly make sense; but an argument can be made, for instance, that Managing Self and Managing Career are overlapping (and the two scales are, in fact, significantly correlated). Similarly, I could argue for a variety of other equally plausible distinctions that might have been included on the test, such as managing time and managing personal versus professional life.

The Tacit Knowledge Test.   There are several intriguing features of Wagner and Sternberg's approach to assessing tacit knowledge, including the use of constructed scenarios and sampled responses to those scenarios, as well as the emphasis on expert knowledge (e.g., as reflected in Wagner's deviation-from-prototype approach). Neither of these techniques is exactly novel (see the "critical incidents" approach—e.g., Flanagan, 1954—to assessing job competencies, as well as my discussion of the study of expert–novice differences). However, the combination of the two *is* certainly novel.

At the same time, this technique also raises some questions. First, the selection and writing of items for the tacit knowledge scales is not very clearly described. For example, in the initial construction of the test for psychologists, situations were generated by interviews with five Yale psychologists, plus a review of relevant theory and research. One of the results of this otherwise unspecified procedure is that the initial tacit knowledge scale contained only three items on the Managing Others subscale (vs. 51 and 69 for the Managing Self and Managing Career subscales). Wagner and Sternberg (1985) suggested that this imbalance may reflect the fact that managing others is less important for academic psychologists than it is for business managers. Although that may very well be the case, there also can be no doubt that interpersonal relations are of great significance to the career of faculty members as well, whether it be in teaching or supervising research assistants or making professional contacts. The fact that few items were generated in this area by the interviews does not necessarily mean that this is not an important area for academics. In fact, if this area is to be posited as a major component of tacit knowledge—as it undoubtedly is—then clearly it should be more adequately represented on the tacit knowledge test.

A second issue raised by Wagner and Sternberg's test is that there are multiple items based on the same scenario, and hence these items are not truly independent of each other. It would be interesting to know, for instance, how the items that successfully discriminate between experts and novices are distributed across different scenarios. (For example, for one scenario reproduced in Sternberg, 1986, there is only one "correct" response option out of X alternatives.) Similarly, it would be nice to know how items falling on the different subscales are distributed across scenarios.

Evaluation of Results. Wagner and Sternberg present a number of interesting and compelling results in support of their tacit knowledge viewpoint. For example, the correlations with research-related criteria versus teaching and administrative work certainly squares with most psychologists' view of "success" and status within the academic world. At the same time, such a result seems almost predetermined by the investigators' operational definition of expertise—that is, faculty and graduate students at the top ranked schools, whose ranking is itself determined primarily by research-related criteria.[6] By way of contrast, I would argue that there is also tacit knowledge involved in successful teaching and in successful administrative work that some faculty *choose* to pursue; and I can certainly think of people who are successful at research who have little acumen for either teaching or administration. Furthermore, there is clearly a great deal of variation among psychology departments in the types of tacit knowledge that they model and encourage. (Sternberg himself, 1994, alluded to the differences between his own department's emphasis on empirical research and publications vs. the emphasis at another prominent university on critical thinking.)

A related issue here is that some of the knowledge tapped by the Tacit Knowledge scale—and by the Managing Career subscale in particular—is rather political. For example, two of the items on this subscale are knowing what is valued in the field and "being alert to opportunities to increase your visibility in the field" (Wagner & Sternberg, 1985, p. 442). I do not want to argue that political awareness is unimportant for success in academia or in business. However, I *do* feel that Wagner and Sternberg focused on professions in which the importance of this form of tacit knowledge is exaggerated. (I wonder, for example, whether such "political savvy" would play the same role in most blue collar or civil service occupations, in the latter of which the rules for advancement are far from tacit.) Furthermore, as I argue later, such knowledge is clearly different from the kinds of practical intelligence I have reviewed in previous sections.

In some sense, the most impressive finding of Wagner and Sternberg's research is the lack of relation (except for Wagner's revised questionnaire for psychologists) between IQ and tacit knowledge and the related finding of higher correlations between tacit knowledge and academic and business management criteria than for IQ. These findings were not all that compelling when they were restricted to Yale undergraduates, the group that scored lowest in tacit knowledge (and that likely showed a restricted range of IQs; see Williams & Sternberg, 1995). However, in their recent research, Wagner and Sternberg also reported nonsignificant correlations for both managers and executives and for Air Force recruits.

---

[6]It is somewhat ironic that in recent years there has been a movement (e.g., within the University of California system) toward a greater focus on faculty teaching and against the overemphasis on research.

A related question is how general tacit knowledge itself is. I noted that Wagner (1987) found a relationship between tacit knowledge in psychology and business management among undergraduates, as well as significant correlations among the different facets of tacit knowledge and a general factor underlying such knowledge. These results are clearly of interest to the ongoing debate (see chap. 7) over the issue of domain-specificity or generality of expertise, although it is rather ironic that an approach that began distinguishing among different types of intelligence and that emphasizes (Sternberg, 1985) the role of context, experience, and personal relevance should end up supporting the generality of tacit knowledge itself.

The Relation to Other Research.   As a final note, it is worth mentioning some of the similarities and differences between Wagner and Sternberg's formulation and other approaches to practical intelligence that I have discussed. On the one hand, Wagner and Sternberg (1985, 1986) are clearly concerned with the differences between *practical* and *academic* intelligence, as are Scribner and Ceci and Liker. Tacit knowledge is also clearly "practical" in the sense that it facilitates individuals' purposive adaptation to their work environments.

At the same time, Wagner and Sternberg's conception of practical intelligence or tacit knowledge clearly operates at a rather different level from that of Scribner, the researchers on street math, the observations of Ceci and Liker, and even the cross-cultural research that I discussed. That is, tacit knowledge appears to deal with a higher order kind of *strategic* knowledge—a form of meta-knowledge—or knowledge of how to succeed or handle oneself in general, rather than with one's skill at a particular type of task. Tacit knowledge is not some kind of specialized skill; it is not simply a set of heuristics for processing information or performing tasks; and it is not a procedure that is run off in some kind of automatized, routinized fashion. Rather tacit knowledge is a set of higher order rules or procedures, partly social and partly self-monitoring, that enable the individual to succeed in the broader scheme of things. None of this makes tacit knowledge any less interesting or significant; in fact, as a higher level form of skill, it is in some sense the *most* interesting form of practical intelligence. It *does* suggest, however, that Wagner and Sternberg are studying something rather different from the other researchers I have presented in this chapter.

One final point is worth noting: Wagner and Sternberg's approach to studying tacit knowledge clearly does not amount to either a simple ethnographic study nor a simulation. Rather it constitutes what Wagner (1986) labeled a *second-order ethnography,* where information is obtained from expert witnesses, and an equally second-order, paper-and-pencil simulation. Both of these resemble the methods used by Ceci and Liker, although with a rather different *kind* of simulation and for a very different end. Once again, such an approach underlines the wide array of techniques available for studying everyday knowledge, as well as the variety of forms that such knowledge itself can take.

SUMMARY

Some Common (and Some Different) Themes in Research on Practical Intelligence

Although I have reviewed a number of diverse examples of practical intelligence, it is possible to discern several recurring themes in these different research projects. Probably the most obvious of these is the pervasive emphasis on the differences between such practical intelligence and academic or traditional conceptions of intelligence and reasoning. This distinction has been raised either conceptually or empirically by nearly every project that I have discussed. Another common theme is the domain-specificity or contextual nature of such reasoning, as highlighted in the work of Lave and her associates, in the theorizing of Ceci and Liker, and in the writings of Cole and his associates. Still another issue is the relative flexibility–inflexibility of such problem solving, as reflected in the formulations of Scribner and Cole et al. There is the common concern, expressed most clearly in cross-cultural research, as well as in the research by Saxe and by Carraher et al. on street math, with the social–cultural context of such practical reasoning. Finally, on a methodological level I have noted the common emphasis on beginning with an ethnographic and/or observational stage, followed by an experimental or simulation phase making use of the information gained in the earlier stage.

In addition to these similarities, I have also touched on some of the differences among the several research projects. For example, I have noted some of the differences in the types of practical intelligence studied, for instance, by Scribner, Gladwin, and Wagner and Sternberg. There is the difference in domain-specificity assumed, for example, by Lave versus Wagner and Sternberg. Finally, I have noted some of the differences in methods used by, for example, Ceci and Liker and Wagner and Sternberg on the one hand, and by Scribner and the cross-cultural researchers on the other.

Relationship to More General Issues in Expertise and Problem Solving

Although most of the research projects I have considered in this chapter have stressed the way in which their viewpoints and findings *diverge* from traditional models of reasoning and problem solving, most nevertheless share certain commonalities with traditional conceptions, and, in particular, with the issues raised in chapter 7. The most obvious of these is the emphasis in the research by Scribner, Ceci and Liker, and Wagner and Sternberg on expert–novice differences, although these three research projects have defined expertise in slightly different ways. In addition, there is the concern, already noted, by Lave as well as Wagner and Sternberg with the domain-specificity-generality issue, although again, these different researchers have reached somewhat different conclusions on this issue. Finally, at least in the case of the research by Carraher, Schliemann, et al. and by Ceci and Ruiz (1993), there is a concern with the transfer-of-knowledge issue.

In the next chapter I consider theory and research on everyday judgment and decision making, with a particular emphasis on an issue that has been implicit in much of the material that I have discussed in this and the previous chapter: namely, whether everyday reasoning and practical "intelligence" are, in fact, rational or intelligent on the one hand, or irrational and crude on the other.

Chapter 9

The Study of Heuristics and Judgment Biases: How Rational or Irrational Are We?

Suppose that Pete Sampras reaches the Wimbledon finals in the year 2002. Please rank order the following outcomes from most to least likely.
Sampras will win the match. ———
Sampras will lose the first set. ———
Sampras will win the first set but lose the match. ———
Sampras will lose the first set but win the match. ———

—Example illustrating the conjunction fallacy
(adapted from Kahneman & Tversky, 1982c, p.96)

It has often been observed by sports enthusiasts that baseball or basketball or football players who perform exceptionally well during their first year of play typically have a letdown during their second year. This lowered performance has even been labeled the "sophomore jinx."

Introduction

The General Nature of Judgment Heuristics and Their Applicability to Everyday Judgment and Decision Making

Confirmation Biases and Covariation Assessment

The Rationality Debate

Criticisms of Research on Heuristics and Biases

Other Biases in Social Reasoning

Other Judgment Biases

An Aside on Naturalistic Decision Making

Summary

INTRODUCTION

Another research topic that has generated considerable interest over the past three decades is the role of errors and biases in human judgment and reasoning. In contrast to the literature on practical intelligence reviewed in the last chapter, the general emphasis of research on judgment has been on the factors that *interfere* with reasoned thought in statistical and deductive reasoning. Although most of this research has involved traditional laboratory studies, the *content* of the problems used in this research, as well as its apparent applicability to day-to-day judgments, makes it very relevant to the everyday cognition area.

In addition to this research on heuristics and biases, and some reservations voiced about this research, I also examine the issue of whether everyday judgment in general is essentially rational or irrational. I also look at some recent research and theory on naturalistic decision making, or decision making in real-world, natural situations where important outcomes are on the line.

THE GENERAL NATURE OF JUDGMENT HEURISTICS AND THEIR APPLICABILITY TO EVERYDAY JUDGMENT AND DECISION MAKING

As developed in chapter 7, *heuristics* refer to mental shortcuts in reasoning and judgment. In the case of *judgment* heuristics, these shortcuts are involved in reaching conclusions about the likelihood of some event (e.g., a substantial return on your investment or of rain tomorrow or of being infected by the HIV virus) without having to go to all the trouble of applying the formal rules of probability or inductive reasoning. The advantage of such heuristics is that they are obviously easier and quicker to apply than formal rules or algorithms; and in many cases in everyday life, they yield the correct solution. The downside, and the feature that has been the topic of most of the research on this topic, is that heuristics can lead to biased, inaccurate judgments, including judgments in areas that are of particular importance in people's lives (e.g., purchasing a car, gambling judgments, clinical judgments, and job selection decisions, to name just a few).

In their original formulations Tversky and Kahneman (e.g. Tversky & Kahneman, 1974) identified three main heuristics: namely, *availability, representativeness,* and *anchoring and adjustment.* These heuristics were initially intended to account for errors and biases in statistical judgments; but from the beginning, numerous examples from everyday life were included as well. As other psychologists, particularly *social* psychologists, began to appropriate the notion of heuristics, this idea has been increasingly applied to more everyday situations. I develop each of these three heuristics and the relevant research in turn, and then I consider the notion of heuristics and biases as they apply to everyday cognition in general.

The Availability Heuristic

Probably the easiest of the judgment heuristics to understand is the availability heuristic.[1] According to Tversky and Kahneman (1973), "A person is said to employ the availability heuristic whenever he estimates frequency or probability by the ease with which instances or associations could be brought to mind" (p. 208). For example, people may overestimate the frequency of particular causes of death (e.g., shark attacks vs. being killed by falling airplane parts; homicides and car accidents vs. diabetes and stomach cancer—see Lichtenstein et al., 1978) by virtue of the vividness or the public attention given to the former causes. Or people may overestimate the divorce rate within a given population by thinking of all the instances of divorces among their acquaintances (Tversky & Kahneman, 1973). Similarly, people may overestimate the frequency of problems with a given type of car by thinking about a couple of lemons purchased by friends.

As Tversky and Kahneman (1973) pointed out, "Availability is an ecologically valid cue for the judgment of frequency because, in general, frequent events are easier to recall or imagine than infrequent ones" (p. 209). However, availability is also a fallible cue in that it can be affected by a variety of factors (e.g., vividness, recency) that are not clearly related to frequency; thus, use of this heuristic may also lead to biased judgments.

Tversky and Kahneman (1973) cited a number of studies that confirmed the role of an availability heuristic in judgment. For example, in one study participants estimated the frequency of words beginning with the letter k versus those with k as the third letter. It so happens that there are more words in the latter category than in the former; but because it is easier to generate words beginning with k—and thus these words are more available—participants estimated that there were more instances in this former category. Similarly, participants in another study received lists containing differing numbers of male and female names and differing numbers of famous versus less famous names within these gender groups (e.g., Richard Nixon vs. William Fulbright, and Elizabeth Taylor vs. Lana Turner). Participants in a memory condition were found to recall more of the famous names than of the less famous ones, suggesting that the former were more available. When the fame of the figures within a given gender list was varied

---

[1]Thanks to Baruch Fischhoff for suggesting this order of presentation.

in opposition to the actual gender frequency (i.e., greater fame for the less frequent gender), another group of participants made their frequency estimates (i.e., of the numbers of men vs. women) on the basis of the former rather than the latter cue.

There are a number of different biases that can be accounted for by the availability heuristic (Tversky & Kahneman, 1974). For instance, one of these is the bias resulting from the ease of retrieving instances. The example of basing your frequency estimates of presented names on the ease with which you retrieve famous versus less famous names is one example of this. Other examples include overestimating events or classes of events on the basis of vivid or salient instances (e.g., vivid stories of homicide or of car accidents or diseases in newspapers or on television), or on the basis of recent exposure to such examples (see Combs & Slovic, 1979). Still another set of biases is concerned with how well people's memory search strategy works, as in the word search example given earlier or a search of memory for examples of a particular type of former high school classmate (e.g., the number who continued on to college).

A more important source of bias is the relative *imaginability* of instances or events. Thus, the ease with which an individual can imagine a scenario by which their favorite sports team can win its next game will influence their estimated probability of such an outcome. To use the example given by Tversky and Kahneman (1974), the ease with which you can imagine a dangerous outcome for a given activity will influence the estimated risk of this activity. (I return to this particular case later in this section.) Finally, Tversky and Kahneman (1974) also cited the case of illusory correlation, whereby the frequency of co-occurrence between two events is judged by, among other things, the strength of the association between the two events (e.g., between Blacks or Hispanics and crime). I discuss research on illusory correlation in a later section of this chapter.

A number of different examples of the role of the availability bias in social judgment and attribution have been provided (e.g., Nisbett & Ross, 1980; M. Ross & Sicoly, 1979; Taylor, 1982). For example, Taylor and her associates (e.g., Taylor & Fiske, 1978; see also McArthur, 1981) have shown that salience can have a major impact on observers' causal attributions—for instance, more salient actors are afforded greater causal status, presumably because of the greater "availability" of the actor (see Nisbett & Ross, 1980, for a further discussion of this hypothesis). Similarly, M. Ross and Sicoly (1979) suggested that certain *egocentric attributions* (e.g., remembering more and assigning more causal significance to one's own contributions to a project than to those of one's coworkers) can be accounted for by the fact that one's own contributions are simply more "available" or memorable.

Another area of research that relates to the availability heuristic is the work by Nisbett, Ross, and their associates (e.g., Nisbett & Ross, 1980) on the impact of vivid and concrete information versus abstract, statistical data on judgment. For example, Borgida and Nisbett (1977) reported a study in which participants were presented with course evaluations in one of two forms: (a) in a face-to-face presentation by a panel of students who voiced their own evaluations and comments on the course they had taken or (b) in the form of statistical summaries of evaluations by all students who had taken the course over the previous semester. Although the latter information should have been more informative, participants were more convinced to take the recommended courses by the former method. In another study Reyes et al. (1980) found that vivid pieces of evidence presented for either the prosecution or the defense in a mock jury study had more of an influence on jurors' verdicts than did more "pallid" evidence. This effect, however, held only for a verdict delivered after a 48-hour delay (vs. one made immediately after receiving the evidence), presumably because such vivid evidence is easier to recall at a later point.

As these several examples suggest, one possible problem with the concept of an availability heuristic is that the term has frequently been used, especially by social psychologists, as more of a redescription of a given phenomenon than a carefully worked out explanation. In other words, rather than specifying the exact cognitive mechanisms involved in determining availability, that concept is sometimes simply invoked as an attempt to link a puzzling phenomenon to a more familiar one.

The Representativeness Heuristic

The Nature of the Heuristic.   A second, perhaps more widely applicable decision rule (or set of rules), is the so-called representativeness heuristic. As outlined by Tversky and Kahneman (1982; see also Kahneman & Tversky, 1972), representativeness refers to the degree to which one thing is similar to or resembles another. More specifically, representativeness has to do with (a) the similarity between a specific exemplar and some broader class (e.g., the degree to which the O. J. Simpson trial was representative of criminal trials in general); (b) the similarity between the value of that exemplar and the value in the population as a whole (e.g., the degree to which Shaquille O'Neal's salary is representative of the salaries of basketball players in general); (c) the similarity between a subset and a larger set or class (e.g., the degree to which the political stances of college students are representative of those of the American public in general); and (d) the similarity between an event or state and a process that may have generated it (e.g., the likelihood that John F. Kennedy's death was a result of a mafia conspiracy; see Tversky & Kahneman, 1982). It is apparent, then, that the term *representativeness* refers to a variety of different phenomena.

As one frequently cited example of judgment by representativeness, consider the following scenario (from Kahneman & Tversky, 1973):

> Tom W. is of high intelligence, although lacking in true creativity. He has a
> need for order and clarity, and for neat and tidy systems in which every detail

finds its appropriate place. His writing is rather dull and mechanical, occasionally enlivened by somewhat corny puns and by flashes of imagination of the sci-fi type. He has a strong drive for competence. He seems to have little feel and little sympathy for other people and does not enjoy interacting with others. Self-centered, he nonetheless has a deep moral sense. (p. 238)

Participants were then presented with a list of nine majors (e.g., business administration, computer science, humanities and education, social science and social work, etc.), and they were then asked to rank order these nine in terms of Tom W.'s similarity to majors in that category. A second group was instructed to indicate the likelihood that Tom W. would major in each, given that the above description was generated by a clinical psychologist using a projective test. Finally, a third group was asked to estimate the percentage of students who majored in each of the nine categories.

The results of this study indicated that participants' likelihood estimates were highly correlated (.97) with their similarity judgments, suggesting that such likelihood judgments were based on judgments of representativeness (i.e., the degree to which participants viewed Tom W. as representative of majors in that particular category). Of equal importance, such likelihood estimates were *negatively* correlated (–.65) with the *base rates,* or the number of individuals that the third group expected to major in each category. This latter finding suggests that participants were ignoring such critical information in making their likelihood judgments, even though Bayes's theorem[2] specifies that one factor in judging the likelihood of a major given a piece of information about the person is the prior probability or base rate of that major in the population as a whole. This failure to consider base rates held even though participants in the likelihood estimation task did not place great stock in the information provided about Tom. In a separate experiment (Kahneman & Tversky, 1973) participants were found to take the base rates provided into consideration when no *individuating* information (i.e., specific details about the stimulus person) was provided; but these same base rates were again ignored when such information was provided, even when it was completely uninformative (i.e., did not allow participants to make any kind of discrimination between occupations).

Errors Resulting From the Heuristic.   One of the major fallacies resulting from judgments based on representativeness is this tendency to ignore base rates in the face of specific, individuating information. Such a failure

---

[2]Bayes's theorem can be stated as follows:

$$p\{A \,/\, B\} = \frac{(p\{B \,/\, A\})(p\{A\})}{p\{B\}}$$

where $p\{A\}$ refers to the prior probability or base rate of A (e.g., Tom majoring in computer science), $p\{B\}$ refers to the probability of B (i.e., Tom having the characteristics described), $p\{A/B\}$ refers to the probability that A given B (e.g., Tom having the characteristics described given that he is a computer science major), and $p\{B/A\}$ refers to the probability of B given A.

can be found in the tendency of clinical psychologists and physicians to base their diagnoses on the degree to which a patient's symptoms resemble the prototype of a given disorder, while ignoring the incidence of that problem or disorder (e.g., suicide, schizophrenia, or some rare medical condition) in the population as a whole. It can also be observed in the above-mentioned tendency to judge the likelihood of a person belonging to a given social category (e.g., a personality type or a given profession) on the basis of his or her representativeness of that category (i.e., without considering the number of individuals in the population as a whole who fall in such a category). There has been a great deal of research on this so-called *base-rate fallacy* (see Borgida & Brekke, 1981, for a review), including the provocative finding by Ajzen (1977) that base rates are more likely to be considered when they fit the judge's intuitive theory of cause and effect (e.g., that schizophrenia *causes* a particular set of symptoms).

Another error produced by depending on representativeness is the tendency of individuals to ignore sample size in making probability judgments, a tendency that Tversky and Kahneman (1971) referred to as *the law of small numbers,* or the tendency to see small samples as being equally representative of the population as large ones. For example, Kahneman and Tversky (1972) cited a problem in which participants were asked to compare the likelihood of a large versus a small hospital recording more days in which 60% of the births were boys. The results indicated that participants judged the probability of such a deviation from the population mean (i.e., the mean of 50% male births) to be equally likely in the large sample as in the small samples. Kahneman and Tversky (1972) also described a study in which a group of mathematical psychologists greatly overestimated the likelihood of replicating the results of a previous study even when the second sample was quite small (cf. the evidence by Bar-Hillel, 1979, and Kassin, 1979, on situations in which participants are, in fact, sensitive to sample size).

A number of other errors result from representativeness judgments (see Tversky & Kahneman, 1974). I focus on one of these: namely, a faulty conception of chance. The most obvious example of this is the so-called *gambler's fallacy,* the belief that runs of, say, tails in a coin toss, will be followed by a run of heads, or in other words, the belief that chance is self-correcting. In everyday life this misperception is reflected in the common belief that runs of bad luck will be followed by some good luck, or vice versa. A related observation is what Kahneman and Tversky (1972) have referred to as the belief in *local representativeness,* the belief that randomness (or the characteristics of the population in general) will be reflected in local, short-term sequences (or in small samples from the population). Thus, for example, most people believe that a sequence of HTHTTH is more likely than the sequence HHHTTT because the former sequence seems more random in the short run. Similarly, when asked to estimate the mean IQ of a group of 50 students sampled from a population with a mean IQ of 100, where the first student sampled has an IQ of 150, most participants esti-mate the mean value in the sample to still be 100, as if the other 49 students will somehow correct the bias introduced by that first student. In point of fact, the expected value of the remaining 49 students is now 100, leading to an average IQ of 101 in the sample as a whole (Tversky & Kahneman, 1971). As Tversky and Kahneman put it, chance does not correct; it merely dilutes.

A related example of misperceptions of chance is found in an article by Gilovich, Vallone, and Tversky (1985) on the perception of the *hot hand* or streak-shooting in basketball. The phenomenon of interest here is the percep-tion by basketball fans and by players themselves that a player is sometimes "hot" or "in a zone" such that anything he or she shoots will go in. In other words, players are perceived as shooting in streaks, much like the runs in a se-quence of coin flips, and these streaks cannot be accounted for by sheer chance or the laws of probability. Gilovich et al. (1985) approached this phenomenon in several different ways. First, they demonstrated that, contrary to the assessed expectations of basketball fans, NBA players were no more likely to make a shot after making 1–3 previous shots than they were to make a shot after *miss-ing* the same number of shots. Second, they demonstrated that shooters did *not* show a greater number of streaks of 4, 5, or 6 shots than would be expected by chance. Third, to rule out such things as greater defensive pressure applied to hot shooters or other factors that might detract from successful streak shoot-ing, Gilovich et al. examined free throw shooting, a form of shooting where de-fensive pressure would not play a role. Here they found that the probability of making a second free throw after making the first was identical to the probabil-ity of making the second free throw after *missing* the first. Finally, Gilovich et al. showed basketball fans randomly generated sequences of X's and O's (e.g., OXXXOXXXOXXOOOXOOXXOO), presumably referring to made and missed shots, and found that the fans perceived these sequences as reflecting streak shooting. Once again, these results suggest that perceivers have a faulty perception of chance.

The Conjunction Fallacy. A more recent example of an error presum-ably produced by the representativeness heuristic is the *conjunction fallacy.* As an example of this fallacy, consider the following scenario (adapted from Tversky & Kahneman, 1983):

Linda is 31 years old, single, outspoken, and very bright. She majored in phi-losophy. As a student, she was deeply concerned with issues of discrimination and social justice, and also participated in antinuclear demonstrations. Please rate the likelihood of the following alternatives:

—Linda is a bank teller.
—Linda is a bank teller and is active in the feminist movement. (pp. 297, 299)

The critical finding here was that participants judged the second alterna-tive to be more likely than the first, even though it is impossible for the conjunction of two events or classes (e.g., bank teller and feminist) to be more likely than the likelihood of either one separately—hence, the term the *conjunction fallacy*. (The same principle can be applied to the first example given at the beginning of this chapter.) Such a finding can obviously be accounted for by the representativeness heuristic in that the background information about Linda is more representative of a feminist activist and of a feminist bank teller than it is of a bank teller. In general, the representativeness heuristic leads to the interesting result that adding more relevant detail produces the illusion of greater likelihood or greater confidence, when in fact, such detail can only *reduce* the likelihood of the event. Tversky and Kahneman (1982) argued that such conjunction effects cannot be accounted for by linguistic factors, such as the possibility that participants interpreted the statement "Linda is a bank teller" presented in the context of the "feminist" and "bank teller" as meaning "Linda is a bank teller and is *not* active in the feminist movement." To control for such linguistic factors, Tversky and Kahneman included a between-subjects condition in which the simple events and the compound events were presented to two separate groups. In this study, greater belief in the compound event was again found.

In another set of studies, Tversky and Kahneman (1983) reported evidence for the conjunction fallacy when the two elementary events were causally related—that is, when one event was an outcome that was representative of the causal event, rather than that event being representative of a "model" (e.g., the description of Linda's personality in the example given above). Thus, for example, in the context of a health survey, participants judged the proposition that "Mr F. has had one or more heart attacks and he is over 55 years of age" as being more probable than "Mr. F. has had more than one heart attack." Tversky and Kahneman (1983) reported that the conjunction error here was reduced by having participants judge the relative percentage of men in the survey who had had one or more heart attacks and the percentage who satisfied the conjunction, rather than the probability for a single individual (see Gigerenzer, 1991, for a similar distinction).

Despite these attempts by Tversky and Kahneman (1982, 1983) to address this issue, one of the major criticisms of research on the conjunction fallacy (e.g., Dulany & Hilton, 1991; Fiedler, 1988; Markus & Zajonc, 1985) has been that the observed effects may be due to linguistic difficulties (i.e., in translating or construing the constituent events and/or their conjunction). For example, Fiedler (1988) found that changing the response measure from "probability" to "frequency," on the assumption that participants found the word "probability" to be ambiguous, produced a substantial reduction in the conjunction fallacy. Similarly, Dulany and Hilton (1991) found that participants interpreted the conjunction in a different way from that assumed by Tversky and Kahneman, and these different interpretations "absolve the conjunction effect of fallacy" (p. 86).

One criticism of the representativeness heuristic in general (e.g., Oswald, 1986, cited in Rehm & Gadenne, 1990) implied by the preceding discussion is that the term represents a somewhat vague, catchall term that is used by Tversky, Kahneman, and others in a variety of different ways (see my later discussion of uses of the representativeness heuristic to account for social psychological biases). In the same vein, Sherman and Corty (1984) observed that it is sometimes difficult to distinguish between the representativeness and availability heuristics and that several phenomena described by Kahneman and Tversky can be accounted for by either of the two heuristics. Finally, like its availability counterpart, the representativeness heuristic has often been used as a mere redescription of a phenomenon.

The Anchoring and Adjustment Heuristic

The third heuristic identified by Tversky and Kahneman (1974; see also Lopes, 1982), and the one to which these investigators have given the least attention, is the anchoring and adjustment heuristic alluded to in chapter 1. The argument here is that when judges are given a particular starting point or anchor for making a judgment, and they subsequently attempt to adjust their estimate from that anchor in the light of new information, this adjustment is typically insufficient. Thus, in a frequently cited example (Tversky & Kahneman, 1974), participants in one study were asked to estimate the percentage of African nations in the United Nations, after being given an arbitrary anchor of 65% or 10%. Participants given the 65% anchor gave significantly higher estimates than those who were given the 10% one. In other words, a knowingly arbitrary anchor had an undue influence on participants' judgments because of insufficient adjustment from that anchor. Similarly, when participants were asked to estimate the product of an ascending sequence of numbers (e.g., $1 \times 2 \times 3 \times 4 \times 5 \times 6 \times 7 \times 8$), their estimates were significantly lower than for those who were asked to estimate the product of these numbers presented in descending order, presumably because participants started off calculating the product from the first numbers in the sequence and then extrapolated from there.

These two examples clearly do not qualify as "everyday" or "real world." Plous (1989), on the other hand, reported a study in which respondents were asked to estimate the probability of nuclear war given an initial anchor of 1% or 99%. A clear effect of this anchoring manipulation was found, suggesting that the way in which a political scenario or event is presented (e.g., a worst case scenario) will have an effect on subsequent judgments of the probability of that event (e.g., the likelihood of a political victory or of the use of biological warfare by Iraq). A second example of a real-world application is found in a study by Northcroft and Neale (1987) on the effects of anchors on the appraisal by real estate agents of a set of houses. Specifically, agents were given ten pages of information about a house in which the only factor that was varied was the listing price, which was either substantially or moderately above or substantially or moderately below the true appraised price. This single piece of information had a significant effect on these agents' appraised value of the house, even though the agents did not view listing price as a major factor in their appraisals.

In a recent extension of the anchoring and adjustment heuristic, Wilson, Houston, Etting, and Brekke (1996) demonstrated that the anchoring process can occur even when an individual has not explicitly been asked to or attempted to consider that alternative. Thus, Wilson et al. made the intriguing suggestion that an anchor can have its effect unintentionally and even nonconsciously. As I discuss later in this chapter, this argument is consistent with discussions of some social judgment biases (e.g., Gilbert & Malone, 1995) that suggest that the initial anchoring occurs automatically, whereas the adjustment component is more controlled.

The Simulation Heuristic

In 1982, Kahneman and Tversky introduced another heuristic called the *simulation heuristic*. Originally included under the availability heuristic, the simulation heuristic says that the judged probability of an outcome is based on the ease with which an individual can run a mental simulation that may produce such an outcome. For example, Kahneman and Tversky (1982a) gave participants a scenario in which two men arrive at the airport 30 minutes late for their flights. One man finds that his flight left on time, whereas the other finds that his flight was delayed and left just 5 minutes ago. When participants judged which of the two men would be more disappointed, 96% picked the one who just missed his plane (even though both missed their planes, and both expected to be late), presumably because it seems more likely, based on a mental alteration of the scenario, for this second man to have made his flight. (See the similar results by Turnbull, 1981, dealing with closeness to lottery picks to winning, and Medvac, Madey, & Gilovich, 1995, for an example from the facial reactions of silver vs. bronze medalists in the Olympics; see also Kahneman & Varey, 1990, and Roese & Olson, 1995.) Kahneman and Miller (1986) referred to this ease of constructing a counterfactual from an existing state as *mutability*.

Mutability. Mutability of scenarios is based on a number of different "rules" (Sherman & McConnell, 1995). For example, Kahneman and Tversky (1982a; see also Kahneman & Miller, 1986) argued that in constructing simulations, it is easier to substitute a more likely (normal) event for a less likely (abnormal) one, than to replace a normal event with an unlikely one. Thus, for example, it is easier for basketball fans to conceive of Vince Carter having made a last minute shot that he in fact missed than it is to imagine a member of the Los Angeles Clippers, a team that typically has a losing record (and that typically loses leads in the fourth quarter) doing the same. Kahneman and Tversky (1982a) gave another example in which participants were given a scenario describing a fatal car crash in which the victim had either taken a different route home at his regular time, or had left earlier than usual by the same route. The unsurprising finding was that when participants were asked to complete the sentence "if only ... ," they were more likely to mention the component that was atypical in that particular scenario.

Another implication of this argument is that it should be easier to produce an explanation for action than for inaction (Kahneman & Miller, 1986; Kahneman & Tversky, 1982a)—for instance, why he or she drives a Porsche versus why he or she does not. Stated differently, individuals should show stronger affect—positive or negative—in response to matters of commission than to those of omission (e.g., Kahneman, 1995). Baron and his colleagues (e.g., J. Baron & Ritov, 1994; Spranca, Minsk, & Baron, 1991) labeled this phenomenon the *omission bias*. The general prediction has been confirmed by Gleicher et al. (1990) and by Landman (1987; though see Roese & Olson, 1995). Similarly, Keren and Wagenaar (1985) found that experienced blackjack players tended to hold when their cards totaled 16 even though an optimal, well-known strategy would be to ask for another card if certain face cards showed for the house. Taylor (1991; see also Miller & Taylor, 1995) has speculated that this nonoptimal strategy results from the fact that people experience stronger regret following errors of commission than for ones of omission. In this connection Taylor (1991) found that in a computer simulated blackjack game, players overestimated their losses from acts of commission more than they did their losses from acts of omission.

In contrast to this view, Gilovich and Medvec (1994, 1995b) reported that when people look back at their lives at different ages, they show greater *long-term* regret for inaction than for action. These researchers explain their results in terms of the greater range of potential omitted actions, which are bound only by our imagination, as opposed to the possibilities of action, which are bound by our memory. In addition, the factors leading to omission may appear less reasonable or justifiable when looked at from a later point in our lives, and more kinds of omissions may come to mind in retrospect.

Kahneman (1995), on the other hand, argued that the difference between early and later regrets amounts to the difference between loss and foregone gain. In an earlier classic paper, Kahneman and Tversky (1984) developed the idea of *loss aversion*, or the view that people feel greater regret at losses than at foregone gains (e.g., one would feel worse about losing $1000 than about failing to make an investment that would have netted $1000). This principle accounts for the immediate regret, or what Kahneman (1995) described as *hot regret*. In the long term, however, such pain gives way to what Kahneman calls *wistful regret*, or "the emotion associated with pleasantly sad fantasies of what might have been" (p. 391). Although Kahneman's account does not really "explain" the underlying temporal dynamics of such change, it does suggest that there are two different phenomena in the two situations.

In a recent joint article, Gilovich, Medvec, and Kahneman (1998) concluded that both of their positions are partially right. Specifically, these authors reported research suggesting that whereas regrets over actions lead to hot emotions such as anger, regrets over inactions led to both wistful feelings such as nostalgia, as suggested by Kahneman, and "troublesome" feelings (e.g., of despair), as Gilovich and Medvec argued. Thus, there are two different responses to inaction in the long term, confirming both of these two points of view

In trying to sort out these various accounts, I cannot resist commenting that I have more regrets about the authors' inaction (i.e., what they do not say) than about their actions (i.e., what they *do* say). At least from the standpoint of everyday cognition, it seems clear that some account of memory processes, as well as the relationship between memory and judgment (as in my discussion of the on-line vs. memory conditions described by Hastie & Park, 1986) is needed here. Thus, for example, it may be that in the short term, individuals may remember more clearly their reasons and their gains and losses, and they may focus on the losses, as in Kahneman and Tversky's notion of loss aversion. On the other hand, in long-term retrospect, such evaluations may be more clearly based on their memory for these actions (or inactions) and outcomes; and as their memory for actions fades, their attention may focus more on inaction.

Relation to Other Heuristics. Sherman and McConnell (1995) pointed out that some of the negative outcomes resulting from simulations or faulty counterfactual reasoning are quite similar to those observed with the other heuristics. For example, because some features are more easily changed or mutated than others, and because such mutability (like availability) is a fallible guide to causality, individuals may draw incorrect causal inferences. For instance, because individuals may find it easier to think of how their partner might appreciate them more or how other partners *have* appreciated them more, they may be more prone to attribute their partner's lack of appreciation of them to that partner, rather than to themselves. In general, Kahneman (1995), following Dawes (1988), argued that simulations are frequently given more confidence than they deserve. Finally, thinking about alternatives (e.g., "what might have been") can obviously lead to negative feelings of regret, self-blame, and so forth.

Constraints on Simulations. Seelau, Seelau, Wells, and Windschitl (1995) distinguished among three different types of constraints on mental simulations: namely, those imposed by *natural law* (e.g., it is hard to conceive of objects falling upward because of the knowledge of the law of gravity), those of *availability* (i.e., the difficulty of thinking up alternative outcomes), and those of *purpose* (i.e., certain alternatives may not be considered because they are not relevant to one's current purpose). These three types of constraints not only limit the number of alternatives considered, thus reducing the demand on individuals' processing capacities, but they also place constraints on which alternatives are considered plausible.

It is the second of these constraints that I have illustrated in previous examples—that is, on the mutability of events and the distinction between events and nonevents; this category is obviously related to the availability heuristic from which the simulation heuristic derived. In a later formulation, referred to as *norm theory*, Kahneman and Miller (1986) focused on the simple imaginability of alternatives. Seelau et al., on the other hand, argued for the full range of availability considerations (e.g., recency, salience, familiarity). Seelau et al. also argued that whereas natural law and availability constraints operate at an automatic level, purpose constraints operate at a controlled level. That is, alternatives that spring to mind by virtue of their availability may be overridden if they do not serve one's present purpose. In the example given by Seelau et al., a different set of alternatives may be relevant if one is trying to assign blame from those that will if one is trying to console another person. In general, Seelau et al. cited four categories of purposes that may affect choice of alternatives: determining causality, controlling future outcomes, assigning blame (e.g., for an accident), and consoling a person (cf. the similar concepts of interactional goals [Jones & Thibant, 1958; Hilton & Darley, 1919] and the processing objectives cited in chap. 2).

It is worth noting that this discussion of constructing alternatives bears a resemblance to the emphasis in the text comprehension literature on constructing a situation model (Kintsch, 1988), or a model of the situation being portrayed in the text (including people and events; see my discussion of this topic in chap. 3). Graesser and Zwaann (1995) recently reviewed some of the evidence on inference generation (e.g., of causes, goals, character emotions) in the construction of a situational model. In addition, Zwaan and his associates (Zwaan, Langston, & Graesser, 1995; Zwaan & Radvansky, 1998) proposed an *event-indexing model* in which the reader monitors various features (e.g., temporality, causality, intentionality, protagonists) in trying to make sense out of the text.

The question that arises from this comparison is whether research on text comprehension can shed any light on the construction of simulations and their comparison with the current state of affairs. Most of the research on the construction and comparison of simulations has focused on a simple feature-by-feature analysis (e.g., Dunning & Madey, 1995; Tversky, 1977), though I have also noted a handful of "rules" for and constraints on mutation of scenarios. In addition, there have been a few more general considerations examined. For example, Shafir (1993) showed that people give more weight to factors that facilitate outcomes than to those that interfere with them. Along similar lines, Taylor and Pham (1996) explicitly distinguished between what they call *outcome simulation* and *process simulation*. In the former case, individuals simply simulate the possible outcome of an action or event sequence, whereas in the latter, individuals simulate the entire action sequence.[3]

---

[3]Recently, Taylor, Phan, and Rivkin (1998) proposed still another function of mental simulations: to establish links to action and self-regulation, as in mental simulations in sports and cognitive behavior therapy.

The text comprehension literature suggests that other, more general structural characteristics (e.g., compatibility of goals with actions, general rules of causal inference, overall rules of rhetorical or narrative style) may be involved. A mental simulation is, after all, usually a kind of narrative. For example, to what extent are sexual fantasies (vs. plans for an actual sexual liaison) constrained by laws of causal relations and rules of goal–subgoal relations? Is it easier to imagine a form of sexual activity that is possible but unfamiliar than it is one that is physically, personally, or socially impossible (or at least highly unlikely)? To what extent does a given feature have to fit with the structure of the overall episode or scenario, and how readily are specific features abstracted out from that scenario? (Recall Abelson's [1976a] distinction between episodic and hypothetical scripts.)

Reservations.   As I have suggested for the representativeness and availability heuristics, the concept of a simulation heuristic is not entirely clear. First, by relating such simulations to (and sometimes equating them with) counterfactual thinking in general, it appears that it is not only scenarios or event sequences that can be simulated; but also states or objects. Thus, for example, one can imagine owning a different house or car or having a different body or a different look, as well as thinking about how each of these states or objects might make his or her life better. Along these lines, the question arises whether one can simulate components of a scenario such as the actors and their motives (e.g., the motives of Monica Lewinsky or Linda Tripp) without constructing the whole scenario (cf. my discussion of autobiographical memory)?

Furthermore, the process by which the simulation is carried out is not entirely clear. Is it an active, constructive, effortful process of imagination or is it a passive result of some kind of availability mechanism, or an entirely local process of transforming one actual situation to another hypothetical one on a feature-by-feature basis? How does one draw on background or real-world knowledge in generating this scenario? For example, on the first point, Kahneman (1995) recently proposed that "the most important aspect of the phenomenology of mental simulations is that it is experienced as an act of observation, not as an act of construction" (p. 379; cf. my discussion of the phenomenology of AM). Furthermore, such scenarios are "highly schematic" (p. 379), that is, not all of the details are fleshed out (cf. my discussion of AM on this). On the second point, Kahneman argued that such mental simulations may be instructive in that they represent forms of implicit knowledge—something different from both declarative and procedural knowledge—that cannot be accessed in any other way. The question arises from my earlier discussion of dynamic memory, of course, of what form this implicit knowledge takes— that is, can it exist in prepackaged form, or is it constructed in the course of the simulation?

For the purposes of this book, the simulation heuristic is probably the most interesting of the heuristics in that it relates to several other ideas that I have discussed or will consider (e.g., my discussion of planning and event memory in chap. 4, my discussions later in this chapter of the role of mental simulations and model construction in naturalistic decision-making and of constructing explanations and counterexplanations).

In addition, there has been a good deal of research on the effects of constructing explanations of events or of imagining scenarios on the judged likelihood of outcomes (see Koehler, 1991, for a review). For example, Sherman (e.g., Sherman, Skov, Hervitz, & Stock, 1981; Sherman, Zehner, Johnson, & Hirt, 1983) showed that when participants are asked to generate arguments for one outcome over another, their estimates of the probability of the explained outcome are increased—a phenomenon that L. Ross, Lepper, Strack, and Steinmetz (1977) referred to as the *explanation effect*. For instance, Sherman et al. (1983) found that when participants were to explain why one football team would win over another, they came to believe that the first team's victory was more likely. Along similar lines, Levi and Pryor (1987) showed that among participants who were going to watch a Presidential debate between Walter Mondale and Ronald Reagan, those who were given a set of reasons why one or the other candidate had won the debate (or generated such reasons for themselves) were more likely to predict that that candidate *would* win the debate, whereas those who were simply asked to imagine that the same candidate had won were not. At the same time, there is evidence that being required to generate counterexplanations (i.e., explanations for alternative outcomes) can *reduce* the judged probability of the original outcome (see my later discussion of counterexplanations and my discussion of the development of argumentation in chap. 10). All of this evidence would seem to be in agreement with the arguments of the simulation heuristic.

CONFIRMATION BIASES AND COVARIATION ASSESSMENT

Another set of biases in both inductive and deductive reasoning involve the task of covariation assessment, or determining the degree to which two variables are related. In a general review of research in this area, Crocker (1981) outlined some six steps in the process of such assessment. These six steps are (a) knowing what information to gather in order to test out a presumed correlation; (b) actually sampling this information; (c) classifying the instances (e.g., as members of class A or class B, or as confirming or disconfirming); (d) remembering these instances and classifications, and determining the degree of confirmation or disconfirmation; (e) integrating the evidence to form an overall estimate of covariation; and (f) using the overall estimate of covariation to predict relationships between or among instances. In the discussion that follows, I start with research on Stage 1, followed by research paradigms addressing Stages 3, 4, and 5.

Research on the Confirmation Bias

Wason's Rule Discovery Task.   Probably the most widely researched form of "bias" in this area, and one that has been studied in the context of both inductive and deductive reasoning, is the *confirmation bias*. The confirmation bias refers to the observation that individuals seem to seek out and base their judgments on information that confirms their hypotheses, or "positive" evidence, rather than on "negative" evidence, or information that may disconfirm these hypotheses. Although this term has been applied to a variety of different forms of hypothesis testing (see Fischhoff & Beyth-Marom, 1983, and Klayman & Ha, 1987, for reviews), the most widely cited paradigms are those introduced by Peter Wason (1960, 1966; Wason & Johnson-Laird, 1972).

The first of these paradigms consisted of a *rule discovery*, a hypothesis-testing task in which Wason attempted to simulate a scientific problem-solving exercise. In this task participants were given a set of three numbers—2, 4, and 6—and were asked to generate additional triplets that the experimenter would specify as being or not being an instance of the rule that he or she had in mind. This task is basically the same as that involved in many earlier studies of concept formation (see Bourne, Dominowski, & Loftus, 1979; Bruner et al., 1956) except that in this particular case the universe of possible instances consisted of all possible sets of three numbers rather than some more restricted set of stimulus patterns, and the experimenter's rule consisted of a very general "all ascending sequences of numbers" rather than some more restricted hypothesis (e.g., large red triangles).

The critical finding of this particular paradigm was that participants quickly settled on a hypothesis (e.g., trios of consecutive even numbers), tested out positive examples of that hypothesis, and showed strong confidence in the hypothesis without testing negative instances (i.e., instances that might disconfirm that hypothesis). Thus, for example, participants with a "consecutive even numbers" hypothesis might select 8, 10, and 12 as their next three numbers, rather than 7, 8, and 9, or 8, 10, and 16—each of which would have been consistent with the experimenter's hypothesis but not with the participants'. (An example of an expanded protocol from one of Wason's participants is given in Table 9.1.) Such a confirming strategy clearly violates the generally accepted norm in formal logic and in the philosophy of science (e.g., Popper, 1959) as well as critical reasoning in general (e.g., Baron, 1994; Kuhn, 1991), of seeking falsifying evidence in testing hypotheses, and in the present case, it is at best a rather inefficient and ineffective manner of information search. (Participants also frequently failed to give up hypotheses after receiving negative feedback.)

There have been a number of variations on the original Wason rule induction study. For example, Penrose (1962, cited in Wason, 1968) conducted a study in which instead of a numerical sequence, the exemplar

TABLE 9.1

Examples of Protocols From Rule Discovery Task*

No. 4. Female, aged 19

8 10 12: two added each time; 14 16 18: even numbers in order of magnitude; 20 22 24: same reason; 1 3 5: two added to preceding number.

The rule is that by starting with any number two is added each time to form the next number.

2 6 10: middle number is the arithmetic mean of the other two; 1 50 99: same reason.

The rule is that the middle number is the arithmetic mean of the other two.

3 10 17: same number, seven, added each time; 0 3 6: three added each time.

The rule is that the difference between two numbers next to each other is the same.

12 8 4: the same number is subtracted each time to form the next number.

The rule is adding a number, always the same one to form the next number.

1 4 9: any three numbers in order of magnitude.

The rule is any three numbers in order of magnitude (17 minutes).

No. 5. Female, aged 19

1 3 5: add two to each number to give the following one; 16 18 20: to test the theory that it is simply a progression of two. These are chosen so that they are more complex and not merely simple numbers; 99 101 103: to test the progression of two theory, using odd numbers.

As these numbers can hardly have any other connection, unless it is very remote, the rule is a progression of adding two, in other words either all even or all odd numbers.

1 5 9: the average of the two numbers on the outside is the number between them.

The rule is that the central figure is the mean of the two external ones.

6 10 14; the difference between the first two numbers, added to the second number gives the third; 7 11 15: to test this theory; 2 25 48: to test this theory.

The rule is that the difference between the first two figures added to the second figure gives the third.

7 9 11, 11 12 13, 12 9 8, 77 75 71.

Subject gives up (45 minutes).

Note.   *Data adapted from "'On the Failure to Eliminate Hypotheses ...'—A Second Look" by P. C. Wason, 1968a. In *Thinking and Reasoning* (pp. 168–169) edited by P. C. Wason & P. N. Johnson-Laird. Baltimore, MD: Penguin Books.

given was a verbal description of "a Siamese cat," where the rule being instantiated was "all living things." A similar search for positive instances was found in this version of the task. Wason (1968a) reported that neither monetary incentives nor explicit instructions to consider alternative hypotheses led participants to eliminate hypotheses. One manipulation that *did* have some effect (Thompson, 1962, cited in Wason, 1968a; see also Wetherick, 1962) was to present negative instances first. This is a point that I return to later.

Two other interesting variations on the rule discovery task have been reported by Mynatt, Tweney, and their associates. In one interactive computer version of the task, Mynatt, Doherty, and Tweney (1977, 1978) found that participants continued to seek confirming evidence for their (incorrect) hypothesis, but when they *did* encounter disconfirming evidence, they *did* reject the incorrect hypothesis. In another version, Tweney et al. (1980) presented participants with the basic Wason problem, but instead of yes–no feedback, they gave them the feedback of either DAX for positive examples of the rule, or MED for all triplets that failed to satisfy that rule. This version of the problem is thus structurally identical to the original one except that participants treated the two types of feedback as if they represented two different hypotheses. (Wharton, Cheng, & Wickens, 1993, refer to this variation as a *dual goal,* as opposed to the usual *one goal* instructions.) Thus, even though participants sought out positive instances of both rules, in the process they also received information that disconfirmed or offered negative evidence for each in contrast to the other. As a result, participants were quicker or more successful at discovering the correct rule.

One possible conclusion from these two studies is that the tendency to show biased sampling of information in testing out a hypothesis is reduced when one is motivated to examine alternative possibiilities. This examination of alternative possibilities, of course, is one of the presumed functions of a university education. I also discuss a similar proposal later in this chapter, when I talk about research on belief perseverance.

Klayman (1995; Klayman & Ha, 1987) have questioned the label "confirmation bias," which falsely implies that we cannot deal with disconfirming information. These commentators argued that Wason's results may be restricted to a specific paradigm, one in which participants' rules are a *subset* of the experimenter's rules. Specifically, a rule such as "consecutive even numbers" is embedded within the experimenter's rule of "ascending sequences of numbers," or the rule "pediatrician" is embedded within the broader rule of "physician" or "health care professional." (See Fig. 9.1.) One of the results of this particular problem type is that falsification can only be achieved by seeking out negative instances of a rule. As Fig. 9.1 indicates, however, there are other circumstances in which falsification can be obtained by seeking out *positive* instances; thus, Klayman and Ha proposed the term *positive test strategy* as an alternative to the conformation bias.

One interesting application of the notion of a confirmation bias in *social* cognition is found in a widely cited study by Snyder and Swann (1978). In this study participants were allowed to choose questions to ask a target person in order to find out if that person was an introvert or an extravert. The finding that Snyder and Swann interpreted as reflecting a confirmation bias (or confirmation "strategy") was that participants who were asked to test whether the target person was an extravert tended to select questions that emphasized extraversion (e.g., "What would you do if you wanted to liven up a party?") and were thus likely to confirm their initial hypothesis, rather than seeking information that might be more suited to an introvert (e.g., "What factors make it hard for you to really open up to people?").

In response to Snyder and Swann's findings, Trope and Bassok (1982, 1983) argued that hypothesis-testing strategies, in social interaction or elsewhere, are *diagnosing*, that is, seeking out information that is more probable under one hypothesis than under an alternative one, rather than a simple confirming one. In a direct test of these two possible strategies, Trope and Bassok (1982) used an information-gathering task similar to Snyder and Swann's, and found no evidence for a confirming strategy and clear evidence for a diagnosing one. That is, participants sought out information that allowed them to support one hypothesis in contrast to another rather than seeking out information that was supportive of just one. In a second set of studies, Trope and Bassok (1983) found that a confirming strategy was engaged in only when the hypothesis was an extreme one (e.g., an extreme extrovert), where confirming information was itself diagnostic.

Problems in Covariation Assessment

A second issue that has sparked a great deal of research has to do with one's ability to *interpret* covariation. Research on this topic has come from a number of different sources, including experimental (e.g., Smedslund, 1963; Ward & Jenkins, 1965), social (e.g., Hamilton & Gifford, 1976; Jennings, Amabile, & Ross, 1982), developmental (e.g., Inhelder & Piaget, 1958; Shaklee & Mims, 1981), and clinical psychologists (e.g., L. J. Chapman & Chapman, 1967, 1969). To take two frequently cited examples, Smedslund (1963) gave nurses a set of 100 cards describing the presence or absence of a symptom and presence or absence of a disease. Of these 100 cases, 37 showed the joint presence of symptom and disease, 33 showed the presence of the disease in the absence of the symptom, 17 showed the absence of the disease in the presence of a symptom, and 13 showed the joint absence of symptom and disease. The important finding here was that the nurses interpreted this pattern of results

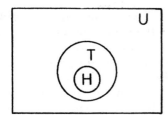

Figure 1: Representation of a situation in which the hypothesized rule is embedded within the correct rule, as in Watson's (1960) "2, 4, 6" task. (U = the universe of possible instances [e.g., all triples of numbrs]; T = the set of instances that have the target property [e.g., they fit the experimenter's rule: increasing]; H = the set of instances that fit the hypothesized rule [e.g., increasing by 2].)

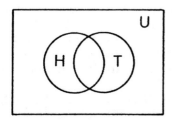

Figure 2: Representation of a situation in which the hypothesized rule overlaps the correct rule.

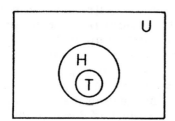

Figure 3: Represnetation of a situation in which the hypothesized rule surrounds the correct rule.

FIG. 9.1. Klayman and Ha's set theory of conception of Wason's rule discovery task, under three different assumptions. From "Confirmation, Disconfirmation, and Information in Hypothesis Testing" by J. Klayman, & Y. Ha, 1987, *Psychological Review, 94*, 213-214. Copyright © 1987 by the American Psychological Association. Reprinted with permission.

as showing a correlation between symptom and disease, even though 50% of the cases failed to show a covariation (see Berger, 1994, for a similar result with physicians). The accounts given by nurses suggested that they had focused primarily on the present–present cell.

In another classic study, Ward and Jenkins (1965) presented participants with information about the relationship between cloud seeding and rain—a set of conditions that was expected to highlight the possible role of chance in producing outcomes. This information was presented in one of three ways: in terms of a general summary of the data; in the form of serial, trial-by-trial instances; and in both trial-by-trial and summary forms. Participants' judgments in the first condition were responsive to covariation, suggesting that we do show some understanding of contingency tables (see Crocker, 1981, vs. Nisbett & Ross, 1980), whereas judgments of participants in the other two conditions were not. For those participants who did not use the normatively correct strategy, 68% seemed to focus on confirming instances.

In their reviews of the literature on covariation assessment, Crocker (1981) and Alloy and Tabachnik (1984) reviewed some of the factors that influence such judgments. For example, participants show greater accuracy for judgments based on nonbinary variables than for those based on binary ones (such as those used in the two studies just reviewed). Similarly, participants make more accurate judgments of covariation when the variables are causally related (see the Azjen study cited earlier) or when the related instances occur close together in time. Finally, when some of the factors that may distort covariation judgments at earlier stages are eliminated (e.g., having to sample cases or to ensure that these cases are randomly selected, or having to recall instances and estimate their frequencies), accuracy is increased (Crocker, 1981). Viewed from a different perspective, Crocker (1981) suggested that most studies of covariation assessment that eliminate these factors by presenting the data in some kind of precoded form may actually underestimate the amount of bias or inaccuracy in full covariation judgments.

One interesting variation on the covariation paradigm has been reported by Harkness, DeBono, and Borgida (1985). These authors argued that when participants are not really *involved* in a decision task, they may use less effortful, less time-consuming strategies of covariation assessment (see my earlier discussion of judgment heuristics). Therefore, Harkness et al. included a condition in which participants would be more involved (i.e., they were going to date the person described in the contingency task). The information that each female participant received about their prospective date was his reactions to several other women with particular characteristics (e.g., attractive, good sense of humor). Thus, the judgment task consisted of participants' estimates of covariation (presented in tabular form) between these characteristics and their prospective dates' dating choices; the dependent variable was the complexity of the covariation strategy that participants used in making their judgments.

The interesting results of the Harkness et al. study were that participants in the high-involvement condition used more complex covariation strategies (e.g., a complete conditional probability strategy vs. a single cell, positive-confirming-instances strategy) and were more accurate in their judgments than those in a low-involvement condition (i.e., where participants did not believe that they would be dating the person described). These results speak to some extent to the issue of the applicability of laboratory studies of covariation assessment to real-world tasks (although it may be argued that information about dates is seldom presented in tabular form).

Another popular paradigm that has examined the issue of covariation assessment involves the phenomenon of *illusory correlation*. As the label suggests, illusory correlation refers to the fact that people often perceive and remember a correlation between events or categories when none, in fact, exists. The first research on this topic was conducted by L. J. Chapman and

Chapman (1967, 1969; L. J. Chapman, 1967). In his initial study, L. J. Chapman (1967) proposed two different factors that affect this faulty judgment: namely, an associative connection between events or categories, and the co-occurrence of two distinctive events. Chapman varied both of these factors in a paired association task in which two pairs of words in each series had a high word association (e.g., lion–tiger, bread–butter), whereas another pair consisted of words that were three or four letters longer than the others (e.g., magazine-building). When participants were asked to go back and estimate the degree of co-occurrence between the two members of a word pair, where each word was actually paired with every other word equally often, they overestimated the degree of co-occurrence of the associatively related words and those that were distinctive by virtue of their greater length.

One of Chapman and Chapman's interests was in the role of illusory correlation in clinical diagnoses from projective tests. Specifically, L. J. Chapman and Chapman (1967, 1969) sought to explain why clinicians continue to use tests with no evidence of validity, and why they see a connection between responses to the tests and specific disorders, when no such relationship exists. One possible explanation for these false perceptions is associatively based illusory correlation. Specifically, L. J. Chapman and Chapman (1967) asked practicing clinicians with experience in the Draw-A-Person test to indicate what symptoms were associated with what features of the drawings (e.g., paranoia associated with large eyes). A group of college students was then presented with 45 drawings paired with two symptom statements, each an equal number of times, and were asked to indicate which features of the drawings were most frequently paired (in the study) with which symptoms. Chapman and Chapman (1967) found that the college students overestimated the frequency of pairing of particular symptoms with certain characteristics of the drawing, that these pairings were consistent with the clinicians' diagnostic judgments, and that both could be predicted from a third group's ratings of the associative strength (i.e., of the words) between the description of the characteristic and the symptom description. In other words, the clinicians' judgments could be predicted from illusory correlations, which could in turn be predicted from associative connections. A similar set of findings was reported by L. J. Chapman and Chapman (1969) for the Rorschach Inkblot Test.

The concept of illusory correlation has also been applied by Hamilton and his students (e.g., Hamilton & Gifford, 1976; Hamilton & Rose, 1980; see Hamilton & Sherman, 1989, for a review) to the development and maintenance of social stereotypes. In this case, the primary explanatory principle has been the co-occurrence of distinctive events. Thus, in the initial study on this topic, Hamilton and Gifford (1976) presented participants with 39 behavioral descriptions that applied to either Group A (26 descriptions) or Group B (13 descriptions). Thus, Group B was made distinctive by virtue of being in the minority. In addition, each group was described by an equal ratio (9:4) of desirable to undesirable descriptions. Thus, undesirable behaviors were made distinctive by virtue of being less frequent, even though they occurred in the same ratio for both groups. As predicted by the concept of the co-occurrence of distinctive events, participants were found to overestimate the correlation of Group B with undesirable behaviors, and they gave more unfavorable evaluations of Group B. Hamilton and Gifford drew an analogy between these findings and the formation of stereotypes, that is, linking a minority or infrequently encountered group with undesirable (and hence infrequent) behaviors (e.g., crime). To make sure that these results were due to paired distinctiveness rather than to a preexisting assumption of the undesirability of minority groups, Hamilton and Gifford repeated the experiment, but this time with desirable behaviors in the minority. Again, an illusory correlation was found, this time between Group B and *desirable* behaviors.

In the original Hamilton and Gifford study and most of the studies that have followed, distinctiveness has been defined in terms of infrequency. In at least two other subsequent studies, however, distinctiveness has been operationalized in other ways. For example, Spears, van der Plight, and Eiser (1985) defined distinctiveness in terms of both infrequency and the incongruence of a set of expressed opinions with participants' own attitudes. These investigators found that such incongruence contributed to an observed illusory correlation. In another study Sanbonmatsu, Sherman, and Hamilton (1987) found that simply giving participants instructions to pay attention to a particular group produced an illusory correlation. From these results, Hamilton concluded that anything that "draws attention to a stimulus" (Hamilton & Sherman, 1989, p. 71) can produce an illusory correlation.

In contrast, in a critique of research on illusory correlation, Fiedler (1991) found fault with this notion of distinctiveness. Fiedler argued that it is typically simply assumed, but not directly tested, that infrequency can somehow be equated with distinctiveness. Furthermore, he argued that the other ways of operationalizing distinctiveness (e.g., instructions to pay attention or consistency with one's own opinions) are complex and multifaceted, and thus it is not clear that the effects are due to distinctiveness and only distinctiveness. I return to this topic when I discuss salience effects later in this chapter.

One proposed explanation of this illusory correlation (Hamilton, 1981; Tversky & Kahneman, 1974) is in terms of the availability heuristic. Specifically, the stronger the associative connection between items or events, the greater the availability of that associated item for subsequent judgments. Similarly, events that are more distinctive are also more available. In support of this view, Hamilton and Gifford (1976) reported a correlation between memory and frequency judgments. In addition, Johnson and Mullen (1994) reported faster reaction times for recall of negative behaviors in the minority group in the illusory correlation paradigm, suggesting greater accessibility of the distinctive behaviors in this condition.

Another explanation of illusory correlation effects is in terms of schema- (e.g., Hamilton, 1981) or expectancy-based confirmation (e.g., Hamilton, 1981; Kayne & Alloy, 1988). That is, stereotypes represent knowledge structures that include expectancies about groups (e.g., about women or ethnic minorities). These expectancies affect the processing of incoming information relevant to these structures (e.g., about women's performance in the military) and may be maintained through a kind of confirmation bias. For example, Kayne and Alloy (1988) suggested that the effects of illusory correlations might occur in at least three different ways: namely, producing overrecall of expectancy-consistent information, underrecall of expectancy-disconfirming information, and over*weighting* of expectancy-confirming information when combining such information. One problem with this account is that, as I discussed in chapter 3, there is a good deal of debate about the relative recallability of schema- or expectancy-consistent or inconsistent information. In addition, such an account would seem to apply primarily to existing knowledge, such as associatively-based illusory correlation, rather than to distinctive or salient input, although Hamilton (1981) suggested that distinctively based illusory correlation may also serve as the basis for schemas or stereotypes.

Wason's Selection Task and the Role of Pragmatic Reasoning Schemas

Another challenging reasoning task introduced by Wason (1966) is the *selection problem*. In this classic task, which Evans, Newstead, and Byrne (1993) described as "the most intensively researched single problem in the history of the psychology of reasoning" (p. 99), participants were given the four cards illustrated in Fig. 9.2, along with a conditional rule: "If there's an A on one side of the card, then there must be a 3 on the other side." The task was to indicate what cards must be turned over in order to test out whether the rule is correct or not—hence the term "selection" (as opposed to passive reception—see Bruner et al., 1956). The logical solution to the problem is to turn over the A and the 7 in order to test out the rule, because a falsifying result on the other side of either (i.e, a non-3 on the other side of the A, or an A on the other side of the 7) would serve to disconfirm the rule. In actual fact, participants typically chose to turn over only the A, or to turn over both the A and the 3, both of which amount to confirmation strategies (and both of which are fallacious).

The selection task is of interest for a number of reasons. First, it suggests that participants have difficulties with deductive, conditional reasoning, as well as with inductive reasoning tasks, although this is certainly not a great revelation in and of itself (see Evans, 1983, 1984; Wason & Johnson-Laird, 1972). More important, there are some obvious similarities between the findings for this task and some of the observations made on the rule discovery task (see Evans, 1982; Wason & Johnson-Laird, 1972; see also Gorman, 1995, for an explicit comparison between the two tasks). Specifically, participants clearly show what may be construed as a confirmation bias (i.e., seeking out confirming or positive instances to test). They also show great confidence in their answers, although they are quick to recognize the value of falsification when it is pointed out to them.

A number of different explanations have been offered of the types of errors made on this selection task. The original account proposed by Wason (1966), in keeping with his account of the rule discovery task, was in terms of a verification bias. That is, participants seemed to seek out information that confirmed their original hypothesis of A *and* 3. However, other commentators (e.g., Evans, 1989; Klayman & Ha, 1987) found fault with such an account; Wason himself (e.g., Wason & Evans, 1975) has given up on such an explanation, on the selection task at least. Evans (e.g., 1989), in particular, argued that the problem encountered by participants is not a focus on confirming a rule, but rather a difficulty in dealing with negative tests or negative information (e.g., not 3) in reasoning tasks in general, a difficulty that Evans (1972) referred to as the *matching bias.* In support of this latter view, Evans and Lynch (1973) presented the selection task with either a positive or negative item in either the antecedent (e.g., "If there's *not* an A on the

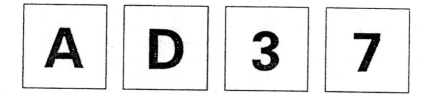

The subject is then told that "the following rule applies to these four cards and may be true or false"

**If there is an A on one side of the card,
then there is a 3 on the other side of the card**

The subject is then asked to decide which of the four cards would need to be turned over in order to decide whether the rule is true or false.

FIG. 9.2. The cards used in Wason's selection task. From *Human Reasoning: The Psychology of Deduction,* (p. 100) by J. St. B. T. Evans, S. E. Newstead, & R. M. J. Byrne, (Eds.), 1993, Hillsdale, NJ: Lawrence Erlbaum Associates. Copyright © 1993 by Lawrence Erlbaum Associates. Reprinted with permission.

front ...") or the consequent (e.g., "... then there is *not* a 4 on the other side"). These investigators found that participants tended to choose the positive instances, thus supporting the matching bias over a verification bias account; in fact, the study actually found some evidence for falsification rather than verification.

   Content Effects in the Selection Task.   One of the most interesting results from D selection task—and the one that is most relevant to the concerns of this book—is the observation that specific types of content can facilitate or inhibit performance on that task (see Evans, 1989; Evans et al., 1993; Griggs, 1983). This effect was first observed by Wason and Shapiro (1971), who replaced the A and 3 with "Manchester" and "car," so that the rule became "Every time I go to Manchester I travel by car." In this case, many participants chose to test out "Manchester" and "train," rather than "Manchester" and "car," although it has been difficult to replicate these results (e.g., Griggs & Cox, 1982; Manktelow & Evans, 1979; Yachinin & Tweney, 1982). Another, more powerful variation on this effect came in a study by Johnson-Laird, Legrenzi, and Legrenzi (1972), where the rule was "If the letter is sealed then it has a 50 lire stamp on it," referring to an actual rule then in effect in the British postal system (even though the rule was stated in terms of Italian currency). In this particular case, Manktelow and Evans (1979) attributed these results to participants simply drawing on previous knowledge—what Griggs and Cox (1982) called *memory cuing* or what Pollard (1982) referred to as an *availability account* (à la Tversky & Kahneman, 1973)—rather than an actual reasoning effect. In fact, Manktelow and Evans (1979) and Yachinin and Tweney (1982) reported failures to replicate this finding with American participants. In addition, Golding (1981) later found that the facilitating effect held only for *older* British participants who presumably had experience with the (then defunct) postal rule.

   A more reliable effect of content on selection test performance has been reported by Griggs and Cox (1982). These investigators used a rule that was presumed to be familiar to their Florida participants, to wit, "If a person is drinking beer then that person must be over 19 years of age." This rule has been found to facilitate performance on the selection task, although Griggs and Cox attributed such effects to sheer knowledge effects (i.e., of the drinking rule) on performance rather than to any effects of reasoning per se. At the same time, however, these investigators were willing to acknowledge that such knowledge factors may have their effects via analogy—for instance, facilitation in performance with a novel rule (i.e., "If a person is wearing blue then that person must be over 19 years of age" [Cox & Griggs, 1982]) is found if that rule comes after the drinking age rule. Perhaps more important, participants' performance is also facilitated on a problem or rule with which they have no *direct* experience, e.g., "If the purchase exceeds $30 then the receipt must be approved by the departmental manager" (D'Andrade, cited in Griggs, 1983; see also Dominowski, 1990,

1995), because these participants can bring some analogous experience to bear (see my discussion of the role of analogy in transfer in chap. 7). This result is of importance in that it suggests that one may use more than just direct experience or simple, specific memory structures in solving the selection problem.[4]

The notion that thematic content can have an impact on cognition is certainly not a new idea. For example, Bruner et al. (1956) showed that couching traditional concept formation tasks in terms of real-world, thematic content had a significant effect on participants' hypothesis-testing strategies. Similarly, there is a long history (see Evans, 1982, 1989) on the effects of concrete content on syllogistic reasoning, or the *belief bias* effect. What is perhaps more apparent in the case of the selection problem, though, is that specific types of real-world content may serve to *facilitate* performance and *reduce* errors, whereas others may not.

Dominowski (1995) recently reviewed some of the specific factors that may account for the facilitating effects of thematic content. These factors include the use of more concrete terms, the use of instructions to "check for violations" (of a normative rule) rather than instructions to determine truth or falsity, the use of a familiar scenario (e.g., the drinking age scenario), and the use of a plausible rationale or a personally relevant rule. Dominowski concluded that all four of these factors make a difference.

The Concept of Pragmatic Reasoning Schemas. One concept that has been proposed to account for these content effects (and for why some work and other do not) is the notion by Cheng and Holyoak (1985) of a *pragmatic reasoning schema*. Pragmatic reasoning schemas are intended as a compromise between models of abstract, logical, syntactic (i.e., contentless) rules on the one hand, and content-specific rules or knowledge on the other (see my discussion of domain-specificity in chap. 7). As the term "schema" suggests, pragmatic reasoning schemas refer to abstract *knowledge* structures that also serve as *reasoning* structures—and hence entail procedural as well as declarative knowledge. Such schemas are assumed to be "induced from everyday experiences" (p. 395) with, for example, obligations and permissions. These schemas are pragmatic in the sense that they specify what rules are useful, as well as which are valid (Cheng & Holyoak, 1985). They also extend beyond mere logical rules because they apply to such contents as causality rather than to mere logical rules such as the conditional. Most important, differences between schemas account for the differential effects of specific contents on logical reasoning.

Specifically, Cheng and Holyoak (1985) claimed that the situations that show successful facilitation are ones entailing a *permission schema* (as op-

---

[4]This debate over whether specific contents or knowledge versus more abstract reasoning structures are used is reminiscent of the distinction discussed in chapter 4 between case-based and more abstract forms of memory structures like MOPs and TOPs.

posed to other possibilities such as causal or covariation schemas). A permission schema entails the following four rules:

1. "If the action [e.g., drinking beer] is to be taken, then the precondition [e.g., being over nineteen] must be satisfied"
2. "If the action is not to be taken, then the precondition need not be satisfied"
3. "If the precondition is satisfied, then the action may be taken"
4. "If the precondition is not satisfied, then the action must not be taken." (Cheng & Holyoak, 1985, p. 397)

The relevance of this permission schema (which is called that because it deals with situations involving gaining permission), and of pragmatic reasoning schemas in general, is that by virtue of the pragmatic rules involved, certain logical inferences are "made available" and others are blocked. Thus, in the case of the permission schema, Rules 1 and 4, by virtue of their "must" and "must not" components, make available the logical modus ponens (Rule 1) and contrapositive (Rule 4), whereas Rules 2 and 3, with their nonimperative "need not" and "may," block the denying-the-antecedent (Rule 2) and affirming-the-consequent (Rule 3) errors. The same does not hold for other reasoning schemas, such as covariation or causation. For example, Cheng and Holyoak cited an example from Reich and Ruth (1982) using the causal schema "if the fruit is yellow, then it is ripe," which stresses affirming the consequent, or inferring that the fruit is yellow from the fact that it is ripe.

Cheng and Holyoak (1985) tested out this notion of a permission schema in a series of experiments. The first of these presented two different versions of the permission schema—a postal version such as the one presented earlier, and a permission-to-enter-the-country version (i.e., "If a passenger's form says 'Entering' on one side, then the other side must include 'cholera'"; Cheng & Holyoak, 1985, p. 399)—to two different groups of participants, one from Ann Arbor and the other from Hong Kong. The latter group was included because they actually had experience with the postal rule; neither group had experience with the entering-the-country rule. These two different scenarios were presented with or without a rationale. For example, a rationale for the entering-the-country version was that one side indicated whether the bearer was entering the country or was in transit, whereas the other side indicated what diseases the person has been inoculated for (i.e., either cholera, typhoid, and hepatitis or just typhoid and hepatitis). Thus, the person must have been inoculated if he or she was to enter the country.

The hypotheses in this study were that having a rationale would facilitate performance on both problems for both groups. On the other hand, in the no-rationale condition the prediction was that the Hong Kong students would do better on the postal problem (because of their experience with this scenario) than would the Ann Arbor students, but this would not hold for the entering-the-country one. In other words, the permission schema is context-sensitive. Both of these hypotheses were confirmed by Cheng and Holyoak.

In a second experiment Cheng and Holyoak (1985) presented participants with both an abstract permission schema (i.e., asking them to play the role of an authority checking to see if certain regulations of the "if p then q" form were being followed) and a concrete arbitrary rule (i.e., the original Wason problem). In this study Cheng and Holyoak (1985; see also Cheng & Holyoak, 1989) found better performance on the permission schema than on the arbitrary rule problem, suggesting that people really do have a permission schema apart from any specific knowledge or content and from general logical rules.

Pragmatic reasoning schemas and permission rules are clearly relevant to the study of everyday cognition in that they take reasoning out of the realm of the abstract and contentless (as well as the con*text*less), and place it back in the domain of *practical* reasoning (see chap. 8) and *practical,* voluntary action (see Holyoak & Cheng, 1995). It also places such reasoning back in the *social* realm, with its emphasis on social, normative rules, morality, and even legal perspectives (Holyoak & Cheng, 1995; see Cosmides, 1989, for a more recent emphasis on social contracts).

Although the permission schema has been the most prominent model for content effects in selection problems,[5] there have also been several criticisms of this concept. Jackson and Griggs (1990), for example, argued that there are two factors that can account for Cheng and Holyoak's results without having to invoke the permission schema. The first of these is that Cheng and Holyoak's presentation of the permission schema, unlike the original Wason selection task, involves two explicit negatives in the antecedent and consequent; this feature in itself can account, at least in part, for Cheng and Holyoak's findings. In fact, Jackson and Griggs showed that including explicit negatives in the original selection task improved performance. Second, the permission schema works best when instructions to look out for violations are included (as in the Griggs and Cox [1982] drinking age problem, where the context of a policeman checking for violations was included), rather than instructions to determine whether the rule was true or false. Pollard and Evans (1987; see also Jackson & Griggs, 1990) reported that when these violation instructions were left out, facilitation by the permission schema was no longer found.

---

[5]In recent years another related model has emerged as a competitor to the pragmatic reasoning schema notion. Specifically, Cosmides (1989) has proposed an evolutionarily based "social contract" account of the selection task results, along with a "cheater detection algorithm." Cosmides (1989) and Gigerenzer and Hug (1992) presented evidence that supports this alternative account. (See also Gigerenzer & Hug [1992], Manktelow & Over [1991], and Politzer & Nguyen-Xuan [1992] for discussions of the role of perspective-taking in the social contract situation.)

Another related argument by Manktelow and Over (1990, 1995) is that the abstract selection and the permission problems involve two different logical rules: (a) the indicative conditional and (b) a *deontic* conditional, or an emphasis on imperatives (must) and permission (may) or "practical" human action. Griggs and Cox (1993; see also Griggs, 1995) reached the same conclusion after finding that factors that affect performance on permission schema problems (e.g., the violation instructions) do not have any effect on the abstract selection problem. In addition, Manktelow and Over (1991) showed that not all permission problems lead to a logical conclusion, as defined by the indicative conditional. These arguments raise the more general question of whether everyday content simply adds or subtracts something from existing rules and strategies of reasoning, or, in fact, fundamentally *changes* these rules and strategies. For example, Dominowski and Dallob (1991) presented evidence that the abstract and thematic versions tap the same basic reasoning processes. Alternatively, Evans and Over (1996) argued that the use of thematic or familiar material enables participants to consider hypotheses that *combine* different values on cards (see Bruner et al., 1956, for a similar argument in the area of concept formation). This is an issue I return to in the next chapter.

THE RATIONALITY DEBATE

The Varied Meanings of "Rationality"

One problem with the research on heuristics and biases that I have reviewed is the difficulty in establishing an agreed-upon definition of the term *bias* or, by implication, of *rationality*. If a particular judgment is to be labeled as an error or irrational, then some standard of truth or rationality must be assumed. The most typical position in the literature has been to compare a judgment with some normative standard such as probability theory in general, or Bayes's theorem in particular. In the case of Wason's research on the selection task, the standard has been the rules of propositional logic, whereas for his rule discovery task, it has been Popper's falsificationist logic.

A number of problems with this normative approach have been raised. For one thing, there is more than one conception of probability (e.g., the distinction between relative frequency and single event probability; Gigerenzer, 1991; Gigerenzer & Murray, 1987; though see Shafer & Tversky, 1985). L. J. Cohen (1981) also pointed out that models of logic and probability are constantly changing; in fact, probability theory only emerged with the formulations of Bernoulli and Bayes in the 17th and 18th centuries. In general, Gigerenzer (1991) argued that because there is often more than one correct answer to a given statistical problem, it is misleading to view a deviation from some particular norm as something to be explained. There are also different models of logic (e.g., Manktelow & Over's [1990, 1992] distinction between propositional and deontic logic, and the various conceptions of propositional logic).[6] The general point here is that it is difficult to make a clear-cut determination of what is and is not an error or how reasoning or judgment does or does not deviate from rationality if one does not have a clear, consensual conception of these terms.[7]

These distinctions between different models of probability and logic have resulted in specific criticisms of research on so-called biases. For example, Gigerenzer (1991) argued that one of the problems with Tversky and Kahneman's research is that it has often posed the problems in terms of the probability for single persons or events (e.g., the probability of Tom W. being a computer science major), whereas most peoples' conception of probability has to do with the frequency of multiple objects or events. Similarly, as I have discussed, Manktelow and Over (1990, 1992) argued that Cheng and Holyoak's (1985) research on the permission schema cannot be compared with research on the abstract selection task in that the former involves deontic logic, or an emphasis on "may" statements (or permission), "must" statements (obligation), or both, and with violation of norms, rather than a concern with truth or logic.

Perhaps a more significant objection to the research on bias is that overreliance on a formalist or logical conception of rationality ignores another equally important alternative: namely, *adaptive rationality* (J. R. Anderson, 1990), or the ability to get along in the (real) world (or what Gigerenzer & Todd, 1999, have labeled *ecological rationality*). Although a number of commentators have made this same distinction (e.g., Anderson, 1993; Oaksford & Chater, 1994), perhaps the clearest and most detailed account is that offered by Evans (1993; Evans & Over, 1996). Evans and Over distinguished between two senses of rationality: a rationality according to some formalist or *impersonal* criterion (Evans & Over, 1996)—what Evans has referred to as rationality$_2$—versus rationality according to a *personal* criterion (Evans & Over, 1996), or rationality$_1$. Evans defined this latter form of rationality in two slightly different ways: (a) as an argument that "people reason in such a way as to achieve intelligent (i.e., goal-seeking) actions, within the constraints of their cognitive capacity" (Evans, 1993, p. 15) or (b) as "acting in a way that is generally reliable and efficient for achieving one's

---

[6]Kahneman and Tversky's biases have sometimes been referred to as *cognitive* illusions (Edwards & von Winterfeldt, 1986; Kahneman & Tversky, 1982b, 1996), suggesting that such cognitive errors are analogous to *perceptual* illusions). Funder (1987) and Lopes (1991) both commented on the misleading connotations of that term. However, although this term fits in with the discussion of *memory* illusions in chapter 4, such a term has not been widely used by Kahneman and Tversky themselves, who have not implied a strictly empirical criterion of truth.

[7]The cultural psychologist Richard Shweder (1990) voiced another criticism of the normative model of, for example, decision making: that such rational models remove decision making from one's everyday participation in the world, where factors such as intentions, attitudes, and interpretations also play a role in influencing one's decisions (see chap. 1).

goals" (Evans & Over, 1996, p. 8). Both of these descriptions emphasize the suitability of reasoning for planning actions to accomplish goals. The first, however, underlines individuals' restricted cognitive abilities (cf. Simon's [1969] concept of "bounded rationality"), whereas the latter implicates the "reliability" and "efficiency" of individuals' judgments.

This distinction between rationality$_1$ and rationality$_2$ is of importance because, first of all, it suggests that there is another sense of rationality apart from the formalist conception. More important, it accounts for a kind of paradox in the everyday cognition literature. Specifically, in chapter 8 I discussed how in the area of practical intelligence, the emphasis was on the *wisdom* or practicality of everyday reasoning, whereas the emphasis in the everyday *judgment* literature is on bias and errors. One explanation of this apparent paradox is that researchers in the former area have emphasized rationality$_1$, whereas researchers in human judgment have, for the most part, focused on rationality$_2$. Evans and Over (1996) themselves coined the term *rationality paradox* to refer to the broader contrast between the superior intelligence of humans over other species, and the picture of irrationality derived from laboratory studies. In general, Evans and Over argued that "the notion of rationality$_1$ is embedded in the concept that people have evolved in an adaptive manner that allows them to achieve real-world goals, not to solve laboratory problems" (p. 61) (These authors have pointed out the similarity of this distinction between rationality$_1$ and rationality$_1$, to the distinction made in chap. 8 between theoretical and practical thinking.)

A quick reflection on Evans' definitions suggests that it is possible to meet the criterion of rationality$_1$ without qualifying for rationality$_2$; and, in fact, individuals often do so. As Evans and Over (1996) put it, "we do not naturally reason in order to be logical, but generally are logical (to the extent that we are) in order to achieve our goals" (p. 16). Clearly, very different views of the quality of human thought result from adopting these two different conceptions. It is clearly easier to *define* and demonstrate a deviation from a formal model of reasoning than it is to show rationality$_1$; but at the same time, it is not completely clear why it is significant to demonstrate that people in general often ignore the tenets of Bayes's theorem or the rules of logic. That is, it may be of interest to show that people who are *trained* in formal disciplines such as logic or probability theory continue to make fundamental errors in logical deduction or in ignoring base rates in everyday problems; and Kahneman and Tversky have sometimes included psychologists, statisticians, and mathematical psychologists in their research (e.g., Kahneman & Tversky, 1972; Tversky & Kahneman, 1971; 1982; though see the evidence by Fong, Krantz, & Nisbett, 1986, to be examined in chap. 10). However, if the average person does not operate according to the rules of probability or deductive logic because he or she has not been *taught* these rules, then such a demonstration seems fairly trivial (although it *does* provide for some striking demonstrations of apparent "irrationality$_2$").

One possible argument here, of course, is that people may possess a kind of "natural logic" (e.g., Braine, 1978; Braine & O'Brien, 1998; Rips, 1983, 1994; see also Cosmides, 1989, for a generally similar point of view) that does not require training. On the other hand, Kahneman and Tversky (1982b) made the intriguing argument that one encounters many examples of probability theory in everyday life (e.g., base rates, sample size), but these examples come in a form that cannot be readily encoded, or that such encoding is inaccessible when it comes to making judgments. (This certainly holds for the kind of judgments required in lab studies of inductive reasoning.) Such an argument is certainly plausible and would seem to be a natural topic for researchers on everyday cognition to investigate further.

Evans and Over (1996) *have* approached the results of research on both the base-rate fallacy and the confirmation bias in terms of their distinction between rationality$_1$ and rationality$_2$, and also through a general concept of *relevance*. For example, regarding the latter concept, Bar-Hillel (1980) argued that participants in base-rate studies often may not find such base rate information relevant. Furthermore, as I have discussed, when *causally* relevant information is provided (e.g., Ajzen, 1977), participants' estimates more closely approximate Bayesian rules. Similarly, Evans and Over (1996; see also Klayman & Ha, 1987) argued that people adopt positive test strategies because, for a variety of reasons, these usually work in real-world settings, and thus serve rationality$_1$.

The Optimists Versus the Pessimists

In his chapter on the question of rationality, Jungermann (1983) distinguished between two "camps" on the issue of biases and errors: namely, the so-called *optimists* and the *pessimists*. The pessimists, including Kahneman and Tversky as well as Nisbett and Ross (1980) argued for the limitations of human reasoning and for the impact of biases on judgment and decision making. The optimists, on the other hand, emphasized the underlying rationality and capabilities of human thought, and argued that the finding of pervasive influences of heuristics is an artifact of the experimental situation.

The three different versions of this optimist camp reviewed by Jungermann are the *meta-rationality* argument (Beach & Mitchell, 1987; Jungermann, 1983), the *continuity* argument (Hogarth, 1981), and what Jungermann has called the *structure* argument (Berkeley & Humphreys, 1982; L. D. Phillips, 1983). The meta-rationality position claims that what may seem to be irrational on the face of it is actually *rational* or at least adaptive when factors such as effort and time pressures are taken into account (cf. Evans' concept of rationality$_1$). Thus, for example, there are occasions on which time pressures may make it maladaptive or even impossible to go through all the steps of systematic decision making, such as making on-the-spot decisions (such as the decisions of firefighters or other examples of naturalistic decision making to be reviewed in a later section). In Jungermann's (1983) example, it is unlikely that a person will systematically search through all the books displayed at a store in looking for a book to read on a long trip. Similarly, there may be situations in which the individual is reluctant to put in the mental effort to reach the optimal decision. (Recall that one of the original justifications for the concept of heuristics is that they provide shortcuts to reduce mental effort.) Thus, decision making in its broader context involves a cost–benefit analysis in which a number of factors are considered in addition to specific decision-making strategies.

The continuity position argues that the apparent irrationalities and biases found in lab research are due to the fact that this research has looked at discrete, isolated judgments, rather than viewing decision-making as a continuous, ongoing process in a changing environment. Thus, according to Hogarth (1981), lab research fails to take into consideration things such as feedback from the environment, the existence of redundant information in the real world, and the important relationship between decisions and action. An example in the area of heuristics is the case of the anchoring and adjustment heuristic where insufficient adjustments make sense if the person believes that he or she will be able to make additional corrections or adjustments later.

Finally, the so-called structure position maintains that research on heuristics and biases has failed to consider the participant's cognitive representation of the problem. Thus, for example, I mentioned that Dulany and Hilton (1991) reported that participants seemed to interpret conjunction problems differently from the way assumed by Kahneman and Tversky, and hence their decisions were not really irrational, "given the layperson's assumptions and interpretations of the judgment task" (p. 108; see a similar point by M. S. Cohen, 1993). Dulany and Hilton also made the important point that judgments of rationality or fallacy should be made on the basis of whether participants' conclusions follow from their own premises, "rather than in a departure from someone else's interpretation of the conclusions or premises" (p. 88). Once again, a similar argument has been made by L. J. Cohen (1981).

CRITICISMS OF RESEARCH ON HEURISTICS AND BIASES

There have been a variety of other methodological issues raised by commentators on heuristics research. For example, a number of psychologists have commented on the careful selection and construction of problems in the Kahneman and Tversky research (and as I have discussed, in the Wason rule discovery task as well). Lopes (1991), for instance, has pointed out that the materials in several of Kahneman and Tversky's problems were deliberately chosen so as to set up a competitive test between the heuristics approach and a more "rational" probability theory position. For example, a problem in which participants were to guess whether Rs occur more frequently in the first or third position of words, R was chosen because it was one of the eight (out of 20) consonants that showed greater frequency in the third position. Along similar lines, M. S. Cohen (1993) suggested that the tasks used in the Kahneman and Tversky studies are "systematically nonrepresentative of domains in which heuristics and normative methods generally give the same answer" (p. 53). Finally, W. Edwards (1983) listed a number of different dimensions on which tasks of reasoning and judgment may vary (e.g., degree of realism, amount of time pressure, degree of importance of the task, the availability of tools) and pointed out that only a small percentage of these qualities have, in fact, been sampled in research on judgment biases.

Certainly one of the main issues in the selection of problems is the degree to which these problems are representative of real-world judgments. On the face of it, a number of the problems posed by Kahneman and Tversky seem to deal with realistic content and judgments; in fact, this everyday content is one of the most appealing features of the heuristics research. However, even these problems were chosen to make a point rather than as a representative sample. Furthermore, these problems are presented in compacted, decontextualized form rather than in the full context of a naturalistic environment. As M. S. Cohen (1993) observed, "biases should be exacerbated in a spare laboratory environment (where each cue is essential ...)" (p. 56). Oaksford and Chater (1993) have expressed the same point as follows, it is "likely that people 'scale' down their everyday strategies to deal with laboratory tasks, and this is the source of the systematic biases observed in human reasoning" (p. 55). Similarly, Cohen suggested a number of ways in which laboratory research on heuristics differs from research on everyday cognition. For instance, "'decisions' are typically ... made in information rich environments, for example, they are stretched out in time, with redundant cues, incremental stages of commitment, feedback from earlier actions, and shared responsibility" (p. 55). Needless to say, some of these points are ones raised earlier by Beach and Mitchell (1978) and Hogarth (1981), as well as in my general discussion of the study of everyday cognition in chapter 1. In addition, using real-world materials allows individuals to use their own domain-specific knowledge, which is different from the domain-independent knowledge of probability theory assessed by Kahneman and Tversky.

It is obvious that the original tasks used by Wason and his associates in the rule discovery and selection paradigms were also of questionable ecological validity. Not only were the materials in the original rule discovery task decontextualized and remote from participants' everyday experience, but the relationship between the experimenter's rule and the universe of instances in this problem was only one of several possibilities (see Klayman & Ha, 1987), and one that was most likely to elicit the kinds of responses observed by Wason. And of course, I have pointed out the major effects of problem content on results in the selection problem.

Another related criticism is that Kahneman and Tversky (and those who have been influenced by them), as well as Wason, have overemphasized the role of biases and irrationality in human judgment and reasoning; and in the process, these investigators have constructed problems that highlight the role of such bias. On the first point, Evans (1995) stressed how Wason was "fascinated" with irrationality. Similarly, Lopes (1991) noted how the tone of the classic Tversky and Kahneman (1974) article became increasingly negative and changed from an emphasis on heuristic processing to an emphasis on bias and error. Christensen-Szalanski and Beach (1982) also documented a citation bias according to which articles reporting poor performance, although comparable in number to those citing good performance, were nevertheless cited over 6 times as frequently as their more positive counterparts. At the very least, the original research on heuristics and biases by Kahneman and Tversky (and, to a lesser degree, the research by Wason) has engendered what Lopes (1991) described as a "rhetoric of irrationality," reflected particularly in the social psychological literature (e.g., Gilovich, 1991; Ross, 1977) to be discussed later in this chapter.

One of the results of this overemphasis on biases is that most researchers have failed to focus on the cognitive processes underlying these biases (see Gigerenzer & Murray, 1987, and Wallsten, 1980, on this issue). Recall that one of the noteworthy features of Tversky and Kahneman's research is that it has focused on the judgmental processes (i.e., the heuristics) underlying these biases, rather than simply looking at the accuracy of statistical intuitions. At the same time, Tversky and Kahneman's account does not amount to a completely coherent or thoroughgoing *cognitive* account of these judgmental heuristics (though see Tversky, 1977). For example, Gigerenzer and Murray (1987) pointed out that by presenting problems with preset probabilities, Tversky and Kahneman failed to consider the all-important processes by which participants seek out and evaluate information for themselves. In addition, if one looks closely at the different heuristics, it is apparent that the three (or four) identified are really very different animals (even though they often have overlapping effects—see Sherman & Corty, 1984). The representativeness heuristic, for instance, involves some kind of similarity judgment based on an active, rule-based mental calculation. Availability, on the other hand, involves, for the most part, a kind of passive "bringing" or "coming to mind" of an exemplar, requiring no mental calculation other than the implicit assumption that availability implies frequency. (In their original article on availability, Tversky & Kahneman [1973] also included the ease of mental *construction* as a factor in availability judgments, but this part subsequently evolved into the separate simulation heuristic.) On a slightly different level, Sherman and Corty (1984) suggested that the representativeness and availability heuristics involve a prototype versus an exemplar matching procedure, respectively (see chap. 3). Finally, the anchoring and adjustment "heuristic" does not seem to clearly qualify as a *heuristic* at all.

Shortly before Amos Tversky's death, Kahneman and Tversky (1996) authored a final reply to at least one of their critics. In response to some of Gigerenzer's (1991, 1993; Gigerenzer, Hell, Blank, 1988; Gigerenzer, Hoffrage, & Kleinbolting, 1991; Gigerenzer & Murray, 1987) objections, Kahneman and Tversky argued once again that their major intent all along was to study the cognitive processes involved in judgments, that the concern with error and bias evolved simply out of the observation that so many judgments involved such error. Furthermore, contrary to Gigerenzer's characterization of their research, Kahneman and Tversky pointed out that in probably their most widely cited reference (i.e., Tversky & Kahneman, 1974), only 2 of the 12 biases they reviewed involved subjective probability estimates of unique (rather than repeated) events, so Gigerenzer's criticism that Kahneman and Tversky ignore the frequentists and are "narrowly Bayesian" is wrong. In addition, these authors argued (and I think I agree), contrary to Gigerenzer, that most people have no problem with the idea of predicting the probability of single events.

In general, Kahneman and Tversky emphasized that many of the criticisms raised by Gigerenzer were answered in other studies of their own and others that Gigerenzer failed to mention. For instance, Gigerenzer (1991) argued that there would be less neglect of the base rates if participants were informed that, for example, Tom W., in the example of the engineer given early in this chapter, was presented as randomly sampled from the population. Kahneman and Tversky argued that, in point of fact, they did present that condition in the same article (Kahneman & Tversky, 1993). Similarly, in the study of the conjunction error, Kahneman and Tversky accused Gigerenzer of *normative agnosticism,* in that he claims that it is meaningless to speak of an "error" when referring to probabilities of single events, whereas they (Kahneman & Tversky) believe that it is clearly an error, in a sense understandable "in everyday discourse," to believe that an event dominated by another can be more likely than the dominating event, as in the Linda-as-feminist-bankteller example cited earlier. Again, in response to Gigerenzer's criticism that the conjunction error applies only when estimates of the probability of a single event are used. Kahneman and Tversky pointed out that one of their earliest demonstrations of the availability heuristic (i.e., asking participants at one point to estimate the number of seven-letter words ending in "ing" and then a later judgment of words with "n" in the sixth position) is, in fact, an example of the conjunction error using frequencies.

Now Kahneman and Tversky are certainly justified in some of these criticisms. At the same time, however, there is still a central problem remaining in their discussion of heuristics, as Gigerenzer (1996) suggested in his reply. These two important innovators still do not, in my opinion, provide a clear account of the cognitive processes or structures involved in the various heuristics, an account that Kahneman and Tversky insisted was their main goal. For example, is representativeness just a simple matter of pattern matching? Certainly, it doesn't occur automatically; but does it involve a conscious calculation of similarity? (See Medin, 1989; Murphy & Medin, 1985, for arguments against similarity judgments in accounting for categorization.) Does judging representativeness of an exemplar to a category involve the same calculations as judging the degree to which an effect is representative of a causal process? Does it occur as a part of a natural process of pattern recognition, or is it based on some cultural norm to look for similarities? What are the mechanisms behind the availability heuristic? Does generating an image involve the same processes as simply reacting to what "comes to mind"? (Recall my earlier discussion of mental construction.) How do availability and representativeness relate to Schank's (1982a) notion of "remindings" and research on analogical reasoning discussed in chapter 4? How does the anchoring and adjustment heuristic relate to primacy effects in general, and does the "nonconscious" anchoring effect work in the same way as the deliberate or instructed one? Finally, how do the several factors that reduce different biases have their effect? (Again, see Gigerenzer, 1996, for a similar point.)

It seems to me that Kahneman and Tversky's approach is more of a descriptive approach than a cognitive one. Furthermore, as Gigerenzer (1996; Gigerenzer & Todd, 1999) argued, and as I have suggested earlier, Tversky and Kahneman's description of the heuristics is overly vague. (On this issue, Kahneman & Tversky, 1996, made the peculiar argument that "representativeness [like similarity] can be assessed experimentally; hence it does not need to be defined a priori" [p. 585]). This view sounds suspiciously similar to the long-rejected concept of operationism (Bridgman, 1928), that is, that a concept can be defined in terms of a set of experimental operations (or a set of measures). In point of fact, however, representativeness as a theoretical description of a cognitive process or set of standards is *not* sufficiently "defined" in terms of a single judgment that correlates with probability judgments, and it is not clearly enough defined by Kahneman and Tversky on a conceptual level.

In the case of the research by Wason and his associates, there have been several different cognitive models proposed for the selection problem (see Evans, 1989, and Evans et al., 1993, for reviews), although the most prominent of these (i.e., the pragmatic-reasoning schema model) was motivated primarily by research on content effects. When it comes to the rule discovery problem, on the other hand, there have been relatively few cognitive models (though see Fischhoff & Beyth-Marom, 1983, and Klayman & Ha, 1987), at least in part because of the emphasis in this area on correct versus erroneous responses.

Other commentators have criticized the Kahneman and Tversky research on methodological grounds. For example, Kahneman and Tversky themselves (1982b) suggested the role of *conversational postulates* (Grice, 1975) and suggestibility in general in the heuristics paradigm. Specifically, two of Grice's maxims of conversation are that the speaker will only say things that are relevant (*maxim of relation*) and will only include as much information as is necessary (*maxim of quantity*). In the context of the heuristics research, these maxims suggest that when the experimenter provides information such as a personality profile or some sort of anchor, the participant may assume that this information is relevant to the problem at hand and is to be taken seriously. Thus, for example, Schwarz (1996) argued that participants in the initial research on the representativeness heuristic may have been led to believe that they were to depend more on the individuating information about the person (i.e., the description given by psychological experts) than on base rates. Consistent with this view, Schwarz, Strack, Hilton, and Naderer (1991) demonstrated that the base-rate fallacy was greatly reduced when the personality judgments were presented as randomly selected by computer or as selected by statisticians. Similarly, Schwartz et al. showed that varying the order of the base rate and the individuating information influences the degree to which participants pay attention to or ignore base-rate information. One implication of these arguments is that information that would not otherwise be considered may, under these conditions, be given undue weight.[8]

OTHER BIASES IN SOCIAL REASONING

In addition to the research discussed thus far, there is also a related set of *social* biases that have been studied by social psychologists. In this section I review some of these biases and see how they are similar to and different from the heuristics and biases developed in the first section.

The Correspondence Bias or the Fundamental Attribution Error

The Nature of and Research on the Bias. One of the most widely researched phenomena, and, as described by Jones (1990), "a candidate for

---

[8]Donovan and Epstein (1997; see also Epstein, Donovan, & Denes-Raj, 1999; Epstein & Pacini, 1999) recently presented evidence that they believe argues against a conversational maxims account, and that argues instead for a dual representational system in which the "experiential–intuitive" mode often is "more compelling" than the "rational-analytic" one (Donovan & Epstein, 1997, p. 1).

the most robust and repeatable finding in social psychology" (p. 138) is the so-called *fundamental attribution error* (FAE; Ross, 1977), or *correspondence bias* (Jones, 1990), or *overattribution effect* (Jones, 1979). Jones (1990) defined the correspondence bias as "the tendency to see behavior as caused by a stable disposition when it can be just as easily explained as a natural response to more than adequate situational pressures" (p. 138). Thus, for example, if you meet another individual for the first time who is acting within the constraints of a given role (e.g., teacher, physician, psychotherapist) you are likely to underestimate the influence of that role on the individual's behavior (e.g., you may overestimate the intelligence or competence of the teacher or physician in many different areas of his or her life). Alternatively, if a given individual expresses an attitude under conditions that make it likely that such an attitude is not his or her own (e.g., a politician expressing a politically expedient view or a teacher explicitly playing the role of devil's advocate), observers are likely to give too little weight to those situational factors and assume that these viewpoints are actually the actor's.

It is probably not surprising that the lay observer places greater emphasis on dispositions than on situational factors. After all, for a variety of reasons (to be discussed later), people generally play a more apparent role in one's life than do situations; and the predictability or consistency of the people in one's life is a major part of his or her implicit theory of the world (at least in some societies—see Shweder & Bourne, 1982). What *is* particularly impressive and perhaps surprising about research on this topic is the *degree* to which participants discount (see Kelley, 1972) or fail to take into account seemingly obvious situational influences on actors' behavior. For example, in their initial study on the attribution of attitudes, Jones and Harris (1967) found that even when participants were explicitly informed that a confederate had been *told* what to write in an essay on a given topic, these participants nevertheless believed that the essay reflected that confederate's true attitudes. Furthermore, Jones (1979) reviewed evidence suggesting how resistant this person bias is to situational explanations. For instance, M. L. Snyder and Jones (1974) demonstrated that the FAE is found (i.e., participants attribute the sentiments expressed in an actor's essay to that actor's attitude) even when they (participants) themselves were asked to write a counterattitudinal essay in the same way as the confederate presumably did, and even when participants knew that the substance of the essay had actually been dictated by someone else (Miller, 1976), though this error is *not* found when participants actually observe the confederate *copying* the essay. In addition, there is evidence that people sometimes infer dispositions from sheer situational factors. For example, Snyder and Frankel (1976) reported that when participants were told that a woman they observed on a silent videotape was being interviewed about sexual topics, these participants inferred greater anxiety from that woman's ambiguous behavior, and this dispositional attribution was then *generalized* to other situations as well.

I should note that the FAE is related to another "bias" or effect described by Jones and Nisbett (1972): namely the *actor–observer* effect. According to these researchers, actors are more likely to appeal to *situations* in explaining their own actions, but are more likely to appeal to others' *dispositions* in explaining *their* actions. Stated differently, when a person is in the role of observer, he or she takes a very different perspective from the one he or she takes as an actor. Thus, if observers are asked to explain why another person is enjoying a party, they are likely to focus on the attributes of that other that may contribute to this enjoyment (e.g., that person is highly sociable or a "party animal"). On the other hand, if these same observers are asked to explain why they themselves are enjoying that party, they are likely to focus on characteristics of the party (e.g., the people present, the atmosphere). In a review of the evidence on this effect, Watson (1982) concluded that *both* actors and observers showed a preference for dispositional explanations, and that actor–observer differences occurred in *situational* attributions but not in dispositional ones.

Another experimental example of the FAE that is similar to the everyday illustration given above is a study by L. Ross, Amabile, and Steinmetz (1977). In this study participants were assigned to the role of either questioner or contestant (or in a second experiment, the role of a third-party observer) in a quiz game format. In this situation, the questioners were to come up with as difficult and esoteric questions as possible and thus to draw on whatever area of expertise they had at their disposal. The premise here was that the contestant was put at a distinct disadvantage based solely on the "luck of the draw," because assignment of roles was made at random; yet that manipulation of roles was lost on the contestants who attributed significantly more ability and knowledge to the questioner than to themselves. The same was true for the neutral, third-party observer, but not for the questioner, who *knew* that this sampling of questions was not necessarily representative of his or her knowledge in general.

The argument here (L. Ross, Amabile, et al., 1977) is that both contestants and observers ignored the "role-conferred advantages" of the questioners, as well as the fact that the situationally specific expertise of the questioners might not generalize to a consistent dispositional advantage. Also, an implicit assumption of this experimental paradigm is that such role-defined inequities resemble those that can be found in other real-world situations (e.g., in teacher–student or doctor–patient relationships), where the individual in the inferior role (and oftentimes the one in the superior role), tends to ignore the obvious disadvantages of the role with which he or she has been provided.

Relation of the FAE to the Judgment Heuristics. The FAE is certainly significant enough in its own right to merit consideration in a book on everyday cognition. However, what makes it *particularly* relevant for my purposes is the fact that this "error" or bias has been explained by its proponents in terms of at least three of the different heuristics reviewed earlier. For example, Nisbett and Ross (1980) proposed that actions are more representative of the actor than of the situation, both conceptually and linguistically. Thus, for instance, most individuals have observed that different people act differently in the same situation, and thus may have concluded that actions are more diagnostic of the person than of the situation. Furthermore, actors and their actions tend to be similarly described—for instance, an honest action is produced by honest actors.

Another account proposed by Nisbett and Ross (1980) is in terms of the availability heuristic. In this case, the actor is assumed to be more *perceptually* available in that he or she is closer to the action and is more salient than is the situation. In fact, in one of the early formulations of attribution theory, Heider (1958) suggested that the actor stands out in our perceptual field against a situational background, or, in other words, that "behavior ... has such salient properties it tends to engulf the total field" (p. 54). A good deal of evidence exists to suggest that various manipulations of perceptual salience (e.g., manipulations of brightness, movement, focus of the observer's attention) produce increases in the causal significance of the actor (see McArthur, 1981, and Taylor & Fiske, 1978, for reviews; see also Gilbert & Malone, 1995, for a critique of this body of evidence).

Probably a more convincing account of the FAE or the correspondence bias is in terms of the anchoring and adjustment heuristic. This explanation (Gilbert & Malone, 1995; Jones, 1990), which actually complements instead of offering a complete alternative to the two accounts just reviewed, proposes that observers start off by making dispositional attributions as the natural starting point or "anchor" for their explanations of behavior. When these observers are asked to make "adjustments" by taking into account possible situational contingencies, they fail to make *sufficient* adjustments, and hence continue to overemphasize dispositional factors. In this connection, Quattrone (1982) showed that it is also possible to make the *situation* the anchor; in this case participants turn out to have a difficult time taking into account *dispositional* explanations of the actor's consistent behavior (although Jones, 1979, pointed out that this situational attribution error is the exception rather than the rule).

More recently, Gilbert (1989; Gilbert, Pelham, & Krull, 1988) argued that the initial stages of the attribution process—that is, *behavior identification* (identifying the behavior as an example of a trait category) and *dispositional inference*[9]—are automatic, whereas the *situational correction* phase is reasoned and "controlled," and hence requires greater cognitive resources. It follows from this distinction (Gilbert et al., 1988) that anything that distracts the observer or makes him or her *cognitively busy* (e.g., trying to

---

[9]See also Hamilton (1988), Newman and Uleman (1993), and Trope and Liberman (1993) for recent discussions of the differences between the simple categorization of behavior in terms of traits versus inferences about the *causal* influence of such traits.

think of something to say in a conversation, or rehearsing word strings while watching the aforementioned anxious woman) will reduce the correction process—as it, in fact, does (Gilbert et al., 1988)—and hence will exaggerate the correspondence bias. In this connection, Krull (1993) replicated this cognitive busyness effect with initial *situational* rather than dispositional attributions and suggested (contrary to Quattrone, 1982) that this focus on situations is as easily accomplished as the dispositional bias (e.g., by giving observers a situational goal; Krull & Erickson, 1995).

Some Unanswered Questions About the FAE.   As developed thus far, the FAE or correspondence bias is certainly a rather plausible concept and one that has important implications for everyday social interaction. On closer examination, however, a number of questions arise about the concept itself, its theoretical underpinnings, and the research evidence collected in its support.

To begin with, the very fact that investigators disagree about whether the phenomenon is an "error," a "bias," or just an "effect" (see Harvey, Town, & Yarkin, 1981) is noteworthy. For example, Funder (1987) distinguished between an error and a mistake, where an error is defined as "a judgment of an experimental stimulus that departs from a model of the judgment process" (p. 75), or perhaps more generally, a failure of that judgment to conform to some standard arrived at by some scientist or authority (cf. Evans's [1993] discussion of rationality$_2$). In the case of the FAE, that standard involves some conception of reality or judgmental truth imposed by the experimenter in a specific experimental context. As suggested by Funder, such a standard may or may not be applicable in the real world; hence the judgment labeled as an "error" cannot necessarily be considered to be a "mistake." (I would prefer to simply distinguish between an error as defined by an experimenter in the lab and one involving an objective or consensual standard of reality.) In any case, this questioning of the real-world significance of judgmental "errors" is clearly consistent with the discussions throughout this chapter.

As an example, in the Ross et al. (1977) study cited earlier, I might argue that the contestants' inferences represent errors only in the sense that they did not take into account all of the different factors considered by the experimenters (who were themselves at a distinct "role conferred advantage"). Whether such inferences are mistaken or will cause problems in the real world (e.g., placing undue confidence in the general expertise of physicians or teachers) is an open question. Stated differently, the FAE is not an error in the same sense as a perceptual illusion (Funder, 1987) or a logical fallacy is an error—that is, it does not violate any objective or consensual standard of truth or reason. (See my earlier discussion of this point.)

Along these same lines, Gilbert and Malone (1995) proposed three different circumstances or "constraints" under which the FAE may not lead trouble in real-world situations. Specifically, in the first instance, one may constrain onself in the kinds of situations or roles that he or she chooses to be in or to which he or she is drawn. Thus, for example, an extrovert is probably more likely to enjoy parties; and thus, if one fails to consider the party situation in explaining his or her behavior, such a failure may not make any practical difference. Second, there are certain *omnipresent constraints* that may be ignored without causing an individual any problems. For example, one may see people in a relatively circumscribed range of situations and may only be interested in *circumscribed accuracy* (Swann, 1984), for instance, simply seeking to predict a student's or teacher's behavior within the classroom setting. In addition, when situations are long-term or enduring and thus help to shape one's dispositions (e.g., growing up in a particular type of environment), then dispositional and situational accounts may be redundant. Finally, situational constraints may sometimes be "superfluous"; that is, they may influence an individual to do things that he or she would have done anyway (e.g., an extroverted salesman who shows a "gift of gab" in the salesman role). In all of these cases, ignoring situational factors may constitute an "error" in terms of some normative standards (i.e., rationality$_2$, in the broad sense of that term), but it will probably not have a major deleterious effect on judgments (i.e., rationality$_1$).

Gilbert (1989; see also Gilbert & Malone, 1995) also made an effective case, along the same general lines as that made for heuristics, for why it is adaptive for the cognitive system to make fairly standard, automatic dispositional inferences if these inferences do, in fact, "work" in most situations. As Gilbert put it, it makes sense for the "stupid tailors of teleology"[10] to turn out a standard size-34 uniform (or standard dispositional inference) rather than "tailoring" each uniform (or inference) to the situation at hand. It then remains for a single bright supervisor (or controlled process) to make alterations to that standard uniform (or inference) when necessary.

It is also the case that the FAE really consists of two different parts: that is, an overemphasis on dispositional factors and a failure to take situational constraints into account. It can certainly be argued that the dispositional inference stage is a perfectly reasonable one and that it is the failure to take situational factors into account that is a possible error (and one that is exaggerated in lab research on the FAE). In addition, there is evidence (Fein, Hilton, & Miller, 1990) that participants who are provided with alternative personal explanations (e.g., an ulterior motive to be ingratiating or to avoid a task), show a reduction in the correspondence bias, whereas those given situational alternatives do not. Thus, it appears that the FAE does not result from a simple failure to keep more than one hypothesis in mind at once (see the earlier discussion of the confirmation bias), but instead it may be primarily *situational* factors that people have difficulty with.

Gilbert's (1989) argument that dispositional inferences are automatic and spontaneous whereas situational "corrections" require some cognitive effort is certainly reasonable, particularly in view of the evidence (e.g., Tetlock, 1985a, 1992) that asking participants to think more intently about or to justify their judgments mitigates the FAE, whereas interfering with this adjustment process by making participants cognitively busy *increases* it (Gilbert et al., 1988). One *problem* with Gilbert's account is that the situational manipulations involved in many studies of the FAE have been fairly strong, and the "errors" involved have appeared to be fairly egregious. It seems unlikely that a simple failure to call into play one's powers of reasoning, or the momentary failure of the intelligent "supervisor" to make the necessary corrections, can account for the FAE (though it may provide a reasonable account of Gilbert's "cognitive busyness" manipulation).

The question also arises as to exactly why individuals make dispositional inferences so spontaneously (cf. Winter & Uleman's [1984] work on spontaneous trait inference cited in chap. 3). One possibility that I have already discussed is that the actor is more salient or available and therefore "springs to mind" more readily as an explanation of the behavior. This is certainly the kind of explanation that Heider (1958) originally proposed. However, there is evidence (see Kassin & Pryor, 1985; Ross, 1981) that younger children do not commit the FAE, or are less likely to attribute behavior to dispositional causes. The same holds for members of non-Western cultures (J. G. Miller, 1984; M. W. Morris & Peng, 1994): For example, Hindu adults are less likely to explain behaviors, particularly deviant behaviors, in terms of dispositions, and are more likely to explain these behaviors in terms of situational factors than their American counterparts (J. G. Miller, 1984). Such findings argue against some kind of natural tendency based on perceptual salience or other ecological factors (see Fiske & Taylor, 1991, for a similar argument).

An alternative, more likely explanation is that dispositional attributions are learned judgments, ones that have apparently been so *over*learned as to become automatic. Consistent with this account is the research by E. R. Smith (1984, 1990), discussed in chapter 1, on the proceduralization or automatization of social inferences and judgments—including *dispositional* inferences—with increasing practice.

A word is also in order about attempts to explain the FAE in terms of judgment heuristics. First, the accounts of the FAE in terms of the representativeness and availability heuristics offered by Nisbett and Ross (1980) really amount to little more than redescriptions rather than meaningful explanations. Thus, for example, to say that actions are somehow more representative of actors than they are of situations is to beg the question "*Why* are they more representative of actors?" (See Nisbett & Ross, 1980, for an attempted account.) It certainly can be argued that sociable behaviors are more representative of parties than they are of specific partygoers (i.e., behaviors can be just as diagnostic of situations as they are of a person's dispositions). Yet individuals do not seem to make this kind of inference as readily (though see Krull, 1993). Similarly, persons may be more perceptually "available" than situations in most day-to-day interactions; however, I can certainly conceive of more perceptually salient situations as well (e.g., rowdy bars or nightclubs or opening ceremonies at Chicago Bulls basketball games). Furthermore, there is evidence that other types of availability (e.g., availability in memory) do *not* have a clear impact on attributions (see Fiske, Kenny, & Taylor, 1982; Taylor & Fiske, 1975). Finally, although I have suggested that the anchoring and adjustment heuristic makes more sense, I have also argued that the major attraction of Gilbert's account lies in its treatment of the insufficient adjustment phase, rather than the initial dispositional, anchoring phase.

Finally, it should be apparent from this discussion that almost all of the research on the FAE has been carried out in the lab; therefore, many of the criticisms raised against lab studies of heuristics apply to the FAE as well. For example, Funder (1987) argues that the FAE may be a product of conversational postulates or invited inferences that adhere in the experimental situation, but not in the real world (cf. my discussion of similar arguments regarding heuristics in general). For instance, the very fact that the experimenter gave participants the essay in the original Jones and Harris (1967) study may have conveyed the message that the experimenter found this essay to be relevant, even though A. G. Miller, Schmidt, Meyer, and Colella (1984) found that participants in this paradigm did not assign any diagnostic value to the essays. In this connection, Wright and Wells (1988) showed that when warnings were included about the random selection of the essays and their possible irrelevance to their judgments, the FAE was significantly reduced. Thus, one of the sources of the FAE may be that participants read the experimental situation as calling for certain inferences that are not actually made in the real world (or are not made in exactly the same way). If this is in the case, then it certainly speaks to the need to design more real-world studies of this effect.

False Consensus Effect

Still another attributional bias is the *false consensus effect* (FCE) or *egocentric bias*. As defined by L. Ross, Greene, and House (1977), the FCE is the tendency of individuals to "see their own behavioral choices and judgments as relatively common and appropriate to existing circumstances while viewing alternative responses as uncommon, deviant, or inappropriate" (p. 280). In their initial research on this topic, L. Ross et al. (1977) asked students to walk around campus for 30 minutes wearing a sandwich board saying "Eat at Joe's." Some students agreed to do so, and others did not. When asked to estimate the percentage of other students who would also agree to wear the sandwich board, the students who had themselves agreed to do so gave much higher estimates (62%) of how many others would than did those who refused, who judged that most students (67%) would refuse.

In general, subsequent research indicates that the FCE is a reliable phenomenon. For example, B. Mullen et al. (1985) conducted a meta-analysis of the numerous studies on this topic and reported a moderate effect size of .32 for the FCE. It should also be noted, though, that in certain areas such as abilities, participants actually show a false *uniqueness* effect (e.g., Kernis, 1984)—that is, they underestimate others' abilities in comparison to their own, presumably in order to place a greater premium on their own unique talents.

Explanations of the FCE.   In their review of the literature on the FCE, Marks and Miller (1987) offered four different explanations of this phenomenon. The first of these argues that similarities between individuals and others may be more accessible because individuals associate with similar others. Thus, Sherman et al. (1983) found that participants estimated that more people did not smoke if these participants associated with friends who did not smoke. Here beliefs or judgments are a product of interpersonal influences. A second explanation is the salience position, or the argument that one's own attitudes are more salient, and hence have a greater influence on estimates of others' opinions. For example, Marks and Miller (1985) found that willingness to generalize one's own opinions to others is related to the certainty—and hence, the salience—of one's opinions.

A third explanation sees the FCE as a result of reasonable inferences, rather than being due to bias. According to this position, if individuals attribute their opinions or judgments to situational influences, then it is reasonable to expect that others' opinions will be subject to the same influences, and hence similarities in those opinions are rational. For example, Gilovich, Jennings, and Jennings (1983) showed that the FCE is more likely to be found when a situational attribution is made (e.g., attributing preference for city or country life to features of those environments) than when a dispositional one is. The final set of proposed explanations involves motivational factors that might influence the FCE, such as self-enhancement (when comparison to a favorable target is made), or some kind of self-esteem maintenance (e.g., Tesser, 1988). For example, Suls and Wan (1987) showed that participants who had negative qualities or who held minority positions were more likely to show the FCE. The previously described false uniqueness effect for abilities is also consistent with this self-esteem-maintenance argument. (See Marks & Miller, 1987, for a review of the evidence for these different explanations.)

Finally, Fiske and Taylor (1991) offered an account of the FCE in terms of the anchoring and adjustment heuristic. According to this view, people start with their own view as an anchor and then fail to make a sufficient adjustment in trying to take others' positions into account. As I suggested earlier, it is not clear that this account "explains" the phenomenon, that is, it does not say exactly why individuals take our their positions as an anchor (e.g., rather than their colleagues') or why people do not make a sufficient adjustment.

In contrast to these social psychological accounts, Robyn Dawes (1989) presented an argument along Bayesian lines for why the so-called FCE may not really be a bias at all. Dawes argued that it is perfectly justifiable to draw inductive inferences from a single piece of diagnostic information, whether it be about oneself, another person, or a group of people, particularly in the absence of other information. Such inferences can be faulted on the basis of sample size, but there is nothing intrinsically "more biased" about judging other people's opinions on the basis of one's own than in using any other piece of individuating information. In fact, there is evidence (e.g., Hoch, 1987) that individuals' estimates are actually significantly correlated with the true base rates. What *would* make such inferences biased is if they resulted in systematic over- or underestimates of the opinion in the population as a whole. The question is whether the estimates are sufficiently or insufficiently regressive with regard to the base rates (cf. Tversky & Kahneman, 1974), that is, whether individuals conclude that others' opinions are sufficiently different from or too close to their own. Dawes presented evidence to suggest that participants' estimates are, if anything, *too* regressive (i.e., they assume too much difference, indicating a false uniqueness effect rather than an FCE).

Belief Perseverance

Initial Research and the Overt Explanation Paradigm. A final form of bias described by Ross and Anderson (see L. Ross & Anderson, 1982, for a review) is called the *belief perseverance* effect. This effect holds that even after the evidence for one's beliefs has been explicitly discredited, he or she will nevertheless tend to hang on to those beliefs. One of the first studies on this topic was conducted by L. Ross, Lepper, and Hubbard (1975) using a debriefing paradigm. In this study participants were given false feedback about their ability to distinguish between authentic and fictitious suicide notes. After receiving that feedback, these participants were given a thorough debriefing indicating that the feedback was false. Despite this debriefing, participants continued to hold onto a belief in the feedback. The assumption here is that this paradigm can be generalized to real-life maintenance of previous beliefs in the face of disconfirmation.

Nisbett and Ross (1980) proposed three main factors that may underlie such belief perseverance, including a kind of biased memory for and interpretation of new information (cf. Snyder & Cantor, 1979), as well as the familiar self-fulfilling prophecy. The most important of these factors, though, is that individuals construct explanations or engage in causal analyses (Nisbett & Ross, 1980) to support their beliefs, and this rationalization (in the broad sense) of these beliefs makes them more difficult to challenge.

To test out this notion, L. Ross, Lepper, Strack, and Steinmetz (1977) conducted a study in which participants read two psychiatric case studies and were asked to explain why the people described acted in a certain way (e.g., committing suicide) later in life. Participants were then told that the facts about this event had been made up and that nothing was really known of the patients' later lives. Participants were then asked to estimate the likelihood that each of several different events had occurred later in life, including the one they had previously explained. The central finding here was that participants who had explained the target event and had been debriefed still rated that event as more probable than did those who explained an alternative event or were not exposed to the target event until the estimation phase.

This overt explanation paradigm has produced confirmation for the belief perseverance effect in a number of studies (e.g., C. A. Anderson, 1983; Anderson, Lepper, & Ross, 1980). Such results provide suggestive evidence that belief perseverance may result from generating an explanation in support of one's beliefs. However, not all studies have found this effect (e.g., C. A. Anderson, 1982; Jennings, Lepper, & Ross, 1981). This fact led Jennings et al. (1981) to propose that even participants not *induced* to generate explanations may do so spontaneously (see C. A. Anderson, Krull, & Weiner, 1996; and Weiner, 1985, for discussions). In addition, Koehler (1991; see also Gilbert, 1991) argued that simply *accepting* a particular belief on a temporary basis is sufficient in and of itself (i.e., without the need for explanation) to increase one's confidence in that belief.

Counterexplanation. Just as generating an explanation may bolster a given belief or make it harder to refute, so does considering or defending an alternative appear to *reduce* one's confidence in that belief (C. A. Anderson, 1982; Lord, Lepper, & Preston, 1984). The evidence on explicit counterargument is generally consistent with this conclusion, but there is nevertheless some question about how far such counterexplanation actually goes in overcoming the initial belief perseverance effect. There is some evidence (C. A. Anderson & Sechler, 1986) that a subsequent counterexplanation can reverse the effects of the initial explanation; however, other evidence (e.g., C. A. Anderson, 1982) suggests that the original belief is not completely overcome, but simply reduced in strength. The second of these findings suggests that initial beliefs continue to have some priority over later arguments—a kind of primacy effect (see Koehler, 1991; Nisbett & Ross, 1980)—though there is debate about the exact mechanisms underlying such an effect (see Koehler vs. Nisbett & Ross; also see C. A. Anderson et al., 1996, for a detailed model of the explanation process).

The concept of belief perseverance is certainly a fascinating one, and one that can be related to a number of phenomena I have considered, such as the notion of a confirmation bias in general, the simulation heuristic, and counterfactual reasoning. The *problem* I have with this phenomenon is simply that I am not convinced that this concept can be adequately tested with the paradigms used. The most obvious example of this is the debriefing paradigm used in the initial research on this topic. How far can researchers generalize from participants' failure to respond adequately to debriefing in a psychological experiment? How representative is this paradigm of other everyday occasions of belief perseverance? Some of the other studies on this topic are a bit more convincing—such as predicting the outcome of a football game (Sherman et al., 1983) or generating reasons why a participant would or would not buy a videorecorder (Hoch, 1984)—though even here the prediction task is lifted out of its real-world context and the participants' overall belief system; and of course, the conversational postulates critique raised earlier applies here as well.

There is a related set of findings from the text comprehension literature that seem to be consistent with the belief perseverance effect, as well as with a variety of other observations in cognitive psychology and social cognition, including Loftus's research on misleading questions reviewed in chapter 4. I am referring here to research by Wilkes and Leatherbarrow (1988; Wilkes & Reynolds, 1999) on the editing of episodic memory. These investigators looked at the process of directly or indirectly correcting information provided in a previous scenario and then examined the inferences that participants drew from the revised version of that scenario (i.e., with the correction). Thus, for example, in one of the scenarios a description was presented of a fire in a commercial building, where an early indication was that the fire may have been caused by "carelessly stored paint cans and gas cylinders" (Wilkes & Leatherbarrow, 1988, p. 365) in a side room. This explanation was subsequently corrected by information that the room had actually been empty.

The results of this research indicated that later editing, whether direct or indirect, did not successfully prevent inferences from being drawn from the earlier corrected material, even though participants clearly recalled the revisions. Wilkes and Leatherbarrow accounted for this discrepancy between recall and inferences in terms of the distinction made by van Dijk and Kintsch (1983), discussed earlier, between readers' model of the text on the one hand, and readers' situation model on the other. Specifically, this view suggests a dual coding process in which the model of the text retains both old and new information as well as the corrections in memory; however, inferences are contained in the situation model induced from this text. (Notice that this dual level coding also bears a similarity to the two-systems model of the memory–judgment relationship discussed in chap. 2.) Editing of the situation model is difficult to accomplish on-line because it requires a good deal of complex inferential work. As a result, such editing is only done when the reader is directly questioned about an incident (cf. the contrary view by Graesser, Zwaan, and their associates, discussed earlier). Thus, editing is more effective when participants are probed more extensively or when less salient points or themes are addressed, and hence less editing is required (Wilkes & Leatherbarrow, 1988).

Wilkes and Reynolds (1999) also showed that participants continue to make incorrect inferences even when the correction is made in the midst of a sequence of messages, rather than at the end, or even when the correction addresses only one part of the scenario. In a similar vein, H. M. Johnson and Seifert (1994) reported that even when a message in the sequence was immediately corrected, participants continued to draw inferences compatible with that message. Wilkes and Reynolds, following Johnson and Seifert and the argument for minimal inferences in reading by McKoon and Ratcliff (1992), interpreted these results as suggesting that readers defer the process of editing, including correcting causal inferences, until later because of the demanding task of following through all the implications of such a correction, including in particular, rethinking causal inferences. (It should be noted, however, that H. M. Johnson & Seifert, 1998, recently showed that the discredited information continues to have an effect even at delayed test.) Notice that this account is generally consistent with Nisbett and Ross's account of the belief perseverence effect cited earlier.

A Reconsideration of the Rationality Issue

Returning to the issue of rationality and bias, it is apparent that many of the reservations raised earlier regarding the judgment heuristics and the confirmation bias also apply to the social psychological biases. First, the research on these latter biases has focused too heavily on comparing participants' responses to a normative criterion—in this case, some rationally constructed standard of how participants *should* have responded (although Gilbert, 1998, argued that what he calls the *critique of standards* is less applicable to social psychologists because the problems dealt with in that area are clearly open to more than one solution). Second, I (and others, e.g., Funder, 1987, 1995; Gilbert, 1998) believe that social cognitivists in general, and the discussions by Ross, Nisbett, and their associates in particular, have overemphasized the role of error and bias in human judgment to an even greater extent than Kahneman and Tversky. Whereas Kahneman and Tversky (e.g., 1982b) have been primarily concerned with the way in which particular intuitions deviate from the rules of probability theory, social psychological researchers have been intent on demonstrating *general* cognitive limitations, irrationalities, and biases in reasoning in general, including *everyday* reasoning. One result of this overemphasis on error, as I discussed earlier, is that investigators in this area have paid insufficient attention to the cognitive processes underlying these biases. (Two possible exceptions here are the model of the correspondence bias proposed by Gilbert as well as Anderson et al.'s process model of explanation.) Rather, investigators (see especially Nisbett & Ross, 1980) have typically been content to simply link these biases to Kahneman and Tversky's heuristics.

At the same time, the study of these biases in social reasoning raises a separate set of considerations and concerns. First, on the plus side, the former research makes the important point that cognitive biases are partly a product of social influences as well as of cognitive limitations (see Plous, 1993, on this point). The most obvious example of this is the recent interest in the impact of cultural factors on the FAE. This contrast in turn raises the question of the relative importance of each of these factors. For example, does salience or visual orientation or limited processing capacities play the major role in determining biases, or are they primarily a product of social learning and cultural influences? There is also the question of whether the traditional social psychological research paradigms reviewed in this section (e.g., assessing participants' reactions to wearing a signboard, to being told about false feedback, or to watching a person present a speech) can really hope to shed light on the cognitive processes underlying the biases. On the positive side, these sorts of manipulations expand the study of biases to include real-world (or at least "experimentally realistic" [Aronson & Carlsmith, 1968]; see chap. 1) social situations. On the negative side, however, such complex, distal manipulations make it difficult to draw strong inferences about the precise nature of the cognitive processes involved.

OTHER JUDGMENT BIASES

Two other biases that have received considerable attention within both cognitive psychology and social cognition are the *overconfidence effect* (e.g., Lichtenstein & Fischhoff, 1977; Oskamp, 1965) and *hindsight bias* (e.g., Fischhoff, 1975; Fischhoff & Beyth, 1975). These two phenomena have in common the fact that both are concerned with a failure to calibrate accurately our estimates of the probabilities of events with the actual probabilities.

Overconfidence Effects

The overconfidence effect refers to the finding that the confidence that individuals place in their judgments typically exceeds the actual accuracy of those judgments. One of the first studies on this topic was reported by Oskamp (1965). In this study Oskamp presented, in succession, four excerpts from a case history to groups of clinical psychologists, graduate students, and undergraduate students. These participants were asked to make two types of judgments after each new excerpt of the case study: namely, answers to questions about factual material or clearly supported conclusions about the case study as well as estimates of their confidence in the accuracy of these answers. Oskamp found that the three different groups of participants did not differ in their accuracy on the first set of questions. More important, Oskamp found that participants showed increasing confidence in their answers with increasing information, even though they did not show increasing accuracy. As a result, by the end of the case study, more than 90% of the participants showed overconfidence in their judgments. This general finding has been replicated using student counselors in an encounter group situation (Geddes, 1985) and members of a videodating service finding out additional information about potential dates (Woll & Cozby, 1987).

A number of other examples of the overconfidence effect have been reported by Fischhoff and his associates (e.g., Fischhoff, Slovic, & Lichtenstein, 1977; Lichtenstein & Fischhoff, 1977) and more recently by Ross and his associates (e.g., Dunning, Griffin, Milojkovic, & Ross, 1990; Vallone, Griiffin, Lin, & Ross, 1990). For example, Lichtenstein and Fischhoff asked participants to say whether each of a set of drawings came from Europe or Asia; these participants were also asked to rate their confidence in these judgments. Although participants performed at a near chance level on their initial judgments, they showed a mean confidence rating of 68%, suggesting an overconfidence effect. Similarly, Lichtenstein and Fischhoff (1977) also reported a study in which participants judged whether a set of stocks would go up or down. In this case participants actually performed at a *below* chance level, but their confidence ratings averaged 63%.

Ross and his associates have focused on participants' prediction of more real-life criteria (i.e., their own and other people's behavior). For example, Dunning et al. (1990) asked participants to predict a target persons' behavior on the basis of differing amounts of information. These participants were only slightly more accurate when they had greater amounts of information than when they had little, and were overconfident in both conditions. Vallone et al. (1990) asked Stanford students to predict various aspects of their own lives or behavior (e.g., their choice of a major, predicting how much they would like their roommate) and those of their roommates. Students were more accurate in predicting their own behavior than they were in predicting others', but they were overconfident of their predictions in both cases.

One exception to this effect worth noting is the evidence from real-world experts, including bridge players (e.g., Keren, 1987), racetrack handicappers (e.g., Lichtenstein, Fischhoff, & Phillips, 1982), and meteorologists or weather forecasters (e.g., Lichtenstein et al., 1982; Murphy & Brown, 1984). These experts, who of course receive frequent feedback about their judgments, do not show significant overconfidence.

One account of the overconfidence effect is in terms of the confirmation bias. Specifically, Koriat, Lichtenstein, & Fischhoff (1980) proposed, in a manner similar to Nisbett and Ross (1980), that once participants have chosen a given alternative, they proceed to search their memories in a selective manner for confirming evidence. As a result of evidence collection, participants develop strong confidence in their original choice, and hence, *over*confidence. In this connection Koriat et al. (1980) showed that when participants were asked to make lists of the reasons why their answer (to a general information question) might be wrong, these participants showed less overconfidence. Although this finding is consistent with my earlier discussion of the counterexplanation paradigm, note that such evidence bears only indirectly on the notion of a confirmation bias (see Gigerenzer, 1991).

The overconfidence effect appears to be a reliable phenomenon (see Von Winterfeldt & Edwards, 1986), and one that is of clear significance for the study of everyday cognition. It is certainly of interest to know that people tend to place more confidence in their judgments than is warranted. The research on this topic is not without its critics, though. Gigerenzer (1991; Gigerenzer et al., 1991), for example, has argued that the overconfidence paradigm confounds two different types of judgments: confidence in a single event (i.e., a judgment for a given item), and judgments of relative *frequencies* of events (e.g., the frequency of different diseases in one test question; cf. Gigerenzer's [1991] similar critique of research on the representativeness heuristic). When participants are asked to make a confidence estimate about how many items they answered correctly (a frequency judgment), and this estimate is compared with their actual score on these questions (another frequency judgment), no overconfidence effect is found (Gigerenzer et al., 1991). The question addressed in this second case seems rather different, however, from the one examined in overconfidence studies (i.e., where the frequency judgment refers to the content of specific item, such as the disease item, rather than to the questions as a whole).

Hindsight Bias

A second (related) bias examined by Fischhoff (e.g., 1975) is the so-called *hindsight bias,* or the "I-knew-it-all-along" effect. The hindsight bias can be defined as the tendency to overestimate, in retrospect, our prior ability to predict an event. As Fischhoff (1982) has stated it, "in hindsight, people consistently exaggerate what could have been anticipated in foresight. They not only tend to view what has happened as inevitable but also to view it as having appeared 'relatively inevitable' before it happened" (p. 341). Fischhoff (1975) referred to this sense of inevitability or the rapid, unconscious role of outcome data in participants' judgments as *creeping determinism.* Taking this one step further, Hawkins and Hastie (1990) argued that the hindsight bias is distinct from other after-the-fact increases in confidence in that it involves a *"denial that the outcome information has influenced judgment"* (p. 311).

One of the original studies on this topic was conducted by Fischhoff (1975). In this study five different groups of participants read descriptions of clinical case histories and historical events. The first of these groups, the foresight group, was to estimate the probability of each of four outcomes. The other four groups, the hindsight groups, were told that one of the four outcomes had, in fact, occurred (one outcome per group); and they were asked to estimate the likelihood that they would have predicted this outcome, disregarding their knowledge of that outcome. Fischhoff found that the hindsight groups gave much higher estimates of the outcome likelihood than did the foresight group. Similar results have been reported by Arkes, Wortmann, Saville, and Harkness (1981) in the area of medical diagnoses, by Powell (1988) in the area of political predictions, and by Casper and Benedict (1989) in the area of legal decisions, to name just a few (see Hawkins & Hastie, 1990, for a review). In fact, one of the interesting features of the literature on the hindsight bias for the purposes of this book is that a good deal of the research has dealt with real-world events, often in real-world settings.

In another early study, Fischhoff and Beyth (1975) asked participants to predict a set of events regarding Nixon's 1972 trips to the Soviet Union and China (e.g., whether Nixon would meet with Chairman Mao). Then, 2 to 6 months after the trip, these same participants were asked to recall their prior estimates and to indicate whether they thought that each of the events actually did occur. Consistent with the notion of a hindsight bias, Fischhoff and Beyth found that participants recalled having given higher estimates of events that had actually occurred than was the case, while at the same time giving lower probabilities for events that did not occur (cf. Ross's [1989] research on individuals' reconstruction of their life histories, discussed in chap. 5).

Hawkins and Hastie (1990) reviewed a number of possible accounts of the processes involved in the hindsight bias. These explanations include using current belief as an anchor and then trying to adjust that belief, reconstructing the earlier belief, and some kind of motivated change in response. The first explanation is clearly an application of the anchoring and adjustment heuristic, where one's current judgment represents the anchor, and as usual, the adjustment is insufficient. Hawkins and Hastie argued that this viewpoint, although plausible, cannot account for certain findings, such as the fact that knowledge of the occurrence of the outcome leads to greater hindsight bias than does nonoccurrence (cf. the similar asymmetry found for mental simulation), even though both options should have equal status as anchors.

A more complete explanation is that, for a variety of different reasons, individuals may reinterpret the original judgment or belief. Such a reinterpretation may be due to the fact that after knowing the outcome, people may engage in a biased sampling of evidence (e.g., sampling only evidence relating to the obtained outcome as opposed to the initial sampling which was done for more than one outcome; cf. Slovic & Fischhoff, 1977). Alternatively, people may engage in a biased evaluation of that evidence (i.e., interpreting ambiguous information in such a way as to support the outcome; cf. Fischhoff, 1975), or biased combining of the implications of the evidence (e.g., changing the weights attached to the outcome-relevant or outcome-irrelevant pieces of information, or altering one's view of the causal relations among variables).

Finally, the so-called motivated change at the response stage suggests that individuals change their judgments in order to appear more accurate (Fischhoff, 1975) or to convey a favorable self-presentation (Tesser & Campbell, 1983). Hawkins and Hastie concluded that although this factor may play some role, it cannot account for all examples of hindsight bias. For example, attempts to reduce such motivation (to be reviewed in the next chapter) do not have much effect on the hindsight bias, and ego involvement in the task does not always have a major effect on the bias (Leary, 1981, 1982). Along similar lines, Hoffrage, Hertwig, and Gigerenzer (2000) recently proposed what they refer to as the *Reconstruction After Feedback with Take the Best* (RAFT) model of the hindsight bias. According to this model, feedback results in the updating of knowledge, and this updated version serves as the basis for the subsequent postdiction (cf. the related "failure-to-update" account for belief perseverance in the previous section). The RAFT model also predicts (and research confirms) that having participants report their knowledge prior to feedback cuts down on the hindsight bias.

The overall conclusion reached by Hawkins and Hastie is that all three of the proposed explanations play some role under different circumstances. This conclusion is, in some sense, not entirely satisfying because it suggests that the hindsight bias is not a unitary phenomenon. At the same time, however, unlike many of the other biases that I have considered, this review of the hindsight bias focuses more clearly on the underlying cognitive processes involved. This is particularly true for the reinterpretation account, though Hawkins and Hastie also concluded that it is impossible to completely distinguish between cognitive and motivational explanations.

Hindsight errors, like the other biases demonstrated by Tversky and Kahneman, are certainly intriguing and are of particular relevance in some areas (e.g., to historians [Fischhoff, 1980] and political pundits). It is not clear to me, however, how large a role they play in everyday life. Hawkins and Hastie (1990) argued that "hindsight phenomena are prevalant in the real world" (p. 323), and they suggested that everyone can think of examples in our own or other people's lives of such a bias. However, hindsight *phenomena* (e.g., regrets over previous choices) are not the same as hindsight *biases*. I myself am hard-pressed to think of many examples in my personal life (or in most friends and acquaintances). For example, when I think about what went wrong with previous relationships, I may think that I *should* have known it all along, but not that I *did* know. The same holds for political predictions and the like. Hawkins and Hastie do cite one practical example that is fairly convincing, that is, when individuals seek a second opinion in medical diagnosis, it is important that the second opinion be made independently of the first.

Fischhoff (1982) also reviewed research on attempts to reduce or eliminate the hindsight bias. I discuss these "debiasing" techniques in the next chapter; however, the most interesting finding of this review for the purposes of this chapter is that a technique that does have an effect on this bias is to ask participants to explain how some *other* outcome could have occurred. In other words, the same counterexplanation approach described earlier appears to be effective in reducing the hindsight bias as well, presumably because counterexplanation helps individuals to see that other outcomes are indeed possible.

AN ASIDE ON NATURALISTIC DECISION MAKING

Throughout this chapter (and throughout this book) I have been emphasizing the problems of depending exclusively on laboratory research to study everyday cognition. There is one current approach to decision making, which I alluded to in chapter 1, that is a particularly clear illustration of this point, an approach that has been labeled *naturalistic decision making* (NDM; e.g., G. A. Klein et al., 1993; Zsambok & Klein, 1997). As defined by Zsambok (1997), *"NDM is the way in which people use their experience in making their decisions in field settings"* (p. 4), as opposed to the study of decision making in the rarefied atmosphere of the lab. NDM research is concerned primarily with decisions made by experienced people or experts in a given domain, such as firefighters, military commanders, software designers, pilots, and physicians; as such, this research is clearly related to the research discussed in chapter 7 on expert–novice differences.

In a manner similar to the classic research on chess experts, research on NDM tends to focus on the act of recognizing a situation as being of a certain sort (see G. A. Klein's [1989, 1993] *recognition-primed decision* [RPD] model), rather than considering a set of decision options. Thus, a firefighter must recognize that a given set of features is characteristic of a particular type of fire or rescue situation, and anti-aircraft personnel must recognize that a given set of cues suggests an enemy attack or a friendly aircraft flying off course. As these two examples suggest, many NDM situations do not allow for an exhaustive, rational consideration of alternatives; for this and other reasons, NDM models stand in opposition to standard rational models of decision making applied in the lab. To state things differently, Zsambok (1997) mentions four "markers" of NDM research that distinguish it from traditional research on decision making: (a) task and setting (i.e., ill-structured tasks or problems in dynamic environments), (b) the participants (i.e., experienced decision makers in a given domain rather than naive participants), (c) the purpose of the research (i.e., a concern with how these experienced decision makers actually make their decisions rather than with some normative prescription of rationality), and (d) an emphasis on the process of *situation assessment* (G. A. Klein, 1989, 1993; i.e., the recognition component just alluded to, rather than just the process of selecting options).

To illustrate these points, consider a couple of research examples. One of the first models of naturalistic decision making was Gary Klein's RPD model (G. A. Klein, 1989, 1993, 1997; see Fig. 9.3). In their initial study of urban fire ground commanders, G. A. Klein, Calderwood, and Clinton-Cirocco (1986; Klein, 1989) observed that these commanders, who were required to make immediate decisions, did not take time to consider a variety of different courses of action, but rather performed a quick situational assessment and identified, on the basis of their past experience, a situation from which a particular course of action would follow. (See Table 9.2

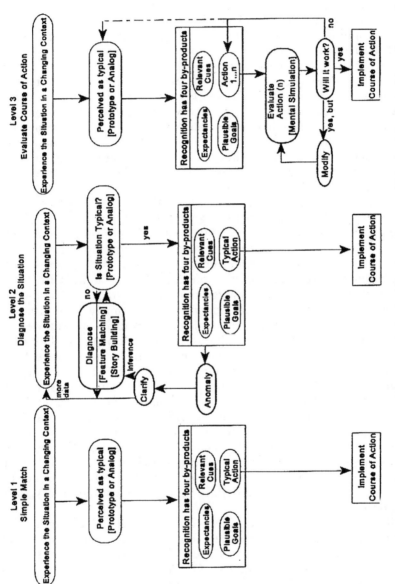

FIG. 9.3. Klein's Recognition-Primed Decision (RPD) model. From "The Recognition-primed Decision (RPD) Model: Looking Back, Looking Forward" by G. A. Klein, 1997. In Naturalistic Decision Making (p. 286) edited by C. E. Zsambok & G. Klein, Mahwah, NJ: Lawrence Erlbaum Associates. Copyright © 1997 by Lawrence Erlbaum Associates. Reprinted with permission.

for a scenario in this fire command study.) As G. A. Klein (1997) put it, "The most critical assertion of the RPD model is that people can use their experience to generate a plausible option as the first one they consider" (p. 288).

It is apparent from Fig. 9.3 that there are four major aspects of the recognition phase: (a) understanding reasonable goals for the situation, (b) focusing on relevant cues, (c) forming expectancies that can be tested, and (d) picking a course of action. Thus, in the scenario described in Table 9.2, the successive goals were to contain the fire, and then, when that was not feasible, to pursue a search-and-rescue goal. The cues included the flames coming from the laundry chute and the smoke coming from the eaves. Expectancies included the initial belief that the fire could be controlled, which was invalidated by later information. Finally, the courses of action were using hoses to put out the fire, followed by evacuating all residents.

This first stage of pattern matching clearly resembles the research discussed in chapter 7 on chess masters, as well as the model of expertise proposed by H. L. Dreyfus and Dreyfus (1986). In fact, some of Klein's own research (e.g., Calderwood et al., 1988; G. A. Klein, Wolf, Militello, & Zsambok, 1995) focused on chess experts, and H. L. Dreyfus (1997) contributed to a conference on NDM. For that matter, the major difference between the models of expertise I reviewed in chapter 7 and Klein's model is that the latter places a greater emphasis on "courses of action," though such action is also obviously implied in research on, for example, chess masters.

If and when this simple matching process fails or is inadequate, then a further process of mental simulation is invoked; recently, Klein and his associates (e.g., Kaempf, Wolf, Thordsen, & Klein, 1992; G. A. Klein, 1997) also

TABLE 9.2

Scenario for Fire Commander Decisions

A firefighting crew arrives at the scene of a reported fire in a four story apartment building. The commander of the crew surveys the front of the building, sees no smoke or flames, and goes around the side. There he sees through a basement window that the laundry shoot is on fire, and that fire has spread to the basement ceiling. He orders his crew into the first and second stories of the building to extinguish the fire from above with hoses. As they enter, the crew reports that the fire has spread above the second floor. Back at the front of the building, the commander sees that smoke is now pouring from the eaves. The fire must have spread via the laundry shoot to the fourth floor and down the corridor from the back to the front of the building. The commander realizes that he will need help, and calls in another unit. He also orders his crew to drop their efforts at suppressing the fire, and to concentrate instead on a room-by-room search for people trapped in the burning building. They succeed in evacuating all the occupants, but the building is gutted, despite the arrival within 10 minutes of a second unit.

Note. From "The Reinvention of Decision Making," by J. Orasanu & T. Connolly, 1993. In *Decision Making in Action: Models and Methods* (p. 3), edited by G. A. Klein, J. Orasanu, R. Calderwood, & C. E. Zsambok, Norwood, NJ: Ablex.

introduced a *diagnostic* function between the matching and mental simulation phases (see Level 2 of Fig. 9.3), where diagnosis refers to an assessment somewhat beyond simple matching. The differences among these three components is not entirely clear, especially because, as I mentioned in my earlier discussion of mental simulation, simulations involve a kind of feature-matching procedure as well. Construction of a simulation, however, would seem to be different from simple pattern matching (see earlier discussion).

In support of this RPD model, G. A. Klein (1989, 1997) cited studies from a variety of sources. For example, Kaempf et al. (1992) examined 78 occasions on which Navy officers involved in anti-aircraft maneuvers had to make actual decisions about how to react to potentially hostile forces. These incidents were probed by retrospective interviews (see Flanagan's [1954] *critical incidents technique* discussed in chap. 8). The researchers found that 78% of these decisions were made without any explicit deliberation, and another 18% involved mental simulations. An even greater percentage of RPDs was found in Klein's study (G. A. Klein et al., 1986) of urban fire commanders, where according to Klein it was actually the less experienced ones who used more analytical approaches. In a study using more on-line assessment Randel, Pugh, Reed, Schuler, and Wyman (1994) looked at the decisions made by Navy electronic technicians in simulated tasks, and found that 93% of these decisions were made in a serial, rather than a several-options-at-a-time manner.

Another example of NDM models and research is found in Lipshitz's (1993; Lipshitz & Ben-Shaul, 1997) research on officers in the Israeli Defense Force. In one study Lipshitz and Ben-Shaul (1997) studied the differences between expert (some of whom were commanders with experience) and novice trainees on a sea combat simulator. The simulator presented information on a radar screen as well as providing simulated radio messages, both of which were similar to the types of situations and information that might actually occur in a real-life combat situation. Specifically, in the particular simulation observed, "The trainees ... 'commanded' three fast gunboats on coastal patrol with the mission of identifying and intercepting suspected targets" (p. 294), and the trainees had to determine the best action. The results of this comparison were similar to those reported in chapter 7 on expert–novice differences in general—for instance, experts collected more information about the situation before considering response options, they searched the presented information more efficiently, and they were more accurate in their understanding of the situation.

Lipshitz and Ben-Shaul's model of the decision-making process (see Fig. 9.4) is similar, but not identical, to Klein's RPD model. In addition to the recognition + action structure, this alternative model (Lipshitz & Ben-Shaul, 1997) includes higher order reasoning and knowledge structures. Specifically, Lipshitz and Ben-Shaul discussed the role of both mental models and schemas in NDM. Mental models refer in this context to the trainees' construction of the situation, or what Klein referred to as *situa-*

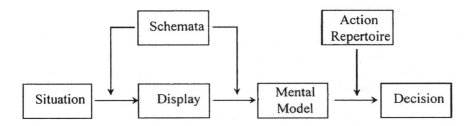

FIG. 9.4. Lipshitz and Ben-Schaul's model of naturalistic decision-making. From "Schemata and Mental Models in Recognition-primed Decision Making" by R. Lipshitz & O. B. Ben-Schaul, 1997. In *Naturalistic Decision Making* edited by C. E. Zsambok & G. A. Klein (p. 298), Mahwah, NJ: Lawrence Erlbaum Associates. Copyright © 1997 by Lawrence Erlbaum Associates. Reprinted with permission.

tional assessment. This mental model is the product of input (or what Lipschitz calls *display*) plus schemas, or general knowledge structures, and serves as the basis for determining action. Lipshitz and Ben-Shaul (1997) also emphasized that action plans are oftentimes worked out before the fact (e.g., various responses to invading forces are well-rehearsed and may be fairly automatic).

Although this is a very brief summary of the NDM approach (see G. A. Klein et al., 1993, and Zsambok & Klein, 1997), I believe that this summary underlines several relevant features of that approach. First, NDM research is more clearly connected to previous research on memory and reasoning, and on expertise in particular, than is traditional decision-making research. Second, this research focuses on fascinating real-world decisions rather than lab simulations or experimental microcosms. (It should be noted that NDM may also deal with more everyday decisions such as which job offer to take or whether to have another child [see Beach, 1990; Beach & Mitchell, 1987]). Finally, NDM research uses rather different methods from those used in traditional decision-making research (e.g., interviews, simulations, think-aloud protocols, and cognitive task analysis in general; see Gordon & Gill, 1997; Woods, 1993). In all three of these respects (see also my discussion in chap. 1 of other distinctive features of NDM research), NDM represents a good example of research on everyday cognition.

SUMMARY

In this chapter I have reviewed a number of apparent errors in human judgment and reasoning and have shown how these biases do (and do not) relate to everyday situations. I have also demonstrated how most of these errors can be related to a set of common heuristics and biases studied by Kahneman and Tversky and by Wason and his associates; I have also examined the debate over rationality versus error in this literature. Finally, I have developed some recent models and research on naturalistic decision making.

There is a sense in which the research discussed in this chapter is, with a few notable exceptions, least clearly related to other research on everyday cognition that I have discussed in previous chapters. (These notable exceptions are research on the simulation heuristic, the concept of pragmatic reasoning schemas, and the more general emphasis on the effects of everyday content on reasoning as well as the research just described on naturalistic decision making.) In fact, in this chapter there has been little mention of the seven models of everyday cognition. (The exception here is the schema model.) This does not mean that all the models in this area have been insufficiently "cognitive"; indeed, the research of Wason and his associates has held a central place in cognitive psychology. It is just that research on judgment and decision making has, for the most part, been pursued in relative isolation from the other topics examined in this book (though see chap. 10). In particular, I have suggested some parallels between research on a couple of the judgment heuristics and biases and research on text comprehension.

For a number of years research on heuristics and biases and its applications dominated the field of human judgment, just as rational models of judgment and decision making dominated research before that. In more recent years there have been growing reservations about these so-called biases, and I have tried to capture this reaction as well. In the end, the picture that will emerge will undoubtedly fall somewhere in between the optimist and the pessimist camps. Indeed, I hope that this picture will include a more systematic account of the cognitive mechanisms underlying everyday judgment rather than simply focusing on whether people are rational or irrational. I have also contrasted the emphasis on error in the judgment and reasoning area with the emphasis on wisdom and adaptiveness in the literature on practical intelligence and have tried to reconcile these two different positions. In the next chapter I examine research on the prospects of improving reasoning and judgment through various forms of training.

Chapter 10

Instructional Implications of Everyday Reasoning

Introduction

Situated Cognition and Education

Authentic Assessment

The Adequacy (or Inadequacy) of Informal Reasoning

Teaching Formal Skills Through Informal Reasoning (and Vice Versa)

Conclusions

INTRODUCTION

In this section I explore some of the implications of my discussions of everyday cognition for learning and instruction. I first review the concept of situated cognition developed in chapters 1 and 8 and a variety of related concepts, and indicate how they pertain to both traditional instruction and to various proposed alternative approaches to education. In addition, I examine the related concept of authentic assessment, or the use of natural, everyday situations and problems to assess a student's competencies and academic progress. I then look at research on the adequacy of informal reasoning and the effectiveness of various interventions to improve such reasoning. Next, I review some research by Richard Nisbett and his associates on the use of everyday knowledge and everyday situations as aids to instruction in formal (i.e., statistical and deductive) reasoning as well as the converse (i.e., the effects of instruction in formal reasoning on our everyday

431

reasoning). This latter research obviously follows from the studies on reasoning and judgment heuristics discussed in chapter 9, as does the research on debiasing to be discussed in the final section of this chapter. In general, most of the research and applications to be discussed in this chapter follow from my discussions in the preceding chapters.

SITUATED COGNITION AND EDUCATION

One currently popular viewpoint on the relationship between everyday cognition and instruction has been labeled *situated cognition* or situated learning (J. S. Brown et al., 1989; Lave, 1988; Lave & Wenger, 1991). I have referred to this viewpoint on several occasions (i.e., in chaps. 1, 7, and 8). In this section I review several different formulations of this position in greater detail, along with some related research and some of the implications of this position for the study of everyday cognition.

The J. S. Brown, Collins, and Duguid (1989) Position

J. S. Brown et al. (1989) appealed to the notion of situated cognition in the context of a general critique of traditional classroom instruction. This critique took issue with the idea that knowing can somehow be abstracted out of either the activity through which it is acquired or that through which it is demonstrated, as well as the *situation* in which it is learned or enacted. Thus, language or mathematical knowledge cannot be distinguished from the particular kinds of activity through which such knowledge is typically acquired (i.e. everyday activity). To do so, by using decontextualized teaching methods, is self-defeating.

Too often, Brown et al. argued, classroom instruction fails to make contact with such everyday cognition. J. S. Brown et al. (1989) expressed it as follows:

> The student enters the school culture while ostensibly being taught something else. And the general strategies for intuitive reasoning, resolving issues, and negotiating meanings that people develop through everyday activity are superseded by the precise, well-defined problems, formal definitions, and symbol manipulation of much school activity. (Brown et al., p. 35)

Rather, Brown et al. argued that learning and doing are inseparable. Thus, for example, vocabulary is typically learned in school in terms of a dictionary definition and a few isolated examples, when in fact word meanings are always dependent on context, both linguistic and extralinguistic.

I have raised this same point earlier in my discussion of Lave et al.'s (1984) research on the use of math in grocery shopping and the way in which this usage differs from school math. Brown et al. cited the example from Lave et al. (1984) of a man in a Weight Watchers program faced with the problem of measuring out 3/4 of the daily 2/3 cup of cottage cheese allotted on the Weight Watchers' plan. Instead of drawing on his school knowledge of fractions and following the accepted procedure of multiplying the two fractions to obtain a product of 1/2 cup, this participant, while muttering that he had taken calculus, proceeded to empty out the 2/3 cup on a cutting board, and then divided this amount up into four sections or quadrants, and then emptied three of these quadrants into the measuring bowl.[1]

The point of Lave's example is that (a) it involves using the resources present in the environment rather than trying to solve the problem in your head, and (b) it reflects the way in which individuals solve mathematical problems in the real world. Once again, traditional schooling ignores these preexisting heuristics, although students use them anyway. (I have also shown these heuristics at work in the street vendors of Brazil and in Scribner's [1984a, 1986] studies of the everyday activities of dairy workers.)

Another part of Brown et al.'s situated cognition position is its emphasis on a kind of apprenticeship whereby learners are exposed to the accepted practices in a given area. "They [students] need to be exposed to the use of a domain's conceptual tools in authentic activity—to teachers acting as practitioners and using these tools in wrestling with *problems of the world*" (Brown et al., 1989, p. 34, italics added). I return to this issue in my discussion of related positions.

Resnick (1987a), in her comparison of school learning and learning in the real world (referred to in chap. 1), also emphasized the difference between the abstracted "symbol manipulation" taught in school and the contextualized knowledge or skills learned outside of school. Not only do people not use their formal training outside of school, but they are also "somehow discouraged from bringing to school their informally acquired knowledge" (1987a, p. 15). For example, research on mathematics learning (Resnick, 1987b) indicates that the kinds of mistakes that children make in math result from these students' failure to understand the meaning of the problem, which is due, at least in part, to the way math is taught in schools—it does not "engage students' interpretative and meaning-construction capacities" (p. 14). On this issue, Resnick (1987a), like Brown et al., argued for the return of apprenticeships (or what she calls

---

[1] I initially thought that this was a silly example (i.e., how many people would actually do this?). Then I remembered that I had recently tried to convert the number of pages I had written for other chapters in this book into the number of pages in the final book. I knew that the formula on the word processor I would be printing out from was three quarters of the number of pages on the processor I was currently using. I also knew that the formula for converting manuscript pages into book pages was 3:2 pages. Thus, in order to calculate the number of book pages, I computed 3/4 of the current number, and then multiplied this product by 2/3—in other words, essentially the same procedure used by the Weight Watchers member, although I used pencil and paper rather than dumping out cottage cheese! With that said, on another real-world occasion within a couple of days, in which I was trying to determine the expenses I had incurred during my sabbatical in England, I made the correct school mathematics calculations, confirming the situational specificity of reasoning (and probably the impact of the problem format).

bridging apprenticeship). Resnick's own research (1987b) indicated that the best programs for teaching cognitive skills are those that include elements that are common to everyday reasoning (e.g., practicing in groups, some form of apprenticeship, and contextualization). At the same time, she stresses the importance of schooling that encourages higher order thinking and reflection.

One other theorist who emphasized the role of situated cognition is James Greeno (e.g., 1989, 1991a, 1991b; Greeno & Moore, 1993; see also Clancey, 1991, 1992, 1993). Greeno argued that knowledge cannot be equated with representations, but rather with "abilities to find and use the concepts in constructive processes of reasoning" (Greeno, 1991a, p. 175). Thus, for example, learning computer software usually involves the ability to use that software or interact with it rather than learning some set of static cognitive symbols. Stated differently, "Cognitive processes are ... interactions with materials and other people, rather than operations on symbols *contained in an individual's mind*" (Greeno, 1991b, p. 212, italics added). Thus, the emphasis is on activity and use rather than on static symbols; or as Kirshner and Whitson (1997) put it, in situated cognition viewpoints, the unit of analysis changes from thoughts within the person's head to the "person-in situation" or "person in activity."

In addition, learning always occurs in the context of *social* activity with peers and, in particular, with teachers (who serve as guides to that new environment), as well as with cultural artifacts such as mathematical notation or calculators. As Resnick, Pontecorvo, and Saljo (1997) stated it, with the idea of situated cognition "comes a revised definition of *reasoning* as a fundamentally social activity in which ideas and concepts are literally *constituted* in interactive discourse" (p. 4). Similarly, Roschelle and Clancey (1992) argued that representations involve a "dialectic between the social and the neural" (p. 435).

Cognitive Apprenticeship. A related alternative to traditional instruction is what Collins, Brown, and Newman (1989; see also J. S. Brown et al., 1989) called *cognitive apprenticeship,* which is based on the practice of apprenticeship in learning trades and crafts, as studied by Lave (e.g., 1993; Lave & Wenger, 1991) and others (e.g., Hutchins, 1995; Jordan, 1989). The argument here is that in traditional schooling "skills and knowledge have become abstracted from their uses ... [whereas] apprenticeship embeds the learning of skills and knowledge in their social and functional context" (Collins et al., 1989, pp. 453–454). Such apprenticeship involves a stage of observation where the master models the desired skills or activities, followed by attempts by the apprentice to recreate the process with the guidance and support—what Wood, Bruner, and Ross (1976; see also Greenfield, 1984) called *scaffolding*—of the master. These two stages are followed by the relatively independent practice of the apprentice, in which the master plays a minor role.

As a cross-cultural example of this concept. Lave (1993, cited in Lave & Wenger, 1991) has examined the way in which the Vai and Gola tailors of Liberia learn their craft. According to Lave, apprentices learn the trade from the last step back to the first—from working on the final product (e.g., sewing buttons and hemming cuffs on trousers) to learning to sew the different parts of the trousers, and then learning to cut out the garment in the beginning. Within each of these stages apprentices start with observation and a first stab at the skill, followed by a practice phase in which the apprentice tries to reproduce the particular skill from beginning to end.

The particular form of apprenticeship proposed by Collins et al. (1989) is a *cognitive* apprenticeship. Rather than learning physical skills as in tailoring or midwifery, a cognitive apprenticeship involves learning cognitive skills via "guided experience" (Collins et al., 1989, p. 457). Unlike traditional apprenticeships, the skills to be learned are not immediately observable; thus cognitive apprenticeship methods serve to externalize these "tacit processes," where the student can observe and practice them and can be helped by teachers and other students. Also involved is the student learning to monitor and correct his or her own thought processes because the teacher cannot see what the student is thinking (or vice versa). The techniques involved include students repeatedly comparing their performance with that of an expert and alternating between producing or generating on the one hand, and evaluation or criticism on the other. The desired result is a kind of "internal" dialogue between the apprentice as generator and the apprentice as critic.

Collins et al. (1989) cited a number of different "success models" of cognitive apprenticeships in action. One such example is Lampert's (1986) research on math instruction with elementary school students. Lampert's approach is to start off with everyday content (e.g., coin problems for teaching multiplication) to try to tap into students' everyday, implicit knowledge and show its relevance to unfamiliar problems. Then students are encouraged to come up with their own word problems to illustrate particular multiplicative relations (e.g., make up a story for the multiplication of 12×4). In this latter exercise students are encouraged to try out different decompositions (e.g., 6×8 and 3×16) to show them that there is no one single "right" solution. Finally, students are taught the standard algorithm, which now has some meaning for them. According to Lampert (1986), this sort of instruction combines four different types of knowledge: (a) intuitive knowledge (the kind that people use in their everyday math), (b) computational knowledge, (c) concrete knowledge (or the concrete applications to students' own made-up problems), and (d) principled knowledge (i.e., the specific mathematical principles, such as commutativity, exemplified by the multiplication problems).

This example and others cited by Collins et al. (e.g., Schoenfeld, 1985) illustrate the application of two different premises of the cognitive apprenticeship rationale. These two premises are introducing students to the "culture" of mathematics on the one hand, and making contact between the student's everyday knowledge of math and mathematics instruction on the other.

Anchored Instruction. Another variation on the situated cognition theme is the concept of *anchored instruction* proposed by the Cognition and Technology Group at Vanderbilt (CTGV; 1991). Like the situated cognition viewpoint, Bransford, Franks and their associates in the CTGV (1991) argued for the importance of presenting information in "the context of meaningful activities … [where students] are likely to perceive the new information as a tool rather than as an arbitrary set of procedures or facts" (p. 3). Such "arbitrary" information represents the problem of *inert knowledge* raised by Whitehead (1929), referring to knowledge—particularly school knowledge—that is acquired but never really used. The importance of "meaningful activities" is particularly clear for young children who need to learn in "meaningful, socially organized contexts" (CTGV, 1991, p. 3). Furthermore, like the advocates of cognitive apprenticeship, the Vanderbilt group stresses the importance of providing learning environments that introduce students to problems of the sort that experts in an area face and the knowledge that these experts use for approaching these problems.

One specific feature of anchored instruction is its emphasis on the importance of providing *macrocontexts* or "complex situations that require students to formulate and solve a set of interconnected subproblems" (CTGV, 1992b, p. 284). Specifically, CTGV stresses the use of video, and in particular, videodisc technology because this medium provides for a more realistic presentation of everyday events. Such a medium also works better for low-achievement students and novices, and videodisc technology has the advantage of allowing both teachers and students to access material anytime they want.

CTGV (1991) cited a couple of examples of research on anchored instruction. In the first of these, called the Young Sherlock Project, the investigators were concerned with helping 5th-grade students to learn language arts and social studies. In this study, students received either regular instruction (e.g., in writing stories or learning historical material) or instruction on these topics anchored in the movies *Young Sherlock Holmes* and *Oliver Twist*. Thus, for example, in teaching students the elements of a good story, the experimental (Sherlock Holmes) group examined these points in the context of the *Young Sherlock Holmes* movie, whereas the control group examined them in a set of stories that varied from element to element—what the Vanderbilt group referred to as *microcontexts*. The result was that the experimental (movie) group wrote stories that "contained many more story elements; their plots were more likely to link character actions and events to goal statements and goal resolution" (p. 4). This group also showed better memory for the historical context (or setting) of the movie after focusing on the historical accuracy of that movie and doing research on historical points (e.g., the nature of the Victorian era). Unfortunately, the variety of differences between the movie and the traditional instruction group make it difficult to know what the exact sources of the superiority of the movie group were.

Another frequently cited example of the CTGV's emphasis on transfer of learning from these discs is the *Jasper series* (CTGV, 1992a, 1992b, 1993). The Jasper series consists of a set of episodes or tapes that incorporate the following seven features: (a) use of a video format, (b) use of realistic problems, (c) use of a format in which students must generate problems rather than simply solve problems presented to them, (d) providing all of the information that the student needs for problem solution, (e) use of complex problems, (f) presentation of pairs of related adventures, and (g) an attempt to draw from and connect different content areas.

As an example of this sort of problem, consider the following scenario (CTGV, 1992a). A character named Larry located in Cumberland City teaches another character named Emily to fly an ultralight airplane, including a description of the plane's features (e.g., fuel capacity, the effect of the shape of the wing on the airplane's lift). Emily then has dinner with Jasper, who in turn heads off on a fishing trip, stopping first at Hilda's house before hiking to Boone's Meadow for fishing. Once at the meadow, Jasper discovers a wounded eagle, uses his CB radio to contact Hilda, who in turn contacts a veterinarian. The veterinarian gives her information about eagles and informs her that there are no roads from Boone's Meadow to Cumberland City (where Emily is located). The video ends with Emily musing about "the fastest way to rescue the eagle and how long will that take?" (p. 70).

There are a variety of ways in which teachers have used this exercise to teach problem solving. For example, many teachers start with large group discussion to generate ideas before dividing up into smaller groups to test or evaluate these ideas (e.g., by discussion or by replaying the videodisc). Although students are typically allowed to generate solutions on their own, teachers often pose questions as well. In the small groups students discuss the various solutions; after two class sessions, they present their conclusions to the class as a whole along with their reasoning or justifications. This last feature gives students experience with presenting their views and responding to questions. Finally, students may be asked to proceed to analogue problems (which vary certain features of the problem already solved to get students to try out their knowledge of math or physics) or extensions (i.e., integrating the material with other areas of curriculum, such as with Charles Lindbergh's flight or the moon landing; see CTGV, 1993). Students may also be encouraged to explore issues raised in the tapes in greater detail, to pose their own problems, or even to create their own videodiscs.

The Jasper series has a number of features that are of interest. First, the series solves the problem of inert knowledge by treating knowledge as a tool for problem solving. The problem used is deliberately complex because real-world problems are often complex and cannot always be resolved in 5 minutes (although in this case, there clearly is a solution). The emphasis is on what CTGV calls a *guided generation* model, in which learning to generate problems, questions, ideas, as well as solutions is encouraged, rather than simple reproduction of the correct answer. Scaffolding plays a major role in such exercises, particularly at the beginning of problem generation and solution; such scaffolding is both encouraged and necessary in view of the complexity of the Jasper problems. Finally, in the Jasper exercises students eventually get to see the solution, even if they are not able to generate it themselves.

CTGV also stresses the overlap between anchored instruction and situated cognition. The first similarity is that both viewpoints emphasize everyday content, authentic tasks, and apprenticeships. Students in the *Young Sherlock Holmes* exercise, for example, do the kinds of research and ask the kinds of questions that a screenwriter would ask; as such, the exercise can be viewed as a kind of apprenticeship, as described by Collins et al. (1989). The exercise can also be viewed as authentic in that the material is in line with "ordinary practices of the culture" (Brown et al., 1989, p. 34). This exercise also involves active research rather than passive reading of assigned materials, and the opportunity to achieve expertise on a given topic. Finally, the tasks become more authentic as the children learn from several exercises, how to do "Jasper-like" tasks and begin to develop Jasper-like, "'intelligence-enhancing' tools" for others. The use of videodiscs and other kinds of visual media (e.g., CD-ROM or interactive computergraphics) makes it possible to give students more real-world, interactive experience than might be provided in either traditional classroom experiences or traditional apprenticeships. The fact that students can go back and visit the same problem from multiple perspectives and that they are involved in problem selection as well as problem solving certainly makes the tasks more authentic as well.

Reservations About Situated Cognition: Cognitive Apprenticeship and Anchored Cognition

A number of criticisms have been raised regarding the concepts of situated cognition and cognitive apprenticeship. For example, in the very next issue of *Educational Researcher,* Palincsar (1989) and Wineberg (1989) voiced reservations about the Brown et al. (1989) article. Both found fault, for instance, with the example of the Weight Watchers' client using situational resources as tools for solving a practical math problem. As Palincsar (1989) put it, "the authors [Brown et al.] regard the dieter's ineptitude with fractions as giving rise to an 'inventive resolution.' ... Instead, it was an act of desperation, born of ignorance. Although the authors laud this activity, I question whether it was learning at all" (p. 7). Wineberg (1989) wondered what the dieter would have done if he had been measuring chocolate syrup or molasses!

Palincsar and Wineberg also found fault with the emphasis in the Brown et al. article on enculturation into the teacher–practitioner's discipline.

Palincsar suggested that in many instances there may be substantially less agreement on the "culture" of that discipline than Brown et al. assume. Second, Palincsar argued that "what we expect of students is substantially different from what we expect of practitioners, with good reason" (p. 6). That is, people typically want students in an area to learn certain basic skills, such as critical or convergent thinking, rather than knowledge or skills that are specific to a given discipline (e.g., learning APA style, or how to write grant proposals; though see my discussion of tacit knowledge in chap. 8). Along similar lines, Wineberg (1989) questioned the value of apprenticeship. As Wineberg put it, "no doubt some apprentices find their apprenticeships absolutely authentic, but I can imagine others who find it absolutely tedious, inefficient, repressive, servile, tradition-bound, and in some cases, even downright mean" (p. 9). That is, some people may find the activities of apprenticeship to be meaningful and significant, whereas others may not.

A couple of other possible reservations should be noted. First, as I discuss later in this chapter, the problem of defining "authenticity" is a difficult one (just as was the term *real world* in chap. 1). For example, is watching a videogame of the Teenage Mutant Ninja Turtles more "authentic" than a textual account of a family interaction? Is a film or video of a gang fight likely to be equally "authentic" for a student from the middle class suburbs as it is for someone from the projects? There is also a potential conflict between the aims of "authenticity" and apprenticeship. That is, being sure that an exercise is representative of the activities of the master may conflict with making the exercise authentic to the student. Thus, for example, having a student practice the skills of a historian or geographer or even a mathematician may, as Wineberg suggested, make that exercise tedious and completely inauthentic for the student. Finally, it is not clear that enough is known about the thought processes of different "masters" or experts to be able to model those processes for the apprentice (though see chap. 7).

One potential risk of this emphasis on everyday knowledge is that it may deflect attention away from traditional skills and academic subject matters and instead place the focus of education on simply reinforcing existing "intuitive" knowledge and preconceptions. Stated differently, making contact with everyday thought is valuable insofar as such thinking and knowledge are used to facilitate acquisition of higher order reasoning and of knowledge that goes beyond students' current situation, but not if it is encouraged *in lieu* of such skills, particularly given the mixed evidence on the validity of everyday reasoning (to be reviewed later in this chapter).

Lave and Wenger: From Situated Learning to Legitimate Peripheral Participation and Communities of Practice

Undoubtedly the most widely cited conception of situated cognition is that of Jean Lave (1988; Lave & Wenger, 1991). Lave, whose work spans the disciplines of anthropology, education, and everyday cognition (see Rogoff &

Lave, 1984, and also my discussion in chap. 8), has described her viewpoint in a number of different ways. On the one hand, Lave (1993; Lave & Wenger, 1991), like Collins et al., looked at apprenticeship, both in her own study of the tailoring trade in Liberia, and also in Lave and Wegner's review of apprenticeships for Yucatec midwifes (Jordan, 1989), naval quartermasters (Hutchins, 1995), and the like. In addition, Lave has been interested in apprenticeship as a metaphor for alternative forms of learning.

The lessons to be learned from the examples reviewed by Lave and Wenger (1991) are that (a) learning often occurs without explicit instruction; (b) learning involves active participation rather than simply observation (as Brown et al. suggested); (c) the so-called learning curriculum of the student or apprentice is not set by instructors, but rather by "the community of practice" (pp. 91–92), such as of midwives or tailors, and the learner's own "peripheral point of view" (see later discussion); (d) artifacts, including technology, are linked to both "cultural practices and social organization" (p. 102); (e) apprenticeship involves learning *to* talk (e.g., learning to tell appropriate stories about one's experiences; cf. Schank & Abelson, 1995), rather than just learning *from* talk; and (f) increasing participation in a practice leads to "an increasing sense of identity as a master practitioner" (p. 111). At least the first four of these lessons are ones that have been touched on in the other positions I have discussed in this chapter.

Lave (1990) also stated the case for apprenticeship in simpler terms. According to Lave, the increased interest in apprenticeship "for theoretical inspiration" is because this concept provides an alternative to the "culture of acquisition" (p. 310), or the position that culture is to be "acquired in the abstract by way of decontextualized school learning" (p. 310). By way of contrast, the concept of apprenticeship emphasizes the fact that knowledge and understanding are "generated in *practice*" (p. 310, italics added) and in situations where that practice takes place (e.g., the situation or context in which street math is practiced). One reason that school math, for example, is not frequently used in everyday life is that math learning in school is abstracted out of the situations in which it is to be used.

This emphasis on the role of situations led to a more general theory of *situated learning*, which emphasizes "the relational character of learning and knowledge, [and makes claims] about the negotiated character of meaning, about the concerned (engaged, dilemma-driven) nature of learning activity for the people involved. That perspective meant that there is no activity that is not situated" (Lave & Wenger, 1991, p. 33). That is, knowledge and learning involve a relationship with the environment, including other people (rather than the material existing in some objective or objectified state); and they involve some active engagement of the person with the material or practice (rather than passively taking in information). Furthermore, the "meaning" of the material to be learned is "negotiated" by the learner him- or herself (rather than existing independently of that learner).

Along similar lines, Lave (1993a) also underlined the critical importance of context and the view that knowledge or activity cannot be decontextualized. Rather, Lave's (1988) emphasis is on the dialectic between the agent and the context; one cannot be separated from the other. Trying to decontextualize learning or knowing, as in searching for general, abstract principles that apply across situations or contexts, results in distancing the knower from his or her "engagement in the world" (p. 23). Such a view assumes that we live in an objective world with objective institutions such as schools, as well as with formalized knowledge. Furthermore, there is the assumption of a literal, unambiguous meaning that can be conveyed in explicit language (e.g., as in a lecture by a teacher).

There is also a good deal of ambiguity, however, about the exact meaning of the terms "situated" and "context," ranging from a concern with the spatial-temporal context, to an emphasis on *social* context, to an emphasis on the context-dependence of meaning, to name just a few interpretations. This ambiguity has led to the recent introduction of two new terms: *legitimate peripheral participation* (Lave & Wenger, 1991) and *communities of practice* (Wenger, 1998). The first, rather awkward construction seems to imply that participation (in some practice) is "always based on situated negotiation and renegotiation of meanings in the world" (Lave & Wenger, 1991, p. 51). Thus, for example, becoming a member of some professional group, or becoming familiar with a new course will often require learning (or negotiating) new terms and rules (see Glick, 1997). Learning is conceived of as increasing participation in a social practice and, as a result, being transformed as a person, including an evolving sense of identity. The notion of *peripheral* participation connotes the process by which newcomers peripheral to the group become transformed into full members (see Pontecorvo & Fasulo, 1997, for a study on the way in which children are socialized into the family around the dinner table).

The concept of communities of practice shows a good deal of overlap with legitimate peripheral participation. To begin with, as outlined by Wenger (1998), knowing always entails participation or an "active engagement in the world" (p. 4). Such participation is always social and always involves some kind of social *practice*. Social practice and communities of practice (where the emphasis is on *practice*) include both implicit as well as explicit materials:

> It [social practice] includes the language, tools, documents, images, symbols, well-defined roles, specified criteria, codified procedures, regulations, and contracts that various practices make explicit for a variety of purposes. But it also includes all the implicit relations, tacit conventions, subtle cues, untold rules of thumb, recognizable intuitions, specific perceptions, well-tuned sensitivities, embodied understanding, underlying assumptions, and shared world views. (Wenger, 1998, p. 47)

At several points, Wenger stresses that the concepts of learning and knowing are located in everyday activities and real-world settings.

As an example of such a community of practice, Wenger (1998) cited the activities of an office of insurance claims processors where workers worked with institutionalized rules and forms (e.g., claims forms), but are also involved in "inventing and maintaining ways of squaring institutional demands with the shifting demands of actual situations" (p. 46). The latter activity is what Wenger calls *local practice*. For example, claims processors must complete a certain number of correct claims per week (i.e., ones that are not voided or disputed by quality reviewers). Because different types of claims take greater or lesser amounts of time and effort, as well as having different likelihoods of being awarded, these processors must work out strategies for which claims to pursue immediately and which to hold off on. For example, there is one type of claim that is particularly difficult and complicated, referred to by the processors as "junk claims," which these processors are likely to save until they have already met their daily quotas. Processors must also learn to negotiate with both clients and "higher ups" (e.g., supervisors and quality reviewers), when to dispute decisions, when to seek out the help of others, and so forth. Thus, just as students often negotiate their own ways of meeting the requirements of school—oftentimes in ways unanticipated by "the system"—and Scribner's (1986) dairy workers devise strategies that minimize their physical or mental work, so do these processors negotiate their own solutions—in this case, sometimes joint solutions—to the tasks with which they are faced.

As far as learning is concerned, Wenger's view, like Lave's, is that learning is *"inherent in human nature"* (p. 226), that it is part of social practice, as in the claims processing office, even if some do not recognize it as such, and that it is best approached within such social practice rather than in some separate, isolated decontextualized arena. In addition, thought cannot be separated from action (cf. Scribner, 1986):

> ... if we believe that information stored in explicit ways is only a small part of knowing, and that knowing involves primarily active participation in social communities, then the traditional format [i.e., of classroom lecturing] does not look so productive. What does look promising are inventive ways of engaging students in meaningful practices, of providing access to resources that enhance their participation, ... and of involving them in actions, discussions, and reflections that make a difference in the communities that they value. (p. 10)

On this note, Wenger made a distinction between participation and *reification,* or turning experiential or social processes into some kind of objectified product. Reification is not a problem in and of itself so long as it is balanced with practice, which it complements. Treating knowledge as some kind of objectified subject matter leads to "a kind of brittle understanding with very narrow applicability. This is especially true if the delivery of codified knowledge takes place away from practice, with a focus on instructional structure and pedagogical authority that discourages negotiation" (Wenger, 1998, p. 265). The learner must participate in that negotiation and must "gain some ownership of the meaning" (Wenger, 1998, p. 265).

Wenger (1998) also emphasized, as did Lave and Wenger (1991), the fact that learning changes one's identity: "Because learning transforms who we are and what we can do [competence], it is an experience of identity. It is not just an accumulation of skills and information" (p. 215). The "student" must not only be engaged in or participate in the practice, but must be able to incorporate "information" into his or her identity:

> What makes information knowledge—what makes it empowering—is the way in which it can be integrated within an identity of participation. When information does not build up to an identity of participation, it remains alien, literal, fragmented, unnegotiable. It is not just that it is disconnected from other pieces of relevant information, but that it fails to translate into a way of being in the world coherent enough to be enacted in practice. (Wenger, 1989, p. 220)

What are the implications of this social practice viewpoint for "designing" education? First, Wenger argued that "*learning cannot be designed:* it can only be designed *for*—that is, facilitated or frustrated" (p. 229). In other words, if learning is inherent in social practice, the best or worst that institutionalized education can do is to enhance that process or interfere with it. The student's engagement or active participation is what determines learning, and he or she may or may not learn what the instructor intended. In this view, "the primary focus must be on negotiation of meaning than on the mechanics of information transmission and acquisition" (p. 265). Stated in more common terms, it is critical to get the student involved, not only in problem-solving, but also in terms of relating it to her or his identity.

One final implication of this emphasis on engagement and identity is that many students do not benefit from institutionalized instruction. Wenger (1989) said it as follows:

> One problem of the traditional classroom format is that it is too disconnected from the world and too uniform [i.e., the same for all students] to support meaningful forms of identification. ... Focusing on an institutionalized curriculum without addressing issues of identity thus runs the risk of serving only those who already have an identity of participation with respect to the material in other contexts. Others must be willing to abandon their claim to ownership of meaning. ... (p. 269)

Thus, as suggested by Lave and Wenger, institutionalized instruction may actually alienate students insofar as it fails to make contact with their worlds or to engage or fit into their existing identities. Thus, education, which is supposed to democratize and give power—information is power, you know—may, in fact, be both alien and alienating. As Wenger (1989) put it, "information by itself, removed from forms of participation, is not knowledge; it can actually be disempowering, overwhelming, and alienating. ... Access to information without negotiability serves only to intensify the alienating effects of non-participation" (p. 220; see Brown & Duguid, 2000, for a similar argument).

Although the *specific* implications of these viewpoints for schooling are not completely clear, the *general* lesson includes the fact that we must pay attention to the social, cultural, and situational context of learning. Thus, for example, as I have discussed, to teach students without considering their everyday experiences or the role of others is problematic. In fact, Wenger (1998) stated explicitly that learning is located in everyday activities and real-world situations. In their recounting of the various studies of apprenticeship, Lave and Wenger (1991) also clearly included the communities of the apprentices' masters; and Wenger placed his major emphasis on communities of practice in general. In addition, both the "legitimate peripheral participation" and the "communities of practice" viewpoints clearly say that the instructor's agenda is not necessarily the same as the student's; Wenger situated learning in social practice and participation rather than in some artificial school "learning" environment. Last but not least, the emphasis here is on learning through active participation rather than through passive note-taking or observation.

Although I return to a critique of situated cognition theories in a later section, at this point let me make a couple of observations. First, as you may have noted, Lave's presentation seems more obscure and opaque than it might be. (Wenger's recent book is somewhat more accessible, but then it is intended for a somewhat different audience from the original Lave & Wenger book.) In part, this can be attributed to the rather different perspective from which Lave's views derive—that is, Soviet activity theory (e.g., Engeström, 1987; Wertsch, 1981), the German school of critical psychology (e.g., Holzkamp, 1987), and European theories of social practice (e.g., Bourdieu, 1977). In part, it can be attributed to her eclecticism (i.e., drawing from psychology, anthropology, and social history), and in part, it can be attributed to the several revisions that her viewpoint has undergone. In any case, one of the results of this obscurity is that Lave's viewpoint has been interpreted in different ways by different writers—as a political statement, as a call for educational reform, as a particular critique of traditional learning theory or developmental theory (see chap. 8).

In point of fact, both Lave's and, to some extent, Wenger's positions can be approached on several different levels. Some of Lave's writings (e.g., 1988; Lave et al., 1984) can be interpreted as a critique of a set of empirical findings (e.g., her critique of research on transfer or of Piagetian approaches to development); in fact, that is the level on which some critics (to be discussed below) have focused. On the other hand, Lave's position can be viewed as a theoretical statement about the nature of learning, or it can be viewed as a meta-theoretical statement (i.e., about how to do psychology or how to structure education) or even as a political statement. From a different perspective, Lave's position can be viewed as an assertion about situations or about our engagement in those situations or about people's relations to objects in general. Such a multilevel (and fairly unsystematic at that[2]) viewpoint is rather difficult to fully comprehend or critique in a thoroughgoing way. This is a point I return to shortly.

Suchman's Situated Action Position

One final approach to situated action is that of Suchman (1987). As discussed in chapter 4, Suchman focused on planning, and argued that "however planned, purposeful activities are inevitably *situated actions* ... [or] actions in the context of particular, concrete circumstances" (p. viii).

Suchman has approached the topic of situated action from a rather different perspective from Lave or Collins et al. (see Suchman, 1993). Specifically, Suchman's concern is with the way in which a communicator calls on his or her understanding of the situation in trying to make sense out of other people's intended (communicated) meanings. As an obvious example, the same question can be interpreted as either a request for information or as sarcasm depending on the conversational context and the recipient's point of view.

Such commonsense knowledge, however, is difficult to formulate in a general, cross-situational way. Any such formulation is necessarily post hoc, and "run[s] up against the fact that there is no *fixed* set of assumptions that underlies a given statement" (Suchman, 1987, p. 61, italics added). Stated differently, whereas many words such as "she" or "he" or "there" are said to be *indexical* in that they depend on the context for their interpretation, so Suchman and others (e.g., Garfinkel, 1967) argued that *all* language, or at least all *communication,* is indexical. All communication depends on the situational context and on the "mutual intelligibility of action" (Suchman, 1987, p. 62), that is, the mutual understanding that participants work out in the process of communication.

What does all of this have to do with education? First, Suchman's emphasis on the "mutual intelligibility of action" obviously fits in with Wenger's notion of "negotiated meaning." More important, Suchman's position suggests that lectures or instructions depend on students sharing in the background knowledge of the instructor (because this knowledge cannot be fully articulated). As a result, most lectures, especially those couched in abstract, decontextualized language, will not be fully comprehended. This problem is exacerbated in the case of noninteractive instruction (e.g., in the descriptions of a textbook writer or in the instructions of an expert to a machine.) Some

---

[2]Kirshner and Whitson (1997) pointed to the importance of developing a more coherent and rigorous theory of situated cognition.

kind of interactive negotiation is necessary. On this point, Suchman (1987) cited research on human–computer interaction in which it appears that the provision of a general help system on the computer does not allow for answers to all of the user's queries because the computer cannot be sensitive to the situated questions of the user. "Due to the constraints on the machine's access to the situation of the user's inquiry, breaches in understanding that for face-to-face interaction would be trivial in terms of detection and repair become 'fatal' for human–computer communication" (p. 170). Thus, situated action points to some of the limitations of noninteractive instruction (such as the current discussion).

Critique of Lave, Wenger, Suchman, and Other Theories of Situated Action

The Rebuttal by Vera and Simon. In a recent review of the literature on situated action (including a number of formulations from artificial intelligence [e.g., Greeno, 1989; T. Winograd & Flores, 1986], as well as Suchman's and Lave's formulations), Vera and Simon (1993a) attempted to show that traditional artificial intelligence (AI) approaches can, in fact, account for situational differences in thought and behavior. The general point made by these authors is that physical symbol systems such as the computer or the human brain can handle situational variables by building patterns of symbols that refer to external objects and then, by a process of pattern matching, determining whether these external objects resemble patterns that have been previously encountered. Vera and Simon (1993a) pointed out that problems in robotics have forced artificial intelligence researchers to pay greater attention to such external, situational patterns and to the feedback resulting from matches or mismatches.

With respect to pedagogical issues, Vera and Simon (1993a) argued against Lave on a couple of different grounds. On the one hand, they argued that traditional symbolic architectures can, in fact, handle interactions with complex, ambiguous environments, including real-world environments (e.g., P. R. Cohen, Greenberg, Hart, & Howe's [1980] simulation of a fire fighting system, or Vera et al.'s [1993] simulation of a postal facility). On the other hand, Vera and Simon argued that, contrary to Lave's (1988) objections, the pedagogical problem is the old issue of transfer of training; and as I discussed in chapter 7, that turns out to be an (extremely complex) empirical question.

Both Suchman (1993) and Agre (1993), in speaking for their own positions and for Lave, argued that Vera and Simon's symbolic "world view"[3]

---

[3]Hutchins (1995) also argued against the symbol systems approach, at least in part because of its inside–outside distinction and its implication that symbols are always inside the head. In his discussion of Western navigation (and navigation in the U. S. Navy in particular), Hutchins pointed out how symbolic representations and symbolic activities occur out in the "world" as well (e.g., in maps and logbooks) and how cognitive science's overreliance on laboratory research has resulted in a relative "ignorance" of "cognition in other culturally constituted activities" (p. 371).

(Agre, 1993), has led those authors to misinterpret Lave's more "profound" point. Specifically, it is not a question of transfer from the neutral, decontextualized environment of the school, but rather it must be recognized that action and thought in school are themselves *situated* and not neutral (see a similar point made by Wenger, 1998). Both Agre (1993) and Clancey (1993) argued that Vera and Simon erred by trying to translate Lave's ideas into symbolic terms, when, in fact, Lave's position is that interactions and culture are often not represented in individual symbolic systems, and that intelligent behavior does not always require such symbolic representation (though see my discussion of procedural representations). Furthermore, it should not be assumed that the abstract symbolic representations taught in schools are the only way of formulating a problem or that all cultural practices and social interactions are explicitly represented cognitively.

The crux of the debate (if there is one "crux") between situated cognitivists and symbol systems theorists such as Simon and his associates appears to be whether it is necessary to represent all cognitive activity as symbols. As Greeno and Moore (1993) expressed it, "a symbol ... is a structure—physical or mental—that is interpreted as a *representation of something*" (p. 50, italics added). The position taken by Vera and Simon (and many cognitive scientists; see chap. 1) is that all cognitive activity involves symbols. The position taken by the situated cognitivists, on the other hand, is that activity, physical or cognitive, need not require symbols (or in the most extreme cases, *never* involve symbols), but that all activity *is* situated. Of course, this debate itself hinges on how one construes the term symbol—for instance, does a procedure for tying your shoes or for improvising a basketball shot constitute a symbol? Is knowledge that is not consciously represented still symbolic (see Bereiter, 1997; Vera & Simon, 1993a)?

The Critique by Anderson, Reder, and Simon.   One other general critique of situated cognition has recently been put forward by J. R. Anderson et al. (1996). Anderson et al. suggested that there are four basic assumptions of situated learning approaches, none of which are clearly supported by the empirical evidence. The first of these assumptions is that cognition and action are "situationally grounded" (J. R. Anderson et al., 1996, p. 6). In Anderson et al.'s view, this assertion is certainly true in its weak sense, that is, that a complete description of cognition and action requires a specification of the situational context. Too often, however, this assertion is exaggerated to suggest that cognition or knowledge cannot be transferred from one situation to the next (e.g., from school to some real-world situation). Anderson et al. cited empirical evidence (e.g., Godden & Baddeley, 1975) in which some skills transfer to real-world situations (e.g., divers applying what they have learned in class to their experiences while actually diving), whereas others do not. They also cited some skills (e.g., reading and writing) which clearly *do* transfer; they argued that there are many lab studies that indicate that mathematics transfers or generalizes from school to the lab (although this does not really speak to the issue of transfer to real-world situations). Anderson et al. also took exception to Lave's conclusion that the knowledge acquired in school is not "legitimate," or that it is used to reinforce existing class structure (see also Wenger, 1998). In this connection, Anderson et al. cited research that suggests that school performance does correlate with work performance (though see my discussion in chap. 8 of Sternberg's contrasting interpretation of the same evidence).

The second, related assumption is that, as I just suggested, knowledge or learning does not transfer. I have discussed this claim, along with the more general question of transfer of training, in chapter 7. Here it is sufficient to note that Anderson et al. cited instances in the literature in which transfer has, in fact, been demonstrated, as well as cases in which it has not. Simply stated, Anderson et al.'s argument is that transfer occurs more frequently, and we know more about such transfer than commentators such as Lave would claim. Interestingly, St. Julien (1997) pointed out that the problem for situated cognition is the exact opposite of that for traditional learning theorists (i.e., explaining how transfer *does* occur when it does).

The third assumption is that learning by means of abstract principles is of little use, and that apprenticeships are a more valuable form of learning. Once again, Anderson et al. gave examples of studies in which abstract learning *has* been successful and has even improved on traditional apprenticeship. For instance, Biederman and Shiffrar (1987) reported a study in which the difficult task of learning to sex-type chickens, a skill that takes many years of apprenticeship to master, could be taught within 20 minutes to participants via abstract training to bring them up to the level of experts. Anderson et al. also cited a number of examples, as I did in chapter 7 (and as I do later in this chapter), of studies in which the optimal training has proven to be a combination of abstract training and a number of specific examples rather than either one alone. Finally, Anderson et al. argued that rather than being concerned with how "authentic" a task is, researchers should instead be concerned with the cognitive processes entailed in such a problem.

The final assumption is that learning should occur in complex, real-world social environments. Without going into detail on this issue, I will simply note that Anderson et al. argued that many skills are practiced in nonsocial situations (in the strict sense of that term); they also cited evidence suggesting that learning component skills in isolation from each other often leads to the best results. In addition, many skills (or parts of such skills) that will eventually require teamwork are better learned in nonsocial situations.

A Personal Observation.   I have mixed feelings about the situated cognition position. On the one hand, the idea that knowledge is dependent on situational rules or environmental cues and that schooling should take these everyday, situational influences into account is an appealing one, although one that is hardly new (see St. Julien, 1997; Wineberg, 1989). The emphasis on negotiated meanings and collaborative problem solving or reasoning (e.g., Resnick, Pontecorvo, & Saljo, 1997b) is a valuable addition to cognitive psychology's (and social cognition's) overemphasis on individual thought processes. On the other hand, there is something rather offputting about the more radical version offered by commentators such as Lave and Suchman to the effect that knowledge and planning do not exist apart from the situation and that knowledge somehow emerges only out of one's interaction with that situation. (Of course, this situationism can be stretched to cover a multitude of possibilities. For example, Wegner, 1998, gives the example of a person rehearsing a speech in his or her hotel room; and Clancey, 1993, has even suggested that "we are situated in an empty darkroom, we are situated in bed when dreaming" [p. 100].) Certainly individuals adapt their knowledge to situational rules and demands; it would be absurd to think that people carry knowledge of the world around and apply it in the same way in every situation. In fact, as Bereiter (1997) suggested, as an individual becomes more and more skilled in a given situation, his or her knowledge becomes more and more situation-specific.

On the other hand, it seems equally absurd to argue that people do not transfer knowledge about one situation or occasion to another, or that people do not represent these situations, in some form, to themselves. (See Resnick et al., 1997a, for a somewhat awkward attempt to account for transfer in terms of brain tunings.) To take a trivial example, this morning I watched the replays of Mark McGuire hitting his 61st home run. The U.S. public has been deluged with stories about this impending event for some time now. Do I only have knowledge of it when I see it happening, or when I read a story about it, or when I discuss it with friends? In this connection, Bereiter (1997) gave the example of space missions to the moon, where, he argued, some transfer of knowledge must occur, rather than knowledge being completely situated.

Bereiter (1997) suggested that one of the problems with the situated cognition view is that writers in this area failed to make a critical distinction between process (i.e., of knowing or thinking) and product (i.e., the knowledge produced) or, stated differently, between the "knowledge implicit in the process [i.e., of knowledge construction] from the knowledge that is the product" (p. 296). (Of course, situated cognition writers choose not to make this distinction.) It is the process of knowledge construction that is situated, according to Bereiter, not the product (though the latter *can* be situated too). Once again, it seems to me that one of the critical points of contention here is the question of "what does or does not qualify as a symbol?" (though the transfer issue comes in a close second).

Of all the writings on situated cognition, the most compelling is the recent book by Wenger (1998). Wenger made the point clearly that learning occurs in everyday experiences and that the best that school can do is to try to enhance that informal learning. School learning should draw on everyday learning; in fact, when such school learning becomes reified and alienated from that everyday experience, so does the student become alienated from the school situation. Finally, Wenger made the point clearly that the current structure of education is likely to alienate students who do not already include school learning as part of their identity. It seems to me that all of these are valuable points for educators to consider, as well as underlining the importance of everyday cognition for education.

The critique by J. R. Anderson et al. (1996) is effective insofar as it addresses empirical problems with the situated cognition viewpoint. Unfortunately, many of the examples given by these commentators involve decontextualized lab research, which is unlikely to convince many critics who question the value of lab research as much as they do the decontextualized format of traditional schooling. In addition, as I suggested earlier, situated cognition, at least in the case of some writers (e.g., Lave, Clancey, and Suchman), operates at several different levels, only one of which (and the one that is probably least important) is the level of empirical predictions.

Lave and Suchman frequently seem to be writing about what is possible or impossible *in principle*. For example, Suchman (1987) suggested that it is probably impossible *in principle* to simulate actions or thought in a given situation because the computer cannot predict all of the dynamic cues or reactions of its interaction partner or of the situation. Vera and Simon's critique takes on some of these "in principle" issues, such as whether it is possible in principle to operate in a situation without symbols; however, the issues they focus on fail to make contact with those deemed important by their critics. Furthermore, in her book on legitimate peripheral participation, Lave's position increasingly took on a political tone (e.g., the gradual indoctrination of peripheral members of a group into fully participating ones in terms of both thought and social identity, the tendency of traditional schooling to perpetuate social inequities; this viewpoint is implied in Wegner's book as well.) The *problem* with this multifaceted viewpoint is that it is not formulated in a clear, systematic fashion, so that discussions of situated cognition often seem to move between levels, as happened in the Suchman (1993) and Clancey (1993) rebuttals to Vera and Simon (1993a).

I am not sure if it helps to refer to the opposing positions as having different "world views" (see Vera & Simon, 1993b, for a strong objection to this characterization), but it is certainly true that the two sides are talking past each other. Part of the problem is the variety of different situated cognition theorists and positions, both within cognitive science and from other disciplines. Another part is the rather different assumptions made by the different camps. For example, Simon and his associates believe that the debate can be settled on empirical grounds, whereas the situated cognitivists see it as more of a conceptual debate. I have also argued that, at least in the case of Lave, as well as Clancey (1993, 1997), any given position is presented on several different levels (see Agre, 1997, for a similar observation; see also Table 10.1 for a summary of these different levels.) Vera and Simon's position itself is not presented with absolute clarity either.

TABLE 10.1

Levels of Situated Cognition Position

Level	Argument
1. Empirical	Knowledge (or learning) does not transfer from one situation to another.
2. Methodological	Research on transfer suffers from the fact that the problems examined are separated from their everyday social context.
3. Theoretical	Understanding is generated by and is inseparable from activity rather than being a matter of the accumulation of knowledge.
4. Critique of traditional cognitive science	Cognitive science has been too concerned with cognitions "in the head" and too little concerned with the "lived-in world" (Lave, 1993, p. 7).
5. Critique of traditional learning theory	Traditional learning theory has been exclusively concerned with the transmission of knowledge rather than with its invention (Lave, 1993).
6. Critique of educational practice	Schools fail to take students' everyday knowledge and reasoning strategies into consideration, even though these find their way into school (e.g., solving arithmetic problems) anyway.
7. In principle	It is impossible in principle to predict knowledge from one situation to another because knowledge emerges from a given situation.
8. Sociopolitical	Learners start off as a "peripheral" member of a culture or "community of practitioners" (Lave & Wenger, 1991, p. 29), and learning is therefore a process of becoming enculturated into and becoming a full member of that culture or community.
	Learning involves actors with different positions, goals and perspectives rather than the kind of homogeneity assumed by most learning theories.

I have suggested that one valid criticism raised by Lave, Resnick, Wenger, and others is that school learning fails to take into account (different) students' everyday knowledge, and, as a result, fails to engage students' attention. This is certainly a reasonable point, particularly in view of the changing demographics of American schools and universities. However, the implication that everyday reasoning (e.g., in math) or the way in which *just plain folks* (JPFs; Lave, 1988) reason is good or wise enough (i.e., in that people are able to get along in their everyday world) is certainly open to debate. (See my discussion of rationality$_2$ in chap. 9.) For example, Kirshner and Whitson (1997) suggested that "One source of inspiration for situated cognitivists is the *robust expertise* that ordinary folks regularly display in ordinary situations" (p. 4, italics added) as opposed to the demonstrated failure of formal schooling to have an effect. Even though school must make some kind of contact with students' everyday knowledge in order to be maximally effective, certainly the purpose of education is not to simply reinforce existing knowledge and abilities, but rather to enable individuals to acquire more generalizable skills that extend beyond, and are superior to their skills as JPFs. It is one thing to criticize educational *practice*; it is quite another thing to accept lay reasoning and knowledge as "good enough." (See my later discussion of research on the adequacy of informal reasoning.)

The Concept of Distributed Cognition

Another clearly related concept is that of *distributed cognition* (e.g., Salomon, 1993a). Although this concept has been used in a variety of different ways, the general idea is that cognitions do not exist solely as isolated events inside the head of the individual:

> People appear to *think in conjunction or partnership* with others and with the help of culturally provided tools and implements. Cognitions, it would seem, are not content-free tools that are brought to bear on this or that problem; rather they emerge in a situation tackled by teams of people and the tools that are available to them. (Salomon, 1993b, p. xiii)

The overlap of these ideas with situated cognition should be clear.

The thrust of distributed cognition theory is clearest when one interacts with technological devices (as well as directly with other people). As I sit here with my word processor, I am not only dependent on the words of Gavriel Salomon and other writers on this topic; I am also dependent on the people who developed WordPerfect 7.1 and the knowledge they built into their software, as well as the people who developed the hardware for my notebook computer so that I can transport this knowledge from one location to another, not to mention the colleagues and students with whom I have discussed some of these ideas. As a relatively isolated scholar, I am nevertheless making use of the distributed knowledge of those whose work I am discussing.

The "Radical" Version.   Salomon (1993b, 1993c) argued that there are at least two different versions of the distributed cognition viewpoint (just as there were for situated cognition): a *radical* version, which suggests that all cognitions should be reconceptualized as social–cultural transactions, and a more traditional one, which proposes that there are cognitions in the head, but that there are also cognitions that are distributed over a number of people.

One position that falls in the former category is Pea's (1993) view of distributed intelligence. According to this position, external tools and resources such as the abacus or the hand calculator, and certainly the advent of computer technology, change the nature of intelligence:

> Knowledge is commonly socially constructed, through collaborative efforts toward shared objectives or by dialogues and challenges brought about by differences in persons' perspectives. Intelligence may also be distributed for use in designed artifacts as diverse as physical tools, representations such as diagrams, and computer-user interfaces. In these cases, intelligence is often distributed by off-loading what would be elaborate and error-prone mental reasoning processes as action constraints of either the physical or symbolic environments. (Pea, 1993, p. 48)

Another way of putting this, as Pea himself did, is that intelligence exists out there in these artifacts and tools. This argument is clearly similar to some situated cognition viewpoints (e.g., Clancey, 1993; Hutchins, 1995), and the emphasis on social construction is also similar to both situated cognition and my discussion of social representations theory (e.g., Moscovici, 1961) in chapter 1. In general, Pea emphasized the degree to which individuals depend on props in the environment rather than symbols "in the head" (cf. my discussion in chap. 8).

This distribution is particularly apparent in the computer age, where, as I indicated earlier, a seemingly solitary activity in fact involves an interaction with all the people whose knowledge went into the development of the software. (Such distribution is even clearer with interactive computing.) People offload their memory limitations to the memory of the computer; they offload spelling to a spellcheck, mathematics and statistics to statistical packages, and so forth. With the advent of the World Wide Web, distributed knowledge becomes an even more integral part of learning and education. At the same time, the computer also allows people to develop new skills and to augment existing ones.

The Conservative Version.   Two examples of the more conservative view of distributed cognition are offered by Perkins (1993) and Salomon (1993c; Salomon, Perkins, & Globerson, 1991). Perkins called his viewpoint the *person-plus* position (as opposed to a *person-solo* one). The example Perkins gave is of the knowledge acquired by a student in a class, *plus* the notes he or she has taken, which, strictly speaking, are not part of that individual's knowledge, but can be consulted. Salomon et al. (1991) emphasized the "residue" of peoples' interaction with technology, a residue that exists not only in the person's head (e.g., an acquired skill or change in knowledge), but in the environment (e.g., in some hard copy or disk copy) as well. In addition to generating this residue, the resources in the environment (e.g., a computer, a videotape) also serve as "vehicles of thought."

One implication of the person-plus versus person-solo distinction for education, according to Perkins (1993), is that schools typically place too much emphasis on the latter (or at best on "person plus paper and pencil"), and not enough on the former. In Perkins's view, the person-plus model is more likely to be of use in the real world, and "most students have much to learn about the art of distributing cognition, and schools should help" (p. 95). Thus, students typically do not use all (or even many) of the more creative features of word processors (e.g, moving paragraphs, trying out alternative ways of expressing the same idea, as opposed to simple spell checks or correction of grammar) or well-known strategies of note taking or reading.

Salomon (1993c) argued against the radical version of distributed cognition, and stressed instead the importance of maintaining the concept of a separate person. The emphasis should be on the "student's ability to handle *new* situations and meet *new* intellectual challenges" (p. 128; cf. Resnick, 1987b). This is particularly true in the case of technology, where too much dependence on, say, existing computer technology is likely to lead to problems given the rapid changes occurring in that arena. One must learn something besides the specific operations for a given program or a given statistical package. Finally, Salomon argued that rather than producing technology that simply allows the user to "offload" functions onto the computer or the environment, individuals should develop technologies or "intellectual partnerships" that provide guides to the user to develop his or her own skills.

Some Conclusions About Distributed Cognition. The notion of distributed cognition, much like that of situated cognition, expands the conception of everyday cognition in a couple of different ways. First, it suggests that much of "cognition" lies out there in the instructions on the microwave package or the visual displays in a videogame, rather than in individuals' heads (cf. the theorizing of Scribner reviewed in chap. 8). In addition, technology in general, and computer technology in particular, expand the arena of everyday cognition and will continue to do so. The question remains whether offloading more and more of our cognitive functions onto technological aids will have a salutary effect on human thought, which is both enhanced and diminished by such technology (see Pea, 1993, and Salomon, 1993c, for discussions). It is also ironic that a technology that many people feared would isolate people is, in fact, likely to introduce our thinking to more social influences.

Nickerson (1993) also voiced some reservations about the concept of distributed cognition. First, he questioned whether it is meaningful to equate a person's intelligence with the knowledge or intelligence "contained" or implicit in the tools and artifacts that that person uses. For example, Nickerson noted that two different persons using the same tool may use it with different effectiveness. In addition, most people who have used a word processor or statistical package will certainly have experienced frustration at these instruments not "knowing" something about their (the users') work (cf. Suchman's discussion of help menus). Similarly, it is not clear that students' notes, for example, contain distributed intelligence if that student is unable to access or reconstruct that knowledge. Finally, Nickerson, like Perkins, pointed out that one of the implications of the increasingly distributed nature of knowledge is that it is important for schools to provide students with tools—on the computer or elsewhere—for information gathering and access.

AUTHENTIC ASSESSMENT

The Nature of Authentic Assessment. One related approach to the *assessment* of knowledge or achievement (and an approach that also has implications for instruction) is the popular idea of *authentic assessment.* Authentic assessment refers to gathering information or evaluating students' performance on the basis of activities that are meaningful to them, ones that they can relate to or that tap into their interests. Such tests "require that students demonstrate what they can do in the same way that workers do in out-of-school settings: by performing tasks that are complex and that require production of solutions or products" (Darling-Hammond, Ancess, & Falk, 1995, p. 22).

One of the major concerns expressed here is that standardized, multiple-choice tests may not truly assess students' accomplishments, and the use of such tests may also have a deleterious effect on the way students are taught and the way in which they learn to "think" (i.e., focusing on low-level, isolated information). In contrast, authentic assessment usually involves projects that allow students to best demonstrate their skills and that involve a meaningful, usually long-term, active production (e.g., a folder of stories or poems, a science experiment). Furthermore, authentic assessment typically sees the purpose of assessment as giving feedback to students and helping them to plan future learning rather than as a way of "testing" or comparing that student to some normative standard.

A variety of different commentators (e.g., Baker, O'Neill, & Linn, 1993; Newmann, 1997; Wiggins, 1989) have proposed a variety of criteria that define an instrument as authentic or performance-based:

> They [authentic assessments] are designed to be truly representative of performance in the field. Students actually *do* writing. ... They *conduct* science experiments. ... The tasks are contextualized, complex intellectual challenges involving the student's own research or use of knowledge in "ill-structured" tasks. ... They also allow appropriate room for student learning styles, aptitudes, and interests. (Darling-Hammond et al., 1995, p. 12)

Second, assessment is based on and integrated with classroom activities (and hence is situated). Third, authentic assessment involves gathering evidence from multiple activities or products (e.g., multiple forms of literary performance and contexts). Fourth, in authentic assessment learners know what is expected of them, rather than having to guess what is on a multiple-choice test; these expectations are based on decisions made by a teacher familiar with her or his students or a mutual decision made by members of the school, rather than by some outside authority or bureaucrat. Finally, and most important, *"Authenticity* ... [involves] the use of disciplined inquiry that has some value or meaning beyond success in school" (Newmann, 1997, p. 361; see my discussion of the limitations of academic intelligence and intelligence tests in chap. 1).

One of the primary tools of authentic assessment is the use of *portfolios.* Portfolios are collections of students' performance or products (e.g., a sample of their artistic or literary products, or their scores on various math projects, selected by either the student or the teacher or both). Stecher and Herman (1993) identified several features of portfolio assessment, including (a) the material being evaluated is accumulated over an extended time period; (b) students play a role in selecting materials; and (c) students provide commentary on the material included. As in authentic assessment in general, the samples of products are chosen for the portfolio so as to fit in with instruction (see Herman & Winters, 1994, for evidence). Although portfolios have been widely trumpeted as a highly desirable alternative to standard ability assessment, as yet there has been relatively little systematic empirical research on the topic (Herman & Winters, 1994).

Some Reservations About Authentic Assessment.   Herman and Winters (1994; Stecher & Herman, 1997) argued that advocates of portfolio assessment are typically unconcerned with such things as reliability and validity:

> Many portfolio advocates, bridling against the measurement experts who, they believe, have long defined assessment practice and used it to drive curriculum and instruction, do not seem to give much weight to technical quality. These advocates accept at face value the belief that performance assessments in general and portfolio assessments in particular are better than traditional multiple-choice tests ... and are more suitable for the thinking and problem-solving skills that students will need for future success. (pp. 48–49)

Yet if educators wish to present results that serve as accurate measures for public decision making (and not just to facilitate student learning and curriculum planning), then criteria such as reliability and validity must be considered. Herman and Winters pointed out that there has been relatively little evidence collected on reliability; and the evidence that *does* exist is inconsistent (e.g., Hambleton et al., 1995; Koretz, Stecher, Klein, & McCaffrey, 1994). In those cases where reasonable interrater reliability has been found (e.g., Herman, Gearhart, & Baker, 1993), an attempt was made to provide clear criteria, rigorous training, and guidelines that express a common understanding of student performance (Herman & Winters, 1994). When it comes to validity, it is often the case that there are no acceptable outside criteria (because standardized ability tests are not acceptable).

Herman and Winters (1994) also argued that portfolios and other forms of authentic assessment may actually overestimate students' abilities, rather than standardized tests underestimating them. For example, different students get differing amounts of support in school in, for example, writing;

students also get different amounts of help from family and outside sources (which undoubtedly places minority and lower class students at a disadvantage). Furthermore, Webb (1993) found that students were judged to perform better when this judgment was based on group collaboration than when it was based on individual performance, and that this was particularly true for low-ability students. It should also be clear that there are numerous other alternatives to multiple-choice tests (e.g., essay exams, in-class writing assignments) that are not subject to these criticisms.

Stecher and Herman (1997) also raised the question of how to compare different students' performance on portfolio assessment (or on authentic assessment in general; Baker et al., 1993). That is, whereas standardized tests give scores on a common set of problems, portfolios are individualized for specific students' needs and capabilities. This personalized approach is fine for the purpose of instruction (assuming that the teachers can, in fact, assess their own student's capabilities and needs). However, for the purpose of selection of students or for school districts to justify their programs, the lack of comparability among students is a real obstacle.

One other major problem with authentic assessment is the difficulty of determining what tasks are or are not authentic (see Valencia et al., 1994, for a similar point), just as I noted the difficulty in defining "everyday" in chapter 1. Clearly, what is authentic will depend on what activities are typically engaged in by a given culture, subculture, or group. For example, the uses of mathematics will be very different for lower class street vendors in Brazil versus upper- or middle-class Brazilians; and the relevance of computers will differ for different classes or ethnic groups as well. Trying to tailor assessment to the environment and needs of a given student is an attractive ideal, but an objective that is difficult to achieve in practice. For example, in chapter 9 I reviewed a number of judgment biases (e.g., the representativeness heuristic, the confirmation bias) that may interfere with accurate judgments. There is also the question of whether teachers can draw accurate conclusions about students based on multiple, diverse, and oftentimes qualitative indicators. Although the call for using multiple indicators has a nice ring to it, there is a good deal of evidence from research on clinical judgment (e.g., Dawes, Faust, & Meehl, 1989, 1993; Grove & Meehl, 1996) that suggests that professionals are neither very reliable nor accurate in combining the results of multiple pieces of information. In point of fact, Gearhart, Herman, Baker, and Witaker (1993) reported that half of the students who were classified as "masters" on the basis of overall summary scores for their portfolios were not so classified when an average based on scores of the individual components of this portfolio was used. In this connection M. M. Voss (1992) cited an example of an elementary school teacher who found that the entries in her portfolios were too overwhelming, and so in filling out a report card, she "relied [in her narrative] on her general knowledge of the students rather than documentation" (p. 28). For that matter, it is not even clear what the criterion of accuracy might be in authentic assessment (see Herman & Walters, 1994).

All of these factors suggest that there may be major difficulties in interpreting the results of such assessment (cf. Valencia et al., 1994, for a similar warning).

There are also some obvious administrative problems posed by authentic assessment, particularly in the present political, economic climate. First, there is an apparent dilemma in trying to provide feedback to students and teachers on the one hand, and the need for accountability to policymakers on the other (see Stecher & Herman, 1997). Second, Baker and O'Neil (1994; Baker et al., 1993) wrote extensively about the problem of inequity in the use of portfolios. For example, one difficulty is that "Tasks likely to appeal to the majority culture will ... more probably be represented in assessments with comparative or accountability purposes" (Baker & O'Neil, 1994, p. 16). In addition, lower-class children are less likely to have had instruction in higher-level reasoning; therefore, they are likely to have a harder time adjusting to the authentic assessment approach. Furthermore, different types of tasks must be designed "that uniquely stimulate their interest, relate to their particular world and prior knowledge, and otherwise adapt to their special backgrounds" (Baker & O'Neil, 1994, p. 16). Finally, if one believes that school is a means for social and economic advancement (contra Lave), then teaching to a particular group of students' current social status would seem to be discriminatory.

None of this is to suggest that authentic assessment is an unworthy endeavor. In fact, the general idea of authentic assessment has much to recommend that. Certainly most teachers have had the feeling that if they could somehow harness the same abilities and motivation that students show in everyday activities and apply these to their classroom learning, most of these students would perform at a higher level in school. This point obviously relates to my discussion of situated cognition earlier in this chapter. Of course, one of the major points of this chapter is to underline the value of making contact with students' everyday experience. Similarly, because education is designed in part to provide students with the skills to cope with life experiences in general, it makes sense to try to provide "genuine" rather than contrived learning experiences. Nevertheless, it is important to recognize some of the difficulties raised by such idealistic efforts as well.

THE ADEQUACY (OR INADEQUACY) OF INFORMAL REASONING

If, in fact, we choose to appeal to students' everyday reasoning or knowledge in teaching academic subjects (or in lieu of these), it is important to evaluate the adequacy of such reasoning. In chapter 9 I discussed some of the different views of rationality, and the different conclusions reached when judgment or reasoning is evaluated in terms of standards of formal reasoning on the one hand, or in terms of pragmatic value on the other.

Perkins' Research on Informal Reasoning

A somewhat different approach to the evaluation of informal, everyday reasoning has been presented by David Perkins and his associates (e.g., Perkins, 1989; Perkins, Allen, & Hafner, 1983; Perkins et al., 1991). Perkins (1985a; Perkins et al., 1991) suggested that informal reasoning involves *situation modeling* (cf. Kintsch, 1988), or building a conception of the situation and then constructing alternative scenarios, along with arguments (e.g., causal, intentional) for each (see my discussion of counterfactual reasoning and counterexplanation in chap. 9). The criteria for judging the soundness of informal reasoning, then, are the balance or one-sidedness of the arguments and their completeness (i.e., the number of different arguments raised) as well as the occurrence of certain errors in such reasoning.

More specifically, Perkins's research has focused on what he called *vexed* issues, or issues where there are two opposing positions that can be defended. For example, one of the issues posed in Perkins' studies was "does violence on television significantly increase the likelihood of violence in real life?" (Perkins, 1985a, p. 564). Participants, who ranged from high school to graduate students, were typically given two issues of this sort and were asked to make some kind of "snap judgment" of the right answer to such a question. Then they were asked to take a position and develop arguments for that position. Finally, participants received prompts or scaffolding to get them to make more complete and less biased arguments. Participants' answers were scored in terms of the number of arguments presented, the number of arguments on either side of the issue, the number and type of errors, and an overall rating of the quality of the reasoning.

The major finding of this research was that participants, even when prompted or guided, were able to produce very few arguments; those arguments that they did produce tended to be their own position (what Perkins et al., 1991, have labeled "my side" arguments) rather than producing counterarguments (or "other-side" arguments). For example, Perkins (1985a) found that high school students produced a total of 2.4 lines of argument per issue, with 1.8 lines being my-side arguments. First-year college students produced four lines, 2.9 of which were my-side arguments, whereas graduate students produced 4.6 lines, with 3.3 lines being my-side arguments. Perkins (1985a) reported a finding from pilot work that 6.0 lines of argument for each side were readily "accessible," suggesting that participants' reasoning was incomplete as well as biased. In addition, Perkins (1985b) found that when fourth year high school, college, and graduate students were compared with their first year counterparts, only the high school students showed improvement over the four years (and this gain was only 0.4 lines). This suggests that reasoning does not show a great deal of improvement with greater education.

Perkins (1985a, 1985b; Perkins, Bushey, & Farady, 1986) examined a number of factors that may influence the quality of informal reasoning. Degree of interest in a topic was not correlated with lines of argument, though participants who were asked to present arguments for an issue that was personally important and also "vexing" to them (e.g., a career or marital choice) produced over 9 lines of argument and a more balanced set of my-side and other-side arguments. However, because these participants were self-selected based on them indicating that they had a vexed personal issue (and because participants indicated that they had spent an average of 125 hours thinking about the issue), these results do not necessarily mean that reasoning about personal issues is always characterized by extensive and balanced arguments. (You can undoubtedly think of issues that are of personal interest on which your arguments are completely one-sided and not well thought out; see Woll & Loukides, 2000, and Perkins, 1989). Prior knowledge does not seem to be related to elaborateness or balance of participants' arguments. Although IQ is related to number of arguments, this holds only for my-side arguments.

One other factor examined by Perkins is "know how," that is, knowing how to produce arguments or how to debate (see my discussion of tacit knowledge in chap. 8). Perkins et al. (1986) reported that explicit instructions to generate more arguments and more balanced ones produced a 150% increase in other-side arguments. Perkins et al. also compared four different types of training: a semester in a debating class, the first year at a liberal arts college (which emphasized reasoning skills), a semester of graduate school in education (again, at a school emphasizing general reasoning), and a year in law school. The major finding was that the debating experience, as well as the first year at a liberal arts school, led to "modest" improvement in reasoning, but only in my-side arguments. There were no effects of graduate school or law school. When metacognitive prompts (e.g., asking participants to provide more arguments when they seemed to have exhausted their store of arguments) were provided, participants showed a 100% increase in my-side arguments and a 700% increase in other-side ones. Finally, providing a course in situation modeling produced a more modest increase (100%) in other-side arguments.

Perkins (1989) also reported the results of a study in which scaffolding was provided to high school students consisting of requests for more other-side arguments, followed by asking for five more of both my-side and other-side arguments and a detailed consideration of students' own arguments and a counterarguing procedure. Under these conditions, participants showed a significant increase in both my-side and other-side arguments (109% and 700% increases, respectively).

Perkins et al. (1983) suggested that the reason for our generally poor everyday reasoning is that instead of working for good, thorough situation modeling, most people instead use what they call a *makes sense epistemology*. That is, they are concerned with constructing a position that "makes sense," that "hangs together well and displays good congruence with one's most prominent prior beliefs" (Perkins et al., 1991, p. 98; cf. the similar concept of *satisficing* by Simon, 1956). Thus, once individuals have convinced themselves that their arguments "make sense," they stop generating arguments, own-side or other-side, resulting in biased and incomplete reasoning. (Perkins, 1989, correctly pointed out the similarity of this observation to research on the confirmation bias, reviewed in chap. 9.) In later publications, Perkins, Jay, and Tishman (1993) linked these limitations to the notion of *learning dispositions,* or students' "abiding tendencies to [not] be mindful, invest mental energy, explore, inquire, organize thinking, take intellectual risks, and so on" (Perkins et al., 1993, p. 75).

The reasons for maintaining such a "makes sense" viewpoint are similar to those reviewed in chapter 9 for judgment heuristics: "It is quick, easy, and, for many purposes, perfectly adequate" (Perkins et al., 1991, p. 99); it is well-suited to people's limited processing capacity; and it provides people with a defense against possible threats to their strongly held beliefs. Such a viewpoint, however, cannot deal with new, inconsistent information and thus must falsify reality to maintain a consistent outlook. The alternative is to adopt a more *critical epistemology,* which, if it is coherent, allows us to take more factors into account, be open to more possibilities, and to make better decisions because more information is available.

One possible problem with the Perkins findings and conclusions—which I am sure squares with many college professors' impressions—is that it is difficult to clearly distinguish between "learning dispositions" and mere rhetorical style (see Tetlock, Hannum, & Micheletti, 1984). That is, the questioning procedure used by Perkins does not explicitly ask for other-side arguments, and therefore, it is at least possible that participants simply do not understand the importance of articulating these counterarguments. Alternatively, they may be so used to defending or advocating a particular side of an issue that they do not even feel the need to articulate the arguments on the other side. For example, the simple act of asking participants to generate more arguments or more other-side arguments leads to a significant increase in both types of argument. In addition, in our own research (e.g., Wilson & Woll, 2000; Woll, Navarrete, Sussman, & Marcoux, 1998), to be described later, we asked participants to give both pro and con arguments to everyday issues, and found that with these instructions participants generated nearly as many con as pro arguments.

It is also worth noting that Perkins's conclusion about the small number of arguments generated by participants is somewhat misleading. This is because his operational definition of an argument is rather stringent. Specifically, a participant could state an argument that additional funding for education would allow schools to buy more computers and then give a number of different justifications for why more computers would benefit learning. All of these justifications would be scored simply as elaborations on the single argument of "buying computers." This is a perfectly justifiable definition or criterion of an argument, but it may give a somewhat misleading picture of the adequacy of students' reasoning abilities.

Voss's Research and Model of Informal Reasoning

Another related approach to commonsense reasoning is that of James Voss. In chapter 7, I alluded to Voss's research on knowledge of social sciences and international relations on the one hand, and on baseball on the other. In recent years J. F. Voss (1991; J. F. Voss et al., 1989) has turned to the study of more informal types of reasoning. J. F. Voss et al. (1989) adapted and combined two models put forward by the philosophers Angel (1964) and Toulmin (1958) to evaluate such informal reasoning. In the resulting model (see Fig. 10.1) there is a *conclusion,* which is divided up into a *claim* or argument and a *datum,* or the evidence for that claim. A *condition* is a factor that might influence the datum, the claim, or both (e.g., the breakup of the Soviet Union might influence calls for a large military budget), and the data that back these arguments. A *qualification* refers to a specific condition under which the claim can be made (e.g., a deduction can be made on your income tax only if a particular condition holds), and an *enabling* condition refers to a condition that permits the claim to be made (e.g., having a baby enables a woman to be a mother). The *reasons* in Fig. 10.1 refer to counterarguments that contradict the original claim.

In Voss et al.'s initial research on this topic, participants from six different groups (all combinations of high and low education, high and low formal coursework in economics, and employment in an economically related area or not[4]) were given three different economic topics; interest rates, automobile prices, and the federal deficit. Participants were first to mention as

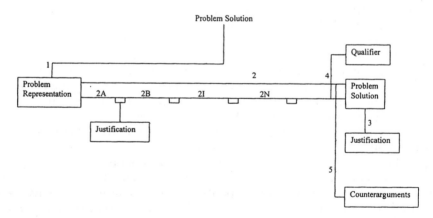

FIG. 10.1. A representation of Toulmin's (1985) model of informal reasoning. Adapted from "Informal Reasoning and Subject Matter Knowledge in the Solving of Problems by Naive and Novice Individuals," by J. F. Voss, J. Blais, M. L. Means, T. R. Green, & E. Ahwesh, 1986, *Cognition and Instruction, 3,* p. 273. Copyright © 1986 by Lawrence Erlbaum Associates. Reprinted with the permission.

---

[4]Because participants who had not gone to college could not have taken a formal economics course, two of the eight combinations were not possible.

many factors as they could that might influence these three issues and indicate how or why these factors could produce change. Next, they were asked to say which of these factors would have the greatest impact. Finally, participants received 28 problems dealing with the three different topics and were asked to indicate what would happen, and why—for instance, "if health care costs rise considerably, what effect, if any, do you think this would have on the size of the federal deficit, and why?" (J. F. Voss et al., 1989, p. 226).

Participants' answers to these questions were analyzed in a number of different ways. First, the six different groups gave approximately the same number of arguments, with the exception of the college educated group with no economic coursework and no economically related jobs. This group gave a significantly greater number of arguments on the automobile price question only. Second, three out of the four groups with a college education gave more abstract answers than did the two groups without such an education. Third, all four college educated groups gave better, sounder reasons (i.e., better in terms of economic theory) than did those groups without a college education; but economic coursework in and of itself did not make a difference.

When it came to the concepts outlined in Fig. 10.1, all groups appeared to represent the questions appropriately; but the groups who lacked a college education tended to show either deletions (e.g., converting "steel imports" to "importing" in general) or substitution of concepts (e.g., talking about "automobile imports" instead of "steel imports"). There were no group differences in the frequency of either direct answers (i.e., ones that directly stated a claim plus a reason) or indirect ones (i.e., those that followed some line of reasoning to get to a claim), although the reasons given by the college group for their claims were judged to be sounder than those given by the group without a college education. The latter group showed more distortions in their "line of argument" (e.g., unconnected arguments) and in their indirect answers, and they included fewer qualifiers and counterarguments.

The major finding of this study, at least from Voss et al.'s point of view, is the failure to find differences between those with and without specific formal economic coursework (what Voss et al. referred to as novices vs. *naive* participants). This finding suggests that coursework did not have an impact on participants' everyday reasoning about economic matters, a finding that contrasts with previous research by McCloskey and his associates (McCloskey & Kohl, 1983; McCloskey, Washburn, & Felch, 1983) on the positive effects of high school or college courses in physics on students' reasoning about everyday physics problems. One interpretation of these results offered by Voss et al. is that there was a better fit between the everyday physics problems and students' coursework, whereas the economics problems in their study involved issues that naive participants could have picked up from their personal experience or the media or other everyday sources. (After a reading of the questions used in this study, I find this interpretation unconvincing.)

The finding that college students performed better in most respects than did noncollege students could be the result of a number of different factors (e.g., differences in IQ). Voss et al. pointed out, however, that these results are seemingly contrary to the findings by Perkins et al., who, you will recall, found that four years of college did not make a difference in participants' everyday reasoning (although Perkins et al. *did* find a difference between those with a high school education and those with a college education). The fact that college students showed a greater proficiency at informal reasoning mechanisms suggested to Voss et al. (1989) that college course work should be concerned with "the utilization of informal reasoning in acquiring and utilizing knowledge" (p. 245), as well as imparting knowledge per se, because these two factors are interrelated in the Voss et al. study. Voss et al. even suggested that testing for such informal reasoning might be tried, both for its own sake and as a possible predictor of college aptitude. Finally, in a later paper on informal reasoning, Voss (1991) emphasized the importance of teaching such reasoning in the social sciences in the same way that problem solving is taught in math and the natural sciences, and that such training in reasoning must also involve greater *knowledge* of social science material.

Kuhn on Argumentation Skills

One final approach to everyday reasoning that focuses directly on the development of argumentation skills is that of Deanna Kuhn (1991, 1992, 1993). Kuhn began her discussion with a distinction between two senses of the term "argument." On the one hand, a *rhetorical* argument conforms to the dictionary definition—a claim or assertion and a justification (see Voss's model described above). What is more important to Kuhn, however, as it was to Perkins, is the notion of a *dialogic* argument, or an argument as an assertion that has an opposite. In her own research Kuhn examined not only participants' assertions and justifications on a set of "everyday" issues, but also their alternative arguments, counterarguments, and rebuttals. Equally important, Kuhn's position is that *all* arguments are implicitly dialogic.

In her qualitative research study, Kuhn posed three questions to participants, and then conducted interviews designed to elicit arguments on both sides of the issue. The three issues were "What causes prisoners to return to prison after they've been released?" "What causes children to fail in school?" and "What causes unemployment?" Notice that all three of these questions ask for causal explanations, and also that all three are subject to the criticisms raised earlier about the definition of "everyday" issues, although Kuhn (1991) argued that all three were selected "as ones people are likely to have occasion to think and talk about" (p. 16). The interview involved eliciting a participant's causal account, followed by probes for that participant to justify his or her arguments. This in turn was followed by a question about possible counterarguments. Finally, participants were asked to give a rebuttal to either the direct counterarguments or alternative theories specified in the preceding question. It should be noted that these probe questions were typically posed as an attempt to convince or answer the arguments from another person; and Kuhn, following Vygotsky (1978), Piaget (1950), and others, explicitly argued for the internal reasoning being the product of internalized social discourse. In addition, Kuhn's study is notable in that it sampled four groups ranging from teenage high school students to 60-year-old retirees.

Of particular interest in this essentially descriptive study is Kuhn's distinction between *pseudoevidence* and *genuine evidence,* the former of which simply reinforces the "plausibility" of the causal account, whereas the latter speaks to the "correctness" of that account (i.e., that the cause does, in fact, produce the result, rather than just showing that the cause makes sense; cf. Perkins). Stated differently, pseudoevidence, which was the most frequent form of justification "takes the form of a scenario, or script [either generalized of in terms or specific instances], depicting how the phenomenon might occur" (Kuhn, 1991, p. 64). Such pseudoevidence amounts to a redescription or illustration of the original causal assertion. Both of these types can be distinguished from nonevidence, which includes evidence that is not necessary or relevant to the causal theory, citing evidence that does not relate to that theory, or "cit[ing] the phenomenon itself as evidence regarding its cause" (Kuhn, 1991, p. 82; see Table 10.2 for examples of both types of evidence and nonevidence.)

In looking at the use of genuine evidence, Kuhn found that the frequency of such evidence differed, though not significantly, from topic to topic, with the greatest percentage (40%) coming for the topic that participants were likely to have the most personal experience with (i.e., failure in school) and the smallest (28%) for the topic that they presumably had the least personal experience with (i.e., the return to prison). No significant differences were found across different age groups, but educational level did make a difference. Specifically, those with a college education were significantly more likely to give genuine evidence than were those without (60% vs. 24%, respectively). This evidence clearly speaks to Perkins's and Voss's arguments about the effect of a college education on the quality of informal reasoning.

Another set of findings that relates to Perkins's research concerns the frequency with which participants offered alternative theories and counterarguments. The percentage of participants who were able to provide alternative theories—which is obviously critical to the notion of a dialogic argument—was substantially higher (64%) than the percentage for genuine evidence, though there was a significant relationship between the former and the latter. As in the previous analysis, there were no significant differences among the topics, though the same trend held. Once again, the differences among age groups was nonsignificant, whereas college educated participants were significantly more likely to generate alternative theories than were those without a college education.

TABLE 10.2

Examples of Genuine Evidence, Pseudoevidence, and Nonevidence
from the Kuhn (1991) Study

---

1. Genuine evidence

a. Covariation evidence

[Participant is asked how he might give evidence for his arguments that school failure is the result of a lack of family support.] "Well, I think that they can look at kids that are failing in school and see if the parent is present or parents are doing their job." (What do you think they would find out?) "Well, I think they would find out that the parents weren't there." (p. 46)

b. Evidence external to the causal sequence

[Participant asked to give evidence for why returning to the same environment might be the cause of prisoners returning to prison.] "Perhaps if older brothers and sisters, or peers, or people close to prisoners, have been in prison before, that might show that this is the sort of environment that one was brought up in and knows and can easily return to." (p. 55)

c. Indirect evidence

(What causes prisoners to return to crime after they're released?) [Participant's answer was returning to the same environment.] "Human beings are very much creatures of habit, and I don't think that there's such a habit as committing a crime, but everything up to committing a crime is probably a habit." (How do you know that this is the cause?) "I'm not certain, but it just seems pretty obvious from all the other spheres of life, people are so set in their ways." (p. 60)

2. Pseudoevidence

(How do you know that this [i.e., the fact that crime is rewarding] is the cause?) "Because I think if they want to become a good citizen, they would. But if they go to jail and come back out and are on the street again and are back in crime, you can't go back to their case histories to check on what they did. One crime is committed. That is put aside and they start a new one. I mean the judge can review it, but it isn't told to the jury or anything else or anything like that. And these are repeat offenders." (If you were trying to convince someone else that your view that wanting to stay in crime is the cause, what evidence would you give to try to show this?) "Well, I would get some evidence of people that did commit crimes and went to jail and now are good, honest citizens. And there are. There are many. ..." (Just to be sure that I understand, can you explain exactly how this shows that wanting to stay in crime is the cause?) "Well, they always blame the environment and how they are brought up, and I can remember, I can state that crime and the burning of buildings that you have throughout the United States today ..." [proceeds to a comparison of how things were in his day.] (pp. 71–72)

3. Nonevidence

(If you were trying to convince someone else that your view is right, what evidence would you give to try to show this?) "Well, I'd look up in books what percentage of people did crimes, just to get the percentage, and the I'd check out the seriousness of the crime. I might see what type of crime it was. And, I don't know, I might if possible, try to get to meet the people. I mean just through information. I mean give him more facts and more facts. To back up the facts I'd give him more facts. I think I could convince someone." (pp. 83–84)

From *The Skills of Argument,* by D. Kuhn, 1991, New York: Cambridge University Press. Copyright © 1991 by Cambridge University Press. Reprinted with permission.

With regard to counterarguments, as one might expect from Perkins's research findings, participants had a difficult time coming up with such arguments, even though Kuhn's notion of a dialogic argument presupposes that the ability to see such counterarguments is an essential component of successful argumentation. Less than half (47%) of participants were able to generate such counterarguments, and many of these were weak counterarguments (i.e., they left the original causal account partially intact, or did not completely invalidate the original argument). Amongst those who were unsuccessful or only partially successful at generating counterarguments, the greatest percentage tended to offer alternative theories as counterarguments. Nearly 25% of participants were not able or willing to generate counterarguments for any of the three issues. On questioning, the most frequent reason for this was that because the antecedent and consequent frequently occurred together, no consideration of an alternative cause was necessary. (Kuhn pointed out the obvious similarity of this situation to the confirmation bias discussed in chap. 9; but I might also cite the research on covariation assessment, as well as Perkins's notion of a "makes sense epistemology.") Finally, there was, once again, a relationship between ability to generate a counterargument and ability to produce genuine evidence, although this relationship was weaker than that for the ability to generate alternative theories. As before, participants with a college education were better able to generate counterarguments than were those without, with the exception of the presumably familiar school-failure topic where the two groups did equally well.

The third step in Kuhn's interviews was to ask participants to give rebuttals to their counterarguments. Here Kuhn distinguished between two types of successful rebuttals: namely, *simple* and *integrative rebuttals*. (These successful rebuttals can themselves be distinguished from a variety of unsuccessful rebuttals, including simply reasserting the original argument or rebuttals that contradict the original theory, as well as from "nonattempts" to rebut.) Simple rebuttals are just specific arguments against the counterarguments generated in the previous stage, whereas integrative rebuttals refer to ones that try to connect or integrate the counterargument with the original theory, in the process of arguing for the superiority of the latter. As I discuss later, this distinction bears a certain similarity to the notion of integrative complexity used by Tetlock and his associates (e.g., Tetlock & Hannum, 1983) in the area of political reasoning. Kuhn's findings indicate that 47% of participants gave rebuttals, and 25% of these gave integrative rebuttals. Once again, those with a college education were more likely to give successful rebuttals in general and integrative rebuttals in particular than were those without a college education.

Kuhn also emphasized a point that was stressed by Perkins: namely, that individuals must take an attitude that such argumentation is of value in the first place. In her questioning of participants on this issue, Kuhn identified what she considered to be three different attitudes or *epistemological theories*. The most frequent attitude, accounting for over half of the participants, was what Kuhn refers to as an *absolutist* viewpoint. According to this view, it is possible to have an absolute truth, and experts can know this truth (such as the answers to the three issues described earlier) with certainty. The second attitude is the *multiplist* viewpoint, which argues *against* absolute certainty and *for* a kind of epistemological relativism where all opinions are equally valid and are more of a matter of taste than of validity. Finally, there is the *evaluative* viewpoint, which also argues against absolute certainty, but which sees the expert position as more certain than the participant's own. Clearly, the preferred scientific or rational position is the last of these. Not surprisingly, though, only 15% of participants showed this sort of position. Equally unsurprising, the greatest number of participants (51%) showed an absolutist epistemology. Although those with a college education were less likely to be absolutist than those without (41% vs. 65%, respectively), this viewpoint was still the dominant one for the college students as well (except in the case of school failure issue where absolutist and multiplist views were about equally frequent). Finally, the relationships between theses epistemological theories and the other argumentation skills reviewed were nonsignificant.

In a separate session of this same study participants were asked to evaluate two different types of evidence about the return-to-prison and the school-failure issues. These two types were labeled *underdetermined* and *overdetermined* evidence. Underdetermined evidence involved simply giving participants a description of the issue with a specific instance, with no other evidence or mention of possible causes at all. Overdetermined evidence, on the other hand, involved presenting three different possible causes advocated by three different authorities along with the outcome.

The results of this interrogation are not very encouraging. For underdetermined evidence, where no causal accounts were given, participants tended to impose their own theory or causal account on the evidence. Perhaps even more discouraging was the fact that when participants were given overdetermined evidence, they tended to focus on the causal account that was most consistent with their own theory, though participants showed lower levels of certainty in their position in this condition than in the underdetermined one. Kuhn interpreted these results as suggesting that people frequently do not see a "boundary" between evidence and their theories or do not evaluate the evidence in its own right, apart from how it might be interpreted through their theory. Another way to think about this is that people have a hard time dealing with information that is inconsistent with their schema.[5] Such findings also support the notion of a confirmation bias discussed in chapter 9. Fortunately, those with a college education were less

---

[5]There is also evidence by Tyler and Voss (1982) on the effect of amount of knowledge on the processing of information congruent and incongruent with their political position about the USSR.

likely to express certainty in response to the evidence and were more likely to acknowledge alternative causes than were those without a college education.

In connection with my discussion of expertise in chapter 7, Kuhn also included an analysis of the responses of 15 "experts": 5 philosophers without domain-specific knowledge, 5 "expert" (i.e., experienced) parole officers with domain-specific knowledge on the return-to-prison issue, and 5 "expert" school teachers with domain-specific knowledge on the school-failure issue. The results of this small sample comparison are seemingly at odds with the findings from the expertise literature. Specifically, the philosophers performed better at the various components of effective argumentation despite their lack of domain-specific knowledge, whereas the two groups of domain-specific experts actually performed worse (e.g., at generating counterarguments and in showing evaluative epistemologies) in their own area of expertise. These results suggest that when it comes to higher order reasoning, rather than everyday problem solving, high domain knowledge can actually serve as an impediment to systematic reasoning (cf. Greenwald, Pratkanis, Leippe, & Baumgartner, 1986, for a similar observation for theory testing in psychology as a discipline). It should be noted, however, that these results are somewhat inconsistent with other evidence (e.g., Fiske, Kinder, & Larter, 1983; Tyler & Voss, 1982) on the weighing of schema-inconsistent evidence by experts. Recall also that in chapter 7 I noted that when experts in physics move into a domain with which they are less familiar, they are more likely to use general methods or heuristics to solve problems. Of course, philosophers are specifically trained in the use of general, domain-independent reasoning skills.

In her summary of these various findings, Kuhn argued that the most significant result is the degree to which participants showed certainty about their viewpoints and were absolutist in their views. This tendency is, if anything, exaggerated in the case of topics with which they are familiar. Although I have pointed out some conflicting findings here, I must say that this finding squares to some extent with my personal impression that people seem to be more confident and more dogmatic about everyday, personal issues with which they have experience than about, say, political or economic ones. According to Kuhn's evidence, everyday reasoners too often do not think of their theories as theories, do not consider alternative positions, and do not view evidence except in terms of their own theories. Kuhn clearly sees these findings and the kind of tasks and issues used in her research as reflecting the kinds of reasoning that goes on in many, if not most everyday situations (see Kuhn et al., 1994, for an extension of these results to jurists' justification of their verdicts in a reproduction of a murder trial). On this note, Kuhn tries to relate her results to such everyday judgment phenomena as the belief bias, the overconfidence effect, and the belief perseverance phenomenon, as well as to the aforementioned confirmation bias—all topics that I considered in chapter 9. She also related her findings to the domain-specificity debate, which I discussed in chapter 7, claiming that her results argue for the possibility of reasoning skills and deficiencies that apply across different topics or domains. (In so doing, Kuhn overlooked the fact that she also found some differences in reasoning styles across different problems, particularly when the personal relevance or expertise of a topic was varied.) Finally, and most obviously, Kuhn drew a connection between her results and the viewpoint reviewed earlier by Perkins and his students.

The comparison to research on judgment biases offers a clear reminder of the issue raised in chapter 9 about the different forms and models of rationality. Specifically, Kuhn's model of argumentation and her comparison of everyday reasoning to scientific reasoning (e.g., Kuhn, 1989, 1993) clearly suggest another model of rationality$_2$, one that is consistent with the similar model put forth by Piaget (1952, and thus, the question that is raised is: Should such a model of rationality$_2$ be used as a standard against which the rationality of everyday reasoning, or rationality$_1$, should be evaluated? There is certainly a sense in which Kuhn's model of argumentation and systematic reasoning seems to be a more appropriate one for education to aspire to, but then some philosophers and psychologists interested in deductive reasoning may consider traditional models of propositional logic or analytic reasoning to be more suitable, and those interested in inductive reasoning may reasonably argue for the laws of probability to be a more appropriate one. In fact, in the most frequently used psychological text on critical reasoning (Halpern, 1996) includes chapters on each of these models.

More important, though, is the question of whether systematic, reflective reasoning, of the sort advocated by Kuhn, is either necessary or even desirable in an individual's everyday commerce with the world. For example, as I asked in chapter 9, is it always desirable to engage in a thorough-going consideration of alternative viewpoints and counterarguments and an unbiased consideration of new information? Recall the discussion on naturalistic decision-making, where choices have to be made on the spot, or the account of time pressures by Jungermann (1983) in chapter 9. Certainly Kuhn's model is an admirable one for making long-term, serious decisions such as career choices, investment decisions, marital selection, political decisions, and the like. But what about deciding where to go lunch, or whether to take your umbrella today, or how to respond to a request made by a friend or colleague? (See Gigerenzer & Todd, 1999, for an interesting variation on this argument—and a rather different view of marital choice!—in their defense of "fast and frugal heuristics.") Earlier I examined the value of heuristics so long as they lead to favorable outcomes; in chapter 9 I also discussed the concept of adaptive rationality. If a given "theory" or style of thinking works to promote good outcomes and also conserves cognitive resources, is that not in some way preferable in many or most everyday activities to a deliberative consideration of all alternatives? Certainly as issues become more personal, as Kuhn herself found, systematic, unbiased thinking becomes more unlikely.[6]

Once again, this should certainly not be interpreted as a condemnation of all instruction in rational, deliberative thought. I am a major advocate of teaching critical thinking both in the context of social science content and in separate critical reasoning course work. My aim here is simply to raise the question of whether a model of rigorous, systematic thought is really a meaningful model of everyday reasoning in general.

There is also the question raised earlier of whether the issues used by Kuhn really do represent issues of personal relevance, or "everyday" issues for most people. Although the question of school failure may be one that impinges on many people's—students' and parents'—lives, the causes of unemployment and of recidivism in crime probably do not, or at least not in this particular decontextualized form. Rather, these are rather abstract issues that people probably think about primarily when they are brought up in thoughtful discussions or when queried by inquisitive researchers or academics.

One thing, I believe, is clear: At best, the kinds of issues explored in Kuhn's (as well as Perkins's and Voss's) research represent only one small part of what can reasonably be called "everyday reasoning."

Some Complications, and Is It Really Everyday Reasoning?

Results somewhat at variance with Voss's and Kuhn's were reported by Woll and Loukides (2000; see also Woll, Kernes, Wentsel, & Raymond, 1992). In this study political novices (Introductory Psychology students) were compared with relative experts, or what Voss would label as naive participants (i.e., political campaign workers and political science majors) on a variety of different dimensions, including political reasoning. In this study reasoning was assessed by giving participants a set of political dilemmas (e.g., what the United States should do if there were a Communist takeover of the Philippines), which they were to respond to within seven sentences. The major relevant results of this study for the current discussion were that experts differed from novices not only in their political knowledge, but also in terms of different dimensions of reasoning. Specifically, "experts" included more politically relevant facts; their justifications followed a more logical se-

---

[6]I am reminded here of the somewhat similar, though more skeletal theory of personal constructs by George Kelly (1955). Kelly's view, which is frequently described as a model of the human scientist, argues for a particular type of scientific construct called the *propositional* construct, or a construct that leaves open other dimensions on which an object or event may be interpreted. However, even Kelly acknowledged that sometimes you need to stop leaving options open and preempt further construing, even though in other situations such *preemptive* or close-minded constructs are undesirable. And of course, there is the comment by Jerome Bruner (1956), in his review of Kelly's volumes, that he rather thought that "when some people get angry or inspired or in love" (p. 356), he assumed that they were interested in something other than simply extending their construct systems.

quence; they were more likely to justify their answers in terms of some abstract ethical or political principle; and they were more likely to refer to alternative viewpoints in their answers. Experts' answers were also more integratively complex (Tetlock & Hannum, 1983): that is, they took more dimensions into consideration and were more likely to try to integrate these different dimensions. Thus, both coursework and work in the field seemed to lead to increases in political expertise (though sheer interest in politics cannot be ruled out as a factor).

There is a clearly some disagreement among the results of these three studies. First, the Woll and Loukides study agreed with Perkins et al. in that introductory psychology students showed relatively poorly argued justifications of their positions, giving very few and poorly organized arguments. On the other hand, the Woll and Loukides results disagree with the results of the Voss et al. study, because it appeared that coursework in political science improved participants' reasoning in that domain, and it did so on dimensions similar to those used by Voss et al. (i.e., logic of argument sequence and justification in term of higher order principles).

What was needed here was a study of reasoning on more *everyday* topics, such as personal relationships, life decisions, important purchases (see Denney, 1989; Hartley, 1989), rather than on less immediately relevant, more academic topics such as the federal deficit or a Communist takeover of the Philippines. (These may represent everyday topics for academics, but I suspect that they are not major concerns for many college students.) Stated differently, although the terms "everyday" and "informal" have been used more or less interchangeably in the literature, it is obviously possible for reasoning to be informal without being about everyday issues.

In a recent study designed along the lines of the Perkins et al. research, Woll, Navarrete, Sussman, and Marcoux (1998; see also Navarrete, Woll, Sussman, & Marcoux, 1998) presented college students with a set of everyday dilemmas, for instance, whether to forego your BA to take a well-paying job, whether to take a romantic partner back if he or she has been cheating on you. Participants were asked to state their position on each issue and then give both pro and con arguments regarding that position. The interesting finding in this research was that, contrary to the results of Perkins and his associates, our participants generated as many counterarguments as pro ones. In fact, it was frequently difficult to determine which of these two positions represented the participants' "true" viewpoint based on their arguments, although preliminary judgments rated pro arguments as more convincing than con arguments.

There are two possible reservations about these results that are currently being examined. The first, as mentioned earlier, is that, unlike most of Perkins' studies, participants in the Woll et al. study were instructed to give both pro and con arguments. In this sense, the Woll et al. results can be compared with the Perkins (1989) scaffolding study where increases in both pro and con arguments were found. This pattern of results raises the question of whether participants' difficulties in the Perkins studies were due to the content of the issues used or the nature of the questioning technique.

In order to tease apart these two possibilities, Wilson and Woll (2000) used the Woll et al. (1998) procedure to examine reasoning with Perkins's (1985) issues. Initial findings indicated that although our explicit probing of con arguments resulted in an increase in the number of con arguments over that reported by Perkins, the former number was still smaller than the number reported by Woll et al. (1998) for more everyday issues. Thus, although the difference in procedure made some difference, it did not entirely account for the Woll et al. findings for more everyday issues.

The second reservation regarding the Woll et al. results is that the arguments given by participants were rather uniform and predictable and could have resulted from previous discussions or from simply overhearing these issues, rather than being generated by these students in response to the question. Therefore, current research is looking at issues that have everyday content but are presented in novel, less familiar contexts (e.g., what if a friend or business partner absconded with the company finances and then begged for forgiveness, or what if a loved one became ill and needed you to care for him or her even though it required dropping out of school).

TEACHING FORMAL SKILLS THROUGH INFORMAL REASONING (AND VICE VERSA)

Thus far, I have focused on the role of everyday knowledge and informal reasoning in academic learning and on the adequacy of such reasoning. Another question raised in chapter 9 is the degree to which individuals are actually sensitive to certain formal rules of inductive and deductive reasoning and the degree to which training in these formal principles facilitates *in*formal reasoning.

Statistical or Inductive Reasoning

A program of research on the latter question has been conducted by Richard Nisbett (e.g., 1993) and his associates. In an initial article, Nisbett, Krantz, Jepson, and Kunda (1983) took some of the observations made by Kahneman and Tversky, discussed in chapter 9, and showed that individuals are more likely to use statistical concepts such as sample size and the nature of the sampling process when these factors are more evident. For example, in one study Nisbett et al. (1983) presented the following scenario:

> David L. was a senior in high school on the East Coast who was planning to go to college. He had compiled an excellent record in high school and had been admitted to his top two choices: a small liberal arts college and an Ivy League university. David had several older friends who were attending the liberal arts college and several who were attending the Ivy League university.

They were all excellent students like himself and had interests similar to his. The friends at the liberal arts college all reported that they liked the place very much and that they found it very stimulating. The friends at the Ivy League university reported that they had many complaints on both personal and social grounds and on educational grounds.

David initially thought that he would go to the smaller college. However, he decided to visit both schools himself for a day. He did not like what he saw at the private liberal arts college. Several people whom he met seemed cold and unpleasant; a professor he met with briefly seemed abrupt and uninterested in him; and he did not like the "feel" of the campus. He did like what he saw at the Ivy League university. Several of the people he met seemed like vital, enthusiastic, pleasant people; he met with two different professors who took a personal interest in him; and he came away with a very pleasant feeling about the campus. (p. 353)

Participants were asked to rate, on a 5-point scale, which of the two schools they thought David should choose, with the issue being whether they would be influenced more by David's one time impression or by the more representative sampling of his friends. In one condition, participants received the scenario as is, whereas in another condition a section was added which emphasized the possibility of error in David's sampling by portraying him as drawing up lists of classes, places, and activities he wanted to examine, and then having him pick out a sample of these fairly randomly (i.e., by him dropping a pencil and selecting the item that it fell on).

In the control condition (i.e., where participants did not receive the emphasis on randomness), 74% indicated that David should attend the Ivy League school, whereas only 56% of the participants who received the additional text made this choice. In addition, a significantly greater percentage of the latter participants mentioned statistical considerations than did the former group. Thus, it appears that when the statistical properties of a sample or the sampling process are highlighted, albeit in a rather artificial way, some individuals do, in fact, take these statistical properties into consideration in making their judgments.

If this is true, then it should be possible to influence judgments through training in statistical principles. Contrary to the heuristics and biases tradition reviewed in chapter 9, Nisbett, Krantz, Jepson, and Fong (1982) suggested that there is reason for optimism because many statistical principles are of fairly recent origin (i.e., 300 years ago or less), and because many times principles of proper or "good" reasoning (e.g., causal reasoning) are quicker and/or easier to follow than incorrect ones (though see my earlier discussion of the counterintuitive nature of many statistical principles). Nisbett et al. also cited the example of one participant unskilled in probability theory who responded to the David problem with a justification that seemed to take into account sampling biases (i.e., that David's experiences may have constituted an unrepresentative sample of events at the two colleges). (See a similar example by Voss et al., 1989, of an extended rationale by one participant without economics coursework or experience although both of these observations obviously involve a very small sample size!)

In this connection, Fong, Krantz, and Nisbett (1986) conducted several different experiments on the effects of instruction on students' use of probability concepts. The first experiment dealt with the law of large numbers, or the principle that the larger the sample, the more clearly that sample reflects the properties of the overall population. In this study participants received three types of test problems, each of which incorporated one of six types of formats. The three problem types were (a) probabilistic, where the sample was clearly generated in a random manner; (b) the presentation of objective data, but with no indication that the sample was randomly generated; and (c) subjective data from which participants were to draw conclusions about a population of subjective data. (See Table 10.3 for examples of these three different sorts of problems.)

Another factor in this first experiment was the role of instructions. All instructions included an initial paragraph introducing the law of large numbers. In one condition, the "rules" condition, this introduction was followed by a detailed account of the law of large numbers. In a second, "examples" condition, the introduction was followed by a set of three example problems in which the correct conclusion was presented along with an explanation of the applicability of the law of large numbers to these problems. A third condition, called the "full training" condition, included a combination of rules and examples training. Finally, there were two different control conditions, one in which no instructions were given, and a "demand" condition in which the examples were given without the accompanying rule. (This last condition was included to control for demand characteristics and the effects of simply making the rule more salient by the examples.) Answers to the various questions were scored on a 3-point scale ranging from 1 (*completely deterministic response*) to 2 (*a poor statistical response*) to 3 (*good statistical response*).

The first major finding of this study was that participants who received full training were more likely to give a statistical response (i.e., a greater proportion of 2 or 3 responses) than were those who received either rules or examples training alone, both of whom in turn showed more statistical responses than participants in the two control conditions (see Table 10.4). The second finding was a similar trend for appropriateness of statistical consideration (i.e., proportion of 3s out of the total statistical responses), although in this case the difference between the full training condition on the one hand, and the rules and the examples conditions on the other, was only marginally significant. There was also an effect of problem type, with the greatest evidence for statistical reasoning (75%) in the case of probabilistic problems, followed by objective (48%) and subjective problems (33%). These latter two findings suggest that it is simply a matter of whether the participants saw the relevance of statistical reasoning that was important. Finally, there was no interaction of training with problem type (see Fig. 10.2) for statistical reasoning (i.e., training had an equal effect across prob-

TABLE 10.3

Examples of Problem Types

Type of Problem	Example
Probabilistic	At Stanbrook University, the Housing Office determines which of the 10,000 students enrolled will be allowed to live on campus the following year. At Stanbrook, the dormitory facilities are excellent, so there is always great demand for housing. Unfortunately, there are only enough on campus spaces for 5000 students. The Housing Office determines who will get to live on campus by having a Housing Draw; every student picks a number out of a box over a 3-day period. These numbers range from 1 to 10,000. If the number is 5000 or under, the student gets to live on campus. If the number is over 5000, the student is not be able to live on campus.
	On the first day of the draw, Joe talks to five people who have picked a number. Of these, four people got low numbers. Because of this, Joe suspects that the numbers in the box were not properly mixed, and that the early numbers are more favorable. He rushes over to the Housing Draw and picks a number. He gets a low number. He later talks to four people who drew numbers on the second or third day of the draw. Three got high numbers. Joe says to himself, "I'm glad that I picked when I did, because it looks like I was right that the numbers were not properly mixed."
	What do you think of Joe's reasoning. Explain.
Objective	A talent scout for a professional basketball team attends two college games with the intention of observing carefully the talent and skill of a particular player. The player looks generally excellent. He repeatedly plays worthy of the best professional players. However, in one of the games, with his team behind by 2 points, the player is fouled while shooting and has the opportunity to tie the game by making both free throws. The player misses both free throws and then tries too hard for the rebound from the second one, committing a foul in the process. The other team then makes two free throws, for a 4-point lead, and goes on to win by 2 points.
	The scout reports that the player in question "has excellent skills, and should be recruited. He has a tendency to misplay under extreme pressure, but this will probably disappear with more experience and better coaching."
	Comment on the thinking embodied in the scout's opinion that the player (a) "has excellent skills" and that the player has (b) "a tendency to misplay under extreme pressure." Does the thinking behind either conclusion have any weaknesses?

Subjective

Gerald M. has a 3-year-old son, Timmy. He told a friend: "You know, I've never been much for sports, but I think Timmy will turn out the same. A couple of weeks ago, an older neighbor boy was tossing a ball to him, and he could catch it and throw it all right, but he just didn't seem interested in it. Then the other day, some kids his age were kicking a little soccer ball around. Timmy could do it as well as the others, but he lost interest very quickly and started playing with some toy cars while the other kids went on kicking the ball around for another 20 or 30 min."

Do you agree with Gerald's reasoning that Timmy is likely not to care much for sports? Why or why not?

Note. Within each type of problem there were six different problem structures. For the clearest comparison, I have selected examples with the same structure. All of the examples are taken from "The Effects of Statistical Training on Thinking About Everyday Problems" by G. T. Fong, D. H. Krantz, & R. E. Nisbett, 1986, *Cognitive Psychology, 18, pp. 253-292.* Copyright © 1986 by Academic Press, reproduced by permission of the publisher. All rights of reproduction in any form reserved.

TABLE 10.4

Frequency and Quality of Statistical Answers in Experiment 1

Condition	n	Frequency		Quality	
		Overall Proportion	Log-Linear Effect	Overall Proportion	Log-Linear Effect
Control	68	.421	−0.515	.542	−0.501
Demand	73	.440	−0.420	.577	−0.316
Rule	69	.557	0.188	.666	0.165
Examples	69	.535	0.074	.659	0.181
Rull training	68	.643	0.673	.708	0.471

Note. From "The Effects of Statistical Training on Thinking About Everyday Problems" by G. T. Fong, D. H. Krantz, & R. E. Nisbett, 1986, *Cognitive Psychology, 18,* pp. 263. Copyright © 1986 by Academic Press, reproduced by permission of the publisher. All rights of reproduction in any form reserved.

lem types, suggesting that formal training not only has an effect on statistical reasoning, but this effect is an across-the-board one).

In two other studies Fong et al. (1986) examined the effects of amount of training on statistical reasoning. In the first of these, the researchers looked at the performance of four different groups with differing amounts of training, ranging from those with no background in statistics to participants who had had several statistics courses (and most of whom were PhDs). These four groups received one of two different versions of an everyday problem about restaurant quality, one of which emphasized the randomness of a patron's selection of restaurants and one of which did not. The result was that the amount of statistical background had a significant effect on amount and quality of statistical reasoning, whereas the presence of a cue of randomness had an effect on amount but not on quality of such reasoning.

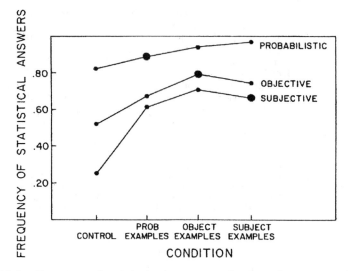

FIG. 10.2. Frequency of statistical responses as a function of training condition and problem type. From "The Effects of Statistical Training on Thinking About Everyday Problems" by G. T. Fong, D. H. Krantz, & R. E. Nisbett, 1986, *Cognitive Psychology, 18,* p. 273. Copyright © 1986 by Academic Press, reproduced by permission of the publisher. All rights of reproduction in any form reserved.

However, for those trained in experimental design, it should be clear that there were other possible factors apart from statistical training that could have been the source of these differences. Therefore, Fong et al. conducted a fourth experiment to look at the effects of an introductory statistics course on everyday reasoning about statistical concepts. In this case male participants were given a questionnaire on sports issues during either the first or the last week of the class. Within this questionnaire there were statistical questions asking, for example, about the reasons why Rookies of the Year in baseball so frequently show a decrease in performance during the second year. There were four such problems in the questionnaire, and participants' answers were scored in terms of the same three categories described earlier. The central finding (see Fig. 10.3) was that the statistics course led to a significantly higher proportion of statistical answers and a higher quality of statistical answers for two out of the four problems. Thus, training again appears to have an effect on everyday reasoning, although the failure to find effects on responses to two of the questions argues against drawing too strong a conclusion.

In a subsequent study, Fong and Nisbett (1991) demonstrated that training in the law of large numbers, using either sports examples or examples of ability testing (e.g., determining whether an applicant could indeed speak Spanish), showed clear transfer from one domain to the other on immediate testing. Interestingly, when tested 2 weeks later, the training in the original domain showed good retention (see Fig. 10.4), whereas performance in the untrained domain declined significantly, though participants still performed

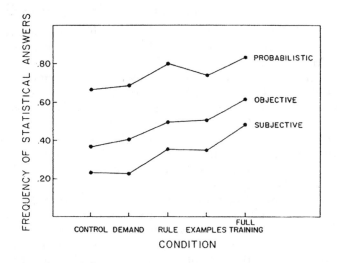

FIG. 10.3. Effects of statistical training on four statistical problems. From from "The Effects of Statistical Training on Thinking About Everyday Problems" by G. T. Fong, D. H. Krantz, & R. E. Nisbett, 1986, *Cognitive Psychology, 18*, p. 267. Copyright © 1986 by Academic Press, reproduced by permission of the publisher. All rights of reproduction in any form reserved.

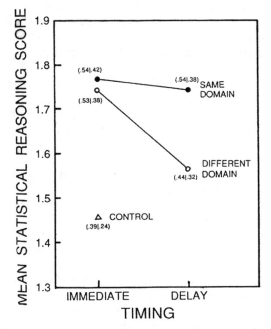

FIG. 10.4. Retention of the law of large numbers after two weeks. From "Immediate and Delayed Transfer of Training Effects in Statistical Reasoning" by G. T. Fong & R. E. Nisbett, 1991, *Journal of Experimental Psychology: General, 120*, p. 38. Copyright © 1991 by the American Psychological Association. Reprinted with permission.

signficantly higher in this domain than did those in a no-training control group. Fong and Nisbett concluded that these results demonstrate that participants learned an abstract rule, rather than simply the concrete examples—a conclusion reinforced by testing participants' memory for those examples at delay—which they could then apply to a new domain and to a second set of problems in the same domain 2 weeks later. Other commentators (e.g., Ceci & Ruiz, 1993), however, have interpreted the significant decline for the transfer problems as indicating that the effects of training on transfer are short-lived. The glass is either half-full or half empty.

Fong et al. (1986; see also Nisbett, Fong, Lehman, and Cheng, 1987) concluded from these findings that formal training in statistics does, in fact, improve everyday statistical reasoning. They also argued that their research emphasizes the importance of including everyday examples or applications in statistics courses. Along these lines, Nisbett et al. (1987) argued that "subjects' failure to use the law of large numbers reflects not so much the lack of a general rule, but rather the difficulty of seeing its applicability to events of various kinds" (p. 627). Nisbett et al. (1987) proposed a *codability hypothesis,* according to which certain events such as the behavior of a slot machine are more readily seen in terms of randomizing devices and statistical principles, whereas other events such as social behavior or subjective events are not. Other objective events, such as a baseball player's batting average or a student's GPA fall somewhere in between in that they are codable, but are seen in causal terms as well. In addition, as I have discussed, Nisbett et al. (1983) showed that presenting problems in such a way that participants could see the randomness or uncertainty involved led to increased use of statistical principles to explain the events. (Note the similarity here to observations made by Kahneman & Tversky, 1982b, cited in chap. 9.) Along similar lines, Kunda and Nisbett (1986) reported results for peoples' understanding of covariation (see chap. 9) indicating that participants' estimates of such covariation are more accurate when they are more familiar with the domain under consideration (e.g., estimates of agreement in course evaluations) and when the information is more codable (e.g., ability estimates in terms of grades versus units of social behavior).

It is possible, however, to conceive (à la Perkins and Kuhn) of an opposing argument. It is my observation that people in general (or at least Westerners exposed to pop psychology) tend to resist probabilistic reasoning when it comes to psychological states and social behaviors, not only because these phenomena are generally less codable in probabilistic terms, but also because our own personal experience gives us the impression that we are "experts" on these topics. (You need only watch any Oprah-style talk show to see the degree to which people are willing to impose, with great confidence, their own lay theories of psychology and social behavior on others.) Therefore, I suspect that for the everyday reasoner (including those educated in psychology), statistical training will have less of an influence, particularly in comparison with individuating information that has personal relevance.

Along similar lines, Einhorn (1986) suggested that clinical psychologists are unwilling to accept the statistical stance of "accepting error to make less error" (p. 387) because they take a more deterministic view of human nature, and are also more interested in understanding (and treating) the individual person than in making general predictions. (This is a strange kind of individual determinism!) To this I would add the fact that this deterministic viewpoint or theory of psychological functioning is based largely on these psychologists' own clinical (and personal) experiences.

Additional research on this topic has been reported by Lehman, Lempert, and Nisbett (1988). The concern of these investigators was with the effects of graduate training in different disciplines (i.e,., law, medicine, psychology, and chemistry) on statistical reasoning in everyday life. The major findings of this article for the purposes of this chapter concern the changes between first and third year students in statistical and methodological reasoning (i.e., questions about confounding variables and controls) using both cross-sectional and longitudinal designs. Both psychology and medical students showed significant increases from the first to the third years in both designs, whereas law and chemistry students did not (see Fig. 10.5). Interestingly, in a subsequent replication at UCLA (the original study was performed at the University of Michigan), it was found that students in the social science areas of psychology (e.g., social and developmental psychology) showed improvement comparable with the Michigan students, whereas students in the natural science areas (e.g., physiological, learning, and experimental psychology) did not.

The apparent explanation for these findings is that psychology graduate students have a good deal of training in both statistics and experimental design, whereas law and chemistry students do not. Medical students, it turns out, at least at Michigan, are trained on the topic of judgment under uncertainty, as well as having experience with statistical concepts, both of which may account for their performance on the statistical problems. In addition, Lehman et al. speculated that psychology students majoring in the social science areas are more accustomed to applying statistical and methodological concepts to everyday problems than are those majoring in the natural sciences. Finally, chemistry students deal primarily with deterministic rather than probabilistic cases and do not have to deal with "messy problems that contain substantial uncertainty and a tangled web of causes" (Lehman et al., 1988, p. 441).

The most important conclusion from this research, however, is, once again, that formal training has an impact on everyday reasoning, contrary to the theorizing of many psychologists (see chap. 7). Even though some rules may not transfer, as some psychologists have found, others apparently do:

Importantly, none of the studies that have led to this pessimistic perspective on the value of formal discipline have examined situations in which people learn through immersion in a field of study and have numerous occasions to apply

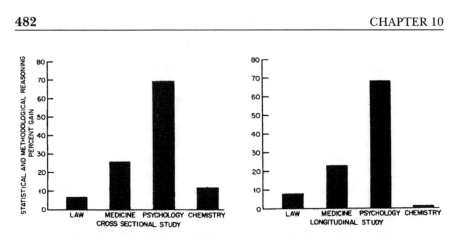

FIG. 10.5. Improvement in statistical and methodological reasoning by graduate students in different disciplines. From "The Effects of Graduate Training on Reasoning: Formal Discipline and Thinking About Everyday-life Events," by D. R. Lehman, R. O. Lempert, & R. E. Nisbett, 1988, *American Psychologist, 43*, p. 441. Copyright © 1988 by the American Psychological Association. Reprinted with permission.

the rules of the discipline to problems that arise both inside and outside their course of study. Yet this seems to be how disciplinary learning naturally occurs. (Lehman et al., 1988, p. 441)

In particular, Lehman et al. (1988) argued that the rules that can be most usefully taught are those "that people have induced ... in the course of their daily existence" (p. 441; see the discussion of pragmatic reasoning schemas in chap. 9). These include rules of causality and generalization, and of the validity of arguments and the "probativeness of evidence" (p. 441).

A similar conclusion was reached in a study by Lehman and Nisbett (1990) on the effects of *under*graduate training in the social sciences, natural sciences, and humanities on statistical and methodological thinking on the one hand, and conditional reasoning on the other. As in the Lehman et al. (1988) study, these investigators found that training in the social sciences (over the course of a 4-year education) had a substantial influence on statistical and methodological thinking, but not on conditional reasoning, whereas training in the natural sciences and humanities had a significant effect on conditional reasoning versus a small but marginally significant effect on statistical reasoning.

Deductive Reasoning

The evidence for teaching deductive reasoning is less encouraging. For example, Cheng, Holyoak, Nisbett, and Oliver (1986) conducted a study analogous to the Fong et al. (1986) study reviewed earlier. Specifically, Cheng et al. gave participants only abstract rule training on the conditional rule, only a few examples of correct solutions (using the kinds of concrete materials reviewed in chap. 9), or a combination of the two. These participants then received eight Wason-type selection problems. Two of these contained the kind of arbitrary content included in most research on deductive reasoning; two were examples of the permission schema; two were designed to encourage the *converse bias* (i.e., inferring that the converse of the rule is also true, e.g., "If a washing label has 'silk' on one side, then it has 'dry clean only' on the other side" [Cheng et al., 1986, p. 301]); and two were biconditional (i.e., they explicitly encouraged the converse) with arbitrary material. As usual, participants were asked to select which of the terms (i.e., p, q, $not\ p$, and $not\ q$) were necessary for testing the rule and then to judge the degree to which four different transformations of the conditional rule (i.e., $if\ q\ then\ p$) maintained the same meaning as the conditional.

The basic finding of this study was that only the training that included both abstract rules and concrete examples had an effect on reasoning performance; rules or examples alone did not. This result is slightly different from those reported by Fong et al. (1986) for inductive reasoning, where training in both rules and examples alone resulted in greater statistical reasoning than the control conditions. This discrepancy suggested to Cheng et al. that unlike statistical rules, the conditional rule does not actually exist in everyday reasoning. In addition, differences in performance were found for the different problem types, with permission schemas leading to the fewest errors, followed by the converse bias problems, followed by the two kinds of problems with arbitrary content.

In a second study, Cheng et al. provided an entire semester course in logic in order to see if more extensive training might improve conditional reasoning. In point of fact, there was no overall effect of training for any problem type; the only error type on which any improvement was found was the frequency of (erroneously) choosing q (i.e., affirming the consequent). There was an effect of problem type, with the permission problems producing fewer errors than either the converse bias or arbitrary content problem, but there was no interaction between training and problem type.

In general, these results suggest that even intensive training in deductive reasoning is ineffective. Interestingly, to the extent that there *were* effects of such training, it was on the nonarbitrary permission schema problems rather than on the arbitrary symbols problems. It is also of interest to note that the simple wording of the problems (i.e., expressing them in the form of a permission or obligation schema) had a strong effect on problem solution, as did brief training on the obligation schema. This was presumably due to the fact that permission and obligation represent natural or common pragmatic reasoning schemas (though see the reservations by Manktelow & Over, 1990, 1995, discussed in chap. 9). "Education in reasoning is likely to be effective when it serves to refine pragmatically useful rules that most people will have naturally induced in at least a rudimentary form from everyday experiences" (Cheng et al., 1986, pp. 520–521). Thus, the conclusion here is essentially the same as that for inductive reasoning (i.e., training works best with either familiar or pragmatically useful rules and content, or both).

Somewhat more encouraging results were reported by Lehman et al. (1988), who included conditional reasoning problems in their comparison of the effects of graduate training in four different areas. Here participants received the same four kinds of conditional and biconditional problems used in the Cheng et al. study. The basic finding in this study was that graduate students in psychology, medicine, and law all showed some improvement in such conditional reasoning. Furthermore, this improvement held across all four reasoning problems. Lehman et al. argued that both psychology and medical students have to engage in evidence testing of the sort that is involved in the conditional and that law students are clearly exposed to problems involving permission and obligation (though again, no interaction with type of problem was found here).

Conclusion

The evidence reviewed in this section indicates that training in statistics can, in fact, transfer to everyday situations, whereas training in logic or deductive reasoning apparently does not. This suggests that courses in statistics or elementary probability theory would be a useful addition to a general college education, though such a course should include plenty of real-world examples (and if my nonstatistical observations are correct, they may not transfer to real-life human relations problems very well either). Whether such instruction would be equally useful for all majors (e.g., for students in the natural sciences and the arts, as well as for social science majors—see my discussion of Voss's proposal) or for individuals who do not go to college remains to be seen.

Fischhoff (1982) on Debiasing

A more pessimistic view of the prospect of improving human judgment and reasoning has been put forth by Fischhoff (1982) in a chapter on *debiasing*. In this chapter Fischhoff reviewed the many attempts that have made to reduce the biases discussed in chapter 9, with particular reference to the hindsight and overconfidence biases. As listed in Table 10.5, Fischhoff divided the possible sources of biases into three categories: faulty tasks, faulty judges, and a mismatch between judges and tasks. Within each of these categories there are two different subtypes, each of which includes a variety of different approaches to debiasing. For example, under the category of faulty tasks is the possibility that the tasks are unfair—for instance, in that participants may not be motivated by the task, may find the task confusing, or there may be some kind of misunderstanding between judge and experimenter. Under the category of faulty judges are the notions that judges need improvement or that they are incapable of improvement, or both. Finally, under mismatches there is the possibility that the task simply needs

TABLE 10.5

Presumed Sources of Bias and Possible Debiasing Techniques

Source	Debiasing Technique
Faulty tasks	
Unfair tasks	
Lack of motivation	Raise stakes
Confusion about task	Clarify instructions/stimuli
Disbelief about nature of task or payoffs	Discourage second-guessing
Failure to express knowledge	Use better response modes
Too many questions	Ask fewer questions
Misunderstood tasks	
Behavior serves unrecognized goal	Demonstrate alternative goal
Misunderstanding of key terms	Demonstrate semantic
Task impossible unless judges make additional assumptions	disagreement
	Demonstrate impossibility of task
Behavior reflects unseen distinction	Demonstrate overlooked distinction
Faulty judges	
Perfectible individuals	(In order of increasing effort)
	Warn of problem (in general)
	Describe problem (to judge)
	Provide personalized feedback
	Train extensively
Incorrigible individuals	Replace them
	Recalibrate their responses
	Plan on error (in judgment or action)
Mismatch between judge and task	
Restructuring	
Knowledge implicit but not expressed	Make knowledge explicit
Ignoring discrepant information	Search for discrepant information
Problem overwhelming	Decompose problem
Too narrow a focus	Consider alternative situations
Failure to consider alternative conceptions	Offer alternative formulations
Education (of alternative judges)	Rely on substantive experts
	Educate from childhood

Note. From "Debiasing," by B. Fischhoff, 1982. In *Judgment Under Uncertainty: Heuristics and Biases* (p. 424), edited by D. Kahneman, P. Slovic, & A. Tversky, New York: Cambridge University Press. Copyright © 1982 by Cambridge University Press. Adapted with permission.

to be restructured to make it more compatible for the judge or that new judges need to be educated in the skill.

For each of these sources, there is a suggested debiasing technique. For example, to deal with lack of motivation, one may try "raising the stakes," whereas for confusing tasks, one may try making the instructions or the task clearer. These debiasing techniques are also given in Table 10.5.

The conclusion of Fischhoff's review is that both the hindsight and overconfidence biases are "moderately robust, resisting attempts to interpret them as artifacts and eliminate them by 'mechanical' manipulations, such as making subjects work harder" (p. 440). Of particular relevance for the purposes of this section is the finding that education in general does not serve to reduce these biases. As noted in chapter 9, one method that *has* proved to be effective in debiasing is to have participants explain or consider alternative outcomes. This strategy has been effective for both the hindsight bias (Slovic & Fischhoff, 1977) and overconfidence effects (Koriat et al., 1980).

CONCLUSIONS

Once again, in this chapter, as in chapter 9, my review has found the pessimists aligned against the optimists, the critics against the defenders. I have reviewed the criticisms raised against traditional educational practice by those advocating situated cognition, and I have discussed the attempts by the defenders of traditional cognitive psychology and education to answer these critics. I have examined some of the arguments for authentic assessment and distributed cognition, and I have voiced some reservations about these two positions. Finally, I have examined some of the mixed evidence concerning the adequacy of informal reasoning and regarding the "trainability" of inductive and deductive reasoning and the debiasing of human judgment.

What can be concluded from these mixed results? One apparent conclusion is that training in reasoning works best when it makes contact with everyday experience and with rules that are useful and adaptive. The same seems to apply to schooling in general, though use of examples or everyday experience alone does not seem to be the answer here. Conversely, there is evidence that everyday reasoning can itself be improved via formal training or schooling, although this works better for inductive than for deductive reasoning, and it does not necessarily apply to all inductive reasoning or judgment biases.

What do these results suggest about the proper uses and objectives of education? On the one hand, Nisbett and his colleagues interpreted their results as supporting some variation on formal education. On the other hand, these and other results also suggest the importance of making greater contact with everyday experience in teaching reasoning.

Although it would be presumptuous of me to try to set forth some general prescription for education on the basis of the mixed evidence reviewed here, it is nevertheless clear that the major lesson from this chapter is that the educational enterprise needs to establish better connections with everyday experience, not only as a resource from which to draw, but also as a target domain to which educational lessons can be applied. Drawing on such experience can facilitate the acquisition of new forms of reasoning or learning dispositions; as I have discussed, at least some types of formal training can then be applied back to everyday experience. This does not mean sacrificing traditional education to the exercise of mere common sense or the substitution of apprenticeships or "radical" models of distributed cognition for traditional education, although the increasing role of computers and other technological innovations (e.g., the Internet, virtual reality) in education does suggest that the concept of distributed cognition will be of increasing importance. Finally, there may be some role for authentic assessment in the form of using more personally meaningful materials and posing more personally meaningful questions if such materials can be better integrated with traditional views of education and assessment.

It is now time to try to tie together and draw some general conclusions from the several different topics that I have reviewed throughout this book. That is indeed the task for the final chapter of this book.

Chapter 11

A Reconsideration of the Field of Everyday Cognition

Introduction

Common Themes and Issues

Conclusions

Suggestions for the Future

INTRODUCTION

In this book I have examined a variety of different types of everyday cognition, ranging from memory for people and life events to everyday reasoning and judgment to instructional implications of such knowledge and reasoning. I hope that the preceding chapters have convinced you that there really is a substantial literature on everyday cognition and that this literature is of considerable interest from both a practical and theoretical standpoint.

Not surprisingly, such a wide variety of topics has raised a number of different topic-specific questions regarding such topics as the "specialness" of face recognition, the phenomenon of childhood amnesia, the relative influence of evaluative versus descriptive information in impression formation. What is perhaps more noteworthy, and of course, what I have tried to underline throughout this book, is the degree of *commonality* among the concerns and central themes in these different areas.

In this last chapter I review some of these common themes, as well as some of the differences among these various topics. I then try to draw some

488

conclusions about the current status of everyday cognition and where I think the study of everyday cognition will (or should) go from here.

COMMON THEMES AND ISSUES

Let me begin with a few issues that I introduced in chapter 1 and that I have been explicitly tracking throughout this book.

Theoretical–Conceptual Commonalities

The Models of Everyday Cognition. In chapter 1, I introduced seven models of everyday cognition—the associative network model, the procedural model, the schema or knowledge structure viewpoint, the exemplar model, the information processing or computational viewpoint, the connectionist or PDP model, and the situated cognition viewpoint. I have tried to show how these seven models are relevant to the different topics that I have reviewed. To summarize, in Table 11.1 I have listed the seven models and the specific topics to which they have been applied. In this summary and in my reviews throughout this book, I have tried not to *force* either theory or research into these categories, and you have probably noticed that much of what I have discussed does not fall into one or the other category.

Now mere frequency counts are obviously a rather crude measure of the relevance or significance of a model to everyday cognition. It is nevertheless apparent from this listing that the schema or constructivist model was by far the most frequently applied of the seven, followed by the computational model. Both of these were also applicable to a wide *variety* of topics, although the primary focus of the schema model is clearly in the memory area. Connectionist and exemplar models are making definite inroads into the area of everyday cognition, whereas the procedural and situated cognition viewpoints have a smaller and more restricted influence, the former being primarily a function of the work of John Anderson on skilled performance, and the latter the result of the work of Jean Lave on the divergence of everyday thinking from academic schooling.

The broad applicability of the schema model may be due to a variety of different factors. On the positive side, it may reflect the fact that, as Minsky (1975) suggested (see chap. 1), everyday thinking simply involves more structured patterns of thought, or as Bartlett (1932) argued, more reconstructive processes than have typically been studied in the experimental literature on memory and reasoning. Along these lines, it is worth noting that the schema model was particularly prominent in the areas of event and autobiographical memory, two areas where traditional lab research has had the least impact. At the same time, these are also the two areas where there has been the greatest debate over the relative role of abstract structures versus specific instances.

TABLE 11.1

Summary of the Applications of the Seven Models

Model	Applications
1. Associative network	Carlston's associated systems model of person memory (chap. 2)
	Wyer and Srull's person memory model (chap. 2)
	The featural model of face recognition (chap. 3)
	Einstein and McDaniel's simple activation model of prospective memory (chap. 4)
	The copy model (W. F. Brewer) of autobiographical memory (chap. 5)
	The trace integrity model of childhood amnesia (Howe & Courage; chap. 6)
2. Procedural	Anderson's proceduralization model of skill acquisition (chap. 7)
	Singley and Anderson's identical elements and procedures of transfer (chap. 7)
	The rules in Cheng and Holyoak's pragmatic reasoning schemas (chap. 9)
3. Schema, constructivist	Schema and prototype models of person memory (e.g., M. B. Brewer and Woll & Graesser; chap. 2)
	Wyer and Radvansky's emphasis on the construction of situation models in impression formation (chap. 2)
	The categorization process in M. B. Brewer's and Fiske and Neuberg's dual process models of impression formation (chap. 3)
	Schema and prototype models of face recognition (e.g., Ellis) (chap. 3)
	Schank and Abelson's script model of event memory (chap. 4)
	Graesser's script- (or schema-) copy—plus—tag model (chaps. 2 and 4)
	Nelson's model of general event representations (chap. 4) Schank's model of MOPs, TOPs, and dynamic memory (chap. 4)
	Kolodner's E-MOP model of event memory (chap. 4)
	E. Loftus's overwriting or updating account of eyewitness memory (chap. 4)
	The schema or reconstructive memory model of autobiographical memory (W. F. Brewer, Barclay, M. Ross, Thompson, et al. (chap. 5)
	Reiser et al.'s context-plus-index model of autobiographical memory (chap. 6)
	Conway and Bekerian's A-MOP model of autobiographical memory (chap. 6)
	The role of themes in autobiographical memory (chap. 6)
	Conway's hierarchical model of autobiographical memory (chap. 6)
	The emphasis on the role of narrative formats in the development of autobiographical memory (chap. 6)

	The emphasis in the expertise literature on experts seeing and thinking in terms of patterns (chap. 7)
	Rumelhart and Norman's schema model of skill acquisition (chap. 7)
	Kahneman and Tversky's judgment heuristics (chap. 9)
	Cheng and Holyoak's pragmatic reasoning schema view of deductive reasoning (chap. 9)
4. Exemplar or case-based	Bruce and Young's concept of a Face Recognition Unit (chap. 3)
	The instance-based connectionist model of face recognition (chap. 3)
	Kolodner's case-based reasoning model of event memory (chap. 4)
	Hammond's case-based model of planning (chap. 4)
	Nelson's later episodic view of the origins of autobiographical memory (chap. 5)
	Klein and Loftus's pure exemplar and exemplar–summary models of self-judgments (chap. 6)
5. Computational, information processing	M. B. Brewer's dual process model of impression processing formation (chap. 2)
	Fiske's continuum model of impression formation (chap. 2)
	Bruce and Young's model of face processing (chap. 3)
	Shallice and Burgess's supervisory system model of prospective memory (chap. 4)
	Hayes-Roth and Hayes-Roth's model of planning (chap. 4)
	Williams and Hollan's as well as Conway's cyclic retrieval models of retrieval of autobiographical memory (chap. 6)
6. Connectionist, PDP	Connectionist models (Kunda & Thagard, Read & Miller, and Smith & DeCoster) of impression formation (chap. 2)
	Connectionist models (the interaction–activation, WISARD, and Kohenen et al.'s model of face recognition (chap. 3)
	Connectionist models of case-based reasoning reviewed by Barnden and Holyoak (chap. 4)
7. Situated cognition	Suchman's conception of planning as situational (chap. 4)
	Lave et al.'s research and formulation of everyday math in grocery shopping (chap. 8)
	Scribner's model of practical thinking in the workplace (chap. 8)
	The application of situated cognition arguments by Brown et al., Lave, Greeno, and others, to education (chap. 10)

Note. MOP = memory organization packet; TOP = thematic organization pattern; E-MOP = event memory organization packet; A-MOP = autobiographical memory organization packets; PDP = parallel distributed processing.

On the negative side, the schema or constructive memory or knowledge structure viewpoint has frequently been criticized for its vagueness; and, as the labels suggest, is also the one which, at least in my presentation, encompasses the widest variety of different emphases. For example, it is certainly possible to argue for the role of constructive or reconstructive memory without emphasizing patterned knowledge structures; in fact, some of the PDP models that I discussed did exactly that. On the other hand, it is possible to emphasize structure without stressing abstract structures; again, much of Gestalt psychology and the exemplar model often fit the bill here. Thus, although constructive inference, abstract knowledge structures, and patterned thinking and memory typically go together in schema theories, they do entail somewhat different emphases.

The same can be said, of course, to a somewhat lesser degree, for the associative network models, for which I have emphasized the featural, componential emphasis in face recognition research, the concrete, reproductive emphasis of the copy model in research on AM, the simple (passive) activation emphasis of MacDaniel and Einstein in research on prospective memory, and, of course, the associationist assumption reflected primarily in the literature on person memory. Once again, each of these various features or assumptions can be found in other models as well (e.g., the associationist notion in connectionist models, the concrete, reproductive assumption in the exemplar model). Thus, even though the associative network model has waned in popularity itself over the past decades, many of its assumptions remain in other current models.

It is apparent that information processing models have been widely deployed across a variety of different topics, both within everyday cognition and within cognitive psychology and social cognition in general. In fact, for many years, information processing or computational models were part of the very definition of social cognition and cognitive psychology. Such models have played a less influential role in everyday cognition, with the main emphasis coming primarily in the areas of person memory and face recognition.

The alternative and now very influential connectionist models were originally restricted to lower level processes with clear biological and neurological underpinnings (e.g., letter and word processing, speech processing, and, in everyday cognition, face processing). In recent years, however, as I have discussed, connectionism has also been applied to higher level processes such as impression formation and case-based reasoning. At the same time, however, as I have touched on in the discussion of Kunda and Thagard's and Smith and DeCoster's models of impression formation, these models are still restricted to relatively automatic processing. The main exception here is the applications to analogical reasoning, a feature that has now been included in models of impression formation (e.g., Spellman & Holyoak, 1992; Thagard & Kunda, 1998). The degree to which connectionism resolves the problems posed by such higher order cognitive processes will be a major factor in whether connectionism proves to be a major force in everyday cognition.[1] (Also recall that most of the connectionist models that I have reviewed have been localist versions rather than full-scale PDP models.)

With all of this said, it should be noted that much of the research on practical intelligence or informal reasoning that I have reviewed has not been theoretically motivated (or at least not by the models that I developed). For that matter, my selection of topics in this area has been somewhat unsystematic, in part because this area lacks a systematic framework, theoretical or otherwise. (The one possible exception here is the general discussion by Scribner of practical thinking.) In addition, with the major exception of Cheng and Holyoak's discussion of pragmatic reasoning schemas, the applicability of our models to research on everyday judgment is not entirely clear, primarily because of the somewhat ambiguous cognitive status of Kahneman and Tversky's judgment heuristics (as well as the fact that, as I have argued, the different heuristics seem to have somewhat different statuses).

Some Conceptual Issues Raised by the Seven Models. The discussion of the overall models of everyday cognition also raises several general conceptual issues that I have been tracking over the different topics in this book. These issues include (a) the relative importance of abstract versus specific knowledge; (b) the related issue of the role of hierarchical versus other less structured forms of knowledge organization; (c) the domain-specificity versus generality of everyday knowledge and processes; (d) the relative importance of context in everyday cognition; (e) the separateness or inseparability of process and representation; (f) the degree to which memory, reasoning, and judgment are accurate or rational versus error-prone; and (g) the degree to which everyday cognition can be meaningfully separated into two different systems.

On the first of these, I have described debates over the primacy of abstract versus specific knowledge not only in the general contrast of the schema and exemplar models, but also in some form in nearly every chapter of this book. Specifically, in chapter 4 I examined the debate between the notions of scripts, themes, and abstract plans, on the one hand, and Kolodner's case-based reasoning viewpoint on the other. In my discussion of autobiographical memory, I reviewed Conway's distinction between higher order themes or A-MOPS on the one hand, and event-specific knowledge on the other, and the debate over the different modes of access to AM (i.e., via themes or extended event timelines vs. concrete experiences or sensory cues). The same general idea was repeated in Berntsen's (1998) distinction between the different sources of voluntary versus involuntary

---

[1]Outside the area of everyday cognition, connectionism has been applied to a variety of higher order processes such as language processing, categorization, and decision making, though the models reviewed in this book are based on more lower level processes such as word recognition.

memories, in Pillemer and White's two-systems account of childhood amnesia, in W. F. Brewer's (1986, 1996) emphasis on memory for irrelevant details and on phenomenological qualities of AM, in Nelson's (1993a) distinction between general event representations and specific AMs, and even in S. B. Klein and Loftus's (1993) comparison of a pure abstraction model and a pure exemplar model of the relationship between the self and autobiographical memories.

In the area of person memory, I have discussed the distinction between categories and prototypes on the one hand, and exemplars on the other, a theme that carried over into both M. B. Brewer's (1988) and Fiske and Neuberg's (1990) distinction between categorical and individuating or piecemeal processes and representations, as well as my own distinction between individual and generic person schemas. In the area of face recognition I examined the distinction between face recognition units for specific faces versus face prototypes or schemas. In everyday judgment, there is research by Nisbett, Borgida, and their associates (Borgida & Nisbett, 1977; Nisbett, Borgida, Crandall, & Reed, 1976) that I did not discuss on the greater power of concrete instances over abstract statistical information; and in chapter 10 I also looked at the influence of concrete everyday knowledge on the use of abstract rules of reasoning. Finally, in chapter 10 I discussed the importance of combining concrete, everyday examples along with more general, abstract rules and principles.

Now it is clear that this concrete-versus-abstract issue is not restricted to the study of everyday cognition. In fact, it is a question that pervades cognitive psychology, psychology in general, and the entire field of epistemology. It seems to me, however, that this is a particularly relevant question for *everyday* cognition, for the simple reason that people live their everyday lives in the concrete world—they remember specific episodes in their lives, their decisions are usually about concrete issues, they usually reason about specifics—and yet they cannot get by, adapt, make their way in the world without some kind of generic knowledge about this in their everyday lives (see Nelson, 1993a, for a discussion of this issue). In addition, as I discussed in chapter 10, most traditional instruction tends to focus on general principles that students are then expected to apply to the concrete situations they encounter everyday. Thus, the relative mix of these two different forms of cognition and representation, and the points of contact between them are clearly critical issues in the study of everyday cognition.

The emphasis on hierarchical organization is somewhat more restricted. First, I suggested that both prototype and schema conceptions presuppose some kind of hierarchical organization. This idea was most obvious in the area of person memory. (In fact, even Wyer & Srull's associative network model assumes a certain amount of hierarchical organization, e.g., traits or evaluative person concepts subsuming a set of behaviors). In chapter 4 I discussed the notion of plan hierarchies; to a lesser extent, hierarchies are involved in both models of planning as well. The notion of hierarchical organization is implicit in the concept of MOPs and explicit in that of E-MOPs, as well in the very structure of belief systems, with the concepts of scripts and themes. The clearest statement of hierarchical structures was found in the area of autobiographical memory, where both Conway and Neisser explicitly proposed hierarchical models of AM, and Huttenlocher and her associates (as well as other commentators on forward telescoping) proposed a hierarchical rather than a linear representation of time (as well as of space). Finally, there is also Ellis and Shallice's (1993) distinction between brute retrieval and hierarchical retrieval of delayed intentions.

In addition to this handful of examples of hierarchical organization, it is also interesting to note how many investigators in the area of everyday cognition have proposed alternatives to this form of representation. For example, S. Klein argued against the hierarchical conception of person memory proposed by Wyer and Srull in favor of a one-behavior–one-trait model. Certainly, PDP models eschew hierarchical models in favor of *parallel distributed* representations (though see Clark, 1993). More to the point, research on FRUs, event specific knowledge (insofar as it exists in a separate knowledge store), CBR, separate autobiographical episodes, and the like, focus more on the individual object or event in its own right rather than on their organization, although obviously some sort of organization of even concrete instances is necessary.

The next two issues (i.e., domain specificity and context-specificity) clearly go hand in hand as well. I reviewed the evidence on domain-specificity in chapter 7 and found that some compromise between complete specificity and complete generality seems to be the current "consensus," although there are still advocates of the specificity position as well. This same question of domain specificity was also apparent in my discussion of practical intelligence and everyday problem solving where an attempt was made by several investigators (e.g., Lave, Ceci & Liker, Cole et al., Wagner & Sternberg, and the cross-cultural researchers) to distinguish between task-specific skills and the misleading notion of *general* intelligence. In chapter 10 I looked at the debate between advocates of general syntactic rules versus the cuing of specific memories in deductive reasoning. Finally, in chapter 9 I alluded to Kahneman and Tversky's (1984) concept of framing effects; and in their rebuttal to Gigerenzer, Kahneman and Tversky (1996) emphasized the importance of context on the use of judgmental heuristics.

In everyday cognition it seems likely that there is going to be less generalizability than in formal reasoning or academic intelligence. At the same time, however, complete situational specificity such as that proposed by Lave and Suchman is also rather dubious. I have mentioned a variety of compromises such as those proposed by Pennington and Behder in the transfer literature, by Salomon and Perkins regarding domain specificity, and by Cheng and Holyoak in the area of reasoning and judgment. It seems likely that some such compromise will eventually be reached for everyday cognition, and that compromise will involve some combination of generalizable skills and domain-specific knowledge, as in the study of expertise. (Perkins and Salomon's [1989] metaphor of the "gripping device for retrieving and wielding domain-specific knowledge" seems appropriate here.)

In my discussions of everyday *memory*, the emphasis was more on *context* or situational specificity. This emphasis was most apparent in the area of face recognition, where Thomson (1986) in particular emphasized the role of context in such recognition. Context is also clearly a point of interest in the study of autobiographical organization and retrieval, to wit, Reiser et al.'s (1985) context-plus-index model and Williams and Hollan's emphasis on "find-a context," although the term *context* here is a bit more general than some other conceptions of that term. On a somewhat more pedestrian level, research on both flashbulb memories and AM have emphasized being able to specify the spatial and temporal context of a memory. Context has always been an issue in impression formation (e.g., Asch, 1946; see also Woll et al., 1980), and context-sensitivity played a role in Schank's (1982a) decision to move from scripts to MOPS and in the formulation of the concept of E-MOPs.

The theme of context sensitivity and even situational sensitivity is also apparent in my discussion of everyday problems solving and decision making. This theme is clearly illustrated in the situated cognition view of Lave, Suchman, Clancey, and others. Furthermore, the idea that thinking depends on constraints and opportunities (or affordances; cf. Gibson, 1966, 1979; Neisser, 1976) provided by the environment is part of both Scribner's (e.g., 1986) viewpoint and also the distributed cognition view of Pea (1993) and Salomon (1993b; Salomon et al., 1991). Along similar lines, Hutchins (1995) emphasized the role of the environment, in the form of charts and instruments, in Western navigation. In the previous chapter I discussed the emphasis placed by Klein and by Lipshitz an Ben-Shaul on situational assessment in their models of naturalistic decision making. Finally, I reviewed the emphasis on opportunism in the two models of planning reviewed in chapter 4, a concept that certainly entails a sensitivity to environment and situations.

The fifth issue that I have been tracking is the common concern with the distinction (or lack thereof) between mental representations and the processes or procedures that operate on those representations. This issue is most apparent in the areas of everyday memory, where every topic that I considered (i.e., memory for faces, person memory, memory for events, and autobiographical memory) raised this distinction; but it is also an issue in the area of expertise, where there is some disagreement over whether it is a greater store of background knowledge or a set of cognitive skills that distinguishes experts from novices. On the other side, I indicated that proponents of situated cognition have questioned any distinction between representation and practice; and, as I pointed out in chapter 1 and have followed through the immediately succeeding chapters, connectionist or PDP models have strongly questioned the distinction between representation and process. Finally, in my discussion of research on everyday judgment, and the work on Wason's selection problem in particular, I have examined the debate over the relative role of judgment heuristics and pragmatic reasoning schemas on the one hand, versus more specific forms of cognitive representation in producing everyday judgment errors on the other.

The sixth issue to be considered is, indeed, the relative error-proneness of everyday cognition. The most explicit example of this concern is the debate over the role of bias and error versus rationality in everyday judgment, but I also looked at the issue raised in the area of everyday reasoning and problem solving as well as in the debate over distortion and "memory illusions" in event memory. In chapter 5, I alluded to the problem of accuracy in autobiographical memory; and in chapter 3, I briefly mentioned the study of errors in everyday face recognition. (There is also a recently revived literature on accuracy of personality judgments that I have chosen not to discuss.) In these latter cases the issue is some *objective* standard of empirical truth. Finally, in the previous chapter I looked at the "adequacy" of everyday reasoning in the research of Perkins, Kuhn, and Voss; and I looked at the degree to which such reasoning could be improved by some kind of formal training.

In chapter 9 I noted some of the difficulties entailed in trying to define rationality and in placing too great an emphasis on our susceptibility to error and distortion. I have argued throughout this book that although the prevalence of error in human cognition is of some interest, particularly when it comes to evaluating the skills of so-called experts or the effectiveness of education, it is a mistake to place *too* much of an emphasis on this feature, particularly when it comes to the study of *everyday* cognition, just as it would be an error to be too impressed by evidence of accuracy or rationality. Everyday cognition undoubtedly contains a good deal of error, and it is undoubtedly possible (and in fact, rather easy) to provide demonstrations of such error. It is also possible to find evidence for accuracy, creativity, perspicacity, and wisdom, if we are so inclined. The more important question, as Kahneman and Tversky (1996) pointed out on more than one occasion, is *how* and *why* individuals generate the answers or judgments that are considered to be errors or insights, whether these processes serve other adaptive functions, whether they are the product of erroneous social beliefs or faulty information, and whether they are a matter of faulty processing or a limited database (see Abelson's [1976] discussion of "limited subjective rationality"). In other words, instead of looking for errors in everyday cognition, researchers need to understand the logic or *psycho*logic (Abelson & Rosenberg, 1958) behind these errors, the representations and the operations performed on everyday knowledge that produce these responses.

The final issue, which has been of lesser but growing importance, is the dual-process or dual-system viewpoint. I first developed this position in the dual-process models of impression formation, in E. R. Smith and DeCoster's (1998a) and Kunda and Thagard's (1996) discussions of PDP models of this process, and in the memory versus judgment distinction in this same area. I also discussed a similar distinction raised by Pillemer (1998) and by Pillemer and White (1989), and I suggested that the distinction between voluntary and involuntary memories might fit this distinction as well (see Dulany's [1997] distinction between the *deliberative* and *evocative* mode). This sort of distinction is clearly related to the automatic versus controlled processing (e.g., Bargh, 1994, 1997; Shiffrin & Schneider, 1977; Wegner & Bargh, 1998) and implicit versus explicit memory distinctions (e.g., Schacter, 1987), as well as to the dozen and one other dual-process models now popular in social psychology. Finally, as I indicated in chapter 9, Epstein (1991) and his associates (e.g., Donovan & Epstein, 1997) proposed a distinction between "experiential–intuitive" and "rational–analytic" modes and suggested that the conjunction error results from the greater power of the former. Although this distinction is not currently central to everyday cognition, it will be interesting to see if it emerges as such, as it has in *social* cognition, in the next several years.

The Significance of These Commonalities.   The main reason for raising these commonalities is to demonstrate that there is, in fact, a surprisingly coherent "field" of everyday cognition, that even though research on everyday memory, everyday reasoning and problem-solving, and everyday judgment have proceeded in relative isolation from each other, there are nevertheless a number of important connections among the three areas of research, as well as the literature on education and instruction. It is true, of course, that these issues, as well as the models that I reviewed, are also common to cognitive psychology in general. In fact, one of the connections that I have been stressing throughout this book is to the research literature on text comprehension.

At the same time, however, it seems to me that at least some of these issues are more salient in the study of everyday cognition than in other areas of cognitive psychology or social cognition. For example, as I suggested earlier, the concrete versus abstract issue seems particularly salient in the everyday cognition area because so many of the "stimuli" (e.g., faces, specific events, specific events in your own life, everyday tasks and problems) are themselves concrete and even episodic in nature. Similarly, the issue of error-proneness plays a particluarly significant role in everyday cognition for the simple reason that many of the critiques of bias and error have focused on everyday sorts of judgment. (I hardly think that the work of Kahneman and Tversky would have been as widely cited and as influential as it has been if they and those who followed them had simply focused on the errors made in formal statistical judgment.) Finally, even though the context specificity issue is one that has pervaded research on language and memory in general, it seems particularly pertinent to everyday cognition, where, unlike traditional experimental psychology, the materials (for the most part) are not presented in decontextualized form.

Research Methods

Another factor that I have been stressing throughout this book is the relative emphasis on alternative research procedures versus controlled experimental research. In the course of my discussions, I have touched on a wide variety of alternative techniques, from the use of diaries and mailed-in postcards in the study of autobiographical and prospective memory, to ethnographic and cross-cultural research in the study of practical intelligence, to think-aloud protocols and critical incidents sampling in the study of expertise and naturalistic decision making, to studying amnesiacs and propsopagnosics and examining surveillance tapes in face recognition, to the analysis of archival data in eyewitness identification, to a variety of different types of computer simulations in a variety of different areas. There are undoubtedly a greater number and a greater variety of nonexperimental techniques in the study of everyday cognition than in most other areas of cognitive psychology. This is certainly not surprising, because one of the major ways in which everyday memory research has staked out its territory is by its opposition to the restrictions of traditional experimental research.

At the same time, however, it is clear that experimental studies still play a major role in nearly all areas of everyday cognition. For example, experimental research dominates the areas of face and person memory, as well as research on prospective memory; it also plays a major role in the study of biases in human judgment and errors in eyewitness memory. Such experimental research is of least importance in the areas of autobiographical and event memory and in research on practical intelligence.

It should be noted, however, that much of the experimental research on the topic of everyday cognition has been of the analogue variety rather than the "basic research" sort. For example, Loftus's research on eyewitness memory reviewed in Chapter 4 has clearly attempted to create an analogue of real-world eyewitness situations (as has research on eyewitness identification), although I also argued that recent research on that topic has focused on more basic memory principles and more basic stimuli in accounting for problems in eyewitness memory. Similarly, Fiske and Neuberg explicitly referred to their research on impression formation and stereotyping as involving the creation of "microcosms" of real-world social situations, and much of the research on biases in social reasoning discussed in chapter 9 can be viewed as analogue studies as well. For that matter, even Wason's research on the rule discovery task was an attempt to create an analogue to scientific reasoning.

In Chapter 1, I discussed some of the desirable (and some of the problematic) uses of experimental research in the study of everyday cognition. For example, when observations in the real world suggest some set of competing explanations or hypotheses that can only be tested in the lab or with experimental manipulations, or when researchers have collected enough data to warrant construction of a model (such as Conway's model in the area of autobiographical memory, or the Bruce and Young model in the area of face recognition), then lab research or simulations are probably in order. One other example of this is the research reviewed in chapters 3 and 4 on eyewitness memory, although I have also noted that some commentators (e.g., Yuille, 1986, 1993) viewed this lab research on face memory as failing to make contact with actual cases of real-world eyewitness testimony. On the other hand, the areas of prospective memory and person memory are, I believe, good examples of areas where investigators have moved too quickly into the lab. For example, I discussed in chapter 4 how some investigators (e.g., Kvavilashvili & Ellis, 1996) argued that lab studies of short-delay intentions do not really make contact with real-world studies of longer delays. Similarly, I have argued that research on person memory has focused too much on experimental studies and has failed both to collect sufficient observations and to test their principles in real-world settings.

As a kind of model of how everyday cognition research might proceed, it seems to me that the research strategies of Sylvia Scribner, of researchers on street math, and of Cole's experimental anthropology have much to recommend them. Specifically, beginning with ethnographic research trying to get "the lay of the land," followed by mini-simulations or mini-experiments to test out hypotheses derived from such ethnographic beginnings seems like a reasonable strategy for at least some areas of everyday cognition. Similarly, testing out experimental findings in the real world (e.g., findings from face recognition research as they apply to eyewitness identification or just to everyday cases of recognition; e.g., Young, Hay & Ellis, 1985b), or findings from experimental studies of human judgment to real-life judgment contexts, or even my own research (Woll & Van Der Meer, 1996) on the influence of processing goals on person memory in a videodating context,[2] seem to be reasonable contributions. Still another possibility is to pursue lab research and naturalistic research on the same topic in parallel, allowing each to inform the other. For example, lab research and more naturalistic research on eyewitness testimony might be used together to triangulate that topic. The *problem* with this strategy, as I discussed in chapter 4 in regard to research on prospective memory, is that naturalistic and experimental research often focus on such different *parts* of the same phenomenon that never the twain shall meet.

---

[2]This research on videodating is an interesting example in that it could be argued that videodating, where participants watch and make judgments on the basis of videotapes of prospective matches, is not really a real-world setting either. That is, we do not frequently meet people or make judgments about people as passive observers of an interview with the person. This, of course, speaks to the question of just what is and what is not real world. We chose this setting because it involved a modicum of control (in that the tapes we used had a certain common structure), but also dealt with real-world relationship issues, where the judgments made were from people with real motives to find a partner.

As I indicated in chapters 1 and 3, there is a certain irony in the fact that the area of person memory, of all topics, has been most dependent on experimental techniques and has made the least use of alternative methods. People are undoubtedly the most important, most common, and most complex of everyday "objects," and one would certainly expect for there to be a greater use of more naturalistic materials and settings in the study of how we form impressions and how we represent them. Pepitone (1999) recently suggested that Kurt Lewin, one of the founders of social psychology, would probably not be happy with the overemphasis of social psychology in general on laboratory research, particularly because Lewin himself did relatively little lab research. I have suggested that this overemphasis on experimental methods and experimental control represents a real shortcoming of the person memory area because, as a general rule, such studies are unlikely to engage either the real motivation or the extensive background knowledge that everyone has about full-bodied, complex people with real-world behaviors, real-world expressive behavior, real-world physical characteristics, real-world speech, and so forth.

In the study of face recognition, controlled experimental research seems to be a more reasonable strategy because the face is a more circumscribed pattern and can be brought directly into the lab, although even here one might expect situational factors to play a role (see Davies, 1988). At the same time, critics of face recognition research in the area of eyewitness testimony (e.g., Yuille, 1993) have complained about the artificiality of Photofit and other techniques used for facial identification in criminal cases; even more mainstream researchers (e.g., Ellis & Shepherd, 1992) have emphasized the importance of using videotapes and live presentations rather than just still photographs. In addition, Bahrick (1984; Bahrick et al., 1979) showed how it is possible to study memory for faces with naturalistic tasks and designs as well.

Bahrick's research raises another question: In the era of sophisticated multivariate statistics and state-of-the-art video and interactive computer technology, should the traditional 2 × 2 lab study really still be the model of psychological research? With video technology, researchers can replay an interaction or an episode numerous times under a variety of conditions (see, e.g., the Burton, Wilson, et al., 1999, study using surveillance tapes with face and other parts of the body covered up, or Woll & Van Der Meer's [1996] presentation of videodating interviews with different processing goals). Such tapes can be edited to create variations of the original. Similarly, with regression analyses such as those used by Bahrick et al., or structural equations modeling (e.g., Bentler & Wu, 1994), it is possible to distinguish among several different patterns of causal influence.[3] These and other computer-based modeling procedures can, in my opinion, go a long way to legitimizing nonexperimental forms of research.

---

[3]There is currently some debate about the degree to which so-called causal modeling can, in fact, show causal influences.

Another common methodological approach which I have described in several chapters is the prevalence of computer simulations. For example, we encountered three PDP simulations of person memory and three more of face recognition. In Chapter 4 I also alluded to some different PDP simulations of event memory and planning. Such simulations have also been advocated in social psychology in general (Hastie, 1988; Ostrom, 1988; E. Smith, 1988); and of course, simulations are a staple in the cognitive sciences. At the same time, we have encountered criticisms of such models by Suchman (1987) and other situated cognitivists; and I have questioned whether existing models of word processing represent an appropriate basis for modeling processes such as impression formation.

It seems clear that simulations provide a valuable tool in testing out the viability of major assumptions or hypotheses; and it seems certain that such simulations, whether of the computational or connectionist variety, will become increasingly popular in the future. At the same time, it remains an open question, whether everyday cognition presents any new and/or intractable problems for the simulation approach or for the cognitive sciences in general.

Interdisciplinary Focus. One other commonality among most of these different areas is their interdisciplinary nature. This feature is clearest in the areas of face recognition, where cognitive, developmental, and forensic psychologists, as well as researchers in neuroscience and computer modeling, have all contributed; and in event memory, where psychologists such as Robert Abelson and researchers in artificial intelligence such as Roger Schank have forged profitable alliances and have influenced a generation of students. We have also seen an interdisciplinary emphasis in other areas, e.g., the influence of anthropologists and cross-cultural researchers in the area of practical intelligence, the input from social, clinical, and cognitive psychologists, as well as philosophers in the area of judgment biases, the joint role of cognitive psychologists, educational researchers, workers in artificial intelligence and anthropologists on the question of instructional implications. Autobiographical memory has also drawn upon research in cognitive, developmental, and social psychology, as well as material from literature, philosophy, and psychoanalysis.

It seems to me that this interdisciplinary flavor is one of the strong suits of everyday cognition, as well as the cognitive sciences in general. In writing this book, I have consulted books and journals in cognitive, social, developmental, and physiological psychology, as well as references in education, anthropology, psychoanalysis, law, and artificial intelligence. Casting such a broad net has been both demanding and very exciting. If nothing else, it is refreshing to break out of a narrow, disciplinary rut and look at the "bigger picture."

One particular interdisciplinary connection that I have been trying to make throughout this book is between everyday cognition and research on text comprehension. Thus, for example, I discussed how Wyer has recently added a situation model component to his person memory model, and I also pointed out the similarity of Hastie and Park's online versus memory distinction to the debate in the reading comprehension literature about what inferences are made at what point in the reading process. The research reviewed in chapter 4 regarding event memory was clearly generated by investigators in the areas of text or natural language comprehension. In chapter 5 I discussed the fact that many commentators believe that AM begins with the development of narrative language; in chapter 6 it is clear that the context-plus-index model emerged from the text comprehension literature. Finally, in chapter 9, I drew a connection between research on counterfactual thinking and the belief perseverance on the one hand, and research on text comprehension on the other. The lesson here, as I see it, is that the concerns of research in text comprehension and question answering with the causal, temporal, goal-directed features of human thought has much to offer to the conceptualization of everyday thought. After all, in order to comprehend text, or at least narrative text, one must bring to the situation some kind of everyday knowledge about how people and the world operate. Conversely, although I think that Schank and Abelson's (1995) proposal that all thought is storytelling takes this point a bit too far, certainly there is a narrative component to everyday thought, as reflected in the event and autobiographical memory areas and maybe even the person memory literature (e.g., see Read, Jones, & Miller, 1990, for a goal-based view of traits).

CONCLUSIONS

As stated earlier, one major aim of this book has been to demonstrate that everyday cognition is a viable and a valuable topic for psychological research and that there is, in fact, already a surprisingly large amount and variety of evidence on this topic. Nearly all of the specific topics I have covered have seen an upsurge or resurgence of interest in the past decade or two. In addition, I have attempted to show that even though many of these topics (i.e., everyday memory, practical intelligence or informal reasoning, everyday judgment and decision-making, recent developments in education using everyday cognition) have been pursued separately from each other, they nevertheless show a surprising similarity, both in the kinds of issues they raise and in the conceptual models put forward to account for their findings. It really *is* meaningful to talk about a discipline or area of everyday cognition. That discipline is not yet as coherent or integrated as it might be, but that remains for future consideration.

It is undoubtedly premature at this point to think about a single theory or model to apply to all areas; I certainly do not propose to do that here. On this issue I agree, more or less, with Rubin (1988) that in the early stages of research on this topic investigators should not tie everyday cognition too closely to any single theory, but rather should be open to a variety of different viewpoints (as in the seven different models). My intent in this book has simply been to bring together a variety of areas and point out some commonalities among them. I obviously believe that there is some value in such an exercise, so long as people do not allow the specific phenomena under consideration to be swallowed up by some all-encompassing process theory or one particular issue.

At the same time, it is also clear that the various topics I have considered differ greatly in the degree to which research on each topic has been theoretically or empirically motivated—top-down or bottom-up—as well as in the degree of coherence of research on that topic. For example, in the area of event memory, we saw that research and observations have been guided primarily by Schank and Abelson's script theory and by Schank's later theory of dynamic memory. In other words, the theory preceded the data collection, although that theory has also been revised in light of the results of both simulations and empirical research. On the other hand, research in areas such as prospective memory and practical intelligence have been generated more by the intrinsic interest of the phenomena themselves (as well as some practical concerns in the former case), and higher level theory is generally hard to come by. Research on face recognition and autobiographical memory has involved a combination of empirical, theoretical, and model-based approaches. Finally, there is Wyer and Srull's Person Memory model, which aspires to be a general, all-purpose model of memory, but which at the same time (until the most recent revision) is more data-driven than it is theory- or conceptually-driven. That is, the major assertions in this model have been more in the way of summaries of research findings than conceptually driven arguments.

One possible compromise between these theory-motivated versus topic- or data-motivated positions can be found in the taxonomy of prospective memory studies proposed by Kvavilashvili and Ellis (1996), or in the proposal by Ceci and Bronfenbrenner (1991) that individuals develop a theory or taxonomy of situations in everyday cognition. Another possibility is to compare and attempt to consolidate some of the specific models in different areas—for instance, the restricted information processing models put forward by M. B. Brewer (1988) and Fiske and Neuberg (1990) in the area of impression formation and the similar model put forward by Bruce and Young (1986) in the area of face processing. (As I discussed in chap. 3, the common form of the latter set of models allows some sort of integration of impression formation and face-processing research.) Alternatively, it is possible to bring together the connectionist models that I reviewed on each of these topics. For example, the lower level units of Read and Miller's Social Dynamics Model (i.e., the feature and identification levels) can be related both to the initial levels of the Bruce and Young information-processing model and to portions of the IAC and WISARD models of face recognition. In any case, it seems important to also establish some coherence *within* individual topic areas (e.g., on practical intelligence, in autobiographical memory; though see S. J. Anderson & Conway, 1997), as well as trying to find commonalities *across* areas.

As indicated earlier, another lesson of this book is that it is possible to combine traditional experimental research with a variety of naturalistic alternatives. I believe that my review has produced convincing evidence that naturalistic methods and research in natural settings can be used profitably to study everyday cognition, and that there are a variety of such methods to choose from. However, I certainly would not go as far as Neisser (1978) and reject traditional experimental research out of hand. Nor would I go along with Shiffrin's (1996) argument in the other direction that phenomena such as expertise must be broken down into component parts so that these parts can be studied experimentally (though see my discussion of J. R. Anderson et al., 1996, in chap. 10).

I have reviewed a good deal of experimental research in this book and have tried to show that this research has made valuable contributions to the field of everyday cognition. What I hope is clear from my review is that no one method is the be-all or end-all of research on everyday cognition. Unfortunately, in many of the areas I have reviewed, the results of experimental research have been at odds with those of more naturalistic studies, or vice versa. What is needed, then, is more *integrated* research, research in which the naturalistic observations inform the experimental (or quasi-experimental) like that carried out by Scribner (1986) in work environments, or in which naturalistic and experimental research occur in *parallel,* where both inform each other, as in research on autobiographical memory.

SUGGESTIONS FOR THE FUTURE

My proposals for the future study of everyday cognition follow rather directly from the conclusions just reviewed.

An Integrated Discipline

The clearest need is to establish a more coherent discipline of everyday cognition. This discipline might start with the several commonalities that I have outlined and then proceed to a deeper analysis of the literature that I have reviewed; or it might start with some alternative integrative framework emphasizing the points of contact among these different topics. For example, I have discussed the relationship between AM and event memory, and W. F. Brewer (1997) has recently suggested connections between AM and children's eyewitness memory. I have also suggested the possible links between research on person memory and event memory, on the one hand, and the literature on text processing on the other; there have also recently been a couple of attempts to tie decision making closer to reasoning (e.g., Johnson-Laird & Shafir, 1993) and cognitive psychology in general (e.g., Busemeyer, Hastie, & Medin, 1995).

An example of how *not* to accomplish this integration, in my opinion, is found in the various *Practical Aspects of Memory* (PAM) volumes (Gruneberg, Morris, & Sykes, 1978, 1988; Herrmann, McEvoy, Hertzog, Hertel, & Johnson, 1996). These conferences *have* helped to "loosen up" traditional experimental psychology and have been influential in establishing the field of everyday memory as a viable topic. The conferences have also contributed a number of important papers to this field, not the least of which is the opening paper by Neisser (1978). Nevertheless, the resulting volumes have offered such a loosely organized smorgasbord of topics that they have made it difficult to define or circumscribe the subject matter of everyday cognition. In addition, the rather uneven quality of the papers presented at the PAM conferences has given many psychologists the wrong impression of everyday cognition research and, as discussed in chapter 1, has provided ammunition for the critics of such research. In sum, these conferences have been useful as first steps; but they are certainly not the means in and of themselves for establishing an integrated discipline.

While establishing such a discipline, however, everyday cognition should maintain its contacts with the "traditional" disciplines of cognitive science and social cognition. Indeed, I have argued that social cognition has (or should have) more in common with everyday cognition than it does with some of the more "basic" topics of cognitive psychology (e.g., word recognition, category clustering). At the same time, though, the cognitive sciences are an umbrella under which there is room for the study of everyday cognition topics as well. For that matter, cognitive science may serve as a model of interdisciplinary study that the study of everyday cognition might emulate.

Naturalistic Research and Phenomena

The other point emphasized in this book is the need to give greater attention to how cognitive processes and knowledge structures operate in the real world and to use more naturalistic methods for studying these phenomena (i.e., rather than always seeking out laboratory tests or tests that *have to* follow from some grand existing theory). As I have indicated on several occasions, I believe that naturalistic research is particularly needed in the area of person memory, where everyone has such a wealth of knowledge or beliefs (accurate or inaccurate), as well as on the topics of event memory and human judgment. On the last of these, the recent interest in naturalistic decision making (e.g., G. A. Klein, 1998; Zsambok & Klein, 1997) is a step in the right direction.

Researchers also need to be more open to everyday observations of interesting phenomena, whether it be flashbulb memories (e.g., of the death of John F. Kennedy, Jr. by individuals with differing kinds of interests and different types of background information about him), expert knowledge (e.g., of crossword puzzle experts [Hambrick, Salthouse, & Meinz, 1999]), everyday problem solving (e.g., on the Internet), memory for TV programs, and the like, while at the same time not allowing themselves to get *too* wrapped up in the phenomena themselves. (The middle ground between studying a bunch of isolated interesting phenomena and being *too* focused on just theory testing is going to be an interesting one to negotiate.) Finally, as I have argued on several occasions, experimental research clearly has its place in the mix of everyday cognition, so long as it is not always the *first* option.

Eclecticism

Another suggestion that follows from the literature reviewed in this book is the value of researchers becoming familiar with areas different from their own, a lesson that can be learned from the cognitive sciences as well. Too often researchers get stuck in their own little bailiwick, and, as a result, fail to see the commonalities and connections of that one topic to others. This is undoubtedly a problem in all areas of psychology; but in everyday cognition, where questions such as flashbulb memories or childhood amnesia or failures at face recognition are so fascinating in their own right, it is particularly easy to get caught up in them as isolated phenomena. Yet it would be a shame to overlook or lose sight of the many points of common interest among these different topics.

There is also a clear downside to this emphasis on similarities and to keeping track of more than one area at once. First, it's damn difficult to keep up with the literatures in several different areas simultaneously, particularly since a premium is usually placed in academia on becoming an expert, with detailed knowledge, in some specific, narrow topic. (In other words, academics are usually encouraged to be domain specific.)

Often, when psychologists *do* attempt to establish contact with areas outside their own, there is a temptation for researchers (or practitioners) in the one area to borrow methods, concepts, and/or models from the other area without fully appreciating what they're borrowing or their appropriateness for the particular phenomena being addressed. Thus, for instance, I have noted that early on at least, researchers in person memory borrowed methods such as category clustering (e.g., Hamilton et al., 1980) and concepts such as associative networks (e.g., Wyer & Srull, 1989) and simple categorization principles (e.g., Cantor & Mischel, 1979) to study topics such as organization in impression formation. In my opinion, category clustering does not provide an appropriate measure of the particular form of organization involved in impression formation (particularly as proposed by Asch, 1946); and neither associative network nor simple categorization models (e.g., Kunda, 1999) are adequate for representing the patterned, dynamic nature of impression formation or person memory (see Murphy & Medin, 1985). It is interesting to note that these latter models have recently been superseded or extended by a concern with situation models by Wyer and Radvansky (1999) and by connectionist models (though see Kunda, 1999, chap. 2), the latter of which, as we saw, are mostly taken from simulations of word and letter recognition. It remains to be seen whether these new models will provide an appropriate fit for person memory.

In summary, simply borrowing methods, measures, or models from other areas without fully examining the assumptions involved or the implications of such applications does not seem to me be very useful in and of itself. Psychologists and other researchers in everyday cognition need to become familiar with both the area which they are borrowing *from* and the area which they are applying these principles *to*. I hope that I have generally succeeded at that in this book.

Interdisciplinary Emphasis

As implied by the emphasis on eclecticism, I think that the material presented in this book, as well as the cognitive sciences in general, underlines the importance of a truly interdisciplinary approach, including, of course, greater interchange among the various subdisciplines of psychology. The study of everyday cognition should draw from anthropology, sociology, philosophy, and education, even literature and history—the so-called cultural sciences (e.g., Cole, 1996)—as well as the cognitive, information, and neurosciences.

In summary, I hope that this book has convinced you that everyday cognition is a topic that should be of interest to scholar and layperson alike, that it can be studied in a rigorous, systematic way, and that it, in fact, calls out for further investigation. It will be interesting to see how research and theory on this topic progress over the next decade.

References

Abelson, R. P. (1966). Psychological implication. In R. P. Abelson, E. Aronson, W. J. McGuire, T. M. Newcomb, M. J. Rosenberg, & P. H. Tannenbaum (Eds.), *Theories of cognitive consistency: A source book* (pp. 112–139). Chicago: Rand McNally.

Abelson, R. P. (1968). Computers, polls, and public opinion—some puzzles and paradoxes. *Transaction, 5,* 20–27.

Abelson, R. P. (1973). The structure of belief systems. In R. C. Schank & K. M. Colby (Eds.), *Computer models of thought and language* (pp. 287–339). San Francisco: Freeman.

Abelson, R. P. (1975). Concepts for representing mundane reality in plans. In D. G. Bobrow & A. Collins (Eds.), *Representation and understanding: Studies in cognitive science* (pp. 278–308). New York: Academic Press.

Abelson, R. P. (1976a). Script processing in attitude formation and decision making. In J. S. Caroll & J. W. Payne (Eds.), *Cognition and social behavior* (pp. 33–45). Hillsdale, NJ: Lawrence Erlbaum Associates.

Abelson, R. P. (1976b). Social psychology's rational man. In S. I. Benn & G. W. Mortimer (Eds.), *Rationality and the social sciences: Contributions to the philosophy and methodology of the social sciences* (pp. 58–89). Boston: Routledge.

Abelson, R. P. (1981). Psychological status of the script concept. *American Psychologist, 36,* 715–729.

Abelson, R. P., & Black, J. B. (1986). Introduction. In J. A. Galambos, R. P. Abelson, & J. B. Black (Eds.), *Knowledge structures* (pp. 1–18). Hillsdale, NJ: Lawrence Erlbaum Associates.

Abelson, R. P., & Kanouse, D. E. (1966). Subjective acceptance of verbal generalizations. In S. Feldman (Ed.), *Cognitive consistency: Motivational antecedents and behavioral consequents* (pp. 173–199). New York: Academic Press.

Abelson, R. P., & Lalljee, M. (1988). Knowledge structures and causal explanation. In D. Hilton (Ed.), *Contemporary science and natural explanation; Common sense conceptions of causality* (pp. 175–203). New York: New York University Press.

Abelson, R. P., & Rosenberg, M. J. (1958). Symbolic psycho-logic: A model of attitudinal cognition, *Behavioral Science, 4,* 1–12.

Abernethy, B., Thomas, K. T., & Thomas, J. T. (1993). Strategies for improving understanding of motor expertise (or mistakes we have made and things we have learned).

In J. L. Starkes & F. Allard (Eds.), *Cognitive issues in motor expertise* (pp. 317–356). Amsterdam: North-Holland/Elsevier.

Agre, P. E. (1993). The symbolic worldview: Reply to Vera and Simon. *Cognitive Science, 17,* 61–69.

Agre, P. E. (1997). *Computation and human experience.* New York: Cambridge University Press.

Ajzen, I. (1977). Intuitive theories of events and the effects of base-rate information on prediction. *Journal of Personality and Social Psychology, 35,* 303–314.

Alba, J. W., & Hasher, L. (1983). Is memory schematic? *Psychological Bulletin, 93,* 203–231.

Allard, F., & Starkes, J. L. (1991). Motor-skill experts in sports, dance, and other domains. In K. A. Ericsson & J. Smith (Eds.), *Toward a general theory of expertise: Prospects and limits* (pp. 126–152). New York: Cambridge University Press.

Alloy, L. B., & Tabachnik, N. (1984). Assessment of covariation by humans and animals: The joint influence of prior expectations and current situational information. *Psychological Review, 91,* 112–149.

Allport, G. W. (1937). *Personality: A psychological interpretation.* New York: Holt.

Amabile, T. M., & Kabat, L. G. (1982). When self-descriptions contradict behavior: Actions do speak louder than words. *Social Cognition, 1,* 311–335.

Andersen, S. M., & Cole, S. W. (1990). "Do I know You?" The role of significant others in general social perception. *Journal of Personality and Social Psychology, 59,* 384–399.

Andersen, S. M., & Glassman, N. S. (1996). Responding to significant others when when they are not there: Effects on interpersonal inference, motivation, and affect. In R. M. Sorrentino & E. T. Higgins (Eds.), *Handbook of motivation and cognition, vol. 3: The interpersonal context* (pp. 262–321). New York: Guilford.

Andersen, S. M., & Klatzky, R. L. (1987). Traits and social stereotypes: Levels of categorization in person perception. *Journal of Personality and Social Psychology, 53,* 235–246.

Anderson, C. A. (1982). Inoculation and counter-explanation: Debiasing techniques in the perseverance of social theories. *Social Cognition, 1,* 126–139.

Anderson, C. A. (1983). Abstract and concrete data in the perseverance of social theories: When weak data lead to unshakeable beliefs. *Journal of Experimental Social Psychology, 19,* 93–108.

Anderson, C. A., Krull, D. S., & Weiner, B. (1996). Explanations: Processes and consequences. In E. T. Higgins & A. W. Kruglanski (Eds.), *Social psychology: Handbook of basic principles* (pp. 271–296). New York: Guilford.

Anderson, C. A., Lepper, M. R., & Ross, L. (1980). Perseverance of social theories: The role of explanation in the persistence of discredited information. *Journal of Personality and Social Psychology, 39,* 1037–1049.

Anderson, C. A., & Sechler, E. S. (1986). Effects of explanation and counter-explanation on the development and use of social theories. *Journal of Personality and Social Psychology, 50,* 24–34.

Anderson, C. A., & Sedikides, C. (1991). Thinking about people: Contributions of a typological alternative to associationistic and dimensional models of person perception. *Journal of Personality and Social Psychology, 60,* 203–217.

Anderson, J. R. (1976). *Language, memory, and thought.* Hillsdale, NJ: Lawrence Erlbaum Associates.

Anderson, J. R. (Ed.). (1981). *Cognitive skills and their acquisition.* Hillsdale, NJ: Lawrence Erlbaum Associates.

Anderson, J. R. (1982). Acquisition of cognitive skill. *Psychological Review, 89,* 369–406.

Anderson, J. R. (1983). *The architecture of cognition.* Cambridge, MA: Harvard University Press.

Anderson, J. R. (1987). Skill acquisition: Compilation of weak-method solutions. *Psychological Review, 94,* 192–208.

Anderson, J. R. (1990). *The adaptive character of thought.* Hillsdale, NJ: Lawrence Erlbaum Associates.

Anderson, J. R. (1993). *Rules of the mind.* Hillsdale, NJ: Lawrence Erlbaum Associates.

Anderson, J. R., & Bower, G. H. (1973). *Human associative memory.* Washington, DC: V. H. Winston & Sons.

Anderson, J. R., Reder, L. M., & Simon, H. A. (1996). Situated learning and education. *Educational Researcher, 25*(4), 5–11.

Anderson, N. H. (1968). Application of a linear-serial model to a personality impression formation task using serial presentation. *Journal of Personality and Social Psychology, 10,* 354–362.

Anderson, N. H., & Hubert, S. (1963). Effects of concomitant verbal recall on order effects in personality impression formation. *Journal of Verbal Learning and Verbal Behavior, 2,* 379–391.

Anderson, S. J., & Conway, M. A. (1993). Investigating the structure of autobiographical memories. *Journal of Experimental Psychology: Learning, Memory, and Cognition, 19,* 1178–1196.

Anderson, S. J., & Conway, M. A. (1994). *Are autobiographical memories stable?* Unpublished paper, Lancaster University.

Anderson, S. J., & Conway, M. A. (1997). Representations of autobiographical memories. In M. A. Conway (Ed.), *Cognitive models of memory: Studies in cognition* (pp. 217–246). Cambridge, MA: MIT Press.

Angel, R. B. (1964). *Reasoning and logic.* New York: Appleton-Century Crofts.

Arbib, M. A. (Ed.). (1995). *The handbook of brain theory and neural networks.* Cambridge, MA: MIT Press.

Arkes, H. R., Wortmann, R. L., Saville, R. D., & Harkness, A. R. (1981). Hindsight bias among physicians weighing the likelihood of diagnosis. *Journal of Applied Psychology, 66,* 252–254.

Aronson, E., & Carlsmith, J. M. (1968). Experimentation in social psychology. In G. Lindzey & E. Aronson (Eds.), *Handbook of social psychology* (2nd ed., Vol. 2, pp. 1–79). Reading, MA: Addison-Wesley.

Asch, S. E. (1946). Forming impressions of personality. *Journal of Abnormal and Social Psychology, 41,* 258–290.

Asch, S. E., & Zukier, H. (1984). Thinking about persons. *Journal of Personality and Social Psychology, 46,* 1230–1240.

Atkinson, R. C., & Shiffrin, R. M. (1968). Human memory: A proposed system and its control processes. In K. W. Spence and J. T. Spence (Eds.), *The psychology of learning and motivation: Advances in research and theory* (Vol. 2, pp. 89–105). New York: Academic Press.

Baddeley, A. D. (1992a). Is memory all talk? *The Psychologist, 5,* 447–448.

Baddeley, A. D. (1992b). What is autobiographical memory? In M. A. Conway, D. C. Rubin, H. Spinnler, & W. A. Wagenaar (Eds.), *Theoretical perspectives on autobiographical memory* (pp. 13–29). Dordrecht, The Netherlands: Kluwer Academic.

Baddeley, A. D. (1993). Commentary: Holy war or wholly unnecessary? Some thoughts on the "conflict" between laboratory studies and everyday memory. In G. M. Davies & P. H. Logie (Eds.), *Memory in everyday life* (pp. 532–536). Amsterdam: North-Holland/Elsevier Science.

Baddeley, A. D., & Hitch, G. (1977). Recency re-examined. In S. Dornic (Ed.), *Attention and performance VI* (pp. 646–667). Hillsdale, NJ: Lawrence Erlbaum Associates.

Baddeley, A. D., Lewis, V., & Nimmo-Smith, I. (1978). When did you last ...? In M. M. Gruneburg, P. E. Morris, & R. N. Sykes (Eds), *Practical aspects of memory: Current research and issues. Vol. 1: Memory in everyday life* (pp. 77–83). London: Academic Press.

Baddeley, A. D., & Wilkins, A. J. (1984). Taking memory out of the laboratory. In J. E. Harris & P. E. Morris (Eds.), *Everyday memory, actions and absent-mindedness* (pp. 1–17). London: Academic Press.

Baddeley, A. D., & Wilson, B. (1986). Amnesia, autobiographical memory, confabulation. In D. C. Rubin (Ed.), *Autobiographical memory* (pp. 225–252). New York: Cambridge University Press.

Baddeley, A. D., & Woodhead, M. M. (1983). Improving face recognition ability. In S. M. A. Lloyd-Bostock and B. R. Clifford (Eds.), *Evaluating witness evidence* (pp. 125–136). Chichester, England: Wiley.

Bahrick, H. P. (1984a). Semantic memory content in permastore: Fifty years of memory for Spanish learned in school. *Journal of Experimental Psychology: General, 113*, 1–29.

Bahrick, H. P. (1984b). Associations and organization in cognitive psychology: A reply to Neisser. *Journal of Experimental Psychology: General, 113*, 36–37.

Bahrick, H. P. (1991). A speedy recovery from bankruptcy for ecological memory research. *American Psychologist, 46*, 76–77.

Bahrick, H. P. (1996). Synergistic strategies for memory research. In D. Herremann, C. McEvoy, C. Hertzog, P. Hertel, & M. Johnson (Eds.), *Basic and applied memory research: Theory in context* (Vol. 2, pp. 51–62). Mahwah, NJ: Lawrence Erlbaum Associates.

Bahrick, H. P. (1998). Loss and distortion in autobiographical memory content. In C. P. Thompson, D. J. Herrmann, D. Bruce, J. D. Read, D. G. Payne, & M. P. Toglia (Eds.), *Autobiographical memory: Theoretical and applied perspectives* (pp. 69–78). Mahwah, NJ: Lawrence Erlbaum Associates.

Bahrick, H. P., Bahrick, L. E., Bahrick, A. S., & Bahrick, P. E. (1993). Maintenance of foreign language vocabulary and the spacing effect. *Psychological Science, 4*, 316–321.

Bahrick, H. P., Bahrick, P. E., & Wittlinger, R. P. (1975). Fifty years of names and faces: A cross sectional approach. *Journal of Experimental Psychology: General, 104*, 54–75.

Bahrick, H. P., & Hall, L. K. (1991). Preventive and corrective maintenance of access to knowledge. *Applied Cognitive Psychology, 5*, 1–18.

Bahrick, H. P., Hall, L. K., & Berger, S. A. (1996). Accuracy and distortion in memory for high-school grades. *Psychological Science, 7*, 265–271.

Bahrick, H. P., & Phelps, E. (1988). The maintenance of marginal knowledge. In U. Neisser & E. Winograd (Eds.), *Remembering reconsidered: Ecological and traditional approaches to the study of memory* (pp. 178–192). New York: Cambridge University Press.

Baker, E. L., & O'Neil, H. F. (1994). Performance assessment and equity: A view from the USA. *Assessment in Education, 1*, 11–26.

Baker, E. L., O'Neil, H. F., & Linn, R. L. (1993). Policy and validity prospects for performance based assessment. *American Psychologist, 48*, 1210–1218.

Banaji, M. R., & Crowder, R. G. (1989). The bankruptcy of everyday memory. *American Psychologist, 44*, 1185–1193.

Barclay, C. R. (1986). Schematization of autobiographical memory. In D. C. Rubin (Ed.), *Autobiographical memory* (pp. 82–99). New York: Cambridge University Press.

Barclay, C. R. (1993a). Remembering ourselves. In G. M. Davies & R. H. Logie (Eds.), *Memory in everyday life* (pp. 285–309). Amsterdam: North-Holland/Elsevier Science.

Barclay, C. R. (1993b). Rejoinder: Reflections on Professors Robinson's and Larsen's comments. In G. M. Davies & R. H. Logie (Eds.), *Memory in everyday life* (pp. 321–323). Amsterdam: North-Holland/Elsevier Science.

Barclay, C. R. (1994). Composing protoselves through improvisation. In U. Neisser & R. Fivush (Eds.), *The remembering self: Construction and accuracy in the self-narrative* (pp. 55–77). New York: Cambridge University Press.

Barclay, C. R. (1996). Autobiographical remembering: Narrative constraints on objectified selves. In D. C. Rubin (Ed.), *Remembering our past: Studies in autobiographical memory* (pp. 94–125). New York: Cambridge University Press.

Barclay, C. R., & Smith, T. S. (1992). Autobiographical remembering: Creating personal culture. In M. A. Conway, D. C. Rubin, H. Spinnler, & W. A. Wagenaar (Eds.), *Theoretical perspectives on autobiographical memory* (pp. 75–97). Dordrecht, The Netherlands: Kluwer Academic.

Barclay, C. R., & Subramaniam, G. (1987). Autobiographical memories and self-schemata. *Applied Cognitive Psychology, 1,* 169–82.

Barclay, C. R., & Wellman, H. M. (1986). Accuracies and inaccuracies in autobiographical memory. *Journal of Memory and Language, 25,* 93–103.

Barclay, J. R., Bransford, J. D., Franks, J. J., McCarrell, N. S., & Nitsch, K. E. (1974). Comprehension and semantic flexibility. *Journal of Verbal Learning and Verbal Behavior, 13,* 471–481.

Bargh, J. A. (1994). The Four Horsemen of automaticity: Awareness, efficiency, intention, and control in social cognition. In R. S. Wyer, Jr. & T.K. Srull (Eds.), *Handbook of social cognition* (2nd ed., pp. 1–40). Hillsdale, NJ: Lawrence Erlbaum Associates.

Bargh, J. A. (1997). The automaticity of everyday life. In R. S. Wyer, Jr. (Ed.), *The automaticity of everyday life: Advances in social cognition* (Vol. 10, pp. 1–61). Mahwah, NJ: Lawrence Erlbaum Associates.

Bargh, J. A., & Chartrand, T. L. (1999). The unbearable automaticity of being. *American Psychologist, 54,* 462–479.

Bar-Hillel, M. (1973). On the subjective probability of compound events. *Organizational Behavior and Human Performance, 9,* 396–406.

Bar-Hillel, M. (1979). The role of sample size in sample evaluation. *Organizational Behavior and Human Performance, 24,* 245–257.

Bar-Hillel, M. (1980). The base-rate fallacy in probability judgments. *Acta Psychologica, 44,* 211–233.

Barlow, H. B. (1972). Single units and sensation: A neuron doctrine for perceptual psychology? *Perception, 1,* 371–394.

Barnden, J. A. (1995). Artificial intelligence and neural networks. In M. A. Arbib (Ed.), *Handbook of brain theory and neural networks* (pp. 98–102). Cambridge, MA: MIT Press.

Barnden, J. A., & Holyoak, K. J. (Eds.) (1994). *Advances in connectionist and neural computation theory. Vol. 3: Analogy, metaphor, and reasoning.* New York: Academic Press.

Baron, J. (1994). *Thinking and deciding* (2nd ed.). New York: Cambridge University Press.

Baron, J., & Ritov, I. (1994). Reference points and omission bias. *Organizational Behavior and Human Decision Processes, 59,* 475–498.

Baron, R. J. (1981). Mechanisms of human facial recognition. *International Journal of Man–Machine Studies, 15,* 137–178.

Baron, R. M. (1988). An ecological framework for establishing a dual-mode theory of social knowing. In D. Bar-Tal & A. W. Kruglanski (Eds.), *The social psychology of knowledge* (pp. 48–82). New York: Cambridge University Press.

Barsalou, L. W. (1983). Ad hoc categories. *Memory & Cognition, 11,* 211–227.

Barsalou, L. W. (1987). The instability of graded structure: Implications for the nature of concepts. In U. Neisser (Ed.), *Concepts and conceptual development* (pp. 101–140). New York: Cambridge University Press.

Barsalou, L. W. (1988). The content and organization of autobiographical memories. In U. Neisser & E. Winograd (Eds.), *Remembering reconsidered: Ecological and traditional approaches to the study of memory* (pp. 193–243). New York: Cambridge University Press.

Barsalou, L. W. (1991). Deriving categories to achieve goals. In G. H. Bower (Ed.), *The psychology of learning and motivation: Advances in research and theory* (Vol. 27, pp. 1–64). New York: Academic Press.

Barsalou, L. W., & Bower, G. H. (1984). Discrimination nets as psychological models. *Cognitive Science, 8,* 1–26.

Bartlett, F. C. (1932). *Remembering.* Cambridge, UK: Cambridge University Press.

Bartlett, F. C. (1958). *Thinking: An experimental and social study.* New York: Basic Books.

Bartlett, J. C., & Searcy, J. (1993). Inversion and configuration of faces. *Cognitive Psychology, 25,* 281–316.

Bass, E., & Davis, L. (1988). *The courage to heal: A guide for women survivors of child sexual abuse.* New York: Harper & Row.

Bassok, M. (1990). Transfer of domain-specific problem–solving procedures. *Journal of Experimental Psychology: Learning, Memory, and Cognition, 16,* 522–533.

Bassok, M., & Holyoak, K. J. (1985, November). *Transfer between isomorphic topics in algebra and physics.* Paper presented at the meeting of the Psychonomic Society, Boston.

Bassok, M., & Holyoak, K. J. (1989). Interdomain transfer between isomorphic topics in algebra and physics. *Journal of Experimental Psychology: Learning, Memory, and Cognition, 15,* 153–166.

Bassok, M., & Holyoak, K. J. (1993). Pragmatic knowledge and conceptual structure: Determinants of transfer between quantitative domains. In D. K. Detterman & R. J. Sternberg (Eds.), *Transfer on trial: Intelligence, cognition, and instruction* (pp. 68–98). Norwood, NJ: Ablex.

Bauer, P. J. (1993). Identifying subsystems of autobiographical memory: Commentary on Nelson. In C. A. Nelson (Ed.), *Memory and affect in development: The Minnesota Symposium on Child Psychology* (Vol. 26, pp. 25–37). Hillsdale, NJ: Lawrence Erlbaum Associates.

Bauer, P. J. (1996). What do infants recall of their lives? Memory for specific events by one- to two-year-olds. *American Psychologist, 51,* 29–41.

Bauer, P. J., & Hertsgaard, L. A. (1993). Increasing steps in recall of events: Factors facilitating immediate and long term memory in 13.5- and 16.5-month-old children. *Child Development, 64,* 1204–1223.

Bauer, P. J., & Mandler, J. M. (1989). One thing follows another: Effects of temporal structure on 1- to 2-year-olds' recall of events. *Developmental Psychology, 25,* 197–206.

Beach, L. R. (1990). *Image theory: Decision making in personal and organizational settings.* West Sussex, England: John Wiley.

Beach, L. R., & Mitchell, T. R. (1978). A contingency model for the selection of decision strategies. *Academy of Management Review, 3,* 439–449.

Beach, L. R., & Mitchell, T. R. (1987). Image theory: Principles, goals, and plans in decision making. *Acta Psychologica, 66,* 201–220.

Bedard, J., & Chi, M. T. H. (1992). Expertise. *Current Directions in Psychological Science, 1,* 135–139.

Bekerian, D. A., & Bowers, J. M. (1983). Eyewitness testimony: Were we misled? *Journal of Experimental Psychology: Learning, Memory, and Cognition, 9,* 139–145.

Bekerian, D. A., & Dritschel, P. H. (1992). Autobiographical remembering: An integrative approach. In M. A. Conway, D. C. Rubin, H. Spinnler, & W. A. Wagenaar (Eds.), *Theoretical perspective on autobiographical memory* (pp. 135–150). Dordrecht, The Netherlands: Kluwer Academic.

Belli, R. F. (1989). Influences of misleading post event information: Misinformation interference and acceptance. *Journal of Experimental Psychology: General, 118,* 72–85.

Belli, R. F., & Loftus, E. F. (1996). The pliability of autobiographical memory: Misinformation and the false memory problem. In D. C. Rubin (Ed.), *Remembering our past: Studies in autobiographical memory* (pp. 157–179). New York: Cambridge University Press.

Belli, R. F., Windshitl, P. D., McCarthy, T. T., & Winfrey, S. E. (1992). Detecting memory impairment with modified test procedure: Manipulating retention interval with centrally presented event items. *Journal of Experimental Psychology: Learning, Memory, and Cognition, 18,* 356–367.

Benner, P. E. (1984). *From novice to expert: Excellence and power in clinical nursing*. Menlo Park, CA: Addison-Wesley.

Benner, P. E., Tanner, C. A., & Chesla, C. A. (1996). *Expertise in nursing practice: Caring, clinical judgment, and practice*. New York: Springer.

Bennett, D. J., & Woll, S. B. (1980). Some social psychological influences on the linguistic performances of Black teenagers. *Discourse Processes, 3*, 73–97.

Benson, K. A., Jarvi, S. D., Arai, Y., Thielbar, P. R. S., Frye, K. J., & Goracke McDonald, B. L. (1992). Socio-historical context and autobiographical memories: Variations in the reminiscence phenomenon. In M. A. Conway, D. C. Rubin, H. Spinnler, & W. A. Wagenaar (Eds.), *Theoretical perspectives on autobiographical memory* (pp. 313–322). Dordrecht, The Netherlands: Kluwer Academic.

Bentler, P. M., & Wu, E. J. (1994). *EQS 5 users guide*. BMOP Software, Inc., Los Angeles, CA.

Bereiter, C. (1991). Implications of connectionism for thinking about rules. *Educational Researcher, 20*(3), 10–16.

Bereiter, C. (1997). Situated cognition and how to overcome it. In D. I. Kirshner & J. A. Whitson (Eds.), *Situated cognition: Social, semiotic, and psychological perspectives* (pp. 281–300). Mahwah, NJ: Lawrence Erlbaum Associates.

Berkeley, D., & Humphreys, P. (1982). Structuring decision problems and the bias heuristic. *Acta Psychologica, 50*, 201–252.

Berliner, D. C. (1994). The wonder of exemplary performance. In J. N. Mongieri & C. C. Black (Eds.), *Creating powerful thinking in parents and students* (pp. 161–186). Fort Worth, TX: Holt Brace.

Bernstein, B. (1958). Some sociological determinants of perception: An enquiry into sub-cultural differences. *British Journal of Sociology, 9*, 159–174.

Berntsen, D. (1996). Involuntary autobiographical memories. *Applied Cognitive Psychology, 10*, 435–454.

Berntsen, D. (1998). Voluntary and involuntary access to autobiographical memory. *Memory, 6*, 113–141.

Berry, D. S. (1990). Taking people at face value: Evidence for the kernel of truth hypothesis. *Social Cognition, 8*, 343–361.

Berry, D. S., & McArthur, L. Z. (1986). Perceiving character in faces: The impact of age-related craniofacial changes on social perception. *Psychological Bulletin, 100*, 3–18.

Berry, J. W., & Irvine, S. H. (1986). Bricolage: Savages do it daily. In R. J. Sternberg & R. K. Wagner (Eds.), *Practical intelligence: Nature and origins of competence in the everyday world* (pp. 271–306). New York: Cambridge University Press.

Biederman, I., & Shiffrar, M. M. (1987). Sexing day-old chicks: Expert systems analysis of a difficult perceptual-learning task. *Journal of Experimental Psychology: Learning, Memory, and Cognition, 13*, 640–645.

Binet, A. (1894). *The psychology of great calculators and chess players*. Paris: Hochette.

Bisiacchi, P. S. (1996). A neuropsychological approach in the study of prospective memory. In M. A. Brandimonte, G. O. Einstein, & M. A. McDaniel (Eds.), *Prospective memory: Theory and applications* (pp. 297–317). Mahwah, NJ: Lawrence Erlbaum Associates.

Bloom, B. S. (Ed.). (1985). *Developing talent in young people*. New York: Basic Books.

Bodenhausen, G. V., Macrae, C. N., & Sherman, J. W. (1999). On the dialectics of discrimination: Dual processes in social stereotyping. In S. Chaiken & Y. Trope (Eds.), *Dual-process theories in social psychology* (pp. 271–290). New York: Guilford.

Bodenhausen, G. V., & Wyer, R. S., Jr. (1985). Effects of stereotypes on decision making and information strategies. *Journal of Personality and Social Psychology, 48*, 267–282.

Bonissonc, P. P., Ran, L. F., & Berg, G. (1994). The case for nonconnectionist associative retrieval in case-based reasoning systems. In J. A. Barnden & K. J. Holyoak (Eds.),

Advances in connectionist and neural computation theory. Vol. 3: Analogy, metaphor, and reminding (pp. 169–202). New York: Academic Press.

Borgida, E., & Brekke, N. (1981). The base rate fallacy in attribution and prediction. In J. H. Harvey, W. J. Ickes, & P. F. Kidd (Eds.), *New directions in attribution research* (Vol. 3, pp. 66–97). Hillsdale, NJ: Lawrence Erlbaum Associates.

Borgida, E., & Nisbett, R. E. (1977). The differential impact of abstract vs. concrete information on decisions. *Journal of Applied Psychology, 7*, 258–271.

Bornstein, B. (1963). Prosopagnosia. In L. Halpen (Ed.), *Problems of dynamic neurology* (pp. 283–317). Jerusalem: Hadassah Medical Organization.

Bornstein, B., Sroka, H., & Munita, H. (1969). Prosopagnosia with animal face agnosia. *Cortex, 5*, 164–169.

Bothwell, R. K., Deffenbacher, K. A., & Brigham, J. C. (1987). Correlation of eyewitness accuracy and confidence: Optimality hypothesis revisited. *Journal of Applied Psychology, 72*, 691–695.

Bourdieu, P. (1977). *Outline of a theory of practice.* New York: Cambridge University Press.

Bourne, L. E., Dominowski, R. L., & Loftus, E. F. (1979). *Cognitive processes.* Englewood Cliffs, NJ: Prentice-Hall.

Bousfield, W. A. (1953). The occurrence of clustering in the recall of randomly arranged associates. *Journal of General Psychology, 49*, 229–240.

Bower, G. H., Black, J. B., & Turner, T. J. (1979). Scripts in memory for text. *Cognitive Psychology, 11*, 177–220.

Bower, G. H., & Karlin, M. B. (1974). Depth of processing pictures of faces and recognition memory. *Journal of Experimental Psychology, 103*, 751–757.

Bowers, K. S., & Farvolden, P. (1996). Revisiting a century-old Freudian slip—from suggestion disavowed to the truth repressed. *Psychological Review, 119*, 355–380.

Bowlby, J. (1969). *Attachment and loss. Vol. 1: Attachment.* New York: Basic Books.

Bradburn, N. M., Huttenlocher, J., & Hedges, L. V. (1994). Telescoping and temporal memory. In N. Schwarz & S. Sudman (Eds.), *Autobiographical memory and the validity of retrospective reports* (pp. 203–215). New York: Springer-Verlag.

Bradburn, N. M., Rips, L. J., & Shevell, S. K. (1987, April). Answering autobiographical questions: The impact of memory and inference on surveys. *Science, 236*(4798), 157–161.

Bradshaw, J. L., & Wallace, G. (1971). Models for the processing and identification of faces. *Perception and Psychophysics, 9*, 443–448.

Braine, M. D. S. (1978). On the relation between the natural logic of reasoning and standard logic. *Psychological Review, 85*, 1–21.

Braine, M. D. S., & O'Brien, D. P. (Eds.). (1998). *Mental logic.* Mahwah, NJ: Lawrence Erlbaum Associates.

Brainerd, C. J., & Reyna, V. F. (1993). Memory independence and memory interference in cognitive development. *Psychological Review, 100*, 42–67.

Brainerd, C. J., & Reyna, V. F. (1995). Learning rates, learning opportunities and the development of forgetting. *Developmental Psychology, 31*, 251–262.

Brandimonte, M. A., Einstein, G. O., & McDaniel, M. A. (Eds.). (1996). *Prospective memory: Theory and applications.* Mahwah, NJ: Lawrence Erlbaum Associates.

Brandimonte, M. A., & Passolonghi, M. C. (1994). The effect of cue-familiarity, cue-distinctiveness, and retention interval on prospective remembering. *Quarterly Journal of Experimental Psychology: Human Experimental Psychology, 47A*, 565–587.

Bransford, J. D., & Franks, J. J. (1972). The abstraction of linguistic ideas: A review. *Cognition, 1*, 211–249.

Bransford, J. D., & Johnson, M. K. (1973). Consideration of some problems of comprehension. In W. G. Chase (Ed.), *Visual information processing* (pp. 383–438). New York: Academic Press.

Bransford, J. D., Nitsch, K. E., & Franks, J. J. (1977). Schooling and the facilitation of knowledge. In R. C. Anderson, R. J. Spiro, & W. E. Montague (Eds.), *Schooling and the acquisition of knowledge* (pp. 31–55). Hillsdale, NJ: Lawrence Erlbaum Associates.

Breakwell, G. M., & Canter, D. V. (Eds.). (1993). *Empirical approaches to social representations*. Oxford, England: Clarendon Press.

Bredart, S., & Bruyer, R. (1994). The cognitive approach to familiar face processing in human subjects. *Behavioral Processes, 33,* 213–232.

Brennen, T., & Bruce, V. (1991). Context effects in the processing of familiar faces. *Psychological Research, 53,* 296–304.

Brewer, M. B. (1988). A dual process model of impression formation. In T. K. Srull & R. S. Wyer, Jr. (Eds.), *A dual process model of impression formation: Advances in social cognition* (Vol. 1, pp. 1–36). Hillsdale, NJ: Lawrence Erlbaum Associates.

Brewer, M. B., Dull, V., & Lui, L. N. (1981). Perceptions of the elderly: Stereotypes as prototypes. *Journal of Personality and Social Psychology, 41,* 656–670.

Brewer, M. B., & Feinstein, A. S. H. (1999). Dual processes in the cognitive representation of persons and social categorization. In S. Chaiken & Y. Trope (Eds.), *Dual-process theories in social psychology* (pp. 255–270). New York: Guilford.

Brewer, M. B., & Lui, L. N. (1989). The primacy of age and sex in the structure of person categories. *Social Cognition, 7,* 262–274.

Brewer, W. F. (1986). What is autobiographical memory? In D. C. Rubin (Ed.), *Autobiographical memory* (pp. 25–49). New York: Cambridge University Press.

Brewer, W. F. (1988). Memory for randomly sampled autobiographical events. In U. Neisser & E. Winograd (Eds.), *Remembering reconsidered: Ecological and traditional approaches to the study of memory* (pp. 21–90). New York: Cambridge University Press.

Brewer, W. F. (1992). Phenomenal experience in laboratory and autobiographical memory tasks. In M. A. Conway, D. C. Rubin, H. Spinnler, & W. A. Wagenaar (Eds.), *Theoretical perspectives on autobiographical memory* (pp. 31–51). Dordrecht, The Netherlands: Kluwer Academic.

Brewer, W. F. (1993). The theoretical and empirical status of the flashbulb memory hypothesis. In E. Winograd & U. Neisser (Eds.), *Affect and accuracy in recall: Studies in "flashbulb" memories* (pp. 274–305). New York: Cambridge University Press.

Brewer, W. F. (1994). Autobiographical memory and survey research. In N. Schwarz & S. Sudman (Eds.), *Autobiographical memory and the validity of retrospective reports* (pp. 11–20). New York: Springer-Verlag.

Brewer, W. F. (1995). To assert that essentially all human knowledge and memory is represented in terms of stories is certainly wrong. In R. S. Wyer (Ed.), *Knowledge and memory: The real story. Advances in social cognition* (Vol. 8, pp. 109–119). Hillsdale, NJ: Lawrence Erlbaum Associates.

Brewer, W. F. (1996). What is recollective memory? In D. C. Rubin (Ed.), *Remembering our past: Studies in autobiographical memory* (pp. 19–66). New York: Cambridge Univeristy Press.

Brewer, W. F. (1997). Children's eyewitness memory research: Implications from schema memory and autobiographical memory research. In N. L. Stein, P. A. Ornstein, B. Tversky, & C. Brainerd (Eds.), *Memory for everyday and emotional events* (pp. 453–466). Mahwah, NJ: Lawrence Erlbaum Associates.

Brewer, W. F., & Dupree, D. A. (1983). Use of plan schemata in the recall and recognition of goal-directed actions. *Journal of Experimental Psychology: Learning, Memory, and Cognition, 9,* 117–129.

Brewer, W. F., & Nakamura, G. V. (1984). The nature and functions of schemas. In R. S. Wyer & T. K. Srull (Eds.), *Handbook of social cognition* (1st ed., Vol. 1, pp. 119–160). Hillsdale, NJ: Lawrence Erlbaum Associates.

Brewin, C. R., Andrews, B., & Gottlib, I. H (1993). Psychopathology and early experiences: A reappraisal of retrospective reports. *Psychological Bulletin, 113,* 82–98.

Bridgman, P. W. (1928). *The logic of modern physics.* New York: Macmillan.

Brigham, J. C. (1988). Is witness confidence helpful in judging eyewitness accuracy? In M. M. Gruneberg, P.E. Morris, & R. N. Sykes (Eds.), *Practical aspects of memory: Current research and issues: Vol. 1. Memory in everyday life* (pp. 77–82). Chichester, England: Wiley.

Brigham, J. C., Maass, A., Snyder, L. D., & Spaulding, K. (1982). Accuracy of eyewitness identification in a field setting. *Journal of Personality and Social Psychology, 42,* 673–681.

Brigham, J. C., & Ready, D. J. (1985). Own-race bias in line up construction. *Law and Human Behavior, 9,* 415–424.

Broadbent, D. E. (1989). Lasting representations and temporary processes. In H. L. Roediger, III & F. I. M. Craik (Eds.), *Varieties of memory and consciousness: Essays in honor of Endel Tulving* (pp. 211–228). Hillsdale, NJ: Lawrence Erlbaum Associates.

Brooks-Gunn, J., & Lewis, M. (1984). The development of early visual self-recognition. *Developmental Review, 4,* 215–239.

Brown, A. L. (1990). Domain-specific principles affect learning and transfer in children. *Cognitive Science, 14,* 107–133.

Brown, J. S., Collins, A., & Duguid, P. (1989). Situated cognition and the culture of learning. *Educational Researcher, 18,* 32–42.

Brown, J. S., & Duguid, P. (2000). *The social life of information.* Cambridge, MA: Harvard Business School Press.

Brown, N. R., Rips, L. J., & Shevell, S. K. (1985). The subjective dates of natural events in very-long-term memory. *Cognitive Psychology, 17,* 139–177.

Brown, N. R., Shevell, S. K., & Rips, L. J. (1986). Public memories and their personal context. In D. C. Rubin (Ed.), *Autobiographical memory* (pp. 137–158). New York: Cambridge University Press.

Brown, R., & Kulik, J. (1977). Flashbulb memories. *Cognition, 5,* 73–99.

Brown, R., & McNeill, D. (1966). The "tip of the tongue" phenomenon. *Journal of Verbal Learning and Verbal Behavior, 5,* 325–337.

Bruce, D. (1988). Mechanistic and functional explanations of memory. *American Psychologist, 46,* 46–48.

Bruce, D., & Read, J. D. (1988). The how and why of memory for frequency. In M. M. Gruneberg, P. E. Morris, & P. N. Syker (Eds.), *Practical aspects of memory: Current research and issues, Vol. 1: Memory in everyday life* (pp. 317–322). New York: Wiley.

Bruce, V. (1979). Searching for politicians: An information-processing approach to face recognition. *Quarterly Journal of Experimental Psychology, 31,* 373–395.

Bruce, V. (1983). Recognising faces. *Philosophical Transactions of the Royal Society, B302,* 423–436.

Bruce, V. (1988). *Recognising faces.* Hove, UK: Lawrence Erlbaum Associates.

Bruce, V., & Burton, A. M. (1989). Computer recognition of faces. In A. W. Young & H. D. Ellis (Eds.), *Handbook of research on face processing* (pp. 487–506). Amsterdam: North Holland/Elsevier Science.

Bruce, V., Doyle, T., Dench, N., & Burton, A. M. (1991). Remembering facial configurations. *Cognition, 38,* 109–144.

Bruce, V., & Humphreys, G. W. (1994). Recognizing objects and faces. In V. Bruce & G. W. Humphreys (Eds.), *Object and face recognition: Special issue of Visual Cognition* (pp. 141–180). Hove, UK: Lawrence Erlbaum Associates.

Bruce, V., & Valentine, T. (1985). Identity priming in the recognition of familiar faces. *British Journal of Psychology, 76,* 373–383.

Bruce, V., & Valentine, T. (1986). Semantic priming of familiar faces. *Quarterly Journal of Experimental Psychology, 38A,* 125–150.

Bruce, V., & Young, A. W. (1986). Understanding face recognition. *British Journal of Psychology, 77*, 305–327.

Bruce, V., & Young, A. W. (1998). *In the eye of the beholder: The science of face perception*. Oxford, England: Oxford University Press.

Bruck, M., Cavanagh, P., & Ceci, S. J. (1991). Forty something: Recognizing faces at one's 25th reunion. *Memory & Cognition, 19*, 221–228.

Bruhn, A. R. (1990). *Earliest childhood memories: Vol. 1. Theory and application to clinical practice*. New York: Praeger.

Brunas, J. S., Young, A. W., & Ellis, A. W. (1990). Repetition priming from incomplete faces: Evidence for part to whole completion. *British Journal of Psychology, 81*, 43–56.

Bruner, J. S. (1956). A cognitive theory of personality [Review of the book *The psychology of personal constructs*]. *Contemporary Psychology, 1*, 355–357.

Bruner, J. S. (1986). *Actual minds, possible worlds*. Cambridge, MA: Harvard University Press.

Bruner, J. S. (1987). Life as narrative. *Social Research, 54*, 11–32.

Bruner, J. S. (1990). *Acts of meaning*. Cambridge, Ma: Harvard University Press.

Bruner, J. S. (1994). The "remembered" self. In U. Neisser & R Fivush (Eds.), *The remembering self: Construction and accuracy in the self-narrative* (pp. 41–54). New York: Cambridge University Press.

Bruner, J. S., Goodnow, J. J., & Austin, G. A. (1956). *The study of thinking*. New York: Wiley.

Bruner, J. S., & Tagiuri, P. (1954). The perception of people. In G. Lindzey (Ed.), *The handbook of social psychology* (1st ed, Vol. 2, pp. 634–654). Reading, MA: Addison-Wesley.

Brunswik, E. (1956). *Perception and the representative design of psychological experiments* (2nd ed.). Berkeley, CA: University of California Press.

Bruyer, R. (1991). Covert face recognition in prosopagnosia: A review. *Brain and Cognition, 15*, 223–235.

Bruyer, R., & Scailquin, J. C. (1994). Person recognition and aging: The cognitive status of addresses. An empirical question. *International Journal of Psychology, 29*, 351–366.

Bryson, M., Bereiter, C., Scardamalia, M., & Joram, E. (1991). Going beyond the problem as given: Problem solving in expert and novice writers. In R. J. Sternberg & P. A. Frensch (Eds.), *Complex problem solving: Principles and mechanisms* (pp. 61–84). Hillsdale, NJ: Lawrence Erlbaum Associates.

Burgess, P. W., & Shallice, T. (1997). The relationship between prospective and retrospective memory: Neuropsychological evidence. In M. A. Conway (Ed.), *Cognitive models of memory: Studies in cognition* (pp. 247–272). Cambridge, MA: MIT Press.

Burton, A. M., & Bruce, V. (1992). I recognize your face but I can't remember your name: A simple explanation? *British Journal of Psychology, 83*, 45–60.

Burton, A. M., Bruce, V., & Hancock, P. J. B. (1999). From pixels to people: A model of familiar face recognition. *Cognition, 23*, 1–31.

Burton, A. M., Bruce, V., & Johnston, R. A. (1990). Understanding face recognition with an interactive activation model. *British Journal of Psychology, 81*, 361–380.

Burton, A. M., Wilson, S., Cowan, M., & Bruce, V. (1999). Face recognition in poor-quality video: Evidence from security surveillance. *Psychological Science, 10*, 243–248.

Burton, A. M., Young, A. W., Bruce, V., Johnston, R. A., & Ellis, A. W. (1991). Understanding covert recognition. *Cognition, 39*, 129–166.

Busemeyer, J., Hastie, R., & Medin, D. L. (Eds.). (1995). *The psychology of learning and motivation: Decision-making from a cognitive perspective* (Vol. 32). San Diego, CA: Academic Press.

Byrne, R. W. (1977). Planning meals: Problem-solving on a real data-base. *Cognition, 5,* 287–332.

Calderwood, R., Klein, G. A., & Crandall, B. W. (1988). Time pressure, skill, and move quality in chess. *American Journal of Psychology, 101,* 481–493.

Camerer, C. F., & Johnson, E. J. (1991). The process-performance-paradox in expert judgment: How can experts know so much and predict so badly? In K. A. Ericsson & J. Smith (Eds.), *Toward a general theory of expertise: Prospects and limits* (pp. 195–217). New York: Cambridge University Press.

Campbell, D. T. (1958). Common fate, similarity, and other indices of the status of aggregates of persons as social entities. *Behavioral Science, 3,* 14–25.

Campbell, R., Heywood, C. A., Cowey, A., Regard, M., & Landis, T. (1990). Sensitivity to eye gaze in prosopagnosic patients and monkeys with superior temporal sulcus ablation. *Neuropsychologia, 28,* 1123–1142.

Campbell, R., Walker, J., & Baron-Cohen, S. (1995). The development of differential use of inner and outer face features in familiar face identification. *Journal of Experimental Child Psychology, 59,* 196–210.

Cantor, N., & Kihlstrom, J. F. (1989). Social intelligence and cognitive assessment of personality. In R. S. Wyer, Jr. & T. K. Srull. (Eds.), *Social intelligence and cognitive assessment of personality: Advances in social cognition* (Vol. 2, pp.1–59). Hillsdale, NJ: Lawrence Erlbaum Associates.

Cantor, N., & Mischel, W. (1979). Prototypicality and personality: Effects on free recall and personality impressions. *Journal of Research in Psychology, 13,* 187–205.

Capon, N., & Kuhn, D. (1979). Can consumers calculate best buys? *Journal of Consumer Research, 8,* 449–453.

Capon, N., & Kuhn, D. (1982). Logical reasoning in the supermarket: Adult females' use of a proportional reasoning strategy in an everyday context. *Developmental Psychology, 15,* 450–452.

Carbonell, J. (1981). Counterplanning: A strategy-based model of adversary planning in the real world. *Artificial Intelligence, 16,* 295–329.

Carbonell, J. G. (1978). POLITICS: Automated ideological reasoning. *Cognitive Science, 2,* 27–51.

Carey, S. (1981). The development of face processing. In G. Davies, H. D. Ellis, & J. Shepherd (Eds.), *Perceiving and remembering faces* (pp. 9–38). London: Academic Press.

Carey, S. (1992). Becoming a face expert. In V. Bruce, A. Cowey, A. W. Young, & D. L. Perrett (Eds.), *Processing the human face* (pp. 95–110). Oxford, England: Clarenda Press.

Carey, S., & Diamond, R. (1994). Are faces perceived as configurations more by adults than by children? In V. Bruce & G. W. Humphreys (Eds.), *Object and face recognition. Special issue of Visual Cognition* (pp. 253– 274). Hove, England: Lawrence Erlbaum Associates.

Carlston, D.E. (1980). The recall and use of traits and events in social inference processes. *Journal of Experimental Social Psychology, 16,* 303–328.

Carlston, D. E. (1992). Impression formation and the modular mind: The associated systems theory. In L. L. Martin & A. Tesser (Eds.), *The construction of social judgments* (pp. 301–341). Hillsdale, NJ: Lawrence Erlbaum Associates.

Carlston, D. E. (1994). Associated systems theory: A systematic approach to cognitive representations of persons. In T. K. Srull & R. S. Wyer (Eds.), *Associated systems theory: A systematic approach to cognitive representations of persons: Advances in social cognition* (Vol. 7, pp. 1–78). Hillsdale, NJ: Lawrence Erlbaum Associates.

Carlston, D. E., & Skowronski, J. J. (1994). Savings in the relearning of trait information as evidence for spontaneous inference generation. *Journal of Personality and Social Psychology, 66,* 840–856.

Carraher, T. N. (1986). From drawings to buildings: Working with mathematical scales. *International Journal of Behavioral Development, 9,* 527–544.

Carraher, T. N., Carraher, D. W., & Schliemann, A. D. (1985). Mathematics in the streets and in schools. *British Journal of Developmental Psychology, 3,* 21–29.

Carris, M., Zaragoza, M., & Lane, S. (1992, May). *The role of visual imagery in source misattribution errors.* Poster presented at the annual meeting of the Midwestern Psychological Association, Chicago.

Casper, J. D., & Benedict, K. P. J. L. (1989). Juror decision-making, attitudes, and the hindsight bias. *Law and Human Behavior, 13,* 291–310.

Caudill, M., & Butler, C. (1990). *Naturally intelligent systems.* Cambridge, MA: Bradford Books.

Ceci, S. J. (1991). How much does schooling influence general intelligence and its cognitive components? A reassessment of the evidence. *Developmental Psychology, 27,* 703–722.

Ceci, S. J., & Bronfenbrenner, U. (1985). "Don't forget to take the cupcakes out of the oven": Prospective memory, strategic time-monitoring, and context. *Child Development, 56,* 152–164.

Ceci, S. J., & Bronfenbrenner, U. (1991). On the demise of everyday memory: "The rumors of my death are much exaggerated" (Mark Twain). *American Psychologist, 46,* 27–31.

Ceci, S. J., & Bruck, M. (1993). Suggestibility of the child witness: A historical review and synthesis. *Psychological Bulletin, 113,* 403–439.

Ceci, S. J., & Bruck, M. (1995). *Jeopardy in the courtroom: A scientific analysis of children's testimony.* Washington, DC: American Psychological Association.

Ceci, S. J., & Liker, J. K. (1986a). A day at the races: A study of IQ, expertise, and cognitive complexity. *Journal of Experimental Psychology: General, 115,* 255–266.

Ceci, S. J., & Liker, J. K. (1986b). Academic and nonacademic intelligence: An experimental separation. In R. J. Sternberg & R. K. Wagner (Eds.), *Practical intelligence: Nature and origins of competence in the everyday world.* (pp. 119–142). New York: Cambridge University Press.

Ceci, S. J., & Liker, J. K. (1988). Stalking the IQ expertise relation: When the critics go fishing. *Journal of Experimental Psychology: General, 117,* 96–100.

Ceci, S. J., & Ruiz, A. (1993). Transfer, abstractness, and intelligence. In D. K. Detterman & R. J. Sternberg (Eds.), *Transfer on trial: Intelligence, cognition, and instruction* (pp. 168–191). Norwood, NJ: Ablex.

Chaiken, S., & Trope, Y. (Eds.). (1999). *Dual-process theories in social psychology.* New York: Guilford Press.

Chance, J. E., & Goldstein, A. G. (1996). The other race effect and eyewitness identification. In S. L. Sporer & R. S. Malpass (Eds.), *Psychological issues in eyewitness identification* (pp. 153–176). Mahwah, NJ: Lawrence Erlbaum Associates.

Chandler, C. C. (1989). Specific retroactive interference in modified recognition test: Evidence for an unknown cause of interference. *Journal of Experimental Psychology: Learning, Memory, and Cognition, 15,* 256–265.

Chandler, C. C. (1991). How memory for an event is influenced by related events: Interference in modified recognition tests. *Journal of Experimental Psychology: Learning, Memory, and Cognition, 17,* 115–125.

Chapman, L. J. (1967). Illusory correlation in observational report. *Journal of Verbal Learning and Verbal Behavior, 6,* 151–155.

Chapman, L. J., & Chapman, J. P. (1967). Genesis of popular but erroneous diagnostic observations. *Journal of Abnormal Psychology, 72,* 193–204.

Chapman, L. J., & Chapman, J. P. (1969). Illusory correlation as an obstacle to the use of valid psychodiagnostic signs. *Journal of Abnormal Psychology, 74,* 271–280.

Charness, N. (1976). Memory for chess positions: Resistance to interference. *Journal of Experimental Psychology: Learning, Memory, and Cognition, 2*, 641–653.

Charness, N. (1981). Search in chess: Age and skill differences. *Journal of Experimental Psychology: Human Perception and Performance, 7*, 467–476.

Charness, N. (1989). Expertise in chess and bridge. In D. Klahr & K. Kotovsky (Eds.), *Complex information processing: The impact of Herbert A. Simon* (pp. 183–208). Hillsdale, NJ: Lawrence Erlbaum Associates.

Charness, N. (1991). Expertise in chess: the balance between knowledge and search. In K. A. Ericsson & J. Smith (Eds.), *Toward a general theory of expertise: Prospects and limits* (pp. 39–63). New York: Cambridge University Press.

Chase, W. C., & Ericsson, K. A. (1981). Skilled memory. In J. R. Anderson (Ed.), *Cognitive skills and their acquisition* (pp. 141–189). Hillsdale, NJ: Lawrence Erlbaum Associates.

Chase, W. C., & Ericsson, K. A. (1982). Skill and working memory. In G. Bower (Ed.), *The psychology of learning and motivation: Advances in research and theory* (Vol. 16, pp. 1–58). New York: Academic Press.

Chase, W. G., & Simon, H. A. (1973a). Perception in chess. *Cognitive Psychology, 4*, 55–81.

Chase, W. G., & Simon, H. A. (1973b). The mind's eye in chess. In W. G. Chase (Ed.), *Visual information processing* (pp. 215–281). New York: Academic Press.

Cheng, P. W., & Holyoak, K. J. (1985). Pragmatic reasoning schemas. *Cognitive Psychology, 17*, 391–416.

Cheng, P. W., & Holyoak, K. J. (1989). On the natural selection of reasoning theories. *Cognition, 33*, 285–313.

Cheng, P. W., Holyoak, K. J., Nisbett, R. E., & Oliver, L. M. (1986). Pragmatic versus syntactic approaches to training deductive reasoning. *Cognitive Psychology, 18*, 293–328.

Chi, M. T. H., (1978). Knowledge structures and memory development. In R. Siegler (Ed.), *Children's thinking: What develops?* (pp. 73–96). Hillsdale, NJ: Lawrence Erlbaum Associates.

Chi, M. T. H., & Bassok, M. (1989). Learning from example via self-explanations. In L. B. Resnick (Ed.), *Knowing, learning, and instruction: Essays in honor of Robert Glaser* (pp. 252–282). Hillsdale, NJ: Lawrence Erlbaum Associates.

Chi, M. T. H., Bassok, M., Lewis, M. W., Reimann, P., & Glaser, R. (1989). Self-explanations: How students study and use examples in learning to solve problems. *Cognitive Science, 13*, 145–182.

Chi, M. T. H., Feltovich, P. J., & Glaser, R. (1981). The classification and representation of physics problems by experts and novices. *Cognitive Science, 5*, 121–152.

Chi, M. T. H., Glaser, R., & Farr, M. J. (Eds.). (1988). *The nature of expertise*. Hillsdale, NJ: Lawrence Erlbaum Associates.

Chi, M. T. H., & Van Lehn, K. A. (1991). The content of physics self-explanations. *Journal of the Learning Sciences, 1*, 69–105.

Chiesi, H. L., Spilich, G. J., & Voss, J. F. (1979). Acquisition of domain-related information in relation to high and low domain knowledge. *Journal of Verbal Learning and Verbal Behavior, 18*, 257–273.

Christensen-Szalanski, J. J., & Beach, L. R. (1984). The citations bias: Fad and fashion in the judgement and decision literature. *American Psychologist, 39*, 75–78.

Christianson, S. A. (1992). Emotional stress and eyewitness memory: A critical review. *Psychological Review, 112*, 284–309.

Clancey, W. J. (1988). Acquiring, representing, and evaluating a competence model of diagnostic strategy. In M. T. H. Chi, R. Glaser, & M. J. Farr (Eds.), *The nature of expertise* (pp. 343–418). Hillsdale, NJ: Lawrence Erlbaum Associates.

Clancey, W. J. (1991). Situated cognition: Stepping out of representational flatland. *AI Communications, 4*, 109–112.

Clancey, W. J. (1992). Representations of knowing: In defense of cognitive apprenticeship. *Journal of Artificial Intelligence and Education, 3,* 139–168.

Clancey, W. J. (1993). Situated cognition: A neuropsychological interpretation: Response to Vera and Simon. *Cognition Science, 17,* 87–116.

Clancey, W. J. (1997). *Situated cognition: On human knowledge and computer representations.* New York: Cambridge University Press.

Clark, A. (1993). *Associative engines: Connectionism, concepts, and representational change.* Cambridge, MA: MIT Press.

Clement, J. J. (1989). Generation of spontaneous analogies by students solving science problems. In D. M. Topping, D. C. Crowell, & V. N. Kobayashi (Eds.), *Thinking across cultures: The Third International Conference on Thinking* (pp. 303–308). Hillsdale, NJ: Lawrence Erlbaum Associates.

Clement, P. W. (1982). Practitioner-model programs? *American Psychologist, 37,* 339–340.

Cockburn, J. (1995). *Dissociation between prospective and retrospective memory in amnesia.* Paper presented at the British Psychological Society annual conference, Warwick, England.

Cognition and Technology Group at Vanderbilt. (1991). Anchored instruction and its relationship to situated cognition. *Educational Researcher, 19*(4), 2–10.

Cognition and Technology Group at Vanderbilt. (1992a). The Jasper experiment: An exploration of issues in learning and instructional design. *Educational Technology Research and Development, 40,* 65–80.

Cognition and Technology Group at Vanderbilt. (1992b). The Jasper series as an example of anchored instruction: Theory, program description, and assessment data. *Educational Psychologist, 27,* 291–315.

Cognition and Technology Group at Vanderbilt. (1993). Toward integrated curricula: Possibilities from anchored instruction. In M. Rabinowitz (Ed.), *Cognitive science foundations of instruction* (pp. 33–56) Hillsdale, NJ: Lawrence Erlbaum Associates.

Cohen, C. E. (1981) Goals and schemas in person perception: Making sense out of the stream of behavior. In N. Cantor & J. Kihlstrom (Eds.), *Personality, cognition, and social interaction* (pp. 45–68) Hillsdale, NJ: Lawrence Erlbaum Associates.

Cohen, D. B. (1974). Toward a theory of dream recall. *Psychological Bulletin, 81,* 138–154.

Cohen, G. (1989). *Memory in the real world.* Hove, England: Lawrence Erlbaum Associates.

Cohen, J. (1988). *Statistical power analysis for the behavioral sciences* (2nd ed.). Hillsdale, NJ: Lawrence Erlbaum Associates.

Cohen, L. J. (1981). Can human irrationality be experimentally demonstrated? *Behavioral and Brain Sciences, 4,* 317–331.

Cohen, M. S. (1993). The naturalistic basis of decision biases. In G. A. Klein, J. Orasanu, R. Calderwood, & C. E. Zsambok (Eds.), *Decision making in action: Models and methods* (pp. 51–99). Norwood, NJ: Ablex.

Cohen, P. C. (1982). *A calculating people: The spread of numerosy in early America.* Chicago: University of Chicago Press.

Cohen, P. R., Greenberg, M. L., Hart, D. M., & Howe, A. E. (1980). Trial by fire: Understanding the design requirements for agents in complex environments. *AI Magazine, 10,* 34–48.

Cole, M. (1990). Cultural psychology: A once and future discipline? In J. J. Bergman (Ed.), *Nebraska symposium on motivation, 1989: Cross-cultural perspectives* (pp. 279–335). Lincoln, NE: University of Nebraska Press.

Cole, M. (1996). *Cultural psychology: A once and future discipline?* Cambridge, MA: Harvard University Press.

Cole, M., & Bruner, J. S. (1971). Cultural differences and inferences about psychological processes. *American Psychologist, 26,* 867–876.

Cole, M., Dore, J., Hall, W. S., & Dowley, G. (1978). Situational variability in the speech of preschool children. *Annals of the New York Academy of Science, 318,* 63–105.

Cole, M., Gay, J., Glick, J. A., & Sharp, D. W. (1971). *The cultural context of learning and thinking.* New York: Basic Books.

Cole, M., & Griffin, P. (1980). Cultural amplifiers reconsidered. In D. R. Olson (Ed.), *The social foundations of language and thought: Essays in honor of J. S. Bruner* (pp. 343–363). New York: Norton.

Cole, M., & Scribner, S. (1974). *Culture and thought: A psychological introduction.* New York: Wiley.

Collins, A. M., Brown, J. S., & Newman, S. (1989). Cognitive apprenticeship: Teaching students the craft of reading, writing, and mathematics. In L. B. Resnick (Ed.), *Knowing, learning, and instruction: Essays in honor of Robert Glaser* (pp. 453–494). Hillsdale, NJ: Lawrence Erlbaum Associates.

Collins, A. M., & Loftus, E. F. (1975). A spreading activation theory of semantic processing. *Psychological Review, 82,* 407–428.

Combs, B., & Slovic, P. (1979). Newspaper coverage of causes of death. *Journalism Quarterly, 54,* 837– 843, 849.

Connors, E., Lundregan, T., Miller, N., & McEwen, T. (1996). *Convicted by juries, exonerated by science: Case studies in the use of DNA evidence to establish innocence after trial.* Washington, DC: Department of Justices, Office of Justice Programs.

Conway, M., & Ross, M. (1984). Getting what you want by revising what you had. *Journal of Personality & Social Psychology, 47,*738–748.

Conway, M. A. (1988). Images in autobiographical memory. In M. Denis, J. Engelkamp, & J. T. E. Richardson (Eds.), *Cognitive and neuropsychological approaches to mental imagery* (pp. 337–346). Dordrecht, The Netherlands: Martinus Nijhoff.

Conway, M. A. (1990a). *Autobiographical memory: An introduction.* Milton Keynes, UK: Open University Press.

Conway, M. A. (1990b). Associations between autobiographical memories and concepts. *Journal of Experimental Psychology: Learning, Memory, and Cognition, 16,* 799–812.

Conway, M. A. (1991). In defense of everyday memory. *American Psychologist, 46,* 19–26.

Conway, M. A. (1992). A structural model of autobiographical memory. In M. A. Conway, D. C. Rubin, H. Spinnler, & W. A. Wagennar (Eds.), *Theoretical perspectives on autobiographical memory* (pp. 167–194). Dordrecht, The Netherlands: Kluwer Academic.

Conway, M. A. (1993). Method and meaning in memory research. In G. M. Davies & R. H. Logie (Eds.), *Memory in everyday life* (pp. 499–524). Amsterdam: North-Holland/Elsevier Science.

Conway, M. A. (1995). *Flashbulb memories.* Hove, England: Lawrence Erlbaum Associates.

Conway, M. A. (1996). Autobiographical knowledge and autobiographical memories. In D. C. Rubin (Ed.), *Remembering our past: Studies in autobiographical memory* (pp. 67–93). New York: Cambridge University Press.

Conway, M. A. (1997a). The inventory of experience: Memory and identity. In J. W. Pennebaker, D. Paez, & B. Rimé (Eds.), *Collective memory of political events: Social psychological perspectives* (pp. 21–45). Mahwah, NJ: Lawrence Erlbaum Associates.

Conway, M. A. (1997b). Past and present: Recovered memories and false memories. In M. A. Conway (Ed.), *Recovered memories and false memories* (pp. 150–191). Oxford, England: Oxford University Press.

Conway, M. A. (Ed.). (1997c). *Recovered memories and false memories.* Oxford, England: Oxford University Press.

Conway, M. A. (1999, April). *The construction of autobiographical memories in the self-memory system.* Paper presented at the meeting of the Western Psychological Association, Irvine, CA.

Conway, M. A., & Bekerian, D. A. (1987). Organization in autobiographical memory. *Memory & Cognition, 15*, 119–132.

Conway, M. A., Collins, A. F., Gathercole, S. E., & Anderson, S. J. (1996). Recollections of true and false autobiographical memories. *Journal of Experimental Psychology: General, 125*, 69–95.

Conway, M. A., & Fthenaki, A. (2000). Disruption and loss of autobiographical memory. In L. Cermak (Ed.), *Handbook of neuropsychology: Memory and its disorders* (2nd ed., pp. 257–288). Amsterdam: Elsevier.

Conway, M. A., & Hague, S. (1999). Overshadowing the reminiscence bump: Memories of a struggle for independence. *Journal of Adult Development, 6*, 35–44.

Conway, M. A., & Montgomery, S. (1990). *On the intersection of public and private history: Recency and autobiographical memory.* Unpublished manuscript, University of Lancaster, England.

Conway, M. A., & Pleydell-Pearce, C. W. (2000). The construction of autobiographical memory in the self-memory system. *Psychological Review, 107*, 261–288.

Conway, M. A., & Rubin, D. C. (1993). The structure of autobiographical memory. In A. E. Collins, S. E. Gathercole, M. A. Conway, & P. E. Morris (Eds.), *Theories of memory* (pp. 103–137). Hove, England: Lawrence Erlbaum Associates.

Conway, M. A., Rubin, D. C., Spinnler, H., & Wagenaar, W. A. (Eds). (1992). *Theoretical perspectives on autobiographical memory.* Dordrecht, The Netherlands: Kluwer Academic.

Cosmides, L. (1989). The logic of social exchange: Has natural selection shaped how humans reason? Studies with the Wason selection task. *Cognition, 31*, 187–276.

Cox, J. R., & Griggs, R. A. (1982). The effects of experience on performance in Wason's selection task. *Memory & Cognition, 10*, 496–502.

Craik, F. I. M., & Lockhart, R. S. (1972). Levels of processing: A framework for memory research. *Journal of Verbal Learning and Verbal Behavior, 11*, 671–684.

Crawford, J., Kippax, S., Onyx, J., Gault, U., & Benton, P. (1992). *Emotion and gender: Constructing meaning from memory.* London: Sage.

Crocker, J. (1981). Judgment of covariation by social perceivers. *Psychological Bulletin, 90*, 272–292.

Crovitz, H. F., Harvey, M. T., & McKee, D. C. (1980). Selecting retrieval cues for early-childhood amnesia: Implications for the study of shrinking retrograde amnesia. *Cortex, 16*, 305–310.

Crovitz, H. F., & Quina-Holland, K. (1976). Proportion of episodic memories from early childhood by age. *Bulletin of the Psychonomic Society, 7*, 61–62.

Crovitz, H. F., & Schiffman, H. (1974). Frequency of episodic memories as a function of their age. *Bulletin of the Psychonomic Society, 4*, 517–518.

Crowder, R. G. (1993). Commentary: Faith and skepticism in memory research. In G.M. Davies & R. H. Logie (Eds.), *Memory in everyday life* (pp. 525–531). Amsterdam: North Holland/Elsevier Science.

Crowder, R. G. (1996). The trouble with prospective memory: A provocation. In M. A. Brandimonte, G. O. Einstein, & M. A. McDaniel (Eds.), *Prospective memory: Theory and applications* (pp. 143–148). Mahwah, NJ: Lawrence Erlbaum Associates.

Csikszentmihalyi, M., & Beattie, O. V. (1979). Life themes: A theoretical and empirical exploration of their origins and effects. *Journal of Humanistic Psychology, 19*, 45–63.

Cutler, B. L., & Penrod, S. D. (1995). *Mistaken identification: The eyewitness, psychology, and the law.* New York: Cambridge University Press.

Cutshall, J., & Yuille, J. C. (1989). Field studies of eyewitness memory of actual crimes. In D. C. Raskin (Ed.), *Psychological methods in criminal investigation and evidence* (pp. 97–124). New York: Springer.

Damasio, A. R. (1989). Neural mechanisms. In A.W. Young & H.D. Ellis (Eds.), *Handbook of research on face processing* (pp. 405–425). Amsterdam: North Holland/Elsevier Science.

D'Andrade, R. (1995). *The development of cognitive anthropology*. New York: Cambridge University Press.

Darling-Hammond, L., Ancess, J., & Falk, B. (1995). *Authentic assessment in action: Studies of students and schools at work*. New York: Teachers College Press.

Davies, G. M. (1986). The recall and reconstruction of faces: Implications for theory and practice. In H. D. Ellis, M.A. Jeeves, F. Newcombe, & A. Young (Eds.), *Aspects of face processing* (pp. 388–397). Amsterdam: North Holland/Elsevier Science.

Davies, G. M. (1988). Faces and places: Laboratory research on context and face recognition. In G. M. Davies & D. M. Thomson (Eds.), *Memory in context: Context in memory* (pp. 35–53). Chichester, England: Wiley.

Davies, G. M. (1989). The applicability of facial memory research. In A.W. Young & H. D. Ellis (Eds.), *Handbook of research on face processing* (pp. 557–562). Amsterdam: North Holland/Elsevier Science.

Davies, G. M., & Dalgleish, T. (Eds.). (in press). *Recovered memories: Seeking the middle ground*. Sussex, England: Wiley.

Davies, G. M., Ellis, H. D., & Shepherd, J. W. (1978). Face recognition accuracy as a function of mode of representation. *Journal of Applied Psychology, 63*, 180–187.

Davies, G. M., & Logie, R. H. (Eds.). (1993). Memory in everyday life. Amsterdam: North Holland, Elsevier Science.

Davies, G. M., Shepherd, J. W., & Ellis, H. D. (1979). Effects of interpolated mug shot exposure on accuracy of eyewitness identification. *Journal of Applied Psychology, 64*, 232–237.

Dawes, R. M. (1979). The robust beauty of improper linear models in decision making. *American Psychologist, 34*, 571–582.

Dawes, R. M. (1988). You can't systematize common sense: Dyslexia. In J. Dowic & A. S. Elstein (Eds.), *Professional judgment: A reader in clinical decision making* (pp. 150–162). Cambridge, England: Cambridge University Press.

Dawes, R. M. (1989). Statistical criteria for establishing a truly false consensus effect. *Journal of Experimental Social Psychology, 25*, 1–17.

Dawes, R. M., Faust, D., & Meehl, P. E. (1989, March). Clinical versus actuarial judgment. *Science, 243*(4899), 1668–1674.

Dawes, R. M., Faust, D., & Meehl, P. E. (1993). Statistical prediction versus clinical prediction: Improving what works. In G. Keron & C. Lewis (Eds.), *A handbook for data analysis in the behavioral sciences: Methodological issues* (pp. 351–367). Hillsdale, NJ: Lawrence Erlbaum Associates.

Dawson, V. L., Zeitz, C. M., & Wright, J. C. (1989). Expert–novice differences in perception: Evidence of experts' sensitivities to the organization of behavior. *Social Cognition, 7*, 1–30.

de Groot, A. D. (1965). *Thought and choice in chess*. New York: Basic Books.

de Groot, A. D. (1966). Perception and memory versus thought: Some old ideas and recent findings. In B. Kleinmuntz (Ed.), *Problem solving* (pp. 19–50). New York: Wiley.

de Haan, E. H., Young, A. W., & Newcombe, F. (1991). A dissociation between the sense of familiarity and access to semantic information concerning familiar people. *European Journal of Cognitive Psychology, 3*, 51–67.

de Renzi, E. (1986). Current issues on prosopagnosia. In H. Ellis, M.A. Jeeves, F. Newcombe, & A. Young (Eds.), *Aspects of face processing* (pp. 243–252). Dordrecht, The Netherlands: Martinus Nijhoff.

de Renzi, E. (1986). Prosopagnosia in two patients with CT scan evidence of damage confined to the right hemisphere. *Neuropsychologia, 24*, 385–389.

de Renzi, E., Faglioni, P., Grossi, D., & Nichelli, P. (1991). Apperceptive and associative forms of prosopagnosia. *Cortex, 27,* 213–221.

de Renzi, E., Liotti, M., & Nichelli, N. (1987). Semantic amnesia with preservation of autobiographic memory. A case report. *Cortex, 23,* 575–597.

Deffenbacher, K. A. (1988). Eyewitness research: The next ten years. In M.M. Gruneberg, P. E. Morris, & R. N. Sykes (Eds.), *Practical aspects of memory: Current research and issues: Vol. 1: Memory in everyday life* (pp. 20–26). Chichester, England: Wiley.

Deffenbacher, K.A. (1989). Forensic facial memory: Time is of the essence. In A.W. Young & H. D. Ellis (Eds.), *Handbook of research on face processing* (pp. 563–570). Amsterdam, The Netherlands: Elsevier Science.

Denney, N. W. (1989). Everyday problem solving: Methodological issues, research findings, and a model. In L.W. Poon, D. C. Rubin, & B. A. Wilson (Eds.), *Everyday cognition in adulthood and late life* (pp. 330–351). New York: Cambridge University Press.

Desimone, R. (1991). Face-selective cells in the temporal cortex of monkeys. *Journal of Cognitive Neuroscience, 3,* 1–8.

Detterman, D. K. (1993). The case for the prosecution: Transfer as an epiphenomenon. In D. K. Detterman & R. J. Sternberg (Eds.), *Transfer on trial: Intelligence, cognition, and instruction* (pp. 1–24). Norwood, NJ: Ablex.

Devenport, J. L., Penrod, S. D., & Cutler, B. L. (1997). Eyewitness identification evidence: Evaluating commonsense evaluations. *Psychology, Public Policy, and Law, 3,* 338–361.

Devine, P. G., & Baker, S. M. (1991). Measurment of racial stereotype subtyping. *Personality and Social Psychology Bulletin, 17,* 44–50.

Devine, P. G., Sedikides, C., & Fuhrman, R. W. (1989). Goals in social information processing: The case of anticipated interaction. *Journal of Personality and Social Psychology, 56,* 680–690.

Diamond, R., & Carey, S. (1977). Developmental changes in the representation of faces. *Journal of Experimental Child Psychology, 23,* 1–22.

Diamond, R, & Carey, S. (1986). Why faces are not special: An effect of expertise. *Journal of Experimental Psychology: General, 115,* 107–117.

Diges, M. (1988). Stereotypes and memory for real traffic accidents. In M. M. Gruneberg, P. E. Morris, & R. N. Sykes (Eds.), *Practical aspects of memory: Current research and issues. Vol. 1: Memory in everyday life* (pp. 59–65). New York: Wiley.

Domeshek, E. A. (1994). A case study of case indexing: Designing index feature sets to suit task demands and support parallelism. In J. A. Barnden & K. J. Holyoak (Eds.), *Advances in connectionist and neural computation theory. Vol. 3: Analogy, metaphor, and reminding* (pp. 126–168). New York: Academic Press.

Dominowski, R. L. (1990). Problem solving and metacognition. In K. J. Gilhooly, M. T. G. Keene, R. H. Logie, & G. Erdos (Eds.), *Lines of thinking* (Vol. 2, pp. 313–328). New York: Wiley.

Dominowski, R. L. (1995). Content effects in Wason's selection task. In S. E. Newstead & J. St. B. T. Evans (Eds.), *Perspectives on thinking and reasoning* (pp. 41–65). Hillsdale, NJ: Lawrence Erlbaum Associates.

Dominowski, R. L., & Dallob, A. (1991, September). *Reasoning abilities, individual differences, and the four card problem.* Paper presented at the eighth annual conference of the Cognitive Psychology Section, British Psychological Society. Oxford, England.

Donovan, S., & Epstein, S. (1997). The difficulty of the Linda conjunction problem can be attributed to its simultaneous concrete and unnatural representation, and not to conversational implicature. *Journal of Experimental Social Psychology, 33,* 1–20.

Dreben, E. K., Fiske, S. T., & Hastie, R. (1979). The independence of evaluative and item information: Impression and recall order effects in behavior-based impression formation. *Journal of Personality and Social Psychology, 37,* 1758–1768.

Dreyfus, H. L. (1979). *What computers can't do.* New York: Harper.

Dreyfus, H. L. (1997). Intuitive, deliberative, and calculative models of expert performance. In C. E. Zsambok & G. A. Klein (Eds.), *Naturalistic decision making* (pp. 17–28). Mahwah, NJ: Lawrence Erlbaum Associates.

Dreyfus, H. L., & Dreyfus, S. (1986). *Mind over machine: The powers of human intuition and expertise in the age of the computer.* New York: Free Press.

Dukes, W. F., & Bevan, W. (1967). Stimulus variation and repetition in acquisition of naming responses. *Journal of Experimental Psychology, 74*, 178–181.

Dulany, D. E. (1997). Consciousness in the explicit (deliberative) and implicit (evocative) mode. In G. D. Cohen & J. W. Schooler (Eds.), *Scientific approaches to consciousness* (pp. 179–210). Mahwah, NJ: Lawrence Erlbaum Associates.

Dulany, D. E. (1998). *A note on modeling: Mathematical and computional.* Unpublished manuscript, University of Illinois at Urbana-Champaign.

Dulany, D. E. (1999). Consciousness, connectionism, and intentionality. *Behavioral and Brain Sciences, 22*, 154–155.

Dulany, D. E., & Hilton, D. J. (1991). Conversational implicature, conscious representations, and the conjuction fallacy. *Social Cognition, 9*, 85–110.

Duncker, K. (1945). On problem-solving. *Psychological Monographs, 58*, (No. 270).

Dunning, D., Griffin, D. W., Milojkovic, J. D., & Ross, L. (1990). The overconfidence effect in social prediction. *Journal of Personality and Social Psychology, 58*, 568–581.

Dunning, D., & Madey, S. F. (1995). Comparison processes in counterfactual thought. In N. J. Roese & J. M. Olson (Eds.), *What might have been: The social psychology of counterfactual thinking* (pp. 103–131). Mahwah, NJ: Lawrence Erlbaum Associates.

Duveen, G., & Lloyd, B. (1993). An ethnographic approach to social representations. In G. M. Breakwell & D. V. Canter (Eds.), *Empirical approaches to social representations* (pp. 90–109). Oxford, England: Clarendon Press.

Dyer, M. G. (1983). *In-depth understanding: A computer model of integrated processing for narrative comprehension.* Cambridge, MA: MIT Press.

Eacott, M. J. (1999). Memory for the events of early childhood. *Current Directions in Psyhological Science, 8*, 46–49.

Eacott, M. J., & Crawley, R. A. (1998). The offset of childhood amnesia: Memory for events that occurred before age 3. *Journal of Experimental Psychology: General, 127*, 22–33.

Ebbinghaus, H. (1964). *Memory: A contribution to experimental psychology.* New York: Dover. (Original work published 1885)

Edwards, D., & Middleton, D. (1988). Conversational remembering and family relationships: How children learn to remember. *Journal of Social and Personal Relationships, 5*, 3–26.

Edwards, D., & Potter, J. (1992). The chancellor's memory: Rhetoric and truth in discursive remembering. *Applied Cognitive Psychology, 6*, 187–215.

Edwards, W. (1983). Human cognitive capabilities, representativeness and ground rules for research. In P. C. Humphreys, O. Svenson, & A. Vari (Eds.), *Analysing and aiding decision processes* (pp. 507–513). Amsterdam: North Holland/Elsevier Science.

Edwards, W., & von Winterfeldt, D. (1986). On cognitive illusions and their implications. In H. R. Arkes & K. R. Hammond (Eds.), *Judgment and decision making: An interdisciplinary reader* (pp. 642–679). New York: Cambridge University Press.

Eddy, A. S. (1988). *The relationship between the Tacit Knowledge Inventory for Managers and the Armed Services Vocational Aptitude Battery. Unpublished master's thesis.* St. Mary's University, San Antonio, TX.

Egan, O., Pittner, M., & Goldstein, A. D. (1977). Eyewitness identification: Photographs vs. live models. *Law and Human Behavior, 1*, 199–206.

Egeth, H. E., & McCloskey, M. (1984). Expert testimony about eyewitness behavior: Is it safe and effective? In G. L. Wells & E. F. Loftus (Eds.), *Eyewitness testimony: Psychological perspective.* New York: Cambridge University Press.

Einhorn, H. (1986). Accepting error to make less error. *Journal of Personality Assesment, 50*, 387–395.

Einstein, G. O., Holland, L. J., McDaniel, M. A., & Guynn, M. J. (1992). Age related deficits in prospective memory: The influence of task complexity. *Psychology and Aging, 7*, 471–478.

Einstein, G. O., & McDaniel, M. A. (1990). Normal aging and prospective memory. *Journal of Experimental Psychology: Learning, Memory, and Cognition, 15*, 717–726.

Einstein, G. O., McDaniel, M. A., Richardson, S. L., Guynn, M. J., & Cunfer. (1995). Aging and prospective memory: Examining the influences of self-initiated retrieval processes. *Journal of Experimental Psychology: Learning, Memory, and Cognition, 21*, 996–1007.

Einstein, G. O., & McDaniel, M. A. (1996). Retrieval processes in prospective memory: Theoretical approaches and some new empirical findings. In M. A. Brandimonte, G. O. Einstein, & M. A. McDaniel (Eds.), *Prospective memory: Theory and applications* (pp. 115–142). Mahwah, NJ: Lawrence Erlbaum Associates.

Ekman, P. (Ed.). (1972). *Emotion in the human face*. New York: Cambridge University Press.

Ellis, A. W., Flude, B. M., Young, A. W., & Burton, A. M. (1996). Two loci of repetition priming in the recognition of familiar faces. *Journal of Experimental Psychology: Learning, Memory, and Cognition, 22*, 295–308.

Ellis, A. W., Shepherd, J. W., & Davies, G. M. (1979). Identification of familiar and unfamiliar faces from internal and external features: Some implications for theories of face recognition. *Perception, 8*, 431–439.

Ellis, A. W., & Young, A. W. (1989). Are faces special? In A. W. Young & H. D. Ellis (Eds.), *Handbook of research on face processing* (pp. 1–26). Amsterdam: North Holland/Elsevier Science.

Ellis, A. W., Young, A. W., Flude, B. M., & Hay, D. C. (1987). Repetition priming of face recognition. *Quarterly Journal of Experimental Psychology: Human Experimental Psychology, 39*A, 193–210.

Ellis, H. D. (1981). Theoretical aspects of face recognition. In G. Davies, H. Ellis, & J. Shepherd (Eds.), *Perceiving and remembering faces* (pp. 171–197). London: Academic Press.

Ellis, H. D. (1986). Introduction: Processes underlying face recognition. In R. Bruyer (Ed.), *The neuropsychology of face perception and facial expression* (pp. 1–27). Hillsdale, NJ: Lawrence Erlbaum Associates.

Ellis, H. D., & Deregowski, J. B. (1981). Within-race and between-race recognition of transformed and untransformed faces. *American Journal of Psychology, 94*, 27–35.

Ellis, H. D., & Shepherd, J. W. (1992). Face memory—theory and practice. In M. M. Gruneberg & P. E. Morris, (Eds.), *Aspects of memory, Vol. 1: The practical aspects* (2nd ed., pp. 51–85). London: Routledge.

Ellis, H. D., & Young, A. W. (1989). Are faces special? In A. W. Young & H. D. Ellis (Eds.), *Handbook of research on face processing* (pp. 1–26). Amsterdam: North-Holland/Elsevier.

Ellis, J. A. (1988). Memory for future intentions: Investigating pulses and steps. In M. M. Gruneberg, P. E. Morris, & R. N. Sykes (Eds.), *Practical aspects of memory: Current research and issues. Vol. 1: Memory in everyday life* (pp. 371–376). New York: Wiley.

Ellis, J. A. (1996). Prospective memory or the realization of delayed intentions: A conceptual framework for research. In M. A. Brandimonte, G. O. Einstein, & M. A. McDaniel (Eds.), *Prospective memory: Theory and applications* (pp. 1–22). Mahwah, NJ: Lawrence Erlbaum Associates.

Ellis, J. A., & Nimmo-Smith, I. (1993). Recollecting naturally-occurring intentions: A study of cognitive and affective factors. *Memory, 1*, 107–126.

Ellis, J. A., & Shallice, T. (1993). *Memory for, and the organization of, future intentions*. Unpublished manuscript. University of Reading, England.

Endo, M., Takahashi, K., & Maruyama, K. (1984). Effects of observer's attitude on the familiarity of faces: Using the difference in cue value between central and peripheral facial elements as an index of familiarity. *Tohoku Psychologica Folia, 43,* 23–24.

Engeström, Y. (1987). *Learning by expanding: An activity-theoretical approach to developmental research.* Helsinki: Orenta-Konsultit.

Epstein, S. (1991). Cognitive-experiential self-theory: An integrative theory of personality. In R. C. Curtis, (Ed.), *The relational self: Theoretical convergences in psychoanalysis and social psychology* (pp. 111–137). New York: Guilford.

Epstein, S., Donovan, S., & Denes-Raj, V. (1999). The missing link in the paradox of the Linda conjunction problem: Beyond knowing and thinking of the conjunction rule, the intrinsic appeal of heuristic processing. *Personality and Social Psychology Bulletin, 25,* 204–214.

Epstein, S., & Pacini, R. (1999). Some basic issues regarding dual-process theories from the perspective of cognitive-experiential self-theory. In. S. Chaiken & Y. Trope (Eds.), *Dual-process theories in social psychology* (pp. 462–480). New York: Guilford.

Erber, R., & Fiske, S. T. (1984). Outcome dependency and attention to inconsistent information. *Journal of Personality and Social Psychology, 47,* 709–726.

Ericsson, K. A. (1996a). The acquisition of expert performance: An introduction to some of the issues. In K. A. Ericsson (Ed.), *The road to excellence: The acquisition of expert performance in the arts and sciences, sports, and games* (pp. 1–50). Mahwah, NJ: Lawrence Erlbaum Associates.

Ericsson, K. A. (Ed.). (1996b). *The road to excellence: The acquisition of expert performance in the arts and sciences, sports, and games.* Mahwah, NJ: Lawrence Erlbaum Associates.

Ericsson, K. A., & Charness, N. (1994). Expert performance: Its structure and acquisition. *American Psychologist, 49,* 725–747.

Ericsson, K. A., & Harris, M. (1989). *Acquiring expert memory performance without expert knowledge: A case study in the domain of chess.* Unpublished manuscript. University of Colorado.

Ericsson, K. A., & Kintsch, W. (1995). Long-term working memory. *Psychological Review, 102,* 211-245.

Ericsson, K. A., Krampe, R. T., & Tesch-Roemer, C. (1993). The role of deliberate practice in the acquisition of expert performance. *Psychological Review, 100,* 363-406.

Ericsson, K. A., & Lehmann, A. C. (1996). Experts and exceptional performance: Evidence of maximal adaptation to task constraints. *Annual Review of Psychology, 47,* 273-305.

Ericsson, K. A., & Pennington, N. (1993). The structure of memory performance in experts: Implications for memory in everyday life. In G. M. Davies & R. H. Logie (Eds.), *Memory in everyday life* (pp. 241–272). Amsterdam: North Holland/Elsevier.

Ericsson, K. A., & Polson, P. G. (1988a). An experimental analysis of the mechanisms of a memory skill. *Journal of Experimental Psychology: Learning, Memory, and Cognition, 14,* 305–316.

Ericsson, K. A., & Polson, P. G. (1988b). A cognitive analysis of exceptional memory for restaurant orders. In M. T. H. Chi, R. Glaser, & M. J. Farr (Eds.), *The nature of expertise* (pp. 23–70). Hillsdale, NJ: Lawrence Erlbaum Associates.

Ericsson, K. A., & Smith, J. (1991a). Prospects and limits of the empirical study of expertise: An introduction. In K. A. Ericsson & J. Smith (Eds.), *Toward a general theory of expertise: Prospects and limits* (pp. 1–38). New York: Cambridge University Press.

Ericsson, K. A., & Smith, J. (Eds.) (1991b). *Toward a general theory of expertise: Prospects and limits.* New York: Cambridge University Press.

Ericsson, K. A., & Staszewski, J. J. (1989). Skilled memory and expertise: Mechanisms of exceptional performance. In D. Klahr & K. Kotovsky (Eds.), *Complex information processing: The impact of Herbert A. Simon* (pp. 235–267). Hillsdale, NJ: Lawrence Erlbaum Associates.

Erikson, E. (1950). *Childhood and society*. New York: Norton.

Ernst, G. W., & Newell, A. (1969). *GPS: A case study in generality and problem-solving*. New York: Academic Press.

Estes, W. K. (1988). Toward a framework for combining connectionist and symbol-processing models. *Journal of Memory and Language, 27*, 196–212.

Evans, J. St. B. T. (1972). Interpretation and matching bias in a reasoning task. *British Journal of Psychology, 24*, 193–199.

Evans, J. St. B. T. (1982). *The psychology of deductive reasoning*. London: Routledge & Kegan Paul.

Evans, J. St. B. T. (1983). Selective processes in reasoning. In J. St. B. T. Evans (Ed.), *Thinking and reasoning: Psychological approaches* (pp. 135–163). London: Routledge Kegan Paul.

Evans, J. St. B. T. (1984). Heuristic and analytic processes in reasoning. *British Journal of Psychology, 75*, 451–468.

Evans, J. St. B. T. (1989). *Bias in human reasoning: Causes and consequences*. Hove, England: Lawrence Erlbaum Associates.

Evans, J. St. B. T. (1993). Bias and rationality. In K. I. Manktelow & D. E. Over (Eds.). *Rationality: Psychological and philosophical perspectives* (pp. 6–30). London: Routledge & Kegan Paul.

Evans, J. St. B. T. (1995). Relevance and reasoning. In S. E. Newstead & J. St. B. T. Evans (Eds.), *Perspectives on thinking and reasoning* (pp. 147–171). Hillsdale, NJ: Lawrence Erlbaum Associates.

Evans, J. St. B. T., & Lynch, J. S. (1973). Matching bias in the selection task. *British Journal of Psychology, 64*, 391–397.

Evans, J. St. B. T., Newstead, S. E., & Byrne, R. M. J. (Eds). (1993). *Human reasoning: The psychology of deduction*. Hillsdale, NJ: Lawrence Erlbaum Associates.

Evans, J. St. B. T., & Over, D. E. (1996). *Rationality and reasoning*. Hove, UK: Psychology Press.

Farah, M. J. (1996). Is face recognition 'special'? Evidence from neuropsychology. *Behavioural and Brain Research, 76*, 181–189.

Farah, M. J., Levinson, K. L., & Klein, K. L. (1995). Face perception and within-category discrimination in prosopagnosia. *Neuropsychologia, 33*, 661–674.

Farah, M. J., Tanaka, J. W., & Drain, H. M. (1995). What causes the face inversion effect? *Journal of Experimental Psychology: Human Perception and Performance, 21*, 628–634.

Farah, M. J., Wilson, K. D., Drain, H. M., & Tanaka, J. R. (1995). The inverted face inversion effect in prosopagnosia: Evidence for mandatory, face-specific perceptual mechanisms. *Vision Research, 35*, 2089–2093.

Farah, M. J., Wilson, K. D., Drain, H. M., & Tanaka, J. N. (1998). What is 'special' about face perception? *Psychological Review, 105*, 482–498.

Fein, S., Hilton, J. L., & Miller, D. T. (1990). Suspicion of ulterior motivation and the correspondence bias. *Journal of Personality and Social Psychology, 58*, 753–764.

Feltovich, P. I., Johnson, P. E., Moller, J. H., & Swanson, D. E. (1984). LCS: The role and development of medical knowledge in medical expertise. In W. J. Clancey & E. H. Shortliffe (Eds.), *Readings in medical artificial intelligence* (pp. 275–319). Reading, MA: Addison Wesley.

Fiedler, K. (1988). The dependence of the conjunction fallacy on subtle linguistic factors. *Psychological Research, 50*, 123–129.

Fiedler, K. (1991). The tricky nature of skewed frequency tables: An information loss account of distinctiveness-based illusory correlations. *Journal of Personality and Social Psychology, 60,* 24–36.

Field, T. M., Cohen, D., Garcia, R., & Greenberg, R. (1984). Mother-stranger face discrimination by the new born. *Infant Behavior and Development, 7,* 19–25.

Fischhoff, B. (1975). Hindsight ≠ foresight: The effects of outcome knowledge on judgment under uncertainty. *Journal of Experimental Psychology: Human Perception and Performance, 1,* 288–299.

Fischhoff, B. (1980). For those condemned to study the past: Reflections on historical judgment. In R. A. Shweder & D. W. Fiske (Eds.), *New directions for methodology of social and behavioral science: No. 4. Fallible judgment in behavioral research* (pp. 79–93). San Francisco: Jossey-Bass.

Fischhoff, B. (1982). Debiasing. In D. Kahneman, P. Slovic, & A. Tversky (Eds.), *Judgment under uncertainty: Heuristics and biases* (pp. 422–444). New York: Cambridge University Press.

Fischhoff, B., & Beyth, R. (1975). "I knew it would happen": Remembered probabilities of once-future things. *Organizational Behavior and Human Performance, 13,* 1–16.

Fischhoff, B., & Beyth-Marom, R. (1983). Hypothesis evaluation from a Bayesian perspective. *Psychological Review, 90,* 239–260.

Fischhoff, B., Slovic, P., & Lichtenstein, S. (1977). Knowing with certainty: The appropriateness of extreme confidence. *Journal of Experimental Psychology: Human Perception and Performance, 3,* 552–564.

Fisher, R. P., & Geiselman, R. E. (1988). Enhancing eyewitness memory with the cognitive interview. In M. M. Gruneberg & P. E. Morris (Eds.), *Practical aspects of memory: Current research and issues. Vol: 1. Memory in everyday life* (pp. 34–39). New York: Wiley.

Fiske, S. T. (1988). Compare and contrast: Brewer's dual process model and Fiske et al's continuum model. In T. K. Srull & R. S. Wyer, Jr. (Eds.), *A dual process model of impression formation: Advances in social cognition* (Vol. 1, pp. 65–76). Hillsdale, NJ: Lawrence Erlbaum Associates.

Fiske, S. T. (1992). Thinking is for doing: Portraits of social cognition from Daguerreotype to laser photo. *Journal of Personality and Social Psychology, 63,* 877–889.

Fiske, S. T. (1993). Controlling other people: The impact of power on stereotyping. *American Psychologist, 48,* 621–628.

Fiske, S. T. (1998). Stereotyping, prejudices, and discrimination. In D. T. Gilbert, S. T. Fiske, & G. Lindzey (Eds.), *The handbook of social psychology* (4th ed., Vol. 1, pp. 357–441). New York: McGraw-Hill.

Fiske, S. T., & Cox, M.G. (1979). Person concepts: The effects of target familiarity and descriptive purpose on the process of describing others. *Journal of Personality, 47,* 136–161.

Fiske, S. T., Kenny, D.A., & Taylor, S.E. (1982). Structural models for the mediation of salience effects on attribution. *Journal of Experimental Social Psychology, 18,* 105–127.

Fiske, S. T., Kinder, D. R., & Larter, W. M. (1983). The novice and the expert: Knowledge-based strategies in political cognition. *Journal of Experimental Social Psychology, 19,* 381–400.

Fiske, S. T., Lin, M., & Neuberg, S. I. (1999). The continuum model: Ten years later. In S. Chaiken & Y. Trope (Eds.), *Dual-process theories in social psychology* (pp. 231–254). New York: Guilford.

Fiske, S. T., & Linville, P.W. (1980). What does the schema concept buy us? *Personality and Social Psychology Bulletin, 6,* 543–557.

Fiske, S. T., & Neuberg, S.L. (1990). A continuum of impression formation, from category-based to individuating processes: Influences of information and motivation on attention and interpretation. In M.P. Zanna (Ed.), *Advances in experimental social psychology* (Vol. 23, pp. 1–74). New York: Academic Press.

Fiske, S. T., Neuberg, S. L., Beattie, A. E., & Milberg, S. J. (1987). Category-based and at-tribute-based reactions to others: Some informational conditions of stereotyping and individuating processes. *Journal of Experimental Social Psychology, 23,* 399–427.

Fiske, S. T., & Pavelchak, M. A. (1986). Category-based versus piecemeal-based affective responses: Developments in schema-triggered affect. In R. M. Sorrentino & E. T. Higgins (Eds.), *Handbook of motivation and cognition: Vol. 1 Foundations of social behavior* (pp. 167–203). New York: Guilford.

Fiske, S. T., & Taylor, S. E. (1984). *Social cognition* (1st ed.). Reading, MA: Addison-Wesley.

Fiske, S. T., & Taylor, S. E. (1991). *Social cognition* (2nd ed.). New York: McGraw-Hill.

Fitts, P. M. (1964). Perceptual-motor skill learning. In A. W. Melton (Ed.), *Categories of human learning* (pp. 243–285). New York: Academic Press.

Fitzgerald, J. M. (1988). Vivid memories and the reminiscence phenomenon: The role of a self narrative. *Human Development, 31,* 261-273.

Fivush, R. (1988). The functions of event memory: Some comments on Nelson and Barsalou. In U. Neisser & E. Winograd (Eds.), *Remembering reconsidered: Ecological and traditional approaches to the study of memory* (pp. 277–282). New York: Cambridge University Press.

Fivush, R. (1994a). Constructing narrative, emotion, and self in parent-child conver-sations about the past. In U. Neisser & R. Fivush (Eds.), *The remembering self: Con-struction and accuracy in the self narrative* (pp. 136–157). New York: Cambridge University Press.

Fivush, R., (1994b). Young children's event recall: Are memories constructed through discourse? *Consciousness and Cognition, 3,* 356–373.

Fivush, R., & Fromhoff, F.A. (1988). Style and structure in mother-child conversations about the past. *Discourse Processes, 11,* 337–355.

Fivush, R., Gray, J. T., & Fromhoff, F. A. (1987). Two year olds talk about the past. *Cogni-tive Development, 2,* 393–410.

Fivush, R., Haden, C., & Reese, E. (1996). Remembering, recounting, and reminiscing: The development of autobiographical memory in social context. In D. C. Rubin (Ed.), *Remembering our past: Studies in autobiographical memory* (pp. 341–359). New York: Cambridge University Press.

Fivush, R., & Hamond, N. R. (1990). Autobiographical memory across the preschool years: Toward reconceptualizing childhood amnesia. In R. Fivush & J. A. Hudson (Eds.), *Knowing and remembering in young children* (pp. 223–248). New York: Cam-bridge University Press.

Fivush, R., Hudson, J., & Nelson, K. (1984). Children's long-term memory for a novel event: An exploratory study. *Merrill-Palmer Quarterly, 30,* 303–316.

Fivush, R., & Reese, E. (1992). The social construction of autobiographical memory. In M. A. Conway, D. C. Rubin, H. Spinnler, & W. A. Wagenaar (Eds.), *Theoretical perspec-tives on autobiographical memory* (pp. 115–132). Dordrecht, The Netherlands: Kluwer Academic.

Fivush, R., & Schwartzmueller, A. (1998). Children remember childhood: Implications for childhood amnesia. *Applied Cognitive Psychology, 12,* 455–473.

Flanagan, J. C. (1954). The critical incident technique. *Psychological Bulletin, 51,* 327-358.

Flin, R. H. (1985). Development of visual memory: An early adolescent regression. *Jour-nal of Early Adolescence, 5,* 259–266.

Fodor, J. A. (1983). *The modularity of mind.* Cambridge, MA: MIT Press.

Fodor, J. A., & Pylyshyn, Z. W. (1988). Connectionism and cognitive architecture: A criti-cal analysis. *Cognition, 28,* 3–71.

Fong, G. T., Krantz, D. H., & Nisbett, R. E. (1986). The effects of statistical training on thinking about everyday problems. *Cognitive Psychology, 18,* 253–292.

Fong, G. T., & Nisbett, R. E. (1991). Immediate and delayed transfer of training effects in statistical reasoning. *Journal of Experimental Psychology: General, 120*, 34–45.

Franklin, H. C, & Holding, D. H. (1977). Personal memories at different ages. *Quarterly Journal of Experimental Psychology, 29*, 527–532.

Franks, J. J., & Bransford, J. D. (1971). Abstraction of visual patterns. *Journal of Experimental Psychology: General, 90*, 65–74.

Freedman, J. L., & Loftus, E. F. (1971). Retrieval of words from long-term memory. *Journal of Verbal Learning and Verbal Behavior, 10*, 107–115.

Freud, S. (1924). Remembering, repeating and working through. In J. Strachey (Ed. & Trans.), *Standard edition of the complete psychological works of Sigmund Freud* (Vol. 12, pp.147–156). London: Hogarth Press. (Original work published 1914)

Freud, S. (1950). Screen memories. In J. Strachey (Ed. & Trans.), *Standard edition of the complete psychological works of Sigmund Freud* (Vol. 3, pp. 303–322). London: Hogarth Press. (Original work published 1899)

Freud, S. (1953a). Fragment of an analysis of a case of hysteria. In J. Strachey (Ed. & Trans.), *The standard edition of the complete psychological works of Sigmund Freud* (Vol. 7, pp. 123–243). London: Hogarth Press. (Original work published 1905)

Freud, S. (1953b). Three essays on the theory of sexuality. In J. Strachey (Ed. & Trans.). *Standard edition of the complete psychological works of Sigmund Freud* (Vol. 7, pp. 3–122). London: Hogarth Press. (Original work published 1905)

Freud, S. (1963). Introductory lectures on psychoanalysis. In J. Strachey (Ed. & Trans.), *Standard edition of the complete psychological works of Sigmund Freud* (Vol. 15, pp. 1–242). London: Hogarth. (Original work published 1916)

Friedman, S., & Scholnick, E. K. (1997). The planning construct in the psychological literature. In S. Friedman & E. K. Scholnick (Eds.), *Blueprints for thinking: The role of planning in cognitive development* (pp. 3–38). New York: Cambridge University Press.

Friedman, W. J. (1987). A follow up to "scale effects in memory for the time of events": The earthquake study. *Memory & Cognition, 15*, 518 520.

Friedman, W. J. (1993). Memory for the time of past events. *Psychological Bulletin, 113*, 44–66.

Friedman, W. J., & Wilkins, A. J. (1985). Scale effects in memory for the time of events. *Memory & Cognition, 13*, 168–175.

Fromholt, P., & Larsen, S. F. (1992). Autobiographical memory and life-history narratives in aging and dementia (Alzheimer type). In M. A. Conway, D. C. Rubin, H. Spinnler, & W. A. Wagenaar (Eds.), *Theoretical perspectives on autobiographical memory* (pp. 413–426). Dordrecht, The Netherlands: Elsevier.

Fryback, D., & Edwards, W. (1973). Choices among bets by Las Vegas gamblers: Absolute and contextual effects. *Journal of Experimental Psychology: General, 98*, 271-278.

Funder, D. (1987). Errors and mistakes: Evaluating the accuracy of social judgment. *Psychological Bulletin, 101*, 75–90.

Funder, D. (1995). On the accuracy of personality judgment: A realistic approach. *Psychological Review, 102*, 652–670.

Gage, N. L., & Berliner, D. C. (1988). *Educational Psychology* (4th ed.). Boston: Houghton Mifflin.

Galambos, J. A., Abelson, R. P., & Black, J. B. (Eds.). (1986). *Knowledge structures*. Hillsdale, NJ: Lawrence Erlbaum Associates.

Galotti, K. M. (1989). Approaches to studying formal and everyday reasoning. *Psychological Bulletin, 105*, 331–351.

Galton, F. (1879). Generic faces. *Proceedings of the Royal Institution, 9*, 161–170.

Galton, F. (1883). *Inquiries into human faculty and its development* (1st ed.). London: Macmillan.

Gardner, H. (1983). *Frames of mind: The theory of multiple intelligences.* New York: Basic Books.

Garfinkel, H. (1967). *Studies in ethnomethodology.* Englewood Cliffs, NJ: Prentice-Hall.

Gates, S. A., & Colburn, D. K. (1976). Lowering appointment failures in a neighborhood health center. *Medical Care, 14,* 263–267.

Gauthier, I., & Tarr, M. J. (1997). Becoming a 'greeble' expert: Exploring mechanisms for face recognition. *Vision Research, 37,* 1673–1682.

Gearhart, M., Herman, J. L., Beker, E. L., & Witaker, A. (1993). *Whose work is it? A question for the validity of large scale portfolio assessment.* (Tech. Rep. No. 363). Los Angeles: University of California, CRESST Center for the Study of Education.

Geddes, J. C. (1985). *The development of overconfidence in clinical judgment as a function of clinical training.* Unpublished masters thesis, California State University, Fullerton.

Geiselman, R. E. (1988). Improving eyewitness memory through mental reinstatement of context. In G. M. Davies & D. M. Thomson (Eds.), *Memory in context: Context in memory* (pp. 245–266). Chichester, England: Wiley.

Geiselman, R. E., & Fisher, R. P. (1996). Ten years of cognitive interviewing. In D. G. Payne & F. G. Conrad (Eds.), *Intersections in basic and applied memory research* (pp. 291–310). Mahwah, NJ: Lawrence Erlbaum Associates.

Gentner, D. (1983). Structure-mapping: A theoretical framework for analogy. *Cognitive Science, 7,* 155–170.

Gentner, D., & Gentner, D. R. (1983). Flowing waters or teeming crowds: Mental models of electricity. In D. Gentner & A. L. Stevens (Eds.), *Mental models* (pp. 99–129). Hillsdale, NJ: Lawrence Erlbaum Associates.

Gentner, D., & Landers, R. (1985). *Analogical reminding: A good match is hard to find.* Proceedings of the International Conference on Cybernetics and Society (pp. 607–613). Tucson, AZ.

Gentner, D. R. (1987). Timing of skilled motor performance: Tests of the proportional duration model. *Psychological Review, 94,* 255–276.

Gentner, D. R. (1988). Expertise in typewriting. In M. T. H. Chi, R. Glaser, & M. J. Farr (Eds.), *The nature of expertise* (pp. 1–21). Hillsdale, NJ: Lawrence Erlbaum Associates.

Gentner, D. R., Grudin, J. T., & Conway, E. (1980). Finger movements in transcription typing (Tech Rep. 8601). La Jolla: University of California, San Diego, Center for Human Information Processing.

Gergen, K. J. (1973). Social psychology as history. *Journal of Personality and Social Psychology, 26,* 309–320.

Gergen, K. J. (1994). Mind, text, and society: Self-memory in social context. In U. Neisser & R. Fivush (Eds.), *The remembering self: Construction and accuracy in the self-narrative* (pp. 78–104). New York: Cambridge University Press.

Gibson, J. J. (1966). *The senses considered as perceptual systems.* Boston: Houghton Mifflin.

Gibson, J. J. (1979). *The ecological approach to visual perception.* Boston: Houghton Mifflin.

Gick, M. L., & Holyoak, K. J. (1980). Analogical problem solving. *Cognitive Psychology, 12,* 306–355.

Gick, J. J., & Holyoak, K. J. (1983). Schema induction and analogical transfer. *Cognitive Psychology, 15,* 1–38.

Gigerenzer, G. (1991). How to make cognitive illusions disappear: Beyond 'heuristics and biases'. In W. Stroebe & M. Hewstone (Eds.), *European review of social psychology* (Vol. 2, pp. 83–115). Chichester, England: Wiley.

Gigerenzer, G. (1993). The bounded rationality of probabilistic mental models. In K. I. Manktelow & D. F. Over (Eds.), *Rationality: Psychological and philosophical perspectives* (pp. 284–313). London: Routledge.

Gigerenzer, G. (1996). On narrow norms and vague heuristics: A reply to Kahneman and Tversky (1996). *Psychological Review, 103,* 592–596.

Gigerenzer, G., Hell, W., & Blank, H. (1988). Presentation and content: The use of base rates as a continuous variable. *Journal of Experimental Psychology: Human Perception and Performance, 14*, 513–525.

Gigerenzer, G., Hoffrage, U., & Kleinbolting, H. (1991). Probabilistic mental models: A Brunswikian theory of confidence. *Psychological Review, 98*, 506–528.

Gigerenzer, G., & Hug, K. (1992). Domain specific reasoning: Social contracts, cheating, and perspective change. *Cognition, 43*, 127–171.

Gigerenzer, G., & Murray, D. J. (1987). *Cognition as intuitive statistics*. Hillsdale, NJ: Lawrence Erlbaum Associates.

Gigerenzer, G., & Todd, P. M. (1999). Fast and frugal toolbox. In G. Gigerenzer, P. M. Todd, & the ABC Research Group, *Simple heuristics that make us smart* (pp. 1–34). New York: Oxford University Press.

Gilbert, D. T. (1989). Thinking lightly about others: Automatic components of the social inference process. In J. S. Uleman & J. A. Bargh (Eds.), *Unintended thought* (pp. 189–211). New York: Guilford.

Gilbert, D. T. (1991). How mental systems believe. *American Psychologist, 46*, 107–119.

Gilbert, D. T. (1998). Ordinary personology. In D. T. Gilbert, S. T. Fiske, & G. Lindzey (Eds.), *The handbook of social psychology* (4th Ed., Vol. 2, pp. 89–150). Boston: McGraw-Hill.

Gilbert, D. T., & Malone, P. S. (1995). The correspondence bias. *Psychological Bulletin, 117*, 21–38.

Gilbert, D. T., Pelham, B. W., & Krull, D. S. (1988). On cognitive busyness: When person perceivers meet persons perceived. *Journal of Personality and Social Psychology, 54*, 733–739.

Gilovich, T. (1991). *How do we know what isn't so: The fallibility of human reason in everyday life*. New York: Free Press.

Gilovich, T., & Medvec, V. H. (1994a). Some counterfactual determinants of satisfaction and regret. In N. J. Roese & J. M. Olson (Eds.), *What might have been: The social psychology of counterfactual thinking* (pp. 259–282). Mahwah, NJ: Lawrence Erlbaum Associates.

Gilovich, T., & Medvec, V. H. (1994b). The temporal pattern to the experience of regret. *Journal of Personality and Social Psychology, 67*, 357–365.

Gilovich, T., & Medvec, V. H. (1995). The expression of regret: What, when, and why. *Psychological Review, 102*, 379–395.

Gilovich, T., Medvec, V. H., & Kahneman, D. (1998). Varieties of regret: A debate and final resolution. *Psychological Review, 105*, 602–605.

Gilovich, T., Jennings, D. L., & Jennings, S. (1983). Causal focus and estimates of consensus: An examination of the false-consensus effect. *Journal of Personality and Social Psychology, 45*, 550–559.

Gilovich, T., Vallone, R., & Tversky, A. (1985). The hot hand in basketball: On the misperception of random sequences. *Cognitive Psychology, 17*, 295–314.

Gladwin, T. (1970). *East is a big bird: Navigation and logic on Puluwat atoll*. Cambridge, MA: Harvard University Press.

Glaser, R. (1996). Changing the agency for learning: Acquiring expert performance. In K. A. Ericsson (Ed.), *The road to excellence: The acquisition of expert performance in the arts and sciences, sports, and games* (pp. 303–311). Mahwah, NJ: Lawrence Erlbaum Associates.

Glaser, R., & Chi, M. T. H. (1988). Overview. In M. T. H. Chi, R. Glaser, & M. J. Farr (Eds.), *The nature of expertise* (pp. xv–xxviii). Hillsdale, NJ: Lawrence Erlbaum Associates.

Gleicher, F., Kost, K. A., Baker, S. M., Strathman, A. J., Richman, S. A., & Sherman, S. J. (1990). The role of counterfactual thinking in judgments of affect. *Personality and Social Psychological Bulletin, 16*, 284–295.

Glick, J. (1997). Discourse and development: Notes from the field. In L. B. Resnick, R. Saljo, C. Pontecorvo, & B. Burge (Eds.). *Discourse, tools, and reasoning: Essays on situated cognition* (pp. 243–264). New York: Springer.

Gluck, M. A., & Rumelhart, D. E. (Eds.). (1990). *Neurosciences and connectionist theory*. Hillsdale, NJ: Lawrence Erlbaum Associates.

Gobet, F., & Simon, H. A. (1995). *Role of presentation time in recall of game and random positions*. (Tech. Rep. C.I.P. 524). Pittsburgh, PA: Carnegie-Mellon University, Department of Psychology.

Gobet, F., & Simon, H. A. (1996). The roles of recognition processes and look ahead search in time-constrained expert problem solving: Evidence from grand-master-level chess. *Psychological Science, 7,* 52–55.

Godden, D. R., & Baddeley, A. D. (1975). Context-dependent memory in two natural environments: On land and underwater. *British Journal of Psychology, 66,* 325–331.

Goldberg, L. R. (1968). Simple models or simple processes? Some research on clinical judgments. *American Psychologist, 23,* 483–496.

Golding, E. (1981). *The effect of past experience on problem solving.* Paper presented at the annual conference of the British Psychological Society. University of Surrey, England.

Goldstein, A. G., & Chance, J. E. (1981). Laboratory studies of face recognition. In G. Davies, H. Ellis, & J. Shepherd (Eds.). *Perceiving and remembering faces* (pp. 81–104). London: Academic Press.

Gollwitzer, P. M., & Bargh, J. A. (Eds.). (1996). *The psychology of action: Linking cognition and motivation to behavior.* New York: Guilford.

Goodman, J., & Loftus, E. F. (1989). Implications of facial memory research for investigative and administrative criminal procedures. In A. W. Young & H. D. Ellis (Eds.), *Handbook of research on face processing* (pp. 571–579). Amsterdam: North-Holland/Elsevier Science.

Goodman, G. S., Quas, J. A., Batterman-Faunce, J. M., Riddlesberger, M. M., & Kuhn, J. (1994). Predictors of accurate and inaccurate memories of traumatic events experienced in childhood. *Consciousness and Cognition, 3,* 369–394.

Gordon, S. E. (1993). Implications of cognitive theory for knowledge acquisition. In R. R. Hoffman (Ed.), *The psychology of expertise: Cognitive research and empirical AI* (pp. 99–120). New York: Springer-Verlag.

Gordon, S. E., & Gill, R. T. (1997). Cognitive task analysis. In C. B. Zambok & G. Klein (Eds.), *Naturalistic decision making* (pp. 131–140). Mahwah, NJ: Lawrence Erlbaum Associates.

Goren, C. C., Sarty, M., & Wu, B. W. K. (1975). Visual following and pattern discrimination of face-like stimuli by newborn infants. *Pediatrics, 56,* 544–559.

Gorman, M. E. (1995). Hypothesis testing. In S. E. Newstead & J. St. B. T. Evans (Eds.), *Perspectives on thinking and reasoning* (pp. 217–240). Hillsdale, NJ: Lawrence Erlbaum Associates.

Goschke, T., & Kuhl, J. (1993). Representations of intentions: Persisting activation in memory. *Journal of Experimental Psychology: Learning, Memory, and Cognition, 19,* 1211–1226.

Gott, S. P., Hall, E. P., Pokorny, R. A., Dibble, E., & Glaser, R. (1993). A naturalistic study of transfer: Adaptive expertise in technical domains. In D. K. Detterman & R. J. Sternberg (Eds.), *Transfer on trial: Intelligence, cognition, and instruction* (pp. 258–288). Norwood, NJ: Ablex.

Graesser, A. C. (1981). *Prose comprehension beyond the word.* New York: Springer-Verlag.

Graesser, A. C., & Clark, L. F. (1985). *Structures and procedures of implicit knowledge.* Norwood, NJ: Ablex.

Graesser, A. C., Gordon, S. E., & Sawyer, J. D. (1979). Recognition memory for typical and atypical actions in scripted activities: Test of a script pointer + tag hypothesis. *Journal of Verbal Learning and Verbal Behavior, 18,* 319–332.

Graesser, A. C., & Nakamura, G. V. (1982). The impact of a schema on comprehension and memory. In G. Bower (Eds.), *The psychology of learning and motivation: Advances in research or theory* (Vol. 16, pp. 99–135), New York: Academic Press.

Graesser, A. C., Robertson, S. P., & Clark, L. F. (1983). Question answering: A method for exploring the on-line construction of prose representation. In J. Fein & R. O. Freedle (Eds.), *New directions in discourse processing in prose comprehension* (pp. 41–68). Norwood, NJ: Ablex.

Graesser, A. C., Singer, M., & Trabasso, T. (1994). Constructing inferences during narrative text comprehension. *Psychological Review, 101,* 371–395.

Graesser, A. C., Woll, S. B., Kowalski, D. J., & Smith, D. A. (1980). Memory for typical and atypical actions in scripted activities. *Journal of Experimental Psychology: Human Learning and Memory, 6,* 503–515.

Graesser, A. C., & Zwaan, R. A. (1995). Inference generation and the construction of situation models. In C. A. Weaver & S. Mannes (Eds.), *Discourse comprehension: Essays in honor of Walter Kintsch* (pp. 117–139). Hillsdale, NJ: Lawrence Erlbaum Associates.

Green, C. (1998). Are connectionist models theories of cognition? *Psycoloquy, 9*(4), 1–11.

Greenfield, P. (1984). A theory of the teacher in the learning activities of everyday life. In B. Rogoff & J. Lave (Eds.), *Everyday cognition: Its development in social context* (pp. 117–138). Cambridge, MA: Harvard University Press.

Greeno, J. G. (1989). Situations, mental models, and generative knowledge. In D. Klahr & K. Kotovsky (Eds.), *Complex information processing: The impact of Herbert A. Simon* (pp. 285–318). Hillsdale, NJ: Lawrence Erlbaum Associates.

Greeno, J. G. (1991a). Number sense as situated knowing in a conceptual domain. *Journal of Research in Mathematics Education, 22,* 170–218.

Greeno, J. G. (1991b). Environments for situated conceptual learning. In L. Birnbaum (Ed.), *The international conference on the learning sciences: Proceedings of the 1991 conference.* AACE (pp. 211–216).

Greeno, J. G., & Moore, J. L. (1993). Situativity and symbols: Response to Vera and Simon. *Cognitive Science, 17,* 49–59.

Greenwald, A. G., Pratkanis, A. R., Leippe, M. R., & Baumgartner, M. H. (1986). Under what conditions does theory obstruct research progress? *Psychological Review, 93,* 216–229.

Gregg, L. W., & Simon, H. A. (1967). Process models and stochastic theories of simple concept formation. *Journal of Mathematical Psychology, 4,* 246–266.

Grice, H. P. (1975). Logic and conversation. In P. Cole & J. L. Morgan (Eds.), *Syntax and semiotics 3: Speech acts* (pp. 95–113). New York: Academic Press.

Griggs, R. A. (1983). The role of problem content in the selection task and THOG problem. In J. St. B. T. Evans (Ed.), *Thinking and reasoning: Psychological approaches* (pp. 16–43). London: Routledge & Kegan Paul.

Griggs, R. A. (1995). The effects of rule clarification, decision justification, and selection instruction on Wason's abstract selection task. In S. E. Newstead & J. St. B. T. Evans (Eds.), *Perspectives on thinking and reasoning* (pp. 17–39). Hillsdale, NJ: Lawrence Erlbaum Associates.

Griggs, R. A., & Cox, J. R. (1982). The elusive thematic-materials effect in Wason's selection task. *British Journal of Psychology, 73,* 407–420.

Griggs, R. A., & Cox, J. R. (1993). Permission schemas and the selection task. *Quarterly Journal of Experimental Psychology: Human Experimental Psychology, 46A,* 637–651.

Gross, C. G. (1992). Representation of visual stimuli in inferior temporal cortex. In V. Bruce, A. Cowey, A. W. Young, & D. L. Perrett, (Eds.), *Processing the facial image* (pp. 3–10). Oxford, UK: Clarendon Press.

Gross, C. G., & Sergent, J. (1992). Face recognition. *Current Opinion in Neurobiology, 7,* 156–161.

Grove, W., & Meehl, P. (1996). Comparative efficacy of informal (subjective, impressionistic) and formal (mechanical, algorithmic) prediction procedures: The clinical statistical controversy. *Psychology, Public Policy, and Law, 2,* 293–323.

Gruber, H. (1991). *Qualitative aspekte von expertise in schach: Begriffe, modellen unter-suchungen und perspectiven der expertise forschung.* [Qualitative aspects of expertise in chess: Terminology, models, empirical studies, and outlooks on expertise research]. Germany: Feenschach.

Grudin, J., & Conway, E. (1980). Finger movements in transcription typing (Tech Rep. 8601). La Jolla, CA: University of California, San Diego, Center for Human Information Processing.

Grudin, J. T., & Larochelle, S. (1982). *Diagraph frequency effects in typewriting*. (Tech Rep. CHIP 110). La Jolla: University of California, San Diego, Center for Human Information Processes.

Gruneberg, M. M., Morris, P. E., & Sykes, R. N. (Eds.). (1978). *Practical aspects of memory*. London: Academic Press.

Gruneberg, M. M., Morris, P. E., & Sykes, R. N. (Eds.). (1988). *Practical aspects of memory: Current research and issues, Vol. 1: Memory in everyday life*. New York: Wiley.

Guynn, M. J., McDaniel, M. A., & Einstein, G. O. (1996). Prospective memory: When reminders fail. *Memory & Cognition, 26*, 287–298.

Halpern D. F. (1996). *Thought and knowledge: An introduction to critical thinking*. (3rd ed.). Mahwah, NJ: Lawrence Erlbaum Associates.

Hambleton, R. K., Jaeger, R. M., Koretz, D., Linn, R. L., Millman, J., & Phillips, S. E. (1995). *Review of the measurement quality of the Kentucky instructional results information system, 1991-1994*. Frankfort, KY: Kentucky General Assembly.

Hambrick, D. Z., Salthouse, T. A., & Meinz, E. J. (1999). Predictors of crossword puzzle proficiency and moderators of age-cognition relations. *Journal of Experimental Psychology: Applied, 128*, 131–164.

Hamilton, D. L. (1977). *Illusory correlation as a basis for social stereotypes*. Paper presented at the annual convention of the American Psychological Association. San Francisco, CA.

Hamilton, D. L. (1981). Illusory correlations as a basis for stereotyping. In D. L. Hamilton (Ed.), *Cognitive processes in stereotyping and intergroup behavior* (pp.115–144). Hillsdale, NJ: Lawrence Erlbaum Associates.

Hamilton, D. L. (1988). Causal attribution viewed from an information processing perspective. In D. Bar-Tal & A. W. Kruglanski (Eds.), *The social psychology of knowledge* (pp. 359–385). Cambridge: Cambridge University Press.

Hamilton, D. L., Driscoll, D. M., & Worth, L. T. (1989). Cognitive organization of impressions: Effects of incongruency in complex representations. *Journal of Personality and Social Psychology, 57*, 925–939.

Hamilton, D. L., Dugan, P. M., & Trolier, T. K. (1985). The formation of stereotypic beliefs: Further evidence for distinctiveness-based illusory correlations. *Journal of Personality and Social Psychology, 48*, 5–17.

Hamilton, D. L., & Gifford, R. K. (1976). Illusory correlation in interpersonal perception: A cognitive basis of stereotype judgments. *Journal of Experimental Social Psychology, 12*, 392–407.

Hamilton, D. L., Katz, L. B., & Leirer, V. O. (1980). Cognitive representation of personality impressions: Organizational processes in first impression formation. *Journal of Personality and Social Psychology, 57*, 925–939.

Hamilton, D. L., & Rose, T. L. (1980). Illusory correlation and the maintenance of stereotypic beliefs. *Journal of Personality and Social Psychology, 39*, 832–845.

Hamilton, D. L., & Sherman, S. J. (1989). Illusory correlations: Implications for stereotype theory and research. In D. Bar-Tal, C. F. Graumann, A. W. Kruglanski, & W. Stroebe (Eds.), *Stereotypes and prejudice: Changing conceptions* (pp. 59–82). New York: Springer-Verlag.

Hamilton, D. L., & Sherman, S. J. (1996). Perceiving persons and groups. *Psychological Review, 103*, 336–355.

Hammond, K. (1989). *Case-based reasoning: Viewing planning as a memory task*. New York: Academic Press.

Hammond, K., & Seifert, C. M. (1994). Opportunistic memory: "Be prepared." In R. C. Schank & E. Langer (Eds.), *Beliefs, reasoning, and decision making: Psycho-logic in honor of Bob Abelson* (pp. 111–142). Hillsdale, NJ: Lawrence Erlbaum Associates.

Hampson, S. E. (1988). The dynamics of categorization and impression formation. In T. K. Srull & R. S. Wyer, Jr. (Eds.), *Dual process model of impression formation: Advances in social cognition*, (Vol. 1, pp. 77–82). Hillsdale, NJ: Lawrence Erlbaum Associates.

Hampson, S. E., John, O. P., & Goldberg, L. R. (1986). Category breadth and hierarchical structure in personality: Studies of asymmetries in judgments of trait implications. *Journal of Personality and Social Psychology, 51,* 37–54.

Hanson, T. (1992). The mental aspects of hitting a baseball: A case study of Hank Aaron. *Contemporary Thought on Performance and Enhancement, 1,* 49–70.

Harasty, A. N., & Brewer, M. B. (1995, May). *Personality traits and social categories as retrieval cues.* Paper presented at the meeting of the Midwestern Psychological Association, Chicago.

Harkness, A. R., DeBono, K. G., & Borgida, E. (1985). Personal involvement and strategies for making contingency judgments: A stake in the dating game makes a difference. *Journal of Personality and Social Psychology, 49,* 22–32.

Harries, M. H., & Perrett, D. L. (1991). Visual processing of faces in temporal cortex: Physiological evidence for a modular organization and possible anatomical correlates. *Journal of Cognitive Neuroscience, 3,* 9–24.

Harris, J. E. (1980). Memory aids people use: Two interview studies. *Memory & Cognition, 8,* 31–38.

Harris, J. E. (1984). Remembering to do things: A forgotten topic. In J. E. Harris & P. E. Morris (Eds.), *Everyday memory, actions and absent-mindedness* (pp. 71–92). London: Academic Press.

Harris, J. E., & Wilkins, A. J. (1982) Remembering to do things: A theoretical framework and an illustrative experiment. *Human Learning, 1,* 123–136.

Hartley, J. T. (1989). Memory for prose: Perspectives on the reader. In L. W. Poon, D. C. Rubin, & B. A. Wilson (Eds.). *Everyday cognition in adulthood and later life* (pp. 135-156). New York: Cambridge University Press.

Hartshorn, K., Rovee-Collier, C., Gerhardstein, P., Bhatt, R. S., Wondoloski, T. L., Klein, P., Gilch, J., Wurtzel, N., & Campos-de-Carvalho, M. (1998). The ontogeny of long-term memory over the first year and a half of life. *Devlopmental Psychobiology, 32,* 69–89.

Harvey, J. H., Town, T. R., & Yarkin, K. L. (1981). How fundamental is the fundamental attribution error? *Journal of Personality and Social Psychology, 40,* 346–349.

Harvey, J. H., Yarkin, K. L., Lightner, J. M., & Town, J. P. (1980). Unsolicited interpretation and recall of interpersonal events. *Journal of Personality and Social Psychology, 38,* 551–568.

Hastie, R. (1980). Memory for behavioral information that confirms or contradicts a personality impression. In R. Hastie, T. M. Ostrom, E. Ebbeson, R. S. Wyer, D. Hamilton, & D. E. Carlston (Eds.), *Person memory: The cognitive basis of social perception* (pp. 155–177). Hillsdale, NJ: Lawrence Erlbaum Associates.

Hastie, R. (1986). A primer of information processing theory for the political scientist. In R. R. Lau & D. O. Sears (Eds.), *Politcal Cognition: The 19th Annual Carnegie Mellon Symposium on Cognition* (pp. 11–39). Hillsdale, NJ: Lawrence Erlbaum Associates.

Hastie, R. (1988). A computer simulation of person memory. *Journal of Experimental Social Psychology, 24,* 423–447.

Hastie, R., & Kumar, P. A. (1979). Person memory: Personality traits as organizing principles in memory for behaviors. *Journal of Personality and Social Psychology, 37,* 25–38.

Hastie, R., & Park, B. (1986). The relationship between memory and judgment depends on whether the judgment task is memory-based or on-line. *Psychological Review, 93*, 258–268.

Hastie, R., Park, B., & Weber, R. (1984). Social memory. In R. S. Wyer & T. K. Srull (Eds.), *Handbook of social cognition* (1st ed., Vol. 2., pp. 151–212). Hillsdale, NJ: Lawrence Erlbaum Associates.

Hastie, R., & Pennington, N. (1989). Notes on the distinction between memory-based versus on-line judgments. In J. N. Bassili (Ed.), *Online cognition in person perception* (pp. 1–17). Hillsdale, NJ: Lawrence Erlbaum Associates.

Hatano, G. (1988). Social and motivational bases for mathematical understanding. *New Directions for Child Development, 41*, 55–70.

Hawkins, S. A., & Hastie, R. (1990). Hindsight: Biased judgments of past events after the outcomes are known. *Psychological Bulletin, 107*, 311–327.

Hay, D. C., & Young, A. W. (1982). The human face. In A. W. Ellis (Ed.), *Normality and pathology in cognitive functions*. London: Academic Press.

Hayes-Roth, B., & Hayes-Roth, F. (1979). A cognitive model of planning. *Cognitive Science, 3*, 275–310.

Hayes-Roth, F., Waterman, D. A., & Lenat, D. B. (1983). *Building expert systems*. Reading, MA: Addison-Wesley.

Heider, F. (1958). *The psychology of interpersonal relations*. New York: Wiley.

Herman, J. L., Gearhart, M., & Baker, E. L. (1993). Assessing writing portfolios: Issues in the validity and meaning of scores. *Educational Assessment, 1*, 201–224.

Herman, J. L., & Winters, L. (1994). Portfolio research: A slim collection. *Educational Leadership, 52*(2), 48–55.

Herrmann, D. J., McEvoy, C., Hertzog, C., Hertel, P., & Johnson, M. K. (Eds.). (1996). *Basic and applied memory research* (Vols. 1 & 2). Mahwah, NJ: Lawrence Erlbaum Associates.

Heuer, E., & Reisberg, D. (1992). Emotion, arousal, and memory for detail. In S. Christianson (Ed.), *The handbook of emotion and memory: Research and theory* (pp. 151–180). Hillsdale, NJ: Lawrence Erlbaum Associates.

Heywood, C. A., & Cowey, A. (1992). The role of the 'face-cell' area in the discrimination and recognition of faces by monkeys. In V. Bruce, A. Cowey, A. W. Young, & D L. Perrett (Eds.), *Processing the facial image* (pp. 31–38). Oxford, England: Clarendon Press.

Hilton, J. L., & Darley, J. M. (1991). The effects of interaction goals on person perception. In M. Zanna (Ed.), *Advances in experimental social psychology (Vol. 24)*, pp. 236–267). San Diego, CA: Academic Press.

Hintzman, D. L. (1986). "Schema abstraction" in a multiple-trace memory model. *Psychological Review, 93*, 411–428.

Hirst, W. (1994). The remembered self in amnesics. In U. Neisser & R Fivush (Eds.), *The remembering self: Construction and accuracy in the self-narrative* (pp. 252–277). New York: Cambridge University Press.

Hirst, W., & Gluck, D. (1999). Revisiting John Dean's memories. In E. Winograd, R. Fivush, & W. Hirst (Eds.), *Ecological approaches to memory: Essays in honor of Ulric Neisser* (pp. 253–281). Mahwah, NJ: Lawrence Erlbaum Associates.

Hirst, W., & Manier, D. (1996). Remembering as communication: A family recounts its past. In D. C. Rubin (Ed.), *Remembering our past: Studies in autobiographical memory* (pp. 271–290). New York: Cambridge University Press.

Hoch, S. J. (1984). Availability and interference in predictive judgment. *Journal of Experimental Psychology: Learning, Memory, & Cognition, 10*, 649–662.

Hoch, S. J. (1987). Perceived consensus and predictive accuracy: The pros and cons of projection. *Journal of Personality and Social Psychology, 53*, 221–234.

Hodges, J. R., & McCarthy, R. A. (1993). Autobiographical amnesia resulting from bilateral paramedian thalamic infarction. *Brain, 116,* 921–940.

Hoffman, C., Mischel, W., & Mazze, K. (1981). The role of purpose in the organization of information about behavior: Trait-based versus goal-based categories in person cognition. *Journal of Personality and Social Psychology, 40,* 211–225.

Hoffrage, U., Herturg, R., & Gigerenzer, G. (2000). Hindsight bias: A by-product of knowledge updating? *Journal of Experimental Psychology: Learning, Memory, and Cognition, 26,* 566–581.

Hogarth, R. M. (1981). Beyond discrete biases: Functional and dysfunctional aspects of judgmental heuristics. *Psychological Bulletin, 90,* 197–217.

Holding, D. H. (1985). *The psychology of chess skill.* Hillsdale, NJ: Lawrence Erlbaum Associates.

Holding, D. H., Noonan, T. K., Pfau, H. D., & Holding, C. S. (1986). Date attribution, age, and the distribution of lifetime memories. *Journal of Gerontology, 41,* 481–485.

Holding, D. H., & Reynolds, R. I. (1982). Recall or evaluation of chess positions as determinants of chess skill. *Memory & Cognition, 10,* 237–242.

Holmes, A., & Conway, M. A. (1999). Generation identity and the reminiscence bump: Memories for public and private events. *Journal of Adult Development, 6,* 21–34.

Holyoak, K. J. (1991). Symbolic connectionism: Toward third-generation theories of expertise. In K. A. Ericsson & J. Smith (Eds.), *Toward a general theory of expertise: Prospects and limits* (pp. 301–335). New York: Cambridge University Press.

Holyoak, K. J., & Cheng, P. W. (1995). Pragmatic reasoning about human voluntary action: Evidence from Wason's selection task. In S. E. Newstead & J. St. B. T. Evans (Eds.), *Perspectives on thinking and reasoning* (pp. 67–89). Hillsdale, NJ: Lawrence Erlbaum Associates.

Holyoak, K. J., & Koh, K. (1987). Surface and structural similarity in analogical transfer. *Memory & Cognition, 15,* 332–340.

Holyoak, K. J., & Thagard, P. (1989). Analogical mapping by constraint satisfaction. *Cognitive Science, 13,* 295–355.

Holzkamp, K. (1987). Critical psychology and overcoming of scientific indeterminacy in psychological theorizing (L. Zusne, trans.). In R. Hogan & W. H. Jones (Eds. and Trans.), *Perspectives in personality* (Vol. 2, pp. 93–123). Greenwich, CT: JAI Press.

Horvath, J. A., Forsythe, G. B., Sternberg, R. J., Bullis, R. C., Sweeney, P. J., Williams, W. M., McNally, J. A., & Wattendorf, J. A. (1999). Experience, knowledge, and military leadership. In R. J. Sternberg & J. A. Horvath (Eds.), *Tacit knowledge in professional practice: Researcher and practioner perspectives* (pp. 39–71). Mahwah, NJ: Lawrence Erlbaum Associates.

Howe, M. J. A., Davidson, J. W., & Sloboda, J. A. (1998). Innate talents: Reality or myth? *Behavioral and Brain Sciences, 21,* 399–407.

Howe, M. L. (2000). *The fate of early memories: Developmental science and the retention of childhood experiences.* Washington, DC: American Psychological Association.

Howe, M. L., & Courage, M. L. (1993). On resolving the enigma of infantile amnesia. *Psychological Bulletin, 113,* 305–326.

Howe, M. L., & Courage, M. L. (1997). The emergence and early development of autobiographical memory. *Psychological Review, 104,* 499–523.

Howe, M. L., Courage, M. L., & Peterson, C. (1994). How can I remember when "I" wasn't there: Long-term retention of traumatic experiences and emergence of the cognitive self. *Consciousness and Cognition, 3,* 327–355.

Howe, M. L., & O'Sullivan, J. T. (1997). What children's memories tell us about recalling our childhoods: A review of storage and retrieval processes in the development of long-term retention. *Developmental Review, 17,* 148–204.

Howes, M., Siegel, M., & Brown, F. (1993). Early childhood memories: Accuracy and affect. *Cognition, 47,* 95–119.

Hudson, J. A. (1986). Memories are made of this: General event knowledge and the development of autobiographical memory. In K. Nelson (Ed.), *Event knowledge: Structure and function in development* (pp. 97–118). Hillsdale, NJ: Lawrence Erlbaum Associates.

Hudson, J. A. (1990). The emergence of autobiographical memory in mother-child conversation. In R. Fivush & J. A. Hudson (Eds), *Knowing and remembering in young children* (pp. 166–196). New York: Cambridge University Press.

Hudson, J., & Nelson, K. (1986). Repeated encounters of a similar kind: Effects of familiarity on children's autobiographical memory. *Cognitive Development, 1,* 253–271.

Huff, C. R. (1987). Wrongful conviction: Societal tolerance of injustice. *Research in Social Problems and Public Policy, 4,* 99–115.

Huff, C. R., Rattner, A., & Sagarin, E. (1996). *Convicted but innocent: Wrongful conviction and public policy.* Thousand Oaks, CA: Sage.

Hull, C. L. (1931). Goal attraction and directing ideas conceived as habit phenomena. *Psychological Review, 38,* 487–506.

Humphrey, G. (1951). *Thinking: An introduction to its experimental psychology.* New York: Wiley.

Hutchins, E. (1980). *Culture and inference: A Trobriand case study.* Cambridge, MA: Harvard University Press.

Hutchins, E. (1983). Understanding Micronesian navigation. In D. Gentner & A. Stevens (Eds.), *Mental models* (pp. 191–225). Hillsdale, NJ: Lawrence Erlbaum Associates.

Hutchins, E. (1995). *Cognition in the wild.* Cambridge, MA: MIT Press.

Hutchins, E., & Hinton, G. (1984). Why the islands move. *Perception, 12,* 629–632.

Huttenlocher, J., Hedges, L.V., & Bradburn, N. M. (1990). Reports of elapsed time: Bounding and rounding processes in estimation. *Journal of Experimental Psychology: Learning, Memory, and Cognition, 16,* 196–213.

Huttenlocher, J., Hedges, L. V., & Duncan, S. (1991). Categories and particulars: Prototype effects in estimating spatial location. *Psychological Review, 98,* 352–376.

Huttenlocher, J., Hedges, L.V., & Prohaska, V. (1988). Hierarchical organization in ordered domains: Estimating dates of events. *Psychological Review, 95,* 471–484.

Huttenlocher, J., Hedges, L. V., & Prohaska, V. (1992). Memory for day of the week: A 5 + 2 day cycle. *Journal of Experimental Psychology: General, 121,* 313–325.

Huttenlocher, J., & Prohaska, V. (1997). Reconstructing the times of past events. In N. L. Stein, P. A. Ornstein, B. Tversky, & C. Brainerd (Eds.), *Memory for everyday and emotional events* (pp. 105–179). Mahwah, NJ: Lawrence Erlbaum Associates.

Hyllegard, R. (1991). The role of baseball seam pattern in pitch recognition. *Journal of Sport and Exercise Psychology, 13,* 80–84.

Hyman, I. E., Jr. (1999). Creating false autobiographical memories: Why people believe their memory errors. In E. Winograd, R. Fivush, & W. Hirst (Eds.), *Ecological approaches to cognition: Essays in honor of Ulric Neisser* (pp. 229–252). Mahwah, NJ: Lawrence Erlbaum Associates.

Hyman, I. E., Jr., & Faries, J. M. (1992). The functions of autobiographical memory. In M. A. Conway, D. C. Rubin, H. Spinnler, & W. A. Wagenaar (Eds.), *Theoretical perspectives on autobiographical memory* (pp. 207–221). Dordrecht, The Netherlands: Kluwer Academic.

Hyman, I. E., Jr., Husband, T. H., & Billings, J. F. (1995). False memories of childhood experiences. *Applied Cognitive Psychology, 9,* 181–187.

Inhelder, B., & Piaget, J. (1958). *The growth of logical thinking from childhood to adolescence: An essay on the construction of formal operational structures.* New York: Basic Books.

Intons-Peterson, M. J., & Best, D. L. (1998). Introduction and a brief history of memory distortions and their prevention. In M. J. Intons-Peterson & D. L. Best (Eds.), *Memory distortions and their prevention* (pp. 1–14). Mahwah, NJ: Lawrence Erlbaum Associates.

Intons-Peterson, M. J., & Fournier, J. (1986). External and internal memory aids: When and how often do we use them? *Journal of Experimental Psychology: General, 115*, 267–280.

Jackson, S. L., & Griggs, R. A. (1990). The elusive pragmatic reasoning schemas effect. *Quarterly Journal of Experimental Psychology: Human Experimental Psychology 42A*, 352–373.

Jacoby, L. L. (1988). Memory observed and memory unobserved. In U. Neisser & E. Winograd (Eds.), *Remembering reconsidered: Ecological and traditional approaches to the study of memory* (pp. 145–177). New York: Cambridge University Press.

Jacoby, L. L., & Kelley, C. M. (1992). Unconscious influences on memory: Dissociations and automaticity. In D. Milner & M. Rugg (Eds.), *The neuropsychology of consciousness* (pp. 201–233). New York: Academic Press.

Jacoby, L. L., Woloshyn, V., & Kelley, C. M. (1989). Becoming famous without being recognized: Unconscious influences of memory produced by dividing attention. *Journal of Experimental Psychology: General, 118*, 115–125.

Janet, P. (1928). *L'evolution de la memoire et de la notion du temps* (The development of memory and of the concept of time) Vol. 1. Paris: Chahine.

Jennings, D. L., Amabile, T. M., & Ross, L. (1982). Informal covariation assessment: Data-based vs. theory-based judgments. In D. Kahneman, P. Slovic, & A. Tversky (Eds.), *Judgment under uncertainty: Heuristics and biases* (pp. 211–230). New York: Cambridge University Press.

Jennings, D. L., Lepper, M. R., & Ross, L. (1981). Persistence of impressions of personal persuasiveness: Perseverance of erroneous self-perceptions outside the debriefing paradigm. *Personality and Social Psychology Bulletin, 7*, 257–263.

Jodelet, D. (1991). *Madness and social representations*. Hemel Hempstead, UK: Harvester Wheatsheaf.

Johnson, C., & Mullen, B. (1994). Evidence for the accessibility of paired distinctiveness in distinctiveness-based illusory correlation in stereotyping. *Personality and Social Psychology Bulletin, 20*, 65–70.

Johnson, H. M., & Seifert, C. M. (1992). The role of predictive features in retrieving analogical cases. *Journal of Memory and Language, 31*, 648–667.

Johnson, H. M., & Seifert, C. M. (1994). Sources of the continued influence effect: When misinformation in memory affects later inferences. *Journal of Experimental Psychology: Learning, Memory, and Cognition, 20*, 1420–1436.

Johnson, H. M., & Seifert, C. M. (1998). Updating accounts following a correction of misinformation. *Journal of Experimental Psychology: Learning, Memory, and Cognition, 24*, 1483–1495.

Johnson, M. H., Dziurawiec, S., Ellis, H. D., & Morton, J. (1991). Newborns' preferential tracking of face-like stimuli and its subsequent decline. *Cognition, 40*, 1–19.

Johnson, M. H., & Morton, J. (1991). *Biology and human development: The case of face recognition*. New York: Basic Books.

Johnson, M. K. (1983). A multiple-entry, modular memory system. In G. H. Bower (Ed.), *The psychology of learning and motivation: Advances in research and theory* (Vol. 17, pp. 81–123). New York: Academic Press.

Johnson, M. K. (1985). The origin of memories. In P. C. Kendall (Ed.), *Advances in cognitive-behavioral research and therapy* (Vol. 4, pp. 1–27). New York: Academic Press.

Johnson, M. K., Hashtroudi, S., & Lindsay, D. S. (1993). Source monitoring. *Psychological Bulletin, 114*, 3–28.

Johnson, M. K., & Raye, C. L. (1981). Reality monitoring. *Psychological Review, 88*, 67–85.

Johnson, P. E., Duran, A. S., Hassebrock, F., Moller, J., Prietula, M., Feltovich, P. J., & Swanson, D. B. (1981). Expertise and error in diagnostic reasoning. *Cognitive Science, 5*, 235–283.

Johnson-Laird, P. N., Legrenzi, P., & Legrenzi, S. M. (1972). Reasoning and a sense of reality. *British Journal of Psychology, 63*, 395–400.

Johnson-Laird, P. N., & Shafir, E. (Eds.). (1993). *Reasoning and decision making.* Amsterdam: Elsevier Science Publishers.

Jones, E. E. (1979). The rocky road from acts to dispositions. *American Psychologist, 34*, 107–117.

Jones, E. E. (1985). Major developments in social psychology during the past five decades. In G. Lindzey & E. Aronson (Eds.), *The handbook of social psychology* (3rd ed., Vol. 1, pp. 47–107). New York: Random House.

Jones, E. E. (1990). *Interpersonal perception.* New York: Freeman.

Jones, E. E., & Harris, V. A. (1967). The attribution of attitudes. *Journal of Experimental Social Psychology, 3*, 1–24.

Jones, E. E., & Nisbett, R. E. (1972). The actor and the observer: Divergent perspectives of the causes of behavior. In E. E. Jones, D. E. Kanouse, H. H. Kelley, R. E. Nisbett, S. Valins, & B. Weiner (Eds.), *Attribution: Perceiving the causes of behavior* (pp. 79–84). Morristown, NJ: General Learning Press.

Jones, E. E., & Thibaut, J. W. (1958). Interaction goals as bases for inference in interpersonal perception. In R. Tagiuri & L. Petrullo (Eds.), *Person perception and interpersonal behavior* (pp. 151–178) Stanford, CA: Stanford University Press.

Jongman, R. W. (1968). *The eye of the master.* Amsterdam: Van Gorcun.

Jordan, B. (1989). Cosmopolitical obstetrics: Some insights from the training of traditional midwives. *Social Science and Medicine, 28*, 925–944.

Jungermann, H. (1983). The two camps on rationality. In R. W. Scholz (Ed.), *Decision making under uncertainty* (pp. 65–86). Amsterdam: Elsevier.

Kaempf, G. L., Wolf, S., Thordsen, M. L., & Klein, G. A. (1992). *Decision making in the AEGIS combat information center.* Fairborn, OH: Klein Associates.

Kahneman, D. (1995). Varieties of counterfactual thinking. In N. Roese & J. Olson (Eds.), *What might have been: The social psychology of counterfactual thinking* (pp. 375–396). Hillsdale, NJ: Lawrence Erlbaum Associates.

Kahneman, D., & Miller, D. T. (1986). Norm theory: Comparing reality to its alternatives. *Psychological Review, 93*, 136–153.

Kahneman, D., & Tversky, A. (1972). Subjective probability: A judgment of representativeness. *Cognitive Psychology, 3*, 430–454.

Kahneman, D., & Tversky, A. (1973). On the psychology of prediction. *Psychological Review, 80*, 237–251.

Kahneman, D., & Tversky, A. (1982a). On the study of statistical intuitions. *Cognition, 11*, 123–141.

Kahneman, D., & Tversky, A. (1982b). The simulation heuristic. In D. Kahneman, P. Slovic, & A. Tversky (Eds.), *Judgment under uncertainty: Heuristics and biases* (pp 201–208). New York: Cambridge University Press.

Kahneman, D., & Tversky, A. (1984). Options, values, and frames. *American Psychologist, 39*, 341–350.

Kahneman, D., & Tversky, A. (1996). On the reality of cognitive illusions. *Psychological Bulletin, 103*, 582–591.

Kahneman, D., & Varey, C. A. (1990). Propensities and counterfactuals: The loser that almost won. *Journal of Personality and Social Psychology, 59*, 1101–1110.

Kanter, R. (1977). *Men and women of the corporation.* New York: Basic Books.

Kanwisher, N., McDermott, J., & Chun, M. M. (1997). The fusiform face area: A module in human extrastriate cortex specialized for face perception. *Journal of Neuroscience, 17*, 4302–4311.

Kapelman, A. S. (1996). A daughter's perspective. In E. Tobach, R. J. Falmagne, M. B. Parlee, L. M. W. Martin, & A. S. Kapelman (Eds.), *Mind and social practice: Selected writings of Sylvia Scribner* (pp. xix–xxv). New York: Cambridge University Press.

Kassin, S. M. (1979). Base rates and prediction: The role of sample size. *Personality and Social Psychology Bulletin, 5,* 210–213.

Kassin, S. M., Ellsworth, P. C., & Smith, V. L. (1989). The "general acceptance" of psychological research on eyewitness testimony: A survey of the experts. *American Psychologist, 44,* 1089–1098.

Kassin, S. M., & Pryor, J. B. (1985). The development of attribution processes. In J. Pryor & J. Day (Eds.), *The development of social cognition* (pp. 3–34). New York: Springer-Verlag.

Kayne, N. T., & Alloy, L. B. (1988). Clinician and patient as aberrant actuaries: Expectation-based distortions in assessment of covariation. In L. Y. Abramson (Ed.), *Social cognition and clinical psychology: A synthesis* (pp. 295–365). New York: Guilford.

Keenan, J. M. (1993). An exemplar model can explain Klein and Loftus' results. In R. S. Wyer, Jr. & T. K. Srull (Eds.), *The mental representation of trait and autobiographical knowledge about the self* (Vol. 5, pp. 111–121). Hillsdale, NJ: Lawrence Erlbaum Associates.

Kelly, C. M., & Jacoby, L. L. (1990). The construction of subjective experience: Memory attribution. *Mind and Language, 5,* 49–68.

Kelly, G. A. (1955). *The psychology of personal constructs.* New York: Norton.

Kelley, H. H. (1972). Causal schemata and the attribution process. In E. E. Jones, D. E. Kanouse, H. H. Kelly, R. E. Nisbett, S. Valins, & B. Weiner (Eds.), *Attribution: Perceiving the causes of behavior* (pp. 151–174). Morristown, NJ: General Learning Press.

Keren, G. M. (1987). Facing uncertainty in the game of bridge: A calibration study. *Organizational Behavior and Human Decision Processes, 39,* 98-114.

Keren, G. B., & Wagenaar, W. A. (1985). On the psychology of playing blackjack: Normative and descriptive considerations with implications for decision theory. *Journal of Experimental: General, 114,* 133–158.

Kernis, M. H. (1984). Need for uniqueness, self-schemas, and thought as moderators of the false-consensus effect. *Journal of Experimental Social Psychology, 20,* 350-362.

Kihlstrom, J. F., & Harackiewicz, J. M. (1982). The earliest recollection: A new survey. *Journal of Personality, 50,* 134–148.

King, A. (1994). Guiding knowledge construction in the classroom: Effects of teaching children how to question and how to explain. *American Educational Research Journal, 31,* 338–398.

Kintsch, W. (1988). The role of knowledge in discourse comprehension: A constructive integration model. *Psychological Review, 95,* 163–182.

Kintsch, W. (1998). *Comprehension: A paradigm for cognition.* New York: Cambridge University Press.

Kirshner, D. I., & Whitson, J. A. (1997). Editors introduction. In D. I. Kirshner & J. A. Whitson (Eds.), *Situated cognition: Social, semiotic, and psychological perspectives* (pp. 1–16). Mahwah, NJ: Lawrence Erlbaum Associates.

Klatzky, R. L. (1991). Let's be friends. *American Psychologist, 46,* 43–45.

Klayman, J. (1995). Varieties of confirmation bias. In J. Busemeyer, R. Hastie, & D. Medin (Eds.), *The psychology of learning and motivation: Decision making from a cognitive perspective* (Vol. 32, pp. 385–418). San Diego, CA: Academic Press.

Klayman, J., & Ha, Y. (1987). Confirmation, disconfirmation, and information in hypothesis testing. *Psychological Review, 94,* 211–228.

Klein, G. A. (1989). Recognition primed decision. In W. B. Rouse (Ed.), *Advances in man–machine systems research* (Vol. 5, pp. 47–92). Greenwich, CT: JAI Press.

Klein, G. A. (1993). A recognition-primed decision (RPD) model of rapid decision making. In G. A. Klein, J. Orasanu, R. Calderwood, & C. E. Zsambok (Eds.), *Decision making in action: Models and methods* (pp. 138–147). Norwood, NJ: Ablex.

Klein, G. A. (1997). The recognition-primed decision (RPD) model: Looking back, looking forward. In C. E. Zsambok & G. Klein (Eds.), *Naturalistic decision making* (pp. 285–292). Mahwah, NJ: Lawrence Erlbaum Associates.

Klein, G. A. (1998). *Sources of power.* Cambridge, MA: MIT Press.

Klein, G. A., Calderwood, R., & Clinton-Cirocco, A. (1986). Rapid decision making on the fire ground. *Proceedings of the 30th annual meeting of the Human Factors Society, 1,* 576–580.

Klein, G. A., & Hoffman, R. R. (1993). Seeing the invisible: Perceptual cognitive aspects of expertise. In M. Rabinowitz (Ed.), *Cognitive science foundations of instruction* (pp. 203–226). Hillsdale, NJ: Lawrence Erlbaum Associates.

Klein, G. A., Orasanu, J., Calderwood, R., & Zsambok, C. E. (Eds.). (1993). *Decision making in action: Models and methods.* Norwood, NJ: Ablex.

Klein, G. A., Wolf, S., Militello, L., & Zsambok, C. E. (1995). Characteristics of skilled option generation in chess. *Organizational Behavior and Human Decision Processes, 62,* 63–69.

Klein, S. B., & Loftus, J. (1990). Rethinking the role of organization in person memory: An independent trace storage model. *Journal of Personality and Social Psychology, 59,* 400–410.

Klein, S. B., & Loftus, J. (1993). The mental representation of trait and autobiographical knowledge about the self. In R. S. Wyer, Jr. & T. K. Srull (Eds.), *The mental representation of trait and autobiographical knowledge about the self. Advances in social cognition* (Vol. 5, pp. 1–49). Hillsdale, NJ: Lawrence Erlbaum Associates.

Klein, S. B., Loftus, J., & Burton, H. A. (1989). Two self-reference effects: The importance of distinguishing between self-descriptiveness judgments and autobiographical retrieval in self-referent encoding. *Journal of Personality and Social Psychology, 56,* 853–865.

Klein, S. B., Loftus, J., & Plog, A. E. (1992). Trait judgments about the self: Evidence from the encoding specificity paradigm. *Personality and Social Psychology Bulletin, 18,* 730–735.

Klein, S. B., Loftus, J., Trafton, J. G., & Fuhrman, R. W. (1992). Use of exemplars and abstractions in trait judgments: A model of trait knowledge about the self and others. *Journal of Personality and Social Psychology, 63,* 739–753.

Koehler, D. J. (1991). Explanation, imagination, and confidence in judgment. *Psychological Bulletin, 110,* 499–519.

Kohonen, T. (1977). *Associative memory: A system-theoretical approach.* Berlin: Springer-Verlag.

Kohonen, T., Oja, E., & Lehtio, P. (1981). Storage and processing of information in distributed associative memory systems. In G. E. Hinton & J. L. McClelland (Eds.), *Parallel models of associative memory* (pp. 105–143). Hillsdale, NJ: Lawrence Erlbaum Associates.

Kolodner, J. L. (1983a). Maintaining organization in a dynamic long term memory. *Cognitive Science, 7,* 243–280.

Kolodner, J. L. (1983b). Reconstructive memory: A computer model. *Cognitive Science, 7,* 281–328.

Kolodner, J. L. (1984). *Retrieval and organization strategies in conceptual memory: A computer model.* Hillsdale, NJ: Lawrence Erlbaum Associates.

Kolodner, J. L. (1994). From natural language understanding to case-based reasoning and beyond: A perspective on the cognitive model that ties it all together. In R. C. Schank & E. Langer (Eds.), *Beliefs, reasoning, and decision making: Psycho-logic in honor of Bob Abelson* (pp. 55–110). Hillsdale, NJ: Lawrence Erlbaum Associates.

Kolodner, J. L., & Simpson, R. L. (1989). The mediator: Analysis of an early case-based problem. *Cognitive Science, 13,* 507–550.

Kolodner, J. T. (1993). *Case-based reasoning.* San Diego: Morgan Kaufmann.

Koretz, D., Stecher, B. M., Klein, S., & McCuffrey, D. (1994). The Vermont portfolio assessment program: Findings and implications. *Educational Measurement: Issues and Practices, 13*(3), 5–16.

Koriat, A., Ben-Zur, H., & Nussbaum, A. (1990). Encoding information for future action: Memory for to be performed task versus memory for to be recalled task. *Memory & Cognition, 18*, 568–578.

Koriat, A., Fischhoff, B., & Razel, O. (1976). An inquiry into the process of temporal orientation. *Acta Psychologica, 40*, 57–73.

Koriat, A., Lichtenstein, S., & Fischhoff, B. (1980). Reasons for confidence. *Journal of Experimental Psychology: Human Learning and Memory, 6*, 107–118.

Kosslyn, S. M., & Koenig, O. (1992). *Wet mind: The new cognitive neuroscience*. New York: Free Press.

Krafka, C., & Penrod, S. D. (1985). Reinstatement of context in a field experiment on eyewitness identification. *Journal of Personality and Social Psychology, 49*, 58–69.

Krampe, R. T. (1994). *Maintaining excellence: Cognitive-motor performance in pianists differing in age and skill level*. Berlin: Edition Sigma.

Krueger, J., & Rothbart, M. (1988). Use of categorical and individuating information in making inferences about personality. *Journal of Personality and Social Psychology, 55*, 187–195.

Krull, D. S. (1993). Does the grist change the mill? The effect of the perceiver's inferential goal on the process of social inference. *Personality and Social Psychology Bulletin, 19*, 340–348.

Krull, D. S., & Erickson, D. J. (1995). Inferential hopscotch: How people draw social inferences from behavior. *Current Directions in Psychological Science, 4*, 35–38.

Kuhn, D. (1989). Children and adults as intuitive scientists. *Psychological Review, 96*, 674–679.

Kuhn, D. (1991). *The skills of argument*. New York: Cambridge University Press.

Kuhn, D. (1992). Thinking as argument. *Harvard Educational Review, 62*, 155–178.

Kuhn, D. (1993). Connecting scientific and informal reasoning. *Merrill-Palmer Quarterly, 39*, 74–103.

Kuhn, D., Weinstock, M., & Fleton, R. (1994). How well do jurors reason? Competence dimensions of individual variation in a juror reasoning task. *Psychological Sciences, 5*, 289–296.

Kunda, Z. (1999). *Social cognition: Making sense of people*. Cambridge, MA: MIT Press.

Kunda, Z., & Nisbett, R. E. (1986). The psychometrics of everyday life. *Cognitive Psychology, 18*, 195–224.

Kunda, Z., & Thagard, P. (1996). Forming impressions from stereotypes, traits, and behavior: A parallel constraint satisfaction theory. *Psychological Review, 103*, 284–308.

Kurucz, J., & Feldmar, G. (1979). Prosopo-affective agnosia as a symptom of cerebral organic disease. *Journal of the American Geriatrics Society, 27*, 225–230.

Kvavilashvili, L. (1987). Remembering intention as a distinct form of memory. *British Journal of Psychology, 78*, 507–518.

Kvavilashvili, L. (1990). *Remembering/forgetting intention as a distinct form of memory and the factors that influence it*. Tablisi, Russia: Metsniereba.

Kvavilashvili, L., & Ellis, J. A. (1996). Varieties of intention: Some distinctions and classifications. In M. A. Brandimonte, G. O. Einstein, & M. A. McDaniel (Eds.), *Prospective memory: Theory and applications* (pp. 23–52). Mahwah, NJ: Lawrence Erlbaum Associates.

Laboratory of Comparative Human Cognition (1980). Culture and intelligence. In R. J. Sternberg (Ed.), *Handbook of human intelligence* (pp. 642–719). New York: Cambridge University Press.

Labov, W. (1972). The logic of non-standard English. In F. Williams (Ed.), *Language and poverty* (pp. 153–189). Chicago: Markham.

Lampert, M. (1986). Knowing, doing, and the teaching of multiplication. *Cognition and Instruction, 3,* 305–342.

Lampinen, J. M. (1996). Recollections of things schematic: The influence of schemas on recollective experience. *Dissertation Abstracts International, 57*(6), 4064B.

Lancaster, J. W., & Barsalou, L. W. (1997). Multiple organizations of events in memory. *Memory, 5,* 569–599.

Landman, J. (1987). Regret and elation following action and inaction: Affective responses to positive versus negative outcomes. *Personality and Social Psychology Bulletin, 13,* 524–536.

Lange, T. E., & Wharton, C. (1994). REMIND: Retrieval from episodic memory by inferencing and disambiguation. In J. A. Barnden & K. J. Holyoak (Eds.), *Advances in connectionist and neural computation theory. Vol. 3: Analogy, metaphor, and reminding* (pp. 29–94). New York: Academic Press.

Langer, E. J. (1989). *Mindfulness.* Reading, MA: Addison-Wesley.

Langer, E. J., & Abelson, R. P. (1972). The semantics of asking a favor: How to succeed in getting a favor without really trying. *Journal of Personality and Social Psychology, 24,* 26–32.

Langer, E. J., Blank, A., & Chanowitz, B. (1978). The mindlessness of ostensibly thoughtful action: The role of "placebic" information in interpersonal interaction. *Journal of Personality and Social Psychology, 36,* 635–642.

Langer, L. L. (1991). *Holocaust testimonials: The ruins of memory.* New Haven, CT: :Yale University Press.

Larkin, J. H. (1983). The role of problem representation in physics. In D. Gentner & A. L. Stevens (Eds.), *Mental models.* (pp. 75–100). Hillsdale, NJ: Lawrence Erlbaum Associates.

Larkin, J. H. (1989). What kind of knowledge transfers? In L. B. Resnick (Ed.), *Knowing, learning, and instruction: Essays in honor of Robert Glaser.* (pp. 283–305). Hillsdale, NJ: Lawrence Erlbaum Associates.

Larkin, J. H., McDermott, J., Simon, D. P., & Simon, H. A. (1980). Models of competence in solving physics problems. *Cognitive Science, 4,* 317–345.

Larsen, S. F. (1992). Personal context in autobiographical and narrative memories. In M. A. Conway, D. C. Rubin, H. Spinnler, & W. A. Wagenaar (Eds.), *Theoretical perspectives on autobiographical memory* (pp. 53–71). Dordrecht, The Netherlands: Kluwer Academic.

Larsen, S. F. (1993). Commentaries: Memory of schemata, details, and selves. In G.M. Davies & R.H. Logie (Eds.), *Memory in everyday life* (pp. 310–315). Dordrecht, The Netherlands: North-Holland/Elsevier Science.

Larsen, S. F., & Plunkett, K. (1987). Remembering experienced and reported events. *Applied Cognitive Psychology, 1,* 15–26.

Larsen, S. F., & Thompson, C. P. (1995). Reconstructive memory in the dating of personal and public news events. *Memory & Cognition, 23,* 780–790.

Larsen, S. F., Thompson, C. P., & Hansen, T. (1996). Time in autobiographical memory. In D. C. Rubin (Ed.), *Remembering our past: Studies in autobiographical memory.* (pp. 129–156). New York: Cambridge University Press.

Lau, R. R. (1986). Political schemata, candidate evaluations, and voting behavior. In R. R. Lau & D. O. Sears (Eds.), *Political cognition* (pp. 95–126). Hillsdale, NJ: Lawrence Erlbaum Associates.

Laufer, E. A., & Glick, J. (1996). Expert and novice differences in cognition and activity: A practical work activity. In Y. Engeström & D. Middleton (Eds.), *Cognition and communication at work* (pp. 177–198). New York: Cambridge University Press.

Laughery, K. R., Alexander, J. F., & Lane, A. B. (1971). Recognition of human faces: Effects of target exposure time, target position, pose position, and type of photograph. *Journal of Applied Psychology, 55*, 477–483.

Laughery, K. R., Duval, C., & Wogalter, M. S. (1986). Dynamics of facial recall. In H. D. Ellis, M. A. Jeeves, F. Newcombe, & A. Young (Eds.), *Aspects of face processing* (pp. 373–387). Dordrecht, The Netherlands: Martinus Nijhoff.

Laughery, K. R., & Wogalter, M. S. (1989). Forensic applications of facial memory research. In A. W. Young & H. D. Ellis (Eds.), *Handbook of research on face processing* (pp. 519–555). Amsterdam: North-Holland/Elsevier Science.

Lave, J. (1988). *Cognition in practice: Mind, mathematics and culture in everyday life.* New York: Cambridge University Press.

Lave, J. (1990). The culture of acquisition and the process of understanding. In J. W. Stigler, R. A. Shweder, & G. Herdt (Eds.), *Cultural psychology: Essays on comparative human development* (pp. 309–327). New York: Cambridge University Press.

Lave, J. (1991). Situating learning in communities of practice. In L. B. Resnick, J. M. Levine, & S. D. Teasley (Eds.), *Perspectives on socially shared cognition* (pp. 63–82). Washington, DC: American Psychological Association.

Lave, J. (1993a). The practice of learning. In S. Chaiklin & J. Lave (Eds.), *Understanding practice: Perspectives on activity and context* (pp. 3–22). New York: Cambridge University Press.

Lave, J. (1993b). *Tailored learning: Education and everyday practice among craftsmen in West Africa.* Unpublished manuscript, University of California, Berkeley.

Lave, J., Murtaugh, M., & de la Rocha, O. (1984). The dialectic of arithmetic in grocery shopping. In B. Rogoff & J. Lave (Eds.), *Everyday cognition: Its development in social context* (pp. 67–94). Cambridge, MA: Harvard University Press.

Lave, J., & Wenger, E. (1991). *Situated learning: Legitimate peripheral participation.* New York: Cambridge University Press.

Leary, M. R. (1981). The distorted nature of hindsight. *Journal of Social Psychology, 115*, 25–29.

Leary, M. R. (1982). Hindsight distortion and the 1980 presidential debate. *Personality and Social Psychology Bulletin, 8*, 257–263.

Leder, H., & Bruce, V. (2000). When inverted faces are recognized: The role of configural information in face recognition. *Quarterly Journal of Experimental Psychology: Human Experimental Psychology, 53A*, 513–536.

Lee, D. D. (1940). A primitive system of values. *Philosophy of Science, 7*, 355–378.

Lee, D. D. (1949). Being and value in a primitive culture. *Journal of Philosophy, 48*, 401–415.

Lehman, D. R., Lempert, R. O., & Nisbett, R. E. (1988). The effects of graduate training on reasoning: Formal discipline and thinking about everyday-life events. *American Psychologist, 43*, 431–442.

Lehman, D. R., & Nisbett, R. E. (1990). A longitudinal study of the effects of undergraduate education on reasoning. *Developmental Psychology, 28*, 952–960.

Lehnert, W. C., Robertson, S. P., & Black, J. B. (1984). Memory interactions during text comprehension. In H. Mandl, N. L. Stein, & T. Trabasso (Eds.), *Learning and comprehension of text* (pp. 355–369). Hillsdale, NJ: Lawrence Erlbaum Associates.

Leont'ev, A. N. (1979). The problem of activity in psychology. In J. Wertsch (Ed.), *The concept of activity in Soviet psychology* (pp. 37–71). White Plains, NY: Sharpe.

Leont'ev, A. N. (1981). *Problems in the development of mind.* Moscow: Progress.

Lesgold, A. M., Rubinson, H., Feltovich, P. J., Glaser, R., Klopfer, D., & Wang, Y. (1988). Expertise in a complex skill: Diagnosing X-ray pictures. In M. T. H. Chi, R. Glaser, & M. Farr (Eds.), *The nature of expertise* (pp. 311–342). Hillsdale, NJ: Lawrence Erlbaum Associates.

Leshowitz, B. (1989). It is time we did something about scientific illiteracy. *American Psychologist, 44*, 1159–1160.

Levi, A. S., & Pryor, J. B. (1987). Use of the availability heuristic in probability estimates of future events: The effects of imagining outcomes versus imagining reasons. *Organizational Behavior and Human Decision Processes, 40*, 219–234.

Levy, R. L., & Claravell, V. (1977). Differential effects of a phone reminder on patients with long and short between-visit intervals. *Medical Care, 15*, 435–438.

Levy, R. L., & Loftus, G. R. (1984). Compliance and memory. In J. E. Harris & P. E. Morris (Eds.), *Everyday memory, actions and absentmindedness* (pp. 93–112). London: Academic Press.

Lewin, K. (1951). Intention, will, and need. In D. Rapaport (Ed. and Trans.), *Organization and pathology of thought* (pp. 95–153). New York: Columbia University Press. (Original work published 1926)

Lewis, D. (1972). *We the navigators.* Honolulu, HI: University Press of Hawaii.

Lewis, M. W., & Anderson, J. R. (1985). Discrimination of operator schemata in problem solving: Learning from examples. *Cognitive Psychology, 17*, 26–65.

Ley, R. G., & Bryden, M. P. (1979). Hemispheric differences in recognising faces and emotions. *Brain and Language, 7*, 127–138.

Leyens, J. P., & Fiske, S. T. (1994). Impression formation: From recitals to symphonie fantastique. In P. G. Devine, D. L. Hamilton, & T. M. Ostrom (Eds.), *Social cognition: Impact on social psychology* (pp. 39–75). San Diego, CA: Academic Press.

Lichtenstein, E. H., & Brewer, W. F. (1980). Memory for goal directed events. *Cognitive Psychology, 12*, 412–445.

Lichtenstein, S., & Fischhoff, B. (1977). Do those who know more also know more about how much they know? *Organizational Behavior and Human Performance, 20*, 159–183.

Lichtenstein, S., Fischhoff, B., & Phillips, L. D. (1982). Calibration of probabilities: The state of the art to 1980. In D. Kahneman, P. Stovic, & A. Tversky (Eds.), *Judgment under uncertainty: Heuristics and biases* (pp. 306–334). New York: Cambridge University Press.

Lichtenstein, S., & Slovic, P. (1973). Response-induced reversals of preference in gambling: An extended replication. *Journal of Experimental Psychology: General, 101*, 16–20.

Lichtenstein, S., Slovic, P., Fischhoff, B., Layman, M., & Combs, B. (1978). Judged frequency of lethal events. *Journal of Experimental Psychology: Human Learning and Memory, 4*, 551–578.

Light, L. L., Kayra-Stuart, F., & Hollander, S. (1979). Recognition memory for typical and unusual faces. *Journal of Experimental Psychology: Human Learning and Memory, 5*, 212–228.

Lindsay, D. S. (1990). Misleading suggestions can impair eyewitnesses' ability to remember event details. *Journal of Experimental Psychology: Learning, Memory, and Cognition, 16*, 1077–1083.

Lindsay, D. S. (1993). Eyewitness suggestibility. *Current Directions in Psychological Science, 2*, 86–89.

Lindsay, D. S. (1994). Memory source monitoring and eyewitness testimony. In D. F. Ross, J. D. Read, & M. Toglia (Eds.), *Adult eyewitness testimony: Current trends and developments* (pp. 27–55). New York: Cambridge University Press.

Lindsay, D. S., & Johnson, M. K. (1989). The eyewitness suggestibility effect and memory for source. *Memory & Cognition, 17*, 349–358.

Lingle, J. H., Geva, N., Ostrom, T. M., Leippe, M. R., & Baumgardner, M. H. (1979). Thematic effects of person judgments on impression organization. *Journal of Personality and Social Psychology, 37*, 674–687.

Lingle, J. H., & Ostrom, T. M. (1979). Retrieval selectivity in memory-based impression judgments. *Journal of Personality and Social Psychology, 37*, 180–194.

Linton, M. (1975). Memory for real-world events. In D. A. Norman & D. E. Rumelhart (Eds.), *Explorations in cognition* (pp. 376–404). San Francisco: Freeman.

Linton, M. (1978). Real world memory after six years: An in vivo study of very long-term memory. In M. M. Gruneberg, P. E. Morris, & R. N. Sykes (Eds.), *Practical aspects of memory* (pp. 69–76). London: Academic Press.

Linton, M. (1982). Transformations of memory in everyday life. In U. Neisser (Ed.), *Memory observed: Remembering in natural contexts* (pp. 77–81). San Francisco: Freeman.

Linton, M. (1986). Ways of searching and the contents of memory. In D. C. Rubin (Ed.), *Autobiographical memory* (pp. 50–67). New York: Cambridge University Press.

Lipshitz, R. (1993). Decision making as argument-driven action. In G. Klein, J. Urasanu, R. Calderwood, & C. E. Zsambok (Eds.), *Decision making in action: Models and methods* (pp. 172–181). Mahwah, NJ: Lawrence Erlbaum Associates.

Lipshitz, R., & Ben-Shaul, O. B. (1997). Schemata and mental models in recognition-primed decision making. In C. E. Zsambok & G. A. Klein (Eds.), *Naturalistic decision making* (pp. 293–303). Mahwah, NJ: Lawrence Erlbaum Associates.

Livingston, R. B. (1967). Brain circuitry relating to complex behavior. In G. C. Quarton, T. Melnechuck, & F. O. Schmitt (Ed.) *The neurosciences: A study program* (pp. 568–576). New York: Rockefeller University Press.

Locksley, A., Borgida, E., Brekke, N., & Hepburn, C. (1980). Sex stereotypes and social judgment. *Journal of Personality and Social Psychology, 39*, 821–831.

Loftus, E. F. (1975). Leading questions and the eyewitness report. *Cognitive Psychology, 7*, 560–572.

Loftus, E. F. (1977). Shifting human color memory. *Memory & Cognition, 5*, 696–699.

Loftus, E. F. (1979). *Eyewitness testimony*. Cambridge, MA: Harvard University Press.

Loftus, E. F. (1981). Natural and unnatural cognition. *Cognition, 10*, 193–196.

Loftus, E. F. (1991a). The glitter of everyday memory … and the gold. *American Psychologist, 46*, 16–18.

Loftus, E. F. (1991b). Made in memory: Distortions in recollection after misleading information. In G. H. Bower (Ed.), *The psychology of learning and motivation: Advances in research and theory* (Vol. 27, pp. 187–215). San Diego, CA: Academic Press.

Loftus, E. F. (1993). The reality of repressed memories. *American Psychologist, 48*, 518–537.

Loftus, E. F. (1997a). Creating false memories. *Scientific American, 277*, 70–75.

Loftus, E. F. (1997b). Memories for a past that never was. *Current Directions in Psychological Science, 6*, 60–65.

Loftus, E. F., Coan, J. A., & Pickrell, J. F. (1996). Manufacturing false memories based on bits of reality. In L. Reder (Ed.), *Implicit memory and metacognition* (pp. 195–220). Mahwah, NJ: Lawrence Erlbaum Associates.

Loftus, E. F., Donders, K., Hoffman, H. G., & Schooler, J. W. (1989). Creating new memories that are quickly accessed and confidently remembered. *Memory & Cognition, 17*, 607–616.

Loftus, E. F., & Hoffman, H. G. (1989). Misinformation and memory: The creation of new memories. *Journal of Experimental Psychology: General, 118*, 100–104.

Loftus, E. M., & Ketcham, K. (1994). *The myth of repressed memory: False memories and allegations of sexual abuse*. New York: St. Martin's Press.

Loftus, E. M., Korf, N. L., & Schooler, J. W. (1989). Misguided memories: Sincere distortions of reality. In J. Yuille (Ed.), *Credibility assessment* (pp. 155–173). Dordrecht, The Netherlands: Kluwer Academic Press.

Loftus, E. F., & Loftus, G. R. (1980). On the permanence of stored information in the human brain. *American Psychologist, 35*, 421–434.

Loftus, E. F., & Marburger, W. (1983). Since the eruption of Mt. St. Helens, has anyone beaten you up? Improving the accuracy of retrospective reports with landmark events. *Memory & Cognition, 11*, 114–120.

Loftus, E. F., Miller, D. G., & Burns, H. (1978). Semantic integration of verbal information into a visual memory. *Journal of Experimental Psychology: Human Learning and Memory, 4,* 19–31.

Loftus, E. F., & Palmer, J. C. (1974). Reconstruction of automobile destruction: An example of the interaction between language and memory. *Journal of Verbal Learning and Verbal Behavior, 13,* 585–589.

Loftus, E. F., Schooler, J. W., & Wagenaar, W. A. (1985). The fate of memory: Comment on McCoskey and Zaragoza. *Journal of Experimental Psychology: General, 114,* 375–380.

Loftus, E. F., Smith, K. D., Johnson, D. A., & Fiedler, J. (1988). Remembering "when": Errors in the dating of autobiographical memories. In M. M. Gruneberg, P. E. Morris, & R. N. Sykes (Eds.), *Practical aspects of memory: Current research and issues. Vol. 1: Memory in everyday life* (pp. 234–240). New York: Wiley.

Lopes, L. L. (1982). *Toward a procedural theory of judgment.* (Technical report 17). Madison, WI: Wisconsin Human Information Processing Program.

Lopes, L.L. (1991). The rhetoric of irrationality. *Theory & Psychology, 1,* 65–82.

Lord, C. G., Lapper, M. G., & Preston, E. E. (1984). Considering the opposite: A corrective strategy for social judgment. *Journal of Personality and Social Psychology, 47,* 1231–1243.

Lucchelli, F., Muggia, S., & Spinnler, H. (1995). The 'petites madeleines' phenomenon in two amnesic patients: Sudden recovery of forgotten memories. *Brain, 118,* 167–183.

Luria, A. K. (1931). Psychological expedition to central Asia. *Science, 74*(1920), 383–384.

Luria, A. K. (1971). Towards the problem of the historical nature of psychological processes. *International Journal of Psychology, 6,* 259–272.

Luria, A. K. (1976). *Cognitive development: Its cultural and social foundations.* Cambridge, MA: Harvard University Press.

Luszsz, M. A. (1989). Theoretical models of everyday problem solving in adulthood. In J. D. Sinnott (Ed.), *Everyday problem solving: Theory and applications* (pp. 24–39). New York: Praeger.

Lynn, S. J., Lock, T. G., Myers, B., & Payne, D. G. (1997). Recalling the unrecallable: Should hypnosis be used to recover memories in psychotherapy? *Current Directions in Psychological Science, 6,* 79–83.

Lynn, S. J., & McConkey, K. J. (Eds.). (1998). *Truth in memory.* New York: Guilford.

MacLeod, M. (1985). *Perspectives on an assault: Varying accounts by different witnesses.* Paper presented at the NATO Advanced Study Institute on the Role of Psychology in the Selection and Training of Police, Skiathos, Greece.

MacLeod, M. (1987). *Psychological dynamics of the police interview.* Unpublished doctoral dissertation, University of Aberdeen, Scotland.

MacLeod, M. D., Frowley, J. N., & Shepherd, J. W. (1994). Whole body information: Its relevance to eyewitnesses. In D. F. Ross, J. D. Read, & M. Toglia (Eds.), *Adult eyewitness testimony: Current trends and developments* (pp. 125–143). New York: Cambridge University Press.

Maier, R. N. F. (1930). Reasoning in humans I: On direction. *Journal of Comparative Psychology, 10,* 115–143.

Maier, R. N. F. (1931). Reasoning in humans II: The solution of a problem and its appearance in consciousness. *Journal of Comparative Psychology, 12,* 181–194.

Malone, D. R., Morris, H. H., Kay, M. C., & Levin, H. S. (1982). Prosopagnosia: A double dissociation between recognition of familiar and unfamiliar faces. *Journal of Neurology, Neurosurgery, and Psychiatry, 45,* 820–822.

Malpass, R. (1981). Training in face recognition. In G. M. Davies, H. D. Ellis, & J. W. Shepherd (Eds.), *Perceiving and remembering faces* (pp. 271–285). London: Academic Press.

Malpass, R. S. (1996). Enhancing eyewitness memory. In S. L. Sporer & R. S. Malpass (Eds.), *Psychological issues in eyewitness identification* (pp. 177–204). Mahwah, NJ: Lawrence Erlbaum Associates.

Malpass, R. S., & Devine, P. G. (1981). Guided memory in eyewitness identification. *Journal of Applied Psychology, 66,* 343–350.

Malpass, R. S., & Hughes, K. D. (1986). Formation of facial prototypes. In H. D. Ellis, M. A. Jeeves, F. Newcombe, & A. Young (Eds.), *Aspects of face processing* (pp. 373–387). Dordrecht, The Netherlands: Martinus Nijhoff.

Malpass, R. S., & Kravitz, J. (1969). Recognition for faces of own and other-race. *Journal of Personality and Social Psychology, 13,* 330–334.

Mandler, G. (1980). Recognizing: The judgment of previous occurrence. *Psychological Review, 87,* 252–271.

Mandler, G. (1994). Hypermnesia, incubation, and mind popping: On remembering without really trying. In C. Umilta & M. Moscovitch (Eds.), *Attention and performance: Conscious and unconscious information processing* (pp. 3–33). Cambridge, MA: MIT Press.

Mandler, J. M. (1990). Recall and its verbal expression. In R. Fivush & J. A. Hudson (Eds.), *Knowing and remembering in young children* (pp. 317–330). New York: Cambridge University Press.

Mandler, J. M., & McDonough, L. (1995). Long-term recall of event sequences in infancy. *Journal of Experimental Child Psychology, 59,* 457–474.

Mandler, J. M., & McDonough, L. (1997). Nonverbal memory. In N. L. Stein, P. A. Ornstein, B. Tversky, & C. Brainerd (Eds.), *Memory for everyday and emotional events* (pp. 141–164). Mahwah, NJ: Lawrence Erlbaum Associates.

Mandler, J. M., & Murphy, C. M. (1983). Subjective judgments of script structure. *Journal of Experimental Psychology: Learning, Memory, and Cognition, 9,* 534–543.

Manktelow, K, I., & Evans, J. St. B. T. (1979). Facilitation of reasoning by realism: Effect or no effect? *British Journal of Psychology, 70,* 477–488.

Manktelow, K. I., & Over, D. E. (1990). Deontic thought and the selection task. In K. J. Gilhooly, M. T. G. Keane, & G. Erdos (Eds.), *Lines of thinking* (Vol. 1, pp. 153–164). London: Wiley.

Manktelow, K. I., & Over, D. E. (1991). Social roles and utilities in reasoning with deontic conditionals. *Cognition, 39,* 85–105.

Manktelow, K. I., & Over, D. E. (1992). Obligation, permission, and mental models. In V. Rogers, A. Rutherford, & P. Bibby (Eds.), *Models in the mind* (pp. 249–266). London: Academic Press.

Manktelow, K. I., & Over, D. E. (1995). Deontic reasoning. In S. E. Newstead & J. St. B. T. Evans (Eds.), *Perspectives on thinking and reasoning* (pp. 91–114). Hillsdale, NJ: Lawrence Erlbaum Associates.

Mannetti, L., & Tanucci, G. (1993). The meaning of work for young people: The role of parents in the transmission of a social representation. In G. M. Breakwell & D. V. Canter (Eds.), *Empirical approaches to social representations* (pp. 298–314). Oxford, England: Clarendon Press.

Mantyla, T. (1996). Activating actions and interrupting intentions: Mechanisms of retrieval sensitization in prospective memory. In M. A. Brandimunte, G. O. Einstein, & M. A. McDaniel (Eds.), *Prospective memory: Theory and applications* (pp. 93–113). Mahwah, NJ: Lawrence Erlbaum Associates.

Markham, S. (1996). Unpublished raw data. California State University, Fullerton.

Markman, A. B. (1999). *Knowledge representations.* Mahwah, NJ: Lawrence Erlbaum Associates.

Marks, G., & Miller, N. (1985). The effect of certainty on consensus judgments. *Personality and Social Psychology Bulletin, 11,* 165–177.

Marks, G., & Miller, N. (1987). Ten years of research on the false-consensus effect: An empirical and theoretical review. *Psychological Bulletin, 102,* 72–90.

Markus, H. R. (1977). Self-schemata and processing information about the self. *Journal of Personality and Social Psychology, 35,* 63–78.

Markus, H. R., & Nurius, P. (1986). Possible selves. *American Psychologist, 41,* 954–969.

Markus, H. R., & Ruvolo, A. (1989). Possible selves: Personalized representations of goals. In L. Pervin (Ed.), *Goal concepts in personality and social psychology* (pp. 311–343). Hillsdale, NJ: Lawrence Erlbaum Associates.

Markus, H. R., & Zajonc, R. B. (1985). The cognitive perspective in social psychology. In G. Lindzey & E. Aronson (Eds.), *Handbook of social psychology* (3rd ed., Vol. 1, pp. 137–230). Reading, MA: Addison-Wesley.

Massaro, D. W. (1988). Some criticisms of connectionist models of human performance. *Journal of Memory and Language, 27,* 213–234.

Matthews, M. L. (1978). Discrimination of Identikit constructions of faces: Evidence for a dual processing strategy. *Perception and Psychophysics, 23,* 153–161.

Maurer, D. (1985). Infants' perception of facedness. In T. M. Field & N. Fox (Eds.), *Social perception in infants* (pp. 73–100). Norwood, NJ: Ablex.

Mayer, R. E. (1989). Models of understanding. *Review of Educational Research, 59,* 43–64.

Maylor, E. A. (1990). Age and prospective memory. *Quarterly Journal of Experimental Psychology: Human Experimental Psychology 42A,* 471–493.

McAdams, D. F. (1993). *The stories we live by: Personal myths and the making of the self.* New York: Morrow.

McArthur, L. Z. (1981). Judging a book by its cover: A cognitive analysis of the relationship between physical appearance and stereotyping. In A. H. Hastorf & A. M. Isen (Eds.), *Cognitive Social Psychology* (pp. 149–211). Amsterdam: North Holland/Elsevier.

McArthur, L. Z., & Baron, R. M. (1983). Toward an ecological theory of social perception. *Psychological Review, 90,* 215–238.

McCabe, A., & Peterson, C. (1991). Getting the story: A longitudinal study of parental styles in eliciting narratives and developing narrative skill. In A. McCabe & C. Peterson (Eds.), *Developing narrative structure* (pp. 217–253). Hillsdale, NJ: Lawrence Erlbaum Associates.

McCarthy, G., Puce, A., Gore, J. C., & Allison, T. (1997). Face-specific processing in the human fusiform gyrus. *Journal of Cognitive Neuroscience, 9,* 605–610.

McCarthy, R. A., & Hodges, J. R. (1995). Trapped in time: Profound autobiographical memory loss following a thalamic stroke. In R. Campbell & M. A. Conway (Eds.), *Case studies in memory impairment: Broken memories* (pp. 31–44). Oxford, England: Blackwell.

McClelland, J. L., McNaughton, B. L., & O'Reilly, R. C. (1995). Why there are complementary learning systems in the hippocampus and neocortex: Insights from the successes and failures of connectionist models of learning and memory. *Psychological Review, 102,* 419–457.

McClelland, J. L., & Rumelhart, D. E. (1981). An interactive activation model of context effects in letter perception: An account of basic findings. *Psychological Review, 88,* 375–407.

McClelland, J. L., & Rumelhart, D. E. (1986). A distributed model of human learning and memory. In J. L. McClelland & D. E. Rumelhart (Eds.), *Parallel distribual processing: Explorations in the microstructures of cognition* (Vol. 2, pp. 170–215). Cambridge, MA: MIT Press.

McCloskey, M. (1991). Networks and theories: The place of connectionism in cognitive science. *Psychological Science, 2,* 387–395.

McCloskey, M., & Kohl, D. (1983). Naïve physics: The curvilinear impetus principle and its role in interactions with moving objects. *Journal of Experimental Psychology: Learning, Memory, and Cognition, 9,* 146–156.

McCloskey, M., Washburn, A. & Felch, L. (1983). Intuitive physics: The straight-down belief and its origin. *Journal of Experimental Psychology: Learning, Memory, and Cognition, 9,* 636–649.

McCloskey, M., & Zaragoza, M. (1985a). Misleading postevent information and memory for events: Arguments and evidence against memory impairment hypotheses. *Journal of Experimental Psychology: General, 114,* 1–16.

McCloskey, M., & Zaragoza, M. (1985b). Postevent information and memory: Reply to Loftus, Schooler, and Wagenaar. *Journal of Experimental Psychology: General, 114,* 381–387.

McCollough, W. S., & Pitts, W. (1943). A logical calculus of the ideas immanent in nervous activity. *Bulletin of Mathematical Biophysics, 5,* 115–133.

McCormack, P. D. (1979). Autobiographical memory in the aged. *Canadian Journal of Psychology, 33,* 118–124.

McDaniel, M. A. (1995). Prospective memory: Progress and processes. In D. Medin (Ed.), *The psychology of learning and motivation: Advances in research and theory* (Vol. 33, pp. 191–221). San Diego, CA: Academic Press.

McDaniel, M. A., & Einstein, G. O. (1993). The importance of cue-familiarity and cue-distinctiveness in prospective memory. *Memory, 1,* 23–41.

McDonough, L., & Mandler, J. M. (1994). Very long-term recall in infants: Infantile amnesia reconsidered. *Memory, 2,* 339–352.

McFarland, C., & Ross, M. (1987). The relation between current impressions and memories of self and dating partners. *Personality and Social Psychology Bulletin, 13,* 228–238.

McFarland, C., Ross, M., & DeCourville, N. (1989). Women's theories of menstruation and biases in recall of menstrual symptoms. *Journal of Personality and Social Psychology, 57,* 522–531.

McKoon, G., & Ratcliff, R. (1992). Inference during reading. *Psychological Review, 99,* 440–466.

McPherson, S. L. (1993a). The influence of player experience on problem solving during batting preparation in baseball. *Journal of Sport and Exercise Psychology, 15,* 304–325.

McPherson, S. L. (1993b). Knowledge representation and decision-making in sport. In J. L. Starkes & F. Allard (Eds.), *Cognitive issues in motor expertise* (pp. 159–188). Amsterdam: North-Holland/Elsevier.

Meacham, J. A., & Emont, N. C. (1989). The interpersonal basis of everyday problem solving. In J. D. Sinnott (Ed.), *Everyday problem solving: Theory and applications* (pp. 2–23). New York: Praeger.

Meacham, J. A., & Leiman, B. (1982). Remembering to perform future actions. In U. Neisser (Ed.), *Memory observed: Remembering in natural contexts* (pp. 327–336). San Francisco: Freeman.

Meacham, J. A., & Singer, J. (1977). Incentive effects in prospective remembering. *Journal of Psychology, 97,* 191–197.

Medin, D. L. (1988). Social categorization: Structures, processes, and purposes. In T. K. Srull & R. S. Wyer (Eds.), *A dual process model of impression formation: Advances in social cognition* (Vol. 1, pp. 119–126). Hillsdale, NJ: Lawrence Erlbaum Associates.

Medin, D. L. (1989). Concepts and conceptual structure. *American Psychologist, 44,* 1469–1481.

Medin, D. L., & Ross, B. H. (1989). The specific character of abstract thought: Categorization, problem-solving, and induction. In R. J. Sternberg (Ed.), *Advances in the psychology of human intelligence* (vol. 5, pp. 189–223). Hillsdale, NJ: Lawrence Erlbaum Associates.

Medin, D. L., & Schaeffer, M. M. (1978). Context theory and classification learning. *Psychological Review, 85,* 207–238.

Medvec, V. H., Madey, S. F., & Gilovich, T. (1995). When less is more: Counterfactual thinking and satisfaction among Olympic medalists. *Journal of Personality and Social Psychology, 69*, 603–610.

Meltzoff, A. N. (1990a). Towards a developmental cognitive science: The implication of cross-modal matching and imitation for the development of representation and memory in infancy. *Annals of New York Academy of Science, 608*, 1–37.

Meltzoff, A. N. (1990b). Foundations for developing a concept of self: The role of imitation in relating self to other and the value of social mirroring, social modeling, and self practice in infancy. In D. Cicchetti & M. Beeghley (Eds.), *The self in transition: Infancy to childhood* (pp. 139–164). Chicago: University of Chicago Press.

Meltzoff, A. N. (1995). What infant memory tells us about infantile amnesia: Long-term recall and deferred imitation. *Journal of Experimental Child Psychology, 59*, 497–515.

Meltzoff, A. N., & Moore, M. K. (1977). Imitation of facial and manual gestures by human neonates. *Science, 198*, 75–78.

Meltzoff, A. N., & Moore, M. K. (1983). Newborn infants imitate adult facial gestures. *Child Development, 54*, 702–709.

Meltzoff, A. N., & Moore, M. K. (1994). Why faces are special in infants: On connecting the attraction of faces and infants' ability for imitation and cross modal processing. In B. Boyssum-Bardies, S. De Schonen, P. Juseyk, P. McNeilage, & J. Morton (Eds.), *Developmental neural cognition: Speech and language in the first years of life* (pp. 261–265). Dordrecht, The Netherlands: Kluwer Academic.

Metcalfe, J. (1990). Composite holographic associative recall model (CHARM) and blended memories in eyewitness testimony. *Journal of Experimental Psychology: General, 119*, 145–160.

Middleton, D., & Edwards, D. (1990). Conversational remembering: A social psychological approach. In D. Middleton & D. Edwards (Eds.), *Collective remembering: Inquiries in social construction* (pp. 23–45). London: Sage Publications.

Miller, A. G., Schmidt, D., Meyer, C., & Colella, A. (1984). The perceived value of constrained behavior: Pressures toward biased inference in the attitude attribution paradigm. *Social Psychology Quarterly, 47*, 160–171.

Miller, D. T. (1976). Ego-involvement and attributions for success and failure. *Journal of Personality and Social Psychology, 34*, 901–906.

Miller, D. T., & Taylor, B. R. (1995). Counterfactual thought, regret, and superstition: How to avoid kicking yourself. In N. J. Roese & J. M. Olson (Eds.), *What might have been: The social psychology of counterfactual thinking* (pp. 305–331). Mahwah, NJ: Lawrence Erlbaum Associates.

Miller, G. A. (1956). The magical number seven, plus or minus two: Some limits to our capacity for processing information. *Psychological Review, 63*, 81–97.

Miller, J. G. (1984). Culture and the development of everyday social explanation. *Journal of Personality and Social Psychology, 46*, 961–978.

Miller, L. C., & Read, S. J. (1987). Why am I telling you this? Self-disclosure in a goal-based model of personality. In V. Derlega & J. Berg (Eds.), *Self-disclosure: Theory, research, and therapy* (pp. 35–58). New York: Plenum.

Miller, L. C., & Read, S. J. (1991). On the coherence of mental models of persons and relationships: A knowledge structure approach. In G. J. O. Fletcher & F. Fincham (Eds.), *Cognition in close relationships* (pp. 69–99). Hillsdale, NJ: Lawrence Erlbaum Associates.

Minsky, M. (1975). A framework for representing knowledge. In P. Winston (Ed.), *The psychology of computer vision* (pp. 211–280). New York: McGraw-Hill.

Mischel, W. (1968). *Personality and assessment.* New York: Wiley.

Mitchell, K. J., & Zaragoza, M. S. (1996). Repeated exposure to suggestion and false memory: The role of contextual variability. *Journal of Memory and Language, 35*, 246–260.

Miyake, N., & Norman, D. A. (1979). To ask a question, one must know enough to know what is not known. *Journal of Verbal Learning and Verbal Behavior, 18*, 357–364.

Morris, M. W., & Peng, K. (1994). Culture and cause: American and Chinese attributions for social and physical events. *Journal of Personality and Social Psychology, 67*, 949–971.

Morris, P. E. (1992). Prospective memory: Remembering to do things. In M. M. Gruneberg & P. E. Morris (Eds.), *Aspects of memory, Vol. 1: The practical aspects* (2nd ed., pp. 196–222). London: Routledge.

Morris, P. E., Gruneberg, M. M., Sykes, R. N., & Merrick, A. (1981). Football knowledge and the acquisition of new results. *British Journal of Psychology, 72*, 479–483.

Morris, P. E., Tweedy, M., & Gruneberg, M. M. (1985). Interest, knowledge and the memorizing of soccer scores. *British Journal of Psychology, 76*, 415–425.

Morton, J. (1969). Interaction of information in word recognition. *Psychological Review, 76*, 165–178.

Morton, J., & Johnson, M. H. (1989). Four ways for faces to be 'special.' In A.W. Young & H. D. Ellis (Eds.), *Handbook of research on face processing* (pp. 49–56). Amsterdam: North Holland/Elsevier Science.

Morton, J., & Johnson, M. H. (1991). CONSPEC and CONLERN: A two-process theory of infant face recognition. *Psychological Review, 98*, 164–181.

Moscovici, S. (1961). *La psychoanalyse, son image et son public* [Psychoanalysis: Its image and its audience]. Paris: Presses Universitaires de France.

Moscovitch, M., Winocur, G., & Behrmann, M. (1997). What is special about face recognition? Nineteen experiments on a person with visual object agnosia and dyslexia but normal face recognition. *Journal of Cognitive Neuroscience, 9*, 555–604.

Mullen, B., Atkins, J. L., Champion, D. S., Edwards, C., Hardy, D., Story, J. E., & Vanderklok, M. (1985). The false consensus effect: A meta-analysis of 115 hypothesis tests. *Journal of Experimental Social Psychology, 21*, 262–283.

Mullen, M. K., & Yi, S. (1995). The cultural context of talk about the past: Implications for the development of autobiographical memory. *Cognitive Development, 10, 407*–419.

Murphy, A. H., & Brown, B. G. (1984). A comparative evaluation of objective and subjective weather forecasts in the United States. *Journal of Forecasting, 3*, 369–393.

Murphy, G. L., & Medin, D. L. (1985). The role of theories in conceptual coherence. *Psychological Review, 97*, 289–316.

Murray, H. A. (1938). *Explorations in personality.* New York: Oxford University Press.

Mynatt, C. R., Doherty, M. E., & Tweeney, R. D. (1977). Confirmation bias in a simulated research environment: An experimental study of scientific inference. *Quarterly Journal of Experimental Psychology, 29*, 85–95.

Mynatt, C. R., Doherty, M. E., & Tweeney, R. D. (1978). Consequences of confirmation and disconfirmation in a simulated research environment. *Quarterly Journal of Experimental Psychology, 30*, 395–406.

Nachson, I. (1995). On the modularity of face recognition: The riddle of domain specificity. *Journal of Clinical and Experimental Neuropsychology, 17*, 256–275.

Nakamura, G. V., Graesser, A. C., Zimmerman, J. A., & Riha, J. (1985). Script processing in a natural situation. *Memory & Cognition, 13*, 140–144.

Narby, D. J., Cutler, B. L., & Penrod, S. D. (1996). The effects of witness, target, and situational factors on eyewitness identifications. In S. L. Sporer & R. S. Malpass (Eds.), *Psychological issues in eyewitness identification* (pp. 23–52). Mahwah, NJ: Lawrence Erlbaum Associates.

Navarrete, J. N., Woll, S. B., Sussman, L. J., & Marcoux, S. (1998, April). *Understanding informal reasoning through pro and con arguments.* Paper presented at the meeting of Western Psychological Association. Albuquerque, NM.

Neisser, U. (1962). Cultural and cognitive discontinuity. In T. E. Gladwin & V. W. Sturtevant (Eds.), *Anthropology and human behavior* (pp. 54–71). Washington, DC: Anthropological Society of Washington.

Neisser, U. (1967). *Cognitive psychology.* New York: Appleton-Century Crofts.

Neisser, U. (1976). *Cognition and reality: Principles and implication of cognitive psychology.* San Francisco: Freeman.

Neisser, U. (1978). Memory: What are the important questions? In M. M. Gruneberg, P. E. Morris, & R. N. Sykes (Eds.), *Practical aspects of memory* (pp. 3–24). London: Academic Press.

Neisser, U. (1981). John Dean's memory: A case study. *Cognition, 9,* 1–22.

Neisser, U. (1982a). Snapshots or benchmarks? In U. Neisser (Ed.), *Memory observed: Remembering in natural contexts* (pp. 43–48). San Francisco: Freeman.

Neisser, U. (Ed.). (1982b). *Memory observed: Remembering in natural contexts.* San Francisco: Freeman.

Neisser, U. (1986). Nested structure in autobiographical memory. In D. C. Rubin (Ed.), *Autobiographical memory* (pp. 71–81). New York: Cambridge University Press.

Neisser, U. (1988a). Five kinds of self-knowledge. *Philosophical Psychology, 1,* 35–59.

Neisser, U. (1988b). What is ordinary memory the memory of? In U. Neisser and E. Winograd (Eds.), *Remembering reconsidered: Ecological and traditional approaches to the study of memory* (pp. 356–373). New York: Cambridge University Press.

Neisser, U. (1988c). Time present and time past. In M. M. Gruneberg, P. E. Morris, & R. N. Sykes (Eds.), *Practical aspects of memory: Current research and issues* (Vol. 2, pp. 545–560). Chichester, England: Wiley.

Neisser, U. (1992). The psychology of memory and the sociolinguistics of remembering. *The Psychologist, 5,* 451–452.

Neisser, U. (1994a). Self-narratives: True and false. In U. Neisser & R. Fivush (Eds.), *The remembering self: Construction and accuracy in the self-narrative* (pp. 1–18). New York: Cambridge University Press.

Neisser, U. (Ed.). (1994b). *The perceived self: Ecological and interpersonal sources of self knowledge.* New York: Cambridge University Press.

Neisser, U., & Fivush, R. (Eds.). (1994). *The remembering self: Construction and accuracy in the self-narrative.* New York: Cambridge University Press.

Neisser, U., & Harsch, N. (1992). Phantom flashbulbs: False recollections of hearing the news about Challenger. In E. Winograd & U. Neisser (Eds.), *Affect and accuracy in recall: Studies of "flashbulb" memories* (pp. 9–31). New York: Cambridge University Press.

Neisser, U., & Jopling, J. A. (Eds.). (1997). *The conceptual self in context: Culture, experience, and self-understanding.* New York: Cambridge University Press.

Nelson, K. (Ed.). (1986). *Event knowledge: Structure and function in development.* Hillsdale, NJ: Lawrence Erlbaum Associates.

Nelson, K. (1988). The ontogeny of memory for real events. In U. Neisser & E. Winograd (Eds.), *Remembering reconsidered: Ecological and traditional approaches to the study of memory* (pp. 244–276). Cambridge, England: Cambridge University Press.

Nelson, K. (Ed.). (1989). *Narratives from the crib.* Cambridge, MA: Harvard University Press.

Nelson, K. (1990a). *Narratives from the crib.* Cambridge, MA: Harvard University Press.

Nelson, K. (1990b). Remembering, forgetting, and childhood amnesia. In R. Fivush & J. A. Hudson (Eds.), *Knowing and remembering in young children* (pp. 301–316). New York: Cambridge University Press.

Nelson, K. (1993a). The psychological and social origins of autobiographical memory. *Psychological Science, 4,* 7–14.

Nelson, K. (1993b). Explaining the emergence of autobiographical memory in early childhood. In A. M. Collins, S. E. Gathercole, M. A. Conway, & P. E. Morres (Eds.), *Theories of memory* (pp. 355–385). Hillsdale, NJ: Lawrence Erlbaum Associates.

Nelson, K. (1993c). Developing self knowledge from autobiographical memory. In R. S. Wyer, Jr., & T. K. Srull (Eds.), *The mental representation of trait and autobiographical knowledge about the self: Advances in social cognition* (Vol. 5, pp. 69–77). Hillsdale, NJ: Lawrence Erlbaum Associates.

Nelson, K. (1994). Long term retention of memory for preverbal experience: Evidence and implication. *Memory, 2,* 467–475.

Nelson, K., & Gruendel, J. M. (1981). Generalized event representations: Basic building blocks of cognitive development. In M. Lamb & A. Brown (Eds.), *Advances in developmental psychology* (Vol. 1, pp. 131–158). Hillsdale, NJ: Lawrence Erlbaum Associates.

Neter, J., & Waksberg, J. (1964). A study of response errors in expenditures data from household interviews. *Journal of the American Statistical Association, 59,* 18–55.

Neuberg, S. L. (1989). The goal of forming accurate impressions during social interactions: Attenuating the impact of negative expectancies. *Journal of Personality and Social Psychology, 56,* 374–386.

Neuberg, S. L., & Fiske, S. T. (1987). Motivational influences on impression formation: Outcome dependency, accuracy-driven attention, and individuating processes. *Journal of Personality and Social Psychology, 53,* 431–444.

Neves D. M., & Anderson, J. R. (1981). Knowledge compilation: Mechanisms for the automatization of cognitive skills. In J. A. Anderson (Ed.), *Cognitive skills and their acquisition* (pp. 57–84). Hillsdale, NJ: Lawrence Erlbaum Associates.

Newcombe, F., & de Haan, E. (1994). Category specificity in visual recognition. In M. J. Farah & G. Ratcliff (Eds.), *The neuropsychology of higher level vision: Collected tutorial essays* (pp. 103–132). Hillsdale, NJ: Lawrence Erlbaum Associates.

Newell, A. (1973). Production systems: Models of control structures. In W. Chase (Ed.), *Visual information processing* (pp. 463–526). New York: Academic Press.

Newell, A. (1990). *Unified theories of cognition.* Cambridge, MA: Harvard University Press.

Newell, A., & Simon, H. A. (1972). *Human problem solving.* Englewood Cliffs, NJ: Prentice-Hall.

Newman, L. S., & Uleman, J. S. (1993). When are you what you did? Behavior identification and dispositional inference in person memory, attribution, and social judgment. *Personality and Social Psychology Bulletin, 19,* 513–525.

Newmann, F. M. (1997). Authentic assessment in social studies: Standards and examples. In G. D. Phye (Ed.), *Handbook of classroom assessment: Learning, achievement, and adjustment* (pp. 359–380). San Diego, CA: Academic Press.

Newmann, P. G. (1977). Visual prototype formation with discontinuous representation of dimensions of variablity. *Memory & Cognition, 5,* 187–197.

Nickerson, R. S. (1991). Modes and models of informal reasoning: A commentary. In J. F. Voss, D. N. Perkins, & J. W. Segal (Eds.), *Informal reasoning and education* (pp. 291–309). Hillsdale, NJ: Lawrence Erlbaum Associates.

Nickerson, R. S. (1993). On the distribution of cognition: Some reflections. In G. Salomon (Ed.), *Distributed cognitions: Psychological and educational considerations* (pp. 229–261). New York: Cambridge University Press.

Nigro, G., & Neisser, U. (1983). Point of view in personal memories. *Cognitive Psychology, 15,* 467–482.

Nisbett, R. E. (1993). *Rules for reasoning.* Hillsdale, NJ: Lawrence Erlbaum Associates.

Nisbett, R. E., Borgida, E., Crandall, R., & Reed, H. (1976). Popular induction: Information is not necessarily informative. In J. S. Carroll & J. W. Payne (Eds.), *Cognition and social behavior* (pp. 113–133). Hillsdale, NJ: Lawrence Erlbaum Associates.

Nisbett, R. E., Fong, G. T., Lehman, D. R., & Cheng, P. W. (1987, October). Teaching reasoning. *Science, 238*(4827), 625–631.

Nisbett, R. E., Krantz, D. H., Jepson, C., & Fong, G. T. (1982). Improving inductive inference. In D. Kahneman, P. Slovic, & A. Tversky (Eds.), *Judgment under uncertainty: Heuristics and biases* (pp. 445–459). New York: Cambridge University Press.

Nisbett, R. E., Krantz, D. H., Jepson, C., & Kunda, Z. (1983). The use of statistical heuristics in everyday inductive reasoning. *Psychological Review, 90,* 339–363.

Nisbett, R. E., & Ross, L. (1980). *Human inference: Strategies and shortcomings of social judgment.* Englewood Cliffs, NJ: Prentice-Hall.

Nisbett, R. E., & Wilson, T. D. (1977). Telling more than we can know: Verbal reports on mental processes. *Psychological Review, 8,* 231–259.

Noble, C. E. (1952). An analysis of meaning. *Psychological Review, 59,* 421–430.

Norman, D. A. (1981). Categorization of action slips. *Psychological Review, 88,* 1–15.

Norman, D. A., & Shallice, T. (1986). Attention to action: Willed and automatic control of behavior. In R. J. Davison, G. E. Schwartz, & D. Shapiro (Eds.), *Consciousness and self-regulation* (Vol. 4, pp. 1–18). New York: Plenum.

Northcroft, G. B., & Neale, M. A. (1987). Experts, amateurs, and real estate: An anchoring-and-adjustment perspective on property pricing decisions. *Organizational Behavior and Human Decision Processes, 39,* 84–97.

Nosofsky, R. M. (1987). Attention and learning processes in the identification and categorization of integral stimuli. *Journal of Experimental Psychology: Learning, Memory, and Cognition, 13,* 87–108.

Novick, L. R. (1988). Analogical transfer, problem solving, and expertise. *Journal of Experimental Psychology: Learning, Memory, and Cognition, 14,* 510–520.

Nunes, T., Schliemann, A. D., & Carraher, D. W. (1994). *Street mathematics and school mathematics.* New York: Cambridge University Press.

Nuthall, G., & Alton-Lee, A. (1995). Assessing classroom learning: How students use their knowledge and experience to answer classroom achievement test questions in science and social studies. *American Educational Research Journal, 32,* 185–223.

Oakes, P. J., & Turner, J. C. (1990). Is limited processing capacity the cause of social stereotyping? In W. Stroebe & M. Hewstone (Eds.), *European review of social psychology* (Vol. 1, pp. 111–137) Chichester, England: Wiley.

Oaksford, M., & Chater, N. (1993). Reasoning theories and bounded rationality. In K. I. Manktelow & D. E. Over (Eds), *Rationality: Psychological and philosophical perspectives* (pp. 31–60). London: Routledge & Kegan Paul.

Oaksford, M., & Chater, N. (1994). A rational analysis of the selection task as optimal data selection. *Psychological Review, 101,* 608–631.

Ofshe, R. J. (1992). Inadvertent hypnosis during interrogation: False confession due to dissociative state. Misidentified multiple personality and the satanic cult hypothesis. *International Journal of Clinical and Experimental Hypnosis, 40,* 125–156.

Ofshe, R. J., & Watters, E. (1993). Making monsters. *Society, 30,* 4–16.

Okagaki, L., & Sternberg, R. J. (1993). Putting the distance into students' hands: Practical intelligence for school. In R. R. Cocking & K. A. Renninger (Eds.), *The development and meaning of psychological distance* (pp. 237–254). Hillsdale, NJ: Lawrence Erlbaum Associates.

Orasanu, J., & Connolly, T. (1993). The reinvention of decision making. In G. A. Klein, J. Orasanu, R. Calderwood, & C. E. Zsambok (Eds.), *Decision making in action: Models and methods* (pp. 3–20). Norwood, NJ: Ablex.

Ornstein, P. A., Shapiro, L. B., Clubb, P. A., Follmer, A., & Baker-Ward, L. (1997). The influence of prior knowledge on children's memory for salient medical experiences. In N. L. Stein, P. A. Ornstein, B. Tversky, & C. Brainerd (Eds.), *Memory for everyday and emotional events* (pp. 83–111). Mahwah, NJ: Lawrence Erlbaum Associates.

Oskamp, S. (1965). Overconfidence in case study judgments. *Journal of Consulting Psychology, 29,* 261– 265.

Ostrom, T. M. (1977). Between-theory and within-theory conflict in explaining context efforts in impression formation. *Journal of Experimental Social Psychology, 13,* 492–503.

Ostrom, T. M. (1984). The sovereignty of social cognition. In R. S. Wyer & T. K. Srull (Eds.), *Handbook of social cognition* (1st ed., Vol. 1, pp. 1–38). Hillsdale, NJ: Lawrence Erlbaum Associates.

Ostrom, T. M. (1988). Computer simulation: The third symbol system. *Journal of Experimental Social Psychology, 24,* 381–392.

Ostrom, T. M., Pryor, J. B., & Simpson, D. D. (1981). The organization of social information. In E. T. Higgins, C. P. Herman, & M. P. Zanna (Eds.), *Social cognition: The Ontario symposium* (Vol. 1, pp. 3–38). Hillsdale, NJ: Lawrence Erlbaum Associates.

Oswald, M. (1986). Urterle uber der repraesentativitaetsheurismus [Judgments concerning the representativeness heuristics]. *Archive-fur-psychologie, 138,* 113–125.

Palincsar, A. S. (1989). Less charted waters. *Educational Researcher, 18*(4), 5–7.

Papert, S. (1980). *Mind storms: Children, computers, and powerful ideas.* New York: Basic Books.

Park, B. (1986). A method for studying the development of impressions of real people. *Journal of Personality and Social Psychology, 51,* 907–917.

Park, D. C., & Kidder, D. P. (1996). Prospective memory and medication adherence. In M. A. Brandimonte, G. O. Einstein, & M. A. McDaniel (Eds.), *Prospective memory: Theory and applications* (pp. 369–390). Mahwah, NJ: Lawrence Erlbaum Associates

Patalano, A. L., & Seifert, C. M. (1997). Opportunistic planning: Being reminded of pending goals. *Cognitive Psychology, 34,* 1–36.

Paull, G. C., & Glencross, D. J. (1997). Expert perception and decision making in baseball. *International Journal of Sport Psychology, 28,* 35–56.

Payne, D. G., & Blackwell, J. M. (1998). Truth in memory: Caveat emptor. In S. J. Lynn & K. M. McConkey (Eds.), *Truth in memory* (pp. 32–61). New York: Guilford.

Payne, D. G., Neuschatz, J. S., Lampinen, J. M., & Lynn, S. J. (1997). Compelling memory illusions: the qualitative characteristics of false memories. *Current Depictions in Psychological Science, 6,* 56–60.

Pea, R. D. (1993). Practices of distributed intelligence and designs for education. In G. Salomon (Ed.). *Distributed cognitions: Psychological and educational considerations* (pp. 47–87). New York: Cambridge University Press.

Pea, R. D., & Kurland, D. M. (1984). On the cognitive effects of learning computer programming. *New Ideas in Psychology, 2,* 137–168.

Penfield, W., & Roberts, L. (1959). *Speech and brain mechanisms.* Princeton, NJ: Princeton University Press.

Pennington, N., & Hastie, R. (1986). Evidence evaluation in complex decision-making. *Journal of Personality and Social Psychology, 51,* 242–250.

Pennington, N., & Hastie, R. (1988). Explanation-based decision making: Effects of memory structure on judgment. *Journal of Experimental Psychology: Learning, Memory, and Cognition, 14,* 521–533.

Pennington, N., & Hastie, R. (1993a). Reasoning in explanation-based decision making. *Cognition, 49,* 123–163.

Pennington, N., & Hastie, R. (1993b). A theory of explanation-based decision making. In G. A. Klein, J. Orasanu, R. Calderwood, & C. E. Zsambok (Eds.), *Decision making in action: Models and methods* (pp. 188–204). Norwood, NJ: Ablex.

Pennington, N., & Rehder, B. (1995). Looking for transfer and interference. In D. L. Medin (Ed.), *The psychology of learning and motivation: Advances in research and theory* (Vol. 33, pp. 223–289). San Diego, CA: Academic Press.

Penrod, S. D., & Cutler, B. J. (1995). Witness confidence and witness accuracy: Assessing their forensic relation. *Psychology Public Practice and the Law, 1,* 817–845.

Penrose, J. (1962). *An investigation into some aspects of problem-solving behaviour.* Unpublished doctoral dissertation, University of London.

Pepitone, A. (1999). Historical sketches and critical commentary about social psychology in the golden age. In H. Rodrigues & R. V. Levine (Eds.), *Reflections on one hundred years of experimental social psychology* (pp. 170–199). New York: Basic Books.

Perkins, D. N. (1985a). Post primary education has little impact on informal reasoning. *Journal of Educational Psychology, 77,* 562–571.

Perkins, D. N. (1985b). Reasoning as imagination. *Interface, 16,* 4–26.

Perkins, D. N. (1989). Reasoning as it is and could be. In D. Topping, D. Crowell, & V. Kobayashi (Eds.), *Thinking: The third international conference* (pp. 175–194). Hillsdale, NJ: Lawrence Erlbaum Associates.

Perkins, D. N. (1993). Person plus: A distributed view of thinking and learning. In G. Salomon (Ed.), *Distributed cognitions: Psychological and educational considerations* (pp. 88–110). New York: Cambridge University Press.

Perkins, D. N., Allen, R., & Hafner, J. (1983). Difficulties in everyday reasoning. In W. Maxwell (Ed.), *Thinking: The expanding frontier* (pp. 177–189). Philadelphia: Franklin Institute Press.

Perkins, D. N., Bushey, B., & Farady, M. (1986). *Learning to reason.* (Final report for grant NIE-G-83-0028). Cambridge, MA: Harvard Graduate School of Education.

Perkins, D. N., Farady, M., & Bushey, B. (1991). Everyday reasoning and the roots of intelligence. In J. F. Voss, D. N. Perkins, & J. Segal (Eds.) *Informal reasoning and education* (pp. 83–106). Hillsdale, NJ: Lawrence Erlbaum Associates.

Perkins, D. N., Jay, E., & Tishman, S. (1993). New conceptions of thinking: From ontology to education. *Educational Psychology, 28,* 67–85.

Perkins, D. N., & Salomon, G. (1988). Teaching for transfer. *Educational Leadership, 46*(1), 22–32.

Perkins, D. N., & Salomon, G. (1989). Are cognitive skills context bound? *Educational Researcher, 18*(1), 16–25.

Perkins, D. N., Schwartz, S., & Simmons, R. (1988). Instructional strategies for the problems of novice programmers. In R. E. Mayer (Ed.), *Teaching and learning computer programming: Multiple research perspectives* (pp. 153–178). Hillsdale, NJ: Lawrence Erlbaum Associates.

Perner, J., & Ruffman, T. (1995). Episodic memory and autonoetic consciousness: Developmental evidence and a theory of childhood amnesia. *Journal of Experimental Child Psychology, 59,* 516–548.

Perrett, D. I., Hietanen, J. K., Oram, M. W., & Benson, P. J. (1992). Organization and functions of cells responsive to faces in the temporal cortex. In V. Bruce, A. Cowey, A. W. Young, & D. L. Perrett (Eds.), *Processing the facial image* (pp. 23–30). Oxford, England: Clarendon Press.

Perrett, D. I., Mistlin, A. J., & Chitty, A. J. (1987). Visual neurons responsive to faces. *Trends in Neurosciences, 10,* 358–364.

Perrett, D. I., Rolls, E. T., & Caan, W. (1982). Visual neurons responsive to faces in the monkey temporal cortex. *Experimental Brain Research, 47,* 329–342.

Perris, E. L., Myers, N. A., & Clifton, R. K. (1990). Long-term memory for a single infancy experience. *Child Development, 61,* 1796–1807.

Pezdak, K., & Banks, W. P. (Eds.). (1996). *The recovered memory/false memory debate.* San Diego, CA: Academic Press.

Phillips, L. D. (1983). A theoretical perspective on heuristics and biases in probabilistic thinking. In P. C. Humphreys, O. Svenson, & A. Vari (Eds.), *Analyzing and aiding decision processes* (pp. 525–543). Amsterdam: North-Holland/Elsevier Science.

Phillips, L. D., & Wright, G. N. (1977). Cultural differences in viewing uncertainty and assessing probabilities. In H. Jungermann & G. deZeeuw (Eds), *Decision making and change in human affairs* (pp. 507–519). Amsterdam: D. Reidel.

Phillips, W. A., & Smith, L. S. (1989). Conventional and connectionist approaches to face processing by computer. In A.W. Young & H. D. Ellis (Eds.), *Handbook of research on face processing* (pp. 513–518). Amsterdam: North-Holland/Elsevier Science.

Piaget, J. (1926). *The language and thought of the child.* New York: Harcourt Brace.

Piaget, J. (1950). *The psychology of intelligence.* New York: Harcourt Brace.

Piaget, J. (1952). *The origins of intelligence in children.* New York: International University Press.

Piaget, J., & Inhelder, B. (1971). *Mental imagery in the child: A study of development of imaginal representation.* New York: Basic Books.

Piaget, J., & Inhelder, B. (1973). *Memory and intelligence.* London: Routledge & Kegan Paul.

Pigott, M. A., Brigham, J. C., & Bothwell, R. K. (1990). A field study of the relationship between quality of eyewitnesses descriptions and identification accuracy. *Journal of Police Science and Administration, 17,* 84–88.

Pillemer, D. B. (1992). Remembering personal circumstances: A functional analysis. In E. Winograd & U. Neisser (Eds.), *Affect and accuracy in recall: Studies in "flashbulb" memories* (pp. 236–264). New York: Cambridge University Press.

Pillemer, D. B. (1998). *Momentous events, vivid memories.* Cambridge, MA: Harvard University Press.

Pillemer, D. B., Picarillo, M. L., & Pruett, J. C. (1994). Very long-term memories of a salient preschool event. *Applied Cognitive Psychology, 8,* 95–106.

Pillemer, D. B., & White, S. H. (1989). Childhood events recalled by children and adults. In H. Reese (Ed.), *Advances in child development and behavior* (Vol. 21, pp. 297–340). San Diego, CA: Academic Press.

Platz, S. J., & Hosch, H. M. (1988). Cross-racial/ethnic eyewitness identification: A field study. *Journal of Applied Social Psychology, 18,* 972–984.

Plomin, R. (1998). Genetic influence and cognitive abilities. *Behavioral and Brain Sciences, 21,* 420–421.

Plous, S. (1989). Thinking the unthinkable: The effects of anchoring on likelihood estimates of nuclear war. *Journal of Applied Social Psychology, 19,* 67–91.

Plous, S. (1993). *The psychology of judgment and decision making.* New York: McGraw-Hill.

Polanyi, M. (1966). *The tacit dimension.* New York: Doubleday.

Polanyi, M. (1973). *Personal knowledge.* London: Routledge & Kegan Paul.

Politzer, G., & Nguyen-Xuan, A. (1992). Reasoning about conditional promises and warnings: Darwinean algorithms, mental models, relevance judgments or pragmatic schemas? *Quarterly Journal of Experimental Psychology: Human Experimental Psychology, 44A,* 401–421.

Pollard, P. (1982). Human reasoning: Some possible effects of availability. *Cognition, 12,* 65–96.

Pollard, P., & Evans, J. St. B. T. (1987). Content and context effects in reasoning. *American Journal of Psychology, 100,* 41–60.

Polya, G. (1957). *How to solve it: An aspect of mathematical method.* Princeton, NJ: Princeton University Press.

Pontecorvo, C., & Fasulo, A. (1997). Learning to argue in family shared discourse: The reconstruction of past events. In L. B. Resnick, R. Saljo, C. Pontecorvo, & B. Burge (Eds.), *Discourse, tools, and reasoning: Essays on situated cognition* (pp. 406–442). New York: Springer.

Poon, L. W., Welke, D. J., & Dudley, W. N. (1993). What is everyday cognition? In J. M. Puckett & H. W. Reese (Eds.), *Mechanisms of everyday cognition* (pp. 19–32). Hillsdale, NJ: Lawrence Erlbaum Associates.

Popper, K. R. (1959). *The logic of scientific discovery.* New York: Basic Books.

Potter, J., & Wetherell, M. (1987). *Discourse and social psychology: Beyond attitudes and behaviour.* Beverly Hills, CA: Sage.

Powell, J. L. (1988). A test of the knew-it-all along effect in the 1984 presidential and state-wide elections. *Journal of Applied Social Psychology, 18,* 760–773.

Pylyshyn, Z. W. (1979). Validating computational models: A critique of Anderson's indeterminacy of representation claim. *Psychological Review, 86,* 383–394.

Quattrone, G. A. (1982). Overattribution and unit formation: When behavior engulfs the person. *Journal of Personality and Social Psychology, 42,* 593–607.

Randel, J. M., Pugh, H. L., Reed, S. K., Schuler, J. W., & Wyman, B. (1994). *Methods for analyzing cognitive skills for a technical task.* San Diego, CA: Navy Personnel Research and Development Center.

Read, J. D., Tollestrup, P., Hammersley, R., McFadzen, E., & Christensen, H. M. (1990). Unconscious transference effect: Are innocent bystanders ever misidentified? *Applied Cognitive Psychology, 4,* 3–31.

Read, S. J. (1987). Constructing causal scenarios: A knowledge structure approach to causal reasoning. *Journal of Personality and Social Psychology, 52,* 288–302.

Read, S. J., & Cesa, I. L. (1991). This reminds me of the time when: Reminding in explanation. *Journal of Experimental Social Psychology, 27,* 1–25.

Read, S. J., Jones, D. K., & Miller, L. C. (1990). Traits as goal-directed categories: The role of goals in the coherence of dispositional categories. *Journal of Personality and Social Psychology, 58,* 1048–1061.

Read, S. J., & Marcus-Newhall, A. (1993). Explanatory coherence in social explanations: A parallel distributed processing account. *Journal of Personality and Social Psychology, 65,* 429–447.

Read, S. J., & Miller, L. C. (1993). Rapist or "regular guy": Explanatory coherence in the construction of mental models of others. *Personality and Social Psychology Bulletin, 19,* 526–541.

Read, S. J., Vanman, E. J., & Miller, L. C. (1997). Connectionism, parallel constraint satisfaction, and Gestalt principles: (Re)Introducing cognitive dynamics to social psychology. *Personality and Social Psychology Review, 1,* 26–53.

Read, S. J., & Miller, L. C. (1998a). On the dynamic construction of meaning: An interactive activation and competition model of social perception. In S. J. Read & L. C. Miller (Eds.), *Connectionist models of social reasoning and social behavior* (pp. 27–65). Mahwah, NJ: Lawrence Erlbaum Associates.

Read, S. J., & Miller, L. C. (1998b). Preface. In S. J. Read & L. C. Miller (Eds.), *Connectionist models of social reasoning and social behavior* (pp. vii–xxiv). Mahwah, NJ: Lawrence Erlbaum Associates.

Read, S. J., & Miller, L. C. (Eds.). (1998c). *Connectionist models of social reasoning and social behavior.* Mahwah, NJ: Lawrence Erlbaum Associates.

Reed, S. K., Ernst, G. W., & Banerji, R. (1974). The role of analogy in transfer between similar problem states. *Cognitive Psychology, 6,* 436–450.

Reese, E., & Fivush, R. (1993). Parental styles of talking about the past. *Developmental Psychology, 29,* 596–606.

Reeves, L. M., & Weisberg, R. W. (1994). The role of content and abstract information in analogical transfer. *Psychological Bulletin, 115,* 381–400.

Rehm, J. T., & Gadenne, V. (1990). *Intuitive predictions and professional forecasts: Cognitive processes and social consequences.* New York: Pergamon.

Reich, S. S., & Ruth, P. (1982). Wason's selection task: Verification, falsification, and matching. *British Journal of Psychology, 73,* 395–405.

Reiser, B. J., Black, J. B., & Abelson, R. P. (1985). Knowledge structures in the organization and retrieval of autobiographical memories. *Cognitive Psychology, 17,* 89–137.

Reiser, B. J., Black, J. B., & Kalamarides, P. (1986). Strategic memory search processes. In D. C. Rubin (Ed.), *Autobiographical memory* (pp. 100–121). New York: Cambridge University Press.

Reitman, W. (1965). *Cognition and thought.* New York: Wiley.

Renault, B., Signoret, J. L., Debruille, B., Breton, F., & Bolger, G. T. (1989). Brain potentials reveal covert facial recognition in prosopagnosia. *Neuropsychologia, 27,* 905–912.

Resnick, L. B. (1987a). Learning in school and out. *Educational Researcher, 16*(9), 13–20.

Resnick, L. B. (1987b). *Education and learning to think.* Washington, DC: National Academic Press.

Resnick, L. B. (1991). Shared cognition: Thinking as actual practice. In L. B. Resnick, J. M. Livine, & S. Teasley (Eds.), *Perspectives on socially shared cognition.* Washington, DC: American Psychological Association.

Resnick, L. B., Pontecorvo, C., & Saljo, R. (1997a). Discourse, tools, and reasoning. In L. B. Resnick, R. Saljo, C. Pontecorvo, & B. Burge (Eds.), *Discourse, tools, and reasoning: Essays on situated cognition.* New York: Springer.

Resnick, L. B., Pontecorvo, C., Saljo, R., & Burge, B. (Eds.). (1997b). *Discourse, tools, and reasoning: Essays on situated cognition.* New York: Springer.

Reyes, R. M., Thompson, W. C., & Bower, G. H. (1980). Judgmental biases resulting from differing availabilities of arguments. *Journal of Personality and Social Psychology, 39,* 2–12.

Rhodes, G., Brake, S., & Atkinson, A. P. (1993). What's lost in inverted faces? *Cognition, 47,* 25–57.

Rhodes, G., & Tremewan, T. (1993). The Simon then Garfunkel effect: Semantic priming, sensitivity, and the modularity of face recognition. *Cognitive Psychology, 25,* 147–187.

Rhodes, G., & Tremewan, T. (1994). Understanding face recognition: Caricature effects, inversion, and the homogeneity problem. In V. Bruce & G. W. Humphreys (Eds.), *Object and face recognition: Special issue of Visual Cognition* (pp. 275–311). Hove, England: Lawrence Erlbaum Associates.

Ribot, T. (1882). *Diseases of memory: An essay in the positive psychology* (W. H. Smith, Trans.). New York: Appleton.

Riggio, R. E. (1986). Assessment of basic social skills. *Journal of Personality and Social Psychology, 51,* 649–660.

Rips, L. J. (1983). Cognitive processes in propositional reasoning. *Psychological Review, 90,* 38–71.

Rips, L. J. (1994). *The psychology of proof: Deductive reasoning in human thinking.* Cambridge, MA: MIT Press.

Riskey, D. R. (1979). Verbal memory processes in impression formation. *Journal of Experimental Psychology: Human Learning and Memory, 5,* 271–281.

Roberts, P., & McGinnis, D. (1998, August). *The unexpected expression: Passive memories in everyday life.* Paper presented at the 3rd Practical Aspects of Memory Conference, College Park, MD.

Roberts, P., McGinnis, D., Clark, R., & Reyes, R. (1996, April). *When I smelled that cologne....* Paper presented at the 6th Cognitive Aging Conference, Atlanta, GA.

Robertson, S. P. (1986). Conceptual structure, question-answering processes, and the effects of misleading questions. In J. A. Galambos, R. P. Abetson, & J. B. Black (Eds.), *Knowledge structures* (pp. 145–183). Hillsdale, NJ: Lawrence Erlbaum Associates.

Robertson, S. P., Black, J. B., & Lehnert, W. G. (1985). Misleading question effects as evidence for integrated question understanding and memory search. In A. C. Graesser & J. B. Black (Eds.), *The psychology of questions* (pp. 191–218). Hillsdale, NJ: Lawrence Erlbaum Associates.

Robinson, J. A. (1976). Sampling autobiographical memory. *Cognitive Psychology, 8,* 578–595.

Robinson, J. A. (1986). Temporal reference systems and autobiographical memory. In D.C. Rubin (Ed.), *Autobiographical memory* (pp. 159–188). New York: Cambridge University Press.

Robinson, J. A. (1992). First experience memories: Contexts and functions in personal histories. In M. A. Conway, D. C. Rubin, H. Spinnler, & W. A. Wagenaar (Eds.), *Theoretical perspectives on autobiographical memory* (pp. 223–239). Dordrecht, The Netherlands: Kluwer Academic.

Robinson, J. A., & Swanson, K. L. (1990). Autobiographical memory: The next phase. *Applied Cognitive Psychology, 4*, 321–335.

Robinson, J. A., & Swanson, K. L. (1993). Field and observer modes of remembering. *Memory, 1*, 169– 184.

Roediger, H. L., III. (1991). They read an article?: A commentary on the everyday memory controversy. *American Psychologist, 46*, 37–40.

Roediger, H. L., III. (1996a). Memory illusions. *Journal of Memory and Language, 35*, 76–100.

Roediger, H. L., III. (1996b). Prospective memory and episodic memory. In M. A. Brandimonte, G. O. Einstein, & M. A. McDaniel (Eds.), *Prospective memory: Theory and applications* (pp. 149–156). Mahwah, NJ: Lawrence Erlbaum Associates.

Roediger, H. L., III., Jacoby, J. D., & McDermott, K. B. (1996). Misinformation effects in recall: Creating false memories through repeated retrieval. *Journal of Memory and Language, 35*, 300–318.

Roediger, H. L., III., & McDermott, K. B. (1995). Creating false memories: Remembering words not presented in lists. *Journal of Experimental Psychology: Learning, Memory, and Cognition, 21*, 803–814.

Roediger, H. L., III., Wheeler, M. A., & Rajaram, S. (1993). Remembering, knowing, and reconstructing the past. In D. L. Medin (Ed.), *The psychology of learning and motivation: Advances in research and theory* (Vol. 33, pp. 97–134). San Diego, CA: Academic Press.

Roese, N. J., & Olson, J. M. (1995). Counterfactual thinking: A critical overview. In N. J. Roese & J. M. Olson (Eds.), *What might have been: The social psychology of counterfactual thinking* (pp. 1–55). Mahwah, NJ: Lawrence Erlbaum Associates.

Rogers, T. B., Kuiper, N. A., & Kirker, W. S. (1977). Self-reference and the encoding of personal information. *Journal of Personality and Social Psychology, 35*, 667–688.

Rogoff, B., & Lave, J. (Eds.) (1984). *Everyday cognition: Its development in social context.* Cambridge, MA: Harvard University Press.

Rolls, E. T. (1992). Neurophysiological mechanisms underlying face perception within and beyond the temporal cortical visual area. In V. Bruce, A. Cowey, A. W. Young, & D. L. Perrett (Eds.), *Processing the human face* (pp. 11–21). Oxford, England: Clarendon Press.

Rosch, E. H. (1975). Cognitive representations of semantic categories. *Journal of Experimental Psychology: General, 104*, 192–233.

Rosch, E. H. (1978). Principles of categorization. In E. Rosch & B.B. Lloyd (Eds.), *Cognition and categorization* (pp. 29–48). Hillsdale, NJ: Lawrence Erlbaum Associates.

Rosch, E. H., Mervis, C. B., Gray, W., Johnson, D., & Boyes-Braem, P. (1976). Basic objects in natural categories. *Cognitive Psychology, 8*, 382–439.

Rosch, E. H., Simpson, C., & Miller, R.S. (1976). Structural bases of typicality effects. *Journal of Experimental Psychology: Human Perception and Performance, 2*, 491–502.

Roschelle, J., & Clancey, W. J. (1993). Learning as social and neural. *Educational Psychology, 27*, 435– 453.

Rosenbloom, P. S., Laird, J. E., & Newell, A. (Eds.). (1993). *The Soar papers: Research on integrated intelligences.* Cambridge, MA: MIT Press.

Rosenbloom, P. S., Newell, A., & Laird, J. E. (1991). Toward the knowledge level in Soar: The role of the architecture in the use of knowledge. In K. Van Lehn (Ed.), *Architec-*

tures for intelligence: The Twenty-Second Carnegie-Mellon Symposium on Cognition (pp. 75–111). Hillsdale, NJ: Lawrence Erlbaum Associates.

Ross, B. H. (1987). This is like that: The use of earlier problems and the separation of similarity effects. *Journal of Experimental Psychology: Learning, Memory, and Cognition, 13,* 629–639.

Ross, B. H. (1989a). Distinguishing types of superficial similarity: Different effects on the access and use of earlier problems. *Journal of Experimental Psychology: Learning, Memory, and Cognition, 15,* 456–468.

Ross, B. H. (1989b). Some psychological results on case-based reasoning. In K. Hammond (Ed.), *Proceedings of the second workshop on case-based-reasoning* (pp. 144–147). San Mateo, CA: Kaufman.

Ross, B. H., & Murphy, G. L. (1999). Food for thought: Cross-classification and category organization in a complex real-world domain. *Cognitive Psychology, 38,* 495–553.

Ross, B. M. (1991). *Remembering the personal past: Descriptions of autobiographical memory.* New York: Oxford University Press.

Ross, L. (1977). The intuitive psychologist and his shortcomings: Distortions in the attribution process. In L. Berkowitz (Ed.), *Advances in experimental social psychology* (Vol. 10, pp. 174–221). New York: Academic Press.

Ross, L. (1981). The "intuitive scientist" formulation and its developmental implications. In J. H. Flavell & L. Ross (Eds.), *Social cognitive development* (pp. 1–42). New York: Cambridge University Press.

Ross, L., Amabile, T. M., & Steinmetz, J. L. (1977). Social roles, social control, and biases in social-perception processes. *Journal of Personality and Social Psychology, 35,* 485–494.

Ross, L., & Anderson, C. A. (1982). Shortcomings in the attribution process: On the origins and maintenance of erroneous social assessments. In D. Kahneman, P. Slovic, & A. Tversky (Eds.), *Judgment under uncertainty: Heuristics and biases* (pp. 129–152). New York: Cambridge University Press.

Ross, L., Greene, D., & House, P. (1977). The "false consensus effect": An egocentric bias in social perception and attribution processes. *Journal of Experimental Social Psychology, 13,* 279–301.

Ross L., Lepper, M. R., & Hubbard, M. (1975). Perseverance in self-perception and social perception: Biased attribution processes in the debriefing paradigm. *Journal of Personality and Social Psychology, 32,* 880–892.

Ross L., Lepper, M. R., Strack, F., & Steinmetz, J. L. (1977). Social explanation and social expectation: Effects of real and hypothetical explanations on subjective likelihood. *Journal of Personality and Social Psychology, 35,* 817–829.

Ross, M. (1989). Relation of implicit theories to the construction of personal histories. *Psychological Review, 96,* 341–357.

Ross, M. (1997). Validating memories. In N. L. Stein, P. A. Ornstein, B. Tverskey, & C. Brainerd (Eds.), *Memory for everyday and emotional events* (pp. 49–81). Mahwah, NJ: Lawrence Erlbaum Associates.

Ross, M., & Buehler, R. (1994a). Creative remembering: Construction and accuracy in the self-narrative. In U. Neisser & R. Fivush (Eds.), *The remembered self: Construction and accuracy in the self-narrative* (pp. 205–235). New York: Cambridge University Press.

Ross, M., & Buehler, R. (1994b). On authenticating and using personal recollections. In N. Schwarz & S. Sudman (Eds.), *Autobiographical memory and the validity of retrospective reports* (pp. 55–69). New York: Springer-Verlag.

Ross, M., & Conway, M. (1986). Remembering one's own past: The construction of personal histories. In R. M. Sorrentino & E. T. Higgins (Eds.), *Handbook of motivation and cognition. Vol. 1: Foundations of social behavior* (pp. 122–144). New York: Guilford Press.

Ross, M., McFarland, C., & Fletcher, G. J. O. (1981). The effect of attitude on the recall of personal histories. *Journal of Personality and Social Psychology, 10,* 627–634.

Ross, M., & Sicoly, F. (1979). Egocentric biases in availability and attribution. *Journal of Personality and Social Psychology, 37*, 322–337.

Rossi, P. H., & Nock, S. L. (1982). *Measuring social judgments: A factorial survey approach.* Beverly Hills, CA: Sage.

Rovee-Collier, C., & Bhatt, R. S. (1993). Evidence of long-term memory in infancy. In R. Vasta (Ed.), *Annals of child development* (Vol. 9, pp.1–45). London: Jessica Kingsley.

Rovee-Collier, C., & Shyi, G. (1992). A functional and cognitive analysis of infant long-term retention. In M. L. Howe, C. J. Brainerd, & V. F. Reyna (Eds.), *Development of long term retention* (pp. 3–55). New York: Springer-Verlag.

Rowe, D. C. (1998). Talent scouts, not practice scouts: Talents are real. *Behavioral and Brain Sciences, 21*, 421–422.

Rubin, D. C. (1982). On the retention function for autobiographical memory. *Journal of Verbal Learning and Verbal Behavior, 21*, 21–38.

Rubin, D. C. (1988). Issues of regularity and control: Confessions of a regularity freak. In L. W. Poon, D. C. Rubin, & B. A. Wilson (Eds.), *Everyday cognition in adulthood and late life* (pp. 84–103). Cambridge, UK: Cambridge University Press.

Rubin, D. C. (1996). Introduction. In D. C. Rubin (Ed.), *Remembering our past: Studies in autobiographical memory* (pp. 1–15). New York: Cambridge University Press.

Rubin, D. C. (1998). Beginnings of a theory of autobiographical remembering. In C. P. Thompson, D. J. Herrmann, J. D. Read, D. C. Payne, & M. P. Toglia (Eds.), *Autobiographical memory: Theoretical and applied perspectives* (pp. 47–67). Mahwah, NJ: Lawrence Erlbaum Associates.

Rubin, D. C., & Baddeley, A. L. (1989). Telescoping is not time compression: A model of the dating of autobiographical events. *Memory & Cognition, 17*, 653–661.

Rubin, D. C., & Wenzel, A. E. (1996). One hundred years of forgetting: A quantitative description of retention. *Psychological Review, 103*, 734–760.

Rubin, D. C., Wetzler, S. E., & Nebes, R. D. (1986). Autobiographical memory across the lifespan. In D. C. Rubin (Ed.), *Autobiographical memory* (pp. 202–221). New York: Cambridge University Press.

Rumelhart, D. E., & Norman, D. A. (1982). Simulating a skilled typist: A study of skilled cognitive motion performance. *Cognitive Science, 6*, 1–36.

Rumelhart, D. E., McClelland, J. L, & and the PDP Research Group. (1986). *Parallel distributed processing: Explorations in the microstructure of cognition: Vol. 1. Foundations.* Cambridge, MA: MIT Press.

Rumelhart, D. E., & Norman, D. A. (1978). Accretion, tuning, and restructuring: Three modes of learning. In J. W. Cotton & R. L. Klatzky (Eds.), *Semantic factors in cognition* (pp. 37–53). Hillsdale, NJ: Lawrence Erlbaum Associates.

Rumelhart, D. E., & Ortony, A. (1977). The representation of knowledge in memory. In R. C. Anderson, R. J. Spiro, & W. E. Montague (Eds.), *Schooling and the acquisition of knowledge* (pp. 99–135). Hillsdale, NJ: Lawrence Erlbaum Associates.

Saariluoma, P. (1989). Chess players' recall of auditorily presented chess positions. *European Journal of Cognitive Psychology, 1*, 309–320.

Saariluoma, P. (1991). Aspects of skilled imagery in blindfold chess. *Acta Psychologica, 77*, 65–89.

Sacerdoti, E. (1975). *A structure for plans and behavior* (Tech. Rep. No 109). Stanford, CA: Stanford University. SRI Artificial Intelligence Center.

Salaman, E. (1970). *A collection of moments: A study of involuntary memories.* London: Longman.

Salaman, E. (1982). A collection of moments. In U. Neisser (Ed.), *Memory observed: Remembering in natural context* (pp. 49–63). San Francisco: Freeman.

Salomon, G. (1993a). Editor's introduction. In G. Salomon (Ed.). *Distributed cognitions: Psychological and educational considerations* (pp. xi–xxi). New York: Cambridge University Press.

Salomon, G. (1993b). No distribution without individuals' cognition: A dynamic interactional view. In G. Salomon (Ed.), *Distributed cognitions: Psychological and educational considerations* (pp. 111–138). New York: Cambridge University Press.

Salomon, G. (Ed.). (1993c). *Distributed cognitions: Psychological and educational considerations.* New York: Cambridge University Press.

Salomon, G., & Perkins, D. N. (1989). Rocky roads to transfer: Rethinking mechanisms of a neglected phenomenon. *Educational Psychologist, 24*, 113–142.

Salomon, G., Perkins, D. N., & Globerson, T. (1991). Partners in cognition: Extending human intelligence with intelligent technologies. *Educational Researcher, 20*(3), 2–9.

Salthouse, T. A. (1984). Effects of age and skill in typing. *Journal of Experimental Psychology: General, 113*, 345–371.

Salthouse, T. A. (1986). Perceptual, cognitive, and motoric aspects of transcription typing. *Psychological Bulletin, 99*, 303–319.

Salthouse, T. A. (1991). Expertise as the circumvention of human processing limitations. In K. A. Ericsson & J. Smith (Ed.), *Toward a general theory of expertise: Prospects and limits* (pp. 286–300). New York: Cambridge University Press.

Sanbonmatsu, D. M., Sherman, S., & Hamilton, D. L. (1987). Illusory correlation in the perception of individuals and groups. *Social Cognition, 5*, 1–25.

Sanderson, P. M. (1989). Verbalizable knowledge and skilled task performance: Association, dissociation, and mental models. *Journal of Experimental Psychology: Leaning, Memory, and Cognition, 15*, 729–747.

Sarfert, E. (1911). Zur Kenntnis der schiffahrtskunde der karoliner. *Korrespondenzblatt der deutschen Gessellschaft für Anthropologie. Ethnologie, und Urgeschichte, 42.*

Saxe, G. (1988a). Candy selling and math learning. *Educational Researcher, 17*(6), 14–21.

Saxe, G. (1988b). The mathematics of child street vendors. *Child Development, 59*, 1415–1425.

Saxe, G. (1991). *Culture and cognitive development.* Hillsdale, NJ: Lawrence Erlbaum Associates.

Scardamalia, M., & Bereiter, C. (1991). Literate expertise. In K. A. Ericsson & J. Smith (Eds.), *Toward a general theory of expertise: Prospects and limits.* (pp. 172–194). New York: Cambridge University Press.

Schachtel, E. (1947). On memory and childhood amnesia. *Psychiatry, 10*, 1–26.

Schacter, D. L. (1987). Implicit memory: History and current status. *Journal of Experimental Psychology: Learning, Memory, and Cognition, 13*, 501–518.

Schacter, D. L. (1993). Understanding implicit memory: A cognitive neuroscience approach. In A. F. Collins, S. E. Gathercole, M. A. Conway, & P. E. Morris (Eds.), *Theories of memory* (pp. 387–412). England: Lawrence Erlbaum Associates.

Schacter, D. L. (1995). Memory distortion: History and current status. In D. L. Schacter, J. T. Coyle, G. D. Fischback, M. M. Mesulam, & L. E. Sullivan (Eds.), *Memory distortion: How minds, brains, and societies reconstruct the past* (pp. 1–43). Cambridge, MA: Harvard University Press.

Schacter, D. L. (1996). *Searching for memory: The brain, the mind, and the past.* New York: Basic Books.

Schacter, D. L. (1997). False recognition and the brain. *Current Directions in Psychological Science, 6*, 65–70.

Schacter, D. L., Coyle, J. T., Fischback, G. D., Mesulam, M. M., & Sullivan, L. E. (Eds.). (1995). *Memory distortion: How minds, brains, and societies reconstruct the past.* Cambridge, MA: Harvard University Press.

Schacter, D. L., Norman, K. A., & Koutstaal, W. (1998). The cognitive neuroscience of constructive memory. *Annual Review of Psychology, 49*, 289–318.

Schank, R. C. (1975). *Conceptual information processing.* Amsterdam: North-Holland/Elsevier Science.

Schank, R. C. (1982a). *Dynamic memory: A theory of reminding and learning in computers and people.* New York: Cambridge University Press.

Schank, R. C. (1982b). Reminding and memory organization: An introduction to MOPs. In W. G. Lehnert & M. H. Ringer (Eds.), *Strategies for natural language processing* (pp. 455–493). Hillsdale, NJ: Lawrence Erlbaum Associates.

Schank, R. C. (1990). *Tell me a story: A new look at real and artificial memory.* New York: Scribner.

Schank, R. C. (1994). Goal-based scenarios. In R. C. Schank & E. Langer (Eds.), *Beliefs, reasoning, and decision making: Psycho-logic in honor of Bob Abelson* (pp. 1–32). Hillsdale, NJ: Lawrence Erlbaum Associates.

Schank, R. C., & Abelson, R. P. (1977). *Scripts, plans, goals, and understanding.* Hillsdale, NJ: Lawrence Erlbaum Associates.

Schank, R. C., & Abelson, R. P. (1995). Knowledge and memory: The real story. In R. S. Wyer (Ed.), *Knowledge and memory: The real story. Advances in social cognition* (Vol. 8, pp. 1–85). Hillsdale, NJ: Lawrence Erlbaum Associates.

Schiff, W., Banks, L., & Bordes-Galdi, G. (1986). Recognizing people seen in events via dynamic 'mugshots.' *American Journal of Psychology, 99*, 219–231.

Schliemann, A. D., & Acioly, N. M. (1989). Mathematical knowledge developed at work: The contribution of practice versus the contribution of schooling. *Cognition and Instruction, 6*, 185–221.

Schliemann, A., & Nunes, T. (1990). A situated schema of proportionality. *British Journal of Developmental Psychology, 8*, 259–268.

Schneider, D. J. (1973). Implicit personality theory: A review. *Psychological Bulletin, 79*, 294–309.

Schneider, D. J., Hastorf, A. H., & Ellsworth, P. C. (1979). *Person perception.* (2nd ed.). Reading, MA: Addison-Wesley.

Schoenfeld, A. H. (1982). Beyond the purely cognitive: Belief systems, social cognition, and metacognitions as driving forces in intellectual problems. *Cognitive Science, 7*, 329–363.

Schoenfeld, A. H. (1985). *Mathematical problem solving.* New York: Academic Press.

Schoenfeld, A. H., & Herrmann, D. (1982). Problem perception and knowledge structure in expert and novice mathematical problem solvers. *Journal of Experimental Psychology: Learning, Memory, and Cognition, 3*, 484–494.

Schooler, J. W., Bendiksen, M., & Ambodar, Z. (1997). Taking the middle line: Can we accommodate both fabricated and recovered memories of sexual abuse? In M. Conway (Ed.), *False and recovered memories* (pp. 251–292). New York: Oxford University Press.

Schooler, J. W., & Herrmann, D. J. (1992). There is more to episodic memory than just episodes. In M. A. Conway, D. C. Rubin, H. Spinnler, & W. A. Wagenaar (Eds.), *Theoretical perspectives on autobiographical memory* (pp. 241–262). Dordrecht, The Netherlands: Kluwer Academic.

Schuman, H., & Rieger, C. (1992). Collective memory and collective memories. In M. A. Conway, D. C. Rubin, H. Spinnler, & W. A. Wagenaar (Eds.), *Theoretical perspectives on autobiographical memory* (pp. 323–336). Dordrecht, The Netherlands: Kluwer Academic.

Schuman, H., & Scott, J. (1989). Generations and collective memories. *American Sociological Review, 54*, 359–381.

Schwarz, N. (1996). *Cognition and communication: Judgmental biases, research methods, and the logic of conversation.* Mahwah, NJ: Lawrence Erlbaum Associates.

Schwarz, N., Strack, F., Hilton, D. J., & Naderer, G. (1991). Judgmental biases and the logic of conversation: The contextual relevance of irrelevant information. *Social Cognition, 9*, 67–84.

Scribner, S. (1975). Recall of categorical syllogisms: A cross-cultural investigation of error on logical problems. In R. Falmagne (Ed.), *Reasoning: Process and representation* (pp. 153–173). Hillsdale, NJ: Lawrence Erlbaum Associates.

Scribner, S. (1977). Modes of thinking and ways of speaking: Cultural and logic reconsidered. In P. N. Johnson-Laird, & P. C. Wason (Eds.), *Thinking: Essays in cognitive science*. Cambridge University Press.

Scribner, S. (1992). Mind in action: A functional approach to thinking: *Quarterly newsletter of the Laboratory of Comparative Human Cognition, 14*(4), 103–110.

Scribner, S. (1984a). Studying working intelligence. In B. Rogoff & J. Lave (Eds.), *Everyday cognition: Its development in social context* (pp. 9–40). Cambridge, MA: Harvard University Press.

Scribner, S. (1984b). Toward a general model of practical thinking at work. In S. Scribner (Ed.), *Cognitive studies of work: Special issue of the Quarterly Newsletter of the Laboratory of Comparative Human Cognition, 6*(1–2), 37–41.

Scribner, S. (1985). Knowledge at work. *Anthropology and Education Quarterly, 16*, 199–206.

Scribner, S. (1986). Thinking in action: Some characteristics of practical thought. In R. J. Sternberg & R. K. Wagner (Eds.), *Practical intelligence: Nature and origins of competence in the everyday world* (pp. 13–30). New York: Cambridge University Press.

Scribner, S. (1988, April). *Head and hand: An activity approach to thinking*. Occasional Paper No 3. United States Department of Education.

Scribner, S., & Cole, M. (1973). *The psychology of literacy*. Cambridge, MA: Harvard University Press.

Scribner, S., Gauvain, M., & Fahrmeier, E. (1984). Use of spatial knowledge in the organization of work. *The Quarterly Newsletter of the Laboratory of Comparative Human Cognition, 6*, 32–33.

Searleman, A., & Herrmann, D. J. (1994). *Memory from a broader perspective*. New York: McGraw-Hill.

Seelau, E. P., Seelau, S. M., Wells, G. L., & Windschitl, P. D. (1995). Counterfactual constraints. In N. J. Roese & J. M. Olson (Eds.), *What might have been: The social psychology of counterfactual thinking* (pp. 57–79). Mahwah, NJ: Lawrence Erlbaum Associates.

Seidenberg, M. S. (1993). Connectionist models and cognitive theory. *Psychological Science, 4*, 228–235.

Seidenberg, M. S. (1997). Language acquisition and use: Learning and applying probabilistic constraints. *Science, 275*, 1599–1603.

Seidenberg, M. S., & McClelland, J. L. (1989). A distribual, developmental model of word recognition and naming. *Psychological Review, 96*, 523–568.

Seifert, C. M. (1994). The role of goals in retrieving analogical cases. In J. A. Barnden & K. J. Holyoak (Eds.), *Advances in connectionist and neural computation theory. Vol. 3: Analogy, metaphor, and reminding* (pp. 95–125). New York: Academic Press.

Seifert, C. M., Abelson, R. P., & McKoon, G. (1986). The role of thematic knowledge structures in reminding. In J. A. Galambos, R. P. Abelson, & J. B. Black (Eds.), *Knowledge structures* (pp. 185–210). Hillsdale, NJ: Lawrence Erlbaum Associates.

Seifert, C. M., & Black, J. B. (1983). *Thematic connections between episodes*. Proceedings of the Fifth Annual Conference of the Cognitive Science Society. Rochester, New York.

Seifert, C. M., McKoon, G., Abelson, R. P., & Ratcliff, R. (1986). Memory connections between thematically similar episodes. *Journal of Experimental Psychology: Learning, Memory, and Cognition, 12*, 220–231.

Seifert, C. M., & Patalano, A. L. (1991). Memory for interrupted tasks: The Zeigarnik effect. In *Proceedings of the Thirteenth Annual Cognitive Science Society* (pp. 114–119). Hillsdale, NJ: Lawrence Erlbaum Associates.

Sergent, J. (1984). An investigation into component and configural processes underlying face recognition. *British Journal of Psychology, 75*, 221–242.

Sergent, J. (1989). Structural processing of faces. In A. W. Young & H. D. Ellis (Eds.), *Handbook of research on face processing* (pp. 57–91). Amsterdam: North-Holland/Elsevier Science.

Sergent, J., & Bindra, D. (1981). Differential hemispheric processing of faces: Methodological considerations and reinterpretation. *Psychological Bulletin, 89,* 541–554.

Sergent, J., & Signoret, J. L. (1992). Functional and anatomical decomposition of face processing: Evidence from prosopagnosia and PET study of normal subjects. In V. Bruce, A. Cowey, A. W. Young, & D. L. Perrett (Eds.), *Processing the facial image* (pp. 55–62). Oxford, England: Clarendon Press.

Shafer, G., & Tversky, A. (1985). Languages and designs for probability judgment. *Cognitive Science, 9,* 309–339.

Shaffer, L. H. (1973). Latency mechanisms in transcription typing. In S. Kornblum (Ed.), *Attention and performance* (pp. 435–446). New York: Academic Press.

Shaffer, L. H. (1975). Multiple attention in continuous verbal tasks. In P. M. A. Rabitt & S. Dornic (Eds.), *Attention and performance. V* (pp. 157–167). New York: Academic Press.

Shafir, E. (1993). Choosing versus rejecting: Why some options are both better and worse than others. *Memory & Cognition, 21,* 546–556.

Shaklee, H., & Mims, M. (1981). Development of rule use in judgments of covariation between events. *Child Development, 52,* 317–325.

Shallice, T. (1988). *From neuropsychology to mental structure.* Cambridge, England: Cambridge University Press.

Shallice, T., & Burgess, P. W. (1991a). Higher order cognitive impairments and frontal lobe lesions in man. In H. S. Levin, H. M. Eisenberg, & A. L. Benton (Eds.), *Frontal lobe function and injury* (pp. 125–138). Oxford, England: Oxford University Press.

Shallice, T., & Burgess, P. W. (1991b). Deficits in strategy application following frontal lobe damage in man. *Brain, 114,* 727–741.

Shank, M. D., & Haywood, K. M. (1987). Eye movements while viewing a baseball pitch. *Perceptual and Motor Skills, 64,* 1191–1197.

Shapiro, P. N., & Penrod, S. D. (1986). Meta-analysis of facial identification studies. *Psychological Bulletin, 100,* 139–156.

Sharp, D. W., Cole, M., & Lave, C. (1979). Education and cognitive development: The evidence from experimental research. *Monographs of the Society for Research in Child Development, 44,* 1–2 (Serial No. 178).

Shea, J. B., & Paull, G. (1996). Capturing expertise in sports. In K. A. Ericsson (Ed.), *The road to excellence: The acquisition of expert performance in the arts and sciences, sports, and games* (pp. 321–335). Mahwah, NJ: Lawrence Erlbaum Associates.

Sheehan, P. W. (1988). Memory distortion in hypnosis. *International Journal of Clinical and Experimental Hypnosis, 36,* 296–311.

Sheingold, K., & Tenney, Y. J. (1982). Memory for a salient childhood event. In U. Neisser (Ed.), *Memory observed: Remembering in natural contexts.* San Francisco: Freeman.

Shepherd, J. W. (1986). An interactive computer system for retrieving faces. In H. D. Ellis, M. A. Jeeves, E. Newcombe, & A. W. Young (Eds.), *Aspects of face processing* (pp. 398–409). Dordrecht, The Netherlands: Martinus Nijhoff.

Shepherd, J. W. (1989). The face and social attribution. In A. W. Young & H. D. Ellis (Eds.), *Handbook of research on face processing* (pp. 289–320). Amsterdam, The Netherlands: North-Holland/Elsevier Science.

Shepherd, J., Davies, G., & Ellis, H. D. (1981). Studies of cue saliency. In G. Davies, H. Ellis, & J. Shepherd (Eds.), *Perceiving and remembering faces* (pp. 105–131). London: Academic Press.

Shepherd, J. W., & Ellis, H. D. (1996). Face recall—methods and problems. In S. L. Sporer & R. S. Malpass (Eds.), *Psychological issues in eyewitness identification* (pp. 87–115). Mahwah, NJ: Lawrence Erlbaum Associates.

Shepherd, J. W., Ellis, H. D., & Davies, G. (1982). *Identification evidence: A psychological analysis.* Aberdeen, Scotland: Aberdeen University Press.

Sherman, S. J., & Corty, E. (1984). Cognitive heuristics. In R. S. Wyer & T. K. Srull (Eds.), *Handbook of social cognition* (1st ed., Vol. 1, pp.189–286). Hillsdale, NJ: Lawrence Erlbaum Associates.

Sherman, S. J., & McConnell, A. R. (1995). Dysfunctional implications of counterfactual thinking: When alternatives to reality fail us. In N. E. Roese & J. M. Olson (Eds.), *What might have been: The social psychology of counterfactual thinking* (pp. 199–231). Mahwah, NJ: Lawrence Erlbaum Associates.

Sherman, S. J., Skov, R. B., Hervitz, E. F., & Stock, C. B. (1981). The effects of explaining hypothetical future events: From possibility to probability to actuality and beyond. *Journal of Experimental Social Psychology, 17,* 142–158.

Sherman, S. J., Zehner, K. S., Johnson, J., & Hirt, E. R. (1983). Social explanation: The role of timing, set, and recall on subjective likelihood estimates. *Journal of Personality and Social Psychology, 44,* 1127–1143.

Sherry, D. F., & Schacter, D. L. (1987). The evolution of multiple memory systems. *Psychological Review, 94,* 439–454.

Shiffrin, R. M. (1996). Laboratory experimentation on the genesis of expertise. In K. A. Ericsson (Ed.), *The road to excellence: The acquisition of expert performance in the arts and sciences, sports, and games* (pp. 337–345). Mahwah, NJ: Lawrence Erlbaum Associates.

Shiffrin, R. M., & Schneider, W. (1977). Automatic and controlled information processing: II. Perceptual learning, automatic attending, and a general theory. *Psychological Review, 84,* 127–190.

Shweder, R. A. (1990). Cultural psychology. In R. A. Shweder, J. W. Stigler, & G. H. Herdt (Eds.), *Cultural psychology: Essays in comparative human development.* New York: Cambridge University Press.

Shweder, R. A., & Bourne, E. (1982). Does the concept of the person vary cross-culturally? In A. J. Marsella & G. White (Eds.), *Cultural conceptions of mental health and therapy.* Boston: Reidel.

Simon, H. A., (1956). Rational choice and the structure of the environment. *Psychological Review, 63,* 129–138.

Simon, H. A. (1957). *Models of man: Social and rational.* New York: Wiley.

Simon, H. A. (1973). The structure of ill-structured problems. *Artificial Intelligence, 4,* 181–262.

Simon, H. A. (1983). *Reason in human affairs.* Stanford: Stanford University Press.

Simon, H. A. (1989). *Models of thought* (vol. 2). New Haven, CT: Yale University Press.

Simon, H. A. (1990). Invariants of human behavior. *Annual Review of Psychology, 41,* 1–19.

Simon, H. A., & Chase, W. G. (1973). Skill in chess. *American Scientist, 61,* 394–403.

Singer, J. A., & Salovey, P. (1997). *The remembered self.* New York: Free Press.

Singer, J. L. (1993). Experimental study of ongoing conscious experience. In G. R. Bock & J. Marsh (Eds.), *Experimental and theoretical studies of consciousness* (pp. 100–122). Chichester, England: Wiley.

Singley, M. U., & Anderson, J. R. (1989). *The transfer of cognitive skills.* Cambridge, MA: Harvard University Press.

Sinnott, J. D. (Ed.). (1989). *Everyday problem-solving: Theory and applications.* New York, Praeger.

Skinner, B. F. (1990). Can psychology be a science of mind? *American Psychologist, 45,* 1206–1210.

Skowronski, J. J., Betz, A. L., Thompson, C. P., & Shannon, L. (1991). Social memory in everyday life: The recall of self-events and other-events. *Journal of Personality and Social Psychology, 60,* 831–843.

Skowronski, J. J., Betz, A. L., Thompson, C. P., Walker, W. R., & Shannon, L. (1994). The impact of differing memory domains on event-dating processes in self and proxy reports. In N. Schwarz & S. Sudman (Eds.), *Autobiographical memory and the validity of retrospective reports* (pp. 217–231). New York: Springer-Verlag.

Skowronski, J. J., & Thompson, C. P. (1990). Reconstructing the dates of personal events: Gender differences in accuracy. *Applied Cognitive Psychology, 4,* 371–381.

Slavin, R. T. (1983). When does cooperative learning increase student performance? *Psychological Bulletin, 94,* 429–445.

Sloboda, J. (1991). Musical expertise. In K. A. Ericsson & J. Smith (Eds.), *Toward a general theory of expertise: Prospects and limits* (pp. 153–171). New York: Cambridge University Press.

Sloboda, J. A. (1985). *The musical mind: The cognitive psychology of music.* Oxford, England: Oxford University Press.

Sloboda, J. A. (1996). The acquisition of musical performance expertise: Deconstructing the "talent" account of individual differences in musical expressivity. In K. A. Ericsson (Ed.), *The road to excellence: The acquisition of expert performance in the arts and sciences, sports, and games* (pp. 107–126). Mahwah, NJ: Lawrence Erlbaum Associates.

Slovic, P. (1969). Analyzing the expert judge: A descriptive study of a stockbroker's decision process. *Journal of Applied Psychology, 53,* 255–263.

Slovic, P. (1972). From Shakespeare to Simon: Speculations—and some evidence—about man's ability to process information. *Oregon Research Institute Monograph, 12*(2).

Slovic, P., & Fischhoff, B. (1977). On the psychology of experimental surprises. *Journal of Experimental Psychology: Human Perception and Performance, 3,* 544–551.

Smedslund, J. (1963). The concept of correlation in adults. *Scandinavian Journal of Psychology, 4,* 165–173.

Smith, E. E., Adams, N. E., & Schorr, D. (1978). Fact retrieval and the paradox of intelligence. *Cognitive Psychology, 10,* 438–464.

Smith, E. E., & Medin, D. L. (1981). *Categories and concepts.* Cambridge, MA: Harvard University Press.

Smith, E. E., & Nielson, G. D. (1970). Representation and retrieval processes in short term memory: Recognition and recall of faces. *Journal of Experimental Psychology, 85,* 397–405.

Smith, E. R. (1984). Attributions and other inferences: Processing information about the self versus others. *Journal of Experimental Social Psychology, 20,* 97–115.

Smith, E. R. (1988). Category accessibility effects in a simulated exemplar-based memory. *Journal of Experimental Social Psychology, 24,* 448–463.

Smith, E. R. (1990). Content and process specificity in the effects of prior experiences. In T. K. Srull & R. S. Wyer, Jr. (Eds.), *Content and process specificity in the effects of prior experiences: Advances in social cognition.* (Vol. 3, pp. 1–59). Hillsdale, NJ: Lawrence Erlbaum Associates.

Smith, E. R. (1991). Illusory correlation in a simulated exemplar-based memory. *Journal of Experimental Social Psychology, 27,* 107–123.

Smith, E. R. (1996). What do connectionism and social psychology offer each other? *Journal of Personality and Social Psychology, 70,* 893–912.

Smith, E. R. (1998). Mental representations and memory. In D. T. Gilbert, S. T. Fiske, & G. Lindzey (Eds.), *The handbook of social psychology* (4th ed. Vol. 1, pp. 391–445). New York: McGraw-Hill.

Smith, E. R., & DeCoster, J. (1998a). Knowledge acquisition, accessibility, and use in person perception and stereotyping: Simulation with a recurrent connectionist model. *Journal of Personality and Social Psychology, 74,* 21–35.

Smith, E. R., & DeCoster, J. (1998b). Person perception and stereotyping: Simulation using distributed representations in a recurrent connectionist network. In S. J. Read & L. C. Miller (Eds.), *Connectionist models of social reasoning and social behavior* (pp. 71–109). Mahwah, NJ: Lawrence Erlbaum Associates.

Smith, E. R., & DeCoster, J. (1999). Associative and rule-based processing: A connectionist interpretation of dual process models. In S. Chaiken & Y. Trope (Eds.), *Dual-process theories in social psychology* (pp. 323–336). New York: Guilford.

Smith, E. R., & DeCoster, J. (2000). Dual process models in social and cognitive psychology: Conceptual integration and links to underlying systems. *Personality and Social Psychology Review, 4,* 108–132.

Smith, E. R., & Zarate, M. A. (1992). Exemplar-based model of social judgment. *Psychological Review, 99,* 3–21.

Smith, M. E. (1952). Childhood memories compared with those of adult life. *Journal of Genetic Psychology, 80,* 151–182.

Smolensky, P. (1988). On the proper treatment of connectionism. *Behavioral and Brain Sciences, 11,* 1–74.

Snyder, M. L. (1974). Self-monitoring of expressive behavior. *Journal of Personality and Social Psychology, 30,* 526–537.

Snyder, M. J., & Cantor, N. (1979). Testing hypotheses about other people: The use of historical knowledge. *Journal of Experimental Social Psychology, 15,* 330–342.

Snyder, M. J., & Swann, W. B. (1978). Behavioral confirmation in social interaction: From social perception to social reality. *Journal of Experimental Social Psychology, 14,* 148–162.

Snyder, M. J., & Uranowitz, S. W. (1978). Reconstructing the past: Some cognitive consequences of person perception. *Journal of Personality and Social Psychology, 36,* 941–950.

Snyder, M. L., & Frankel, A. (1976). Observer bias: A stringent test of behavior engulfing the field. *Journal of Personality and Social Psychology, 34,* 857–864.

Snyder, M. L., & Jones, E. E. (1974). Attitude attribution when behavior is constrained. *Journal of Experimental Social Psychology, 10,* 585–600.

Solso, R. L., & McCarthy, J. E. (1981). Prototype formation of faces: A case of pseudo-memory. *British Journal of Psychology, 72,* 499–503.

Spears, R., van der Plight, J., & Eiser, J. R. (1985). Illusory correlation in the perception of group attitudes. *Journal of Personality and Social Psychology, 48,* 863–875.

Spears, R., van der Plight, J., & Eiser, J. R. (1986). Generalizing the illusory correlation effect. *Journal of Personality and Social Psychology, 51,* 1127–1134.

Spellman, B. A, & Holyoak, K. J. (1992). If Saddam Hussein is Hitler, then who is George Bush? Analogical mapping between systems of social rules. *Journal of Personality and Social Psychology, 62,* 913–933.

Spence, D. (1988). Passive remembering. In U. Neisser & E. Winograd (Eds.), *Remembering reconsidered: Ecological and traditional approaches to the study of memory* (pp. 311–325). New York: Cambridge University Press.

Spilich, G. J., Vesonder, G. T., Chiesi, H. L., & Voss, J. F. (1979). Text processing of domain-related information for individuals with high and low domain knowledge. *Journal of Verbal Learning and Verbal Behavior, 18,* 275–290.

Sporer, S. L. (1992). Post-dicting, eyewitness accuracy: Confidence, decision times, and person descriptions of choosers and nonchoosers. *European Journal of Social Psychology, 22,* 157–180.

Sporer, S. L. (1996). Psychological aspects of person descriptions. In S. L. Sporer & R. S. Malpass (Eds.), *Psychological issues in eyewitness identification* (pp. 53–86). Mahwah, NJ: Lawrence Erlbaum Associates.

Sporer, S. L., Penrod, S. D., Read, D., & Cutler, B. J. (1995). Choosing, confidence, and accuracy: A meta-analysis of the confidence-accuracy relation in eyewitness identification studies. *Psychological Bulletin, 118,* 315–327.

Spranka, M., Minsk, E., & Baron, J. (1991). Omission and commission in judgment and choice. *Journal of Experimental Social Psychology, 27,* 76–105.

Squire, L. R. (1987). *Memory and brain.* New York: Oxford University Press.

Squire, L. R. (1995). Biological foundations of accuracy and inaccuracy in memory. In D. L. Schacter, J. L. Coyle, G. D. Fischback, M. M. Mesulam, & L. E. Sullivan (Eds.),

Memory distortion: How minds, brains, and societies reconstruct the past. Cambridge, MA: Harvard University Press.

Srull, T. K. (1981). Person memory: Some tests of associative storage and retrieval models. *Journal of Experimental Psychology: Human Learning and Memory, 7,* 440–463.

Srull, T. K. (1983). Organizational and retrieval processes in person memory: An examination of processing objectives, presentation format, and the possible role of self-generated retrieval cues. *Journal of Personality and Social Psychology, 44,* 1157–1170.

Srull, T. K., & Wyer, R. S., Jr. (1979). The role of category accessibility in the interpretation of information about persons: Some determinants and implications. *Journal of Personality and Social Psychology, 37,* 1660–1672.

Srull, T. K., & Wyer, R. S., Jr. (1980). Category accessibility and social perception: Some implications for the study of person memory and interpersonal judgments. *Journal of Personality and Social Psychology, 38,* 841– 856.

Srull, T. K., & Wyer, R. S., Jr. (1986). The role of chronic and temporary goals in social information processing. In R. M. Sorentino & E. T. Higgins (Eds.), *Handbook of motivation and cognition, Vol. 1: Foundations of social behavior* (pp. 503–548). New York: Guilford.

Srull, T. K., & Wyer, R. S., Jr. (1989). Person memory and judgment. *Psychological Review, 96,* 58–83.

St. Julien, J. (1997). Explaining learning: The research trajectory of situated cognition and the implication of connectionism. In D. Kirshner & J. A. Whitson (Eds.), *Situated cognition: Social, semiotic, and psychological prospectives* (pp. 261–279). Mahwah, NJ: Lawrence Erlbaum Associates.

Stangor, C., & McMillan, D. (1992). Memory for expectancy-congruent and expectancy-incongruent information: A review of the social and social developmental literatures. *Psychological Bulletin, 111,* 42–61.

Stanovich, K. E., & Cunningham, A. E. (1991). Reading as constrained reasoning. In R. J. Sternberg & P. A. Frensch (Eds.), *Complex problem solving: Principles and mechanisms* (pp. 3–60). Hillsdale, NJ: Lawrence Erlbaum Associates.

Starkes, J. L., & Allard, F. (Eds.). (1993). *Cognitive issues in motor expertise.* Amsterdam: North- Holland/Elsevier.

Starkes, J. L., Deakin, J. M., Allard, F., Hodges, N. J., & Hayes, A. (1996). Deliberate practice in sports: What is it anyway? In K. A. Ericsson (Ed.), *The road to excellence: The acquisition of expert performance in the arts and sciences, sports, and games* (pp. 81–106). Mahwah, NJ: Lawrence Erlbaum Associates.

Staszewski, J. J. (1987). *The psychological reality of retrieval structures: A theoretical and empirical investigation of expert knowledge.* Unpublished doctoral dissertation, Cornell University.

Staszewski, J. J. (1988). Skilled memory and expert mental calculation. In M. T. H. Chi, R. Glaser, & M. Farr (Eds.), *The nature of expertise* (pp. 91–128). Hillsdale, NJ: Lawrence Erlbaum Associates.

Stecher, B. M., & Herman, J. L. (1997). Using portfolios for large scale assessment. In G. D. Phye (Ed.) *Handbook of classroom assessment: Learning, achievement, and adjustment* (pp. 491–516). San Diego, CA: Academic Press.

Sternberg, R. J. (1985). *Beyond IQ: A triarchic theory of human intelligence.* New York: Cambridge University Press.

Sternberg, R. J. (1986). *Intelligence applied: Understanding and measuring your intellectual skills.* San Diego, CA: Harcourt Brace.

Sternberg, R. J. (1988). *The triarchic mind: A new theory of human intelligence.* New York: Viking.

Sternberg, R. J. (1996). Cost of expertise. In K. A. Ericsson (Ed.), *The road to excellence: The acquisition of expert performance in the arts and sciences, sports, and games* (pp. 347–354). Mahwah, NJ: Lawrence Erlbaum Associates.

Sternberg, R. J., & Caruso, D. (1985). Practical modes of knowing. In E. Eisner (Ed.), *Learning the ways of knowing* (pp. 133–158). Chicago: University of Chicago Press.

Sternberg, R. J., & Frensch, P. A. (1993). Mechanisms of transfer. In D. K. Detterman & R. J. Sternberg (Eds.), *Transfer on trial: Intelligence, cognition, and instruction* (pp. 25–38). Norwood, NJ: Ablex.

Sternberg, R. J., & Horvath, J. A. (1995). A prototype view of expert teaching. *Educational Researcher, 24*(6), 9–17.

Sternberg, R. J., & Wagner, R. K. (1993). The geocentric view of intelligence and job performance is wrong. *Current Directions in Psychological Science, 2*, 1–5.

Sternberg, R. J., Wagner, R. K., & Okagaki, L. (1993). Practical intelligence: The nature and role of tacit knowledge in work and at school. In J. Puckett & H. W. Reese (Eds.), *Mechanisms of everyday cognition* (pp. 205–227). Hillsdale, NJ: Lawrence Erlbaum Associates.

Sternberg, R. J., Wagner, R. K., Williams, W. M., & Horvath, J. A. (1995). Testing common sense. *American Psychologist, 50*, 912–927.

Sternberg, R. J., & Williams, W. M. (1997). Does the Graduate Record Examination predict meaningful success in the graduate training of psychology? A case study. *American Psychologist, 52*, 630–641.

Stevens, L. J., & Fiske, S. T. (1995). Motivation and cognition in social life: A social survival perspective. *Social Cognition, 13*, 189–214.

Stonham, J. (1986). Practical face recognition and verification with WISARD. In H. D. Ellis, M. A. Jeeves, F. Newcombe, & A. Young (Eds.), *Aspects of face processing.* Dordrecht, The Netherlands: Martinus Nijhoff.

Suchman, L. A. (1987). *Plans and situated action: The problem of human–machine communication.* New York: Cambridge University Press.

Suchman, L. A. (1993). Response to Vera and Simon's situated action: A symbolic interpretation. *Cognitive Science, 17*, 71–75.

Suls, J., & Wan, C. K. (1987). In search of the false-uniqueness phenomenon: Fear and estimates of social consensus. *Journal of Personality and Social Psychology, 52*, 211–217.

Swann, W. B. (1984). Quest for accuracy in person perception: A matter of pragmatics. *Psychological Review, 91*, 457–477.

Takane, Y., & Sergent, J. (1983). Multidimensional models for reaction times and same–different judgments. *Psychometrika, 48*, 393–423.

Tanaka, J. W., & Farah, M. J. (1993). Parts and wholes in face recognition. *Quarterly Journal of Experimental Psychology: Human Experimental Psychology, 46*A, 225–245.

Tanaka, J. W., Giles, M., Kremen, S., & Simon, V. (1998). Mapping attractor fields in face space: The atypicality of bias in face recognition. *Cognition, 68*, 199–220.

Tarr, M. J. (1998, August). *Visual object recognition: Can a single mechanism suffice?* Paper presented at the 106th Annual Convention of the American Psychological Association, San Francisco.

Taylor, B. R. (1992). The effects of counter-factual thought on affect, memory, and belief. *Dissertation Abstracts International, 53*(1–B), 611.

Taylor, S. E. (1981a). A categorization approach to stereotyping. In D. L. Hamilton (Ed.), *Cognitive processes in stereotyping and intergroup behavior* (pp. 83–104). Hillsdale, NJ: Lawrence Erlbaum Associates.

Taylor, S. E. (1981b). The interface of cognitive and social psychology. In J. Harvey (Ed.), *Cognition, social behavior, and the environment* (pp. 189–211). Hillsdale, NJ: Lawrence Erlbaum Associates.

Taylor, S. E. (1982). The availability bias in social perception and interaction. In D. Kahneman, P. Slovic, & A. Tversky (Eds.), *Judgment under uncertainty: Heuristics and biases* (pp. 190–200). New York: Cambridge University Press.

Taylor, S. E., & Crocker, J. (1981). Schematic bases of social information processing. In E. T. Higgins, C. P. Herman, & M. P. Zanna (Eds.), *Social cognition: The Ontario symposium* (Vol. 1, pp. 89–134). Hillsdale, NJ: Lawrence Erlbaum Associates.

Taylor, S. E., & Fiske, S. T. (1975). Point-of-view and perceptions of causality. *Journal of Personality and Social Psychology, 32*, 439–445.

Taylor, S. E., & Fiske, S. T. (1978). Salience, attention, and attribution: Top of the head phenomena. In L. Berkowitz (Eds.), *Advances in experimental social psychology* (Vol. 11, pp. 249–288). New York: Academic Press.

Taylor, S. E., & Pham, L. B. (1996). Mental simulation, motivation, and action. In P. M. Gollwitzer & J. A. Bargh (Eds.), *The psychology of action: Linking cognition and motivation to behavior* (pp. 219–235). New York: Guilford.

Taylor, S. E., Pham, L. B., Rivkin, I. D., & Armor, D. A. (1998). Harnessing the imagination: Mental simulation, self-regulation, and coping. *American Psychologists, 53*, 429–439.

Taylor, S. E., & Winkler, J. D. (1980, September). *Development of schemas.* Paper presented at the 88th Annual Convention of the American Psychological Association, Montreal, Quebec, Canada.

Tesser, A. (1988). Toward a self-evaluation maintenance model of social behavior. In L. Berkowitz (Ed.), *Advances in experimental social psychology* (Vol. 21, pp. 181–227). New York: Academic Press.

Tesser, A., & Campbell, J. (1983). Self definition and self-evaluation maintenance. In J. Suls & A. Greenwald (Eds.), *Social psychological perspectives on the self* (pp. 1–31). Hillsdale, NJ: Lawrence Erlbaum Associates.

Tessler, M., & Nelson, K. (1994). Making memories: The influence of joint encoding on later recall by young children. *Consciousness and Cognition, 3*, 307–326.

Tetlock, P. E. (1985). Integrative complexity of American and Soviet foreign policy rhetoric: A time series analysis. *Journal of Personality and Social Psychology, 49*, 1565–1585.

Tetlock, P. E. (1992). The impact of accountability on judgment and choice: Toward a social contingency model. In M. Zanna (Ed.), *Advances in experimental social psychology* (Vol. 23, pp. 331–376). San Diego, CA: Academic Press.

Tetlock, P. E., & Hannum, K. A. (1983). *Integrative complexity coding manual.* Unpublished manuscript, University of California, Berkeley.

Tetlock, P. E., Hannum, K. A., & Micheletti, P. M. (1984). Stability and change in the complexity of senatorial debate: Testing the cognitive versus rhetorical style hypotheses. *Journal of Personality and Social Psychology, 46*, 979–990.

Teuber, H. L. (1978). The brain and human behavior. In R. Held, H. W. Leibowitz, & H. L. Teuber (Eds.), *Handbook of sensory psychology.* (Vol. 8). Berlin: Springer-Verlag.

Thagard, P. (1989). Explanatory coherence. *Behavioral and Brain Sciences, 12*, 435–502.

Thagard, P., & Kunda, Z. (1998). Making sense of people: Coherence mechanisms. In S. J. Read & L. C. Miller (Eds.), *Connectionist models of social reasoning and social behavior* (pp. 3–26). Mahwah, NJ: Lawrence Erlbaum Associates.

Thomas, J. R., French, K. E., & Humphries, C. A. (1986). Knowledge development and sport skill performance: Directions for motor behavior research. *Journal of Sport Psychology, 8*, 259–272.

Thomas, K. T. (1994). The development of sport expertise: From Leeds to MVP legend. *Quest, 46*, 199–210.

Thompson, C. P. (1982). Memory for unique personal events: The roommate study. *Memory & Cognition, 10*, 324–332.

Thompson, C. P. (1985). Memory for unique personal events: Some implications of the self-schema. *Human Learning, 4*, 267–280.

Thompson, C. P., & Cowan, T. (1986). Flashbulb memories: A nicer interpretation of a Neisser recollection. *Cognition, 22*, 199–200.

Thompson, C. P., Skowronski, J. J., & Betz, A. L. (1993). The rise of partial temporal information in dating personal events. *Memory & Cognition, 21*, 352–360.

Thompson, C. P., Skowronski, J. J., Larsen, S. F., & Betz, A. (1996). *Autobiographical memory: Remembering what and remembering when.* Mahwah, NJ: Lawrence Erlbaum Associates.

Thompson, C. P., Skowronski, J. J., & Lee, D. J. (1988a). Reconstructing the date of a personal event. In M. M. Gruneberg, P. E. Morris, & R. N. Sykes (Eds.), *Practical aspects of memory: Current research and issues: Vol. 1. Memory in everyday life* (pp. 241–246). Chichester, England: Wiley.

Thompson, C. P., Skowronski, J. J., & Lee, D. J. (1988b). Telescoping in dating naturally occurring events. *Memory & Cognition, 16*, 461–468.

Thompson, P. (1980). Margaret Thatcher: A new illusion. *Perception, 9*, 483–484.

Thomson, D. M. (1986). Face recognition: More than a feeling of familiarity? In H. D. Ellis, M. A. Jeeves, F. Newcombe, & A. Young (Eds.), *Aspects of face processing* (pp. 118–122). Dordrecht, The Netherlands: Martinus Nijhoff.

Thomson, D. M., Robertson, S. L., & Vogt, R. J. (1982). Person recognition: The effect of context. *Human Learning, 1*, 137–154.

Thorndike, E. L. (1913). *Educational psychology Vol. 2. The psychology of learning.* New York: Bureau of Publications, Teachers College.

Thorndike, E. L., & Woodworth, R. S. (1901). The influence of improvement in one mental function upon the efficiency of other functions: Functions involving attention, observation and discrimination. *Psychological Review, 8*, 553–564.

Tikhomirov, O., & Poznyanskaya, E. D. (1966). An investigation of visual search as a means of analyzing heuristics. *Soviet Psychology, 5*, 3–15.

Tippett, L. J., Miller, L. A., & Farah, M. J. (2000). Prosopamnesia: A selective impairment of face learning. *Cognitive Neuropsychology, 17*, 241–255.

Tobach, E., Falmagne, R. J., Parlee, M. B., Martin, L. M. W., & Kapelman, A. S. (Eds.). (1996). *Mind and social practice: Selected writings of Sylvia Scribner.* New York: Cambridge University Press.

Toland, H. K. (1990). *True belief in misleading postevent information.* Unpublished masters thesis. University of Washington, Seattle.

Tollerstrup, P. A., Turtle, J. W., & Yuille, J. C. (1994). Actual victims and witnesses to robbery and fraud: An archival analysis. In D. F. Ross, J. D. Read, & M. P. Toglia (Eds.), *Adult eyewitness testimony: Current trends and developments* (pp. 144–160). New York: Cambridge University Press.

Tomkins, S. S. (1979). Script theory: Differential magnification of affects. In H. E. Howe, Jr. & R. Dienstbiener (Eds.), *Nebraska symposium on motivation* (pp. 201–236). Lincoln, NE: University of Nebraska Press.

Torff, B. (1999). Tacit knowledge in teaching: Folk pedagogy and teacher education. In R. J. Sternberg & J. A. Horvath (Eds.), *Tacit knowledge in professional practice: Researcher and practitioner perspectives* (pp. 195–213). Mahwah, NJ: Lawrence Erlbaum Associates

Toulmin, S. E. (1958). *The uses of argument.* Cambridge: Cambridge University Press.

Toyama, J. S. (1975). *The effect of orientation on the recognition of faces: A reply to Yin.* Unpublished doctoral dissertation, University of Waterloo, Ontario, Canada.

Tranel, D., & Damasio, A. R. (1985). Knowledge without awareness: An autonomic index of facial recognition by prosopagnosics. *Science, 228*, 1453–1454.

Trope, Y. (1986). Identification and inferential processes in dispositional attribution. *Psychological Review, 93*, 239–257.

Trope, Y., & Bassok, M. (1982). Confirmatory and diagnosing strategies in social information gathering. *Journal of Personality and Social Psychology, 43,* 22–34.

Trope, Y., & Bassok, M. (1983). Information-gathering strategies in hypothesis-testing. *Journal of Experimental Social Psychology, 19,* 560–576.

Trope, Y., & Liberman, A. (1993). The use of trait conceptions to identify other people's behavior and to draw inferences about their personalities. *Personality and Social Psychology Bulletin, 19,* 553–562.

Tulving, E. (1962). Subjective organization in free recall of "unrelated" words. *Psychological Review, 69,* 349–354.

Tulving, E. (1972). Episodic and semantic memory. In E. Tulving & W. Donaldson (Eds.), *Organization of memory* (pp. 382–403). New York: Academic Press.

Tulving, E. (1983). *Elements of episodic memory.* New York: Oxford University Press.

Tulving, E. (1985a). Memory and consciousness. *Canadian Psychologist, 26,* 1–12.

Tulving, E. (1985b). Synergistic ecphory in recall and recognition. *Canadian Journal of Psychology, 36,* 130–147.

Tulving, E. (1991). Memory research is not a zero-sum game. *American Psychologist, 46,* 41–42

Tulving, E., Schacter, D. L., McLachlan, D. R., & Moscovitch, M. (1988). Priming of semantic autobiographical memory: A case study of retrograde amnesia. *Brain and Cognition, 8,* 3–30.

Tulving, E., & Thomson, D. M. (1973). Encoding specificity and retrieval processes in episodic memory. *Psychological Review, 80,* 359–380.

Turnbull, W. (1981). Naive conceptions of free will and the deterministic paradox. *Canadian Journal of Behavioral Science, 13,* 1–13.

Tversky, A. (1977). Features of similarity. *Psychological Review, 84,* 327–352.

Tversky, A., & Kahneman, D. (1971). Belief in the law of small numbers. *Psychological Bulletin, 76,* 105–110.

Tversky, A., & Kahneman, D. (1973). Availability: A heuristic for judging frequency and probability. *Cognitive Psychology, 5,* 207–232.

Tversky, A., & Kahneman, D. (1974). Judgment under uncertainty: Heuristics and biases. *Science, 185,* 1124–1131.

Tversky, A., & Kahneman, D. (1982). Judgments of and by representativeness. In D. Kahneman, P. Slovic, & A. Tversky (Eds.), *Judgment under uncertainty: Heuristics and biases* (pp. 84–98). New York: Cambridge University Press

Tversky, A., & Kahneman, D. (1983). Extensional versus intuitive reasoning: The conjunction fallacy in probability judgment. *Psychological Review, 90,* 293–315.

Tversky, A., & Krantz, D. H. (1969). Similarity of schematic faces: Test of interdimensional additivity. *Perception and Psychophysics, 5,* 124–128.

Tversky, B., & Tuchin, M. (1989). A reconciliation of the evidence on eyewitness testimony: Comments on McCloskey & Zaragoza. *Journal of Experimental Psychology: General, 118,* 86–91.

Tweney, R. D., Doherty, M. E., Worner, W., Pliske, D., Mynatt, C. R., Gross, K. & Arkkelin, D. (1980). Strategies of rule discovery in an inference task. *Quarterly Journal of Experimental Psychology, 32,* 109–123.

Tyler, S. (Ed.). (1969). *Cognitive anthropology.* New York: Academic Press.

Tyler, S. W., & Voss, J. F. (1982). Attitude and knowledge effects in prose processing. *Journal of Verbal Learning and Verbal Behavior, 21,* 524–538.

Uleman, J. S. (1987). Consciousness and control: The case of spontaneous trait inferences. *Personality and Social Psychology Bulletin, 13,* 337–354.

Uleman, J. S. (1999). Spontaneous versus intentional inferences in impression formation. In S. Chaiken & Y. Trope (Eds.), *Dual-process theories in social psychology* (pp. 141–160). New York: Guilford Press.

Uleman, J. S., Newman, L. S., & Moskowitz, G. B. (1996). People as flexible interpreters: Evidence and inferences from spontaneous trait inference. In M. P. Zanna (Ed.), *Advances in experimental social psychology* (Vol. 28, pp. 211–279). San Diego, CA: Academic Press.

Underwood, B. J., & Schulz, R. W. (1960). *Meaningfulness and verbal learning*. New York: Lippincott.

Usher, J. A., & Neisser, U. (1993). Childhood amnesia and the beginnings of memory for four early life events. *Journal of Experimental Psychology: General, 122*, 155–165.

Valencia, S. W., Hiebert, E. H., & Afflerbach, P. P. (1994). Realizing the possibilities of authentic assessment: Current trends and future issues. In S. W. Valencia, E. H. Hiebert, & P. P. Afflerbach (Eds.), *Authentic reading assessment: Practices and possibilities* (pp. 286–300). Newark, NJ: International Reading Association.

Valentine, T. (1988). Upside-down faces: A review of the effect of inversion upon face recognition. *British Journal of Psychology, 79*, 471–491.

Valentine, T. (1991). A unified account of the effects of distinctiveness, inversion, and race in face recognition. *Quarterly Journal of Experimental Psychology: Human Experimental Psychology, 43*A, 161–206.

Vallone, R., Griffin, D. W., Lin, S., & Ross, L. (1990). Overconfident prediction of future actions and outcomes by self and others. *Journal of Personality and Social Psychology, 58*, 582–592.

van Dijk, T. A., & Kintsch, W. (1983). *Structures of discourse comprehension*. New York: Academic Press.

Vera, A. H., Lewis, R. L., & Lerch, F. J. (1993). Situated decision making and recognition based learning: Applying symbolic theories to interactive tasks. In W. Kintsch (Ed) *Proceedings of the 15th annual conference of the cognitive science society* (pp. 84–95). Hillsdale, NJ: Lawrence Erlbaum Associates.

Vera, A. H., & Simon, H. A. (1993a). Situated action: A symbolic interpretation. *Cognitive Science, 17*, 7–48.

Vera, A. H., & Simon, H. A. (1993b). Situated action: Reply to reviewers. *Cognitive Science, 17*, 77–86.

Von Winterfeldt, D., & Edwards, W. (1986). *Decision analysis and behavioral research*. New York: Cambridge University Press.

Voss, J. F. (1991). Informal reasoning and international relations. In J. F. Voss, D. N. Perkins, & J. W. Segal (Eds.). *Informal reasoning and education* (pp. 37–58). Hillsdale, NJ: Lawrence Erlbaum Associates.

Voss, J. F., Blais, J., Means, M. L., Greene, T. R., & Ahwesh, E. (1986). Informal reasoning and subject matter: Knowledge in the solving of problems by novice and naive individuals. *Cognition and Instruction, 3*, 269–302.

Voss, J. F., Greene, T. E., Post, P. A., & Penner, B. C. (1983). Problem solving skills in the social sciences. In G. Bower (Ed.), *The psychology of learning and motivation: Advances in research and theory* (Vol. 17, pp. 165–213). New York: Academic Press.

Voss, J. F., Perkins, D. N., & Segal, J. (Eds.). (1991). *Informal reasoning and education*. Hillsdale, NJ: Lawrence Erlbaum Associates.

Voss, J. F., Tyler, S. W., & Yengo, L. M. (1983). Individual differences in the solving of social science problems. In R. L. Dillon & R. R. Schmek (Eds.), *Individual differences in cognition* (pp. 205–232). New York: Academic Press.

Voss, J. F., Vesonder, G. T., & Spilich, G. J. (1980). Text generation and recall by high-knowledge and low-knowledge individuals. *Journal of Verbal Learning and Verbal Behavior, 19*, 651–667.

Voss, M. M. (1992). Portfolios in first grade: A teacher's discoveries. In D. H. Graves & B. S. Sunstein (Eds.), *Portfolio portraits* (pp. 17–33). Portsmouth, NJ: Heineman.

Vygotsky, L. S. (1978). *Mind in society*. Cambridge, MA: Harvard University Press.

Wagenaar, W. A. (1986). My memory: A study of autobiographical memory over six years. *Cognitive Psychology, 18*, 225–252.

Wagner, R. K. (1986). The search for intraterrestrial intelligence. In R. J. Sternberg & R. K. Wagner (Eds.), *Practical intelligence: Nature and origins of competence in the everyday world* (pp. 361–378). New York: Cambridge University Press.

Wagner, R. K. (1987). Tacit knowledge in everyday intelligent behavior. *Journal of Personality and Social Psychology, 52*, 1236–1247.

Wagner, R. K., & Stanovich, K. E. (1996). Expertise in reading. In K. A. Ericsson (Ed.), *The road to excellence: The acquisition of expert performance in the arts and sciences, sports, and games* (pp. 189–225). Mahwah, NJ: Lawrence Erlbaum Associates.

Wagner, R. K., & Sternberg, R. J. (1985). Practical intelligence in real-world pursuits: The role of tacit knowledge. *Journal of Personality and Social Psychology, 48*, 436–458.

Wagner, R. K., & Sternberg, R. J. (1986). Tacit knowledge and intelligence in the everyday world. In R. J. Sternberg & R. K. Wagner (Eds.), *Practical intelligence: Nature and origins of competence in the everyday world* (pp. 51–83). New York: Cambridge University Press.

Wagner, R. K., & Sternberg, R. J. (1990). Street smarts. In K. E. Clark & M. B. Clark (Eds.), *Measures of leadership* (pp. 493–504). West Orange, NJ: Leadership Library of America.

Wagner, R. K., Sujan, H., Sujan, M., Rashotte, C. A., & Sternberg, R.J. (1999). Tacit knowledge in sales. In R. J. Sternberg & J. A. Horvath (Eds.), *Tacit knowledge in professional practice: Researcher and practitioner perspectives* (pp. 155–182). Mahwah, NJ: Lawrence Erlbaum Associates.

Waldfogel, S. (1948). The frequency and affective character of childhood memories. *Psychological Monographs, 62*, 1–34.

Wallace, M. A., & Farah, M. J. (1992). Savings in relearning face–name associations as evidence for 'covert recognition' in prosopagnosia. *Journal of Cognitive Neuroscience, 4*, 150–154.

Wallace, W. P. (1980). On the use of distractors for testing recognition memory. *Psychological Bulletin, 88*, 696–674.

Wallsten, T. (1980). Processes and models to describe choice and inference behavior. In T. Wallsten (Ed.), *Cognitive processes in choice and decision behavior* (pp. 215–237). Hillsdale, NJ: Lawrence Erlbaum Associates.

Walter, W. R., Vogt, R. J., & Thompson, C. P. (1997). Autobiographical memory: Unpleasantness fades faster than pleasantness over time. *Applied Cognitive Psychology, 11*, 399–413.

Ward, W. C., & Jenkins, H. M. (1965). The display of information and the judgment of contingency. *Canadian Journal of Psychology, 19*, 231–241.

Warrington, E. K., & James, M. (1967). An experimental investigation of facial recognition in patients with unilateral cerebral lesions. *Cortex, 3*, 317–326.

Wason, P. C. (1960). On the failure to eliminate hypotheses in a conceptual task. *Quarterly Journal of Experimental Psychology, 12*, 129–140.

Wason, P. C. (1966). Reasoning. In B. M. Foss (Ed.), *New horizons in psychology* (Vol. 1, pp.135–151). Harmondsworth, England: Penguin.

Wason, P. C. (1968a). 'On the failure to eliminate hypotheses ...'—a second look. In P. C. Wason & P. N. Johnson-Laird (Eds.), *Thinking and reasoning* (pp. 165–174). Baltimore, MD: Penguin Books.

Wason, P. C. (1968b). Reasoning about a rule. *Quarterly Journal of Experimental Psychology, 20*, 273–281.

Wason, P. C., & Evans, J. St. B. T. (1975). Dual processes in reasoning? *Cognition, 3*, 141–154.

Wason, P. C., & Johnson-Laird, P. N. (1972). *Psychology of reasoning: Structure and content.* London: D. T. Batsford.

Wason, P. C., & Shapiro, D. (1971). Natural and contrived experience in a reasoning problem. *Quarterly Journal of Experimental Psychology, 23*, 63–71.

Watkins, M. J., Ho, E., & Tulving, E. (1976). Context effects in recognition memory for faces. *Journal of Verbal Learning and Verbal Behavior, 15*, 505–517.

Watson, D. (1982). The actor and the observer: How are their perceptions of causality divergent? *Psychological Bulletin, 92*, 682–700.

Webb, N. (1993). *Collaborative group versus individual assessment in mathematics: Group processes and outcomes.* Los Angeles: CRESST/UCLA.

Wegner, D. M., & Bargh, J. A. (1998). Control and automaticity in social life. In D. T. Gilbert, S. T. Fiske, & G. Lindzey (Eds.), *Handbook of social psychology* (4th ed., pp. 436–496). Boston: McGraw-Hill.

Weinberger, H. J., Wadsworth, J., & Baron, R. S. (1983). Demand and the impact of leading questions on eyewitness testimony. *Memory & Cognition, 11*, 101–104.

Weiner, B. (1985). "Spontaneous" causal thinking. *Psychological Bulletin, 97*, 74–84.

Weinstein, L. N., Schwartz, D. G., & Arkin, A. M. (1991). Qualitative aspects of sleep mentation. In S. J. Ellman & J. S. Antrobus (Eds.), *The mind in sleep: Psychology and psychophysiology* (2nd ed., pp. 172–213). New York: Wiley.

Wellington, D. B., Nissen, M. J., & Bullemer, P. (1989). On the development of procedural knowledge. *Journal of Experimental Psychology: Learning, Memory, and Cognition, 15*, 1047–1060.

Wells, G. L. (1978). Applied eyewitness-testimony research: System variables and estimator variables. *Journal of Personality and Social Psychology, 36*, 1546–1557.

Wells, G. L. (1984). How adequate is human intuition for judging eyewitness testimony? In G. L. Wells & E. L. Loftus (Eds.), *Eyewitness testimony: Psychological perspectives* (pp. 256–272). New York: Cambridge University Press.

Wells, G. L. (1993). What do we know about eyewitness identification? *American Psychologist, 48*, 553– 571.

Wells, G. L., & Hryeiw, B. (1984). Memory for faces and retrieval operations. *Memory & Cognition, 12*, 338–344.

Wells, G. L., & Lindsay, R. C. (1985). Methodological notes in the accuracy-confidence relation in eyewitness identifications. *Journal of Applied Psychology, 70*, 413–419.

Wells, G. L., & Loftus, E. F. (1984). Eyewitness research: Then and now. In G. L. Wells & E. F. Loftus (Eds.), *Eyewitness testimony: Psychological perspectives* (pp. 1–11). New York: Cambridge University Press.

Wells, G. L. & Loftus, E. F. (Eds.). (1984). *Eyewitness testimony: Psychological perspectives.* (pp. 256–272). New York: Cambridge University Press.

Wells, G. L., & Turtle, J. W. (1986). Eyewitness identification: The importance of lineup models. *Psychological Bulletin, 99*, 320–329.

Wenger, E. (1998). *Communities of practice: Learning, meaning, and identity.* New York: Cambridge University Press.

Wertsch, J. V. (Ed.) (1981). *The concept of activity in Soviet psychology.* Armonk, NY: Sharpe.

West, R. F., Stanovich, K. E., & Mitchell, H. R. (1993). Reading in the real world and its correlates. *Reading Research Quarterly, 28*, 35–50.

Wetherick, N. E. (1962). Elimination and enumerative behavior in a conceptual task. *Quarterly Journal of Experimental Psychology, 14*, 246–249.

Wetzler, S. E., & Sweeney, J. A. (1986a). Childhood amnesia: A conceptualization in cognitive-psychological terms. *Journal of the American Psychoanalytic Association, 34*, 663–685.

Wetzler, S. E., & Sweeney, J. A. (1986b). Childhood amnesia: An empirical demonstration. In D. C. Rubin (Ed.), *Autobiographical memory* (pp. 191–201). New York: Cambridge University Press.

Wharton, C. M, Cheng, P. W., & Wickens, T. D. (1993). Hypothesis-testing strategies: Why two goals are better than one. *Quarterly Journal of Experimental Psychology: Human Experimental Psychology, 46*A, 743–758.

White, R. T. (1982). Memory for personal events. *Human Learning, 1,* 171–183.

White, R. T. (1989). Recall of autobiographical events. *Applied Cognitive Psychology, 3,* 127–135.

White, S. H., & Pillemer, D. B. (1979). Childhood amnesia and the development of a socially accessible memory system. In J. F. Kihlstrom & F. J. Evans (Eds.), *Functional disorders of memory* (pp. 29–73). Hillsdale, NJ: Lawrence Erlbaum Associates.

Whitehead, A. N. (1929). *The aims of education.* Cambridge, England: Cambridge University Press.

Whittlesea, B. W., & Dorken, M. D. (1993). Incidentally, things in general are particularly determined: An episodic processing account of implicit learning. *Journal of Experimental Psychology: General, 122,* 227–248.

Wiggins, G. (1989). Teaching to the (authentic) test. *Educational Leadership, 46*(7), 41–47.

Wilensky, R. (1983). *Planning and understanding: A computational approach to human reasoning.* Reading, MA: Addison-Wesley.

Wilkes, A. L., & Letherbarrow, M. (1988). Editing episodic memory following the identification of error. *Quarterly Journal of Experimental Psychology: Human Experimental Psychology, 40A,* 361–387.

Wilkes, A. L., & Reynolds, D. J. (1999). On certain limitations accompanying readers' interpretations of corrections in episodic text. *Quarterly Journal of Experimental Psychology: Human Experimental Psychology, 52A,* 165–183.

Wilkins, A. J., & Baddeley, A. D. (1978). Remembering to recall in everyday life: An approach to absentimindedness. In M. M. Gruneberg, P. E. Morris, & R. N. Sykes (Eds.), *Practical aspects of memory* (pp. 27–34). London: Academic Press.

Williams, D. M., & Hollan, J. D. (1981). The process of retrieval from very long term memory. *Cognitive Science, 5,* 87–119.

Williams, D. M., & Santos-Williams, S. M. (1980). A method for exploring retrieval processes using verbal protocols. In R. S. Nickerson (Ed.), *Attention and Performance, VIII* (pp. 671–689). Hillsdale, NJ: Lawrence Erlbaum Associates.

Willis, S. L., & Schai, K. W. (1993). Everyday memory: Taxonomic and methodological considerations. In J. M. Puckett, & H. W. Reese (Eds.), *Mechanisms of everyday cognition* (pp. 33–53). Hillsdale, NJ: Lawrence Erlbaum Associates.

Wilson, K., & Woll, S. B. (2000, April). *Pro and con arguments as a measure of informal reasoning.* Paper presented at convention of Western Psychological Association, Portland, OR.

Wilson, T. O., Houston, C. E., Etting, K. M., & Brekke, N. (1996). A new look at anchoring effects: Basic anchoring and its antecedents. *Journal of Experimental Psychology: General, 125,* 387–402.

Wineberg, S. S. (1989). Remembrance of theories past. *Educational Researcher, 18*(4), 7–10.

Winograd, E. (1976). Recognition memory for faces following nine different judgments. *Bulletin of the Psychonomic Society, 8,* 419–421.

Winograd, E. (1988). Some observation on prospective remembering. In M. M. Gruneberg, P. E. Morris, & R. N. Sykes (Eds.), *Practical aspects of memory: Current research and issues. Vol. 1: Memory in everyday life* (pp. 349–353). Chichester: England. Wiley.

Winograd, E., & Killinger, W. A. (1983). Relating age at encoding in early childhood to adult recall: Development of flashbulb memories. *Journal of Experimental Psychology: General, 112,* 413–422.

Winograd, E., & Rivers-Bulkeley, N. T. (1977). Effects of changing context on remembering faces. *Journal of Experimental Psychology: Human Learning and Memory, 3,* 397–405.

Winograd, T., & Flores, F. (1986). *Understanding computers and cognition: A new foundation for design.* Norwood, NJ: Ablex.

Winter, L., & Uleman, J. S. (1984). When are social judgments made? Evidence for the spontaneousness of trait inferences. *Journal of Personality and Social Psychology, 47,* 237–252.

Woll, S. B. (2000). *Social cognition and autobiographical memory: Two divergent approaches to the representation of the self.* Manuscript in preparation, California State University, Fullerton.

Woll, S. B., & Breitenbach, L. (1998, April). *Flashbulb memories for the death of Princess Diana.* Paper presented at the Western Psychological Association convention, Albuquerque, NM.

Woll, S. B., & Clark, L. F. (1989). *The relative impact of scripts and person schemas on social information processing.* Unpublished manuscript. California State University, Fullerton.

Woll, S. B., & Cozby, P. C. (1987). Videodating and other alternatives to traditional methods of relationship initiation. In W. H. Jones & D. Perlman (Eds.), *Advances in personal relationships* (Vol. 1, pp. 69–108). Greenwich, CT: JAI Press.

Woll, S. B., & Graesser, A. C. (1982). Memory discrimination for information typical or atypical of person schemata. *Social Cognition, 1*, 287–310.

Woll, S. B., Kernes, J., Wentsel, C., & Raymond, T. (1992). The effects of political expertise, ideology, and issue on political reasoning. *International Journal of Psychology, 27(3/4)*, 274.

Woll, S. B., & Loukides, Z. (2000). *Components and correlates of political expertise.* Manuscript submitted for publication.

Woll, S. B., Navarrete, J. B., Marcoux, S., & Sussman, L. J. (1998, April). *Understanding informal reasoning using pro and con arguments.* Paper presented at the Western Psychological Association Convention, Albuquerque, NM.

Woll, S. B., & Van Der Meer, A. (1996). *Impression formation in a naturalistic context: The role of processing goals and stimulus characteristics in videodating.* Unpublished manuscript, California State University, Fullerton.

Woll, S. B., Weeks, D. G., Fraps, C. L., Pendergrass, J., & Vanderplas, M. A. (1980). Role of sentence context in the encoding of trait descriptors. *Journal of Personality and Social Psychology, 39*, 59–68.

Wood, D., Bruner, J. S., & Ross, G. (1976). The role of tutoring in problem solving. *Journal of Child Psychology and Psychiatry, 17*, 89–100.

Woodhead, M. M., Baddeley, A. D., & Simmonds, D. C. V. (1979). On training people to recognise faces. *Ergonomics, 22*, 333–343.

Woods, D. D. (1993). Process tracing methods for the study of cognition outside the experimental psychology laboratory. In G. A. Klein, J. Orasanu, R. Calderwood, & C. E. Zsambok (Eds.), *Decision makers in action: Models and methods* (pp. 228–251). Norwood, NJ: Ablex.

Wright, E. F., & Wells, G. L. (1988). Is the attitude-attribution paradigm suitable for investigating the disposition bias? *Personality and Social Psychology Bulletin, 14*, 183–190.

Wyer, R. S. Jr., (1989). Social memory and social judgment. In P. R. Solomon, G. R. Goethals, C. M. Kelley, & B. R. Stephens (Eds.), *Memory: Interdisciplinary approaches* (pp. 243–270) New York: Springer-Verlag.

Wyer, R. S., Jr., Bodenhausen, G. V., & Srull, T. K. (1984). The cognitive representation of persons and groups and its effect on recall and recognition memory. *Journal of Experimental Social Psychology, 20*, 445–469.

Wyer, R. S., & Carlston, D. E. (1994). The cognitive representation of persons and events. In R. S. Wyer & T. K. Srull (Eds.), *Handbook of social cognition* (2nd ed., pp. 41–98). Hillsdale, NJ: Lawrence Erlbaum Associates.

Wyer, R. S., & Gordon, S. E. (1982). The recall of information about persons and groups. *Journal of Experimental Social Psychology, 18*, 1–28.

Wyer, R. S., Jr., Lambert, A. J., Budesheim, T. L., & Gruenfeld, D. H. (1992). Theory and research on person impression formation: A look to the future. In L. L. Martin & A.

Tesser (Eds.), *The construction of social judgments* (pp. 3–36). Hillsdale, NJ: Lawrence Erlbaum Associates.

Wyer, R. S., & Martin, L. L. (1986). Person memory: The role of traits, group stereotypes, and specific behaviors in the cognitive representation of persons. *Journal of Personality and Social Psychology, 50,* 661–675.

Wyer, R. S., & Radvansky, G. A. (1999). The comprehension and validation of social information. *Psychological Review, 106,* 89–118.

Wyer, R. S., & Srull, T. (1989). *Memory and cognition in its social context.* Hillsdale, NJ: Lawrence Erlbaum Associates.

Wyer, R. S., & Srull, T. K. (Eds.). (1994). *Handbook of social cognition, Vol. 2: Applications* (2nd ed.). Hillsdale, NJ: Lawrence Erlbaum Associates.

Yachanin, S. A., & Tweney, R. D. (1982). The effect of thematic content on cognitive strategies in the four-card selection task. *Bulletin of the Psychonomic Society, 19,* 87–90.

Yamane, S., Kaji, S., & Kawano, K. (1988). What facial features activate face neurons in the inferotemporal cortex? *Experimental Brain Research, 23,* 209–214.

Yaniv, I., & Meyer, D. E. (1987). Activation and metacognition of inaccessible stored information: Potential bases for incubation effects in problem solving. *Journal of Experimental Psychology: Learning, Memory, and Cognition, 13,* 187–205.

Yarmey, A. D. (1994). Earwitness evidence: Memory for a perpetrator's voice. In D. F. Ross, J. D. Read, & M. Toglia (Eds.), *Adult eyewitness testimony: Current trends and developments* (pp. 101–124). New York: Cambridge University Press.

Yin, R. K. (1969). Looking at upside-down faces. *Journal of Experimental Psychology, 81,* 141–145.

Yin, R. K. (1970). Face recognition by brain-injured patients: A dissociable ability? *Neuropsychologia, 8,* 395–402.

Young, A. W., & Bion, P. J. (1980). Absence of any developmental trends in right hemisphere superiority for face recognition. *Cortex, 16,* 213–221.

Young, A. W., & Bion, P. J. (1981). Accuracy of naming laterally presented known faces by children and adult. *Cortex, 17,* 97–106.

Young, A. W., & de Haan, E. H. (1988). Boundaries of covert recognition in prosopagnosia. *Cognitive Neuropsychology, 5,* 317–336.

Young A. W., & Ellis, H. D. (1989). Semantic processing. In A. W. Young & H. D. Ellis (Eds.), *Handbook of research in face processing* (pp. 235–262). Amsterdam: North-Holland/Elsevier Science.

Young, A. W., Hay, D. C., & Ellis, A. W. (1985a). The faces that launched a thousand slips: Everyday difficulties and errors in recognizing people. *British Journal of Psychology, 76,* 495–523.

Young, A. W., Hay, D. C., & Ellis, A. W. (1985b). Getting semantic information from familiar faces. In H. D. Ellis, M. A. Jeeves, F. Newcombe, & A. W. Young (Eds.), *Aspects of face processing* (pp. 123–135). Dordrecht, The Netherlands: Martinus Nijhoff.

Young, A. W., Hay, D. C., McWeeny, K. H., Flude, B. M., & Ellis, A. W. (1985). Matching familiar and unfamiliar faces on internal and external features. *Perception, 14,* 737–746.

Young, A. W., Hellawell, D., & Hay, D. C. (1987). Configural information in face perception. *Perception, 16,* 747–759.

Young, A. W., McWeeny, K. H., Hay, D. C., & Ellis, A. W. (1986). Access to identity-specific semantic codes from familiar faces. *Quarterly Journal of Experimental Psychology: Human Experimental Psychology, 38A,* 271–295.

Yuille, J. C. (1986). Meaningful research in the police context. In J. Yuille (Ed.), *Police selection and training: The role of psychology* (pp. 224–243). Dordrecht, The Netherlands: Martinus Nijhoff.

Yuille, J. C. (1993). We must study forensic eyewitnesses to know about them. *American Psychologist, 48*, 572–573.

Yuille, J. C., & Cutshall, J. (1986). A case study of eyewitness of a crime. *Journal of Applied Psychology, 71*, 291–301.

Yuille, J. C., & Kim, C. K. (1987). A field study of the forensic use of hypnosis. *Canadian Journal of Behavioral Psychology, 19*, 418–429.

Zaragoza, M. S., & Koshmider, J. W. (1989). Misled subjects may know more than their performance implies. *Journal of Experimental Psychology: Learning, Memory, and Cognition, 15*, 246–255.

Zaragoza, M. S., & McCloskey, M. (1989). Misleading postevent information and the memory impairment hypothesis: Comment on Belli and reply to Tversky & Tuchin. *Journal of Experimental Psychology: General, 118*, 92–99.

Zaragoza, M. S., McCloskey, M., & Jamis, M. (1987). Misleading postevent information and recall of the original event: Further evidence against the memory impairment hypothesis. *Journal of Experimental Psychology: Learning, Memory, and Cognition, 13*, 36–44.

Zebrowitz, L. A. (1990). *Social perception.* Pacific Grove, CA: Brooks/Cole.

Zsambok, C. E. (1997). Naturalistic decision making: Where are we now? In C. E. Zsambok & G. Klein (Eds.), *Naturalistic decision making* (pp. 3–16). Mahwah, NJ: Lawrence Erlbaum Associates.

Zsambok, C. E., & Klein, G. A. (Eds.). (1997). *Naturalistic decision making.* Mahwah, NJ: Lawrence Erlbaum Associates.

Zukier, H. (1986). The paradigmatic and narrative modes in goal-guided inference. In R. M. Sorrentino & E. T. Higgins (Eds.), *Handbook of motivation and cognition: Vol. 1 Foundations of social behavior* (pp. 465–502). New York: Guilford.

Zwaan, R. A., Langston, M. C., & Graesser, A. C. (1995). Dimensions of situation model construction in narrative comprehension: An event indexing model. *Psychological Science, 6*, 292–297.

Zwaan, R. A., & Radvansky, G. A. (1998). Situation models in language comprehension and memory. *Psychological Bulletin, 123*, 16–185.

Author Index

A

Abelson, R. P., 28, 35, 57, 131, 132, 133, 136, 137, 138, 139, 145, 146, 147, 148, 176, 229, 230, 231, 233, 234, 236, 241, 256, 265, 269, 382, 440, 496, 497, 503, *509, 534, 549, 566, 571, 572*
Abernethy, B., 280, *509*
Acioly, N. M., 321, 333, 335, 336, 337, 339, *571*
Adams, N. E., 277, *575*
Afflerbach, P. P., 457, *582*
Agre, P. E., 446, 447, 450, *510*
Ahwesh, E., 271, 462, 463, 464, 474, *582*
Ajzen, I., 374, 401, *510*
Alba, J. W., 34, 36, 64, 145, 191, *510*
Alexander, J. F., 126, *550*
Allard, F., 279, 281, 284, *510, 577*
Allen, R., 459, 460, *563*
Allison, T., 93, *555*
Alloy, L. B., 389, 392, *510, 546*
Allport, G. W., 47, *510*
Alton-Lee, A. 10, *569*
Amabile, T. M., 52, 387, 409, 411, *510, 544, 568*
Ambodar, Z., 155, *571*
Ancess, J., 455, *526*
Andersen, S. M., 48, 59, 68, *510*
Anderson, C. A., 32, 33, 59, 295, 300, 416, 417, *510, 567*

Anderson, J. R., 31, 32, 33, 274, 294, 295, 296, 299, 300, 301, 302, 304, 311, 399, 417, 447, 450, 505, *510, 511, 551, 560, 574*
Anderson, N. H., 47, 52, 85, *511*
Anderson, S. J., 212, 229, 232, 234, 239, 240, 241, 242, 249, 263, 267, 268, 505, *511, 524*
Andrews, B., 194, *517*
Angel, R. B., 462, *511*
Arai, Y., 200, *515*
Arbib, M. A., 40, *511*
Arkes, H. R., 422, *511*
Arkin, A. M., 190, *583*
Arkkelin, D., 386, *580*
Armor, D. A., 381, 578
Aronson, E., 14, 420, *511*
Asch, S. E., 47, 52, 60, 61, 64, 65, 76, 496, 507, *511*
Atkins, J. L., 415, *558*
Atkinson, A. P., 92, 97, *566*
Atkinson, R. C., 18, 37, *511*
Austin, G. A., xi, 384, 395, 398, *511, 519*

B

Baddeley, A. D., 13, 17, 26, 27, 99, 123, 163, 185, 186, 187, 190, 202, 207, 228, 447, *511, 512, 537, 568, 569, 586*
Bahrick, A. S., 121, *512*

589

Subject Index

A

Accessibility effect, *see* Eyewitness memory

Accessibility principle, *see* Autobiographical memory, dating

Accretion, *see* Skill acquisition, schema view

ACT*, *see* Procedural or production systems model

Action-trigger schema, *see* Schema model

Activity dominance viewpoint 229–233, 243–246, 490, 503, *see also* Autobiographical memory, organization, and Context-plus-index model

activities versus actions or categorical cues 230

failures to recall in 243–244

initial studies of 231–232

Activity theory, *see* Soviet activity theory

Actor-observer effect 409, *see also* Fundamental attribution error

Adaptive control of thought (ACT*) model, *see* Procedural or production systems model

Adaptive rationality, *see* Rationality, types of

Affordances 496

Amnesiacs 227–228, 240, 499, *see also* Childhood amnesia, and Prosopagnosia

A-MOPs, *see* Autobiographical memory, organization of

Analogue studies 499, *see also* Continuum model, experimental microcosms, and Eyewitness memory, for events

Analogy, *see* Skill acquisition, proceduralization account, and Connectionist model of impression formation

Anchoring and adjustment heuristic, *see* Judgment heuristics

Anchored instruction, *see* Situated cognition

Analogy, role of, *see* IMP model, and Transfer of training

Apprenticeship 434–436, 440, *see also* Situated cognition, implications for education

bridging apprenticeship 434

cognitive apprenticeship 434–436

examples of 435

premises 435–436

examples of 434, 440

Archival data 122, 499, *see also* Eyewitness memory, for faces

Associated Systems theory, *see* Associative network models